8000+ BIHAR OBJECTIVE QUESTIONS

USEFUL FOR ALL COMPETITIVE EXAMINATIONS OF BIHAR

DIPTI SHARMA

PRABHAT EXAMS

Publisher

PRABHAT EXAMS

An imprint of Prabhat Prakashan Pvt. Ltd.

4/19 Asaf Ali Road, New Delhi–110 002

Ph. 23289555 • 23289666 • 23289777 • Helpline/ 7827007777

e-mail: prabhatbooks@gmail.com • Website: www.prabhatexam.com

Price

Six Hundred Twenty Five Rupees

ISBN 978-93-7573-021-7

Printed at

Japan Art, Delhi

8000+ BIHAR OBJECTIVE QUESTIONS

by Dipti Sharma

ISBN 978-93-7573-021-7

₹ 625.00

Preface

For a long time readers were requesting a standard book related to Bihar which contains all the authentic information about Bihar. Keeping this demand in mind, the presented book 'Bihar Objective' has been written. The state of Bihar, famous for its Glorious History, is continuously on the path of development. Although it is neither easy nor possible to compile all the information of this diverse state into one book, but after deep study and research, we have tried to collect information from various authentic sources and this book is the result of this effort.

In the presented book more than 8000+ objective type questions have been given, which are from History of Bihar, Freedom Movement, Folk Culture, Fairs and Festivals, Literature, Personalities of Bihar, Health, Sports, Climate and Soil, Forest and Wildlife, Agriculture, Industry, Tourism, Disaster Management, Administrative Structure, Plans, Policies and Naxalism & Others, which are related to Bihar.

For the convenience of the readers, the book is divided into three parts. Part-I consists of objective type questions on various topics related to the state. Part-II consists of 125 Practice Sets, which have been designed keeping in mind the trend of questions in Bihar examinations. In Part-III, previous years' solved papers of various competitive examinations conducted by the state are given, which will be helpful for the candidates preparing for various competitive exams of Bihar.

Hope this book will also be liked by the general readers who want to get information about the state of Bihar.

Simple, comprehensible and clear language is used in the book. Readers' suggestions are always welcomed to improve the quality of the book.

Contents

Part–I
Objective Questions

1 Sources of History

ARCHAEOLOGICAL SOURCES

1. **In which places of Bihar, Archaeological sources of pre-historic age have been found?**
(a) Patna (b) Kaimur
(c) Bhagalpur (d) All of these
2. **In which of the following places, Archaeological sources of pre-historic age have not been found?**
(a) Munger
(b) Gaya
(c) Vaishali
(d) All of the above
3. **In which present day district pre-historic place Chirand is situated?**
(a) Saran (b) Vaishali
(c) Gaya (d) Patna
4. **In which present day district pre-historic place Chechar is situated?**
(a) Madhubani (b) Darbhanga
(c) Vaishali (d) Mujaffarpur
5. **In which of the pre-historic places, bone equipments of Neolithic age have been recovered?**
(a) Chirand (b) Chechar
(c) Sonpur (d) Maner
6. **In which of the pre-historic places of Bihar, equipments and earthwares of copper age have been found?**
(a) Chechar
(b) Maner
(c) Sonpur
(d) All of the above
7. **Which of the following are Bihar's archaeological sources?**
(a) Copper plate engraving
(b) Ruins
(c) Coins
(d) All of the above
8. **Lauriya inscription of Lauriya Areraj and Lauriya Nandangarh belonged to which emperor?**
(a) Chandragupta Maurya
(b) Ashok
(c) Ajatshatru
(d) Dhananand
9. **In which of the following places pillar edicts have been found?**
(a) Rampurva
(b) Chandanpeer Pahadi
(c) Lauriya Areraj
(d) Lauriya Nandangarh
10. **___________ pertaining to Ashoka period have been found from Chandanpur Hill of Sasaram.**
(a) Minor rock edicts
(b) Pillar Edicts
(c) Inscriptions
(d) All of the above
11. **Cave inscriptions of which of the following rulers have been recovered from Barabar Nagarjuna Hill?**
(a) Ashok
(b) Ajatshatru
(c) Dashrath
(d) Chandragupta Maurya

12. The language of Mauryan Inscriptions found in Bihar was_________

(a) Sanskrit (b) Magadhi
(c) Prakrit (d) Awadhi

13. Name the script of the Mauryan Insriptions found in Bihar is–

(a) Brahmi (b) Kharoshthi
(c) Persian (d) Both (a) and (b)

14. From which site in Bihar, 'Yaksha' idol has been recovered?

(a) Gaya (b) Patna
(c) Munger (d) Saran

15. In the __________district of Bihar, two inscriptions related to Goddess Prabhudaya have been recovered.

(a) Patna (b) Gaya
(c) Bhagalpur (d) Vaishali

16. From which of the places below, a seal relating to 'Dhruvswamini' has been recovered?

(a) Chirand (b) Chechad
(c) Sonpur (d) Basad

17. Dhruvswamini is considered wife of which of the following rulers?

(a) Ashok
(b) Chandragupta Maurya
(c) Chandragupta-II
(d) None of the above

18. In which language, Gupta Period inscriptions have been found in Bihar?

(a) Sanskrit (b) Hindi
(c) Awadhi (d) Prakrit

19. In inscriptions found at Bodhgaya, monks of which country are mentioned?

(a) China
(b) Thailand
(c) Indonesia
(d) Srilanka

20. Which monk of Srilanka is mentioned in Bodhgaya inscriptions?

(a) Mahamana-I
(b) Mahamana-II
(c) Adinath-I
(d) Adinath-II

21. In which place Gupta period seal was found, which mentions about Gupta Dynasty?

(a) Vaishali (b) Saran
(c) Nalanda (d) Munger

22. In which of the places, stone inscription related to Gupta period are found?

(a) Patna (b) Gaya
(c) Navada (d) Bhagalpur

23. Who is considered the founder of the post Gupta Period Dyanasty?

(a) Aditya Sen (b) Krishan Gupt
(c) Amar Gupt (d) Chandra Gupt

24. In which of the following ruler's inscriptions, we find knowledge of history from post Gupta dynasty period to Adityasen's period?

(a) Brahmgupt
(b) Krishan Gupt
(c) Adityasen
(d) None of the above

25. Mandar Hill situated in Baunsi from where Adityasen's inscriptions have been recovered, falls in which of the following districts?

(a) Bhagalpur (b) Gaya
(c) Aurangabad (d) Banka

26. In which out of the following inscriptions, there are mentions about digging of ponds and erection of Vishnu idol?

(a) Krishna Gupt
(b) Adityasen
(c) Amargupt
(d) Both (a) and (c)

27. From Dev Varunarka near Arrah, a stone edict of ________has been recovered.

(a) Krishangupt (b) Amargupta
(c) Adityasen (d) Jeev Gupt II

28. In pre-medieval age, inscriptions of the _________ rulers, have been found in various parts of Southern and Middle Bihar, which are in Sanskrit language.
(a) Maurya
(b) Gupt
(c) Pal
(d) All of the above

29. In which of the following Pal Rulers, mention of a person named Keshav is made?
(a) Devpal (b) Dharam pal
(c) Nandpal (d) Mihirpal

30. From which place, Pal Ruler Dharampal's edict was recovered?
(a) Navada (b) Nalanda
(c) Munger (d) Bodhgaya

31. Nalanda Copperplate edict of _______ makes it clear that he had donated one village in Gaya.
(a) Devpal (b) Keshavpal
(c) Dharmpal (d) Adityapal

32. From among the following rulers, whose edict stated Veersen being made the President of Nalanda University?
(a) Dharampal (b) Mahipal
(c) Devpal (d) Adityapal

33. From one of the following rulers, whose edict (Nalanda Stone) states that Nalanda Monastery was burnt?
(a) Mahipal (b) Devpal
(c) Dharmpal (d) Adityapal

34. In which part of Bihar coins of Pratihar King Bhoj have been found?
(a) Patna (b) Gaya
(c) Nalanda (d) Munger

35. Who is the ruler connected with Munger Copperplate edict?
(a) Dharmpal (b) Devpal
(c) Mahipal (d) Both (a) and (c)

36. Which of the following rulers got constructed the fortification wall of Rajgir Fort?
(a) Adityasen (b) Dharmpal
(c) Krishangupt (d) Ajatshatru

37. Who had studied the barricaded wall of the Rajgir Fort and the caves of Barabar?
(a) Mark Cook (b) Buchanan
(c) Hamilton (d) Both (b) and (c)

38. From which place the gold coins of Shashank have been recovered?
(a) Patna (b) Nalanda
(c) Gaya (d) Both (b) and (c)

39. Who had made a mention of the cave built by Ashoka and his grandson Dasrath on the Barabar Hill?
(a) Major Baro
(b) Major Cook
(c) Major Kitto
(d) Hamilton.

40. Who out of the following had got excavation of the hillock of Kurkikar Kuprahar (Patliputra)?
(a) Major Kitto (b) Li-grand
(c) Buchanan (d) David Hop

41. Who is called the father of the National Archaeological Science?
(a) Major Buchanan
(b) George Orwell
(c) Cunningham
(d) Lord Curzon

42. When did Bihar's archaeological places get recognized?
(a) 1855 AD (b) 1857 AD
(c) 1859 AD (d) 1861 AD

43. Who had identified the archaeological places of Bihar?
(a) Cunningham
(b) Major Kitto
(c) Major Baro
(d) Hamilton

44. Who discovered Bodhi Temple situated in Bodh Gaya?
(a) Buchanan (b) Lee Grand
(c) James Hopps (d) Cunningham

45. Who discovered Bargaon at a distance of 11 kms from Rajgir where the ancient Nalanda University is situated?
(a) Cunningham (b) James Cook
(c) David Harse (d) Carl Mazine

46. In which of the following places, the famous stone edict of Kumargupt and Skandgupt has been found?
(a) Munger (b) Patna
(c) Nalanda (d) Gaya

47. When, in Patna University, was the Department of Ancient Indian History and Archaeology established?
(a) 1948 (b) 1949
(c) 1950 (d) 1951

48. Who, in the year 1950 and 1951, got Kuprahar excavated?
(a) K. Dev
(b) Dr. Som Prakash
(c) Dr. Altekar
(d) Both (a) and (c)

49. When did the State Archaeological Directorate establish?
(a) 1960 (b) 1962
(c) 1964 (d) 1966

50. 'Jatak' tales are related to which religion?
(a) Jain (b) Buddha
(c) Sikh (d) Shaiv

51. Which word has been used in 'Jatak' tales to describe gold coin?
(a) Rupak (b) Kanishka
(c) Nishka (d) Karn

52. In which place of Bihar gold coins have been recovered?
(a) Patna
(b) Vaishali
(c) Munger
(d) None of the above

53. The ancient coins are named as ________.
(a) Karn (b) Pann
(c) Aahat (d) Nishk

54. According to Brihadaranyaka Upanishad, the King of Videha ______ had given (gold/cent) coins in donation.
(a) Janak
(b) Kapil
(c) Shudhdhodhan
(d) Sidhartha

55. The ancient coins recovered from Bihar are originally 'The Ahat' coins only which are known by different names.
(a) Parn
(b) Karshapan
(c) Dharan
(d) All of the above

56. In which place of Bihar, silver 'Ahat' coins have been recovered?
(a) Lohanipur
(b) Motihari
(c) Fatuha
(d) All of the above

57. In Gupta period Bihar, coins made of which metal were in use?
(a) Gold (b) Silver
(c) Copper (d) All of these

LITERARY SOURCES

1. Which of the following is a literary source of Bihar?
(a) Rigveda
(b) Atharvaveda
(c) Shatpath Brahmin
(d) All of the above

2. In which text, the word Bihar was used for the first time?
(a) Rigveda
(b) Atharvaveda
(c) Shatpath Brahmin
(d) Brihadaranayak Upanishad

3. In which text, Magadh was mentioned for the first time.
(a) Rigveda
(b) Atharvaveda
(c) Samveda
(d) Shatpath Brahmin

4. Which of the following literatures give us knowledge of the history of Bihar?
(a) Anguttar Nikay
(b) Bhagwati Sutra
(c) Deergha Nikay
(d) All of the above

5. Which religion Anguttar Nikay and Deergha Nikay are associated with?
(a) Buddhism (b) Jain
(c) Vaishnava (d) Shaiva

6. Which religion Bhagwati Sutra is associated with?
(a) Shaiva (b) Vaishnava
(c) Buddhism (d) Jain

7. Knowledge of Mahajanpadas was first acquired from which of these texts?
(a) Bhagwati Sutra
(b) Anguttar Nikay
(c) Deergha Nikay
(d) Both (a) and (b)

8. What was the total number of Mahajanpadas?
(a) 14 (b) 15
(c) 16 (d) 17

9. How many Mahajanpadas were situated in Bihar?
(a) 2 (b) 3
(c) 4 (d) 5

10. Which of the following is not a Bihar situated Mahajanpada?
(a) Ang (b) Magadh
(c) Vajji (d) Vatsa

11. Who was the author of 'Tabaqat-i-Nasiri?
(a) Minhaz-i-Siraz
(b) Dawood Khan
(c) Abbas Khan Shervani
(d) None of the above

12. Which of the following books is written by Abbas Khan Shervani?
(a) Tarikh-i-Dawoodi
(b) Badshahnama
(c) Tarikh-i-Shersshahi
(d) Tarikh-i-Firozesshahi

13. Which of the following books is the first composition in Persian in India?
(a) Tabaqat-i-Nasiri
(b) Kitabul Hind
(c) Gulbagh
(d) Hindnama

14. Which one of following is incorrect?
(a) Ikhtsan Dehlavi (i) Basatinul Uns
(b) Sheikh Kabir (ii) Afsana-a-Shadi
(c) Rizkullah (iii) Kitabul Hind
(d) Ghulam Hussain Salim (iv) Riyaz Ul Salatin

15. Who of the following is the author of 'Waqiat-a-Mushtaqi'?
(a) Sheikh Kabir
(b) Rizkullah
(c) Ikhtsan Dehlavi
(d) Akhtar Hussain Qazi

16. Which of the following is a composition by Ghulam Hussain Tabatabai?
(a) Waqiat-a-Mushtaqi
(b) Hind Som
(c) Siyar-ul-Mutakherin
(d) Hindnama

17. Who is the author of Kirtilata and Kirtipataka?
(a) Kabir (b) Namdev
(c) Nagarjun (d) Vidyapati

18. Which of the following is a composition of Jyotirishwar?
(a) Varna Bhed
(b) Varna Ratnakar
(c) Varna Parichay
(d) Varn Vyavastha

19. **Who is the author of the book named 'Rajniratnakar'?**
(a) Vidyapati
(b) Nagarjun
(c) Chandeshwar
(d) Jyotirishwar

20. **Which of the following is incorrect?**
(a) Kautilya -Arthshastra
(b) Panini -Ashtadhyayi
(c) Ziauddin Barani -Tarikh-i-Firozeshahi
(d) Abul Fazal -Babarnama (Tuzuk-i-Babri)

21. **Who of the following is the author of 'Akbarnama'?**
(a) Ziauddin Barani
(b) Minhas-ul-Siraz
(c) Abul Fazal
(d) Abdul Hamid Lahori

22. **Who of the following composed 'Indica'?**
(a) Hiuen Tsang (b) I Tsang
(c) Faxian (d) Megasthenes

23. **Which of the following is related to Greece?**
(a) Nunez (b) Hamilton
(c) Megasthenes (d) Captain Cook

24. **Whose journey description amongst the following is considered a literary source for Bihar?**
(a) Hiuen Tsang
(b) Faxian
(c) I Tsang
(d) All of the above

25. **Who among the following had visited Bihar in the Mughal Period?**
(a) John Marshall
(b) Peter Mundi
(c) Manucci
(d) All of the above

26. **Whose journey description amongst the following European travelers is a literary source of the history of Bihar?**
(a) Ralph Rich
(b) Edward Terry
(c) Manrick
(d) All of the above

Answers

ARCHAEOLOGICAL SOURCES

1. (a) **2.** (d) **3.** (a) **4.** (c) **5.** (a) **6.** (d) **7.** (d) **8.** (b) **9.** (a) **10.** (a)
11. (c) **12.** (c) **13.** (a) **14.** (b) **15.** (d) **16.** (d) **17.** (c) **18.** (a) **19.** (d) **20.** (b)
21. (c) **22.** (c) **23.** (b) **24.** (c) **25.** (d) **26.** (b) **27.** (d) **28.** (c) **29.** (b) **30.** (d)
31. (c) **32.** (c) **33.** (a) **34.** (c) **35.** (b) **36.** (d) **37.** (d) **38.** (d) **39.** (c) **40.** (a)
41. (c) **42,** (d) **43.** (a) **44.** (d) **45.** (a) **46.** (c) **47.** (b) **48.** (d) **49.** (b) **50.** (b)
51. (c) **52.** (d) **53.** (c) **54.** (a) **55.** (d) **56.** (d) **57.** (d)

LITERARY SOURCES

1. (d) **2.** (b) **3.** (a) **4.** (d) **5.** (a) **6.** (d) **7.** (d) **8.** (c) **9.** (b) **10.** (d)
11. (a) **12.** (c) **13.** (a) **14.** (c) **15.** (b) **16.** (c) **17.** (d) **18.** (b) **19.** (c) **20.** (d)
21. (c) **22.** (d) **23.** (c) **24.** (d) **25.** (d) **26.** (d)

❑❑❑

2 Ancient Period

PRE-HISTORIC AGE

1. **The habitat signs of primitive human in some of the places in Bihar are__________years old.**
   (a) 20000 (b) 50000
   (c) 75000 (d) 100000
2. **On excavation, in which place in Bihar, remains of paleolithic age have been found?**
   (a) Patna
   (b) Munger
   (c) Nalanda
   (d) All of the above
3. **The initial phase of prehistoric age is called_________**
   (a) Pashan (b) Tamra
   (c) Kansya (d) Old stone age
4. **When did the human beings start their culture on the basis of equipments made of stone?**
   (a) Old stone age
   (b) Stone age
   (c) New stone age
   (d) Mid stone age
5. **In which place in Bihar, equipments from old stone age have been recovered?**
   (a) Jethian Valley
   (b) Valmiki Nagar
   (c) Rajpokhar
   (d) All of the above
6. **Which pair out of the following is incorrect?**
   (a) Gaya - Pemar Valley
   (b) Munger - Paisra
   (c) Bhagalpur - Rajpokhra
   (d) All of the above
7. **Where is Jethian Valley, an old stone age place, located in the present day districts?**
   (a) Gaya (b) Munger
   (c) Nalanda (d) Bhagalpur
8. **Which of the following old stone age place is situated in Bhagalpur?**
   (a) Bhimbandh (b) Bhalizor
   (c) Paisra (d) Pemar Valley
9. **Which of the following old stone age equipments have been found from different parts of Bihar?**
   (a) Usak
   (b) Scraper
   (c) Plaque
   (d) All of the above
10. **In old stone age, what was the main source of human livelihood?**
    (a) Collecting root vegetables
    (b) Hunting
    (c) Fishing
    (d) All of the above
11. **In which place of Bihar remains of two rocky housing of prehistoric humans have been recovered?**
    (a) Vaishali (b) Gaya
    (c) Nalanda (d) Munger
12. **In which district of Bihar Sherghati, – a prehistoric place, is situated?**

(a) Saran (b) Patna
(c) Munger (d) Gaya

13. When did humans start agriculture?
(a) Stone age
(b) Paleolithic age
(c) Neolithic age
(d) Mesolithic age

14. Which of the following is Bihar's neolithic place?
(a) Kutubpur (b) Maner
(c) Senuar (d) All of these

15. Which of the following is not correct?
(a) Vaishali - Chechar
(b) Rohtas - Senuar
(c) Gaya - Taradih
(d) Munger - Kear

16. Neolithic place Chirandh is situated on the bank of which river?
(a) Gandak (b) Old Gandak
(c) Sone (d) Ganga

17. When did excavation begin at Chirandh?
(a) 1960 (b) 1961
(c) 1962 (d) 1963

18. Neolithic place Taradih in Gaya District is situated on the bank of which river?
(a) Ganga (b) Gandak
(c) Kosi (d) Falgu

19. Which of the following Neolithic places is situated on the banks of Kurda river?
(a) Senuar (b) Qutabpur
(c) Kear (d) Chechar

20. Which metal did human being used first?
(a) Brass (b) Copper
(c) Iron (d) Bronze

21. In which place in Bihar, signs of copper stone age were found?
(a) Ariyap
(b) Senuar
(c) Maner
(d) All of the above

22. In Antarjee Kheda, in the Ganga Valley (Uttar Pradesh), signs of availability of which metal are found in around 1050 BC?
(a) Iron (b) Copper
(c) Brass (d) None

23. Iron age is the age of_________.
(a) Vaidik
(b) Post-Vaidik
(c) Maurya
(d) Gupta

24. The second phase of iron age is called_________.
(a) Northern Black Pottery age
(b) Gray Pottery age
(c) Black Pottery age
(d) Northern Gray age

25. When did in Bihar for the first time signs of urbanization appear?
(a) Bronze age
(b) Iron age
(c) Vaidik age
(d) None of the above

26. Harappan Civilization age remained from which time to which time?
(a) 2500-1850 BC
(b) 2400-1800 BC
(c) 2300-1750 BC
(d) 2200-1700 BC

27. Rigveda period is considered from which time to which time?
(a) 1600-1100 BC
(b) 1550-1050 BC
(c) 1500-1000 BC
(d) 1500-950 BC

28. Arya Culture in Ganga Valley expanded from which time to which time?
(a) 1200-800 BC
(b) 1100-700 BC
(c) 1000-600 BC
(d) 900-500 BC

29. As per a mention in Shatpath Brahmin, when did Aryans settle in the plains of Gandak (Videh)?
(a) 600 BC (b) 700 BC
(c) 800 BC (d) 900 BC

30. Which period is considered to be the North Vedic period?
(a) 1100-500 BC
(b) 1000-500 BC
(c) 1000-600 BC
(d) 1000-400 BC

31. Which of the following is the most ancient and most exhaustive text?
(a) Shatpath Brahman
(b) Aitray Brahman
(c) Kaushitaki Brahman
(d) None of the above

32. Which of the following was written by Yagyavalakya?
(a) Samveda
(b) Rigveda
(c) Mahabharat
(d) Shatpath Brahman

33. Which of the following literary sources mentions that the Aryans had for the first time entered into India from north-west?
(a) Rigveda
(b) Atharvaveda
(c) Shatpath Brahman
(d) Aitray Brahman

34. On the banks of which river, the Aryans used to perform big Yajnas and rituals?
(a) Ganga (b) Yamuna
(c) Saraswati (d) Sabarmati

35. Story of which one of these is similar to Shatpath Brahman?
(a) Keshav
(b) Madhav Videh
(c) Gautam Rahugan
(d) Both (b) and (c)

36. Who, out of the following, expanded the Aryan culture up till north Bihar?
(a) Gautam Rahugan
(b) Madhav Videh
(c) Keshav
(d) Dipendranath

37. Which of the following rivers is called Sadaneera?
(a) Ganga (b) Gandak
(c) Sone (d) Falgu

38. The____________talks of having had signs of the Aryans settled and expanded in Mithila Videh area.
(a) Rigveda
(b) Samveda
(c) Aitray Brahman
(d) Shatpath Brahman

39. The king of which of the following places was a philosopher and a scholar who had got Upanishads composed?
(a) Ang (b) Videh
(c) Magadh (d) Vajji

SOCIAL AND RELIGIOUS REFORMS MOVEMENT IN ANCIENT BIHAR

BUDDHISM

1. In 6th century BC, it was a centre of religious movement-
(a) Magadh (b) Vats
(c) Ang (d) Mathura

2. In which of the following Vedas a mention of the caste system is made?
(a) Rigveda (b) Samveda
(c) Atharvaveda (d) Yajurveda

3. Which is not the reason of religious movement?
(a) Yajna related rituals
(b) Brahmins' superiority
(c) Animals sacrifice
(d) Political decentralization

4. **By beginning of________century, practices like untouchability had taken a hard shape.**
(a) Sixth (b) Fifth
(c) Fourth (d) Third

5. **In ________age, animal sacrifice was common in big Yajnas.**
(a) Vedic (b) Post Vedic
(c) Maurya (d) Gupta

6. **How many communities emerged in the post Vedic age?**
(a) 58 (b) 60
(c) 62 (d) 64

7. **Which of the following communities had Bihar as its birth place and 'karmbhoomi' (the land where one works).**
(a) Buddhist (b) Jains
(c) Sikhs (d) Both (a) and (b)

8. **At what age, Mahatma Buddha had left his house?**
(a) 29 (b) 30
(c) 31 (d) 32

9. **Who is considered the founder of e Buddhist?**
(a) Mahatma Isha
(b) Mahavir Jain
(c) Kanishka
(d) Gautam Buddha

10. **Where was Gautam Buddha born?**
(a) Sarnath (b) Lumbini
(c) Amravati (d) Lauriya

11. **Gautam Buddha was son of __________King Shudhodhana of the Shakya ancestry of Kapilavastu.**
(a) Brahmin (b) Kayastha
(c) Kshatriya (d) Vaishya

12. **What was the name of the mother of Gautam Buddha.**
(a) Prajapati Gautam
(b) Yashoda Devi
(c) Mahamaya Devi
(d) Kunti Devi

13. **Who out of the following was the step mother of Gautam Buddha?**
(a) Yashoda Devi
(b) Amrapali
(c) Maitrayee
(d) Prajapati Gautami

14. **What was the childhood name of Gautam Buddha?**
(a) Rahul (b) Mahendra
(c) Siddhartha (d) Karan

15. **According to Chinese literature, when was Gautam Buddha born?**
(a) 563 BC (b) 483 BC
(c) 563 AD (d) 483 AD

16. **Which clan did Mahatma Buddha belong to?**
(a) Shakya
(b) Gautam
(c) Mahamaya
(d) None of the above

17. **When did Mahatma Buddha die?**
(a) 487 BC (b) 485 BC
(c) 483 BC (d) 481 BC

18. **At what age, Mahatma Buddha died?**
(a) 74 (b) 76
(c) 78 (d) 80

19. **At the time of Gautam Buddha, an astrologer called________told King Shudhhodhana that this boy will become a hermit.**
(a) Kamaldev (b) Nagarjun
(c) Kaldeval (d) Navaldeval

20. **At what age, did Gautam Buddha marry?**
(a) 18 (b) 16
(c) 14 (d) 12

21. **What was the name of the wife of Gautam Buddha?**
(a) Yashomati Devi
(b) Mahadevi
(c) Apala
(d) Yashodhara

22. What was the name of the son of Gautam Buddha.

(a) Raj (b) Raman
(c) Rahul (d) Ranjan

23. What out of the following was not seen by Buddha in his stream of journey?

(a) A Patient (b) A woman
(c) A hermit (d) A dead body

24. According to Buddhist literature, Gautam Buddha saw four signs in a single journey.

(a) Sutt Pitaka (b) Jatak Tales
(c) Vinay Pitaka (d) Deerghnikaya

25. The renunciation of home by Gautam Buddha is known by which name?

(a) Mahabhinishkramana
(b) Mahaparinirvana
(c) Nirvana
(d) Kaivalya

26. What was the name of the horse of Gautam Buddha?

(a) Chetak (b) Champak
(c) Kanthak (d) Karni

27. On__________Purnima, Gautam Buddha birth, death and awakening took place.

(a) Chaitra (b) Vaishakh
(c) Ashad (d) Kartik

28. When did Gautam Buddha renunciate his house?

(a) Chaitra purnima
(b) Vaishakh Purnima
(c) Jyeshtha Purnima
(d) Ashad Purnima

29. On the banks of which river in Anuvin, Buddha attained renunciation?

(a) Anoma (b) Sorsava
(c) Sikerhana (d) Tilawe

30. Which of the following had his first Guru Alarkalam?

(a) Mahavir Jain
(b) Mahatma Buddha
(c) Kabir Das
(d) Rishabhdev

31. Where did Gautam Buddha meet Alarkalam?

(a) Lumbini (b) Sarnath
(c) Vaishali (d) Lauriya Areraj

32. Which philosophy was mastered by Guru Alarkaman?

(a) Yoga (b) Sankhya
(c) Mimansa (d) Bhotikvadi

33. Where did Gautam Buddha meet his Guru Rudrak Ramputra?

(a) Nalanda (b) Sarnath
(c) Vaishali (d) Satna

34. Which of the following was not Gautam Buddha's Guru?

(a) Yagyavalakya
(b) Nagarjun
(c) Rudrak Ramputra
(d) Both (a) and (b)

35. In the forest of which area Gautam Buddha practised a hard penance?

(a) Uruvela (b) Sarnath
(c) Shrawasti (d) Lumbini

36. Buddha did his penance with how many of his associates?

(a) Three (b) Four
(c) Five (d) Six

37. Who of the following did penance in the forest with Gautam Buddha?

(a) Kautilya (b) Shavak
(c) Chetanya (d) Amar Singh

38. Who of the following performed penance in Uruvela?

(a) Ajj
(b) Bappa
(c) Assigh
(d) All of the above

39. Guatam Buddha achieved penance again on the banks of which river?

(a) Punpun (b) Niranjan
(c) Kosi (d) Sakri

40. At what age did Gautam Buddha achieve enlightenment?
(a) 31 (b) 33
(c) 35 (d) 37

41. On ________ day of penance Buddha achieved enlightenment.
(a) 43rd (b) 45th
(c) 47th (d) 49th

42. Under which tree did Gautam Buddha start his penance?
(a) Ashoka (b) Mango
(c) Banyan (d) Peepal

43. Where did Gautam Buddha achieve enlightenment?
(a) Vaishali (b) Nalanda
(c) Gaya (d) Shrawasti

44. Who served 'kheer' to Gautam Buddha?
(a) Sujata (b) Suchitra
(c) Sumitra (d) Sukanya

45. When was Gautam Buddha called 'Bodhisatva'?
(a) After starting penance
(b) After achieving enlightenment
(c) After renunciation of home
(d) After delivering sermon

46. The incident of enlightenment under the religion is called ________.
(a) Kevalya (b) Sanlekhna
(c) Nirvana (d) Both (a) and (b)

47. Where, for the first time, make his pupil?
(a) Bodh Gaya (b) Vaishali
(c) Nalanda (d) Lumbini

48. Who out of the following Gautam made his pupil at Bodh Gaya?
(a) Jamali (b) Tapas
(c) Bhallik (d) Both (b) and (c)

49. After enlightenment where did Gautam first go?
(a) Vaishali
(b) Sarnath
(c) Amravati
(d) Lumbini

50. Where did Mahatma deliver his first sermon?
(a) Nalanda (b) Bodhgaya
(c) Sarnath (d) Shrawasti

51. What is the first sermon delivered by Buddha called?
(a) Nirvana
(b) Kevalya
(c) Mahabhinishkrmana
(d) Dharmchakra Parivartan

52. Where was Bodh Sangh formed?
(a) Bodhgaya (b) Sarnath
(c) Nalanda (d) Lumbini

53. Where did Buddha go after delivering his first sermon at Sarnath?
(a) Bodhgaya (b) Varanasi
(c) Patliputra (d) Shrawasti

54. In Varanasi, in whose house Mahatma Buddha stay?
(a) Vishishthaputra
(b) Uttamputra
(c) Shreshthiputra
(d) Namakputra

55. Which ruler had given Venuvan Vihar to Gautam Buddha in donation?
(a) Bimbisara (b) Ajatshatru
(c) Udayin (d) Ashok

56. Which of the following was not the disciple of Gautam?
(a) Upali
(b) Sariputra
(c) Modgalyayan
(d) Jamboot

57. Where did Sariputra and Upali become disciples of Gautam Buddha?
(a) Rajgriha (b) Vaishali
(c) Kaushambi (d) Videha

58. Who was the first woman who joined Bodh Sangha?
(a) Mahamaya Devi
(b) Prajapati Gautami
(c) Apala
(d) Amrapali

59. On whose behest did Gautam Buddha allow women to join Bodh Sangha?
(a) Upali (b) Keshav
(c) Sariputra (d) Anand

60. On joining of Bodh Sangha by women, who had said that the religion which would have gone to exist for 1000 years would now extinguish in 500 years?
(a) Anand
(b) Sariputra
(c) Mahavir Swami
(d) Gautam

61. Who of the following was the cousin of Gautam Buddha?
(a) Rahul (b) Anand
(c) Sariputra (d) Devdutt

62. Where did Devdutt become a disciple of Gautam Buddha?
(a) Rajgriha (b) Vaishali
(c) Lumbini (d) Sarnath

63. How many years after Gautam Buddha attained penance, he reached Vaishali?
(a) 6 (b) 7
(c) 8 (d) 9

64. Ruler of which place donated Kutnprashala Vihar to Gautam Buddha?
(a) Magadh (b) Anga
(c) Videh (d) Lichhavi

65. 'Nagarvadhu' of which place became disciple of Gautam Buddha?
(a) Nalanda (b) Vaishali
(c) Sarnath (d) Shrawasti

66. What was the name of the 'Nagarvadhu'of Vaishali?
(a) Sukanya
(b) Amrapali
(c) Mandakini
(d) Apala

67. Wife of the ruler of__________ became disciple of Buddha.
(a) Lichhavi (b) Anga
(c) Videh (d) Magadh

68. What was the name of the wife of the ruler of Magadh, Bimbisar?
(a) Mahamaya Devi
(b) Amrapali
(c) Kshema
(d) Yashodhara

69. 20 years after achieving enlightenment, where did Buddha go?
(a) Champa (b) Vaishali
(c) Kosal (d) Patliputra

70. Which of the following was the capital of Kosal?
(a) Shrawasti (b) Sarnath
(c) Lumbini (d) Champa

71. Where did the dacoit Angulimal become the disciple of Buddha?
(a) Sarnath (b) Vaishali
(c) Bodhgaya (d) Shrawasti

72. Where did Buddha deliver maximum number of his sermons in his life?
(a) Shrawasti
(b) Bodhgaya
(c) Sarnath
(d) Nalanda

73. Where did Buddha die?
(a) Kushinagar (b) Nalanda
(c) Vaishali (d) Shrawasti

74. Consumption of __________meat caused stomach trouble to Buddha which caused his death.
(a) Goat (b) Camel
(c) Cow (d) Pig

75. The incident of Buddha's death is called________
(a) Kaivalya
(b) Sanlekhna
(c) Dharam chakraparivartan
(d) Mahaparinirvan

76. After Buddha's death, who became the guiding figure of Boddhist Religion?
(a) Sariputra (b) Devdutt
(c) Anand (d) Upali

77. Who among the following uttered his last word as 'ápp dipo bhav'?
(a) Mahavir Swami
(b) Gautam Buddha
(c) Rishabhdev
(d) Ajatshatru

78. In how many parts, Buddha's bone remains were distributed?
(a) 6 (b) 7
(c) 8 (d) 9

79. _______ was constructed on the bone-remains of Buddha.
(a) Stupa (b) Maha
(c) Chaitya (d) Vihar

80. None could enter the Sangh without permission from__________.
(a) King
(b) Gram Pradhan
(c) Guru
(d) Mata-Pita

81. Where, from the following places, Stupa was not constructed with the bone remains of Buddha?
(a) Pava
(b) Videh
(c) Piplivan
(d) Ramgram

82. Who among the following was not a follower of Buddhist Religion?
(a) Bimbisar (b) Prasenjit
(c) Ajatshatru (d) Udayin

83. Who among the following was a disciple of Mahatma Buddha?
(a) Jivak
(b) Mahakashyap
(c) Sunit
(d) All of the above

84. Who among the following women was not a follower of Buddhism?
(a) Priyadarshana
(b) Amrapali
(c) Yashodhara
(d) Nanda

85. How many Arya Truths were told by Gautam Buddha?
(a) 2 (b) 3
(c) 4 (d) 5

86. Ashtangik Marg is related to which religion?
(a) Jain
(b) Sikh
(c) Shaiv
(d) Buddhist

87. Which of the following come under the Ashtangik Marg?
(a) Samyak Drishti
(b) Samyak Aajiv
(c) Samyak Vyayam
(d) All of the above

88. Which of the following does not come under the Ashtangik Marg?
(a) Samyak Gyan
(b) Samyak Smriti
(c) Samyak Samadhi
(d) Samyak Karmant

89. How many 'Sheel' have been taught in Buddhist religion to follow the Ashtangik Marg and to follow moral ethics?
(a) 7 (b) 8
(c) 9 (d) 10

90. Which of the following is included in 10 'Sheel' of Buddhism?
(a) Satya
(b) Ahinsa
(c) Vyabhichar na karna
(d) All of the above

91. Which of the following is not included in 10 Sheels of Buddhism?
(a) Ashtey
(b) Aprigrah
(c) Brahmcharya
(d) Sanyas

92. The causes of agony in Buddhism are called_______

(a) Pratityasamutpada

(b) Kaivalya

(c) Saromi

(d) Nskras

93. How many 'Chakras'are there in Pratityasamutpada?

(a) 10 (b) 11

(c) 12 (d) 13

94. Buddism is_________religion.

(a) Theist

(b) Anishwarvadi Atheist

(c) Both (a) and (b)

(d) None of these

95. Followers of Buddhism do not believe in.

(a) Reincarnation

(b) Soul

(c) Karma

(d) Both (a) and (c)

96. Which of the following rulers gave patronage to Buddhism?

(a) Ashoka

(b) Kanishka

(c) Harshvardhan

(d) All of the above

97. In which of the following countries Buddhism was spread?

(a) Srilanka (b) China

(c) Tibet (d) All of these

98. What were the reasons for the success of Buddhism in India?

(a) People's religion

(b) Use of Pali as a language

(c) Moderate approach

(d) All of the above

99. Which of the following persons were banned from entering the Bodh Sangh?

(a) Debtors

(b) Soldiers

(c) Patients

(d) All of the above

100. Which of the following was not allowed to enter Bodh Sangh?

(a) Thief

(b) Murderer

(c) King's servant

(d) All of the above

101. Who among the following rulers gave his patronage to the Mahayan Branch of Buddhism?

(a) Kanishka

(b) Harshvardhan

(c) Pal rulers

(d) All of the above

102. Which of the following places was a centre of Boddhist education?

(a) Nalanda

(b) Odantpuri

(c) Vikramshila

(d) All of the above

103. Which of following was not a major cause of the downfall of Buddhism?

(a) Corruption

(b) Moral degradation

(c) Poverty

(d) Foreign attacks

104. How many Buddhist councils were organized?

(a) 4 (b) 5

(c) 6 (d) 7

105. When was the first Bodh Sangiti organized?

(a) 489 BC (b) 487 BC

(c) 485 BC (d) 483 BC

106. Where was the first Bodh Sangiti organized?

(a) Rajgriha (b) Vaishali

(c) Patliputra (d) Nalanda

107. Who was the President of the first Bodh Sangiti?

(a) Ajatshatru

(b) Vasumitra

(c) Mahakashyap

(d) Sarvkami

108. During whose period was the first Boddhist Council was organized?
(a) Ajatshatru (b) Bimbisara
(c) Udayin (d) Kalashok

109. After which Boddhist Council, Sut and Vinay Pitaka were collected?
(a) Fourth (b) Third
(c) Second (d) First

110. When was the second Boddhist Council organized?
(a) 450 BC (b) 425 BC
(c) 398 BC (d) 383 BC

111. Where was the second Boddhist Council organized?
(a) Vaishali (b) Rajgriha
(c) Kundalvan (d) Patliputra

112. Who had presided over the second Bodhh Sangiti?
(a) Mahakashyap
(b) Sarvakami
(c) Pushyamitra Shung
(d) Kalashok

113. Who among the following was the ruler at the time of the second Boddhist Council?
(a) Ashok (b) Shashank
(c) Kalashok (d) Ajatshatru

114. After which Boddhist Council, Buddhism was divided between 'Sthavir'and 'Mahasanghik'?
(a) First (b) Second
(c) Third (d) Fourth

115. When was the third Boddhist Council organized?
(a) 249 BC (b) 254 BC
(c) 259 BC (d) 264 BC

116. Where was the third Boddhist Council organized?
(a) Nalanda (b) Patliputra
(c) Gaya (d) Vaishali

117. Who had presided over the third Boddhist Council?
(a) Mahakashyap
(b) Sarvakami
(c) Moggaliputta Tissa
(d) Kalashok

118. In whose rule, the third Boddh Snagiti was organized?
(a) Ajatshatru (b) Dhananand
(c) Udayin (d) Ashoka

119. After which Boddhist Councils, Abhidhamm Pitaka was collected?
(a) First (b) Second
(c) Third (d) Fourth

120. When was the fourth Boddhist Council organized?
(a) 85 AD (b) 87 AD
(c) 95 AD (d) 97 AD

121. Where was the fourth Boddhist Council organized?
(a) Kundalvan (b) Nalanda
(c) Patliputra (d) Sarnath

122. Who had presided over the fourth Boddhist Council?
(a) Kalashok (b) Sarvakami
(c) Vasumitra (d) Mahakashyap

123. Who was the vice president of the fourth Boddhist Council?
(a) Ashwaghosh (b) Nagarjun
(c) Anand (d) Upali

124. In whose rule, the fourth Boddhist Council was organized?
(a) Ashoka (b) Dasrath
(c) Kanishak (d) Udayin

125. After which Boddhist Council, Buddhism was divided in Hinyan and Mahayan sects?
(a) Fourth (b) Third
(c) Second (d) First

126. In Indian Art, construction of 'Stupa', 'Chaitya' and 'Vihar' is related to which religion?
(a) Vaishnav (b) Shaiva
(c) Ajivika (d) Buddhist

127. In which religion for the first time idol worship was started?
(a) Buddhist (b) Jain
(c) Ajivika (d) Vaishnav

128. 'Tripitaka' is the text of which religion?
(a) Jain (b) Sikh'
(c) Ajivika (d) Boddhist

129. Which of the following is not a part of the Tripitaka?
(a) Vinay Pitaka
(b) Anand Pitaka
(c) Sutt Pitaka
(d) Abhidham Pitaka

130. In which of the following Gautam Buddha's teachings and sermons are collected?
(a) Sutt Pitaka
(b) Vinay Pitaka
(c) Abhidham Pitaka
(d) Anand Pitaka

131. Who had got collection of the Sutt Pitaka?
(a) Upali (b) Sariputra
(c) Anand (d) Devdutt

132. How many parts are there in Sutt Pitaka?
(a) Three (b) Four
(c) Five (d) Six

133. Which of the following are part of the Sutt Pitaka?
(a) Deergh Nikay
(b) Majjhim Nikay
(c) Anguttar Nikay
(d) All of the above

134. Khuddak Nikay is part of which Pitaka?
(a) Vinay Pitaka
(b) Sutt Pitaka
(c) Abhidham Pitaka
(d) Anand Pitaka

135. In which of the following Nikays, mention of Buddha's teachings, Ashtangik Marg and Mahaparin-irvan is made?
(a) Deergha Nikay
(b) Sanyukta Nikay
(c) Khuddak Nikay
(d) Majjhim Nikay

136. Where was mention of the sixteen mahajanpadas is made for the first time?
(a) Deergha Nikay
(b) Anguttar Nikay
(c) Majjhim Nikay
(d) All of the above

137. In which of the following Nikays collection of 549 Jatak tales related to Buddha's reincarnation is made?
(a) Anguttar Nikay
(b) Sanyukta Nikay
(c) Khuddak Nikay
(d) Majjhim Nikay

138. Who got Vinay Pitaka composed?
(a) Upali (b) Sariputra
(c) Anand (d) Devdutt

139. In which of the following, collec-tion of rules of the Buddhism are contained?
(a) Sutt Pitaka
(b) Vinay Pitaka
(c) Abhidhamb Pitaka
(d) Anand Pitaka

140. How many parts are there in Vinay Pitaka?
(a) 3 (b) 4
(c) 5 (d) 6

141. Which of the following is not a part of the Vinay Pitaka?
(a) Sutt Vibhang (b) Khandak
(c) Majjhim (d) Parivar

142. Which of the following Pitakas was composed in the form of questions-answers?
(a) Sutt Pitaka
(b) Vinay Pitaka
(c) Anand Pitaka
(d) Abhidhamb Pitaka

143. Bodh Darshan is contained in which of the Pitakas?
(a) Abhidhamb Pitaka
(b) Vinay Pitaka
(c) Sutt Pitaka
(d) Anand Pitaka

144. Who among the following was made to compose Abhidhamb Pitaka?
(a) Vasumitra
(b) Ajatshatru
(c) Ashoka
(d) Mogalliputta Tissa

145. How many Jatak tales are there?
(a) 549 (b) 547
(c) 545 (d) 543

146. The Book 'Milindpanho'is related to which sect?
(a) Boddha (b) Jain
(c) Ajivika (d) Shaiva

147. Who is the author of 'Milindpanho'?
(a) Megasthanese
(b) I Tsang
(c) Nagsen
(d) Kautilya

148. In which of the following literatures a mention is made of the conversation between the Greece Ruler Mindar and Bodh Acharya Nagsen?
(a) Deergh Nikay
(b) Sutt Pitaka
(c) Milindpanho
(d) Khuddak Nikay

149. Minandar was the ruler of which place?
(a) Arab (b) Bactriya
(c) Yunan (d) Greece

150. Bodh literature is written in which language?
(a) Avadhi (b) Magadhi
(c) Pali (d) Sanskrit

151. 'Vishuddhi Marg' is literature of which sect?
(a) Bodh (b) Jain
(c) Ajivika (d) Shaiva

152. Who is the author of 'Vishuddhi Marg'?
(a) Vasumitra
(b) Mogaliputta Tissa
(c) Buddhghosh
(d) Jivak

153. In which of the following literatures, philosophical extracts of Buddhism are contained?
(a) Milindpanho
(b) Vishuddhi Marg
(c) Nidan Katha
(d) Sutt Pitaka

154. Nidan Katha is related literature of which religion?
(a) Ajivika (b) Jain
(c) Boddhist (d) Shaiva

155. Who is the author of Nidan Katha?
(a) Vasumitra
(b) Buddhaghosh
(c) Ashvaaghosh
(d) Mogaliputta Tissa

156. Which of the following is the only biography of Gautam Buddha in Pali language?
(a) Milindpanho (b) Nidan Katha
(c) Vinay Pitaka (d) Sutt Pitaka

157. 'Attha' tales are literature related to which sect?
(a) Jain (b) Boddhist
(c) Sikh (d) Ajivika

158. Commentary written on the tripitakas is in which of the following?
(a) Nidan Katha (b) Milindpanho
(c) Attha Tales (d) Jatak Tales

159. Abhdhambkosh is a literature related to which of the religions?
(a) Jain (b) Boddhist
(c) Ajivika (d) Shaiva

160. Who among the following is the author of Abhdhambkosh?
(a) Sariputra
(b) Vasubandhu
(c) Upali
(d) Mogaliputta Tissa

161. Which of the following literatures provide information about calculation of the time and the year?
(a) Abhidhambkosh
(b) Abhidhamb pitaka
(c) Sutt Pitaka
(d) Vinay Pitaka

162. 'Sandarbha Pundrik' is a literature related to which community?
(a) Jain (b) Boddhist
(c) Ajivika (d) Shaiva

163. Who is the author of Sandarbha Pundarik?
(a) Vasubandhu (b) Nagsen
(c) Vasumitra (d) Ashwagosh

164. Sandarbh Pundarik is related to which community?
(a) Hinyan (b) Mahayan
(c) Vajrayan (d) Both (a) and (b)

165. In which of the following literatures, Bhagwan Buddha has been called Amitabh viz., a person who sits in the heaven?
(a) Milindpanho
(b) Abhdhambkosh
(c) Abhidhamb Pitaka
(d) Sandarbha Pundrika

166. 'Pragya Parmita' is a literature related to which community?
(a) Jain (b) Boddhist
(c) Ajivika (d) Shaiva

167. Who is the author of Pragya Parmita?
(a) Nagarjun (b) Vasumitra
(c) Vasubandhu (d) Ashwaghosh

168. Who among the following had given the doctrine of nihilism (Shunyavaad ka siddhant)?
(a) Ashwaghosh (b) Vasubandhu
(c) Vasumitra (d) Nagarjun

169. In which of the following literatures the doctrine of nihilism is found?
(a) Milindpanho
(b) Pragya Parmita
(c) Sandharbha Pundrika
(d) Attha Tales

170. Akutomaya is literature related to which religion?
(a) Jain (b) Shaiva
(c) Ajivika (d) Boddhist

171. Who among the following is the author of Akutomaya?
(a) Vasumitra (b) Nagarjuna
(c) Vasubandhu (d) Ashwaghosh

172. Lalit-vistar is a text related with which community?
(a) Boddhist (b) Jain
(c) Sikh (d) Ajivika

173. Who among the following is the author of Lalit Vistar?
(a) Ashwaghosh (b) Nagsen
(c) Vasumitra (d) Anand

174. Which of the following literatures is called the Light of Asia?
(a) Lalit Vistar (b) Akutomaya
(c) Milindpanho (d) Deerghnikay

175. Bhashassutra is a literature related to which community?
(a) Jain (b) Boddhist
(c) Shaiva (d) Vaishnav

176. Who is the author of Bhasha Sutra?
(a) Vasumitra (b) Ashwaghosh
(c) Nagsen (d) Sariputra

177. Which of the following literatures is related to Chaturtha Bodh Sangiti?
(a) Lalit Vistar (b) Milindpanho
(c) Akutamaya (d) Vibhasha Sutra

178. 'Sondranand' text is related to which community?
(a) Jain (b) Ajivika
(c) Boddhist (d) Sikh

179. Who is the author of Sondranand text?
(a) Vasumitra (b) Ashwaghosh
(c) Nagsen (d) Upali

180. In which of the following literatures, there is a reference of Gautam Buddha's step brother becoming a Bodh follower?
(a) Lalit Vistar (b) Vibhasha Sutra
(c) Sondranand (d) Akutomaya

181. Who is the author of Buddha Charitra?
(a) Ashwaghosh (b) Vasumitra
(c) Upali (d) Sariputra

182. Which of the following is considered an epic of Buddhism?
(a) Lalit Vistar
(b) Akutomaya
(c) Buddha Charitra
(d) Sondranand

183. Deepvansh is a literature associated with which religion?
(a) Bodh (b) Jain
(c) Ajivika (d) Shaiva

184. Which of the following is history of Srilanka's Bodh literature?
(a) Lalit Vistar
(b) Akutomaya
(c) Buddha Charitra
(d) Deepvansh

185. 'Mahavansh' is related to which community?
(a) Jain (b) Ajivika
(c) Boddhist (d) Shaiva

186. Who is the author of Mahavansh?
(a) Vasumitra
(b) Bhdant Mahanama
(c) Ashwaghosh
(d) Upali

187. From which of the following texts knowledge about Ujjain's Viceroy is acquired?
(a) Mahavansh
(b) Deepvansh
(c) Lalit Vistar
(d) Milind Panho

188. Which text reveals the details of the third Boddhist Council?
(a) Buddha Charitra
(b) Lalit Vistar
(c) Akutomaya
(d) Mahavansh

189. The commentary called 'Granth Vanshnathpakshini' is written on which literature?
(a) Deepvansh (b) Mahavansh
(c) Lalit Vistar (d) Akutomaya

190. 'Divyavadan' is a text related to which religion?
(a) Ajivika (b) Shaiva
(c) Boddhist (d) Jain

191. Which of the following Boddhist text is a Nepali literature?
(a) Deepvansh (b) Mahavansh
(c) Akutomaya (d) Divyavadan

192. How many chapters are there in 'Divyavadan'?
(a) 2 (b) 3
(c) 4 (d) 5

193. Which of the following is a part of 'Divyavadan'?
(a) Buddhavadan
(b) Ashokavadan
(c) Kunalavadan
(d) Both (b) and (c)

194. 'Bodh Bhikshu' believing in the original teachings and sermons of Gautam Buddha are called?
(a) Sthavir (b) Hotwar
(c) Jangam (d) Sutta

195. Bodh Bhikshus desiring change are called?
(a) Thervadi
(b) Mahasanghik
(c) Sthavir
(d) Jangam

196. Who was the promoter of the Sthavir community?
(a) Nagsen
(b) Vasumitra
(c) Mahakachhayan
(d) Upali

197. Who was the promoter of 'Mahasangeet' community?
(a) Vasubandhu (b) Mahakashyap
(c) Sarvakami (d) Anand

198. On extinction of the Sthavir community, which community had emerged in India?
(a) Shrawastivad (b) Gayavad
(c) Ashokavad (d) Kunalvad

199. Hinyan was originally a _______ Sangh.
(a) Mahasangh (b) Viharvad
(c) Sthavir (d) Both (a) and (b)

200. Mahayan was a _________Sangh.
(a) Mahasangh (b) Thervad
(c) Upasakvad (d) Rochakvad

201. In which of the following 'Hinyan' followers keep a faith?
(a) Char Arya Satya
(b) Ashtangik Marg
(c) Dus Sheel
(d) All of the above

202. What is the model of 'Hinyan' community?
(a) Aharta (b) Braharta
(c) Anand (d) Oras

203. According to Hinyan, Buddha was a human being and he used to oppose________.
(a) Idol worship
(b) Education
(c) Anthropomorphism
(d) Whammy

204. One is 'Ahart' if only he tries to achieve__________ for himself.
(a) Kaivalya (b) Samadhi
(c) Sanlekhna (d) Nirvana

205. In__________only, Buddha was considered a deity and hence his idol worship started.
(a) Hinyan (b) Mahayan
(c) Karmyan (d) Yogyan

206. What was the language of the literature pertaining to Mahayan?
(a) Pali (b) Magadhi
(c) Prakrit (d) Sanskrit

207. In which community Buddha has been called 'Bodhsatva'?
(a) Hinyan (b) Mahayan
(c) Vajrayan (d) Karamyaan

208. Buddha had with the help of his five disciples established a Bodh Sangh at________.
(a) Bodhgaya (b) Satna
(c) Vaishali (d) Sarnath

209. Bodh Sangh was based on the system of__________.
(a) Rajtantrik
(b) Jantantrik
(c) Tanashah
(d) Anthropomorphism

210. A person of the following minimum age was allowed to adopt Buddhism.
(a) 15 (b) 16
(c) 17 (d) 18

JAINISM

1. Who was the first 'Tirthankar' of Jainism?
(a) Rishabh Dev
(b) Ajitnath
(c) Mahavir Swami
(d) Parshvanath

2. Who among the following is considered to be the founder of Jainism?
(a) Ajitnath
(b) Adinath
(c) Mahavir Swami
(d) Parshvanath

3. How many Tirthankars are there in Jaininsm?

(a) 22 (b) 23
(c) 24 (d) 25

4. **Who among the following was the 23rd, Tirthankar of Jainism?**
(a) Adinath (b) Parshvanath
(c) Ajitnath (d) Mahavir Swami

5. **Who was the 24th Tirthankar in Jainism?**
(a) Mahavir Swami
(b) Rishabhdev
(c) Adinath
(d) Parshvanath

6. **The word Jain is made of 'Jin' word of Sanskrit which means________.**
(a) Kalyani (b) Sewak
(c) Suyodha (d) Vijeta

7. **The one who wins over himself is called ________ in Jainism.**
(a) Veetrag (b) Hotwar
(c) Sthavir (d) Jangam

8. **The promoters of Jainism are called________.**
(a) Swami (b) Pandit
(c) Dev (d) Tirthankar

9. **The details of how many Tirthankars of Jainism are not available in history?**
(a) 20 (b) 21
(c) 22 (d) 23

10. **The historical detail of which of the following tirthankars is available?**
(a) Rishabhdev
(b) Parshvanath
(c) Mahavir Swami
(d) Both (b) and (c)

11. **Parshvanath was the son of which place's king?**
(a) Kashi (b) Mathura
(c) Ayodhya (d) Patliputra

12. **whose father was Ashvadev among the following Tirthankars?**
(a) Rishabhdev (b) Parshvanath
(c) Adinath (d) Ajitnath

13. **At what age Parshvanath had renunciated his house?**
(a) 30 (b) 32
(c) 34 (d) 36

14. **After how many days' penance, Parshvanath was enlightened?**
(a) 75 (b) 78
(c) 83 (d) 85

15. **On which mountain, Parshvanath got enlightened?**
(a) Samved
(b) Mount Abu
(c) Kanchanjunga
(d) Makalu

16. **The disciples of Parshvanath are called.**
(a) Samgranthi (b) Nigranthi
(c) Samrupi (d) Swathir

17. **What was criticized by Parshvanath?**
(a) Wealth accumulation
(b) Vaidik Rituals
(c) Polytheism
(d) Both (b) and (c)

18. **Who was the major disciple of Parshvanath?**
(a) Keshi (b) Sariputra
(c) Upali (d) Anand

19. **Which of the following is the original teaching of Parshvanath?**
(a) Brahmcharya(b) Satya
(c) Astey (d) Both (b) and (c)

20. **The parents of the 24th, Tirthankar were the disciples of whom?**
(a) Parshvanath (b) Ajitnath
(c) Rishabhdev (d) Both (b) and (c)

21. **At which place was Mahavira born?**
(a) Kundgram (b) Kundalvan
(c) Saligram (d) Kumhrar

22. **Kundgram comes under which district of present day Bihar?**
(a) Nalanda (b) Vaishali
(c) Siwan (d) Patna

23. What was the name of the mother of Mahavir Swami?
(a) Kaushalya (b) Yomati
(c) Yashodhara (d) Trishala

24. The mother of Mahavir Swami was the sister of the King of which place?
(a) Lichhavi (b) Videh
(c) Darbhanga (d) Angg

25. What was the name of the father of Mahavir Swami?
(a) Janak (b) Dashrath
(c) Siddhartha (d) Jivak

26. Mahavir Swami's father was related to which clan?
(a) Kshatriya (b) Vaishya
(c) Brahmin (d) Shudra

27. Mahavir Swami was married to the daughter of which clan?
(a) Smargi (b) Udan
(c) Kundian (d) Toppo

28. Who of the following was the wife of Mahavir Swami?
(a) Mahamayadevi
(b) Yashoda
(c) Yashumati
(d) Prajapati Gautami

29. What was the name of the daughter of Mahavir Swami?
(a) Prabhavati (b) Premvati
(c) Priyamvada (d) Priyadarshana

30. Of the following whom did Priyadarshana marry?
(a) Jamali (b) Anand
(c) Gautam (d) Upasen

31. Where did Mahavir Swami die?
(a) Vaishali (b) Nalanda
(c) Pavapuri (d) Patliputra

32. When was Mahavir Swami born?
(a) 540 BC (b) 525 BC
(c) 515 BC (d) 508 BC

33. When did Mahavir Swami die?
(a) 475 BC (b) 470 BC
(c) 468 BC (d) 463 BC

34. At what age did Mahavir Swami die?
(a) 80 (b) 76
(c) 75 (d) 72

35. What was the childhood name of Mahavir Swami?
(a) Sidhharth (b) Devdutt
(c) Anand (d) Vardhman

36. On whose advice did Mahavir Swami renunciate his house?
(a) Father
(b) Mother
(c) Elder Brother
(d) Wife

37. What was the name of the elder brother of Mahavir Swami?
(a) Gopalvardhan
(b) Navinvardhan
(c) Nandivardhan
(d) Gautamvardhan

38. After how many months of leaving his house, Mahavir Swami left clothes?
(a) 18 months (b) 15 months
(c) 13 months (d) 11 months

39. At what age, Mahavir Swami got enlightened?
(a) 45 (b) 43
(c) 42 (d) 40

40. After how many years of penance, Mahavir Swami got enlightened?
(a) 10 (b) 11
(c) 12 (d) 13

41. On the banks of which river, Mahavir Swami got enlightened?
(a) Niranjana (b) Gandak
(c) Punpun (d) Rijupalika

42. Under which tree, Mahavir Swami got enlightened?
(a) Goolar (b) Saal
(c) Peepal (d) Mango

43. In Jainism, the supreme knowledge is called as _________.
(a) Sanlekhna (b) Nirvana
(c) Kaivalya (d) Jain Satva

44. What is the meaning of Kaivalya?
(a) Well-wisher
(b) Incarnation of the deity
(c) A person acquiring supreme knowledge
(d) An unworthy person

45. What was the name given to the disciples of Mahavir Swami?
(a) Mahant (b) Swami
(c) Jaini (d) Sanmargi

46. Who among the following was the main disciple of Mahavir Swami?
(a) Sariputra
(b) Upali
(c) Anand
(d) Indrabhuti Gautam

47. Who among the following was the first disciple of Mahavir Swami?
(a) Anand
(b) Indrabhuti Gautam
(c) Jamali
(d) Rupali

48. Where did Mahavir Swami deliver his first sermon?
(a) Rajgriha (b) Vaishali
(c) Nalanda (d) Patliputra

49. Who among the following was a disciple of Mahavir Swami?
(a) Pradyot Sen
(b) Udayin
(c) Bimbisara
(d) All of the above

50. Who among the following was not a contemporary of Mahavir Swami?
(a) Ashoka
(b) Ajatshatru
(c) Kalashok
(d) Both (a) and (b)

51. 'Triratna' is a principle of which religion?
(a) Jain (b) Ajivika
(c) Shaiva (d) Bodh

52. Who among the following is included in 'triratna' of Jainism?
(a) Samyak Knowledge
(b) Samyak deed
(c) Samyak Faith
(d) All of the above

53. On which of the following 'triratnas', maximum emphasis was given?
(a) Samyak Deed
(b) Samyak Knowledge
(c) Samyak faith
(d) Both (b) and (c)

54. In which of the following, the followers of Jainism have faith?
(a) God
(b) Reincarnation
(c) Soul
(d) Both (b) and (c)

55. In Jainism, for compliance of moral duty, ______ mahavrats have been suggested?
(a) 2 (b) 3
(c) 4 (d) 5

56. Which of the following is not included in the five 'Mahavratas'?
(a) Satya (b) Prem
(c) Astey (d) Aprigriha

57. Which Mahavrata was added by Mahavir Swami?
(a) Satya
(b) Ahimsa
(c) Brahmcharya
(d) Astey

58. Amongst the Jainism followers who were married, what did they need to follow?
(a) Mahavrat (b) Anuvrat
(c) Karamvrat (d) Dharmvrat

59. How many Anuvratas do Jain followers need to comply?
(a) 2 (b) 3
(c) 4 (d) 5

60. In Jainism how many 'Shikshavratas' are provided for?
(a) 2 (b) 3
(c) 4 (d) 5

61. Who among the following rulers had committed his 'Sanlekhna' (fasting to death)?
(a) Ashoka
(b) Ajatshatru
(c) Chandragupt I
(d) Chandragupta Maurya

62. Which religion has propounded the principle of 'Anekatavad' and 'Syadvad'?
(a) Boddhist (b) Jain
(c) Ajivika (d) Shaiva

63. Jains have imagined ________ kind of justice to explain 'Param Tatva' (Supreme Truth)?
(a) Kupbhang (b) Sanvar
(c) Saptbhang (d) Khet

64. What is meant by 'Syadvad'?
(a) Definite
(b) Impossible
(c) Possibly (Sambhavata)
(d) Welfare

65. How many types of 'Karma' Jainism talks about?
(a) 6 (b) 7
(c) 8 (d) 9

66. ______conditions are called an object under Jainism.
(a) 3 (b) 4
(c) 5 (d) 6

67. When was the first Jain Sangiti organized?
(a) 322–298 BC
(b) 320–292 BC
(c) 318–290 BC
(d) 315–288 BC

68. Where was the first Jain Sangiti organized?
(a) Vaishali (b) Nalanda
(c) Pavapuri (d) Patliputra

69. Who had presided over the first Jain Sangiti?
(a) Balbhadra (b) Sthoolbhadra
(c) Nagsen (d) Ashwasen

70. In whose rule, the first Jain Sangiti was completed?
(a) Chandragupt Maurya
(b) Kalashok
(c) Prasenjit
(d) Ajatshatru

71. How many parts were compiled in Jainism after the first Jain Sangiti?
(a) 10 (b) 11
(c) 12 (d) 13

72. How many Sangitis in total were organized in Jainism?
(a) 2 (b) 3
(c) 4 (d) 5

73. Jainism was divided after which of these Sangitis?
(a) First (b) Second
(c) Third (d) Fourth

74. In how many sects, Jainism was divided?
(a) 2 (b) 3
(c) 4 (d) 5

75. Which of the following is a sect of Jainism?
(a) Nilambar (b) Shwetamber
(c) Digamber (d) Both (b) and (c)

76. When was the second Jain Sangiti organized?
(a) 483 AD (b) 498 AD
(c) 507 AD (d) 512 AD

77. Where was the second Jain Sangiti organized?
(a) Vaishali (b) Vallabhi
(c) Kundalvan (d) Pavapuri

78. Who had presided over the second Jain Sangiti?
(a) Devardhi Kshmasharvan
(b) Devkinandan
(c) Kapilmuni
(d) Vedacharya

79. After which Sangiti the principles of Jainism were written?
(a) First (b) Second
(c) Third (d) Fourth

80. Jain literature is called__________.
(a) Aagam (b) Jatak
(c) Padam (d) Chetan

81. What was the language of Jain Literature?
(a) Sanskrit (b) Pali
(c) Prakrit (d) Both (b) and (c)

82. 14 'Poorvas' is literature of which sect?
(a) Digambar
(b) Shwetambar
(c) Both (a) and (b)
(d) None of the above

83. 14 'Poorvas' is literature related to which religion?
(a) Ajivika (b) Jain
(c) Shaiva (d) Boddhist

84. 12 'Ang' is literature of which religion?
(a) Jain (b) Boddhist
(c) Ajivika (d) Vaishnava

85. 'Achrang Sutra' is literature of which religion?
(a) Shaiva (b) Vaishnava
(c) Jains (d) Boddhist

86. In which of the following literatures, rules relating to rearing of the Jain 'Bhikshuks' are compiled?
(a) 14 Poorvas
(b) 12 Ang
(c) Achrang Sutra
(d) Brahm Sutra

87. Bhagwati Sutra is a text related to which community?
(a) Bodh (b) Jains
(c) Ajivika (d) Shaiva

88. Which of the following was compiled by Sthoolbhadra?
(a) Bhagwati Sutra
(b) 14 Poorvas
(c) 12 Ang
(d) Achrang Sutra

89. In which of the texts , there is a mention of 16 Mahajanpadas for the first time?
(a) 14 Poorvas
(b) 12 Ang
(c) Achrang Sutra
(d) Bhagwati Sutra

90. In which Jain Text, imagination of heaven and hell has been made?
(a) Kalpa Sutra (b) Bhagwati Sutra
(c) 12 Ang (d) Achrang Sutra

91. In which of the following literatures, life style of the Jain Tirthankars is mentioned?
(a) Bhagwati Sutra
(b) 12 Ang
(c) 14 Poorvas
(d) Achrang Sutra

92. From which of the following texts, Jainism was developed?
(a) Kalp Sutra
(b) Bhagwati Sutra
(c) Uttradhyan Sutra
(d) 12 Ang

93. In which of the following texts, mention of a conversation between Indrabhuti Gautam and Prajapati is made?
(a) Uttradhyan Sutra
(b) Kalp Sutra
(c) 12 Ang
(d) Bhagwati Sutra

94. Kalp Sutra is a literature related to which religion?
(a) Boddhist (b) Jain
(c) Shiva (d) Ajivika

95. Who had compiled Kalp Sutra?
(a) Mahavir Swami
(b) Chandragupt Maurya
(c) Ashvasen
(d) Bhadrabahu

96. In which of the Jain literatures, mention about 'Gandhars' is made?

(a) Kalp Sutra
(b) Bhagwati Sutra
(c) Uttradhyan Sutra
(d) 12 Ang

97. In Kalp Sutra, how many gandhars are talked about?
(a) 10 (b) 11
(c) 12 (d) 13

98. Parishishtparvan is a text of which religion?
(a) Jain (b) Boddh
(c) Ajivika (d) Shaiva

99. Who compiled the Parishishtparvan?
(a) Bhadrabahu (b) Hemchandra
(c) Paribhuti (d) Sariputra

100. Scholar Hemchandra was the court scholar of which state's dynasty?
(a) Maharashtra (b) Bihar
(c) Gujrat (d) Karnataka

101. Where did Chandragupt Maurya adopt 'Sanlekhna'?
(a) Vallabhi (b) Shravanbelgola
(c) Pawapuri (d) Cylone

102. After Bhadrabahu who was the most popular scholar of Jainism?
(a) Tarasuri (b) Narpat Maharaj
(c) Suripati (d) Hemchandra

103. Which of the following is called the small literature of Jainism?
(a) Bhagwati Sutra
(b) Kalp Sutra
(c) Parishishtparvan
(d) 12 Ang

104. According to which of the following texts, there was a famine for 12 years in the rule of Chandragupt Maurya?
(a) Parishishtparvan
(b) Bhagwati Sutra
(c) Kalp Sutra
(d) Uttradhyan Sutra

105. Which of the following rulers had travelled to Southern India with Bhadrabahu?
(a) Ajatshatru
(b) Ashoka
(c) Chandragupt Maurya
(d) Udayin

106. 'Avsadgavon' is literature of which religion?
(a) Ajivika (b) Jain
(c) Boddhist (d) Shaiva

107. In which of the following texts, there is a tale of 13 wealthy traders joining Jainism?
(a) Kalp Sutra
(b) Avsadgavon
(c) Bhagwati Sutra
(d) Achrang Sutra

THE DIFFERENT SECTS OF JAINISM

1. Who had stayed back at Magadh in the time of famine?
(a) Bhadrabahu
(b) Sampat Sen
(c) Sthool Bhadra
(d) Tara Suri

2. From which of the following communities, people had stayed back at Magadh at the time of famine?
(a) Shwetambar (b) Digamber
(c) Ajivika (d) Akriyavadi

3. What name is given to Shwetambar Jains?
(a) Yati
(b) Sadhu
(c) Acharya
(d) All of the above

4. In which community of Jainism, rules are followed in hard earnest?
(a) Shwetamber
(b) Digambar
(c) Ajivika
(d) Both (a) and (c)

5. In which community people consider Mahavir Swami as unmarried?
(a) Shwetambar (b) Ajivika
(c) Shaiva (d) Digambar

6. In which community, people do not think it necessary to have food after attaining enlightenment?
(a) Shaiva (b) Ajivika
(c) Shwetambar (d) Digamber

7. Which of the following is sub sect of the Shwetamber community?
(a) Pujera (b) Dhudhiya
(c) Karma (d) Both (a) and (b)

8. Which of the following is sub sect of Digambar community?
(a) Bisapanthi
(b) Therapanthi
(c) Samaiyyapanthi
(d) All of the above

9. Which community worships 'Mandirmargi' and Jain Tirathankars?
(a) Pujera (b) Bisapanthi
(c) Therapanthi (d) Samaiyyapanthi

10. Which community accepts only the principles?
(a) Bisapanthi (b) Dhudhiya
(c) Therapanthi (d) Taranpanthi

11. Which community used to worship the idols of jain Tirthankars?
(a) Dhudhiya
(b) Bisapanthi
(c) Therapanthi
(d) Both (b) and (c)

12. Which of the following communities did not perform idol worship?
(a) Taranpanthi (b) Bisapanthi
(c) Therapanthi (d) Pujera

13. 'Akriyavadi' community was founded by whom?
(a) Puranmal
(b) Nagarmal
(c) Puranakashyap
(d) Sariputra

14. According to which community there is no punishment attached with 'Karma'?
(a) Tarapanthi (b) Shwetamber
(c) Digamber (d) Akriyavadi

15. Who was the founder of 'Ajivika' community?
(a) Mahavir Swami
(b) Pushyamitra Shung
(c) Panini
(d) Makhli Gosal

16. Who among the following rulers had given patronage to Ajivika community?
(a) Bindusara
(b) Ashoka
(c) Dasratha
(d) All of the above

17. 'Bhotikvadi' community was founded by whom?
(a) Makhli Gosal
(b) Ajit Keshkambali
(c) Adinath
(d) Nagsen

18. Which of the following communities is called the 'Lokayat' community?
(a) Akriyavadi (b) Bhotikvadi
(c) Ajivika (d) Shaiva

19. Who among the following developed 'Charvak' philosophy?
(a) Ajitnath
(b) Ajit Keshkambali
(c) Rishabh Dev
(d) Mahavir Swami

20. What is meant by 'Charvak'?
(a) Good looking
(b) Group of sweet talking people
(c) Group of truth speaking people
(d) Both (a) and (c)

21. According to whom, Vedas were compiled by the liars, cunning and carnivorous people?
(a) Ajivika (b) Jain
(c) Boddhist (d) Charwak

22. People from Charwak philosophy do not believe in what?
(a) God
(b) Reincarnation
(c) Wealth
(d) Both (a) and (b)

23. 'Anishchayavadi' community was founded by whom?
(a) Sanjay Vethli Putra
(b) Nagsen
(c) Ashwasen
(d) Makhli Gosal

24. Which of the following communities is called 'sandehvadi' community?
(a) Ajivika
(b) Bhotikvadi
(c) Anishchyavadi
(d) Akriyavadi

POLITICAL HISTORY OF BIHAR

1. Who had determined the political history of India for the first time?
(a) James Peter
(b) Pajirter
(c) Norman Wales
(d) David Cooper

2. Which of the following words was used for the people in Rigvedic time?
(a) Jan (b) Lok
(c) Sabha (d) Samiti

3. When was the word 'Janpad' used for an area for the first time?
(a) Vedic Period
(b) Uttar Vedic Period
(c) Maurya Period
(d) Gupta Period

4. Which of the following was not a Janpad?
(a) Kashi (b) Mathura
(c) Kosal (d) Vajji

5. Where did the capital of Kashi Mahajanpad exist?
(a) Prayagraj (b) Varanasi
(c) Shringeri (d) Patna

6. In which present day state, Kashi district is located?
(a) Bihar
(b) Jharkhand
(c) Uttar Pradesh
(d) Madhya Pradesh

7. Where was the capital of Kosal Mahajanpad?
(a) Ayodhya (b) Prayagraj
(c) Shrawasti (d) Both (a) and (c)

8. Where, in the present day states Kosal Mahajanpad is located?
(a) Uttar Pradesh
(b) Rajasthan
(c) Chattisgarh
(d) Odisha

9. Where was the capital of Ang Mahajanpad?
(a) Champa (b) Vaishali
(c) Patliputra (d) Shrawasti

10. Where in the present day states Ang Mahajanpad is located?
(a) Uttar Pradesh
(b) Jharkhand
(c) Maharashtra
(d) Bihar

11. Where was the capital of Magadha Mahajanpad?
(a) Patliputra (b) Rajgriha
(c) Vaishali (d) Pawapuri

12. Where is the present location of Magadh State?
(a) Bihar (b) Karnataka
(c) Assam (d) Maharashtra

13. Where was the 'Vajji' Mahajanpad's capital located?
(a) Giriraj (b) Patliputra
(c) Nalanda (d) Vaishali

14. Where in the present day states, Vajji mahajanpad is located?
(a) Bihar (b) Assam
(c) Jharkhand (d) Uttar Pradesh

15. Where was the capital of 'Mall' Mahajanpad?
(a) Shrawasti (b) Kushinagar
(c) Prayagraj (d) Shringeri

16. Where in the present day states Mall Mahajanpad is located?
(a) Jharkhand
(b) Bihar
(c) Uttar Pradesh
(d) Both (b) and (c)

17. Where was the capital of 'Dakshini Mall' mahajanpad?
(a) Kushinagar (b) Pawapuri
(c) Virat Nagar (d) Rohtashgarh

18. Where was the capital of 'Chedi' mahajanpad?
(a) Mahishmati (b) Kundalvan
(c) Kundgram (d) Shuktimati

19. Where, in the present day states, Chedi mahajanpad is located?
(a) Uttar Pradesh
(b) Haryana
(c) Punjab
(d) Himachal Pradesh

20. Where was the capital of 'Vats' mahajanpad?
(a) Kushinagar (b) Koshambi
(c) Shrawasti (d) Shuptimati

21. Where, in the present day states Vats mahajanpad is located?
(a) Punjab (b) Haryana
(c) Bihar (d) Uttar Pradesh

22. Where was the capital of 'Kuru' Mahajanpad?
(a) Shuptimati (b) Koshambi
(c) Indraprastha (d) Kurukshetra

23. Where, in the present day states, Kuru mahajanpad is located?
(a) Haryana (b) Punjab
(c) Rajasthan (d) Bihar

24. Where was the capital of 'Uttari Panchal'?
(a) Shrawasti (b) Nalanda
(c) Pawapuri (d) Ahichhatra

25. Where was the capital of 'Dakshini Panchal'?
(a) Ahichhatra (b) Kapilya
(c) Shrawasti (d) Vaishali

26. Which of these was the capital of 'Panchal' Mahajanpad?
(a) Patliputra (b) Kapilya
(c) Koshambi (d) Champa

27. Where was the capital of 'Matsya' mahajanpad?
(a) Virat Nagar (b) Ahichhatra
(c) Vaishali (d) Kushinagar

28. In which state, Matsya Mahajanpad is located?
(a) Jharkhand
(b) Bihar
(c) Uttar Pradesh
(d) Rajasthan

29. Where was the capital of 'Shursen' mahajanpad?
(a) Mathura (b) Brindaban
(c) Kushinagar (d) Banaras

30. Where, in the present day states, Shursen mahajanpad is located?
(a) Bihar (b) Uttar Pradesh
(c) Rajasthan (d) Haryana

31. Where was the capital of 'Ashmak' mahajanpad?
(a) Patna (b) Mathura
(c) Patan (d) Vaishali

32. In which state, Ashmak Mahajanpad is located?
(a) Telangana
(b) Karnataka
(c) Tamilnadu
(d) Andhra Pradesh

33. Where was the capital of 'Uttari Avanti'?
(a) Pawapuri (b) Vallabhi
(c) Ujjain (d) Kundalvan

34. Where was the capital of Dakshini Avanti?
(a) Mahishmati (b) Shuptimati
(c) Vallabhji (d) Ujjain

35. In which state Avanti mahajanpad is located?
(a) Uttar Pradesh
(b) Madhya Pradesh
(c) Rajasthan
(d) Bihar

36. Where was the capital of 'Gandhar' Mahajanpad?
(a) Lahore (b) Ujjain
(c) Kashmir (d) Takshila

37. In which country Gandhar mahajanpad is located?
(a) India (b) Afganistan
(c) Bangladesh (d) Pakistan

38. Where was the capital of Kamboj mahajanpad?
(a) Hotwar (b) Pawapuri
(c) Hatak (d) Kundalgram

39. In which country Kamboj Mahajanpad is located?
(a) Afganistan (b) Pakistan
(c) Bangladesh (d) India

40. What was the other name of 'Vajji Sangh'?
(a) Videh (b) Basenagar
(c) Lichhavi (d) Lachhnota

41. Where was the world's first republic?
(a) Lichhavi (b) Videha
(c) Ang (d) Kosal

42. In which country Takshila now comes now?
(a) India (b) Pakistan
(c) Bangladesh (d) Afganistan

43. In which 'Veda', Ang mahajanpad was first mentioned?
(a) Rigveda (b) Samveda
(c) Atharvaveda (d) Yajurveda

44. In 'Ashtadhyayi' what other name has been given to 'Ang' mahajanpad?
(a) Vang
(b) Kalinga
(c) Pundu
(d) All of the above

45. Under which of the following mahajanpads, areas of Manbhum, Veerbhum, Murshidabad and Santhal Pargana were included?
(a) Vajji (b) Magadh
(c) Ang (d) Kosal

46. According to which of the following texts, son of King Bali had established Ang mahajanpad?
(a) Upanishad (b) Mahabharat
(c) Purana (d) Both (b) amd (c)

47. Under whose rule, Ang was completely merged with Magadh mahajanpad?
(a) Ajatshatru
(b) Chandragupt Maurya
(c) Ashoka
(d) Bimbisara

48. Who of the following was the last ruler of Ang mahajanpad?
(a) Sheshnag (b) Nagsen
(c) Devdutt (d) Brahmdutt

49. Who among the following had established 'Haryank' dynasty?
(a) Bimbisara (b) Bindusara
(c) Brahmdutt (d) Ajatshatru

50. The rulers of Haryank dynasty were related to which mahajanpad?
(a) Kosal (b) Chedi
(c) Magadh (d) Angg

51. The ruler of 'Ikshvaku' dynasty were related to which mahajanpad?
(a) Kashi (b) Angg
(c) Champa (d) Kosal

52. Prasenjit was ruler of which dynasty?
(a) Haryank (b) Gupta
(c) Maurya (d) Ikshvaku

53. Porav Dynasty was related to which mahajanpad?
(a) Kosal (b) Kuru
(c) Angg (d) Magadh

54. Udayin was ruler of which dynasty?
(a) Maurya (b) Gupta
(c) Porav (d) Ikshvaku

55. Prodhotsen was ruler of which mahajanpad?
(a) Avanti (b) Kosal
(c) Vajji (d) Angg

56. _________mahajanpad was established in around the year 725 BC .
(a) Angg (b) Kosal
(c) Vajji (d) Chedi

57. Vajji mahajanpad was a union of how many states?
(a) 8 (b) 7
(c) 6 (d) 5

58. Gyatrik, Ugra and Bhog were states of which mahajanpad?
(a) Vajji (b) Kosal
(c) Kashi (d) Angg

59. Which of the following was not a state of Vajji Mahajanpad?
(a) Lichhavi (b) Videha
(c) Ikshvaku (d) Vaishali

60. Where was the capital of the Lichhavis?
(a) Patna (b) Vallabhi
(c) Vaishali (d) Rajgriha

61. Where was the capital of Videha?
(a) Mithila (b) Girivraj
(c) Vaishali (d) Champa

62. Where was the capital of Gyatrik?
(a) Kundalvan (b) Kundgram
(c) Pawapuri (d) Nalanda

63. Where was the capital of Vajji Mahajanpad?
(a) Ujjain (b) Girivraj
(c) Champa (d) Vaishali

64. Vajji Sangh was called __________ sangh.
(a) Mithila
(b) Yatrik
(c) Lichhavi
(d) Ikshvaku

65. The ruler of Magadh Bimbisara had married daughter of the king of which kingdom?
(a) Videh (b) Lichhavi
(c) Gyatrik (d) Ugra

66. Who among the following was the son of Bimbisara?
(a) Bindusara (b) Ashoka
(c) Dasratha (d) Ajatshatru

67. 'Vajjis' had made a Mahasangh against whom with 'Mallons' and Kosal republic?
(a) Bimbisara
(b) Ajatshatru
(c) Dasratha
(d) Chandragupt Maurya

68. According to which of the following, vajjis had made a constitution to run the administration?
(a) Nagsen
(b) Brahmdutt
(c) Buddha Ghosh
(d) Mahakashyap

69. How many kings were there to run the Vajji Mahasangh?
(a) 7504 (b) 7580
(c) 7624 (d) 7707

70. The meeting of the Lichhavi Sangh used to be organized in a building called________?
(a) Naathsheel (b) Pravansheel
(c) Pragatisheel (d) Santhagar

71. The assembly of the Lichhavi Kings used to be called.
(a) Sanstha (b) Samiti
(c) Vidath (d) Mandal

72. 'Ashtkul' were present in which Mahajanpad?
(a) Angg (b) Kosal
(c) Vajji (d) Chedi

73. To look after a village, which official was appointed?
(a) Pradhan (b) Mukhiya
(c) Bhandari (d) Gamgamini

74. To look after the administration of a city, which official was appointed?
(a) Mayor (b) Adhyaksh
(c) Nagar Var (d) Purnagamik

75. For people of which Sangha, Gautam Buddha had said that so long as they would keep complying with the seven 'Dhammas' they would not be defeated by anyone?
(a) Vajji (b) Kosal
(c) Avanti (d) Chedi

76. Who used to preside over the assemblies of Vajji Sangh?
(a) Nagar Pramukh
(b) Gana Pramukh
(c) Nagar Var
(d) Sabhapati

77. What was the number determined for 'Ganapurti' of the assemblies of the Vajji Sangh?
(a) 15 (b) 18
(c) 20 (d) 22

78. In which Sangh, a decision used to be made on the basis of voting?
(a) Kosal (b) Kashi
(c) Ang (d) Vajji

79. Ballet papers of Vajji Sangh used to be made of what?
(a) Stone (b) Bronze
(c) Wood (d) Brass

80. The mention of the word 'Magadh' is made in which of the Vedas for the first time?
(a) Rigveda (b) Samveda
(c) Atharvaveda (d) Yajurveda

81. In which part of the present state of Bihar, Magadh was situated?
(a) North (b) South
(c) East (d) West

82. Which of the following was not a part of Magadh Sangh?
(a) Navada
(b) Aurangabad
(c) Bhagalpur
(d) Gaya

83. Which of the following was the central point of the Magadh Empire?
(a) Gaya (b) Rajgrih
(c) Patliputra (d) Both (b) and (c)

84. Which of the following was not a cause of advancement for Magadh Empire?
(a) Geographical situation
(b) Availability of mineral resources
(c) Downfall of the other republics
(d) Business advancement

85. Under leadership of which clan, Magadh Empire emerged?
(a) Maurya (b) Haryak
(c) Ikshvaku (d) Gupt

86. According to ancient sources, which was the first clan of Magadh?
(a) Lohar (b) Haryak
(c) Vrihdrath (d) Maurya

87. Who was the founder of Vrihdrath dynasty?
(a) Brahmdutt (b) Buddh Ghosh
(c) Vrihdrath (d) Nagsen

88. What was the name of Vrihdrath's father?
(a) Chamanram Basu
(b) Chediram Basu
(c) Chediraj Basu
(d) Brahmraj Basu

89. Where was the capital of Magadh at the time of Vrihdrath?
(a) Kushnagar (b) Shrawasti
(c) Benkunthpur (d) Kushagrapur

90. Who was the most famous king of the Vrihdrath Empire?
(a) Jarasen (b) Jarasangh
(c) Jamali (d) Budh Ghosh

91. Who became the ruler of Magadh after the death of Jarasangh?
(a) Nakuldev (b) Arjundev
(c) Randev (d) Sehdev

92. Who was the last ruler of the Vrihdrath Empire?
(a) Ripunjay (b) Komliprit
(c) Sehdev (d) Ashwasen

93. Bimbisara sat on the throne of Magadh after killing whom?
(a) Pulak (b) Ripunjay
(c) Sehdev (d) Nakuldev

MAGADH EMPIRE

1. For Kashi, there was a war between Ajatshatru and who else?
(a) Pradyot sen (b) Prasenjit
(c) Jeevak (d) Kanishka

2. Where did Prasenjit run away after defeat in the war?
(a) Shrawasti (b) Kashi
(c) Mathura (d) Kashmir

3. According to Bodh text Mahavansh, who was the founder of 'Haryak' dynasty?
(a) Prasenjit (b) Ajatshatru
(c) Pradyotsen (d) Bimbisara

4. At what age Bimbisara took over the throne?
(a) 15 (b) 17
(c) 21 (d) 23

5. Where did Bimbisara make the capital of Magadh?
(a) Rajpur (b) Rajgrih
(c) Vaishali (d) Patliputra

6. Who was the appointed architect of Rajgrih?
(a) Ashwasen (b) Nagasen
(c) Mahagovind (d) Mahakashyap

7. What policy Bimbisara adopted to uplift Magadh?
(a) Marital relations
(b) Policy of friendship
(c) Policy of victory
(d) All of the above

8. Bimbisar had established marital relations with the rulers of which other empires?
(a) Kosal
(b) Lichhavi
(c) Punjab
(d) All of the above

9. Bimbisara got Kashi in dowry on marrying the sister of the king of which empire?
(a) Kosal
(b) Avanti
(c) Lichhavi
(d) None of the above

10. Bimbisara established relationship of friendship with the ruler of which empire?
(a) Kosal (b) Avanti
(c) Lichhavi (d) Angg

11. Bimbisara appointed his son as the ruler of which mahajanpad?
(a) Angg (b) Kosal
(c) Chedi (d) Vajji

12. Who in the history included elephants permanently in his army?
(a) Ajatshatru (b) Vrihdrath
(c) Jarasangh (d) Bimbisara

13. Ajatshatru became the ruler of Magadh after killing whom?
(a) Prasenjit (b) Bimbisara
(c) Vrihdrath (d) Jarasandh

14. State the period of rule of Bimbisara?
(a) 544-492 BC
(b) 530-490 BC
(c) 525-488 BC
(d) 520-485 BC

15. State the period of rule of Ajatshatru.
(a) 495-472 BC
(b) 493-468 BC
(c) 493-461 BC
(d) 490-458 BC

16. Ajatshatru was the follower of which religion?
(a) Jain (b) Shaiva
(c) Boddhist (d) Ajivika

17. What was the surname of Ajatshatru?
(a) Angad (b) Kunik
(c) Samar (d) Anand

18. In whose rule, Kosal was merged permanently with Magadh?
(a) Bimbisara (b) Ajatshatru
(c) Ashoka (d) Vrihdrath

19. Ajatshatru used weapons like 'rathmusal' and 'kantakshila' in war with whom?
(a) Vajji (b) Kosal
(c) Angg (d) Chedi

20. Ajatshatru made a cantonment on the confluence of which of the rivers?
(a) Ganga-Sone
(b) Ganga-Gandak
(c) Gandak-Sone-Gandak
(d) Ganga-Gandak-Sone

21. Ajatshatru had got constructed a security fort at which place?
(a) Patliputra (b) Nalanda
(c) Vaishali (d) Rajgriha

22. Ajatshatru attacked whom after defeating the Lichhavis?
(a) Mull (b) Vajji
(c) Ang (d) Kashi

23. Ajatshatru developed marital relations with which sangh to make it his friend?
(a) Mull (b) Angg
(c) Kosal (d) Vats

24. Who had got constructed 'Stupa' 10 years after 'Mahaparinirvan' of Gautam Buddha?
(a) Bimbisara (b) Vrihdrath
(c) Jarasangh (d) Ajatshatru

25. Where did Ajatshatru get constructed 'Stupa' on the remains of Buddha?
(a) Rajgriha (b) Vaishali
(c) Vallabhi (d) Patliputra

26. Amrapali was 'Nagarvadhu' of which place?
(a) Patliputra (b) Vallabhi
(c) Nalanda (d) Vaishali

27. Who among the following had developed love relations with Amrapali?
(a) Vrihdrath (b) Bimbisara
(c) Ajatshatru (d) Jarasangh

28. In which of the following caves, the first Buddhist council was conducted?
(a) Saptkarini (b) Saptparni
(c) Girnar (d) Barabar

29. Who had become the ruler of Magadh after Ajatshatru?
(a) Udayin
(b) Kalashok
(c) Chandragupt Maurya
(d) Ashoka

30. Who had killed Ajatshatru?
(a) Kalashok (b) Udayin
(c) Brahmdutt (d) Ghananand

31. What relationship Ajatshatru had with Udayin?
(a) Father and son
(b) Son and father
(c) Brothers
(d) Uncle-Nephew

32. Udayin in has father's empire was Governor of which place?
(a) Champa (b) Kashi
(c) Ujjain (d) Vaishali

33. Who among the following had established Patliputra City?
(a) Bimbisara (b) Ajatshatru
(c) Udayin (d) Jarasangh

34. On the confluence of which river, Udayin had developed Patliputra City?
(a) Ganga-Gandak
(b) Gandak-Sone
(c) Ganga-Sone
(d) Gandak-Kosi

35. Which city was made the capital city by Udayin?
(a) Vaishali (b) Vallabhi
(c) Champa (d) Patliputra

36. Udayin was follower of which religion/sect?
(a) Jain (b) Boddhist
(c) Shaiva (d) Ajivika

37. Where did Udayin get constructed one 'Chaityagriha'?
(a) Vaishali (b) Vallabhi
(c) Nalanda (d) Patliputra

38. Palak was king of which area?
(a) Avanti (b) Kashi
(c) Champa (d) Chedi

39. Who killed Udayin?
(a) Ajatshatru
(b) Bimbisara
(c) Jarasangh
(d) None of the above

40. Who was the last ruler of 'Haryak' dynasty?
(a) Nagsen (b) Nagdashak
(c) Nagdutt (d) Nagarjun

41. Nagdashak was killed by whom?
(a) Shishunag (b) Udayin
(c) Ajatshatru (d) Jarasangh

42. Shishunag was 'Amatya' of which place?
(a) Vaishali (b) Patliputra
(c) Nalanda (d) Kashi

43. In 'Purans' what name has been given to Nagdashak?
(a) Pundu (b) Darshak
(c) Jamali (d) Jamboot

44. Who had established 'Shishunag' dynasty?
(a) Vrihdrath (b) Sheshnag
(c) Nagsen (d) Shishunag

45. During which period, Shishunag ruled over his kingdom?
(a) 412-340 BC
(b) 412-345 BC
(c) 415-348 BC
(d) 415-350 BC

46. What was the period of Udayin's rule?
(a) 470-435 BC
(b) 465-430 BC
(c) 461-444 BC
(d) 470-450 BC

47. Shishunag had shifted the capital of Magadh from Patliputra to which place?
(a) Nalanda (b) Pavapuri
(c) Patna (d) Vaishali

48. Over which state Shishunag achieved victory?
(a) Vats
(b) Koshambi
(c) Avanti
(d) All of the above

49. When did Shishunag die?
(a) 398 BC (b) 396 BC
(c) 394 BC (d) 392 BC

50. Who had become ruler of Magadh after Shishunag?
(a) Nagsen (b) Brahmsen
(c) Jarasangh (d) Kalashok

51. What was the surname of Kalashok?
(a) Koshal (b) Kunik
(c) Kakvarn (d) Kaithya

52. Kalashok had developed the capital of Magadh at which place?
(a) Vaishali (b) Patliputra
(c Ujjain (d) Kashi

53. Who was the best ruler of Shishunag dynasty?
(a) Kalashok
(b) Shishunag
(c) Nagsen
(d) Brahmsen

54. Who among the following was the last ruler of Shishunag dynasty?
(a) Nagsen
(b) Kalashok
(c) Nandivardhan
(d) Narayansen

55. Who of the following had ended the Shishunag dynasty?
(a) Nagsen
(b) Mahapadmanand
(c) Nandivardhan
(d) Narayan Sen

56. Who among the following had established 'Nanda' dynasty?
(a) Mahapadmanand
(b) Parmanand
(c) Dhananand
(d) Uttamanand

57. Under whose dynasty rule, Magadh's power reached its highest level?
(a) Haryak (b) Shishunag
(c) Vrihdrath (d) Nand

58. Who was the most famous ruler of Nanda dynasty?
(a) Parmanand
(b) Mahapadmanand
(c) Dhananand
(d) Both (b) and (c)

59. Who of the following is called 'part of Kali'?
(a) Shishunag
(b) Mahapadmanand
(c) Dhananand
(d) Parmanand

60. Who of the following is called the reincarnation of Parshuram, Bhargava and Ekrat etc.?
(a) Chandragupt Maurya
(b) Ashok
(c) Dhananand
(d) Mahapadmanand

61. Who was the first ruler of Magadh who had unfurled his victory flag over the area south of the 'Vindhya' mountains?
(a) Chandragupt Maurya
(b) Mahapadmanand
(c) Dhananand
(d) Kalashok

62. Who was the ruler who had brought a Jain idol from Orissa to Magadh?
(a) Ajatshatru
(b) Udayin
(c) Kalashok
(d) Mahapadmanand

63. Who was the last ruler of Nanda dynasty?
(a) Gopalnand (b) Parmanand
(c) Brihanand (d) Dhananand

64. Under whose reign, Alexander had attacked India?
(a) Ajatshatru (b) Udayin
(c) Dhananand (d) Kalashok

65. Alexander was the ruler of which country?
(a) Yunnan (b) Greece
(c) England (d) Azrbaijan

66. When did Alexander attack India?
(a) 334 BC (b) 328 BC
(c) 326 BC (d) 324 BC

67. Who had defeated Dhananand?
(a) Chandragupta Maurya
(b) Ashoka
(c) Ajatshatru
(d) Udayin

68. When did Chandragupt Maurya defeat Dhananand?
(a) 320 BC (b) 322 BC
(c) 324 BC (d) 326 BC

69. The rulers of the Nanda dynasty were followers of which religion?
(a) Jain
(b) Boddhist
(c) Ajivika
(d) Shaiva

70. The ruler of Nanda dynasty belonged to which caste?
(a) Brahmin (b) Kshatriya
(c) Vaishya (d) Shudra

71. After Nanda dynasty, which dynasty ruled Magadh?
(a) Maurya (b) Shishunag
(c) Vrihdrath (d) Shung

72. Who was the most powerful king of the Maurya dynasty?
(a) Ashoka
(b) Bindusara
(c) Chandragupt Maurya
(d) Both (b) and (c)

73. Who of the following was the founder of Maurya dynasty?
(a) Ashoka
(b) Bindusara
(c) Chandragupta Maurya
(d) Dasrath

74. According to which text, Chandragupt Maurya was a 'Shudra'?
(a) Brahmin Granth
(b) Vishnupuran
(c) Mudrarakshasa
(d) All of the above

75. According to whom Chandragupta Maurya was a 'Parsik'?
(a) Spooner (b) Dollar
(c) James Dot (d) Kevin Radd

76. Chandragupta Maurya was known by which name?
(a) Stratokotus (b) Sandrokotus
(c) Endrokotus (d) Both (b) and (c)

77. With whose co-operation, Chandragupt Maurya won states in Northern-Western areas?
(a) Ashoka (b) Bindusara
(c) Kautilya (d) Dasratha

78. Which of the following states were won by Chandragupt Maurya?
(a) Punjab (b) Sindh
(c) Kalinga (d) Both (a) and (b)

79. According to Jain and Boddhist texts, Chandragupta Maurya was related to which clan?
(a) Morey Kshatriya
(b) Dev Kshatriya
(c) Surya Kshatriya
(d) Maurya Kshatriya

80. After the death of Alexander, who became the ruler of Babylon?
(a) Nicholas (b) Seleucus
(c) Doppler (d) James I

81. When did a treaty take place between Chandragupt Maurya and Seleucus?
(a) 301 BC (b) 302 BC
(c) 303 BC (d) 304 BC

82. What was the name of the daughter of Seleucus?
(a) Helena (b) Mariya
(c) Stiti (d) Camila

83. Which ruler had married the daughter of Celuecus?
(a) Chandragupta I
(b) Chandragupt Maurya
(c) Udayin
(d) Ashoka

84. What places were given to Chandragupt Maurya in dowry?
(a) Kabul
(b) Kandhar
(c) Herat
(d) All of the above

85. How many elephants were gifted by Chandragupt Maurya to Seleucus?
(a) 200 (b) 300
(c) 400 (d) 500

86. Seleucus had sent whom to the court of Chandragupt Maurya?
(a) Megasthanese
(b) James Peter
(c) Thomas Cook
(d) Nooniz

87. Who of the following rulers is called India's Liberator?
(a) Mahapadmanand
(b) Kalashok
(c) Ashoka
(d) Chandragupt Maurya

88. On which mountain, Chandragupta Maurya had performed penance?

(a) Mahendragiri
(b) Chandangiri
(c) Makalu
(d) Nilgiri

89. Who after Chandragupt Maurya became the ruler of Magadh?
(a) Bimbisara (b) Ashoka
(c) Dasrath (d) Bindusara

90. When did Bindusara become ruler of Magadh?
(a) 302 BC (b) 300 BC
(c) 298 BC (d) 296 BC

91. Who of the following rulers was called 'Amitraghat'?
(a) Chandragupt Maurya
(b) Bindusara
(c) Ashoka
(d) Dasratha

92. The Greeks had called 'Amitrochates' to which ruler?
(a) Dasratha
(b) Chandragupt Maurya
(c) Ashoka
(d) Bindusara

93. Which of the following was the other name of Bindusara?
(a) Singhsen (b) Kunik
(c) Kunal (d) Keshav

94. Who was sent to curb the revolution of Taxila?
(a) Chandragupt Maurya
(b) Dasratha
(c) Ashoka
(d) Bindusara

95. Ashoka was administrator of which place?
(a) Ujjain (b) Vaishali
(c) Nalanda (d) Vallabhi

96. The ruler of which place had sent an ambassador to Mauryan Court?
(a) Syria (b) Japan
(c) Thailand (d) Mangolia

97. Which Syrian ruler had sent his ambassador to India?
(a) Seleucus
(b) Antiyok
(c) Nelson Trump
(d) Kevin Red

98. Which of the following was a Syrian ambassador?
(a) Damascus (b) Cooper
(c) Douglas (d) Kevin Red

99. Philadelphus was the ruler of which place?
(a) Yunnan (b) Greece
(c) Rome (d) Thailand

100. For how many years Bindusara ruled?
(a) 40 (b) 35
(c) 30 (d) 25

101. When did Bindusara die?
(a) 275 BC (b) 273 BC
(c) 270 BC (d) 268 BC

102. Who became the heir of Bindusara?
(a) Nagarjun (b) Ajatshatru
(c) Dasratha (d) Ashoka

103. When did Ashoka become the ruler of Magadh?
(a) 273 BC (b) 272 BC
(c) 271 BC (d) 270 BC

104. According to which literature, Ashoka had killed his brothers?
(a) Sinhali (b) Jain
(c) Shaiva (d) Ajivika

105. According to Sinhali literature, Ashoka had killed how many of his brothers?
(a) 90 (b) 95
(c) 97 (d) 99

106. When was Ashoka coronated?
(a) 273 BC (b) 271 BC
(c) 269 BC (d) 267 BC

107. According to Nepali literature, Ashoka was governor of which place before becoming the ruler?
(a) Taxila (b) Angg
(c) Kashi (d) Chedi

108. Who of the following rulers was called 'Chandshok' or 'Kamashok' in the beginning?
(a) Kalashok (b) Ashoka
(c) Udayin (d) Dasratha

109. In how many inscriptions, mention of the name Ashoka is found?
(a) 4 (b) 5
(c) 3 (d) 2

110. In which of the following inscriptions, name of Ashoka is found?
(a) Maski (b) Gurjara
(c) Nettur (d) All of these

111. In which of the following inscriptions, name of Ashoka is found?
(a) Udegolam (b) Kalinga
(c) Patliputra (d) Vaishali

112. In which inscription, Ashoka has been called 'Priyadarshi'?
(a) Maski (b) Gurjara
(c) Nettur (d) Bhabru

113. In maski inscription, what was Ashoka called?
(a) Buddh Ghosh
(b) Buddh Shakya
(c) Buddh Muni
(d) Buddh Sen

114. Where has Ashoka fought the only war of his life?
(a) Taxila (b) Ujjain
(c) Kalinga (d) Nalanda

115. From which of the following stone inscriptions, knowledge about the Kalinga war is obtained?
(a) 10th (b) 11th
(c) 12th (d) 13th

116. In which year of Ashoka rule, Kalinga war was fought?
(a) 8th (b) 9th
(c) 10th (d) 11th

117. When did Ashoka fight Kalinga war?
(a) 267 BC (b) 265 BC
(c) 263 BC (d) 261 BC

118. After which war, Ashoka adopted 'Dhamma' policy?
(a) Ujjain (b) Taxila
(c) Chedi (d) Kalinga

119. According to whom the purpose of the Kalinga war was to capture the elephant areas?
(a) Nagarjun (b) Ashwasen
(c) Kautilya (d) Pliny

120. 'Rajtaringini' was composed by whom?
(a) Pliny (b) Panini
(c) Huen Tsang (d) Kalhun

121. According to 'Rajtaringini', Ashoka was a firm supporter of which religion before accepting Buddhism?
(a) Shaiva (b) Vaishnava
(c) Ajivika (d) Jain

122. Who had initiated Ashoka into Buddhism?
(a) Nagarjun (b) Ashwaghosh
(c) Kalashok (d) Upagupt

123. In how many parts Ashoka had divided his empire?
(a) 3 (b) 4
(c) 5 (d) 6

124. Which of the following was not a part of the empire of Ashoka?
(a) Uttrapath (b) Dakshinapath
(c) Malkangiri (d) Avanti

125. Where was the capital of Uttrapath?
(a) Pathanpur (b) Lukhnoti
(c) Lahore (d) Taxila

126. Swarngiri was capital of which place?
(a) Avanti (b) Paschim Path
(c) Malkangiri (d) Dakshinapath

127. Where was the capital of Avanti?
(a) Indore (b) Ujjain
(c) Vallabhi (d) Vaishali

128. Where was the capital of Kalinga?
(a) Tambook (b) Tamluk
(c) Tosali (d) Cuttack

129. Where was the capital of Poorvi?
(a) Vaishali (b) Nalanda
(c) Pavapuri (d) Patliputra

130. Where was the capital of the entire Maurya dynasty?
(a) Patliputra (b) Pawapuri
(c) Shivneri (d) Ujjain

131. Which Maurya ruler had established Srinagar city in Kashmir?
(a) Chandragupt Maurya
(b) Bindusara
(c) Ashoka
(d) Dasratha

132. Which city was established by Ashoka in Nepal?
(a) Virat Nagar (b) Vir Ganj
(c) Kathmandu (d) Lalit Patan

133. Junagarh inscription is related to which ruler?
(a) Nandivarman
(b) Ashoka
(c) Ajatshatru
(d) Rudradaman

134. Tushashpa was the governor of which place in Ashoka's time?
(a) Tosli (b) Taxila
(c) Ujjain (d) Swarngiri

135. Tushashpa was a citizen of which country?
(a) Greece (b) Yunnan
(c) Rome (d) China

136. Who, after Ashoka, had become the ruler of Poorvi Bhag?
(a) Kunal (b) Kumar
(c) Dasratha (d) Nagarjun

137. Which state was included in the Poorvi Bhag?
(a) Bihar
(b) Bengal
(c) Uttar Pradesh
(d) All of the above

138. Dasratha had made his capital at which place?
(a) Vaishali (b) Nalanda
(c) Patliputra (d) Pavapuri

139. Who became the ruler of the Pashchimi Bhag?
(a) Kunal (b) Samprati
(c) Kusal (d) Mahendra

140. Under Pashchimi Bhag comes which present day state?
(a) Rajasthan
(b) Gujrat
(c) Madhya Pradesh
(d) All of the above

141. After whom, Samprati is called the best ruler of the Mauryan dynasty?
(a) Chandragupt Maurya
(b) Bindusara
(c) Ashoka
(d) Dasratha

142. 'Rajtaringini' is related to the literature of which state?
(a) Rajasthan (b) Bihar
(c) Gujrat (d) Kashmir

143. According to 'Rajtaringini' who became the ruler of Kashmir area?
(a) Jamali (b) Mahendra
(c) Jalouk (d) Udaisen

144. Who of the following was the last ruler of Maurya dynasty?
(a) Kunal (b) Vrihdrath
(c) Dasrath (d) Samprati

145. Vrihdrath, the last Mauryan ruler was killed by whom?
(a) Shashank
(b) Samprati
(c) Pushyamitra Shung
(d) Dasratha

146. When was Vrihdrath killed?
(a) 185 BC (b) 188 BC
(c) 192 BC (d) 195 BC

147. After Mauryan dynasty, whose rule started in Magadh?
(a) Haryak (b) Shishunag
(c) Shung (d) Kanwa

148. Ashoka was the ruler of Maurya dynasty at which number?
(a) First (b) Fourth
(c) Second (d) Third

149. 'Dhamma' word is a 'prakrit' translation of which language?
(a) Pali (b) Sanskrit
(c) Awadhi (d) Magadhi

150. According to which historian, Ashoka's Dhamma was an imagination of his mind to solve the political-social problems?
(a) Romila Thapar
(b) Irfan Habib
(c) Ramchandra Guha
(d) R. S. Sharma

151. In how many parts, Ashoka's inscriptions have been divided?
(a) 2 (b) 3
(c) 4 (d) 5

152. Which of the following is not a part of Ashoka's inscriptions?
(a) Shilalekh (b) Chitralekh
(c) Guhalekh (d) Stambhlekh

153. From how many places, Ashoka's inscriptions have been recovered?
(a) 6 (b) 7
(c) 8 (d) 9

154. What was the script of most of the inscriptions of Ashoka?
(a) Brahmi (b) Kharoshthi
(c) Sanskrit (d) Both (a) and (b)

155. Which of the following inscriptions has been found from Gujrat?
(a) Mansehra (b) Ganjam
(c) Kalsi (d) Girnar

156. 'Dhaulishila' inscription has been found from which state?
(a) Bihar (b) Odisha
(c) Gujrat (d) Rajasthan

157. Which of the following inscriptions has been found from Odisha?
(a) Jogarh (b) Junagarh
(c) Aughad (d) Supara

158. 'Kalsi shilalekh' was recovered from which place?
(a) Haridwar (b) Dehradun
(c) Bhopal (d) Patliputra

159. 'Bherangudhi' inscription has been found from which state?
(a) Andhra Pradesh
(b) Tamilnadu
(c) Karnataka
(d) Kerala

160. From where has 'Supara' inscription been found?
(a) Rajasthan (b) Punjab
(c) Haryana (d) Maharashtra

161. Which of the following inscriptions has been found in 'Kharoshthi' script?
(a) Supara (b) Shahbazgarhi
(c) Mansehra (d) Both (b) and (c)

162. 'Shahbazgarhi' inscription is found in which place in Pakistan?
(a) Peshwar (b) Lahore
(c) Karachi (d) Rawalpindi

163. 'Mansehra' inscriptions has been recovered from which country?
(a) India (b) Afghanistan
(c) Pakistan (d) Bangladesh

164. From which place in Pakistan, 'mansehra' inscriptions has been found?
(a) Baluchistan
(b) Khaibar Pakhtoon
(c) Dera Ghazi Khan
(d) Hajara

165. 'Sasaram'-small inscription has been found from which state?
(a) Bengal (b) Bihar
(c) Odisha (d) Uttar Pradesh

166. 'Roopnath Laghu Shilalekh' has been found from which place?

(a) Jabalpur (b) Vaishali
(c) Pawapuri (d) Patliputra

167. 'Gurjara Laghu shilalekh' has been found in which state?
(a) Rajasthan
(b) Gujarat
(c) Madhya Pradesh
(d) Bengal

168. From which place in Madhya Pradesh, 'Gurjara Laghu shilalekh' has been recovered?
(a) Devas (b) Sagar
(c) Datia (d) Alirajpur

169. 'Bhabru laghu shilalekh' has been found from which place?
(a) Rajasthan (b) Gujarat
(c) Bihar (d) Madhya Pradesh

170. From which place in Rajasthan, 'Bhabru laghu shilalekh' has been recovered?
(a) Jaisalmer (b) Bikaner
(c) Jaipur (d) Sriganganagar

171. 'Maski laghu shilalekh' has been recovered from which place?
(a) Karnataka (b) Madhya Pradesh
(c) Bihar (d) Bengal

172. From which place in Karnataka, 'Maski laghu shilalekh' has been found?
(a) Sindhudurg (b) Shivmoga
(c) Raichur (d) Brahmgiri

173. 'Brahmgiri laghu shilalekh' has been recovered from which state?
(a) Tamilnadu (b) Andhra Pradesh
(c) Maharashtra (d) Karnataka

174. In Mauryan time, coins were referred to as:
(a) Masak (b) Kakni
(c) Aahat (d) All of these

175. 'Sidhpur laghu shilalekh' was recovered from which place?
(a) Brahmgiri (b) Chittaldurg
(c) Raichur (d) Shivmoga

176. In which state the place known as 'Brahmgiri' is situated?
(a) Bengal (b) Andhra Pradesh
(c) Tamil Nadu (d) Karnataka

177. 'Jatingrameshwaram laghu shilalekh' was found from which place?
(a) Shivmoga (b) Chittaldurg
(c) Brahmgiri (d) Raichur

178. 'Gavimath laghu shilalekh' has been recovered from which place?
(a) Patan (b) Mysore
(c) Vallabhi (d) Raichur

179. 'Palkigundu laghu shilalekh' has been recovered from which place?
(a) Brahmgiri (b) Raipur
(c) Raichoor (d) Chittaldurg

180. 'Rajul mandagiri laghu shilalekh' has been found in which place?
(a) Karnataka (b) Andhra Pradesh
(c) Kerala (d) Goa

181. 'Ahrora laghu shilalekh' has been recovered from which place?
(a) Bahraich (b) Shrawasti
(c) Allahabad (d) Mirzapur

182. What is the number of big inscriptions pertaining to Ashoka?
(a) 6 (b) 7
(c) 8 (d) 9

183. 'Delhi-Topra' inscription has been recovered from which place?
(a) Ambala (b) Dehradun
(c) Nalanda (d) Patliputra

184. 'Sirsawa' inscription has been recovered from which place?
(a) Bihar (b) Uttar Pradesh
(c) Bengal (d) Gujarat

185. 'Delhi-Topra' inscription was brought to Delhi by which ruler?
(a) Ferozshah Tughlak
(b) Mohd. Bin Tughlak
(c) Akbar
(d) Shahjahan

186. 'Delhi-Meerut' inscription was brought to Delhi by which ruler?
(a) Aurangzeb
(b) Babur
(c) Iltutmish
(d) Ferozeshah Tughlak

187. 'Lauriya-Areraj' inscription was recovered from which state?
(a) Bihar (b) Punjab
(c) Haryana (d) Gujarat

188. 'Prayag' inscription has been recovered from which state?
(a) Uttar Pradesh
(b) Madhya Pradesh
(c) Bengal
(d) Bihar

189. 'Prayag' inscription was earlier situated at which place?
(a) Shrawasti (b) Kushinagar
(c) Varanasi (d) Koshambi

190. Which ruler had got 'Prayag' pillar inscription placed in Allahabad Fort?
(a) Babur (b) Akbar
(c) Shahjahan (d) Aurangzeb

191. Sarnath small pillar inscription has been recovered from which state?
(a) Bihar
(b) Bengal
(c) Uttar Pradesh
(d) Rajasthan

192. Where is Sarnath small pillar inscription situated?
(a) Varanasi (b) Kushinagar
(c) Koshambi (d) Mathura

193. Koshambi small pillar inscription has been found from which place?
(a) Allahabad (b) Ujjain
(c) Banaras (d) Mathura

194. According to Mahamopadhyaya Hariprasad Shastri, Ashoka's which policy became the major cause of his downfall?
(a) Military policy
(b) Religious policy
(c) Foreign polciy
(d) Diplomacy

195. According to Hemchandra Rai Choudhry, what was the major cause of downfall of Ashoka?
(a) Non-violence
(b) Military
(c) Peacefulness
(d) Both (a) and (c)

196. 'Rummandei' small pillar inscription has been recovered from which country?
(a) India (b) Pakistan
(c) Afganistan (d) Nepal

197. 'Nigaligaon' small pillar inscription has been recovered in which country?
(a) Nepal (b) Bangladesh
(c) Pakistan (d) India

198. Which is the longest pillar inscription of Ashoka?
(a) First (b) Second
(c) Fourth (d) Seventh

199. Which is the smallest pillar inscription of Ashoka?
(a) Ranchi (b) Rummindei
(c) Nigaligaon (d) Sarnath

200. In which pillar inscription, there is a mention of queen of Ashoka, Karuvaki extending donation?
(a) Ranchi (b) Koshambi
(c) Prayag (d) Both (b) and (c)

201. Which of the following inscriptions is also called ' Rani's' inscriptions?
(a) Rummindei (b) Paryag
(c) Koshambi (d) Both (b) and (c)

202. From which pillar inscription, knowledge about Ashoka's religious travels is obtained?
(a) Ranchi (b) Rummindei
(c) Sanchi (d) Nigaligaon

203. In which of the following pillar inscriptions, there is a mention of tax fixation?
(a) Prayag (b) Koshambi
(c) Nigaligaon (d) Rummindei

204. In his 20th coronation year, Ashoka had travelled to which place?
(a) Bodhgaya (b) Lumbini
(c) Nalanda (d) Pawapuri

205. During Lumbini's travel, Ashoka reduced land revenue tax to how much?
(a) 1/8th (b) 1/7th
(c) 1/6th (d) 1/5th

206. Which ruler had in his inscription stated that all humans are his children?
(a) Chandragupt Maurya
(b) Dasratha
(c) Udayin
(d) Ashoka

207. In which inscription Ashoka had stated that all humans are his children?
(a) Ranchi (b) Dhauli
(c) Jogarh (d) Both (b) and (c)

208. Which ruler had got established separate hospitals for humans and animals?
(a) Mahapadmanand
(b) Dhananand
(c) Ashoka
(d) Udayin

209. From which inscription we come to know that Ashoka had got hospitals established for humans and animals?
(a) Sarnath (b) Ranchi
(c) Koshambi (d) Girnar

210. The hunters and the fishermen had left violence against the living beings by getting impressed with which inscription?
(a) Sanchi (b) Kandhar
(c) Prayag (d) Koshambi

211. The inscription obtained from 'Share Kuna' near Kandhar was in which script?
(a) Brahmi (b) Armaik
(c) Yunani (d) Both (b) and (c)

212. Pillar inscriptions obtained from which place contain texts written by Samudragupta and the courtier of Akbar, Birbal apart from those written by Ashoka?
(a) Sarnath (b) Shrawasti
(c) Allahabad (d) Banaras

213. In which pillar inscription, Ashoka orders his 'mahamatyas' to stop 'Sangh-bhed'?
(a) Sanchi
(b) Sarnath
(c) Koshambi
(d) All of the above

214. __________stone inscription is the only inscription which has been engraved on the stone sheets.
(a) Junagarh (b) Bhabhru
(c) Sanchi (d) Sarnath

215. What was the language of Ashoka's inscriptions?
(a) Sanskrit (b) Magadhi
(c) Pali (d) Prakrit

216. In which script, writing from right to left is made?
(a) Armaik (b) Brahmi
(c) Yunani (d) Kharoshthi

217. In which inscription of Ashoka, brahmi script is written from right to left?
(a) Yerragudi (b) Bhabru
(c) Kandhar (d) Koshambi

218. In which district of Bihar, signs of 'Guha' text have been found?
(a) Vaishali (b) Nalanda
(c) Gaya (d) Patliputra

219. In which of the following hills and caves, signs of 'guha' text have been found?
(a) Nagarjuni
(b) Barabar
(c) Karnchaupad
(d) All of the above

220. Which of the following rulers had got inscripted 'guha' text?
(a) Chandragupta Maurya
(b) Udayin
(c) Ashoka
(d) Kalashok

221. Ashoka had given 'guha-daan' to saints of which religion?
(a) Bodh (b) Ajivika
(c) Jain (d) None of these

222. What was the language of 'guha' text?
(a) Sanskrit (b) Magadhi
(c) Pali (d) Prakrit

223. Who of the following had stated the Mauryans' borders as India's scientific and geographical borders?
(a) Kevin Red (b) Mark Cooper
(c) Smith (d) Hawkins

224. At the time of Chandragupta Maurya and Bindusara, Maurya Empire was divided into how many provinces?
(a) 5 (b) 4
(c) 3 (d) 2

225. Under Uttrapath, which of the following states used to fall?
(a) Jammu and Kashmir
(b) Himachal Pradesh
(c) Uttrakhand
(d) All of the above

226. Which of the following states, was under Avanti State?
(a) Gujarat
(b) Rajasthan
(c) Madhya Pradesh
(d) All of the above

227. Under Dakshinapath, which of the states falls?
(a) Maharashtra
(b) Karnataka
(c) Andhra Pradesh
(d) All of the above

228. Under Maurya administration, how many villages fell under a 'Sthanik'?
(a) 500 (b) 600
(c) 700 (d) 800

229. Under Maurya administration, how many villages fell under a 'Dronmukh'?
(a) 400 (b) 300
(c) 200 (d) 100

230. Under Maurya administration, how many villages fell under a 'Kharvatik'?
(a) 300 (b) 250
(c) 200 (d) 150

231. Under Maurya administration, how many villages fell under a 'Sangrahan'?
(a) 300 (b) 250
(c) 200 (d) 100

232. Under Maurya empire, the tax revenue received from rural area was called ___________.
(a) Kar (b) Bonus
(c) Rashtra (d) Mal-guzari

233. Under Maurya empire, the tax revenue received from city areas was called.
(a) Durg (b) Sam
(c) Haat (d) Naam

234. Under Maurya administration, which of the following used to collect revenue?
(a) Gop (b) Amatya
(c) Samaharta (d) Mahamatya

235. Who among the following is the writer of 'Arthshastra'?
(a) Ashwaghosh (b) Nathmuni
(c) Nagsen (d) Kautilya

236. In 'Arthshastra', what was a high official called?
(a) Samaharta (b) Panth
(c) Tirtha (d) Kantak

237. In 'Arthshastra' mention of how many pilgrimages is made?
(a) 16 (b) 17
(c) 18 (d) 19

238. What was the authority over the pilgrimages called?
(a) Mahamatya (b) Kantak
(c) Jamboot (d) Karta

239. Who among the following looked after law and order matters in the district?
(a) Purohit (b) Kantak
(c) Samaharta (d) Yuvraj

240. Who of the following used to be the head of a 'janpad' during Maurya rule?
(a) Yuvraj (b) Amatya
(c) Thewat (d) Samaharta

241. During Maurya's rule, a 'Koshadhyaksha' was called as________.
(a) Samaharta (b) Kantak
(c) Sheel (d) Sunnidhata

242. Who used to be an official of government land?
(a) Sitadhyaksha
(b) Sunnidhata
(c) Kantak
(d) Gop

243. What was a factory and trading superintendent called?
(a) Amatya (b) Gop
(c) Kantak (d) Panyadhyaksha

244. Who used to be called a metal controller?
(a) Keeladhyaksha
(b) Lohaadhyaksha
(c) Dhatuadhyaksha
(d) Kantaksheel

245. Who of the following used to be 'Charagaah Adhyaksha'?
(a) Panyadhyaksha
(b) Charadhyaksh
(c) Vivitadhyaksha
(d) Gop

246. Who used to be called a 'Baat' and 'Taraju' adhikari?
(a) Panyadhyaksha
(b) Vivitadhyaksha
(c) Gop
(d) Potwadhyaksha

247. Who used to be called a 'Sikka Nirikshak' adhikari?
(a) Mudradhyaksha
(b) Sheeladhyaksha
(c) Roopdarshak
(d) Takadhyaksha

248. Regional governor and protector of Peace and Justice used to be called as________.
(a) Gopt (b) Kantak
(c) Rajuk (d) Sheeladhyaksha

249. The private secretary of the King used to be called what?
(a) Sheel (b) Prativadi
(c) Prativedak (d) Hatak

250. A mint officer used to be called what?
(a) Tankansheel
(b) Patadhyaksha
(c) Lakshnadhyaksha
(d) Mudradhyaksha

251. Who used to be called an 'Agronomoi'?
(a) Krishiadhikari
(b) Sinchai Adhikari
(c) Zile ka Adhikari
(d) Both (a) and (b)

252. A City Officer used to be called what out of the following?
(a) Nayak (b) Aristonomoi
(c) Dhawak (d) Kripan

253. In whose description, maximum account is made of cities of mauryan administration?
(a) Buddh Ghosh
(b) Ashwaghosh
(c) Nagsen
(d) Megasthnese

254. The description of how many five members committees is given by Megasthenese about city administration?
(a) 3 (b) 4
(c) 5 (d) 6

255. In Mauryan rule, what was a criminal court called?
(a) Sheel Shodhak
(b) Kantakshodhan
(c) Nyayshodhan
(d) Sheelshodhan

256. In Mauryan times, who used to be the supreme officer of the law & administration?
(a) Samrat (b) Senapati
(c) Peshwa (d) Mahamantri

257. A complete chapter of Economics number__________ was written on 'Kantakshodhan' justice system?
(a) First (b) Second
(c) Third (d) Fourth

258. In Gupta times, what was a spy used to called?
(a) Sheel Purush
(b) Gop Purush
(c) Kantak Purush
(d) Goorh Purush

259. Kautilya had said 'Eye of the King' to whom?
(a) Peshwa
(b) Senapati
(c) Guptchar
(d) Rajasva Adhikari

260. What was the main basis of the Economy during the Mauryan times?
(a) Krishi (b) Pashupalan
(c) Vyapar (d) Khanij Rajsva

261. Agriculture, animal husbandry, trade and commerce jointly are called what in 'Airthshastra'?
(a) Varta (b) Khewat
(c) Kopt (d) Samman

262. What was rate of tax during the Mauryan time?
(a) 1/4th (b) 1/5th
(c) 1/6th (d) 1/8th

263. Which of the following cities was popular for sericulture during the Mauryan time?
(a) Bang (b) Kashi
(c) Pundra (d) Both (b) and (c)

264. Which city was popular during the Mauryan time for muslin industry?
(a) Bang (b) Kashi
(c) Shrawasti (d) Vaishali

265. From where silk used to be imported during the Mauryan time?
(a) China (b) Japan
(c) Thailand (d) Mangolia

266. During the Mauryan time, 'Aahat' coins made of __________ were in circulation.
(a) Gold (b) Silver
(c) Bronze (d) Seesa

267. On 'Aahat' coins, whose picture used to be inscribed?
(a) Peacock
(b) Mountain
(c) Half moon
(d) All of the above

268. Which of the following was a tax during the Mauran Time?
(a) Sheel (b) Naam
(c) Bali (d) Token

269. Which of the following was a salt-tax?
(a) Hiranya (b) Kaitha
(c) Roopak (d) Nabhik

270. People who used to make the coins themselves, had to pay to the state interest at the rate of what percentage?
(a) 12% (b) 12.5%
(c) 13% (d) 13.5%

271. In lieu of making coins themselves, people had to pay to the State which of these taxes?
(a) Lagaan (b) Sapika
(c) Parikshan (d) Both (b) and (c)

272. During Mauryan times, a landlord was called by what name?
(a) Girhat (b) Malikar
(c) Kshetrak (d) Gumasta

273. During Mauryan times, a farmer was called by what name?
(a) Upvaas (b) Sewak
(c) Gupta (d) Mahi

274. According to which of the historians below, the reason for the downfall of Ashoka was 'Centralization of adminstration'?
(a) Irfan Habib
(b) Romila Thapar
(c) Ramchandra Guha
(d) R S Sharma

275. During Mauryan times, irrigation facility provided by the State was known by what name?
(a) Bandhbandh (b) Setubandh
(c) Khetbandh (d) Naharbandh

276. Which of the following taxes, used to be collected onetime from the entire village?
(a) Lagaan (b) Khewat Kar
(c) Gop Kar (d) Pind Kar

277. During Mauryan times, which tax used to be collected for protection of animals?
(a) Pind (b) Pevand
(c) Vivit (d) Khewat

278. During Mauryan times, free labour viz 'begaar' was known by what name?
(a) Disht (b) Vishti
(c) Sheel (d) Kharaj

279. During Mauryan times, what percentage of tax was levied on indigenous goods?
(a) 6% (b) 5%
(c) 4% (d) 3%

280. During Mauryan times, what percentage of tax was levied on the imported goods?
(a) 8% (b) 9%
(c) 10% (d) 11%

281. During Mauryan times, Uttrapath would run from which place to which other place?
(a) Patliputra-Taxila
(b) Patliputra-Ujjain
(c) Ujjain-Taxila
(d) Ujjain-Swarangiri

282. During Mauryan times, in which direction the 'Himwant marg' used to go?
(a) Uttar Himalaya
(b) Poorva Himalaya
(c) Dakshini Himalaya
(d) Paschim Himalaya

283. For mauryans,_________was the major centre for foreign trade?
(a) Patliputra (b) Patan
(c) Taxila (d) Vaishali

284. Which of the following was a port situated on the western Bank?
(a) Supara
(b) Barberikam
(c) Manjurish
(d) All of the above

285. Which of the following is situated as a port on the eastern banks?
(a) Tamralipti
(b) Bharauch
(c) Calicut
(d) Mangluru

286. Which of the following is true?
(a) Shulk - Chungi kar
(b) Vartini - Sadak kar
(c) Gulm dey - Brmar se raksha kar
(d) All of the above

287. In Kautilya's Arthshastra, how many parts of the State have been described?
(a) 4 (b) 5
(c) 6 (d) 7

288. According to Plini, how much Infantry was being kept by Chandragupta in his army?
(a) 4 lakh (b) 5 lakh
(c) 6 lakh (d) 7 lakh

289. In the battlefield, the commanding officer was called by what name?
(a) Nayak (b) Peshwa
(c) Senapati (d) Mahamatya

290. In Mauryan time, the permanent command was known by what name?
(a) Kopt (b) Maul
(c) Kewat (d) Khemat

291. During Mauryan time, 'Janglee sena' was known by what name?
(a) Aaranya Bal (b) Aatvi Bal
(c) Attavi Bal (d) Khewat Bal

292. In Mauryan time, the borrowed army was known by what name?
(a) Aatav (b) Kshudrak
(c) Khewat (d) Bhratak

293. What was the state currency of the Mauryans?
(a) Hun (b) Pan
(c) Kan (d) Moorn

294. In Arthshastra, Kautilya has talked about what?
(a) Brahmin
(b) Vaishya
(c) Shudra
(d) All of the above

295. Which of the following has been mentioned in the inscriptions of Ashoka?
(a) Dass (b) Karmkaar
(c) Sewak (d) Both (a) and (b)

296. During Mauryan times, prostitutes working freely were called by what name?
(a) Nagarvadhu
(b) Roopak
(c) Rupajiva
(d) Kamuk

297. During Mauryan times, widows living off their own used to be known by what name?
(a) Kshemavasini
(b) Vidhavasini
(c) Pativasini
(d) Kshandvasini

POST MAURYAN BIHAR

1. When did Pushyamitra Shung establish Shung Dynasty?
(a) 185 BC (b) 187 BC
(c) 189 BC (d) 192 BC

2. From Dhandeva's Ayodhya text, knowledge is obtained relating to which dynasty?
(a) Haryak (b) Shishunag
(c) Mauryan (d) Shung

3. 'Garuda' Pillar inscription of which place gives description about Shung dynasty?
(a) Basenagar (b) Chittorh
(c) Vaishali (d) Vallabhi

4. 'Malvikagnimitra' was composed by whom?
(a) Narsen (b) Ashwaghosh
(c) Amarsingh (d) Kalidas

5. Who composed 'Mahabhashya'?
(a) Patanjali (b) Kalidas
(c) Ashwasen (d) Brahmdutt

6. Which of the following compositions provide us knowledge about Shung dynasty?

(a) Meghdoot
(b) Malvikagnimitra
(c) Mahabhashya
(d) Both (b) and (c)

7. Pushyamitra Shung saved Magadh from the attack by whom?
(a) The Deutsche
(b) The Chinese
(c) The Iranians
(d) The Yamanese

8. Pushyamitra Shung won the war with whom?
(a) The Deutsche
(b) Vidarbha
(c) Yaman
(d) Both (b) and (c)

9. Who became the ruler of Magadh after Pushyamitra Shung?
(a) Kunalmitra Shung
(b) Agnimitra Shung
(c) Devmitra Shung
(d) Indramitra Shung

10. Agnimitra was the hero of the play of which of the following?
(a) Kalidas (b) Surdas
(c) Brahmgupt (d) Amar Singh

11. Who was the last ruler of the Shung dynasty?
(a) Brahmbhuti (b) Devbhuti
(c) Naambhuti (d) Indrabhuti

12. Who had killed Devbhuti?
(a) Nagsen (b) Vasumitra
(c) Devmitra (d) Indramitra

13. Where was the capital of Shung rulers?
(a) Vaishali (b) Nalanda
(c) Patliputra (d) Vallabhi

14. Who had destroyed 84 thousand 'bodh stupas'?
(a) Shashank
(b) Ashoka
(c) Brahmgupta
(d) Pushyamitra Shung

15. Pushyamitra Shung had given a glorious shape to 'stupas' situated at which place?
(a) Bharhut (b) Bodhgaya
(c) Sanchi (d) All of these

16. During Shung dynasty, what was the name given to 'Swaranmudra'?
(a) Dinar
(b) Nishk
(c) Swaran
(d) All of the above

17. During shung dynasty, what was the name given to a currency made of bronze?
(a) Aahat (b) Dharan
(c) Karshapan (d) Nishk

18. During Shung Dynasty, currency made of silver used to be called by what name?
(a) Dharan (b) Dhara
(c) Puran (d) Both (a) and (c)

19. Bhagawat religion emerged during the period of which dynasty?
(a) Haryak (b) Shung
(c) Shishunag (d) Maurya

20. During Shung dynasty, eminent specimen of architecture were found in which place?
(a) Nalanda (b) Vaishali
(c) Bodhgaya (d) Patliputra

21. Around the grand temple of Bodhgaya, a small 'Vedika' made of stone is found, to which period this pertain does?
(a) Haryak
(b) Shishunag
(c) Shung
(d) Maurya

22. After Shung dynasty, which dynasty took over the rule of Magadh?
(a) Kanva (b) Haryak
(c) Nand (d) Maurya

23. **Who was the founder of 'Kanva' dynasty?**
(a) Vasudev (b) Nagarjun
(c) Kunal (d) Vasumitra

24. **Which of the following was not a ruler of the Kanva dynasty?**
(a) Vasudev (b) Bhumimitra
(c) Narayan (d) Susharma

25. **Who was the last ruler of the 'Kanva' dynasty?**
(a) Vasumitra (b) Narayan
(c) Susharma (d) Bhumimitra

26. **Who had killed Susharma?**
(a) Simuk (b) Nagdutt
(c) Brahmsen (d) Shashank

27. **The rule of Kanva dynasty lasted for which period?**
(a) 75-25 BC
(b) 74-24 BC
(c) 73-23 BC
(d) 72-27 BC

28. **Kushan dynasty was established by whom?**
(a) Kanishka
(b) Vasudev
(c) Veem Kadphisas
(d) Kujul Kadphisas

29. **Who was the most famous ruler of the Kushan dynasty?**
(a) Veem Kadphisas
(b) Kujul Kadphisas
(c) Kanishka
(d) Dev Kadphisas

30. **When did Kanishka became the ruler?**
(a) 75 AD (b) 73 AD
(c) 70AD (d) 68 AD

31. **At which of the following places, Kanishka had his capital?**
(a) Paithan (b) Patan
(c) Pawapuri (d) Purushpur

32. **Kanishka won the war of expansion of his area to which place?**
(a) Ujjain (b) Kashi
(c) Ang (d) Magadh

33. **Kanishka took along with him which Bodh Scholar?**
(a) Budh Ghosh
(b) Nagsen
(c) Ashwaghosh
(d) Brahmdutt

34. **After the downfall of the Kushans, who ruled over Magadh?**
(a) The Shungs
(b) The Kanvas
(c) The Mauryans
(d) The Lichhvavis

GUPTAS PERIOD BIHAR

1. **In the initial years of ________ century, Magadh regained its lost glory with the establishment of rule of Guptas.**
(a) First (b) Second
(c) Third (d) Fourth

2. **The early Gupta rulers had made which place their capital?**
(a) Vaishali (b) Bodhgaya
(c) Patliputra (d) Nalanda

3. **Who of the following was the founder of Gupta dynasty?**
(a) Brahmgupt (b) Devgupt
(c) Samgupt (d) Shrigupt

4. **When was Gupta dynasty established?**
(a) 248 AD (b) 245 AD
(c) 242 AD (d) 240 AD

5. **Who of the following was the father of Chandragupt I?**
(a) Shrigupt (b) Brahmgupt
(c) Devgupta (d) Ghatotkutch

6. **Who is considered the real founder of Gupta dynasty?**
(a) Brahmgupt (b) Chandragupt I
(c) Shrigupt (d) Samudragupt

7. **What was the period of rule by Chandragupt I?**
(a) 319-335 AD
(b) 322-335 AD
(c) 325-335 AD
(d) 328-340 AD

8. **When did Gupta calendar start?**
(a) 318 AD (b) 319 AD
(c) 320 AD (d) 321 AD

9. **Gupta calendar is related to which other calendar?**
(a) Shaka (b) Brahm
(c) Kashi (d) Vallabhi

10. **Chandragupta I had adopted the title of what?**
(a) Rajraja (b) Rajyadhiraj
(c) Mahadhiraj (d) Maharajadhiraj

11. **Who became the ruler of Gupta dynasty after Chandragupt I?**
(a) Brahmgupt (b) Samudragupt
(c) Narsinghgupt (d) Devgupt

12. **State the period of Samudragupta's rule?**
(a) 335-375 AD
(b) 333-373 AD
(c) 330-370 AD
(d) 328-368 AD

13. **Which of the following rulers of Gupta dynasty are known by the text in 'Prayagprashti'?**
(a) Chandragupt I
(b) Shrigupt
(c) Samudragupt
(d) Ghatotkach

14. **Who of the following is called the 'Napoleon of India'?**
(a) Chandragupta I
(b) Shrigupt
(c) Ghatotkach
(d) Samudragupt

15. **Who of the following Gupta rulers, for the first time defeated rulers of Ganga-Doab area and merged it with their kingdom?**
(a) Samudragupt
(b) Shrigupt
(c) Chandragupt I
(d) Ghatotkach

16. **Who was defeated by Samudragupta?**
(a) Maurya (b) Shaka
(c) Kushanas (d) Both (b) and (c)

17. **Who became the heir of Samudragupta?**
(a) Shrigupta
(b) Brahmgupt
(c) Chandragupt II
(d) Bhimgupta

18. **Which state was won by Chandragupt II?**
(a) Andhra (b) Saurashtra
(c) Malwa (d) Both (b) and (c)

19. **Which of the following rulers' time is called the golden years of Gupta rule?**
(a) Chandragupt I
(b) Shrigupt
(c) Samudragupt
(d) Chandragupt II

20. **Which foreign invaders had attacked the heirs of Chandragupt II?**
(a) Shaka (b) Pehlava
(c) Huns (d) Kushans

21. **State the period of rule of Chandragupta II?**
(a) 380-400 AD
(b) 377-404 AD
(c) 375-412 AD
(d) 373-415 AD

22. **Which of the Hun rulers had attacked Patliputa?**
(a) Devbhuti (b) Devmitra
(c) Kunalsen (d) Mihirkul

23. **Mihirkul had defeated which Gupta ruler?**
(a) Narsinhgupt Baladitya
(b) Shrigupt
(c) Upgupt
(d) Devgupt

24. Latter Gupta dynasty rulers had controlled the __________ area uptill the mid-sixth century AD.
(a) Angg (b) Kashi
(c) Magadh (d) Chedi

25. In some of the eastern U.P. and Bihar areas, rule of which dynasty had established during the latter Gupta rulers' time?
(a) Maukhri (b) Shaka
(c) Pehlav (d) Yavan

26. Which of the following were major Gupta period scholars?
(a) Varahmihir
(b) Aryabhatt
(c) Brahmgupt
(d) All of the above

27. During which time, Nalanda Mahavihar was established?
(a) Mauryan (b) Gupta
(c) Maukhari (d) Paul

28. Who was the founder of Nalanda Mahavihar?
(a) Samudragupt
(b) Shrigupt
(c) Chandragupt I
(d) Kumargupt

29. In whose rule, Fa-Hien had visited India?
(a) Shrigupt
(b) Samudragupt
(c) Chandragupt II
(d) Upgupt

30. Fa-Hien was a traveler from which country?
(a) China (b) Japan
(c) Mangolia (d) Yunnan

31. For three years, where did Fa-hein live?
(a) Pawapuri
(b) Nalanda
(c) Patliputra
(d) Vaishali

32. A significant achievement of which rule was the Mahabodhi temple of Bodhgaya and the remains of the Nalanda Mahavihar?
(a) Mauryan (b) Gupta
(c) Pal (d) Shung

33. The inscriptions obtained from Shahbad area indicate about which of the rulers?
(a) Latter Gupta (b) Maukhri
(c) Shaka (d) Pehlav

34. Who was the founder of the latter Gupta dynasty?
(a) Kumargupt (b) Upgupt
(c) Shrigupt (d) Krishangupt

35. Who was the latter Gupta dynasty ruler who had defeated Maukhri dynasty?
(a) Krishangupt (b) Kumargupt III
(c) Upgupt (d) Devgupt

36. Who was the heir of Kumargupta III?
(a) Upgupt
(b) Brahmgupt
(c) Devgupt
(d) Damodargupt

37. Which latter Gupta ruler had expanded his empire up to Magadh after defeating the rulers of the Maukhri dyanasty?
(a) Devgupt
(b) Kumargupt III
(c) Damodargupt
(d) Brahmgupt

38. Which area was attacked by Shashank?
(a) Kashi (b) Chedi
(c) Lichhavi (d) Magadh

39. Who of the following rulers had destroyed Bodh sacred places badly and caused a damage to Mahabodhi Tree in Bodhgaya?
(a) Kumargupt (b) Nagsen
(c) Brahmgupt (d) Shashank

40. Devgupt defeated the Maukhiri ruler of Kannauj after entering into a treaty with which ruler?
(a) Shashank
(b) Brahmgupt
(c) Damodargupt
(d) Upgupt

41. Devgupt defeated which Maukhiri ruler?
(a) Mihirverman (b) Devvarman
(c) Kunalverman (d) Grihvarman

42. Who of the following ruler had defeated and killed Devgupt?
(a) Mihirkul (b) Nagsen
(c) Rajyavardhan (d) Damodargupt

43. Who was the last ruler of the latter Gupta Dynasty?
(a) Dharmagupt (b) Devgupt
(c) Upgupt (d) Jivitgupt

44. When did Huen Tsang visit India?
(a) 635 AD (b) 630 AD
(c) 628 AD (d) 625 AD

45. Huen Tsang came to India in whose rule?
(a) Shashank (b) Jivitgupt
(c) Harshvardhan (d) Chandragupt II

Answers

PRE-HISTORIC PERIOD

1. (d)	**2.** (d)	**3.** (a)	**4.** (b)	**5.** (d)	**6.** (d)	**7.** (c)	**8.** (b)	**9.** (d)	**10.** (d)
11. (b)	**12.** (d)	**13.** (c)	**14.** (d)	**15.** (d)	**16.** (d)	**17.** (c)	**18.** (d)	**19.** (a)	**20.** (b)
21. (d)	**22.** (a)	**23.** (b)	**24.** (a)	**25.** (b)	**26.** (d)	**27.** (c)	**28.** (c)	**29.** (c)	**30.** (c)
31. (a)	**32.** (d)	**33.** (c)	**34.** (c)	**35.** (d)	**36.** (b)	**37.** (b)	**38.** (d)	**39.** (b)	

THE SOCIAL AND RELIGIOUS REFORMATION MOVEMENT IN ANCIENT BIHAR-BUDDHISM

1. (a)	**2.** (a)	**3.** (d)	**4.** (a)	**5.** (b)	**6.** (c)	**7.** (d)	**8.** (a)	**9.** (d)	**10.** (b)
11. (c)	**12.** (c)	**13.** (d)	**14.** (c)	**15.** (a)	**16.** (b)	**17.** (c)	**18.** (d)	**19.** (c)	**20.** (b)
21. (d)	**22.** (c)	**23.** (b)	**24.** (d)	**25.** (a)	**26.** (c)	**27.** (b)	**28.** (d)	**29.** (a)	**30.** (b)
31. (c)	**32.** (b)	**33.** (c)	**34.** (d)	**35.** (a)	**36.** (c)	**37.** (a)	**38.** (d)	**39.** (b)	**40.** (c)
41. (d)	**42.** (d)	**43.** (c)	**44.** (a)	**45.** (b)	**46.** (c)	**47.** (a)	**48.** (d)	**49.** (b)	**50.** (c)
51. (d)	**52.** (b)	**53.** (b)	**54.** (c)	**55.** (a)	**56.** (d)	**57.** (a)	**58.** (b)	**59.** (d)	**60.** (d)
61. (d)	**62.** (c)	**63.** (c)	**64.** (d)	**65.** (b)	**66.** (b)	**67.** (d)	**68.** (c)	**69.** (c)	**70.** (a)
71. (d)	**72.** (a)	**73.** (a)	**74.** (d)	**75.** (d)	**76.** (c)	**77.** (b)	**78.** (c)	**79.** (a)	**80.** (d)
81. (b)	**82.** (d)	**83.** (d)	**84.** (a)	**85.** (c)	**86.** (d)	**87.** (d)	**88.** (a)	**89.** (d)	**90.** (d)
91. (d)	**92.** (a)	**93.** (c)	**94.** (b)	**95.** (b)	**96.** (d)	**97.** (d)	**98.** (d)	**99.** (d)	**100.** (d)
101. (d)	**102.** (d)	**103.** (c)	**104.** (a)	**105.** (d)	**106.** (b)	**107.** (c)	**108.** (a)	**109.** (d)	**110.** (d)
111. (a)	**112.** (b)	**113.** (c)	**114.** (b)	**115.** (a)	**116.** (b)	**117.** (c)	**118.** (d)	**119.** (c)	**120.** (d)
121. (a)	**122.** (c)	**123.** (a)	**124.** (c)	**125.** (a)	**126.** (d)	**127.** (a)	**128.** (d)	**129.** (b)	**130.** (a)
131. (c)	**132.** (c)	**133.** (d)	**134.** (b)	**135.** (a)	**136.** (b)	**137.** (c)	**138.** (a)	**139.** (b)	**140.** (a)

141. (c) 142. (d) 143. (a) 144. (d) 145. (a) 146. (a) 147. (c) 148. (c) 149. (b) 150. (c)
151. (a) 152. (b) 153. (b) 154. (c) 155. (b) 156. (b) 157. (b) 158. (c) 159. (b) 160. (b)
161. (a) 162. (b) 163. (a) 164. (b) 165. (d) 166. (b) 167. (a) 168. (d) 169. (b) 170. (d)
171. (b) 172. (a) 173. (c) 174. (a) 175. (b) 176. (a) 177. (d) 178. (c) 179. (b) 180. (c)
181. (a) 182. (c) 183. (a) 184. (d) 185. (c) 186. (b) 187. (a) 188. (d) 189. (b) 190. (c)
191. (d) 192. (a) 193. (d) 194. (a) 195. (b) 196. (c) 197. (b) 198. (a) 199. (c) 200. (a)
201. (d) 202. (a) 203. (a) 204. (d) 205. (b) 206. (d) 207. (b) 208. (d) 209. (b) 210. (a)

JAINISM

1. (a) 2. (b) 3. (c) 4. (b) 5. (a) 6. (d) 7. (a) 8. (d) 9. (c) 10. (d)
11. (a) 12. (b) 13. (a) 14. (c) 15. (a) 16. (b) 17. (d) 18. (a) 19. (d) 20. (a)
21. (a) 22. (b) 23. (d) 24. (a) 25. (c) 26. (a) 27. (c) 28. (b) 29. (d) 30. (a)
31. (c) 32. (a) 33. (c) 34. (d) 35. (d) 36. (c) 37. (c) 38. (c) 39. (c) 40. (c)
41. (d) 42. (b) 43. (c) 44. (c) 45. (c) 46. (d) 47. (c) 48. (a) 49. (d) 50. (d)
51. (a) 52. (d) 53. (a) 54. (d) 55. (d) 56. (b) 57. (c) 58. (b) 59. (b) 60. (b)
61. (d) 62. (b) 63. (c) 64. (c) 65. (c) 66. (c) 67. (a) 68. (d) 69. (b) 70. (a)
71. (c) 72. (a) 73. (a) 74. (a) 75. (d) 76. (d) 77. (b) 78. (a) 79. (b) 80. (a)
81. (c) 82. (a) 83. (b) 84. (a) 85. (c) 86. (c) 87. (b) 88. (c) 89. (d) 90. (b)
91. (a) 92. (c) 93. (a) 94. (b) 95. (d) 96. (a) 97. (b) 98. (a) 99. (b) 100. (c)
101. (b) 102. (d) 103. (c) 104. (a) 105. (c) 106. (b) 107. (b)

THE DIFFERENT SECTS OF JAINISM

1. (c) 2. (a) 3. (d) 4. (b) 5. (d) 6. (d) 7. (d) 8. (d) 9. (a) 10. (b)
11. (d) 12. (a) 13. (c) 14. (d) 15. (d) 16. (d) 17. (b) 18. (b) 19. (a) 20. (b)
21. (d) 22. (d) 23. (a) 24. (c)

THE POLITICAL HISTORY OF BIHAR

1. (b) 2. (a) 3. (b) 4. (b) 5. (b) 6. (c) 7. (d) 8. (a) 9. (a) 10. (d)
11. (b) 12. (a) 13. (d) 14. (a) 15. (b) 16. (d) 17. (b) 18. (d) 19. (c) 20. (b)
21. (d) 22. (c) 23. (a) 24. (d) 25. (b) 26. (b) 27. (a) 28. (d) 29. (a) 30. (b)
31. (c) 32. (d) 33. (c) 34. (a) 35. (b) 36. (d) 37. (b) 38. (c) 39. (a) 40. (c)
41. (a) 42. (b) 43. (c) 44. (d) 45. (c) 46. (d) 47. (a) 48. (d) 49. (a) 50. (c)
51. (d) 52. (d) 53. (b) 54. (c) 55. (a) 56. (c) 57. (a) 58. (a) 59. (d) 60. (c)
61. (a) 62. (b) 63. (d) 64. (c) 65. (b) 66. (d) 67. (b) 68. (c) 69. (d) 70. (d)
71. (a) 72. (c) 73. (d) 74. (d) 75. (a) 76. (b) 77. (c) 78. (d) 79. (c) 80. (c)
81. (b) 82. (c) 83. (d) 84. (d) 85. (b) 86. (c) 87. (c) 88. (c) 89. (d) 90. (b)
91. (d) 92. (a) 93. (a)

MAGADH EMPIRE

1. (b)	**2.** (a)	**3.** (d)	**4.** (a)	**5.** (b)	**6.** (c)	**7.** (d)	**8.** (d)	**9.** (b)	**10.** (d)
11. (a)	**12.** (d)	**13.** (b)	**14.** (a)	**15.** (c)	**16.** (a)	**17.** (b)	**18.** (b)	**19.** (a)	**20.** (d)
21. (d)	**22.** (a)	**23.** (d)	**24.** (d)	**25.** (a)	**26.** (d)	**27.** (c)	**28.** (b)	**29.** (a)	**30.** (b)
31. (a)	**32.** (a)	**33.** (c)	**34.** (c)	**35.** (d)	**36.** (a)	**37.** (d)	**38.** (a)	**39.** (d)	**40.** (b)
41. (a)	**42.** (b)	**43.** (b)	**44.** (d)	**45.** (b)	**46.** (c)	**47.** (d)	**48.** (d)	**49.** (c)	**50.** (d)
51. (c)	**52.** (b)	**53.** (a)	**54.** (c)	**55.** (b)	**56.** (a)	**57.** (d)	**58.** (d)	**59.** (b)	**60.** (d)
61. (b)	**62.** (d)	**63.** (d)	**64.** (c)	**65.** (a)	**66.** (c)	**67.** (a)	**68.** (b)	**69.** (a)	**70.** (d)
71. (a)	**72.** (d)	**73.** (c)	**74.** (d)	**75.** (a)	**76.** (d)	**77.** (c)	**78.** (d)	**79.** (a)	**80.** (b)
81. (c)	**82.** (a)	**83.** (b)	**84.** (d)	**85.** (d)	**86.** (a)	**87.** (d)	**88.** (b)	**89.** (d)	**90.** (c)
91. (b)	**92.** (d)	**93.** (a)	**94.** (c)	**95.** (a)	**96.** (a)	**97.** (b)	**98.** (a)	**99.** (b)	**100.** (d)
101. (b)	**102.** (d)	**103.** (d)	**104.** (a)	**105.** (d)	**106.** (c)	**107.** (a)	**108.** (b)	**109.** (a)	**110.** (d)
111. (a)	**112.** (d)	**113.** (b)	**114.** (c)	**115.** (d)	**116.** (a)	**117.** (d)	**118.** (d)	**119.** (c)	**120.** (d)
121. (a)	**122.** (d)	**123.** (c)	**124.** (c)	**125.** (d)	**126.** (d)	**127.** (b)	**128.** (c)	**129.** (d)	**130.** (a)
131. (c)	**132.** (d)	**133.** (d)	**134.** (c)	**135.** (b)	**136.** (c)	**137.** (d)	**138.** (c)	**139.** (b)	**140.** (d)
141. (c)	**142.** (d)	**143.** (c)	**144.** (b)	**145.** (c)	**146.** (a)	**147.** (c)	**148.** (d)	**149.** (b)	**150.** (a)
151. (b)	**152.** (b)	**153.** (c)	**154.** (a)	**155.** (d)	**156.** (b)	**157.** (a)	**158.** (b)	**159.** (a)	**160.** (d)
161. (d)	**162.** (a)	**163.** (c)	**164.** (d)	**165.** (b)	**166.** (a)	**167.** (c)	**168.** (c)	**169.** (a)	**170.** (c)
171. (a)	**172.** (c)	**173.** (d)	**174.** (d)	**175.** (a)	**176.** (d)	**177.** (c)	**178.** (b)	**179.** (c)	**180.** (b)
181. (d)	**182.** (b)	**183.** (a)	**184.** (b)	**185.** (a)	**186.** (d)	**187.** (a)	**188.** (a)	**189.** (d)	**190.** (b)
191. (c)	**192.** (a)	**193.** (a)	**194.** (b)	**195.** (d)	**196.** (d)	**197.** (a)	**198.** (d)	**199.** (b)	**200.** (d)
201. (d)	**202.** (b)	**203.** (d)	**204.** (b)	**205.** (a)	**206.** (d)	**207.** (d)	**208.** (c)	**209.** (d)	**210.** (b)
211. (d)	**212.** (d)	**213.** (d)	**214.** (b)	**215.** (c)	**216.** (d)	**217.** (a)	**218.** (c)	**219.** (b)	**220.** (c)
221. (b)	**222.** (d)	**223.** (c)	**224.** (b)	**225.** (d)	**226** (d)	**227.** (d)	**228.** (d)	**229.** (a)	**230.** (c)
231. (d)	**232.** (c)	**233.** (a)	**234.** (c)	**235.** (d)	**236.** (c)	**237.** (c)	**238.** (a)	**239.** (c)	**240.** (d)
241. (d)	**242.** (a)	**243.** (d)	**244.** (b)	**245.** (c)	**246.** (d)	**247.** (c)	**248.** (c)	**249.** (c)	**250.** (c)
251. (c)	**252.** (b)	**253.** (d)	**254.** (d)	**255.** (b)	**256.** (a)	**257.** (d)	**258.** (d)	**259.** (c)	**260.** (a)
261. (a)	**262.** (c)	**263.** (d)	**264.** (a)	**265.** (a)	**266.** (a)	**267.** (d)	**268.** (c)	**269.** (a)	**270.** (d)
271. (d)	**272.** (c)	**273.** (a)	**274.** (b)	**275.** (b)	**276.** (d)	**277.** (c)	**278.** (b)	**279.** (c)	**280.** (c)
281. (a)	**282.** (a)	**283.** (c)	**284.** (d)	**285.** (a)	**286.** (d)	**287.** (d)	**288.** (c)	**289.** (a)	**290.** (b)
291. (c)	**292.** (d)	**293.** (b)	**294.** (d)	**295.** (d)	**296.** (c)	**297.** (d)			

POST MAURYAN BIHAR

1. (a)	**2.** (d)	**3.** (a)	**4.** (d)	**5.** (a)	**6.** (d)	**7.** (d)	**8.** (d)	**9.** (b)	**10.** (a)
11. (b)	**12.** (b)	**13.** (c)	**14.** (d)	**15.** (d)	**16.** (d)	**17.** (c)	**18.** (d)	**19.** (b)	**20.** (c)

21. (c) **22.** (a) **23.** (a) **24.** (a) **25.** (c) **26.** (a) **27.** (d) **28.** (d) **29.** (c) **30.** (a)
31. (d) **32.** (d) **33.** (c) **34.** (d)

GUPTAS PERIOD BIHAR

1. (d) **2.** (c) **3.** (d) **4.** (d) **5.** (d) **6.** (b) **7.** (a) **8.** (b) **9.** (d) **10.** (d)
11. (b) **12.** (a) **13.** (c) **14.** (d) **15.** (a) **16.** (d) **17.** (c) **18.** (d) **19.** (d) **20.** (c)
21. (c) **22.** (d) **23.** (a) **24.** (c) **25.** (a) **26.** (d) **27.** (b) **28.** (d) **29.** (c) **30.** (a)
31. (c) **32.** (b) **33.** (a) **34.** (d) **35.** (b) **36.** (d) **37.** (c) **38.** (d) **39.** (d) **40.** (a)
41. (d) **42.** (c) **43.** (d) **44.** (a) **45.** (c)

❑❑❑

3 Medieval Bihar

PAL DYNASTY

1. **The Medieval period is considered to begin after the death of which ruler?**
   (a) Rajyavardhan
   (b) Tejvardhan
   (c) Harshvardhan
   (d) Karmvardhan
2. **When did Medieval period begin?**
   (a) 641 AD (b) 643 AD
   (c) 645 AD (d) 647 AD
3. **The period from 8th century to 12th century is considered to be which period?**
   (a) Medieval period
   (b) Pre-medieval period
   (c) Post medieval period
   (d) Mid medieval period
4. **The medieval period began from which year and ended in which year?**
   (a) From 8th to 12th century
   (b) From 9th to 12th century
   (c) From 10th to 12th century
   (d) From 11th to 13th century
5. **In pre-medieval Bihar, who had mainly ruled the State?**
   (a) Pal
   (b) Karnat
   (c) Sen
   (d) All of the above
6. **Who was the founder of the Pal dynasty?**
   (a) Dharam Pal (b) Gopal
   (c) Dev Pal (d) Ram Pal
7. **State the period of rule by Gopal.**
   (a) 750 to 770 AD
   (b) 760 to 770 AD
   (c) 755 to 770 AD
   (d) 760 to 775 AD
8. **According to which historian, Gopal belonged to the kshatriya family of Pundvardhan (District Bogra)?**
   (a) Taranath (b) Lamanath
   (c) Ashwasen (d) Nagarjun
9. **Taranath was a historian of which country?**
   (a) Bharat (b) Mangolia
   (c) Thailand (d) Tibet
10. **Which of following states' ancient name was Pundvardhan?**
    (a) Bengal
    (b) Bihar
    (c) Uttar Pradesh
    (d) Rajasthan
11. **Who became the ruler after Gopal?**
    (a) Dev Pal (b) Mihir pal
    (c) Dharam Pal (d) Anant Pal
12. **State the period of rule by Dharam Pal.**
    (a) 775-795 AD (b) 793-797 AD
    (c) 770-810 AD (d) 770-800 AD
13. **Which of the following Pal rulers had attacked Kannauj.**
    (a) Gopal (b) Dev Pal
    (c) Dharam Pal (d) Anant Pal

14. Dharam Pal had appointed whom as the ruler of Kannauj?
(a) Mihir Sen
(b) Mihir Kul
(c) Chakrayudh
(d) Nagsen

15. Which of following Pal rulers had given himself the title of 'Uttrapathswami'?
(a) Gopal (b) Dharam Pal
(c) Anant Pal (d) Dev Pal

16. Who is the composer of 'Udaisundari'?
(a) Gopal (b) Soddal
(c) Brahmdutt (d) Nagsen

17. Which Pal ruler was called the Lord of the North by Soddal in his composition?
(a) Dharam Pal (b) Dev Pal
(c) Anant Pal (d) Gopal

18. Which of the following rulers was a 'Pratihar' ruler?
(a) Khemraj (b) Dharamraj
(c) Vatsraj (d) Harshraj

19. Which of the following was a 'Rashtrakoot' ruler?
(a) Dhruva (b) Mahendra
(c) Harendra (d) Rajyavardhan

20. Which Pal ruler was defeated by Vatsraj and Dhruva?
(a) Gopal (b) Anantpal
(c) Mihir Pal (d) Dharam Pal

21. Who became Pal ruler after Dharma Pal?
(a) Anant Pal (b) Mihir Pal
(c) Vats Pal (d) Dev Pal

22. In which Pal ruler's period, Pal Empire was at its peak?
(a) Dharam Pal (b) Dev Pal
(c) Gopal (d) Anant Pal

23. Which of the following Pal ruler had adopted an expansionist policy?
(a) Gopal (b) Dev Pal
(c) Dharam Pal (d) Anant Pal

24. Which of the following was a Pratihar ruler?
(a) Nagbhatt II (b) Brahmbhatt
(c) Keshavbhatt (d) Devbhatt

25. Which of the Pal rulers had defeated Pratihar ruler and the 'Huns' of Kamboj?
(a) Dev Pal (b) Anant Pal
(c) Mihir Pal (d) Harsh Pal

26. Balputradev was the ruler of which place?
(a) Ceylon (b) China
(c) Thailand (d) Jawa

27. Which Pal ruler had, on the recommendations of the ruler of Jawa, donated five villages to take care of a Vihar in Nalanda?
(a) Gopal (b) Dev Pal
(c) Dharam Pal (d) Anant Pal

28. Which Pal ruler was famous as guardian of Buddhism?
(a) Dev Pal (b) Dharam Pal
(c) Gopal (d) Mahipal

29. Which Pal ruler has been considered the best one by Arabian traveller Suleman?
(a) Mahipal (b) Anantpal
(c) Dharampal (d) Devpal

30. After death of which Pal ruler, the Pratihars, had in the period of Mihirbhoj and Mahendra Pal, captured most of the areas of Eastern Uttar Pradesh and Bihar?
(a) Dharampal (b) Devpal
(c) Mahipal (d) Anantpal

31. Who became the Pal ruler in 11th century?
(a) Mahendrapal (b) Mrigendrapal
(c) Mahipal (d) Manjaypal

32. Who is called the second founder of the Pal dynasty?
(a) Mahipal (b) Devenderpal
(c) Mahenderpal (d) Ajitpal

33. In Mahipal's period, who had attacked Bengal?
(a) Rajendra Chol
(b) Rajesh Chol
(c) Brahmdutt Chol
(d) Keshav Chol

34. Who was the last ruler of Pal dynasty?
(a) Rajendrapal (b) Mahipal
(c) Rampal (d) Gajendrapal

35. Who was the composer of 'Ram-charitra'?
(a) Sandhyakarnandi
(b) Hrendra Nath
(c) Rajnath Sen
(d) Gopal Dutt

36. 'Ramcharitra' is related to which Pal ruler?
(a) Dharampal (b) Devpal
(c) Mahipal (d) Rampal

37. What type of information does the Maner Bronze inscription of the ruler of Gaharwal dynasty Gobindchandra provide us?
(a) Turushkdand
(b) Kurushkdand
(c) Kamrupdand
(d) Damrushkdand

38. Pal rulers were the followers of which religion?
(a) Jain (b) Ajivika
(c) Boddhist (d) Shaiva

39. The rulers of which dynasty had got established the Vikramshila Mahavihar?
(a) Haryak (b) Shung
(c) Pal (d) Kanva

40. Who had got established the Vikramshila Mahavihar?
(a) Dharampal (b) Gopal
(c) Devpal (d) Mahipal

41. How many villages were donated by Dharampal to Nalanda University?
(a) 100 (b) 150
(c) 200 (d) 250

42. The rulers of which dynasty had got established Odantpur and Jagdal Universities?
(a) Maurya (b) Pal
(c) Shung (d) Sen

43. With which country Pal rulers had close relations?
(a) Tibet (b) Ceylon
(c) Thailand (d) Mangolia

44. Which of the following scholars had gone to Tibet?
(a) Shantrakshit (b) Atish Dipankar
(c) Mrigendra (d) Both (a) and (b)

45. After whose campaigns, Bodh Bhikshu Dharmaswami came to Bihar to get educated in Nalanda Mahavihar?
(a) Bakhtiyar Khilji
(b) Alauaddin Khilji
(c) Balban
(d) Akbar

46. A 'Shailendra' dynasty ruler had obtained permission to build a Bodh temple in Nalanda from which of the Pal rulers?
(a) Dharampal (b) Gopal
(c) Mahipal (d) Devpal

47. Pal period was the best in getting __________ idols?
(a) Brass (b) Bronze
(c) Copper (d) Silver

48. Which of the following called Pal dynasty 'Ruhela'?
(a) Suleman (b) Nagsen
(c) Ashwaghosh (d) Amar Singh

49. When there was rule of Pal dynasty in East India, there was rule of __________dynasty in West of India?
(a) Rashtrakoot (b) Gurjar Pratihar
(c) Solanki (d) Satvahan

50. When there was rule of ________ dynasty in East India, there was rule of Rashtrakoot dynasty in south India.
(a) Maurya (d) Sen
(c) Pal (d) Kanva

51. At Harshavardhan's time, _______ had become a centre of power in India.
(a) Vaishali (b) Kannauj
(c) Patliputra (d) Nalanda

52. For capturing of Kannauj, there was a war between whom?
(a) Pals
(b) Pratihars
(c) Rashtrakoots
(d) All of the above

53. Tripartite war completed in how many phases?
(a) 3 (b) 4
(c) 5 (d) 6

54. Which Pal ruler had taken part in the tripartite war?
(a) Dharampal (b) Yashpal
(c) Mahipal (d) Gopal

55. Dharampal had fought a war with which Pratihar ruler?
(a) Karna (b) Mahendra
(c) Devendra (d) Vatsraj

56. After Dharampal, which Pal ruler had taken a part in the tripartite war?
(a) Devpal (b) Vigrahpal
(c) Narayanpal (d) All of these

57. Finally in the Tripartite war, _________ dynasty won?
(a) Pal (b) Gurjar Pratihar
(c) Rashtrakoot (d) Solanki

58. Which dynasty had ruled over Kannauj for the maximum period?
(a) Gurjar Pritihar
(b) Rashtrakoot
(c) Pal
(d) Solanki

59. The inscription of which Gurjar Ruler has been found from Bengal and Bihar?
(a) Anatpal (b) Mahendrapal
(c) Shivendrapal (d) Gautampal

KARNAT DYNASTY

1. In Rampal's time, in Tirhat area in the northern plains of Ganga, which dynasty had come up?
(a) Karnat dynasty
(b) Sen dynasty
(c) Pal dynasty
(d) Kanva dynasty

2. Who was the founder of Karnat dynasty?
(a) Gopal Dev (b) Dhanya Dev
(c) Ramdev (d) Nyaydev

3. Simraon stone inscription is related to which ruler?
(a) Dhanyadev (b) Nyaydev
(c) Gopal Dev (d) Mahant Dev

4. From Maldev's text, knowledge about which dynasty is obtained?
(a) Haryak Dynasty
(b) Gang Dynasty
(c) Kanva dynasty
(d) Karnat dynasty

5. Where was the capital of Karnat dynasty?
(a) Seswagarh
(b) Simraogarh
(c) Mahendragarh
(d) Jaigarh

6. Whose rule is called the golden age of Mithila?
(a) Karnat (b) Maurya
(c) Shung (d) Kanva

7. Narsainghdev, a ruler from Karnat dynasty had fought a war with the ruler of which place?
(a) Vaishali (b) Bengal
(c) Nalanda (d) Kashi

8. Upto which place did the empire of Narsinghdev exist?
(a) Vaishali (b) Darbhanga
(c) Tirhut (d) Both (b) and (c)

9. Who was the last ruler of Karnat dynasty?
(a) Sher Singh
(b) Hari Singh
(c) Mahavat Singh
(d) Dev Singh

10. When did Karnat dynasty extinguish completely?
(a) 1398 AD (b) 1383 AD
(c) 1378 AD (d) 1368 AD

11. In whose time, development of 'panji-prabandh' took place?
(a) Narsinghdev (b) Harisinghdev
(c) Nyaydev (d) Karansingh

12. Vidyapati was a poet of which language?
(a) Pali (b) Maithili
(c) Magadhi (d) Angika

13. Vidyapati was a courtier of which ruler?
(a) Sher Singh (b) Kriti Singh
(c) Kunal Singh (d) Both (a) and (b)

14. Vidyapati was born in which village?
(a) Nalanda (b) Vaishali
(c) Saran (d) Darbhanga

15. When was Vidyapati born?
(a) 1330 AD (b) 1340 AD
(c) 1350 AD (d) 1360 AD

16. Which of the following books was not composed in Sanskrit?
(a) Vibhag Saar (b) Saarsangraha
(c) Varshkritya (d) Gaya Patan

17. Which of following was written by Chandeshwar?
(a) Krityachintamani
(b) Vibhag Ratnakar
(c) Rajniti Ratnakar
(d) All of the above

18. Which of the following was written by Ganpati Thakur?
(a) Adichinta (b) Gadangbhakti
(c) Tarangini (d) Both (b) and (c)

19. Which of the following is the other name of Vidyapati?
(a) Abhinav Thakur
(b) Abhinav Jaidev
(c) Abhinav Singh
(d) Anjani Jaidev

20. Who is the writer of 'Kirtilata'?
(a) Vidyapati (b) Devsingh
(c) Kirtisingh (d) Brahmgupta

21. What is the language of the text called 'Kirtilata'?
(a) Sanskrit
(b) Maithili
(c) Prakrit
(d) All of the above

22. The language mixed with Sanskrit, Maithili and Prakrit was given the name of which language by Vidyapati?
(a) Tribhasha (b) Sangam
(c) Avhatt (d) Sanchay

23. Who composed 'Bhuparikrama'?
(a) Brahmdutt (b) Nagsen
(c) Vidyapati (d) Kalidas

24. 'Likhnawali' was composed by Vidyapati in which language?
(a) Sanskrit (b) Pali
(c) Magadhi (d) Angika

25. Which of the following was composed by Vidyapati?
(a) Ganga Vakyavali
(b) Daan Vakyavali
(c) Durgabhakti Taringini
(d) All of the above

26. Which of the following was not composed by Vidyapati?
(a) Saar Sangriha
(b) Vibhag Saar
(c) Varsh Kritya
(d) Gaya Patan

27. Which of the following text has a relation with the wife of Narsinghdev, Heermati?
(a) Vishwasdevi
(b) Daanvakyavali
(c) Ganga Vakyavali
(d) All of the above

SEN DYNASTY

1. After the fall of the Pal dynasty, which dynasty was established?
(a) Sen (b) Karnat
(c) Kanva (d) Shung

2. Who established the Sen dynasty?
(a) Gauravsen (b) Mahendrasen
(c) Gopalsen (d) Samantsen

3. Samantsen was a feudal lord under which dynasty's ruler?
(a) Karnat (b) Sangam
(c) Pal (d) Kanva

4. Sen Dynasty became fully independent in whose rule?
(a) Gopalsen (b) Hemant sen
(c) Kunalsen (d) Jivaksen

5. Who was the powerful king of Sen dynasty?
(a) Vijay Sen (b) Lakshman Sen
(c) Ballal Sen (d) Samant Sen

6. Which Sen ruler is referred to in the bronze inscription in Devpada (Bengal)?
(a) Samant Sen (b) Kunal Sen
(c) Vijay Sen (d) Dhruva sen

7. Which Sen ruler had defeated 'Nyayadev'?
(a) Lakshman Sen
(b) Mahendra Sen
(c) Ballal Sen
(d) Vijay Sen

8. Vijaysen was follower of which religion?
(a) Shaiva (b) Jain
(c) Bodh (d) Ajivika

9. Who of the following is the writer of 'Geet Govind'?
(a) Lakshman Sen
(b) Jaidev
(c) Kunal Ghosh
(d) Vijay Singh

10. Jaidev was related to the ruler of which dynasty?
(a) Pal (b) Sen
(c) Karnat (d) Kanva

11. Lakshman Sen was the follower of which religion?
(a) Vaishnav (b) Shaiva
(c) Ajivika (d) Jain

12. Where was the capital of the Sen rulers?
(a) Midnapur (b) Lucknauti
(c) Nadiya (d) Both (b) and (c)

13. Bakhtiyar Khilji was running a campaign in Eastern India in the time of which Sen ruler?
(a) Vijay Sen
(b) Lakshman Sen
(c) Mahendra Sen
(d) Ballal Sen

THE TURK INVASION ON BIHAR

1. Which 'Turk' invader had attacked India in the first phase?
(a) Bakhtiyar Khilji
(b) Mohammad Gauri
(c) Mehmood Ghaznavi
(d) Balban

2. Which 'Turk' invader had attacked India in the second phase?
(a) Mohd. Gauri
(b) Bakhtiyar Khilji
(c) Mehmood Ghaznavi
(d) Balban

3. Who was the ruler of Bihar at the time of invasion by Turks?
(a) Gopal (b) Rampal
(c) Devpal (d) Mahipal

4. Which composition tells us about the Turks' invasion?

(a) Shahnama (b) Qutabuddin

(c) Rehala (d) Padmavati

5. Who is the writer of 'Shahnama'?

(a) Azharuddin

(b) Fidausi

(c) Ibnbatuta

(d) Minhas-us-Siraz

6. Shahnama is the famous composition of which language?

(a) Persian (b) Arabic

(c) Urdu (d) Yunani

7. Who is related to the Yamini clan?

(a) Mohd. Gauri

(b) Mehmood Ghaznavi

(c) Bakhtiyar Khilji

(d) Firdausi

8. What was the name of father of Mehmood Ghaznavi?

(a) Subugtgeen (b) Qutabuddin

(c) Burhanuddin (d) Al-Yahya

9. Who had adorned the title of a 'Ghazi'?

(a) Mohd. Gauri

(b) Akbar

(c) Jahangir

(d) Mehmood Ghaznavi

10. When for the first time Mehmood Ghaznavi had attacked India?

(a) 993 AD (b) 100 AD

(c) 1001 AD (d) 1002 AD

11. Which of the Hindu Kingdom ruler was first attacked by Mehmood Ghaznavi?

(a) Jaipal (b) Jaichand

(c) Jaishah (d) Rampal

12. Where did Mehmood Ghaznavi for the second time attack in the year 1011-12?

(a) Kannauj (b) Dwarka

(c) Vaishali (d) Thaneshwar

13. When did Mehmood Ghaznavi attack Punjab?

(a) 1020-21 (b) 1021-22

(c) 1022-23 (d) 1023-24

14. What was the basic purpose of the attack by Mehmood Ghaznavi over Punjab?

(a) Plundering wealth

(b) To rule

(c) To establish military base

(d) All of the above

15. When did Mehmood Ghaznavi attack Somnath Temple?

(a) 1023-24 (b) 1024-25

(c) 1025-26 (d) 1026-27

16. Where do the Somnath Temple exist?

(a) Uttarakhand (b) Rajasthan

(c) Bihar (d) Gujarat

17. The last invasion by Mehmood Ghaznavi was against which rulers?

(a) Rajput (b) Yadav

(c) Jaat (d) Brahmin

18. What was the main purpose of attack by Ghaznavi?

(a) Propaganda of Islam

(b) Plundering wealth

(c) Establishing a military base

(d) Taking away the slaves from here

19. Which of the following rulers' original name was Muizzuddin Muhammad bin Sam?

(a) Mohd. Gauri

(b) Iltutmish

(c) Babur

(d) Mehmood Ghaznavi

20. What was the basic purpose of attack over India by Mohd. Gauri?

(a) Plundering wealth

(b) Establishing political power

(c) Establishing military base

(d) All of the above

21. When did Bakhtiyar Khilji win Odantpuri (Bihar Sharif)?
(a) 1196 AD (b) 1197 AD
(c) 1198 AD (d) 1199 AD

22. Which Turk ruler had destroyed Nalanda University?
(a) Balban
(b) Iltutmish
(c) Mohd. Gauri
(d) Bakhtiyar Khilji

23. Mohd. bin Bakhtiyar Khilji was the commander of which ruler?
(a) Jalalludin Khilji
(b) Alauddin Khilji
(c) Mohd. Gauri
(d) Babur

24. Who got the credit for establishing Turk rule over Bihar?
(a) Bakhtiyar Khilji
(b) Feroze Shah Tughlak
(c) Balban
(d) Iltutmish

25. Lakshman Sen and Indradhumn Pal had opposed the attack by which Turk ruler?
(a) Alauddin Khilji
(b) Qutabuddin Aibak
(c) Balban
(d) Bakhtiyar Khilji

26. When did Bakhtiyar Khilzi attack and win Nadiya, the capital of Sen rulers?
(a) 1202-03 AD
(b) 1203-04 AD
(c) 1204-05 AD
(d) 1205-06 AD

27. Where did Bakhtiyar Khilji make his capital after winning Bihar and Bengal?
(a) Nadiya (b) Patliputra
(c) Vaishali (d) Lucknauti

28. Who had killed Bakhtiyar Khilji?
(a) Qasim Nomani
(b) Mahavat Khan
(c) Isha Shah Durrani
(d) Ali Mardan Khilji

29. When was Bakhtiyar Khilji killed?
(a) 1205 AD (b) 1206 AD
(c) 1207 AD (d) 1208 AD

30. Qutabuddin Aibak was whose commander?
(a) Mohd. Gauri
(b) Mehmood Ghaznavi
(c) Babur
(d) Alauddin Khilji

31. After the murder of Bakhtiyar Khilji, who established his rule in Bengal and Bihar?
(a) Qutabuddin Aibak
(b) Ali Mardan
(c) Mahavat Khan
(d) Iltutmish

32. Who established an independent Turk Rule in Delhi after death of Mohd. Gauri?
(a) Balban
(b) Qutabuddin Aibak
(c) Alauddin Khilji
(d) Iltutmish

33. When did Qutabuddin Aibak establish the Delhi Sultanate?
(a) 1204 AD (b) 1205 AD
(c) 1206 AD (d) 1207 AD

SULTANATE PERIOD

1. How many dynasties had ruled under the Delhi Sultanate?
(a) 3 (b) 4
(c) 5 (d) 6

2. State the period of 'Mamlook' or 'Ghulam' clan.
(a) 1205-60 AD
(b) 1206-90 AD
(c) 1207-85 AD
(d) 1208-80 AD

3. Which dynasty established its rule in Delhi after the Ghulam dynasty?
(a) Khilji (b) Tughlak
(c) Saiyyad (d) Lodhi

4. **Khilji dynasty remained in power in which of the following years?**
(a) 1285-1310 AD
(b) 1290-1310 AD
(c) 1290-1320 AD
(d) 1295-1325 AD

5. **Which dynasty established its rule over Delhi after the Khilji dynasty?**
(a) Mughals (b) Tughlak
(c) Lodhi (d) Saiyyad

6. **Tughlak dynasty remained in power in which of the following years?**
(a) 1310-1402 AD
(b) 1310-1414 AD
(c) 1320-1414 AD
(d) 1325-1425 AD

7. **Which dynasty established its rule over Delhi after the Tughlak dynasty?**
(a) Lodhi (b) Saiyyad
(c) Ghulam (d) Khilji

8. **Saiyyad dynasty remained in power in which of the following years?**
(a) 1414-1451 AD
(b) 1414-1445 AD
(c) 1420-1455 AD
(d) 1425-1460 AD

9. **Which dynasty established its rule over Delhi after the Saiyyad dynasty?**
(a) Ghulam (b) Khilji
(c) Lodhi (d) Mughal

10. **Lodhi dynasty remained in power in which of the following years?**
(a) 1451-1526 AD
(b) 1450-1530 AD
(c) 1455-1526 AD
(d) 1460-1540 AD

11. **Qutabuddin Aibak had a war with which of the following?**
(a) Shahvar (b) Yaldauj
(c) Kubacha (d) Both (b) and (c)

12. **Who became the ruler of Delhi Sultanate after Qutabuddin Aibak?**
(a) Iltutmish
(b) Balban
(c) Alauddin Khilji
(d) Jalaluddin Khilji

13. **Qutabuddin Aibak remained in power in which of the following years?**
(a) 1205-30 AD (b) 1206-30 AD
(c) 1210-36 AD (d) 1210-38 AD

14. **Who established his independent rule over Bengal and started collecting tax from Tirhut area of Bihar?**
(a) Balban
(b) Jalaluddin
(c) Gayasuddin
(d) Ali Mardan Khilji

15. **Iltutumish established two separate states called Bengal and Bihar after defeating whom?**
(a) Gayasuddin (b) Malik Jani
(c) Farajuddin (d) Hisabuddin

16. **Who became the ruler of Delhi Sultanate after Iltutmish?**
(a) Hisabuddin (b) Gayasuddin
(c) Balban (d) Alauddin Khilji

17. **Who crushed the revolution which began under the leadership of Tugril?**
(a) Balban
(b) Hisamuddin
(c) Malik Jani
(d) Qutabuddin Aibak

18. **In whose dynasty's rule after Balban, the rule of the Turks had established in Tirhut including the South Bihar?**
(a) Khilji
(b) Tughlak
(c) Saiyyad
(d) None of the above

19. Which dynasty's rule and administration is known from the composition made by the Sufi Saint Hazrat Sarfuddin Yahiya Maneri?
(a) Ghulam (b) Khilji
(c) Tughlak (d) Saiyyad

20. Which of the following compositions belong to Saint Hazrat Sarfuddin Yahiya Maneri?
(a) Jame-Jehnuma
(b) Malfujat
(c) Mankibul Asfiya
(d) Both (b) and (c)

21. When did Gayasuddin Tughlak defeat the Karnat dynasty ruler Harisingh Dev?
(a) 1322 AD (b) 1323 AD
(c) 1324 AD (d) 1325 AD

22. Which ruler had established market system?
(a) Alauddin Khilji
(b) Mohd. Tughlak
(c) Balban
(d) Sikandar Lodhi

23. What name was given to Mithila when Gayasuddin Tughlak won it?
(a) Gayaspur (b) Tughlakabad
(c) Tughlakpur (d) Gayasabad

24. Which tughlak ruler had got constructed in Darbhanga one mosque and a 'Durg'?
(a) Gayasuddin Tughlak
(b) Jalauddin Tughlak
(c) Mohd. Bin Tughlak
(d) Ferozeshah Tughlak

25. With whose cooperation Harisingh Dev had taken a refuge in the Nepal area after getting defeated?
(a) Vidyapati
(b) Gangdev
(c) Nanyadev
(d) Shanker Mahadev

26. Where was the capital of Bihar in Tughlak period?
(a) Tughlakpur
(b) Lukmanabad
(c) Bihar Sharif
(d) Patliputra

27. When did Ferozeshah Tughlak begin his Bengal campaign?
(a) 1357 AD (b) 1358 AD
(c) 1359 AD (d) 1360 AD

28. Which composition contains the knowledge about Ferozeshah Tughlak's Bengal campaign?
(a) Tarikh-e-Ferozeshahi
(b) Sirat-e-Ferozeshahi
(c) Ferozenama
(d) Feroze-e-Hind

29. Which Karnat ruler adopted a policy of friendship with the Turks?
(a) Harisingh Dev
(b) Narsingh Dev
(c) Gangasingh Dev
(d) Nanyadev Singh

30. In which Karnat dynasty's ruler's time, Tugaril Tugal had invaded Mithila?
(a) Gangadev Singh
(b) Ramsingh Dev
(c) Narsingh Dev
(d) Both (b) and (c) both

THE RISE OF AFGHAN POWER

1. Taimur invaded India in which ruler's rule?
(a) Ghulam (b) Khilji
(c) Tughlak (d) Saiyyad

2. When did Taimur invade Delhi Sultanate?
(a) 1395 AD (b) 1396 AD
(c) 1397 AD (d) 1398 AD

3. Where did the rule of 'Sharki' Empire establish?
(a) Jaunpur (b) Hisar
(c) Ferozabad (d) Daulatabad

4. Where did 'Hussainshahi Dynasty'establish?
(a) Bihar (b) Bengal
(c) Rajasthan (d) Uttar Pradesh

5. In which dynasties, there was war to capture Bihar?
(a) Sharki-Hussainshahi
(b) Hussainshahi-Lodhi
(c) Lodhi-Sharki
(d) Lodhi-Sharki-Hussainshahi

6. Which Lodhi ruler had crushed the revolution by Hussainshah?
(a) Behlol Lodhi
(b) Ibrahim Lodhi
(c) Sikandar Lodhi
(d) Sujat Lodhi

7. Who was appointed by Sikandar Lodhi to collect tax from Bihar area?
(a) Dilawar Khan
(b) Mubarak Khan
(c) Afzal Khan
(d) Mahavat Khan

8. When did a war break out between Sikander Lodhi and the Nawab of Bengal Alluddin?
(a) 1502 AD (b) 1503 AD
(c) 1504 AD (d) 1505 AD

9. Which Landlord of Bihar had revolted against Ibrahim Lodhi?
(a) Dawood Khan
(b) Islam Shah
(c) Bulleshah
(d) Darya Khan Nuhani

10. Which of the following had a name "Bahar Khan'?
(a) Darya Khan Nuhani
(b) Ibrahim Shah
(c) Behlol Lodhi
(d) Mahavat Khan

11. When did Darya Khan Nuhandi die?
(a) 1520 AD (b) 1521 AD
(c) 1522 AD (d) 1523 AD

12. Who had declared Bihar an independent state after the death of Darya Khan Nuhani?
(a) Ibrahim Shah
(b) Mohd. Shah Nuhani
(c) Islam Shah Nuhani
(d) Akbar Shah Nuhani

13. When did the first Battle of Panipat happen?
(a) 1524 AD (b) 1525 AD
(c) 1526 AD (d) 1527 AD

14. Who had defeated Ibrahim Lodhi in the first Battle of Panipat?
(a) Akbar (b) Babur
(c) Jahangir (d) Aurangzeb

15. As a consequence of the first Battle of Panipat, which dynasty was founded in India?
(a) Khilji (b) Mughal
(c) Shah (d) Mangol

16. Which ruler had founded the Mughal dyanasty?
(a) Islam Shah (b) Sher Shah
(c) Babur (d) Humayun

17. When Afghans tried to have a control over Jaunpur, under whose command Babur had sent an army?
(a) Humayun (b) Akbar
(c) Sher Shah (d) Islam Shah

18. In the beginning of the Mughal dynasty, whose rule prevailed in South Bihar?
(a) Islam Shah (b) Sher Shah
(c) Mohd. Shah (d) Ibrahim Shah

19. In the beginning of the Mughal dynasty, whose rule prevailed in the north?
(a) Nusrat Shah (b) Madim Shah
(c) Islam Shah (d) Mahavat Shah

20. When did Babur die?
(a) 1528 AD (b) 1530 AD
(c) 1532 AD (d) 1534 AD

21. When did the battle of Dausa happen?
(a) 1532 AD (b) 1534 AD
(c) 1536 AD (d) 1537 AD

22. Who had defeated the Afghans in the battle of Dausa?
(a) Babur (b) Humayun
(c) Akbar (d) Aurangzeb

23. After the fall of the Nuhanis, whose power re-emerged?
(a) Karani (b) Afghan
(c) Shah (d) Durrani

24. Under whose command, the Afghan's power came back to life again?
(a) Dawood Khan
(b) Dariya Khan
(c) Mahavat Khan
(d) Sher Shah

SUR DYNASTY

1. What was the original name of Sher Shah?
(a) Faraid Khan
(b) Islam Khan
(c) Ibrahim Khan
(d) Mubarak Khan

2. Ibrahim Khan was the son of whom?
(a) Hasan Khan (b) Hussain Khan
(c) Islam Khan (d) Mahavat Khan

3. Hasan Khan had got the Estate of which place?
(a) Sasa Ram
(b) Vaspur
(c) Tanda
(d) All of the above

4. Who had handed over estates to Hasan Khan?
(a) Islam Khan
(b) Jamal Khan
(c) Mahavat Khan
(d) Dilawar Khan

5. Where did the childhood of Farid Khan spend?
(a) Sasaram (b) Saran
(c) Darbhanga (d) Bihar Sharif

6. Sasaram is situated on the banks of which river?
(a) Ganga (b) Sone
(c) Gandak (d) Kosi

7. ________was the main centre of Islam in the fifteenth century.
(a) Jaunpur (b) Agra
(c) Bihar Sharif (d) Hisar

8. Which place was known as the crown of India?
(a) Patna (b) Darbhanga
(c) Bihar Sharif (d) Jaunpur

9. Hasan Khan handed over his estate to whom?
(a) Islam Khan (b) Mahavat Khan
(c) Farid Khan (d) Mubarak Khan

10. When did Farid Khan get the estate of Sasaram?
(a) 1495 AD (b) 1497 AD
(c) 1499 AD (d) 1501 AD

11. Till when Farid Khan was the owner of the estate of Sasaram?
(a) 1514 AD (b) 1516 AD
(c) 1518 AD (d) 1520 AD

12. Where did Farid Khan go from Sasaram?
(a) Agra (b) Delhi
(c) Alwar (d) Chittor

13. When did Hasan Khan die?
(a) 1516 AD (b) 1518 AD
(c) 1520 AD (d) 1522 AD

14. Farid Khan had taken a refuge under which of the rulers of South Bihar?
(a) Bahar Khan
(b) Ibrahim Khan
(c) Dawood Khan
(d) Mahavat Khan

15. Who had given the title of 'Sher Khan'to Farid Khan?
(a) Ibrahim Lodhi
(b) Feroz Khan
(c) Ibrahim Khan
(d) Bahar Khan

16. Which Mughal ruler appointed Sher Khan in his army?
(a) Babur (b) Humayun
(c) Akbar (d) Shahjahan

17. After death of Bahar Khan, who became the guardian of Jalal?
(a) Lohani Khan (b) Sher Khan
(c) Islam Khan (d) Dudu Biwi

18. After the death of Dudu Biwi, who became the real ruler of Bihar?
(a) Dawood Khan
(b) Luhahi Khan
(c) Sher Khan
(d) Islam Khan

19. Which of the following rulers obtained the title of "Hazrat-e-ala"?
(a) Sher Khan (b) Babur
(c) Jahangir (d) Akbar

20. When did Sher Khan marry the widow of Taz Khan, Laad Malika?
(a) 1528 AD (b) 1530 AD
(c) 1532 AD (d) 1534 AD

21. Who had deputed his son Qutab Khan to defend Chunar?
(a) Bahar Khan (b) Jalal Khan
(c) Sher Khan (d) Umar Khan

22. After death of Babur, who became the ruler of Delhi?
(a) Humayun (b) Akbar
(c) Jahangir (d) Shahjahan

23. When did Humayun become the ruler of Delhi?
(a) 1528 AD (b) 1530 AD
(c) 1532 AD (d) 1534 AD

24. Which Mughal ruler had a huge army to invade Chunargarh?
(a) Babur (b) Akbar
(c) Humayun (d) Aurangzeb

25. When did a war break out in Suratgarh?
(a) 1534 AD (b) 1535 AD
(c) 1536 AD (d) 1537 AD

26. Which battle had taken place between Sher Khan and Mehmood Shah?
(a) Chunargarh (b) Surajgarh
(c) Singhgarh (d) Chittorgarh

27. With whose foreign support, Mehmood Shah had attacked Sher Khan?
(a) The French (b) The Dutch
(c) The British (d) The Portuguese

28. Which ruler had defeated Mehmood Shah in Teliagarhi and Sikri Gali battle?
(a) Sher Shah (b) Humayun
(c) Akbar (d) Bahadur Shah

29. Sher Khan had ascended ______ inclusive of Bengal.
(a) Rohtasgarh (b) Kumbhalgarh
(c) Chittorgarh (d) Surajgarh

30. Seeing the expanding power of Sher Khan, Humayun attacked _______?
(a) Bihar (b) Bengal
(c) Islamabad (d) Jaunpur

31. _________was the main competitor of Humayun?
(a) Bahadur Shah
(b) Sher Shah
(c) Rana Sangha
(d) Daulat Khan Lodhi

32. The battle of Chausa took place between Humayun and________.
(a) Sher Khan
(b) Bahar Khan
(c) Dariya Khan Nuhani
(d) Ibrahim Khan

33. In the battle of Chausa, Humayun jumped into which river?
(a) Gandak (b) Ganga
(c) Kosi (d) Sone

34. The place called Chausa comes under which district?
(a) Darbhanga (b) Buxar
(c) Gaya (d) Arrah

35. When did the battle of Kannauj take place?
(a) 1538 AD (b) 1539 AD
(c) 1540 AD (d) 1541 AD

36. The battle of Kannauj took place between Humayun and who else?
(a) Sher Khan (b) Bahar Khan
(c) Jalaj Khan (d) Mubarak Khan

37. After his defeat of Chausa, Humayun went to which place?
(a) Delhi (b) Gujarat
(c) Agra (d) Bihar Sharif

38. Where did Humayun and Sher Khan face each other?
(a) Bilgram (b) Shahbaad
(c) Jamalpur (d) Tajpur

39. Sher Khan established a new dynasty in India after dismissing which Empire?
(a) The Mughal (b) Khilji
(c) Mangol (d) Tughlak

40. The battles of Chausa and Bilgram resulted into making whom a new Emperor of India?
(a) Humayun (b) Sher Khan
(c) Akbar (d) Babur

41. Who had in reality established the 'Soor'dynasty?
(a) Hasan Khan (b) Islam Khan
(c) Sher Khan (d) Ibrahim Khan

42. Who is known as the founder of the second Afghan dynasty?
(a) Humayun
(b) Sher Khan
(c) Ibrahim Lodhi
(d) Hasan Khan

43. Under whose command an army was kept in Rohtasgarh fort to defend the north west border?
(a) Mahavat Khan
(b) Haibat Khan
(c) Khwas Khan
(d) Both (b) and (c)

44. Who crushed the revolt of Khizr Khan in Bengal?
(a) Humayun (b) Sher Khan
(c) Akbar (d) Ibrahim Lodhi

45. Bengal was divided in how many Sarkars (Districts) by Sher Khan?
(a) 19 (b) 20
(c) 21 (d) 22

46. Which ruler had appointed 'Amin-e-Bangla' (Non-military official)?
(a) Humayun (b) Mehmood Shah
(c) Sher Khan (d) Ibrahim Lodhi

47. After the death of Bahadur Shah, who had declared himself a sovereign ruler after adopting a title of 'Kadir Shah'?
(a) Ismat Khan
(b) Bande Nawaj Khan
(c) Mubarak Khan
(d) Mallu Khan

48. After whose campaign, Mallu Khan surrendered?
(a) Ibrahim Lodhi
(b) Islam Khan
(c) Mahavat Khan
(d) Sher Khan

49. Who was appointed the Estate holder of Malwa by Sher Khan?
(a) Shujad Khan
(b) Javed Khan
(c) Murshid Khan
(d) Ajmat Khan

50. Who was the ruler of Raiseen Pradesh (Madhya Pradesh) in 1543 AD?
(a) Puran Mal
(b) Ajit Singh
(c) Nagar Mal
(d) Devendra Chauhan

51. In which Battle, Sher Shah ordered mass murders, which is considered a black spot on the name of Sher Shah in history?

(a) Malwa (b) Bengal
(c) Raiseen (d) Bihar

52. Whose rule prevailed in Marwad area in 1544 AD?
(a) Maldev (b) Jaidev
(c) Amardev (d) Karndev

53. Sher Shah defeated Udai Singh the ruler of which place?
(a) Amer (b) Jodhpur
(c) Chittor (d) Jaipur

54. Which of the following forts were taken over by Sher Shah?
(a) Mount Abu
(b) Ajmer
(c) Chittor
(d) All of the above

55. Who had said, "for just a handful of millets, would have lost the entire Hindustan?"
(a) Babur (b) Sher Khan
(c) Hasan Khan (d) Akbar

56. When did Sher Shah launch his campaign over Kalinjar?
(a) 1540 AD (b) 1542 AD
(c) 1545 AD (d) 1547 AD

57. Which was the last campaign of Sher Shah?
(a) Marwad (b) Kalinjar
(c) Malwa (d) Raiseen

58. Before death, Sher Shah was shooting which fire weapon?
(a) Kantak (b) Tulguma
(c) Ukka (d) Hathgola

59. Who had said that if fortune supported him and the good luck became his friend, he would one day expell the Mughals from India?
(a) Islam Shah (b) Ibrahim Lodhi
(c) Balban (d) Sher Khan

60. At the time of which battle Sher Khan had said that if fortune supported him and the good luck became his friend, he would one day expel the Mughals from India?
(a) Chanderi (b) Kannauj
(c) Raiseen (d) Bengal

61. Sher Shah is called the forerunner of __________.
(a) Babur (b) Humayun
(c) Shahjahan (d) Akbar

62. Which of the following is the department related to taxation and economy?
(a) Diwan-e-wajarat
(b) Diwan-e-ariz
(c) Diwan-e-rasatal
(d) Diwan-e-insha

63. Who of the following used to be the head of the military administration?
(a) Diwan-e-insha
(b) Diwan-e-sainya
(c) Diwan-e-inshaz
(d) Diwan-e-ariz

64. Which of the following used to be the foreign ministry?
(a) Diwan-e-fahim
(b) Diwan-e-valayat
(c) Diwan-e-rasatal
(d) Diwan-e-insha

65. What name was given to the head of Diwan-e-rasatal?
(a) Diwan-e-mahas
(b) Diwan-e-mohtabis
(c) Diwan-e-khas
(d) Diwan-e-naeem

66. Which department was related to the official orders and correspondence?
(a) Diwan-e-jok
(b) Diwan-e-fahm
(c) Diwan-e-insha
(d) Diwan-e-naks

67. Which department was related to judiciary?
(a) Diwan-e-adal
(b) Diwan-e-qazi
(c) Diwan-e-sahaf
(d) Diwan-e-insha

68. Which of the following was Secret Department?
(a) Diwan-e-barid
(b) Diwan-e-rajjuk
(c) Diwan-e-adal
(d) Diwan-e-mohtasib

69. Who of the following used to take care of the different works related to the Shahi Palace?
(a) Diwan-e-rasatal
(b) Diwan-e-insha
(c) Diwan-e-sama
(d) Khan-e-sama

70. At the time of Sher Shah, in how many sarkars the entire empire was divided?
(a) 44 (b) 45
(c) 46 (d) 47

71. Who of the following used to be a major government official apart from being a military officer?
(a) Diwan-e-osaf
(b) Diwan-e-naksh
(c) Shikdar-e-shikdaran
(d) Shikdar-e-khas

72. Who of the following used to be the highest judicial officer?
(a) Munsife-e-munsifan
(b) Munsif-e-adal
(c) Munsif-e-nyaya
(d) Diwan-e-insha

73. Whose taxation system was implemented by Sher Shah Suri in his province?
(a) Iltutmish
(b) Balban
(c) Mohd. Bin Tughlak
(d) Alauddin Khilji

74. On which of the following arrangements, the land revenue of arrangement of Sher Shah was based?
(a) Raiyyatwadi
(b) Permanent arrangement
(c) Mahalwadi
(d) Jagirdari

75. Sher Shah divided the land in ________?
(a) Beegha (b) Kathhah
(c) Gaj (d) Dhur

76. One beegha was equal to how many 'sikandari'yards?
(a) 2500 (b) 2700
(c) 3100 (d) 3600

77. To measure land, Sikandari yard of how many numbers and stick of the 'san' was used by Sher Shah Suri?
(a) 28 (b) 30
(c) 32 (d) 34

78. How much portion of the produce Sher Shah used to recover as land revenue?
(a) 1/6th (b) 1/5th
(c) 1/4th (d) 1/3th

79. Who was the ruler who started the system of 'Patta'and 'Kabuliyat'?
(a) Iltutmish
(b) Qutubuddin Aibak
(c) Balban
(d) Sher Shah

80. What was the name of Sher Shah's father?
(a) Hasan Khan
(b) Qutab Khan
(c) Bugra Khan
(d) Giyasuddin

81. 'Dahshala' system of land revenues is related to which ruler?
(a) Alauddin Khilji
(b) Akbar
(c) Sher Shah Suri
(d) Ferozeshah Tughlak

82. Sher Shah used to sit in his court to deliver justice on the evening of ________ day.
(a) Monday (b) Wednesday
(c) Friday (d) Sunday

83. Which ruler said that to do justice is the best work to do among the religious works?
(a) Sher Shah Suri
(b) Akbar
(c) Qutubuddin Aibak
(d) Mohd. Bin Tughlak

84. Sher Shah had appointed whom in the markets and inns?
(a) Munsif (b) Adal
(c) Harkara (d) Jagdal

85. In which script the name of the mint of Sher Shah was written?
(a) Afghani (b) Persian
(c) Devnagari (d) Both (b) and (c)

86. Sher Shah was the first ruler who started a 'rupaiya' of pure_______.
(a) Copper (b) Bronze
(c) Silver (d) Gold

87. The silver coins of which of the following rulers remained in circulation till 1835 AD?
(a) Iltutmish (b) Sher Shah Suri
(c) Akbar (d) Aurangzeb

88. In times of Sher Shah, one silver rupee coin used to be equal to how many coins made of copper?
(a) 60 (b) 62
(c) 64 (d) 66

89. The gold coin introduced by Sher Singh was called as?
(a) Asharfi (b) Dinar
(c) Dirhim (d) Taka

90. One asharfi was made of how many grains of the gold?
(a) 161 (b) 163
(c) 165 (d) 167

91. Being a _________, Sher Shah had got imprinted the names of four 'Khalifas' on his coins.
(a) Shiya (b) Sunni
(c) Wahabi (d) Barelvi

92. Where did Sher Shah get constructed the fort of Rohtasgarh?
(a) Kannauj (b) Patna
(c) Hisar (d) Sasaram

93. Who of the following Mughal rulers had got established 'Din Panah' city?
(a) Babur (b) Humayun
(c) Akbar (d) Jahangir

94. Which fort got built by Sher Shah?
(a) Nandangarh (b) Surajgarh
(c) Purana (d) Ajmeri

95. When was the mosque called 'Kila-a-Kuhna' built?
(a) 1541 AD (b) 1542 AD
(c) 1543 AD (d) 1544 AD

96. Which ruler had got constructed 'kila-a-kuhna' mosque?
(a) Sher Shah (b) Babur
(c) Akbar (d) Aurangzeb

97. When was Patliputra re-built as Patna?
(a) 1539 AD (b) 1541 AD
(c) 1543 AD (d) 1545 AD

98. Who was the ruler who rebuilt Patliputra as Patna?
(a) Akbar (b) Mohd. Shah
(c) Aurangzeb (d) Sher Shah

99. Where is the tomb of Sher Shah located?
(a) Agra (b) Hisar
(c) Sasaram (d) Jaunpur

100. Who had said about the tomb of Sher Shah that it is a muslim architectural art from outside and Hindu Architectural art from inside?
(a) Cunningham (b) James Cooper
(c) Hamilton (d) Kanugo

101. Who had said about the tomb of Sher Shah that it is more beautiful than the Tajmahal?
(a) James Mill (b) Hawkins
(c) James Patrick (d) Cunningham

102. Which ruler had given a new shape to Kannauj City after destroying it first?
(a) Iltutmish (b) Balban
(c) Humayun (d) Sher Shah

103. Which ruler had got built 'Sadak-e-azam' (Grand Truck Road)?
(a) Sher Shah
(b) Qutabuddin Aibak
(c) Akbar
(d) Aurangzeb

104. 'Sadak-e-azam' started from Sonar village in the east and ended at________in the west.
(a) Sindh
(b) Peshawar
(c) Kabul (Afghanistan)
(d) Lahore

MUGHALS PERIOD IN BIHAR

1. When did Babur start his military campaign in Bihar?
(a) 1527 (b) 1528
(c) 1529 (d) 1530

2. Babur had appointed whom as Diwan of Bengal?
(a) Mursheed Khan
(b) Mursheed Iraqi
(c) Islam Bang
(d) Ismat Khan

3. In which battle Babur defeated the Afghans?
(a) Ghaghra (b) Chanderi
(c) Malwa (d) Buxar

4. When did the battle of Ghaghra take place?
(a) 1526 AD (b) 1527 AD
(c) 1528 AD (d) 1529 AD

5. When did the rulers of Mughal dynasty again capture Delhi?
(a) 1553 AD (b) 1555 AD
(c) 1557 AD (d) 1559 AD

6. Who of the mughal rulers had defeated the ruler of the Soor dynasty and re-instated the Mughal empire?
(a) Humayun (b) Akbar
(c) Jahangir (d) Daulat Beg

7. When did Humayun die?
(a) 1554 AD (b) 1555 AD
(c) 1556 AD (d) 1557 AD

8. When did Sher Shah establish his rule over Bihar?
(a) 1534 AD (b) 1536 AD
(c) 1538 AD (d) 1540 AD

9. Who became the ruler of Delhi after the death of Humayun?
(a) Iltutmish (b) Akbar
(c) Jahangir (d) Aurangzeb

10. Who is considered the real founder of Mughal Empire in India?
(a) Akbar (b) Jahangir
(c) Shahanshah (d) Aurangzeb

11. In the initial period of Akbar becoming a ruler, where did the Afghans keep continuing their control?
(a) Gujarat (b) Bihar
(c) Rajasthan (d) Bengal

12. When did Suleman Qurrani announce his independent rule over Bihar?
(a) 1562 AD (b) 1564 AD
(c) 1566 AD (d) 1568 AD

13. When did Dawood Khan become the ruler of Bihar?
(a) 1568 AD (b) 1570 AD
(c) 1572 AD (d) 1574 AD

14. Who was sent by Akbar to Bihar to demolish the ever increasing power of Dawood Khan?
(a) Munim Khan
(b) Islam Khan
(c) Ismat Khan
(d) Haibat Jung

15. Which Mughal ruler had sent his commander Shahbaz Khan to crush Bairishah, the king of Chhota Nagpur?

(a) Babur (b) Humayun
(c) Akbar (d) Aurangzeb

16. Who attacked the 'Cheras' of Palamu?

(a) Munim Khan
(b) Raja Mansingh
(c) Akbar
(d) Shahbaz Khan

17. When did Raja Mansingh attack the 'cheras' of Palamu?

(a) 1576 AD (b) 1577 AD
(c) 1578 AD (d) 1579 AD

18. When did Akbar defeat the Mithila Rajpoot King?

(a) 1572 AD (b) 1574 AD
(c) 1576 AD (d) 1578 AD

19. Akbar had authorized whom to collect land revenue from Mithila area?

(a) Mahesh Thakur
(b) Brahmdutt Tiwari
(c) Shivshankar Singh
(d) Erawat Singh

20. Man Singh had defeated which of the following local 'Sardars'?

(a) Gidhhaur
(b) Kharagpur
(c) Bhojpur
(d) All of the above

21. Man Singh made which city his capital?

(a) Sasaram (b) Buxar
(c) Rohtas (d) Vaishali

22. Man Singh had given what new name to Rajmahal area?

(a) Akbarganj
(b) Akbarpur
(c) Akbar Nagar
(d) Man Singh Nagar

23. Who of the following used to be the head of the War Department?

(a) Mir Kayam (b) Mir Bakshi
(c) Mir Meham (d) Mir Gadar

24. Who of the following used to collect tax on the ports, custom duty and the navigation tax?

(a) Mir Vayaj (b) Mir Kabar
(c) Mir Behr (d) Mir Chunk

25. According to 'Aaine-a-akbari, Bihar province was divided in how many sarkars (districts)?

(a) 7 (b) 9
(c) 11 (d) 13

26. Which of the following was not a province of Bihar in the Mughal period?

(a) Munger (b) Rohtas
(c) Bhagalpur (d) Saran

27. Which of the following was a province of Bihar in the Mughal period?

(a) Tirhut
(b) Hazipur
(c) Champaran
(d) All of the above

28. Who is the writer of 'Aaine-a-akbari'?

(a) Abul Fazal (b) Firdausi
(c) Ibnbatuta (d) Abdul Rehman

29. Who had appointed prince 'Parvez' the governor of Bihar?

(a) Babur (b) Akbar
(c) Jahangir (d) Aurangzeb

30. When was prince Parvez appointed as governor of Bihar?

(a) 1619 AD (b) 1621 AD
(c) 1623 AD (d) 1625 AD

31. In whose rule, the Mughals established their rule over Khokhradesh (Chhota Nagapur) area?

(a) Babur (b) Humayun
(c) Jahangir (d) Aurangzeb

32. Jahangir was successful in taking control of the__________mines of the Chota Nagpur area.
(a) Silver (b) Gold
(c) Bauxite (d) Diamond

33. Jahangir in his autobiography, had indicated obtaining of which metal from the Chhota Nagpur Area?
(a) Gold (b) Copper
(c) Seesa (d) Tungston

34. Which of the following is the autobiography of Jahangir?
(a) Tabqate-Jahangiri
(b) Jahangirnama
(c) Tarik-e-Jahangiri
(d) Tujuk-e-Jahangiri

35. Shahjahan had captured Bihar area from whom?
(a) Man Singh
(b) Baikunth Thakur
(c) Mahesh Thakur
(d) Parvez

36. When did Shahjahan snatch Bihar area from Parvez?
(a) 1622-23 AD (b) 1623-24 AD
(c) 1624-25 AD (d) 1625-26 AD

37. Who was appointed the Estate owner of Bihar by Aurangzeb?
(a) Tabrez (b) Azeem
(c) Javed (d) Najim

38. When did Aurangzeb appoint Azeem as the estate owner of Bihar?
(a) 1702 AD (b) 1703 AD
(c) 1704 AD (d) 1705 AD

39. What was the changed name of Patna City given by prince Azeem?
(a) Azeem Nagar
(b) Azeem Ganj
(c) Azeemabad
(d) Azeempur

40. How much money in rupees was spent by prince Azeem for the beautification of the city?
(a) 50 lakhs (b) 75 lakhs
(c) 1 crore (d) 1.5 crore

41. Who was the erstwhile Diwan of Bengal in Aurangzeb's time?
(a) Mir Qasim
(b) Mir Jafar
(c) Murshid Kuli Khan
(d) Sirazudaula

42. In Aurangzeb's period, the number of sarkars in Bihar was 8 and how many 'parganas' were there?
(a) 238 (b) 240
(c) 243 (d) 245

43. Which of the following rights were available to the 'Fauzdar'?
(a) Revenue
(b) Police
(c) Military
(d) All of the above

44. Under Mughal period, what was the smallest unit of administration?
(a) Sarkar (b) Zila
(c) Tehsil (d) Pargana

45. The administration relating to revenue was being run by __________?
(a) Aamil (b) Kamil
(c) Qasim (d) Jamil

46. Which of the following used to perform the duty of writing accounts of the 'Pargana'and remit the self collected revenue to the official treasury?
(a) Gumasta (b) Hota
(c) Karkun (d) Manchaseen

47. Who of the following was the authority over the local treasury?
(a) Fauzdar (b) Talukdar
(c) Fotdar (d) Koshdar

48. The Mughal period's Bihar's land was divided in which of the following?

(a) Khalsa
(b) Jagir
(c) Sayurgal
(d) All of the above

49. In whose rule did Todarmal decide the name of Bihar?
(a) Sher Shah (b) Humayun
(c) Akbar (d) Aurangzeb

50. How much was the land revenue decided for Bihar by Todarmal?
(a) 25 lakh (b) 28 lakh
(c) 31 lakh (d) 35 lakh

51. Which of the following taxes was levied on the traders?
(a) Vujuhat
(b) Jihat
(c) Sairjihat
(d) All of the above

52. Which was collected by the Zamindars?
(a) Faruaat (b) Summat
(c) Jaru (d) Tod

53. Which of the following was tax in Bihar in the Mughal period?
(a) Ikhrajat
(b) Abab
(c) Hubutat
(d) All of the above

54. When did Murshid Quli Khan announce Bihar as an independent state?
(a) 1702 AD (b) 1704 AD
(c) 1700 AD (d) 1708 AD

55. Which Mughal prince was born in Patna?
(a) Mohd. Shah (b) Azeem
(c) Parvez (d) Farrukhsiyer

56. Farrukhsiyar had established his rights over the Mughal throne after defeating whom?
(a) Jahandar Shah
(b) Mohd. Shah
(c) Azeem
(d) Parvez

57. Where did Farrukhsiyar organize his coronation ceremony?
(a) Agra (b) Delhi
(c) Hisar (d) Patna

58. Farrukhsiyar became a Mughal emperor after winning the battle at which place?
(a) Agra (b) Bihar
(c) Bengal (d) Gujarat

59. Who was the first Mughal emperor whose coronation was held in Bihar?
(a) Parvez
(b) Azeem
(c) Jahandar Shah
(d) Farrukhsiyar

60. Till when did the successor of Farrukhsiyar rule Bihar?
(a) 1736 AD (b) 1738 AD
(c) 1740 AD (d) 1742 AD

61. Who was the descendant of Farrukhsiyar?
(a) Sarfaraz (b) Sirazuddin
(c) Shujauddin (d) Both (a) and (c)

62. Who was appointed as the first Nayab Nazim of Bihar?
(a) Muqim Khan
(b) Safdar Khan
(c) Mustkim Khan
(d) Alivardi Khan

63. Who announced himself as the Nawab of Bengal after killing Sarfaraj Khan?
(a) Shujauddin (b) Alivardi Khan
(c) Mir Jafar (d) Mir Qasim

64. When did Alivardikhan announce himself to be the Nawab of Bengal?
(a) 1736 AD (b) 1738 AD
(c) 1740 AD (d) 1742 AD

65. Till when Alivardikhan ruled over Bengal?
(a) 1748 AD (b) 1750 AD
(c) 1754 AD (d) 1756 AD

66. **Who was appointed the Nayab-Nazim of Bengal by Alivardi Khan?**
(a) Mubarak Khan
(b) Muqim Khan
(c) Jainuddin Haibat
(d) Haibat Jung

67. **When did Maratha Peshwa attack Bihar?**
(a) 1743 AD (b) 1745 AD
(c) 1747 AD (d) 1749 AD

68. **When was Haibat Jung killed by the Afghans?**
(a) 1744 AD (b) 1747 AD
(c) 1748 AD (d) 1750 AD

69. **Under whose leadership, the Afghans killed Haibat Jung?**
(a) Muqim Khan
(b) Mastkim Khan
(c) Mustafa Khan
(d) Shaista Khan

70. **In the battle at which place, Alivardi Khan defeated Marathas?**
(a) Fatuha (b) Buxar
(c) Supaul (d) Saran

71. **When did Alivardi Khan defeat Marathas?**
(a) 1750 AD (b) 1751 AD
(c) 1752 AD (d) 1753 AD

72. **Who became the successor of Alivardi Khan?**
(a) Shujaudaula
(b) Asifudaula
(c) Sirazudaula
(d) Mir Qasim

73. **When di Sirazudaula become the Nawab of Bengal?**
(a) 1752 AD (b) 1754 AD
(c) 1756 AD (d) 1758 AD

THE SOCIAL STATUS IN THE MEDIEVAL BIHAR

1. **Hindu society was divided mainly in how many classes in Medieval Bihar?**
(a) 3 (b) 4
(c) 5 (d) 6

2. **Which of the following class occupied the highest position in the society?**
(a) Brahmin (b) Kshatriya
(c) Vaishya (d) Shudra

3. **Where is 'Vishnupad' temple located?**
(a) Mujaffarpur (b) Gaya
(c) Hajipur (d) Bhagalpur

4. **Who was initiated in Vaishnav sect by the vaishnava saint, Ishwarpuri?**
(a) Chaitanya (b) Dadu
(c) Rahim (d) Sant Ramdas

5. **In__________Bihar, Brahma Vishnu and Mahesh were worshipped specially as 'Trimurti'?**
(a) Ancient (b) Medieval
(c) Pre-medieval (d) Post Medieval

6. **In which area of Bihar, 'Shakti'was worshipped in particular?**
(a) Mithila (b) Tirhut
(c) Munger (d) Saran

7. **Which of the following occultists was related to Mithila area?**
(a) Devdivya Mandan Mishra
(b) Gangesh Upadhyay
(c) Rampukar Ojha
(d) Both (a) and (b)

8. **Chaitanya Dev was follower of which sect?**
(a) Shaiva (b) Ajivika
(c) Vaishnav (d) Jain

9. **Who was the main disciple of Chaitanya Dev?**
(a) Gangesh Upadhyay
(b) Mandan Mishra
(c) Ramavtar Tiwari
(d) Raghupati Upadhyay

10. **Where, in Bihar, Raghupati Upadhyay was born?**
(a) Saran (b) Champaran
(c) Munger (d) Tirhut

11. Which of the following is a centre in Bihar related to 'Shaiva'sect?
(a) Vaikatpur
(b) Bajidpur
(c) Gaya
(d) All of the above

12. Where, out of the following places, Hariharnath Temple is situated?
(a) Hajipur (b) Sonpur
(c) Hagalpur (d) Mujjaffarpur

13. Which of the following temples is a huge specimen of worship of Vishnu and Shiva jointly?
(a) Vishnupad (b) Koleshwari
(c) Malooti (d) Hariharnath

14. In_________century, muslims arrived in Bihar.
(a) 11th (b) 10th
(c) 9th (d) 8th

15. In medieval time, the emergence of familism in social set-up of_________ was a wonderful incident.
(a) Tirhut (b) Saran
(c) Gaya (d) Mithila

16. Who got the credit for reconstruction of Mithila society on the lines of familism?
(a) Narsingh Dev
(b) Harisingh Dev
(c) Devsingh Dev
(d) Ramsingh Dev

17. In 'Varna Ratnakar,' Jyotirishwar has provided a list the __________ caste.
(a) Yadav
(b) Rajput
(c) Kayastha
(d) Bhumihar

18. Malik Mohd. Jayasi gave information about __________Rajpoot castes.
(a) 32 (b) 34
(c) 36 (d) 38

19. In which of the Mughal rule, 'Sati Pratha' was banned by enacting a law?
(a) Babur (b) Akbar
(c) Shahjahan (d) Aurangzeb

20. Evidence of whose ruler's wife becoming a 'Sati' is available?
(a) Harisingh Dev
(b) Bhav Singh
(c) Shidev Singh
(d) All of the above

21. In whose compositions, there is a clear evidence of the 'Slave System'?
(a) Raghupati Sahay
(b) Vidyapati
(c) Sudhakar
(d) Nagarjun

22. In medieval times in Bihar, people were fully dependent on________.
(a) Animal husbandry
(b) Agriculture
(c) Trade
(d) All of the above

23. Which area of Bihar was famous as a cloth market?
(a) Mithila (b) Tirhut
(c) Saran (d) Champaran

24. In a book called 'Varnratnakar' belonging to the medieval times, mention of ________types of cloth is made.
(a) 26 (b) 28
(c) 30 (d) 32

25. Saint Imam Taj Fakih was a main person in the list of initial 'sufis' living in __________in the 12th century.
(a) Maner (b) Bihar Sharif
(c) Gaya (d) Ajimabad

26. Sufis of which sect have been the most famous ones in Bihar?
(a) Suhravardi (b) Nakshbandi
(c) Chishti (d) Firdausi

27. In Firdausi sect in Bihar, who occupied the most famous position?
(a) Maqdoom Sharfuddin Ahmed Yahya Maneri
(b) Baba Farid
(c) Maqdum Zakir Yahya Maneri
(d) Both (b) and (c)

28. When did Saint Sharfuddin Yahya Maneri die?
(a) 1378 AD (b) 1381 AD
(c) 1384 AD (d) 1387 AD

29. When was saint Sarfuddin Yahya Maneri born?
(a) 1259 AD (b) 1261 AD
(c) 1263 AD (d) 1265 AD

30. Saint Ahmad Chiramposh was a sufi from which series?
(a) Chishti
(b) Firdausi
(c) Nakshbandi
(d) Suhravardi

31. Where is the tomb of Saint Ahmad Chiramposh?
(a) Maner (b) Bihar Sharif
(c) Gaya (d) Darbhanga

32. Who started the 'Sattariya' community in Bihar?
(a) Abdullah Sattar
(b) Hasan Sattar
(c) Nawaj Sattar
(d) Ahmad Sattar

33. Ali Sher was the first saint of which community in Bihar?
(a) Chishti (b) Suhravardi
(c) Nakshbandi (d) Qadri

34. Where was Saint Ali Sher buried?
(a) Bihar Sharif (b) Patna
(c) Maner (d) Aurangabad

35. Makhdum Shah Muhammad Munnam was the most prestigious and influential saint of ________ sect.
(a) Qadri (b) Chishti
(c) Sattari (d) Nakshbandi

36. Where was Saint Maqdum Shah Muhammad Munnar born?
(a) Patna (b) Hajipur
(c) Bhagalpur (d) Bihar Sharif

37. Who got built the Mir Taki Mosque in Mitan Ghat locality of Patna city?
(a) Sharfuddin Yahya Maneri
(b) Saint Maqdum Shah Muhammad Munnar
(c) Bahauddin Zakariya
(d) Abdul Kadir Zilani

38. Saint Sahkale was saint of which sect?
(a) Nakshbandi (b) Sattari
(c) Chishti (d) Firdausi

39. Where is the tomb of Sufi saint Sahkale situated?
(a) Patna (b) Maner
(c) Bihar Sharif (d) Hazipur

40. Aurangzeb was the disciple of sufi saint of which sect?
(a) Nakshbandi (b) Sattari
(c) Firdausi (d) Chishti

41. Mulla Mohan was the main sufi saint of which place?
(a) Agra (b) Ajmer
(c) Kabul (d) Bihar Sharif

42. Mulla Mohan was sufi saint of which sect?
(a) Sattari (b) Firdausi
(c) Nakshbandi (d) Chishti

43. Saint Sheikh Fateh and Barhan were saints of which sect?
(a) Chishti (b) Sattari
(c) Firdausi (d) Nakshbandi

44. In whose period Sheikh Fateh and Burhan arrived in Bihar?
(a) Akbar
(b) Sher Shah
(c) Aurangzeb
(d) Ferozeshah Tughlak

45. Which of the following was the main centre of education for Hindus in medieval Bihar?
(a) Tola
(b) Pathshala
(c) Mandir
(d) All of the above

46. Which of the following was taught by the teachers?
(a) Dharmashastra
(b) Nyayashastra
(c) Jyothishshastra
(d) All of the above

47. In medieval Bihar, what was the language of education?
(a) Pali (b) Magadhi
(c) Sanskrit (d) Persian

48. In medieval Bihar, _________ was the centre of education by which imparting of education to students was more popular?
(a) Tola (b) Pathshala
(c) Mandir (d) Madrasa

49. Which of the following was the main centre of education for the muslims?
(a) Maktab
(b) Madrasa
(c) Khankah
(d) All of the above

50. In Bihar, where was Khankah located?
(a) Sherghati
(b) Bhagalpur
(c) Phulwari Sharif
(d) All of the above

51. Who of the following was the founder of Darbhanga rule?
(a) Mahesh Thakur
(b) Haridev Thakur
(c) Abhay Thakur
(d) Jai Chand Thakur

52. Raghunandan Dass Rai was a scholar of which subject?
(a) Jyotishshastra
(b) Dharmashastra
(c) Nyayashastra
(d) Tarkshastra

53. Thebooknamed 'Tatvachintamani' was composed by whom?
(a) Raghupati Sahay
(b) Vidyapati
(c) Mahesh Thakur
(d) Ganesh Upadhyay

54. Where was 'Dhyot' test in vogue?
(a) Mithila (b) Saran
(c) Champaran (d) Tirhut

55. Which Mughal ruler had gifted Mithila area to Raghunandan Das Rai after getting influenced by his wisdon?
(a) Babur (b) Humayun
(c) Akbar (d) Aurangzeb

56. In the rule of which Mughal ruler, the scholars of Bihar got much respect?
(a) Akbar (b) Aurangzeb
(c) Shahjahan (d) Jahangir

57. Who is the composer of 'Afsana-e-Shasan'?
(a) Sheikh Kabir
(b) Mohd. Sadiq
(c) Abdul Latif
(d) Sheikh Ziauddin

58. For the study of which language, Raja Rammohan Rai had arrived in Patna?
(a) Persian (b) Sanskrit
(c) Maithili (d) Pali

59. When did Ahmad Bahani visit Shaif Khan Madarasa (Patna)?
(a) 1803 AD (b) 1805 AD
(c) 1807 AD (d) 1809 AD

60. Ahmad Bahani was a traveler from which country?
(a) Greece (b) Yunnan
(c) Iraq (d) Iran

61. Who of the following was Bihar's Nayab Nazim?
(a) Ramnarayan Mauju
(b) Shivnandan Sahay
(c) Harisingh Dev
(d) Maheshchandra

62. Who is the composer of the famous book 'Diwan'?
(a) Sheikh Kabir
(b) Sheikh Ali
(c) Altmash Shah
(d) Zaheer Dehalvi

63. 'Diwan' is a composition of which language?
(a) Persian (b) Sanskri
(c) Pali (d) Magadhi

64. Who composed the famous book 'Khulasat-utt-Tawarikh'?
(a) Mahesh Thakur
(b) Sheikh Kabir
(c) Peer Munsi
(d) Kalyan Singh

65. Who of the following was related to Wahabi Movement?
(a) Maulavi Ahmadullah
(b) Zakir Sheikh
(c) Wahab Ansari
(d) Ziauddin Shah

66. Who of the following had established the madrasa called –Is-lah-al-musalmeen?
(a) Sibli Numani
(b) Ahmad Sheikh
(c) Kayam Ali Shah
(d) Maulavi Ahmadullah

THE ARCHITECTURE OF MEDIEVAL BIHAR

1. Which of the following is the most conspicuous speciality of the Islamic architecture?
(a) Minar (b) Mehrab
(c) Gumbad (d) All of these

2. In whose rule, the medieval Bihar remained?
(a) Sharki
(b) Lodhi
(c) Soor
(d) All of the above

3. Where is the tomb of Malik Ibrahim situated?
(a) Patna (b) Bihar Sharif
(c) Nalanda (d) Hajipur

4. When was the tomb of Malik Ibrahim built?
(a) 1349 AD (b) 1351 AD
(c) 1353 AD (d) 1355 AD

5. Where is the Sangi mosque in Bihar situated?
(a) Patna
(b) Bihar Sharif
(c) Munger
(d) Hajipur

6. Under which rulers, Bengal style developed?
(a) Mughal (b) Sharki
(c) Lodhi (d) Soor

7. Where is the tomb of Shah Nafi situated?
(a) Patna (b) Bihar Sharif
(c) Hajipur (d) Munger

8. When was the tomb of Sher Shah built?
(a) 1541 AD (b) 1543 AD
(c) 1545 AD (d) 1547 AD

9. Which of the following is situated within the fort of Rohtasgarh?
(a) Hathiya Pole
(b) Ganesh Mandir
(c) Aaina Mahal
(d) All of the above

10. Which of the following was built in Akbar's rule?
(a) The stone mosque
(b) The mosque of Ivas Khan
(c) The tomb of Saki Sultan
(d) Both (b) and (c)

11. Where is the tomb of Maqdoom Shah situated?
(a) Maner (b) Bihar Sharif
(c) Aurangabad (d) Hajipur

12. When was the tomb of Maqdoom Shah built?
(a) 1637 AD (b) 1639 AD
(c) 1641 AD (d) 1643 AD

13. In whose rule, the tomb of Maqdoom Shah was built?
(a) Sher Shah (b) Humayun
(c) Akbar (d) Jahangir

14. Where is Sher Shah mosque situated?
(a) Patna (b) Bihar Sharif
(c) Aurangabad (d) Hajipur

15. Where is Mir Saheb Tola mosque situated?
(a) Munger (b) Gaya
(c) Aurangabad (d) Bhagalpur

16. Where is the tomb of Hazrat Muhammad Sibastani situated?
(a) Bhagalpur (b) Munger
(c) Patna (d) Bihar Sharif

17. Who had got constructed the Harishchandra Temple?
(a) Raja Mansingh
(b) Baikunth Thakur
(c) Rama Singh
(d) Mahesh Thakur

18. Which of the following is Netherland style building?
(a) Golghar
(b) Patna Collectorate
(c) Patna College
(d) Both (b) and (c)

19. On which of the following buildings, the effect of the European style is visible?
(a) Rajbhavan
(b) Main Secretariat
(c) High Court
(d) All of the above

Answers

PAL DYNASTY

1. (c)	**2.** (d)	**3.** (b)	**4.** (a)	**5.** (d)	**6.** (b)	**7.** (a)	**8.** (a)	**9.** (d)	**10.** (a)
11. (c)	**12.** (c)	**13.** (c)	**14.** (c)	**15.** (b)	**16.** (b)	**17.** (a)	**18.** (c)	**19.** (a)	**20.** (d)
21. (d)	**22.** (b)	**23.** (b)	**24.** a)	**25.** (a)	**26.** (d)	**27.** (b)	**28.** (a)	**29.** (d)	**30.** (b)
31. (c)	**32.** (a)	**33.** (a)	**34.** (c)	**35.** (a)	**36.** (d)	**37.** (a)	**38.** (c)	**39.** (c)	**40.** (a)
41. (c)	**42.** (b)	**43.** (a)	**44.** (d)	**45.** (a)	**46.** (d)	**47.** (b)	**48.** (a)	**49.** (b)	**50.** (c)
51. (b)	**52.** (d)	**53.** (c)	**54.** (a)	**55.** (d)	**56.** (d)	**57.** (b)	**58.** (c)	**59.** (b)	

KARNAT DYNASTY

1. (a)	**2.** (d)	**3.** (b)	**4.** (d)	**5.** (b)	**6.** (a)	**7.** (b)	**8.** (d)	**9.** (b)	**10.** (c)
11. (b)	**12.** (b)	**13.** (d)	**14.** (d)	**15.** (c)	**16.** (b)	**17.** (d)	**18.** (d)	**19.** (b)	**20.** (a)
21. (d)	**22.** (c)	**23.** (c)	**24.** (a)	**25.** (d)	**26.** (a)	**27.** (d)			

SEN DYNASTY

1. (a)	**2.** (d)	**3.** (c)	**4.** (b)	**5.** (a)	**6.** (c)	**7.** (d)	**8.** (a)	**9.** (b)	**10.** (b)
11. (a)	**12.** (d)	**13.** (b)							

THE TURK INVASION ON BIHAR

1. (c)	**2** (a)	**3.** (b)	**4.** (a)	**5.** (b)	**6.** (a)	**7.** (b)	**8.** (a)	**9.** (d)	**10.** (c)
11. (a)	**12.** (d)	**13.** (b)	**14.** (c)	**15.** (c)	**16.** (d)	**17.** (c)	**18.** (b)	**19.** (a)	**20.** (d)
21. (c)	**22.** (d)	**23.** (c)	**24.** (a)	**25.** (d)	**26.** (b)	**27.** (d)	**28.** (d)	**29.** (b)	**30.** (a)
31. (a)	**32.** (b)	**33.** (c)							

THE SULTANATE PERIOD

1. (c)	**2.** (b)	**3.** (a)	**4.** (c)	**5.** (b)	**6.** (c)	7(b)	**8.** (a)	**9.** (c)	**10.** (a)
11. (d)	**12.** (a)	**13.** (c)	**14.** (c)	**15.** (d)	**16.** (c)	**17.** (a)	**18.** (b)	**19.** (c)	**20.** (d)
21. (c)	**22** (b)	**23.** (c)	**24.** (c)	**25.** (a)	**26.** (c)	**27.** (c)	**28.** (b)	**29.** (b)	**30.** (d)

THE RISE OF THE AFGHAN POWER

1. (c)	**2** (d)	**3.** (a)	**4.** (b)	**5.** (c)	**6.** (c)	**7.** (b)	**8.** (c)	**9.** (d)	**10.** (a)
11. (d)	**12.** (b)	**13.** (c)	**14.** (b)	**15.** (b)	**16.** (c)	**17.** (a)	**18.** (c)	**19.** (a)	**20.** (b)
21. (a)	**22.** (b)	**23.** (b)	**24.** (d)						

SUR DYNASTY

1. (a)	**2.** (a)	**3.** (d)	**4.** (b)	**5.** (a)	**6.** (b)	**7.** (a)	**8.** (d)	**9.** (c)	**10.** (b)
11. (c)	**12.** (a)	**13.** (d)	**14.** (a)	**15.** (d)	**16.** (a)	**17.** (d)	**18.** (c)	**19.** (a)	**20.** (b)
21. (c)	**22.** (a)	**23.** (b)	**24.** (c)	**25.** (a)	**26.** (b)	**27.** (d)	**28.** (a)	**29.** (a)	**30.** (b)
31. (b)	**32.** (a)	**33.** (b)	**34.** (b)	**35.** (c)	**36.** (a)	**37.** (c)	**38.** (a)	**39.** (a)	**40.** (b)
41 (c)	**42.** (b)	**43.** (d)	**44.** (b)	**45.** (a)	**46.** (c)	**47.** (d)	**48.** (d)	**49.** (a)	**50.** (a)
51. (c)	**52.** (a)	**53.** (c)	**54.** (d)	**55.** (b)	**56.** (c)	**57.** (b)	**58.** (c)	**59.** (d)	**60.** (a)
61. (d)	**62.** (a)	**63.** (d)	**64.** (c)	**65.** (b)	**66.** (c)	**67.** (b)	**68.** (a)	**69.** (d)	**70.** (d)
71. (c)	**72.** (a)	**73.** (d)	**74.** (a)	**75.** (a)	**76.** (d)	**77.** (c)	**78.** (d)	**79.** (d)	**80.** (a)
81. (b)	**82.** (b)	**83.** (a)	**84.** (c)	**85.** (d)	**86.** (c)	**87.** (b)	**88.** (c)	**89.** (a)	**90.** (d)
91. (b)	**92.** (d)	**93.** (b)	**94.** (c)	**95.** (b)	**96.** (a)	**97.** (b)	**98.** (d)	**99.** (c)	**100.** (d)
101. (d)	**102.** (d)	**103.** (a)	**104.** (a)						

MUGHALS PERIOD IN BIHAR

1. (c)	**2.** (b)	**3.** (a)	**4.** (d)	**5.** (b)	**6.** (a)	**7.** (c)	**8.** (d)	**9.** (b)	**10.** (a)
11. (b)	**12.** (b)	**13.** (c)	**14.** (a)	**15.** (c)	**16.** (b)	**17.** (d)	**18.** (b)	**19.** (a)	**20.** (d)
21. (c)	**22.** (c)	**23.** (b)	**24.** (c)	**25.** (a)	**26.** (c)	**27.** (d)	**28.** (a)	**29.** (c)	**30.** (b)
31. (c)	**32.** (d)	**33.** (a)	**34.** (d)	**35.** (d)	**36.** (b)	**37.** (b)	**38.** (a)	**39.** (c)	**40.** (c)
41. (c)	**42.** (d)	**43.** (d)	**44.** (d)	**45.** (a)	**46.** (c)	**47.** (d)	**48.** (d)	**49.** (c)	**50.** (a)
51. (d)	**52.** (a)	**53.** (d)	**54.** (b)	**55.** (d)	**56.** (a)	**57.** (d)	**58.** (a)	**59.** (d)	**60.** (c)
61. (a)	**62.** (d)	**63.** (b)	**64.** (c)	**65.** (d)	**66.** (c)	**67.** (a)	**68.** (c)	**69.** (c)	**70.** (a)
71. (b)	**72.** (c)	**73.** (c)							

THE SOCIAL STATUS IN MEDIEVAL BIHAR

1. (b)	**2.** (a)	**3.** (b)	**4.** (a)	**5.** (b)	**6.** (a)	**7.** (d)	**8** (c)	**9.** (d)	**10.** (d)
11. (d)	**12.** (b)	**13.** (d)	**14.** (a)	**15.** (d)	**16.** (b)	**17.** (b)	**18.** (c)	**19.** (b)	**20.** (d)
21. (b)	**22.** (b)	**23.** (a)	**24.** (c)	**25.** (a)	**26.** (d)	**27.** (c)	**28.** (b)	**29.** (c)	**30.** (b)
31. (b)	**32.** (a)	**33.** (d)	**34.** (d)	**35.** (a)	**36.** (d)	**37.** (b)	**38.** (a)	**39.** (a)	**40.** (a)
41. (d)	**42.** (c)	**43.** (a)	**44.** (d)	**45.** (d)	**46.** (d)	**47.** (c)	**48.** (a)	**49.** (d)	**50.** (d)
51. (a)	**52.** (d)	**53.** (d)	**54.** (a)	**55.** (c)	**56.** (d)	**57.** (a)	**58.** (a)	**59.** (c)	**60.** (d)
61. (a)	**62.** (b)	**63.** (a)	**64.** (d)	**65.** (a)	**66.** (d)				

THE ARCHITECTURE OF MEDIEVAL BIHAR

1. (d)	**2.** (d)	**3.** (b)	**4.** (c)	**5.** (b)	**6.** (b)	**7.** (d)	**8.** (c)	**9.** (d)	**10.** (d)
11. (a)	**12.** (c)	**13.** (d)	**14.** (a)	**15.** (d)	**16.** (d)	**17.** (a)	**18.** (c)	**19.** (d)	

❑❑❑

4 Modern Period

THE ARRIVAL OF EUROPEAN COMPANIES IN BIHAR

1. The arrival of the European Companies began in Bihar in the beginning of________century?
(a) 15th (b) 16th
(c) 17th (d) 18th

2. Merchants of which country first arrived in Bihar?
(a) Portugal (b) Holland
(c) Britain (d) Spain

3. Where did the Portuguese establish their trade centre?
(a) Patna (b) Agra
(c) Surat (d) Hooghly

4. What did Portuguese bring with them for trading?
(a) Spices
(b) Cotton cloth
(c) Chinese pottery
(d) Both (a) and (c)

5. What Portuguese would take away from India?
(a) Cotton cloth (b) Spices
(c) Salt (d) Saltpetre

6. By the mid 17th century, _______ had established godowns of saltpetre in Bihar?
(a) Portuguese (b) British
(c) Dutch (d) Spanish

7. The people from which country first established a factory in the northern building of the Patna college?
(a) Portugal (b) Holland
(c) Britain (d) Spain

8. When did the Dutch establish a factory in Patna college?
(a) 1628 AD (b) 1630 AD
(c) 1632 AD (d) 1634 AD

9. The Dutch had interest in which of the following items?
(a) Sugar
(b) Saltpetre
(c) Poppy
(d) All of the above

10. When did the Dutch Trade commander obtain the orders for trading in Bihar, Bengal and Odisha?
(a) 1662 AD (b) 1660 AD
(c) 1658 AD (d) 1656 AD

11. By which time all the 'dennis' godowns and places of Bihar came under the control of the British?
(a) 1845 AD (b) 1843 AD
(c) 1841 AD (d) 1839 AD

12. Who was the Dutch Trade commander who had got an order from Aurangzeb?
(a) Nathias Vagdain Barook
(b) James August
(c) Thomas Book
(d) Nathan Lathal

13. Who revolted and invaded Patna and looted the Dutch factory situated in Fatuha?
(a) Muqim Khan
(b) Shaista Khan
(c) Shamsher Khan
(d) Shahbaz Khan

14. When did Shamsher Khan invade and loot the Dutch factory?
(a) 1842 AD (b) 1844 AD
(c) 18 46 AD (d) 1848 AD

15. In which battle, the British made the Dutch more vulnerable?
(a) Buxar (b) Plassey
(c) Chanderi (d) Khanwa

16. When did the British East India Company establish their solo control over trade of the saltpetre?
(a) 1752 AD (b) 1754 AD
(c) 1756 AD (d) 1758 AD

17. In Battle of Vedra, the British defeated whom?
(a) The Marathas
(b) The Spanish
(c) The Dutch
(d) The Portuguese

18. When did the battle of Vedra take place?
(a) 1753 AD (b) 1755 AD
(c) 1757 AD (d) 1759 AD

19. Major Hardy, the commanding officer of the Patna militia, had captured the Dutch Warehouse of which place?
(a) Agra (b) Delhi
(c) Hugli (d) Patna

20. When did Major Hardy capture the Dutch warehouse?
(a) 1781 AD (b) 1779 AD
(c) 1777 AD (d) 1775 AD

21. From whom Patrick Hitley took charge of the Dutch Factory?
(a) Curzan (b) Cunningham
(c) Maxwell (d) James Cook

22. When did Patrick Hitley take over the charge of the Dutch factory?
(a) 1781 AD (b) 1783 AD
(c) 1785 AD (d) 1787 AD

23. Under Franco-Dutch battle in the year 1795, the dutch bases were handed over to whom?
(a) The Marathas
(b) The Mughals
(c) The English
(d) The Portuguese

24. In 1824-25 AD, the trade centres of which were finally included in the East India Company of the British?
(a) The Dutch
(b) The Portuguese
(c) The Marathas
(d) The Spanish

25. Who had, in India, established the East India Company of the French?
(a) Francis Martin
(b) Frankois Martin
(c) Franceba Holland
(d) Franceba Aukad

26. When, in India, was the French East India Company established?
(a) 1660 AD (b) 1662 AD
(c) 1664 AD (d) 1666 AD

27. When did Martin establish Pondicherry?
(a) 1674 AD (b) 1672 AD
(c) 1670 AD (d) 1668 AD

28. The merchants of which country established Pondicherry?
(a) Holland (b) Spain
(c) France (d) Britain

29. In Mahi and Karaikal which European merchants established trade centres?
(a) The French (b) The Dutch
(c) The Spanish (d) The British

30. Which city was established by the French in Bengal?
(a) Hugli (b) Midnapore
(c) Durgapur (d) Chandranagar

31. In 1734 AD, The French established warehouses in which place?
(a) Delhi (b) Agra
(c) Patna (d) Hugli

32. The French had one major interest to collect _________ from Bihar.
(a) Sugar
(b) Saltpetre
(c) Cotton Clothes
(d) Chinese Pottery

33. When did the British capture Chandranagar?
(a) 1781 AD (b) 1753 AD
(c) 1755 AD (d) 1757 AD

34. The French company head M. Jiyala had to leave Bengal from which market?
(a) Noman (b) Qasim
(c) Jakariya (d) Hasim

35. At the time of the Battle of Plassey, who was the governor of Bihar?
(a) Irekoot
(b) James Lion
(c) Major Hardy
(d) Thomas Hopes

36. When did the French lose Pondicherry Island?
(a) 1757 AD (b) 1759 AD
(c) 1761 AD (d) 1763 AD

37. In 1763 AD, by the Deriff Treaty, who got their lost estates back?
(a) The Spanish
(b) The Dutch
(c) The Portuguese
(d) The French

38. When, in India, the trading activities of the French could remain limited to Pondicherry only?
(a) 1789 AD (b) 1791 AD
(c) 1793 AD (d) 1795 AD

39. In the period of which Governor General, the trading center of the French could remain limited to Pondicherry only?
(a) Cornwallis (b) Reading
(c) Curzon (d) Canning

40. By what time the activities of the French got almost vanished from Bihar and India?
(a) 1810 AD (b) 1812 AD
(c) 1814 AD (d) 1816 AD

41. Among the European companies arriving in India, company of which country is said to have come in the last?
(a) France (b) Italy
(c) Spain (d) Denmark

42. In Bihar, the companies from Denmark had first established factories at which place?
(a) Bihar Sharif (b) Hajipur
(c) Patna (d) Bodhgaya

43. When did the companies from Denmark establish factories in Patna?
(a) 1772-73 AD
(b) 1773-74 AD
(c) 1774-75 AD
(d) 1775-76 AD

44. When did Danish factory Head seek an order from the Governer General and his council?
(a) 1772 AD (b) 1773 AD
(c) 1774 AD (d) 1775 AD

45. Who was the Head of Danish factories in 1775 AD?
(a) George Lloyd
(b) George Burner
(c) Dennis Cooper
(d) Mc Holland

46. The Danish Company mainly did trading of _________ in Bihar.
(a) Sugar (b) Cotton clothes
(c) Salt Petre (d) Grains

47. When did a war break out between Great Britain and Denmark?
(a) 1798 AD (b) 1799 AD
(c) 1800 AD (d) 1801 AD

48. __________captured the Danish factory of Patna and the bunglow in Serampur?
(a) The Marathas
(b) The Dutch
(c) The British
(d) The Portuguese

49. When did the treaty of 'Amiyan' take place?
(a) 1799 AD (b) 1800 AD
(c) 1801 AD (d) 1802 AD

50. Under which Treaty, the Danish areas in India were regained?
(a) Vedra (b) Aamu
(c) Dariya (d) Aamiya

THE ARRIVAL OF EAST INDIA COMPANY

1. Where was the permanent warehouse of East India Company established in the year 1691 AD?
(a) Patna (b) Agra
(c) Hugali (d) Chandranagar

2. East India Company used to manufacture calico clothes on a large scale at_______near Lakhbar?
(a) Bihar Sharif (b) Vaishali
(c) Patna (d) Nalanda

3. Who was appointed the Head of the English factory in Patna?
(a) Wales
(b) George-III
(c) Job Charnak
(d) Hamilton

4. When did Job Charnak become the Head of the English factory in Patna?
(a) 1664 AD (b) 1662 AD
(c) 1660 AD (d) 1658 AD

5. When did Shaista Khan levy tax on the English factory?
(a) 1674 AD (b) 1676 AD
(c) 1678 AD (d) 1680 AD

6. Shaista Khan levied tax on the English factory at what rate?
(a) 2% (b) 5%
(c) 3% (d) 5%

7. Who of the following had looted Hugli city?
(a) Lord Hardinge
(b) Lord Curzon
(c) Alexander Cunningham
(d) Job Charnak

8. When did Job Charnak loot Hugli city?
(a) 1686 AD (b) 1684 AD
(c) 1682 AD (d) 1680 AD

9. Under which Mughal ruler's rule, the English factory in Patna belonging to the British was banned from operations?
(a) Aurangzeb (b) Alam Shah II
(c) Farrukhsiyar (d) Jahandar Shah

10. Under pressure from which Nawab, the factory at Patna was banned from operations?
(a) Mir Qasim
(b) Mir Jafar
(c) Sirajuddaula
(d) Alivardi Khan

11. By whose efforts, the English factory at Patna was re-started in 1755 AD?
(a) Job Charnak
(b) Halwel
(c) Mark Reading
(d) Kevin Dome

12. When did the treaty of Allahabad take place?
(a) 1761 AD (b) 1763 AD
(c) 1765 AD (d) 1767 AD

13. The treaty of Allahabad took place between Lord Clive and which Mughal ruler?
(a) Bahadur Shah Zafar
(b) Shah Alam II
(c) Aurangzeb
(d) Farrukhsiyar

THE ESTABLISHMENT OF THE BRITISH RULE

1. **Who of the following gave a detailed account of the trading activities by visiting various places in Bihar?**
   (a) Edward Terry
   (b) Peter Mundi
   (c) Traver
   (d) All of the above
2. **When did the war of Manihari take place?**
   (a) 1754 AD (b) 1755 AD
   (c) 1756 AD (d) 1757 AD
3. **In the battle of Manihari, Sirajuddaula had defeated whom?**
   (a) Mir Qasim (b) Mir Zafar
   (c) Shujauddola (d) Shaukat Jung
4. **The officers of the British East India Company started fortification of which fort?**
   (a) Fort William
   (b) Rohtasgarh
   (c) Fort St. George
   (d) Fort Douglas
5. **After the battle of Plassey, who was appointed the Nawab of Bengal by the British?**
   (a) Mir Qasim
   (b) Mir Zafar
   (c) Mir Shahid
   (d) Murshid Kuli Khan
6. **After the battle of Plassey, who was appointed the Nayab Nawab of Bengal?**
   (a) Miran (b) Shahbaz Khan
   (c) Haibat Jung (d) Shaukat Jung
7. **After the battle of Plassey, who became the real king of Bihar?**
   (a) Mahesh Thakur
   (b) Jaichand Singh
   (c) Devpal Mishra
   (d) Ram Narayan
8. **When did Mir Qasim become the Nawab of Bengal?**
   (a) 1760 AD (b) 1762 AD
   (c) 1764 AD (d) 1766 AD
9. **With whose support did Mir Qasim become the Nawab of Bengal?**
   (a) Ram Narayan Singh
   (b) Mahesh Thakur
   (c) Alivardi Khan
   (d) The British
10. **Mir Qasim took his capital from Murshidabad to which other place?**
    (a) Bhagalpur (b) Munger
    (c) Bihar Sharif (d) Midnapur
11. **When did Munger become the capital of Bengal?**
    (a) 1757 AD (b) 1759 AD
    (c) 1761 AD (d) 1763 AD
12. **Who with the support of workers of the company stopped the misuse of the concept of adoption?**
    (a) Mir Zafar (b) Mir Qasim
    (c) Meeruch (d) Sirajuddaula
13. **Which English supporter of Mir Qasim was put under house arrest?**
    (a) Jai Chand
    (b) Hira Chand
    (c) Swarup Chand
    (d) Both (b) and (c)
14. **Mir Qasim put Hira Chand and Swarup Chand under house arrest at which place?**
    (a) Murshidabad(b) Munger
    (c) Jehanabad (d) Midnapur
15. **When did Ellis capture Patna and plunder it?**
    (a) 1761 AD (b) 1762 AD
    (c) 1763 AD (d) 1764 AD
16. **Who ordered mass murder of the British officials in Patna?**
    (a) Mir Qasim
    (b) Mir Zafar
    (c) Meeran
    (d) Sirajuddaula

17. **When did the battle of Udvanala of Rajmahal take place?**
(a) 1757 AD (b) 1759 AD
(c) 17 61 AD (d) 1763 AD

18. **In the battle of Udvanala of Rajmahal, the British defeated whom?**
(a) Sirajuddaula
(b) Haibat Jung
(c) Shaukat Jung
(d) Mir Qasim

19. **The defeat at which place ended the fortune of Mir Qasim and at the same time Bihar came under full control of the British?**
(a) Buxar (b) Jehanabad
(c) Munger (d) Murshidabad

20. **Together with whom Mir Qasim started preparation for a war against the british?**
(a) Shaukat Jung
(b) Shah Alam II
(c) Shujauddaula
(d) Both (b) and (c)

21. **Shujauddaula was the ruler of which place?**
(a) Selapur (b) Avadh
(c) Jaipur (d) Munger

MASS MOVEMENT AGAINST THE BRITISH RULE

1. **When did the British take control of Chhota Nagpur?**
(a) 1767 AD (b) 1769 AD
(c) 1771 AD (d) 1773 AD

2. **Tamad Revolution is connected with which tribe?**
(a) Uraon (b) Santhal
(c) Ho (d) Mahali

3. **When did Chero revolution start?**
(a) 1796 AD (b) 1798 AD
(c) 1800 AD (d) 1802 AD

4. **During Chero revolution which king was removed from his throne?**
(a) Harinath Singh
(b) Jainath Singh
(c) Shivnath Singh
(d) Ramnath Singh

5. **Who was appointed the king during the Chero revolution?**
(a) Medini Rai (b) Gopal Shah
(c) Arjun Singh (d) Gopal Rai

6. **Gopal Rai was kept in which jail when taken into prison by the British?**
(a) Ranchi (b) Hazaribagh
(c) Patna (d) Bokaro

7. **After Gopal Rai, who was made the King of that place by the British?**
(a) Chudaman
(b) Yadunath Sahay
(c) Onkar Tiwari
(d) Jogan Majhi

8. **An open revolt began under leadership of which of the following Chero leaders?**
(a) Shashi Singh (b) Arjun Singh
(c) Abhay Singh (d) Bhushan Singh

9. **Who of the following had tried to curb the revolt by the Cheros?**
(a) Major Baro
(b) Lee Grand
(c) Colonel Jones
(d) Major Hardy

10. **When were the Chero revolutionaries hanged?**
(a) 1801 AD (b) 1802 AD
(c) 1803 AD (d) 1804 AD

11. **When did the 'Ho' revolt take place?**
(a) 1818-19 AD (b) 1819-20 AD
(c) 1820-21 AD (d) 1821-22 AD

12. **People of which place had started the Ho revolt?**
(a) Bhagalpur (b) Gaya
(c) Munger (d) Chhota Nagpur

13. **Ho Revolt was conducted against the ruler of which place?**
(a) Singhbhum (a) Manbhum
(a) Tamad (a) Rajmahal

14. Who was the king of Singhbhum at the time of Ho Revolt?
(a) Jagannath Singh
(b) Gopal Singh
(c) Shivraj Singh
(d) Arjun Singh

15. Who sent the army to crush the Ho Revolt?
(a) Major Burrough
(b) James Hardy
(c) Lee Grand
(d) Rufsez

16. The joint revolt of the tribals of which place was called the 'Kol Revolt'?
(a) Palamu (b) Manbhum
(c) Singhbhum (d) All of these

17. Who was the target under the Kol Revolt?
(a) Diku
(b) The British
(c) Local landlords
(d) All of the above

18. Who of the following was leading the Kol Revolt?
(a) Budhu Bhagat
(b) Singh Rai
(c) Surya Munda
(d) All of the above

19. At the time of Kol Revolt, who was the commander of the British Army?
(a) Major Burrough
(b) Colonel Jones
(c) Wilkinson
(d) Lee Grand

20. Which new law was enacted by the Company following the Kol Revolt?
(a) Regulation-X
(b) Regulation-XI
(c) Regulation-XII
(d) Regulation-XIII

21. Which district was divided as a consequence of the Kol Revolt?
(a) Hazaribagh (b) Ramgarh
(c) Ranchi (d) Patna

22. Who was appointed the first Governor under Regulation-XIII?
(a) Thomas Hardy
(b) William Cook
(c) Major Burrough
(d) Wilkinson

23. Which revolt is known as 'Gangaram ka Hungama?'
(a) Chero (b) Bhumij
(c) Kol (d) Santhal

24. 'Bhumij Revolt' was related to which tribal community?
(a) Santhal (b) Kol
(c) Ho (d) Both (b) and (c)

25. Which area used to be called as 'Damin-a-Koh?'
(a) Singhbhum
(b) Manbhum
(c) Santhal Pargana
(d) Bakuda

26. At the time of Santhal Revolt, which police inspector was killed?
(a) Mahesh Lal
(b) Chaman Lal
(c) Devdutt Ram
(d) Bhairav Singh

27. When did Santhal Revolt take place?
(a) 1853-54 AD (a) 1854-55 AD
(a) 1855-56 AD (a) 1856-57 AD

28. Who had led the Santhal Revolt?
(a) Sidhu
(b) Kanhu
(c) Doman Manjhi
(d) Both (a) and (b)

29. Who of the following was killed by bullets?
(a) Jogan Manjhi
(b) Chand
(c) Bhairav
(d) Both (b) and (c)

30. Where were Sidhu-Kanhu hanged?
(a) Barhat (b) Silli
(c) Koderma (d) Palamu

31. When did 'Lota Revolt' take place?
(a) 1852 AD (b) 1854 AD
(c) 1856 AD (d) 1858 AD

32. Who was appointed as the first District Magistrate of Santhal Pargana?
(a) Ashley Eden
(b) Mark Smith
(c) David Cooper
(d) Ashley John

33. 'Hul Revolt' is another name of which revolt?
(a) Bhumik (b) Chero
(c) Kol (d) Santhal

34. When is 'Hul Day' celebrated?
(a) 25th January (b) 23rd April
(c) 30th June (d) 15th November

35. When did 'Neel Revolt' take place?
(a) 1820 AD (b) 1850 AD
(c) 1860 AD (d) 1870 AD

36. Which author has made a mention of 'Sardari Revolt' in his Book?
(a) Nani Gopal Mukherjee
(b) Gopal Rai
(c) S C Rai
(d) Kewal Soren

37. Which of the following is a Book of S C Rai?
(a) The Mundas
(b) The Santhals
(c) The Hul
(d) The Jharkhand

38. The prisoners in __________ jail revolted, which is known as 'Lota Revolt'?
(a) Patna (b) Mujaffarpur
(c) Ranchi (d) Hazaribagh

39. For which of the following revolts, the die-hard supporters were called as 'Safahor'?
(a) Kol (b) Sardari
(c) Bhumij (d) Santhal

40. People indifferent from the Bhumij Revolt were called as _______.
(a) Sabajiya (b) Babajiya
(c) Navbajiya (d) Udbajiya

41. The not so interested worshippers of which of the following movements were known as 'mel-baragar'?
(a) Chuar (b) Tamad
(c) Bhumij (d) Tana Bhagat

42. Which tribal movement is considered to be the most well organized and extensive movement?
(a) Santhals (b) Birsa Munda
(c) Tana Bhagar (d) Sardari

43. The leader of which revolt was considered to be an incarnation of God?
(a) Bhumij (b) Birsa Munda
(c) Sardari (d) Chuar

44. When did Birsa Munda unite around 6000 Mundas for his support?
(a) 1891 AD (b) 1893 AD
(c) 1895 AD (d) 1897 AD

45. Before the 'Lota Revolt', the prisoners used to be given which type of 'Lota'?
(a) Made of Brass
(b) Made of soil
(c) Made of Copper
(d) Made of Bronze

46. When was Birsa Munda born?
(a) 1871 AD (b) 1873 AD
(c) 1875 AD (d) 1877 AD

47. When did Birsa Munda die?
(a) 1897 AD (b) 1899 AD
(c) 1900 AD (d) 1901 AD

48. When was 'Gupla' sub-division created?
(a) 1901 AD (b) 1903 AD
(c) 1908 AD (d) 1918 AD

49. When did 'Khunti' become a sub-division?
(a) 1905 AD (b) 1906 AD
(c) 1907 AD (d) 1909 AD

50. Which of the following movements emerged from the Birsa Movement only?
(a) Chuar (b) Santhal
(c) Bhumij (d) Tana Bhagat

51. When did 'Tana Bhagat Movement' begin?
(a) 1910 AD (b) 1912 AD
(c) 1914 AD (d) 1916 AD

52. Tana Bhagat belonged to which of the tribal communities?
(a) Santhal (b) Uraon
(c) Ho (d) Mahali

53. The disciples of Tana Bhagat followed which religion?
(a) Kuduk (b) Sarna
(c) Harmu (d) Murmu

54. Who was the hero of the 'Tana Bhagat Movement"?
(a) Birsa Bhagat (b) Sukhdev Bhagat
(c) Gaya Bhagat (d) Jatra Bhagat

55. According to a lore, which Uraon deity had appeared before Jatra Bhagat?
(a) Munesh (b) Dharmesh
(c) Kartik (d) Singhbhonga

56. People from which tribal community' had extended their incomparable support and contribution to the independence movement of India?
(a) Tana Bhagat (b) Birsa Munda
(c) Kol (d) Sardari

57. In which part of Bihar 'Noniya revolt' took place between 1770 to 1800 AD?
(a) Tirhut (b) Saran
(c) Purnia (d) All of these

58. Which revolt was related to salt petre producing area?
(a) Chuar (b) Chero
(c) Noniya (d) Sardari

59. The production of salt petre was made to manufacture__________.
(a) Explosives (b) Salt
(c) Paint (d) Lac

60. Which of the following communities used to produce salt petre?
(a) Mahali (b) Binjhia
(c) Kol (d) Noniya

61. Who had led the 'Wahabi Movement' in India?
(a) Sibli Noomani
(b) Nazir Ahmad
(c) Saiyyad Ahmad Bareilwi
(d) Shah Waliullah

62. When was Saiyyad Ahmad Bareilwi born?
(a) 1776 AD (b) 1774 AD
(c) 1772 AD (d) 1770 AD

63. Who was the promoter of the 'Wahabi Movement'?
(a) Danish Wahab
(b) Akram Wahab
(c) Abdul Wahab
(d) Mohd. Wahab

64. When did Saiyyad Ahmad Bareilwi visit Patna?
(a) 1817 AD (b) 1819 AD
(c) 1821 AD (d) 1823 AD

65. Which city in Bihar was the center of the 'Wahabi Movement'?
(a) Patna (b) Bihar Sharif
(c) Hajipur (d) Sonepur

66. Who of the following was connected with the Wahabi Movement?
(a) Vilayat Ali
(b) Inayat Ali
(c) Mohd. Hussain
(d) All of the above

67. Who started a movement against the rich Hindus and Muslim Landlords?
(a) Titu Mir (b) Saiyyad Shah
(c) Karam Shah (d) Gamiya Mir

68. When did the British forces visit Sitna to curb the people of Wahabi Movement?
(a) 1849 AD (b) 1851 AD
(c) 1853 AD (d) 1855 AD

69. Who led the Wahabi movement in Patna?
(a) Farhat Hussain
(b) Vilayat Ali
(c) Inayat Ali
(d) Both (b) and (c)

70. Who made Hyderabad as the center for Wahabi Movement?
(a) Mohd. Hussain
(b) Farhat Hussain
(c) Inayat Ali
(d) Vilayat Ali

71. Where did the Wahabis defeat the English forces?
(a) Sitna (b) Patna
(c) Bareilly (d) Hyderabad

72. After the demise of Vilayat Ali and Inayat Ali, who led the Wahabi Movement?
(a) Farhat Hussain
(b) Maqsood Maulavi Abdullah
(c) Shah Mehmood Qureshi
(d) Shah Wali Ullaha

73. Maqsood Maulavi Abdullaha had made which place the center of Wahabi Movement in 1861 AD?
(a) Bihar Sharif (b) Agra
(c) Nagpur (d) Malka

74. Nevil Chamberlin had sent the leader of the Wahabis to which place after defeating them?
(a) Ladakh
(b) Srinagar
(c) Bombay
(d) Port Blair

Answers

THE ARRIVAL OF EUROPEAN COMPANIES IN BIHAR

1. (c)	**2.** (a)	**3.** (d)	**4.** (d)	**5.** (a)	**6.** (c)	**7.** (b)	**8.** (c)	**9.** (d)	**10.** (a)
11. (a)	**12.** (a)	**13.** (c)	**14.** (d)	**15.** (b)	**16.** (d)	**17.** (c)	**18.** (d)	**19.** (d)	**20.** (a)
21. (c)	**22.** (a)	**23.** (c)	**24.** (a)	**25.** (b)	**26.** (c)	**27.** (a)	**28.** (c)	**29.** (a)	**30.** (d)
31. (c)	**32.** (b)	**33.** (d)	**34.** (b)	**35.** (a)	**36.** (c)	**37.** (d)	**38.** (c)	**39.** (a)	**40.** (c)
41. (d)	**42.** (c)	**43.** (c)	**44.** (d)	**45.** (b)	**46.** (c)	**47.** (d)	**48.** (c)	**49.** (d)	**50.** (d)

THE ARRIVAL OF EAST INDIA COMPANY

1. (a)	**2.** (c)	**3.** (c)	**4.** (a)	**5.** (d)	**6.** (d)	**7.** (d)	**8.** (a)	**9.** (c)	**10.** (d)
11. (b)	**12.** (c)	**13.** (b)							

THE ESTABLISHMENT OF THE BRITISH RULE

1. (d)	**2.** (c)	**3.** (d)	**4.** (a)	**5.** (b)	**6.** (a)	**7.** (d)	**8.** (a)	**9.** (d)	**10.** (b)
11. (c)	**12.** (d)	**13.** (d)	**14.** (b)	**15.** (c)	**16.** (a)	**17.** (d)	**18.** (d)	**19.** (a)	**20.** (d)
21. (b)									

MASS MOVEMENTS AGAINST THE BRITISH RULE

1. (c)	**2.** (a)	**3.** (c)	**4.** (b)	**5.** (d)	**6.** (c)	**7.** (a)	**8.** (d)	**9.** (c)	**10.** (b)
11. (d)	**12.** (d)	**13.** (a)	**14.** (a)	**15.** (d)	**16.** (d)	**17.** (d)	**18.** (d)	**19.** (c)	**20.** (d)
21. (b)	**22.** (d)	**23.** (b)	**24.** (d)	**25.** (c)	**26.** (a)	**27.** (c)	**28.** (d)	**29.** (d)	**30.** (a)
31. (c)	**32.** (a)	**33.** (d)	**34.** (c)	**35.** (a)	**36.** (c)	**37.** (a)	**38.** (b)	**39.** (c)	**40.** (b)
41. (c)	**42.** (b)	**43.** (b)	**44.** (c)	**45.** (a)	**46.** (c)	**47.** (c)	**48.** (c)	**49.** (a)	**50.** (d)
51. (c)	**52.** (b)	**53.** (a)	**54.** (d)	**55.** (b)	**56.** (a)	**57.** (d)	**58.** (c)	**59.** (a)	**60.** (d)
61. (c)	**62.** (a)	**63.** (c)	**64.** (c)	**65.** (b)	**66.** (d)	**67.** (a)	**68.** (c)	**69.** (d)	**70.** (c)
71. (a)	**72.** (b)	**73.** (d)	**74.** (d)						

❑❑❑

5 The Revolt of 1857 and the Freedom Movement

THE REVOLT OF 1857

1. **During which revolt, the British had to face the most powerful mass movement?**
   (a) 1833 AD (b) 1845 AD
   (c) 1857 AD (d) 1868 AD
2. **When did the revolt of 1857 take place in Bihar?**
   (a) 26 January (b) 12 June
   (c) 15 August (d) 15 November
3. **The revolt of 1857 started from which place in Bihar?**
   (a) Deoghar (b) Palamu
   (c) Vaishali (d) Saran
4. **In the 1857 revolt, the soldiers of which regiment were killed?**
   (a) 32nd (b) 34th
   (c) 37th (d) 40th
5. **Who had crushed the revolt of 1857 in Deoghar?**
   (a) Norman Lesley
   (b) Lee Grand
   (c) George Cook
   (d) Mc Donald
6. **The office of the 32nd regiment was shifted from Deoghar Rohini to which other place?**
   (a) Munger (b) Bhagalpur
   (c) Gaya (d) Purnia
7. **When did the revolt of 1857 take place in Patna?**
   (a) 3rd June (b) 3rd July
   (c) 12th August (d) 8th November
8. **From where had Peer Ali led the revolt of 1857?**
   (a) Patna (b) Bhagalpur
   (c) Ranchi (d) Munger
9. **Who was the Mughal emperor at the time of 1857 revolt?**
   (a) Shah Alam II
   (b) Farrukhsiyar
   (c) Jahandar Shah
   (d) Bahadur Shah Zafar
10. **Peer Ali had killed by bullet which British officer?**
    (a) Nathan Brook
    (b) Lee Grand
    (c) Norman Lesley
    (d) Loyal
11. **The revolt of 1857 expanded more fiercely at which place other than Patna?**
    (a) Shahbad
    (b) Arrah
    (c) Tirhut
    (d) All of the above
12. **From Jagdish estate of Shahbad district, who had led the revolt of 1857?**
    (a) Amar Singh
    (b) Abhay Singh
    (c) Veer Kunwar Singh
    (d) Inayat Ali
13. **Veer Kunwar Singh had proceeded towards Arrah with how many soldiers?**
    (a) 5000 (b) 7000
    (c) 8000 (d) 10000

14. British Government had sent the army to Arrah under whose leadership?
(a) Captain Dunber
(b) Mc Donald
(c) Lee Grand
(d) Major Lesley

15. Who had captured Jagdishpur on 12th August?
(a) Irekoot
(b) William Johan
(c) Vincent Ire
(d) Carl Hooper

16. Kunwar Singh had defeated the British along with whom?
(a) Maulvi Ahmudullah
(b) Nana Saheb
(c) Fateh Singh
(d) Haider Ali Khan

17. Where did Nana Saheb and Kunwar Singh defeat the British?
(a) Jagdishpur (b) Azamgarh
(c) Sitab Diyara (d) Hajipur

18. Who had on 2nd August invaded Biwiganj?
(a) Vincent Ire (b) Major Lesley
(c) Lee Grand (d) Irekoot

19. Under whose leadership, British regiment attacked Kunwar Singh and as a consequence, he was killed?
(a) Lee Grand (b) Major Burrough
(c) Irekoot (d) Thomas King

20. When did Kunwar Singh die?
(a) 25 April 1857
(b) 24 April 1858
(c) 26 June 1858
(d) 17 January 1858

21. Where did the revolutionaries attack the jail and got many revolutionaries freed?
(a) Arrah (b) Danapur
(c) Mujaffarpur (d) Gaya

22. Under whose leadership, there was revolt in Rajbir Pargana?
(a) Fateh Singh
(b) Namdar Singh
(c) Namdar Khan
(d) Haider Ali Khan

23. Which area of Bihar remained untouched from the revolt of 1857?
(a) Saran (b) Gaya
(c) Munger (d) Koderma

24. Who was the queen of Britain in the year 1857?
(a) Ellen (b) Victoria
(c) Meghan (d) Camella

THE FREEDOM MOVEMENT

1. When was the Congress established?
(a) 25 December 1884
(b) 28 December 1885
(c) 16 December 1885
(d) 1 January 1886

2. In which city, the Congress was founded?
(a) Delhi (b) Patna
(c) Amritsar (d) Bombay

3. Who of the following British Officers had a main role in establishing Congress?
(a) A. O. Hume
(b) James Lion
(c) Nathan Cook
(d) James Hope

4. Who was the first President of the Congress?
(a) Badruddin Taiyyab Ji
(b) W. C. Banerjee
(c) Baldev Rai
(d) Dada Bhai Naoroji

5. How many delegates participated in the first session?
(a) 72 (b) 74
(c) 70 (d) 78

6. How many delegates from Bihar participated in the first session of the Congress?
(a) 0 (b) 4
(c) 6 (d) 8

7. When did the second session of congress take place?
(a) 1886 AD (b) 1887 AD
(c) 1888 AD (d) 1889 AD

8. How many delegates from Bihar took part in the second session of the Congress?
(a) 30 (b) 31
(c) 34 (d) 36

9. When did the third session of the Congress take place?
(a) 1886 AD (b) 1887 AD
(c) 1888 AD (d) 1889 AD

10. Where did the third session of the Congress take place?
(a) Calcutta (b) Delhi
(c) Madras (d) Meerut

11. When was the first session of the Congress held in Bihar?
(a) 1910 AD (b) 1912 AD
(c) 1914 AD (d) 1916 AD

12. Where did the first session take place in Bihar?
(a) Patna (b) Mujaffarpur
(c) Hajipur (d) Gaya

13. Who presided over the first session of Congress in Bihar?
(a) Rajendra Prasad
(b) Mazharul Haq
(c) Shafi Qureshi
(d) R S Madholkar

14. Which delegation of the Congress was organized in Patna?
(a) 24th (b) 25th
(c) 26th (d) 27th

15. Who was the General Secretary of the Congress session organized in Patna?
(a) Sachchidanand Sinha
(b) Rampukar Singh
(c) Mazharul Haq
(d) Rajendra Prasad

16. Who was the President of the Welcome Committee of the Congress session in Patna?
(a) Mohd. Shafi
(b) Maulana Mazharul Haq
(c) Jaiprakash Narayan
(d) B K Sinha

17. When was the Labour Union constituted in Japla?
(a) 1931 AD (b) 1933 AD
(c) 1935 AD (d) 1937 AD

18. When was the 31st session of the Congress organized?
(a) 1914 AD (b) 1916 AD
(c) 1918 AD (d) 1920 AD

19. Who had presided over the 31st Session of the Congress?
(a) Ambika Charan Majumdar
(b) Dadabhai Naoroji
(c) Mahatma Gandhi
(d) Rajendra Prasad

20. In which session of the Congress, Raj Kumar Shukla met Gandhiji?
(a) Allahabad (b) Patna
(c) Ramgarh (d) Lucknow

21. In which session of the Congress, proposals relating to Patna University Bill and the farmers of the Neel community from Champaran and investigation with regard to their land holdings were passed?
(a) 28th (b) 31st
(c) 34th (d) 37th

22. Where did the 37th session of the Congress take place?
(a) Gaya (b) Bhagalpur
(c) Munger (d) Patna

23. When was the 37th session of the Congress held?
(a) 1918 AD (b) 1920 AD
(c) 1922 AD (d) 1924 AD

24. Who had presided over the 37th session of the Congress?
(a) Rajendra Prasad
(b) Maulana Mazharul Haq
(c) Chitranjan Das
(d) Jatin Das

25. In which of the Congress sessions, the decision of boycotting the legislative assembly was taken?
(a) Gaya (b) Patna
(c) Agra (d) Allahabad

26. When was the 53rd session of the Indian National Congress held?
(a) 1938 AD (b) 1940 AD
(c) 1942 AD (d) 1944 AD

27. Where was the 53rd session of the Congress held?
(a) Ranchi (b) Ramgarh
(c) Patna (d) Gaya

28. Who had presided over the Ramgarh session of the Congress?
(a) Maulana Abul Kalam Azad
(b) R S Madholkar
(c) Rajendra Prasad
(d) Subhash Chandra Bose

29. Which leader of Bihar had organized a meeting against the compromising stand of the Congress with the British in the Ramgarh session of Congress?
(a) Swami Vidyanand
(b) Swami Sahajanand
(c) Narendra Dev
(d) Mahendra Nath

30. Home Rule movement across the country was organized under whose leadership?
(a) Bal Gangadhar Tilak
(b) Annie Besant
(c) Rajendra Prasad
(d) Both (a) and (b)

31. When was the home rule movement held in India?
(a) 1910 AD (b) 1912 AD
(c) 1914 AD (d) 1916 AD

32. Where in Bihar, Home Rule League was established?
(a) Patna (b) Gaya
(c) Munger (d) Hajipur

33. When was the Home Rule League in Bihar established?
(a) 1916 AD (b) 1914 AD
(c) 1912 AD (d) 1910 AD

34. Who was the first President of the Home Rule League formed in Bihar?
(a) Rajendra Prasad
(b) Maulana Mazhrul Haq
(c) Subhash Chandra Bose
(d) Shri Krishna Sinha

35. Who was appointed as the vice president of the Bihar established Home Rule League?
(a) Khan Bahadur Sarfaraz Hussain
(b) Rai Bahadur Purnendu Narayan Sinha
(c) Shri Krishna Sinha
(d) Both (a) and (b)

36. Who was appointed as the Secretary of the Bihar established Home Rule League?
(a) Vaidyanath Narayan Singh
(b) Chandravanshi Sahay
(c) Keshav Chandra Sen
(d) Both (a) and (b)

37. When did Annie Besant visit Patna?
(a) 1914 AD (b) 1916 AD
(c) 1918 AD (d) 1920 AD

38. Except in which district of Bihar, home rule was publicized?
(a) Champaran (b) Saran
(c) Vaishali (d) Munger

39. Champaran was famous for production of which crop?
(a) Sugarcane (b) Poppy
(c) Neel (d) Jute

40. Which of the following is a type of agricultural produce of the neel?
(a) Bayan (b) Jirat
(c) Asamivar (d) Both (b) and (c)

41. The land of the ________ was of the forced possession.
(a) Jirat (b) Asamivar
(c) Batai (d) Hunda

42. In whose company Basavan Singh had established the Cotton Mill Union?
(a) Gandhiji
(b) Jawaharlal Nehru
(c) Subhash Chandra Bose
(d) Maulana Abul Kalam Azad

43. When was it made compulsory to harvest three 'Katthas' of neel in one 'bigha' of land?
(a) 1865 AD (b) 1867 AD
(c) 1869 AD (d) 1871 AD

44. Which crop production was related to the 'teen Kathia system'?
(a) Neel (b) Sugarcane
(c) Rice (d) Corn

45. 'Teen Kathia system' was a major source of exploitation of the farmers of which place?
(a) Saran (b) Bhagalpur
(c) Munger (d) Champaran

46. Before 1867 AD, what price were the farmers paid for production of neel per acre?
(a) ₹ 4.75
(b) ₹ 5.85
(c) ₹ 6.50
(d) ₹ 7.79

47. When did neel producers of Bengal start a movement?
(a) 1854 AD
(b) 1856 AD
(c) 1858 AD
(d) 1860 AD

48. In whose leadership, the neel producers of Bengal launched a revolt?
(a) Subhash Chandra Bose
(b) Jagdish Chandra Basu
(c) Harish Chandra Mukherjee
(d) Dev Chatterjee

49. The farmers of which district of Bihar producing neel had revolted during the period 1866-1888 AD?
(a) Saran (b) Champaran
(c) Darbhanga (d) Both (b) and (c)

50. 'Pan Kharch' used to be collected for which crop?
(a) Sugarcane (b) Mustard
(c) Neel (d) Poppy

51. Which of the following taxes used to be collected as a charge for taking irrigation water from the canals?
(a) Baithmafi (b) Pan Kharch
(c) Madvan (d) Sagaura

52. 'Salami' used to be collected at what rate per 'bigha'?
(a) 3 (b) 4
(c) 5 (d) 6

53. Which of the following taxes was levied at the rate of 1 anna per 1 Rupee of land revenue?
(a) Pan expense (b) Salami
(c) Bethmafi (d) Bandh Behri

54. Which of the following taxes used to be collected from farmers annually in lieu of their plow?
(a) Bandh Behri
(b) Bethmafi
(c) Pan expense
(d) Land revenue

55. What was the annual bethmafi tax which used to be collected from the farmers?
(a) ₹ 3 (b) ₹ 4
(c) ₹ 5 (d) ₹ 6

56. Which of the following taxes was a heir or successor tax?
(a) Bandh Behri (b) Madvan
(c) Bethmafi (d) Baphi-Putahi

57. Which of the following tax was collected by 'kothiwala' at the time of marriage of a girl at the rate of Rupee 1?

(a) Shagun (b) Kalewa
(c) Sagai (d) Madvan

58. Which of the following taxes used to be collected at the time of a widow's re-marriage at the rate of Rupees 5?

(a) Sagaura (b) Vidhur
(c) Akela (d) Jabti

59. For pressing of which of the following, the presser keeper (Kolhu ka malik) would be charged a tax at the rate of ₹1?

(a) Teaspoon oil
(b) Mustard
(c) Mustasd seeds
(d) Sugarcane

60. 'Batchhapi' tax used to be levied on the sale of which of the following items?

(a) Salt (b) Milk
(c) Oil (d) Both (b) and (c)

61. Which of the following taxes was to be paid by the farmers to the 'Kothidars' for treatment of their sickness?

(a) Havahi (b) Neemat
(c) Sarna (d) Kewat

62. Which of the following taxes used to be collected at the rate of 1 anna per receipt with receipts of the land revenue?

(a) Sondhar (b) Dharai
(c) Seeta (d) Saridavan

63. When was a secret Organization formed by the farmers to protest against the exploitation by the 'Milhas'?

(a) 1905-06 AD
(b) 1907-08 AD
(c) 1908-09 AD
(d) 1909-10 AD

64. By which newspaper the attention of the government was drawn to the misery of the farmers cultivating indigo?

(a) Moonlight (b) Searchlight
(c) Bihari (d) Somprakash

65. In the newspaper 'Bihari', who had written about the plight of the farmers cultivating indigo?

(a) Mahesh Thakur
(b) Mahesh Narayan
(c) Deenbandhu Mitra
(d) Mohd Shafi Ahmad

66. Who apprised Gandhiji about the misery of the farmers cultivating indigo?

(a) Rajkumar Shukla
(b) Maulana Mazharul Haq
(c) Rajendra Prasad
(d) Hasan Imam

67. Rajkumar Shukla met whom in Kanpur to tell about the farmers of Champaran being exploited?

(a) Jawaharlal Nehru
(b) Sardar Vallabh Bhai Patel
(c) Subhash Chandra Bose
(d) Ganesh Shanker Vidyarthi

68. Ganesh Shanker Vidyarthi was editor of which Newspaper?

(a) The Pratap
(b) The Prakash
(c) The Prashant
(d) The Pariksha

69. Where was Raj Kumar Shukla born?

(a) Sitab Diyara (b) Satbariya
(c) Jatva-Janera (d) Sikta

70. When di Gandhiji reach Champaran (Motihari)?

(a) 10 January 1917
(b) 18 March 1917
(c) 15 April 1917
(d) 26 June 1917

71. When was a committee formed to know the condition of the farmers of Champaran?
(a) 10 June 1917
(b) 18 April 1917
(c) 15 March 1917
(d) 11 January 1917

72. Who of the following was a member of the Investigation Committee formed over the farmers?
(a) Rajendra Prasad
(b) Raj Kumar Shukla
(c) Brijkishore Prasad
(d) Mahatma Gandhi

73. When was the report of the committee formed over the farmers of Champaran made public?
(a) 16 May 1917
(b) 20 July 1917
(c) 11 July 1917
(d) 18 October 1917

74. What change came up about the condition of the farmers in Champaran?
(a) The end of the 'Teen Kathia system.'
(b) Land revenue on the 'raiyyats' (farmers) got reduced
(c) The other taxes were declared as illegal
(d) All of the above

75. When did Raj Kumar Shukla die?
(a) 18 January 1929
(b) 12 March 1929
(c) 20 May 1929
(d) 18 June 1929

76. Who has launched 'Khilafat Movement' against the allies in the first world war?
(a) Iran
(b) Turkey
(c) Greece
(d) Arab

77. When did 'Khilafat movement' occur?
(a) 1918 AD (b) 1919 AD
(c) 1920 AD (d) 1921 AD

78. Under whose Presidentship The All India 'Khilafat Conference' was organized?
(a) Hasan Imam
(b) Maulana Johar Ali
(c) Mahatma Gandhi
(d) Maulana Mohd Ali

79. Where was the All India Khilafat conference held?
(a) Delhi (b) Patna
(c) Agra (d) Bombay

80. When was the Khilafat related meeting was organized in Patna's 'Anjuman Islamia Hall'?
(a) 18 March 1919
(b) 12 May 1919
(c) 21 June 1919
(d) 30 November 1919

81. Who was the President at the Meeting held at Anjuman Islamia Hall of Patna?
(a) Shafi Imam
(b) Hasan Imam
(c) Maulana Mazhrul Haq
(d) Mohd. Yunus

82. When did a strike take place in the entire Bihar during the Khilafat movement?
(a) 19 March 1920
(b) 21 June 1920
(c) 11 August 1920
(d) 15 November 1920

83. Which Khilafat leader had visited Patna in April 1920?
(a) Maulana Shad
(b) Maulana Johar Ali
(c) Hasan Imam
(d) Maulana Shaukat Ali

84. Who of the following were supporters of the Khilafat Movement?
(a) Rajendra Prasad
(b) Mohd. Shafi
(c) Dharnidhar Prasad
(d) All of the above

85. When did the 12th session of the Bihar Provincial Committee take place?
(a) 1918 AD (b) 1919 AD
(c) 1920 AD (d) 1921 AD

86. Where did the 12h session of the Bihar Provincial Sabha take place?
(a) Munger (b) Bhagalpur
(c) Gaya (d) Patna

87. Who was the President of the 12th Bihar Provincial conference?
(a) Maulana Mazrul Haq
(b) Hasan Imam
(c) Rajendra Prasad
(d) Shri Krishna Sinha

88. In the 12th conference, who put up the proposal for non cooperation?
(a) Hasan Imam
(b) Babu Dharnidhar
(c) Rajendra Prasad
(d) Shah Muhammad Zuber

89. Who had accepted the proposal for non cooperation in the 12th Bihar Provincial conference?
(a) Shah Muhammad Zuber
(b) Ghulam Imam
(c) Babu Gaurav Prasad
(d) All of the above

90. Which province of the country had passed the proposal of non-cooperation before the Calcutta session of Congress?
(a) Madras (b) Gujrat
(c) Bihar (d) Both (b) and (c)

91. A committee was constituted to work on the practical plan of implementing the non-cooperation programme. Who were the members of this committee?
(a) Rajendra Prasad
(b) Maulana Mazhrul Haq
(c) Shah Muhammad Zuber
(d) All of the above

92. In which session, the non-cooperation programme of Gandhiji was accepted?
(a) Nagpur (b) Bombay
(c) Patna (d) Calcutta

93. In which session, Gandhiji's non-cooperation programme was granted a full acceptance?
(a) Bombay (b) Ahmedabad
(c) Nagpur (d) Delhi

94. Who was the President of the Calcutta (special) session?
(a) Rajendra Prasad
(b) Lala Lajpat Rai
(c) Hasan Imam
(d) Dadabhai Naoroji

95. Who had withdrawn his candidature from the Farmers Council as a result of non-cooperation movement?
(a) Gorakh Prasad
(b) Mohd Shafi
(c) Maulana Mazhrul Haq
(d) All of the above

96. Who had left his practice of law as a result of non cooperation movement?
(a) Shri Krishna Singh
(b) Mathura Prasad
(c) Deep Narayan Singh
(d) All of the above

97. When did Gandhiji visit Bihar and formally inaugurate Bihar National University and Bihar Vidyapeeth?
(a) 1917 AD (b) 1919 AD
(c) 1921 AD (d) 1923 AD

98. Who was appointed the Chancellor of Bihar Vidyapeeth?

(a) Rajendra Prasad
(b) Maulana Mazhrul Haq
(c) Shafi Imam
(d) Brij Kishore Prasad

99. Who was appointed the vice-chancellor of Bihar Vidyapeeth?
(a) Brij Kishore Prasad
(b) Shafi Imam
(c) Rajendra Prasad
(d) Shri Krishna Singh

100. Who was appointed by Gandhiji as the Principal of National University in 1919?
(a) Jai Prakash Narayan
(b) Udit Tiwari
(c) Hasan Imam
(d) Rajendra Prasad

101. By July 1922, where only six national schools were opened?
(a) Bhagalpur (b) Munger
(c) Gaya (d) Patna

102. Who was the convenor of the 'Bihar Tilak Swaraj Kosh Samiti'?
(a) Shri Krishna Singh
(b) Rajendra Prasad
(c) Shah Muhammad Zuber
(d) Hasan Imam

103. When did Prince of Wales visit Patna?
(a) 22 March 1921
(b) 10 June 1921
(c) 18 August 1921
(d) 22 December 1921

104. Where was the 16th session of Bihar Students' Conference held?
(a) Gaya (b) Ranchi
(c) Patna (d) Hazaribagh

105. Who was the President of the 16th session of Bihar Students Conference?
(a) Mahatma Gandhi
(b) Maulana Abul Kalam Azad
(c) Sarla Devi
(d) Rajendra Prasad

106. Maulana Mazhrul Haq was related to which Newspaper?
(a) The Motherland
(b) The Bihari
(c) The Searchlight
(d) The Pratap

107. When did Chauri-Chora scandal happen?
(a) 10 January 1922
(b) 5 February 1922
(c) 8 March 1922
(d) 10 June 1922

108. The place known as Chauri-Chora is situated in which district?
(a) Bhagalpur (b) Munger
(c) Gorakhpur (d) Pratapgarh

109. Which movement ended as a consequence of the Chauri-Chora scandal?
(a) Khilafat
(b) Non Cooperation
(c) Quit India
(d) Champaran

110. When did Basavan Singh become an active member of 'Hindustan Socialist Republican Army'?
(a) 1930 AD (b) 1929 AD
(c) 1927 AD (d) 1925 AD

111. Which of the following was an item under Gandhiji's eleven points proposal?
(a) Complete prohibition
(b) Reduction in exchange rate
(c) Deduction in Salaries
(d) All of the above

112. Which of the following was not a point under Gandhiji's 11 points proposal?
(a) Ban on import of foreign clothes
(b) Elimination of salt tax
(c) Free and compulsory education
(d) Reduction of 50% in army related expenditure

113. On refusal of Gandhiji's proposal by Irwin, Gandhiji decided to start which movement?
(a) Non-Cooperation
(b) Khilafat
(c) Non obedience
(d) Quit India

114. With how many disciples, Gandhiji started his 'Dandi Yatra' from Sabarmati Asharam?
(a) 72 (b) 74
(c) 76 (d) 78

115. When did Gandhiji start 'Dandi March'?
(a) 12 March 1930
(b) 18 May 1930
(c) 10 June 1930
(d) 10 August 1930

116. When did Gandhiji reach Dandi from Sabarmati Ashram?
(a) 31 March 1930
(b) 6 April 1930
(c) 8 June 1930
(d) 11 August 1930

117. What was the distance of Dandi from Sabarmati Ashram?
(a) 80 miles (b) 120 miles
(c) 160 miles (d) 200 miles

118. Under whose Presidentship from the following, a meeting was organized at Patna's Bhavar- Pokhar Ground?
(a) Prof. Abdul Bari
(b) Hasan Imam
(c) Rajendra Prasad
(d) Ali Imam

119. In revolt against the 'Chowkidar Tax', which regular training session of the self-helpers was held on 31 May 1931?
(a) Bhagalpur (b) Munger
(c) Gaya (d) Patna

120. When was the Congress announced as an illegal Organisation?
(a) 2 February 1930
(b) 8 March 1930
(c) 1 May 1930
(d) 30 June 1930

121. When did Bihar Pradesh Congress Committee pass a proposal to stage 'Dharnas' before the shops selling foreign clothes and liquor?
(a) 9 May 1930
(b) 10 May 1930
(c) 8 August 1930
(d) 18 November 1930

122. Prisoners under which jail had refused to wear clothes made of foreign brand?
(a) Hajipur (b) Bhagalpur
(c) Chhapra (d) Munger

123. When was the 'Nangi' strike called?
(a) 1930 AD (b) 1928 AD
(c) 1926 AD (d) 1924 AD

124. Where on 12 March 1931 a meeting was organized in which demand for immediate release of political prisoners from jails was made?
(a) Gaya (b) Patna
(c) Bhagalpur (d) Ranchi

125. Under whose presidentship, on 12 March 1931, the demand for release of all political prisoners from jails was made?
(a) Ali Imam
(b) Shri Krishna Singh
(c) Rajendra Prasad
(d) Anugriha Narayan Singh

126. When were Bhagat Singh and his associates hanged?
(a) 23 March 1931
(b) 23 May 1931
(c) 23 June 1931
(d) 23 August 1931

127. When did a complete strike occurr in Patna after the execution of Bhagat Singh?
(a) 24 March (b) 25 March
(c) 26 March (d) 27 March

128. When was the Independence Day celebrated in the entire province?
(a) 26 January (b) 8 March
(c) 10 June (d) 15 August

129. When was the Communal 'Panchayat' announced?
(a) 1828 AD
(b) 1830 AD
(c) 1832 AD
(d) 1834 AD

130. In how many days Gandhiji completed his 'Dandi' March?
(a) 20 days (b) 22 days
(c) 24 days (d) 26 days

131. Which law was broken by Gandhiji on reaching Dandi?
(a) Education (b) Salt
(c) Sugar (d) Oil

132. In Dandi March, who from Bihar accompanied Gandhiji?
(a) Girivardhari Chaudhary
(b) Rajendra Prasad
(c) Shafi Imam
(d) Shri Krishna Singh

133. Who led the civil disobedience movement in Patna?
(a) Ghulam Imam
(b) Jagat Narayan Lal
(c) Rajendra Prasad
(c) Shafi Imam

134. Who led the civil disobedience movement in Darbhanga?
(a) Abdul Bari
(b) Satya Narayan Sinha
(c) Chaturanand Das
(d) Both (b) and (c)

135. Who led the Civil disobedience movement in Munger?
(a) Shri Krishna Singh
(b) Shah Muhammad Zubaid
(c) Nand Kumar Singh
(d) Both (b) and (c)

136. Who led the civil disobedience movement in Mujaffarpur?
(a) Ram Dayalu Singh
(b) Kanakdhari Prasad Thakur
(c) Ram Nandan Singh
(d) All of the above

137. In 1930 during the civil disobedience movement, the demonstrators had captured which city?
(a) Badahi (b) Pakadi
(c) Sikta (d) Vaihanathpur

138. When was Gandhiji arrested during the civil disobedience Movement?
(a) 4 February (b) 4 March
(c) 4 May (d) 4 June

139. When did Bihar State Congress Committee accept the civil disobedience movement?
(a) 4 March 1930
(b) 9 May 1930
(c) 8 June 1930
(d) 10 August 1930

140. Under whose chairmanship, Bihar state Congress Committee accepted the civil disobedience movement?
(a) Hasan Imam
(b) Anugrah Narayan Singh
(c) Chandravanshi Sahay
(d) Rajendra Prasad

141. In which province the 'chowkidari karbandi movement' became popular during the civil disobedience movement?
(a) Gujarat
(b) Madras
(c) Uttar Pradesh
(d) Bihar

142. Where was Narvaspind movement held during the salt movement?
(a) Gaya
(b) Patna
(c) Munger
(d) Bhagalpur

143. Which British Prime Minister had announced communal award?
(a) Ramsay Mcdonald
(b) Winston Churchill
(c) Mark Brook
(d) Margret Thatcher

144. Which nationalist leader had started fast unto death against the communal award?
(a) Jawaharlal Nehru
(a) Maulana Abul Kalam Azad
(a) Rajendra Prasad
(a) Mahatma Gandhi

145. Poona agreement was reached between Mahatma Gandhi and whom by which the communal award was taken back?
(a) Jagjivan Ram
(b) Hasan Imam
(c) Bhimrao Ambedkar
(d) Jaglal Choudhry

146. Who formed the 'Harijan Sewak Sangh'?
(a) Jaglal Choudhry
(b) Gandhiji
(c) Bhimrao Ambedkar
(d) Jawaharlald Nehru

147. Who had given the slogan of personal 'Satyagrah'?
(a) Gandhiji
(b) Jawaharlal Nehru
(c) Subhash Chandra Bose
(d) Hasan Imam

148. In which session of the Congress Gandhiji had given the slogan of personal 'Satyagrah'?
(a) Patna (b) Gaya
(c) Ramgarh (d) Amritsar

149. When did Gandhiji himself start the personal 'Satyagrah'?
(a) 1938 AD
(b) 1940 AD
(c) 1942 AD
(d) 1944 AD

150. Who were the first 'Satyagrahis'?
(a) Vinoba Bhave
(b) Shri Krishan Singh
(c) Hasan Imam
(d) Rajendra Prasad

151. Who was the first 'Satyagrahi' who came from Bihar?
(a) Anugrah Narayan Sinha
(b) Shri Krishna Singh
(c) Rajendra Prasad
(d) Ali Imam

152. Who was the second 'Satyagrahi' who came from Bihar?
(a) Rajendra Prasad
(b) Shri Krishna Singh
(c) Anugrah Narayan Singh
(d) Maulana Mazhrul Haq

153. When did Cripps Mission come to India?
(a) 1938 AD (b) 1940 AD
(c) 1942 AD (d) 1944 AD

154. Under whose leadership Cripps Mission had come to India?
(a) Patrick Lawrence
(b) Stayford Cripps
(c) Allen Hook
(d) George Cripps

155. Who had called the Cripps Mission as post-dated cheque?
(a) Gandhiji
(b) Motilal Nehru
(c) Subhash Chandra Bose
(d) Maulana Abul Kalam Azad

156. The proposal of Quit India movement was initiated in which session?
(a) Ahmedabad (b) Allahabad
(c) Madras (d) Bombay

157. When was the Quit India proposal passed?
(a) 8 January 1942
(b) 10 March 1942
(c) 11 May 1942
(d) 8 August 1942

158. Who was the President of the Congress at the time of Quit India movement?

(a) Maulana Abul Kalam Azad
(b) Mahatma Gandhi
(c) Subhash Chandra Bose
(d) Hasan Imam

159. Who had said at the time of Quit India movement that "when the future of a community is being decided, it cannot quietly look at it"?

(a) Sardar Patel
(b) Gandhiji
(c) Subhash Chandra Bose
(d) Maulana Abul Kalam Azad

160. Who had presented the Quit India movement?

(a) Lala Lajpat Rai
(b) Hasan Imam
(c) Jawaharlal Nehru
(d) Mahatma Gandhi

161. Who had given the slogan "karo ya maro"?

(a) Mahatma Gandhi
(b) Maulana Abul Kalam Azad
(c) Subhash Chandra Bose
(d) Sardar Patel

162. During which movement Mahatma Gandhi had given the slogan 'karo ya maro"?

(a) Khilafat
(b) Non-Cooperation
(c) Civil disobedience
(d) Quit India

163. Who had given his assent for the quit India movement in the last?

(a) Hasan Imam
(b) Mohd Ali Jinnah
(c) Jawaharlal Nehru
(d) Madan Mohan Malviya

164. During Quit India movement, when was Mahatma Gandhi arrested?

(a) 8 August (b) 9 August
(c) 10 August (d) 11 August

165. During Quit India movement, demonstrators from Bihar were given the punishment of maximum imprisonment of how many years?

(a) 51 years (b) 40 Years
(c) 35 Years (d) 30 Years

166. During Quit India movement when was Rajendra Prasad arrested?

(a) 8 August (b) 9 August
(c) 10 August (d) 11 August

167. Rajendra Prasad was kept in which central jail?

(a) Pirbahor
(b) Kadamkua Bankipur
(c) Fulwari Sharif

168. Who was the Commissioner of Patna at the time of Quit India movement?

(a) Cunningham
(b) W. G. Archer
(c) Major Burrough
(d) David Hedley

169. From which post Baldev Sahay had resigned at the time of quit India movement?

(a) Counsel General
(b) Chancellor
(c) Principal
(d) Commissioner

170. When did the students try to unfurl the flag when the collector had given orders for shooting?

(a) 10 August (b) 11 August
(c) 12 August (d) 13 August

171. During the efforts for unfurling national flag at Maharajganj Police Station in Siwan District, who was killed in the shooting?

(a) Sachindra Sanyal
(b) Phoolchand Jha
(c) Baikunth Sharma
(d) Phulena Prasad

172. Who is the author of the book named 'Unki Yadein'?
(a) Tara Devi
(b) Tara Chand Jha
(c) Sarla Devi
(d) Rama Kant Singh

173. On 13th August, from where a small newspaper named 'Azad Hindustan' was published?
(a) Bhagalpur (b) Gaya
(c) Munger (d) Vaishali

174. From 26th August, which newspaper was started by the British Govt.?
(a) Munger Times
(b) Munger News
(c) Bihar Times
(d) Bihar News

175. On 14th August 1942, where while trying to unfurl the national flag on the government buildings, Aklu Sahu, Ganesh Joshi and Nathuni Shah were martyred?
(a) Gaya (b) Hazaribagh
(c) Saran (d) Madhubani

176. Who of the following had constituted the 'Gandhi Sewa Mandal'?
(a) Keshav Prasad Sinha
(b) Praful Chaki
(c) Batukeshwar Dutt
(d) Khudiram Bose

177. At the time of Quit India movement, in which jail Jai Prakash Narayan was kept?
(a) Ranchi (b) Hazaribagh
(c) Patna (d) Gaya

178. On the night of Dipawali, 8th November 1942, who succeeded in escaping from jail along with Jai Prakash Narayan?
(a) Yogendra Shukla
(b) Gulali Prasad
(c) Shaligram Singh
(d) All of the above

179. After escaping from the jail, where did Jaiprakash Narayan first go?
(a) Gaya (b) Ranchi
(c) Patna (d) Mujaffarpur

180. At which place Jaiprakash Narayan constituted 'Azad Dasta'?
(a) Nepal (b) Saran
(c) Koderma (d) Palamu

181. Where did Siyaram Dal play an important role in Quit India Movement?
(a) Uttar Pradesh
(b) Bihar
(c) Gujarat
(d) Madras

182. Who had constituted the Indian National Army?
(a) Subhash Chandra Bose
(b) Raas Bihari Bose
(c) Jagdish Ghosh
(d) Lallan Mishra

183. Where under the presidentship of Raas Bihari Bose, the Indian Unity League was constituted?
(a) Bangkok (b) Singapore
(c) Kathmandu (d) Tokyo

184. Who of the following had first given the idea of constituting the INA?
(a) Captain Jagjit Singh
(b) Captain Mohan Singh
(c) Subhash Chandra Bose
(d) Raas Bihari Bose

185. When did Subhash Chandra Bose lead the INA?
(a) 4 January 1943
(b) 4 March 1943
(c) 4 June 1943
(d) 4 July 1943

186. Who was the personal secretary of Chitaranjan Das at the time of Gaya session of the Congress?
(a) Subhash Chandra Bose
(b) Raas Bihari Bose
(c) Avnath Shah
(d) Hasan Imam

187. Where had Raas Bihari Bose thrown a bomb on the Viceroy and left for Japan?
(a) Bombay (b) Delhi
(c) Lahore (d) Amritsar

188. After the first world war, where had Mahendra Pratap constituted the provincial government?
(a) Dhaka (b) Lahore
(c) Madras (d) Afghanistan

189. Who is the writer of the newspaper The Voice of India?
(a) Anand Mohan
(b) Subhash Chandra Bose
(c) Sheikh Wahab
(d) Rajendra Prasad

190. Where was the branch of Congress established?
(a) Singapore (b) Bangkok
(c) Thimpu (d) Japan

191. Where was Subhash Chandra Bose kept under hourse arrest?
(a) Lahore (b) Assam
(c) Dhaka (d) Calcutta

192. When did the 'Azad Hind Fauj' capture the Andaman and Nicobar islands?
(a) 1942 (b) 1943
(c) 1944 (d) 1945

193. By 1943 AD, where had the headquarters of 'Azad Hind Fauj' developed?
(a) Singapore (b) Bangkok
(c) Rangoon (d) Lahore

194. When was a trial started over the officers of the Azad Hind Fauj in Delhi?
(a) 1944 AD (b) 1945 AD
(c) 1946 AD (d) 1947 AD

195. When was the division of the Bengal announced?
(a) 1902 AD (b) 1903 AD
(c) 1904 AD (d) 1905 AD

196. At the time of the division of Bengal, who was the Viceroy of Bengal?
(a) Lord Curzon
(b) Lord Cunning
(c) Lord Reading
(d) Lord Chelmsford

197. Who got the credit for starting revolution in Bihar?
(a) Gyanendra Nath Mishra
(b) Khudi Ram Bose
(c) Praful Chaki
(d) All of the above

198. Whose of the following workers bore the name of Brahmanand?
(a) Khudiram Bose
(b) Bhagat Singh
(c) Praful Chaki
(d) Gyanendra Nath Mishra

199. When was the Ramakrishna Society formed?
(a) 1902-03 AD
(b) 1903-04 AD
(c) 1904-05 AD
(d) 1906-07 AD

200. Where in Bihar, Ramakrishna Society was constituted?
(a) Gaya (b) Patna
(c) Hajipur (d) Munger

201. Who had in Patna formed the Ramakrishna Society?
(a) Praful Chaki
(b) Khudiram Bose
(c) Babaji Thakur Das Ji
(d) Lallan Pandey

202. Baba Thakur Das had edited which Newspaper?
(a) The Bihari
(b) The Motherland
(c) The Pratap
(d) The Bihar News

203. Who of the following had thrown a bomb on the district magistrate on 30th April 1908?

(a) Bhagat Singh
(b) Khudiram Bose
(c) Praful Chaki
(d) Both (b) and (c)

204. Where was a bomb scandal on 30 April 1908?
(a) Mujaffarpur (b) Gaya
(c) Munger (d) Bhagalpur

205. Who of the following revolutionaries had committed suicide?
(a) Bhagat Singh
(b) Phulena Singh
(c) Praful Chaki
(d) Khudiram Bose

206. Where is Cellular Jail situated?
(a) Nagpur
(b) Bombay
(c) Daman & Diu
(d) Andaman

207. When was Khudiram Bose hanged?
(a) 11 January 1908
(b) 11 June 1908
(c) 11 August 1908
(d) 16 September 1908

208. Shri Kalidas Bose has fought the trial of who out of the following?
(a) Praful Chaki
(b) Jagdish Chandra Bose
(c) Khudiram Bose
(d) Phulena Shah

209. Which committee was constituted against the 'Bang Bhang Movement'?
(a) Anushilan Samiti
(b) Satya Samiti
(c) Gaurav Samiti
(d) Anubhed Samiti

210. Where was Anushilan Samiti constituted as a consequence of Bang Bhang movement?
(a) Ranchi (b) Hazaribagh
(c) Dhaka (d) Patna

211. Revolutionaries were being trained by which Samiti?
(a) Azad Samiti
(b) Anushilan Samiti
(c) Bagchi Samiti
(d) Satya Samiti

212. Who of the following was a major leader of Anushilan Samiti of Bihar?
(a) Nalini Bagchi
(b) Fani Bhushan Bhattacharya
(c) Kheti Nag
(d) All of the above

213. In the history of Bihar's revolutionary movement, whose contribution is considered a major one?
(a) Baikunth Shukla
(b) Yogendra Shukla
(c) Rahul Shukla
(d) Both (a) and (b)

214. Who of the following had become a government approver in Lahore Conspiracy case?
(a) Sachindra Sanyal
(b) Yogendra Shukla
(c) Fanindra Ghosh
(d) Baikunth Shukla

215. Who had killed Fanindra Ghosh?
(a) Baikunth Shukla
(b) Sachindra Sanyal
(c) Lakshman Singh
(d) Sumit Ghosh

216. When was Baikunth Shukla hanged?
(a) 11 January 1934
(b) 08 February 1934
(c) 10 March 1934
(d) 14 April 1934

217. Where was Yogendra Shukla born?
(a) Nalanda (b) Vaishali
(c) Bhagalpur (d) Munger

218. Who of the following was a member of the Hindustan Socialistic Army?
(a) Yogendra Shukla
(b) Khudiram Bose
(c) Praful Chaki
(d) Subhash Chandra Bose

219. In which jail in 1933 Yogendra Shukla had observed fast unto death?

(a) Ranchi (b) Patna
(c) Andaman (d) Ahmedabad

220. Where in the year 1928, Bihar Students Conference was held?

(a) Motihari (b) Betia
(c) Gaya (d) Hajipur

221. Where was 'Bihar Youth Federation' formed?

(a) Hazaribagh (b) Motihari
(c) Patna (d) Ranchi

222. Under whose leadership Bihar Youth Federation was formed?

(a) Batukeshwar Dutt
(b) Gyan Saha
(c) Suresh Bhattacharya
(d) Yogendra Shukla

223. When was Batukeshwar Dutt born?

(a) 1908 AD (b) 1910 AD
(c) 1912 AD (d) 1914 AD

224. Where was Batukeshwar Dutt born?

(a) Aligarh (b) Kannauj
(c) Kanpur (d) Azamgarh

225. By getting inspired from which of the following revolutions, Hindustan Republic Army was constituted in India?

(a) Germany (b) Italy
(c) France (d) Russia

226. When was a bomb dropped on the central hall of the Delhi assembly?

(a) 8 March 1929
(b) 8 April 1929
(c) 10 May 1929
(d) 11 June 1929

227. Who of the following had dropped a bomb on the Legislative assembly?

(a) Chandrashekhar Azad
(b) Bhagat Singh
(c) Batukeshwar Dutt
(d) Both (b) and (c)

228. When was Batukeshwar Dutt released from Andaman Jail?

(a) 1934 AD
(b) 1936 AD
(c) 1938 AD
(d) 1940 AD

THE ROLE OF THE WOMEN IN FREEDOM MOVEMENT

1. Under whose leadership during the civil disobedience movement, students in large number had boycotted the government schools and colleges?

(a) Sarla Devi
(b) Prabhavati Gupta
(c) Ramkali Devi
(d) Suchitra Devi

2. Who of the following had organized a meeting to protest the arrival of Prince of Wales in India?

(a) Suchitra Devi
(b) Savitri Devi
(c) Sarla Devi
(d) Prabhavati Gupta

3. During the civil disobedience movement, the women of Bihar had constituted which Committee?

(a) Sampark Committee
(b) Umeed Committee
(c) Bihar Committee
(d) Charkha Committee

4. Who of the following was wife of Jai Prakash Narayan?

(a) Suchitra Devi
(b) Urmila Devi
(c) Prabhawati Devi
(d) Sunaina Devi

5. **At the time of civil disobedience in whose leadership in Santhal Pargana area there were demonstrations against the salt law?**
(a) Shailbala Rai
(b) Sarla Devi
(c) Urmila Devi
(d) Jahan Ara

6. **Who of the following was the President of Hazaribagh District Congress?**
(a) Sadhna Devi
(b) Saraswati Devi
(c) Suchitra Devi
(d) Shail Bala Rai

7. **Who of the following inspired many other women by visiting various villages to participate in civil disobedience movement?**
(a) Ram Sarup Devi
(b) Sadhna Devi
(c) Geeta Devi
(d) All of the above

8. **Who of the following had launched a movement against the 'Chowkidari Tax'?**
(a) Sadhna Devi
(b) Amravati Devi
(c) Chandravati Devi
(d) All of the above

9. **Who of the following was the wife of Rajendra Prasad?**
(a) Ram Sarup Devi
(b) Prabha wati Devi
(c) Sheela Devi
(d) Rajvanshi Devi

10. **Who of the following freedom fighter women was popular as a 'Dictator'?**
(a) Chandrawati Devi
(b) Rampreet Devi
(c) Shalu Devi
(d) Pramila Devi

11. **Who of the following was arrested during the personal satyagrah by Mahatma Gandhi?**
(a) Priyamvada
(b) Jagat Rani Devi
(c) Janki Devi
(d) All of the above

12. **Who of the following was arrested from Dumka during course of personal satyagrah?**
(a) Mahadevi Kejriwal
(b) Bhagwati Devi
(c) Sadhna Devi
(d) Ram Sarup Devi

13. **In whose chairmanship, a large meeting was organized in Chhapra on 15 August 1942?**
(a) Bhagwati Devi
(b) Shanti Devi
(c) Suniti Devi
(d) Radhika Devi

THE PEASANT MOVEMENT

1. **Where in 1793 was the permanent settlement system organized?**
(a) Bihar
(b) Bengal
(c) Banaras
(d) All of the above

2. **Which governor general had implemented the Permanent Settlement in Bihar?**
(a) Lord John (b) Cornwallis
(c) Lord Curzon (d) Wellington

3. **Under the permanent settlement system, what percentage of land revenue went to the Company?**
(a) 78% (b) 81%
(c) 85% (d) 89%

4. **When did farmers revolution take place in Pandaul?**
(a) 1861-62 AD
(b) 1864-65 AD
(c) 1866-67 AD
(d) 1870-71 AD

5. In 1883-84, farmers of which place had started a big movement against the King?
(a) Betia (b) Dumraon
(c) Dumka (d) Darbhanga

6. The farmers movement in Bihar is considered to have begun since _________Satyagrah?
(a) Patna (b) Champaran
(c) Saran (d) Bhagalpur

7. When did Champaran Satyagrah begin?
(a) 1913 AD (b) 1915 AD
(c) 1917 AD (d) 1919 AD

8. Champaran Satyagrah movement was launched in whose leadership?
(a) Raj Kumar Shukla
(b) Brij Kishore Sharma
(c) Hasan Imam
(d) Mahatma Gandhi

9. Which of the following movements is connected with "Teenkathia"?
(a) Champaran Satyagrah
(b) Disobedience Movement
(c) Namak satyagrah
(d) Both (b) and (c)

10. Farmers of which place had launched a movement by getting inspired by Champaran Satyagrah?
(a) Gaya (b) Madhubani
(c) Saran (d) Bhagalpur

11. Who had led the Farmers agitation in Madhubani District?
(a) Swami Sahajanand
(b) Swami Vidyanand
(c) Indu Lal Yagnik
(d) Mohd. Zuber

12. In whose leadership, Kisan sabha was organized in Munger?
(a) Shah Muhammad Zuber
(b) Hasan Imam
(c) Shri Krishan Singh
(d) Both (a) and (c)

13. When was Kisan Sabha organized in Munger?
(a) 1918-19 AD
(b) 1920-21 AD
(c) 1921-22 AD
(d) 1922-23 AD

14. Who was the main personality behind the farmers agitation in Bihar?
(a) Rajendra Prasad
(b) Swami Sahajanand Saraswati
(c) Gopal Pandey
(d) Hasan Imam

15. Where was Swami Sahajanand Saraswati born?
(a) Ghazipur (b) Saran
(c) Munger (d) Azamgarh

16. When was Swami Sehajanand Saraswati born?
(a) 1881 AD (b) 1883 AD
(c) 1886 AD (d) 1889 AD

17. What was the childhood name of Swami Sahajanand Saraswati?
(a) Tapan Roy (b) Soman Roy
(c) Navrang Roy(d) Jagroo Shah

18. When was publication of a monthly newspaper called 'Bhumihar Brahman' started?
(a) 1911 AD (b) 1913 AD
(c) 1915 Ad (d) 1917 AD

19. 'Bhumihar Brahman', a monthly Newspaper was published from which place?
(a) Kashi (b) Patna
(c) Delhi (d) Amritsar

20. Who among the following was editor of the monthly newspaper 'Bhumihar Brahmin'?
(a) Madan Mohan Malviya
(b) Chunnu Pandey
(c) Swami Sahajanand
(d) Swami Vidyanand

21. Which of the following is a text composed by Swami Sahajanand?
(a) Bhumihar Brahmin Parichay
(b) Bhumihar Brahmin Sangharsha
(c) Bhumihar Brahman Kootniti
(d) Bhumihar Brahmin Ekta

22. Which of the following was composed by Swami Sahajanand?
(a) Brahmin ki Stithi
(b) Jhootha Bhay aur mithya abhiman
(c) Karmkalap
(d) All of the above

23. Who of the following made Sitaram Kendra as the center of his political struggle?
(a) Swami Vidyanand
(b) Rajendra Prasad
(c) Balram Bhagat
(d) Swami Sahajanand

24. Where was Swami Sahajanand's Sitaram Ashram situated?
(a) Bodhgaya (b) Patna
(c) Vaishali (d) Munger

25. Who of the following had constituted the organization called as "Pashchimi Patna Kisan Sabha'?
(a) Rajendra Prasad
(b) Maulana Mazharul Haq
(c) Hasan Imam
(d) Swami Sahajanand Saraswati

26. When was the organization called 'Pashchimi Patna Kisan Sabha' organized?
(a) 1928 AD (b) 1926 AD
(c) 1924 AD (d) 1922 AD

27. Who of the following had constituted 'Prantiya Kisan Sabha'?
(a) Ramdayalu Singh
(b) Yamuna Karyi
(c) Swami Sahajanand Saraswati
(d) All of the above

28. Who was the first President of 'Prantiya Kisan Sabha'?
(a) Ramdayalu Singh
(b) Swami Sahajanand
(c) Shri Krishna Singh
(d) Mohd. Zuber

29. Who was the first secretary of the 'Prantiya Kisan Sabha'?
(a) Shri Krishan Singh
(b) Hasan Imam
(c) Ramdayalu Singh
(d) Peer Munsi

30. When did Sardar Vallabhbhai Patel arrive in Bihar?
(a) 1927 AD (b) 1928 AD
(c) 1929 AD (d) 1930 AD

31. During the salt movement, salt law was broken in 'Vikram Ashram' situated at which place?
(a) Mujaffarpur (b) Bhagalpur
(c) Munger (d) Patna

32. Who was arrested from 'Vikram Ashram' in Patna for breaking the salt law?
(a) Rajendra Prasad
(b) Mohd. Zuber
(c) Shrikrishna Singh
(d) Swami Sahajanand Saraswati

33. When was the 'All India Kisan Sabha' constituted?
(a) 1932 AD (b) 1934 AD
(c) 1936 AD (d) 1938 AD

34. Who of the following had constituted the 'Red Kisan Sabha'?
(a) Jai Prakash Narayan
(b) Swami Sahajanand
(c) Swami Vidyanand
(d) Mohd. Zuber

35. Who was the first President of the 'All India Kisan Sabha'?
(a) Swami Sahajanand
(b) Swami Vidyanand
(c) Jawaharlal Nehru
(d) Sardar Vallabhbhai Patel

36. Who was the first Secretary of the All India Kisan Sabha?
(a) Sukhdev Bhagat
(b) Moti Lal Nehru
(c) N. G. Ranga
(d) Mohd. Zuber

37. Which of the following was composed by Swami Sahajanand?
(a) How I know Bihar
(b) The Other Side of the Shield
(c) Rent Reduction in Bihar-How it works?
(d) Both (b) and (c)

38. Who of the following had given the slogan 'Danda hamare paas hai, lagan kaise loge'?
(a) Swami Sahajanand
(b) Mahatma Gandhi
(c) Subhash Chandra Bose
(d) Jawaharlal Nehru

39. When did Swami Sahajanand resign from the membership of the Congress?
(a) 4 April 1946
(b) 5 May 1947
(c) 8 June 1948
(d) 6 December 1948

40. When did Swami Sahajanand die?
(a) 26 June 1950
(b) 25 August 1950
(c) 10 September 1956
(d) 18 December 1950

41. When was the Congress Socialist Party constituted?
(a) 1930 AD (b) 1932 AD
(c) 1934 AD (d) 1936 AD

42. Who of the following had constituted the Congress Socialist Party?
(a) Jaiprakash Narayan
(b) Narendra Dev
(c) Swami Vidyanand
(d) Both (a) and (b)

43. Where was 'Bakasht Movement' organized?
(a) Jamunapur (b) Badhiya
(c) Belwa (d) Karamva

THE LABOUR MOVEMENT

1. When did the 'Bolshevik Revolution' take place?
(a) 1911 AD (b) 1913 AD
(c) 1915 AD (d) 1917 AD

2. Where did the 'Bolshevik Revolution' take place?
(a) France (b) Russia
(c) Germany (d) Spain

3. The meeting of Bihar Trade Union Congress on 10 June 1944 took place at which place?
(a) Patna (b) Ranch
(c) Girdih (d) Bhagalpur

4. 'Mang Diwas' (day of demand) was decided to be observed on ____ March 1947.
(a) 8 (b) 12
(c) 16 (d) 20

5. When, in India in Madras, labourers decided to observe a strike for the first time?
(a) 1916 AD (b) 1918 AD
(c) 1920 AD (d) 1922 AD

6. Under whose leadership for the first time in Madras, the Indian Labourers had observed strike to defend their rights?
(a) Jamshedji Tata
(b) Abdul Bari
(c) V. P. Wadia
(d) Taiyyab Ji

7. When was Rowlett Act passed?
(a) 1913 AD (b) 1915 D
(c) 1917 AD (d) 1919 AD

8. In protest of which Act, around 40000 labourers had observed a strike in Jameshedpur?
(a) Simon Act (b) Curzon Act
(c) Rowlett Act (d) George Act

9. On whose assurance in the year 1925, labourers had ended their strike?
(a) Prof. Abdul Bari
(b) Jawaharlal Nehru
(c) Subhash Chandra Bose
(d) Mahatma Gandhi

10. Which party was founded by M. N. Roy?
(a) The Communist Party
(b) The Socialist Party
(c) The Peace Party
(d) The Unity Party

11. When was the Communist Party constituted?
(a) 1921 AD (b) 1923 AD
(c) 1925 AD (d) 1927 AD

12. Where was the Communist Party constituted?
(a) Kanpur (b) Patna
(c) Meerut (d) Allahabad

13. Where in the year 1928 the largest strike of the country took place?
(a) Calcutta (b) Delhi
(c) Bombay (d) Jamshedpur

14. Who had led the strike in Jamshedpur?
(a) Jai Prakash Narayan
(b) C F Andrews
(c) M N Roy
(d) Manik Homi

15. On 18th August 1928 a treaty/compromise occurred between Company and which other person?
(a) Mahatma Gandhi
(b) Jawaharlal Nehru
(c) Subhash Chandra Bose
(d) Jamshedji Tata

16. Who had founded the Jamshedpur Labour Federation?
(a) Manik Homi
(b) Jamshedji Tata
(c) Homi Tata
(d) Subhash Chandra Bose

17. Who had presided over the Jharia conference of All India Trade Union Congress?
(a) Subhash Chandra Bose
(b) Mahatma Gandhi
(c) Prof. Abdul Bari
(d) Jawaharlal Nehru

18. Under whose leadership a trade union known as Tata Workers Union was founded?
(a) Prof. Abdul Bari
(b) Jawaharlal Nehru
(c) Subhash Chandra Bose
(d) Mahatma Gandhi

19. Who led the labourers of the coal mine at Bermo?
(a) Prof Abdul Bari
(b) Satya Narayan Singh
(c) Yogendra Shukla
(d) Both (b) and (c)

20. When was 'Jai Prakash Diwas' was observed in the entire province?
(a) 14 March
(b) 10 May
(c) 12 June
(d) 15 August

21. When did the 'August Revolution' take place?
(a) 1917 AD (b) 1921 AD
(c) 1930 AD (d) 1942 AD

THE SOCIALIST MOVEMENT

1. Movements of which countries inspired the Indian Youth to follow the socialist way?
(a) France (b) Britain
(c) America (d) Russia

2. When was the Socialist Party founded in Bihar?
(a) 1927 AD (b) 1929 AD
(c) 1931 AD (d) 1933 AD

3. **Who was the founder of Bihar Socialist Party?**
   (a) Gangasharan Sinha
   (b) Ramvriksha Benipuri
   (c) Ramanand Mishra
   (d) All of the above
4. **When was the formation of Indian Congress Socialist Party formally announced?**
   (a) 1930 AD (b) 1932 AD
   (c) 1934 AD (d) 1936 AD
5. **Who was appointed as the President of Indian Congress Socialist Party?**
   (a) Minu Masani
   (b) Acharya Narendra Dev
   (c) Hasan Imam
   (d) Jai Prakash Narayan
6. **Who was appointed as the Secretary of the Indian Congress Socialist Party?**
   (a) Jai Prakash Narayan
   (b) Shrikrishna Singh
   (c) Rajendra Prasad
   (d) Maulana Mazhrul Haq
7. **When was Jai Prakash Narayan born?**
   (a) 11 April 1902
   (b) 11 May 1902
   (c) 11 June 1902
   (d) 11 October 1902
8. **Jai Prakash Narayan was born in Sitab Diyara village of __________ district.**
   (a) Saran (b) Champaran
   (c) Munger (d) Patna
9. **Who is known as 'Loknayak'?**
   (a) Karpoori Thakur
   (b) Shrikrishna Singh
   (c) Jai Prakash Narayan
   (d) Maulana Mazhrul Haq
10. **When did Jai Prakash Narayan return from America to India?**
    (a) 1923 AD (b) 1925 AD
    (c) 1927 AD (d) 1929 AD
11. **When did Jai Prakash Narayan leave politics?**
    (a) 1949 AD (b) 1951 AD
    (c) 1953 AD (d) 1957 AD
12. **When was Jai Prakash Narayan awarded with 'Magsaysay Prize'?**
    (a) 1965 AD (b) 1963 AD
    (c) 1961 AD (d) 1959 AD
13. **When was Jai Prakash Narayan honoured with 'Bharat Ratna'?**
    (a) 1992 AD (b) 1994 AD
    (c) 1996 AD (d) 1998 AD
14. **When was emergency imposed in the country?**
    (a) 1971 AD (b) 1973 AD
    (c) 1975 AD (d) 1977 AD
15. **Who had given the slogan of the total revolution?**
    (a) Mahatma Gandhi
    (b) Jai Prakash Narayan
    (c) Jawaharlal Nehru
    (d) Subhash Chandra Bose
16. **When did Jai Prakash Narayan die?**
    (a) 1973 AD (b) 1975 AD
    (c) 1977 AD (d) 1979 AD

THE COMMUNIST MOVEMENT

1. **In Bihar, when did spread of communist views take place in public for the rights of labourers of Jharia coal Mines?**
   (a) 1923 AD (b) 1921 AD
   (c) 1919 AD (d) 1917 AD
2. **Who promoted for the first time the communism in Bihar?**
   (a) Singar Vellu Chettiyar
   (b) Manik Homi
   (c) Subhash Chandra Bose
   (d) Abdul Bari
3. **When was the Bihar branch of Communist Party of India constituted?**
   (a) 1928 AD (b) 1930 AD
   (c) 1932 AD (d) 1934 AD

4. Where was the Bihar Branch of Communist Party of India constituted?
(a) Bhagalpur (b) Munger
(c) Patna (d) Saran

5. Under whose leadership, 'Bakasht Movement' was launched?
(a) Swami Vidyanand
(b) Karyanand Sharma
(c) Rahul Sanskrityayan
(d) Both (b) and (c)

6. 'Bakasht Movement' was related to what?
(a) Landless farmers
(b) Marginal farmers
(c) Landlords
(d) Bataidar

DEVELOPMENT OF EDUCATION IN THE BRITISH PERIOD

1. Nalanda University situated at _________ was a major educational center not only of the country but also of the entire world?
(a) Peshawar (b) Amritsar
(c) Ahmedabad (d) Bihar

2. Where is the acrtual start of western education considered is India?
(a) 1831 AD (b) 1833 AD
(c) 1835 AD (d) 1837 AD

3. In the period of which Governor General, there was promotion of western education in India?
(a) Lord William Bentic
(b) Lord Curzon
(c) Lord Wellington
(d) Lord Reading

4. Where, in Bihar, schools were first opened for the western education?
(a) Purnia
(b) Bihar Sharif
(c) Bhagalpur
(d) All of the above

5. When was Saint Joseph school established in Patna?
(a) 1847 AD (b) 1849 AD
(c) 1851 AD (d) 1853 AD

6. When was Saint michael School established in Patna?
(a) 1850 AD (b) 1852 AD
(c) 1854 AD (d) 1856 AD

7. When, in Bihar, Bengalis established a modern girl school?
(a) 1866 AD (b) 1864 AD
(c) 1862 AD (d) 1860 AD

8. Where, in 1887, Tej Narayan Jubilee College was established?
(a) Munger (b) Bhagalpur
(c) Patna (d) Saran

9. When was B N College established in Patna?
(a) 1881 AD (b) 1883 AD
(c) 1886 AD (d) 1889 AD

10. Who of the following founded the B N College?
(a) Visheshwar Singh
(b) Virendra Singh
(c) Ramnath Singh
(d) Jai Narayan Singh

11. When was Columbus College established in Hazaribagh?
(a) 1893 AD (b) 1895 AD
(c) 1897 AD (d) 1899 AD

12. When was BNR Teachers' Training College in Patna established?
(a) 1909 AD
(b) 1907 AD
(c) 1905 AD
(d) 1903 AD

13. Who had established the BNR Teachers Training College?
(a) Hasan Rizvi
(b) Saiyyad Nawab Rizvi
(c) Hasan Imam
(d) Maulana Mazhrul Haq

14. When was Patna University established?
(a) 1913 AD (b) 1915 AD
(c) 1917 AD (d) 1919 AD

15. Who was appointed the first Chancellor of Patna University?
(a) J. Smith
(b) David Headily
(c) Mark Richards
(d) J. J. Jevingus

16. When was Nalanda College established?
(a) 1916 AD (b) 1918 AD
(c) 1920 AD (d) 1922 AD

17. Who had established Nalanda College of Bihar Sharif?
(a) Sharad Singh
(b) Bahadur Idal Singh
(c) Chandradhari Shah
(d) Narottam Mishra

18. When was Patna Science College established?
(a) 1921 AD (b) 1923 AD
(c) 1925 AD (d) 1927 AD

19. When was the Basic Education Board established?
(a) 1938 AD (b) 1936 AD
(c) 1934 AD (d) 1932 AD

20. The start of higher education in Bihar is considered to have begun from when?
(a) 1859 AD (b) 1861 AD
(c) 1863 AD (d) 1865 AD

21. When was Patna University established?
(a) 1863 AD (b) 1864 AD
(c) 1865 AD (d) 1866 AD

22. Where was 'Animal Reproduction and Dairy Farm' established?
(a) Pusa
(b) Bihar Sharif
(c) Sugauli
(d) Motipur

23. When was Pusa situated Animal Reproduction and Dairy Farm established?
(a) 1900 AD (b) 1902 AD
(c) 1904 AD (d) 1906 AD

24. When was 'Agriculture Research Institute' established?
(a) 1900 AD (b) 1902 AD
(c) 1904 AD (d) 1906 AD

25. In the time of which Viceroy, Agriculture Research Institute was established?
(a) Lord Canning
(b) Lord Curzon
(c) Lord Wellington
(d) Lord Reading

26. When was 'Prince of Wales Medical College' established?
(a) 1921 AD (b) 1923 AD
(c) 1925 AD (d) 1927 AD

27. By which name the Prince of Wales Medical College was known later on?
(a) Patna Medical College
(b) Prasad Medical College
(c) Bihar Medical College
(d) Magadh Medical College

28. When was 'Bihar Scientific Society' established?
(a) 1968 AD (b) 1970 AD
(c) 1972 AD (d) 1974 AD

29. Where was 'Bihar Scientific Society' established?
(a) Champaran
(b) Saran
(c) Bihar Sharif
(d) Mujaffarpur

30. Who had founded the 'Bihar Scientific Society'?
(a) Hasan Imam
(b) Shakil Azmi
(c) Saiyyad Imdad Ali
(d) Saiyyad Ata Hussain

31. When was 'Survey Vidyalaya' for Engineering Education established in Patna?
(a) 1870 AD (b) 1872 AD
(c) 1874 AD (d) 1876 AD

32. When was Bihar College of Engineering designated as 'National Institute of Technology' (NIT) by the Government of India?
(a) 2000 AD (b) 2002 AD
(c) 2004 AD (d) 2006 AD

33. When did Bihar Legislative Council start Ayurvedic Education System by passing a proposal?
(a) 1917 AD (b) 1919 AD
(c) 1921 AD (d) 1923 AD

34. When was Government School of Arts and Crafts established in Patna?
(a) 1939 AD (b) 1937 AD
(c) 1935 AD (d) 1933 AD

35. When was Government Ayurvedic School opened in Patna?
(a) 1920 AD (b) 1922 AD
(c) 1924 AD (d) 1926 AD

36. When was the BIT extension branch of Bihar for Engineering Education started?
(a) 2002 AD (b) 2004 AD
(c) 2006 AD (d) 2008 AD

37. Where in Bihar BIT Extension branch was established?
(a) Gaya (b) Patna
(c) Mujaffarpur (d) Munger

38. Where in Bihar 'Chandragupta Manangement Institute' is situated?
(a) Nalanda (b) Hazipur
(c) Mujaffarpur (d) Patna

39. When was Chandragupta Management Institute established in Bihar?
(a) 2004 AD (b) 2006 AD
(c) 2008 AD (d) 2010 AD

40. When was IIT established in Bihar?
(a) 2008 AD (b) 2006 AD
(c) 2004 AD (d) 2002 AD

41. Where is an IIT situated in Bihar?
(a) Bhagalpur (b) Hajipur
(c) Patna (d) Vaishali

42. When was AIIMS established in Bihar by the Govt of India?
(a) 2006 AD (b) 2008 AD
(c) 2010 AD (d) 2012 AD

43. Where is AIIMS situated in Bihar?
(a) Gaya (b) Bihar Sharif
(c) Hajipur (d) Patna

44. Where is the Eastern Regional Office of Indian Agriculture Research Institute situated?
(a) Patna (b) Calcutta
(c) Ranchi (d) Guwahati

45. Where is Agriculture Research Institute situated in Bihar?
(a) Gaya (b) Patna
(c) Mujaffarpur (d) Vaishali

46. Where was 'Corn Research Institute' established?
(a) Begusarai (b) Nalanda
(c) Siwan (d) Motihari

47. Where is 'Water Management Institute' located in Bihar?
(a) Gaya (b) Begusarai
(c) Patna (d) Betia

MISCELLANEOUS

1. In which village in Deoghar district, the revolt of 1857 was started by the soldiers?
(a) Navadih (b) Rohini
(c) Kalyanpur (d) Dawood Nagar

2. Who led the 1857 revolt in Patna?
(a) Peer Munshi
(b) Inayat Ali
(c) Salman Rizvi
(d) Peer Ali

3. **When did the revolt of 1857 begin in Patna?**
   (a) 1 May (b) 8 June
   (c) 3 July (d) 10 August
4. **When did the rule of East India Company end in India?**
   (a) 1857 AD (b) 1858 AD
   (c) 1859 AD (d) 1860 AD
5. **When did the 'Sardari' fight begin in Bihar?**
   (a) 1856 AD (b) 1858 AD
   (c) 1860 AD (d) 1862 AD
6. **When did the publication of Bihar Times begin?**
   (a) 1888 AD (b) 1890 AD
   (c) 1892 AD (d) 1894 AD
7. **When did the demand for separation of Bihar from Bengal begin?**
   (a) 1902 AD (b) 1904 AD
   (c) 1906 AD (d) 1908 AD
8. **When was Delhi Darbar organized?**
   (a) 1910 AD (b) 1911 AD
   (c) 1912 AD (d) 1913 AD
9. **When was the declaration of separating Bihar made?**
   (a) 1910 AD (b) 1911 AD
   (c) 1912 AD (d) 1913 AD
10. **Who had, in Delhi Darbar, announced about making Bihar a separate state?**
    (a) Queen Victoria
    (b) Lord Curzon
    (c) George-V
    (d) George-VI
11. **When was the proposal for separating Bihar and Odissa from Bengal accepted?**
    (a) 1908 AD (b) 1910 AD
    (c) 1912 AD (d) 1914 AD
12. **Where did Jawaharlal Nehru attend the Congress session for the first time?**
    (a) Patna (b) Gaya
    (c) Ramgarh (d) Nagpur
13. **When did Jawaharlal Nehru attend the Congress session for the first time?**
    (a) 1906 AD (b) 1908 AD
    (c) 1910 AD (d) 1912 AD
14. **When was the High Court established in Patna?**
    (a) 1910 AD (b) 1912 AD
    (c) 1914 AD (d) 1916 AD
15. **Who was appointed the first Chief Justice of Patna High Court?**
    (a) Sir Edward (b) Lord George
    (c) James David (d) Mark Cooper
16. **When did the dual rule begin in Bihar?**
    (a) 1913 AD (b) 1915 AD
    (c) 1917 AD (d) 1919 AD
17. **When did Montagu-Chelmsford reformation take place?**
    (a) 1919 AD (b) 1917 AD
    (c) 1915 AD (d) 1913 AD
18. **When was the 'Hindi Sahitya Sammelan' started in Bihar?**
    (a) 1916 AD (b) 1917 AD
    (c) 1918 AD (d) 1919 AD
19. **When was 'Sadakat Ashram' established?**
    (a) 1916 AD (b) 1918 AD
    (c) 1920 AD (d) 1922 AD
20. **Who established 'Sadakat Ashram' in Patna?**
    (a) Maulana Mazhrul Haq
    (b) Hasan Imam
    (c) Mohd Shafi
    (d) Peer Ali
21. **When was 'Swaraj Dal' established in Bihar?**
    (a) 1919 AD (b) 1921 AD
    (c) 1923 AD (d) 1925 AD
22. **When did Simon Commission arrive in Bihar?**
    (a) 1922 AD (b) 1924 AD
    (c) 1926 AD (d) 1928 AD

23. When did Gandhiji evoke personal Satyagrah in Patna?
(a) 1934 AD (b) 1932 AD
(c) 1930 AD (d) 1928 AD

24. When was Orissa separated from Bihar Province?
(a) 1931 AD (b) 1932 AD
(c) 1933 AD (d) 1934 AD

25. Who was appointed the first Governor of the new Bihar in the year 1936?
(a) David Siften
(b) Jack Kallis
(c) David Hooper
(d) Mark Kallis

26. Who was the first Chief Minister of Bihar?
(a) Mohd Yunus
(b) Shaif Shah
(c) Prof Abdul Bari
(d) Hasan Imam

27. Mohd Yunus of Bihar was related to which party?
(a) Communist Party
(b) Congress Party
(c) Peace Party
(d) Bihar Muslim Independent Party

28. When was Mohd Yunus appointed the Prime Minister of Bihar?
(a) 1937 AD (b) 1935 AD
(c) 1933 AD (d) 1931 AD

29. When was Shrikrishna Singh appointed the Chief Minister of Bihar?
(a) 1931 AD (b) 1933 AD
(c) 1935 AD (d) 1937 AD

30. Who established the Momin Congress?
(a) Hasan Imam
(b) Abdul Qayum Ansari
(c) Maulana Shakat Ali
(d) Wahab Shep

31. When was Momin Congress established in Bihar?
(a) 1932 AD (b) 1934 AD
(c) 1936 AD (d) 1938 AD

32. When was Bihar branch of Forward Block constituted?
(a) 1938 AD (b) 1940 AD
(c) 1942 AD (d) 1944 AD

33. On__________August, during the Quit India movement, there was a shooting scandal in Bihar?
(a) 8 (b) 9
(c) 10 (d) 11

34. On 11 August how many students were martyred in Patna shooting scandal?
(a) 7 (b) 10
(c) 11 (d) 13

35. Under whose leadership in Bihar interim government was constituted?
(a) Shrikant Singh
(b) Anugrah Narayan Singh
(c) Shri Krishna Singh
(d) Mohd. Yunus

36. When was the interim government formed under the leadership of Shri Krishna Singh?
(a) 1944 AD (b) 1945 AD
(c) 1946 AD (d) 1947 AD

37. Who became the first Chief Minister of independent Bihar?
(a) Anugrah Narayan Singh
(b) Ramdayalu Singh
(c) Jai Prakash Narayan
(d) Shri Krishna Singh

38. Who was appointed as the first Governor of independent Bihar?
(a) Ramdayalu Singh
(b) Jai Ramdas Daulatram
(c) Jagjivan Ram
(d) Maulana Mazhrul Haq

39. When did Bihar become a State after it ceased to be a Province?
(a) 15 August 1947
(b) 26 January 1948
(c) 16 November 1949
(d) 26 January 1950

40. When was the landlord abolition Act implemented in Bihar?
(a) 1950 AD (b) 1949 AD
(c) 1948 AD (d) 1947 AD

41. When were the first Legislative Assembly elections held in Bihar?
(a) 1949 AD (b) 1950 AD
(c) 1951 AD (d) 1952 AD

42. When did Shri Krishna Singh die?
(a) 1959 AD (b) 1960 AD
(c) 1961 AD (d) 1962 AD

43. After death of Shri Krishna Singh, who became the acting Chief Minister of Bihar?
(a) Anugrah Narayan Singh
(b) Deep Narayan Singh
(c) Hasan Imam
(d) Jagjivan Ram

44. Where is Oil Refinery Plant situated in Bihar?
(a) Vaishali (b) Baroni
(c) Nalanda (d) Mujaffarpur

45. When is Bihar Day celebrated?
(a) 22 March (b) 22 April
(c) 22 May (d) 22 June

46. When was Bihar Centenary year ceremony organized?
(a) 2009 (b) 2010
(c) 2011 (d) 2012

47. When did Mahamaya Prasad become the Chief Minister of Bihar?
(a) 1967 AD (b) 1965 AD
(c) 1963 AD (d) 1961 AD

48. When was Urdu announced as the second Government language in Bihar?
(a) 1969 AD (b) 1971 AD
(c) 1973 AD (d) 1975 AD

49. When was Janta Party government formed in Bihar under leadership of Karpuri Thakur?
(a) 1977 AD (b) 1975 AD
(c) 1973 AD (d) 1971 AD

50. When was Jharkhand separated from Bihar and became a separate state?
(a) 1998 AD (b) 1999 AD
(c) 2000 AD (d) 2001 AD

51. When was 'Global Meet' organised for the first time in Bihar?
(a) 2001 AD (b) 2003 AD
(c) 2005 AD (d) 2007 AD

52. When was 'Bihar Day' celebrated for the first time?
(a) 2010 AD
(b) 2008 AD
(c) 2006 AD
(d) 2004 AD

Answers

THE REVOLT OF 1857

1. (c) **2.** (b) **3.** (a) **4.** (a) **5.** (d) **6.** (b) **7.** (b) **8.** (a) **9.** (d) **10.** (d)
11. (d) **12.** (c) **13.** (d) **14.** (a) **15.** (c) **16.** (b) **17.** (b) **18.** (a) **19.** (a) **20.** (b)
21. (d) **22.** (c) **23.** (c) **24.** (b)

THE FREEDOM MOVEMENT

1. (b) **2.** (d) **3.** (a) **4.** (b) **5.** (a) **6.** (a) **7.** (a) **8.** (b) **9.** (b) **10.** (c)
11. (b) **12.** (a) **13.** (d) **14.** (d) **15.** (a) **16.** (b) **17.** (d) **18.** (b) **19.** (a) **20.** (d)

21. (b) **22.** (a) **23.** (c) **24.** (c) **25.** (a) **26.** (b) **27.** (b) **28.** (a) **29.** (b) **30.** (d)
31. (d) **32.** (a) **33.** (a) **34.** (b) **35.** (d) **36.** (d) **37.** (c) **38.** (a) **39.** (c) **40.** (d)
41. (a) **42.** (c) **43.** (b) **44.** (a) **45.** (d) **46.** (c) **47.** (d) **48.** (c) **49.** (b) **50.** (c)
51. (b) **52.** (a) **53.** (d) **54.** (b) **55.** (a) **56.** (d) **57.** (d) **58.** (a) **59.** (a) **60.** (d)
61. (a) **62.** (d) **63.** (b) **64.** (c) **65.** (b) **66.** (a) **67.** (d) **68.** (a) **69.** (b) **70.** (c)
71. (a) **72.** (d) **73.** (d) **74.** (d) **75.** (c) **76.** (b) **77.** (b) **78.** (c) **79.** (a) **80.** (d)
81. (b) **82.** (a) **83.** (d) **84.** (d) **85.** (c) **86.** (b) **87.** (c) **88.** (b) **89.** (d) **90.** (d)
91. (d) **92.** (d) **93.** (c) **94.** (b) **95.** (d) **96.** (d) **97.** (c) **98.** (b) **99.** (a) **100.** (d)
101. (b) **102.** (a) **103.** (d) **104.** (d) **105.** (c) **106.** (a) **107.** (b) **108.** (c) **109.** (b) **110.** (d)
111. (d) **112.** (c) **113.** (c) **114.** (d) **115.** (a) **116.** (b) **117.** (d) **118.** (b) **119.** (a) **120.** (d)
121. (a) **122.** (c) **123.** (a) **124.** (b) **125.** (c) **126.** (a) **127.** (c) **128.** (a) **129.** (c) **130.** (c)
131. (b) **132.** (a) **133.** (b) **134.** (d) **135.** (d) **136.** (d) **137.** (a) **138.** (c) **139.** (b) **140.** (b)
141. (d) **142.** (b) **143.** (a) **144.** (d) **145.** (c) **146.** (b) **147.** (a) **148.** (d) **149.** (b) **150** (a)
151. (b) **152.** (c) **153.** (b) **154.** (b) **155.** (a) **156.** (d) **157.** (d) **158.** (a) **159.** (d) **160.** (c)
161. (b) **162.** (d) **163.** (c) **164.** (a) **165.** (a) **166.** (b) **167.** (c) **168.** (b) **169.** (a) **170.** (b)
171. (d) **172.** (a) **173.** (c) **174.** (b) **175.** (d) **176.** (a) **177.** (b) **178.** (d) **179.** (a) **180.** (a)
181. (b) **182.** (b) **183.** (a) **184.** (d) **185.** (d) **186.** (a) **187.** (b) **188.** (d) **189.** (a) **190.** (d)
191. (d) **192.** (b) **193.** (c) **194.** (c) **195.** (d) **196.** (a) **197.** (d) **198.** (d) **199.** (d) **200.** (b)
201. (c) **202.** (b) **203.** (d) **204.** (a) **205.** (c) **206.** (d) **207.** (c) **208.** (c) **209.** (a) **210.** (c)
211. (b) **212.** (d) **213.** (d) **214.** (c) **215.** (a) **216.** (d) **217.** (b) **218.** (a) **219.** (c) **220.** (a)
221. (b) **222.** (b) **223.** (b) **224.** (c) **225.** (d) **226.** (b) **227.** (d) **228.** (c)

THE ROLE OF WOMEN IN FREEDOM MOVEMENT

1. (a) **2.** (b) **3.** (d) **4.** (c) **5.** (a) **6.** (b) **7.** (a) **8.** (c) **9.** (d) **10.** (a)
11. (d) **12.** (a) **13.** (b)

THE PEASANT MOVEMENT

1. (d) **2.** (b) **3.** (d) **4.** (c) **5.** (d) **6.** (b) **7.** (c) **8.** (d) **9.** (a) **10.** (b)
11. (b) **12.** (d) **13.** (d) **14.** (b) **15.** (a) **16.** (d) **17.** (c) **18.** (c) **19.** (a) **20.** (c)
21. (a) **22.** (d) **23.** (d) **24.** (b) **25.** (d) **26.** (a) **27.** (d) **28.** (b) **29.** (a) **30.** (c)
31. (d) **32.** (d) **33.** (c) **34.** (a) **35.** (a) **36.** (c) **37.** (d) **38.** (a) **39.** (d) **40.** (a)
41. (c) **42.** (d) **43.** (b)

THE LABOUR MOVEMENT

1. (d) **2.** (b) **3.** (c) **4.** (c) **5.** (b) **6.** (c) **7.** (d) **8.** (c) **9.** (d) **10.** (a)
11. (c) **12.** (a) **13.** (d) **14.** (d) **15.** (c) **16.** (a) **17.** (d) **18.** (a) **19.** (d) **20.** (a)
21. (d)

THE SOCIALIST MOVEMENT

1. (d) **2.** (c) **3.** (d) **4.** (c) **5.** (b) **6.** (a) **7.** (d) **8.** (a) **9.** (c) **10.** (d)
11. (d) **12.** (a) **13.** (d) **14.** (c) **15.** (b) **16.** (d)

THE COMMUNIST MOVEMENT

1. (b) **2.** (a) **3.** (c) **4.** (b) **5.** (d) **6.** (b)

DEVELOPMENT OF EDUCATION IN THE BRITISH PERIOD

1. (d) **2.** (c) **3.** (a) **4.** (d) **5.** (a) **6.** (d) **7.** (a) **8.** (b) **9.** (d) **10.** (a)
11. (d) **12.** (a) **13.** (b) **14.** (c) **15.** (d) **16.** (c) **17.** (b) **18.** (d) **19.** (a) **20.** (c)
21. (a) **22.** (a) **23.** (b) **24.** (c) **25.** (b) **26.** (c) **27.** (a) **28.** (c) **29.** (d) **30.** (c)
31. (c) **32.** (c) **33.** (c) **34.** (b) **35.** (d) **36.** (c) **37.** (b) **38.** (d) **39.** (c) **40.** (a)
41. (c) **42.** (d) **43.** (d) **44.** (a) **45.** (c) **46.** (a) **47.** (c)

MISCELLANEOUS

1. (b) **2.** (d) **3.** (c) **4.** (b) **5.** (c) **6.** (d) **7.** (c) **8.** (c) **9.** (b) **10.** (c)
11. (c) **12.** (a) **13.** (d) **14.** (d) **15.** (a) **16.** (d) **17.** (b) **18.** (d) **19.** (c) **20.** (a)
21. (c) **22.** (d) **23.** (a) **24.** (d) **25.** (a) **26.** (a) **27.** (d) **28.** (a) **29.** (d) **30.** (b)
31. (d) **32.** (b) **33.** (d) **34.** (a) **35.** (d) **36.** (c) **37.** (d) **38.** (b) **39.** (d) **40.** (a)
41. (d) **42.** (d) **43.** (b) **44.** (b) **45.** (a) **46.** (d) **47.** (a) **48.** (d) **49.** (a) **50.** (c)
51. (d) **52.** (a)

❑❑❑

6 Separation of Bihar

1. The talk of a separate Bihar movement was made in which of the following magazines under the title 'Bihar for Biharis only'?
(a) Samvad
(b) Moordh-e-Suleman
(c) Bihari
(d) Pratap

2. When was it published in the magazine 'Moordh-e-Suleman' that 'Bihar is for Biharis only'?
(a) 1870 AD (b) 1872 AD
(c) 1874 AD (d) 1876 AD

3. Where was the magazine 'Moordh-e-Suleman' publshied from?
(a) Bhagalpur (b) Munger
(c) Vaishali (d) Motihari

4. Which Urdu Newspaper has feverishly advocated for the separation of Bihar from Bengal?
(a) The Qaumi Awaj
(b) The Bhumi Azadi
(c) The Inqlab
(d) The Kasid

5. When did the Urdu Newspaper 'Kasid' advocate strongly for the separation of Bihar from Bengal?
(a) 1873 AD
(b) 1875 AD
(c) 1877 AD
(d) 1879 AD

6. Which of the following had given a solid base to the Bihar Separation movement by way of 'Kayastha Gazette'?
(a) Deep Narayan Singh
(b) Anugrah Narayan Singh
(c) Krishna Sahay
(d) Mahesh Narayan

7. The second session of the Provincial Congress was completed in Bihar by efforts of who of the following persons?
(a) Brij Kishore
(b) Deep Narayan Singh
(c) Ali Imam
(d) Maulana Mazhrul Haq

8. Which Lt. Governor had said that unless the people of Bihar are given means of livelihood, the development of Bihar could not take place?
(a) Campbell (b) Smith
(c) David Heir (d) George Belly

9. Who had demanded reservation in government jobs for the 'Biharis'?
(a) Smith (b) Campbell
(c) Ashley Eden (d) Lee Grand

10. Who is the founder of 'Sadar Anjuman-a-Hind'?
(a) Balraj Sahni
(b) Munshi Pyarelal
(c) Hasan Imam
(d) Maulana Imdad Ali

11. Who had handed over a reminder to the Lt. Governor Charles Elliot and Alexander Mckenzie for creation of a separate Bihar?

(a) Shri Krishna Sahay
(b) Mahesh Narayan
(c) Sachchidanand Sinha
(d) Both (b) and (c)

12. When did the Governor General of India made it clear that separation of Bengal was necessary for the administrative convenience?
(a) 1901 AD (b) 1902 AD
(c) 1903 AD (d) 1904 AD

13. Who was the Governor General of India in the year 1903?
(a) Lord Curzon
(b) Lord Dufferin
(c) Lord Reading
(d) Lord Irwin

14. When was division of Bengal announced by the Home Secretary Herbert Rizley?
(a) 5 January 1903
(b) 6 March 1903
(c) 8 May 1903
(d) 3 December 1903

15. Whose book is it –'the Partition of Bengal, Seperation of Bihar'?
(a) Shri Krishna Singh
(b) Sachchidanand Sinha
(c) Mahesh Narayan
(d) Both (b) and (c)

16. Who was appointed the first Lt. Governor of Bihar in the year 1912?
(a) John Smith
(b) Johan Napier
(c) Charles Belly
(d) David Cameroon

17. Where was the first 'Bihari Students' Conference' held?
(a) Gaya
(b) Motihari
(c) Vaishali
(d) Patna

18. When was the first Bihari Students Conference organized?
(a) 1903 AD
(b) 1904 AD
(c) 1906 AD
(d) 1908 AD

19. Under whose Chairmanship, the first Bihari Students Conference was organized?
(a) Subhash Chandra Bose
(b) Rajendra Prasad
(c) Ali Imam
(d) Sharfuddin

20. Who was the Editor of the magazine 'Bihari Times'?
(a) Shri Krishna Singh
(b) Maulana Mazhrul Haq
(c) Ramdayalu Singh
(d) Mahesh Narayan

21. When did the magazine 'Bihari Times' start to get published by the name 'Bihari'?
(a) 1906 AD (b) 1905 AD
(c) 1904 AD (d) 1903 AD

22. When did Mahesh Narayan die?
(a) 1904 AD (b) 1905 AD
(c) 1906 AD (d) 1907 AD

23. In the year 1908, where was the 'Bihar Pradeshik Sammelan' organized?
(a) Betia (b) Motihari
(c) Patna (d) Mujaffarpur

24. Under whose Chairmanship, Bihar provincial conference was held in the year 1908?
(a) Maulana Mazhrul Haq
(b) Ali Imam
(c) Shri Krishan Singh
(d) Brahm Dev Narayan

25. Who had proposed for separation of Bihar in the Bihar Provincial Conference held in the year 1908?
(a) Mohd Fakhruddin
(b) Hasan Imam
(c) Ali Imam
(d) Maulana Mazhrul Haq

26. When was the proposal for separation of Bihar passed unanimously in the Bihar Provincial Conference?

(a) 1902 AD (b) 1904 AD
(c) 1906 AD (d) 1908 AD

27. Who was chosen for the Central Legislative Council from the side of Bengal Legislative Council?

(a) Mohd Sharfuddin
(b) Hasan Imam
(c) Sachchidanand Sinha
(d) Rajendra Prasad

28. When was Sachchidanand Sinha chosen a member of the Central Legislative Council?

(a) 1908 AD (b) 1910 AD
(c) 1912 AD (d) 1914 AD

29. Who was chosen as the law member of the Executive Council of Governor General?

(a) Sachchidanand Sinha
(b) Shri Krishan Singh
(c) Ali Imam
(d) Imdad Ali

30. Which of the Governor Generals had cancelled the division of Bengal?

(a) Lord Curzon
(b) Lord Harding
(c) Lord Reading
(d) Lord Cornwallis

31. When did Governor General cancel the division of Bengal?

(a) 1908 AD
(b) 1909 AD
(c) 1910 AD
(d) 1911 AD

32. When was the announcement of creation of two states viz Bihar and Orissa from Bengal made?

(a) 1910 (b) 1911
(c) 1912 (d) 1913

Answers

1. (b)	**2.** (d)	**3.** (b)	**4.** (d)	**5.** (c)	**6.** (d)	**7.** (b)	**8.** (a)	**9.** (c)	**10.** (b)
11. (d)	**12.** (c)	**13.** (a)	**14.** (d)	**15.** (d)	**16.** (c)	**17.** (d)	**18.** (c)	**19.** (d)	**20.** (d)
21. (a)	**22.** (d)	**23.** (c)	**24.** (b)	**25.** (a)	**26.** (d)	**27.** (d)	**28.** (b)	**29.** (c)	**30.** (b)
31. (d)	**32.** (b)								

❑❑❑

7 Architecture and Painting

THE MAURYAN ART

1. In the Mauryan and the pre-Mauryan time, ________ was used to produce artistic goods.
(a) Soil (b) Wood
(c) Weed (d) Kanva

2. In which period, the use of stone art was first made extensively due to which this artfare became permanent?
(a) Haryak (b) Shishunag
(c) Maurya (d) Kanva

3. How many types of art is found in the Mauryan period?
(a) 1 (b) 2
(c) 3 (d) 4

4. Which of the following is not a kind of Mauryan period art?
(a) Swatantra Kala
(b) Lok Kala
(c) Murti Kala
(d) Rajkiya kala

5. The 'Rajprasad' of Magadh King Chandragupta obtained from Kumrahar situated in Patliputra is an example of which of the following arts?
(a) Lok Kala
(b) Murti Kala
(c) Swatantra Kala
(d) Rajkiya Kala

6. How many stone pillars have been found in the Assembly Hall of Chandragupta Maurya?
(a) 80 (b) 82
(c) 84 (d) 86

7. Who of the following travelers had named the palace of Chandragupta situated at Kumrahar as the one 'Built by a Deity'?
(a) Huen Tsang
(b) Fa-Hien
(c) Marco Polo
(d) I Tsang

8. Fa-Hien was a traveler from which country?
(a) China (b) France
(c) Spain (d) England

9. The maximum remains of which Mauryan ruler are found?
(a) Chandragupta Maurya
(b) Bindusara
(c) Ashoka
(d) Dasratha

10. The artfare of the period of Emperor Ashoka can be divided into how many parts?
(a) 2 (b) 3
(c) 4 (d) 5

11. Which of the following is the best example of the artfare of the Mauryan period?
(a) Pillar
(b) Stupa
(c) Stone Vedika
(d) Guha Vihar

12. On which of the following pillars, 'Dhamma' scripts are engraved?
(a) Lauriya Areraj
(b) Lauriya Nandangarh
(c) Lumbini
(d) All of the above

13. On which of the following pillars, 'Dhamma' scripts are not engraved?
(a) Sanchi (b) Sarnath
(c) Kosay (d) Allahabad

14. Which of the following are the Ashoka built simple pillars?
(a) Basar
(b) Kosay
(c) Rampurva
(d) All of the above

16. Which pillar built by Ashoka bears a bull picture on its top?
(a) Delhi Topra
(b) Lauriya Areraj
(c) Rampurva
(d) Lauriya Nandangarh

17. Which animal's picture is engraved on the pillar of Sarnath?
(a) Tiger (b) Elephant
(c) Lion (d) Rhinoceros

18. The Lion picture engraved on the Sarnath pillar is a sign of _________ of Ashoka?
(a) Power (b) 'Dhamma'
(c) Sacrifice (d) Friendship

19. 'Stupa' is related to which religion?
(a) Jain (b) Buddhist
(c) Ajivika (d) Both (a) and (b)

20. According to the tradition how many 'stupas' were built by Ashoka?
(a) 84 thousand (b) 82 thousand
(c) 80 thousand (d) 75 thousand

21. Which ruler had got built the great 'stupa of Sanchi'?
(a) Ajatshatru
(b) Chandragupta Maurya
(c) Ashoka
(d) Dhananand

22. Where did Ashoka get built a 'stupa' denoting a state of justice?
(a) Nalanda
(b) Takshila
(c) Allahabad
(d) Sanchi

23. The 'Stupas' of the Mauryan period were surrounded by _______.
(a) Vedika (b) Wall
(c) 'Tat' (d) Cloth

24. The pieces of three 'vedikas' have been recovered in excavation at which place?
(a) Sarnath (b) Takshila
(c) Patliputra (d) Nalanada

25. Which Mauryan ruler had got built 'Vihars' for habitation of the 'Bhikshus'?
(a) Chandragupta Maurya
(b) Ashoka
(c) Dasratha
(d) Both (b) and (c)

26. The evidence of a 'Vihar' are found on which hill?
(a) Kainur (b) Barabar
(c) Nagarjuni (d) Both (b) and (c)

27. The evidences of a 'Vihar' are found in which of the following caves?
(a) Sudama cave
(b) Karan Chopar Cave
(c) Vishwa Jhopri Cave
(d) All of the above

28. The other name of the Sudama Cave is_______cave.
(a) Dhamma (b) Mitray
(c) Nyagrodh (d) Gop

29. Sudama Cave was built in ______ year of the Ashoka's coronation?
(a) 10th (b) 12th
(c) 14th (d) 16th

30. **Lomash Rishi Cave was built in the rule of which ruler?**
(a) Ashoka
(b) Ajatshatru
(c) Bindusara
(d) Dasratha

31. **The statues of the 'Yaksha-Yakshini' were the main basis of which art?**
(a) Lok Kala (b) Rajkiya Kala
(c) Pravasi Kala (d) Swatantra kala

32. **From where was the idol named 'Chamargrihni' recovered?**
(a) Sarnath
(b) Sanchi
(c) Takshila
(d) Didarganj (Patna)

33. **From which place, the idol of a Jain 'Tirthankar' was recovered?**
(a) Sarnath (b) Patliputra
(c) Nalanada (d) Shrawasti

POST-MAURYAN ART

1. **Gupta Art was influenced by which style?**
(a) Gandhar Art
(b) Sarnath Art
(c) Amravati Art
(d) Mathura Art

2. **In Mathura Art style, the effect of which religion is mainly reflected?**
(a) Buddhist (b) Jain
(c) Hindu (d) Ajivika

3. **Whose idol measuring 795 feet has been recovered from Sultanganj in Bhagalpur?**
(a) Buddha
(b) Krishna
(c) Rishabhdev
(d) Mahavir Swami

PALA ART

1. **Pal Art was developed from 8th century till which century?**
(a) 9th (b) 10th
(c) 11th (d) 12th

2. **In which period, an advanced style of stone, bronze and 'Ashtdhatu' made idols was developed?**
(a) Pal (b) Gupta
(c) Maurya (d) Sen

3. **Whose major contribution was there in making of the silver statues?**
(a) Lokpal (b) Dhima
(c) Bithpal (d) Both (b) and (c)

4. **Dhiman and Bithpal were habitants of which place?**
(a) Nalanda (b) Vaishali
(c) Munger (d) Bodh Gaya

5. **Dhiman and Bithhpal were contemporary of which Pal ruler?**
(a) Gopal (b) Dharam Pal
(c) Dev Pal (d) Both (b) and (c)

6. **Which of the following is an example of Pal period's architecture?**
(a) Odantpuri Mahavihar
(b) Nalanda Mahavihar
(c) Sompur Mahavihar
(d) All of the above

7. **Odantpuri Bodh mahavihar was built by which Pal ruler?**
(a) Gopal (b) Anantpal
(c) Dharampal (d) Devpal

8. **Vikramshila Mahavihar was built in whose rule?**
(a) Mauryan (b) Sen
(c) Pal (d) Kanva

9. **The evidences of Pal period cave temples have been recovered from which place?**
(a) Raxaul (b) Betia
(c) Kalyanpur (d) Kahalgaon

10. The 'Ardhmandap' of Vishnupal temple has been recovered from which place?

(a) Gaya (b) Nalanda

(c) Motihari (d) Betia

11. The Pal period's artfare style is popular with the name of_______of the medieval period artfare.

(a) Uttari Style

(b) Poorvi Style

(c) Pashchimi Style

(d) Dakshini Style

12. The specimen recovered from Nalanda belong to the period of which ruler?

(a) Devpal (b) Dharampal

(c) Gopal (d) Anantpal

PATNA KALAM

1. After the fall of Mughal period, which painting art was developed in Bihar?

(a) Bihar Kalam

(b) Patna Kalam

(c) Madhubani Kalam

(d) Pal Kalam

2. The pictures of Patna Kalam used to be made on_________.

(a) Ivory (b) Abhrak

(c) Cloth (d) Both (a) and (b)

3. Which of the following had greatly influenced the Patna Kalam style?

(a) Mughal art (b) Rajput art

(c) Company art (d) Both (a) and (c)

4. The pictures of Patna Kalam are classified under which type of pictures?

(a) Guha chitra

(b) Laghu Chitra

(c) Rajkiya Chitra Lok Chitra

(d) All of the above

5. Which of the following style had its main subject as painting of the normal life of the masses?

(a) Pahari Style

(b) Mughal Style

(c) Madhubani Art

(d) Patna Kalam

6. Ragini Gandhari is an example of which painting style?

(a) Patna Kalam

(b) Paul Chitrakala

(c) Madhubani Art

(d) Vaishali Art

7. Who was the painter from Patna Kalam art who had made the painting of Ragini Gandhari?

(a) Mahadev Lal

(b) Ram Lal

(c) Sohan Lal

(d) Janak Lal

8. Which painter has depicted a muslim marriage in his pictures?

(a) Sewak Ram

(b) Janak Ram

(c) Shiv Lal

(d) Madho Lal

9. Who made a painting depicting the vice of having drinks by the Begums?

(a) Yamuna Prasad

(b) Lakshman Prasad

(c) Shiv Prasad

(d) Bharat Prasad

10. In which painting style, the high nose of a human face, dense eyebrows, dense eyes, thin face and dense moustache are depicted?

(a) Madhubani Art

(b) Mughal Art

(c) Patna Kalam

(d) Manjusha Style

11. Nohar and Manohar were the painters of which painting style?

(a) Pal Art (b) Moughal Art

(c) Sen Art (d) Patna Kalam

12. **Who was an important painter of Patna Kalam?**
(a) Sewak Ram (b) Jagat Ram
(c) Gopi Ram (d) Sohan Ram

13. **State the period of art of Sewak Ram?**
(a) 1760-1798 AD
(b) 1765-1801 AD
(c) 1768-1805 AD
(d) 1770-1830 AD

14. **Who of the following Patna Kalam painters had depicted Holi and Diwali in his paintings?**
(a) Hulas Lal (b) Shiv Lal
(c) Jagat Lal (d) Madho Lal

15. **Dakshi Biwi, Sona Biwi and Gur Sahay Lal were related to which art style?**
(a) Mughal Art (b) British Art
(c) Patna Kalam (d) Manjusha Art

16. **Who was the last important painter of Patna Kalam?**
(a) Ishwari Prasad Verma
(b) Hulas Lal
(c) Mahendra Mishra
(d) Mangal Pandey

17. **Who of the following used to give patronage to Patna Kalam?**
(a) Tailor
(b) Ram Sultan Bahadur
(c) P. C. Manuk
(d) All of the above

18. **At which place is a collection of Patna Kalam painting?**
(a) Patna Museum
(b) Khudabaksh Library
(c) London Museum
(d) Both (a) and (b)

19. **Who of the following was evidently influenced by Patna Kalam style?**
(a) M. F. Hussain
(b) Rabindranath Tagore
(c) Avnindra Nath Thakur
(d) Both (b) and (c)

20. **The pictures of a woman selling fish, a farmer ploughing his field and a carpenter cutting the wood are made in which style?**
(a) Mughal Art
(b) Patna Kalam
(c) Madhubani Art
(d) Manjusha Art

MADHUBANI (MITHILA) PAINTING

1. **The songs of which poet had a great influence on the Madhubani paintings?**
(a) Vidyadhar
(b) Gopal Sahay
(c) Mandan Mishra
(d) Vidyapati

2. **The influence of Vidyapati's songs got started which genre of painting?**
(a) Lakshmi (b) Krishna
(c) Shiva (d) Both (b) and (c)

3. **In which of the following folk arts, women play an important role?**
(a) Patna Kalam
(b) Motihari Painting
(c) Madhubani painting
(d) Both (a) and (c)

4. **Which of the following districts has been the central place of Mithila culture?**
(a) Darbhanga
(b) Madhubani
(c) Khagariya
(d) Supaul

5. **Mithila painting is an art of the life of masses of which district?**
(a) Darbhanga
(b) Saharasa
(c) Purnia
(d) All of the above

6. How many types are there of Madhubani Painting?
(a) 1 (b) 2
(c) 3 (d) 4

7. Which of the following is a type of Madhubani painting?
(a) Bhittichitra (b) Viharchitra
(c) Aripan (d) Both (a) and (c)

8. In which style of Mithila painting the women make paintings of different festivals and pictures depicting the culture of social life?
(a) Bhittichitra
(b) Aripan
(c) Mangal Chitra
(d) Both (a) and (b)

9. The decoration of Gosnidhar are paintings of __________ importance.
(a) Social (b) Religious
(c) Folk (d) Political

10. In making of paintings of Gosnidhar decoration, women of which family play an important role?
(a) Brahmin (b) Rajpoot
(c) Kayastha (d) Both (a) and (c)

11. In Gosnidhar's decoration, whose painting is mainly found?
(a) Durga-Kali
(b) Radha-Krishna
(c) Ram-Sita
(d) All of the above

12. The decoration of Kohvarghar is a painting of which style?
(a) British Art
(b) Patna Kalam
(c) Mithila Style
(d) Pahadi Art

13. ________ writing is a Mithila painting depicting geometrical and occult method.
(a) Kohvar (b) Savan
(c) Manjusha (d) Aayat

14. ________ is actually a place where at the time of marriage family deity is installed.
(a) Mandap (b) Madwa
(c) Aangan (d) Kohvar

15. In Kohvar, which symbols are mainly imprinted?
(a) Bamboo
(b) Fish
(c) Tortoise
(d) All of the above

16. Which of the followings symbols is a symbol of male organ and reproduction?
(a) Fish (b) Bamboo
(c) Tota Gyan (d) Lotus leaf

17. By which of the following symbols, long life of bride and bridegroom is wished for?
(a) Lotus leaf (b) Tota Gyan
(c) Tortoise (d) Fish

18. Which of the following symbols wishes for blessing one with a son?
(a) Fish (b) Lotus Leaf
(c) Tota Gyan (d) Kite

19. In Mithila in the time of Vidayapati, Krishna Leela was painted mainly in __________.
(a) Bhittachitra
(b) Kohvar Chitra
(c) Manjusha Chitra
(d) Aripan

20. Under Aripan, paintings are made on which of the places?
(a) The ceiling
(b) The courtyard
(c) The door
(d) All of the above

21. In paintings of which style, the water of pressed rice is coloured and used?
(a) Guha Chitra (b) Aripan
(c) Manjusha (d) Bhittichitra

22. Under Aripan, paintings are made with________.

(a) Brush made of Bamboo
(b) Brush
(c) Finger
(d) All of the above

23. Under Aripan, how many types of painting are made?

(a) 2 (b) 3
(c) 4 (d) 5

24. In which of the following symbols, paintings are made under Aripan?

(a) Swastik
(b) The painting of fruits, flowers and trees
(c) The paintings of the deities
(d) All of the above

25. At the time of________ in Aripan made for the married girls, the use of geometrical shape is mainly done.

(a) Lakshmi Pooja
(b) Tulsi Pooja
(c) Ganesh Pooja
(d) Shiv Pooja

26. On occasions like marriage and other celebrations, ________ shape is mainly used in Aripan?

(a) Bamboo (b) Peacock
(c) Counch (d) Leaves

27. Which of the following is the main center of Madhubani paintings?

(a) Lehriya Saray
(b) Bhavanipur
(c) Simri
(d) All of the above

28. Who of the following is a main artist of Madhubani paintings?

(a) Siya Devi
(b) Ganga Devi
(c) Jagdamba Devi
(d) All of the above

29. Where was the exhibition of paintings made by Shashikala Devi held?

(a) Singapore (b) Liberia
(c) Japan (d) China

30. Who gave international popularity to Mithila Art?

(a) Tambegawa (b) Hasegawa
(c) Toka Machi (d) Yama Guchi

31. In which city of Japan, there is a museum of Mithila artfare?

(a) Tokyo (b) Hoshu
(c) Hokedo (d) Toka Machi

32. Who has done research work on Mithila artfare?

(a) Smith (b) George Orwell
(c) Campbell (d) David Lemon

33. The researcher of which country has done research work on Mithila artfare?

(a) France (b) Spain
(c) Britain (d) Germany

34. Where was Mithila Paintings Institute established?

(a) Saurashtra (b) Ganganagar
(c) Kalyanpur (d) Baikunthpur

MANJUSHA STYLE

1. In which of the districts, a people celebration is made by-Bihul Pooja, Bisahari Pooja and Mansa Pooja?

(a) Angg (b) Magadh
(c) Kosi (d) Kashi

2. ________ is the gift of society standing on the lowest step on the caste ladder?

(a) Patna Kalam
(b) Madhubani Painting
(c) Manjusha Style
(d) Kohvar Artfare

3. **During festivals these days, where are attractive, paintings on 'Manjusha' used for worshipping are made**
   (a) Bhagalpur (b) Gaya
   (c) Madhubani (d) Arwal
4. **The depiction of love towards the nature gives a special distinction to which artfare?**
   (a) Madhubani Artfare
   (b) Patna Kalam
   (c) Manjusha Style
   (d) Mughal Artfare
5. **Who is the main character painted in Manjusha style artfare?**
   (a) Shakya Muni
   (b) Chando Saudagar
   (c) Tana Bhagat
   (d) Heral Saudagar
6. **In which artfare's pictures, a woman is painted always along with her husband?**
   (a) Manjusha Style
   (b) Patna Kalam
   (c) Pahadi Artfare
   (d) Rajput Artfare
7. **The character from Manjusha style Bisahari is painted always with whom?**
   (a) Peacock (b) Parrot
   (c) Tortoise (d) Snake
8. **Who is given the credit for keeping Manjusha style alive in Bihar?**
   (a) Ramavtar Singh
   (b) Chakravati Devi
   (c) Siya Devi
   (d) Sewak Ram
9. **Who attracted the peoples' attention towards Manjusha style by making a slide on it?**
   (a) Shekhar
   (b) Abhinav Sinha
   (c) Love Ranjan
   (d) Prakash Jha

Answers

MAURYAN ART

1. (d) **2.** (c) **3.** (b) **4.** (a) **5.** (d) **6.** (c) **7.** (b) **8.** (a) **9.** (c) **10.** (c)
11. (a) **12.** (d) **13.** (c) **14.** (d) **15.** (c) **16.** (b) **17.** (c) **18.** (a) **19.** (d) **20.** (a)
21. (c) **22.** (b) **23.** (a) **24.** (c) **25.** (d) **26.** (d) **27.** (d) **28.** (c) **29.** (b) **30.** (d)
31. (a) **32.** (d) **33.** (b)

POST-MAURYAN ART

1. (d) **2.** (c) **3** (a)

PALA ART

1. (d) **2.** (a) **3.** (d) **4.** (b) **5.** (d) **6.** (d) **7.** (a) **8.** (c) **9.** (d) **10.** (a)
11. (b) **12.** (a)

PATNA KALAM

1. (b) **2.** (d) **3.** (d) **4.** (b) **5.** (d) **6.** (a) **7.** (a) **8.** (c) **9.** (a) **10.** (c)
11. (b) **12.** (a) **13.** (d) **14.** (a) **15.** (c) **16.** (a) **17.** (d) **18.** (d) **19.** (d) **20.** (b)

MADHUBANI (MITHILA) PAINTING

1. (d) **2.** (d) **3.** **(c)** **4.** (b) **5.** (d) **6.** (b) **7.** (d) **8.** (a) **9.** (b) **10.** (d)
11. (d) **12.** (c) **13.** (a) **14.** (d) **15.** (d) **16.** (b) **17.** (c) **18.** (a) **19.** (d) **20.** (d)
21. (b) **22.** (c) **23.** (d) **24.** (d) **25.** (b) **26.** (d) **27.** (d) **28.** (d) **29.** (c) **30.** (b)
31. (d) **32.** (a) **33.** (d) **34.** (a)

MANJUSHA STYLE

1. (a) **2.** (c) **3.** (a) **4.** (c) **5.** (b) **6.** (a) **7.** (d) **8.** (b) **9.** (a)

❑❑❑

8 Folk Culture

FOLK SONGS

1. **_______ folk song describes the natural beauty in a sweet manner.**
(a) Magadhi (b) Angika
(c) Bhojpuri (d) Pali

2. **Which folk song describes mutual behavior, love, hate and humour in a family relationship?**
(a) Pali (b) Santhali
(c) Bhojpuri (d) Magadhi

3. **Which folk song is sung at the time of birth?**
(a) Khelauna (b) Sohar
(c) Bidai (d) Jogan

4. **'Khelauna' folk song is sung on which occasion?**
(a) Mundan (b) Gauna
(c) Janeu (d) Ropni

5. **In which of the following areas, 'Pavadiya' dance is performed on birth of a son?**
(a) Munger (b) Magadh
(c) Bhojpur (d) Both (b) and (c)

6. **Who composed 'Sohar Chhand' in the past?**
(a) Kabirdas
(b) Vedvyas
(c) Maharashi Valmiki
(d) Tulsidas

7. **In which area of Bihar, there is a tradition of singing a 'sammary' song?**
(a) Mithilanchal
(b) Magadh
(c) Angg
(d) Bhojpur

8. **The house in which at the time of marriage family deity is worshipped and where the holy act is performed is called _________.**
(a) Madwa (b) Kohvar
(c) Anchal (d) Chitralekha

9. **'Dome Kuchh' is a folk song of which place?**
(a) Uttar Pradesh
(b) Madhya Pradesh
(c) Bihar
(d) Rajasthan

10. **'Dome Kuchh' folk music is organized on which occasion?**
(a) Marriage (b) Birth
(c) Mundan (d) Janeu

11. **In whose composition out of the following, there is evidence of the contexts of 'dome kuchh' tradition?**
(a) Vidyapati (b) Kabirdas
(c) Tulsidas (d) Bhikhari Thakur

12. **In which area, at the time of a daughter's departure, 'Samdavni' song is sung?**
(a) Mithila (b) Bhojpur
(c) Angika (d) Magadh

13. **Which of the following is a 'Ritu geet'?**
(a) Kajri
(b) Hindola
(c) Chaita
(d) All of the above

14. The emergence of which of the following 'ritu' songs occurred in Bihar and Eastern Uttar Pradesh?
(a) Hindola (b) Kajri
(c) Chaita (d) Barahmaas

15. Kajri's another version is popular in Mithila area by which name?
(a) Malar (b) Kajrota
(c) Sohrai (d) Khelna

16. Which of the following folk songs is sung in the rainy season?
(a) Hindola (b) Kajri
(c) Chaita (d) Barahmaas

17. 'Phag' song is sung in which season?
(a) Summer (b) Winter
(c) Autumn (d) Spring

18. During which festival in Bihar, there is a tradition of singing a 'Jogida'?
(a) Holi (b) Dussehra
(c) Diwali (d) Teej

19. Which of the following folk songs is mainly based on 'Shringar'?
(a) Kajri (b) Chaita
(c) Barahmaas (d) Hindola

20. In the males of which area of Bihar, there is a tradition of singing 'Chaita' song?
(a) Angga (b) Bhojpur
(c) Magadh (d) Both (b) and (c)

21. The folk song which is sung based on 'Dholak' and 'Jhanjh' is called ________ ?
(a) Chaita (b) Thumri
(c) Kajri (d) Hindola

22. Which of the following folk songs is actually a song of separation?
(a) Thumri (b) Kajri
(c) Hindola (d) Barahmaas

23. In which area women-centric song-drama 'Samachkeva' is specially sung?
(a) Mithila (b) Bhojpur
(c) Magadh (d) Bhagalpur

24. 'Samachkeva' folk song is sung in which month?
(a) Chaitra (b) Baisakh
(c) Aashad (d) Kartik

25. By which of the following castes, song of separation is sung?
(a) Dhobi (b) Lohar
(c) Ahir (d) Kahar

26. 'Loriki' folk song is related to which caste?
(a) Rajput (b) Kayastha
(c) Brahmin (d) Yadav

27. Which song is sung by women in Bihar when they are milling flour on a stone?
(a) Lagni (b) Bhukkal
(c) Domni (d) Khewat

28. Which song is sung by the farm labourers while sowing of rice seeds?
(a) Lagni (b) Chonchar
(c) Khewat (d) Gopni

29. Which of the following is a 'Sagun' song?
(a) Gosavani
(b) Maheshvani
(c) Parati
(d) All of the above

30. 'Alha' is a folk song which is sung in which area?
(a) Bundelkhand
(b) Magadh
(c) Bhojpur
(d) Angga

31. Which type of song 'Alha udal' is?
(a) Shringar Rasa
(b) Vir Rasa
(c) Manoram
(d) All of the above

32. Who is the hero of 'Nayka Banjara' story?
(a) Surmani (b) Shomyik
(c) Shomyanik (d) Khelkundi

33. To which estate 'Meerayan' folklore is related?
(a) Numaligarh (b) Sirgarh
(c) Nunbolgarh (d) Nunjagarh

34. 'Lorikayan' folk song based mainly on 'Veer Ras' is related to which province?
(a) Bihar (b) Haryana
(c) Punjab (d) Madhya Pradesh

35. 'Dina Bhadri', a folk song is related to the people of which caste?
(a) Mushar (b) Yadav
(c) Harijan (d) Kahar

36. 'Noonachar' is a folklore related to which area?
(a) Magadh (b) Mithila
(c) Bhojpur (d) Bhagalpur

37. Who is the hero of 'Noonachar' song folklore?
(a) Nankoo (b) Karnisen
(c) Karnu (d) Ramalu

38. 'Kshatriya-Chauhan' folklore is sung in which area?
(a) Magadh (b) Bhojpur
(c) Mithila (d) Bhagalpur

39. 'Dhudhli-Dhatma' is sung in which area under different names/titles?
(a) Saran (b) Champaran
(c) Darbhanga (d) Both (b) and (c)

40. Which folklore is related to the son of 'Dhurmal Singh'?
(a) Nagarmal (b) Vijaymal
(c) Hajarmal (d) Kamrupmal

41. Which folklore is related to prem rasa and veer rasa?
(a) Salehi (b) Gumru
(c) Sahles (d) Kanwar

42. Hirni-Birni folklore is related to which person?
(a) Goyal Singh
(b) Vijay Singh
(c) Jagmeet Singh
(d) Posan Singh

43. Which of the following folklore is related to the 'Nath panth'?
(a) Hirni-Birni
(b) Kunwar Brijbhar
(c) Sahles
(d) Vijaymal

44. In Kunwar Brijbhar folklore, there is a prominence of which of the following?
(a) Prem Rasa (b) Veer Rasa
(c) Karuna rasa (d) Both (b) and (c)

45. Kunwar Brijbhar folklore is a folklore of the bravery of a______?
(a) King (b) Queen
(c) Prince (d) Commander

46. Which of the following is a dance folklore?
(a) Kunwar Brijbhar
(b) Raja Vikramaditya
(c) Raja Janak
(d) Raja Chandragupta

47. Which folklore is sung by the use of 'Pakhwaj' musical instrument?
(a) Raja Vikramaditya
(b) Kunwar Brijbhar
(c) Hirni-Birni
(d) Sahles

48. The folklore 'Raja Vikrmaditya' is related to the king of which place?
(a) Vijaynagar (b) Kundlipur
(c) Pratapgarh (d) Sambhalpur

49. Amar Singh Bariya is a singer of which class?
(a) Veer Rasa
(b) Prem Rasa
(c) Karun Rasa
(d) All of the above

50. Which folklore is related to the protest against the injustice done by a king to his people?
(a) Amar Singh Bariya
(b) Raja Vikramaditya
(c) Dudhali Dhatma
(d) Kshatriya-Chauhan

51. Amar Singh Bariya folklore is related to the king of which place?
(a) Saran (b) Bhagalpur
(c) Magadh (d) Tirhut

52. Who of the following is called 'Maithil-Kokil'?
(a) Bhikhari Thakur
(b) Vidyapati
(c) Mandan Mishra
(d) Sharda Sinha

53. The age of whom is considered to be a golden age of the folk songs?
(a) Mandan Mishra
(b) Kunal
(c) Vidyapati
(d) Bhikhari Thakur

54. Which folk dance is performed at the time of sowing and harvesting of crop?
(a) Karma (b) Sarhul
(c) Sohrai (d) Jitiya

55. Which dance is mainly performed by the male dancers?
(a) Donkutch (b) Angnai
(c) Chhau (d) Sohrai

56. Which dance is related to the war?
(a) Chhau (b) Karma
(c) Domkutch (d) Jitiya

57. Chhau dance is prevalent mainly in which state?
(a) Jharkhand
(b) Bihar
(c) Madhya Pradesh
(d) Both (a) and (b)

58. Jhinjhim dance is performed on which occasion?
(a) Durga Pooja
(b) Diwali
(c) Holi
(d) Teej

59. Which dance is based on King Chitrasen and his queen?
(a) Karma (b) Sarhul
(c) Sohrai (d) Jhinjhiya

60. 'Dhobia' dance is most popular in which district?
(a) Bhojpur (b) Saran
(c) Champaran (d) Munger

61. Which folk dance, songs of Shringar Rasa are sung on the rhythm of musical instruments?
(a) Kathdhodwa (b) Sarhul
(c) Dhobiya (d) Karma

62. Which dance is performed by male dancers in women attire?
(a) Pavadiya (b) Jogida
(c) Dhobiya (d) Kathdhodwa

63. Which dance is popular among the muslim community of Bihar?
(a) Pavadiya (b) Nachni
(c) Jharni (d) Jindiya

64. Jharni dance is performed on which occasion?
(a) Muharram (b) Id
(c) Bakr-id (d) Both (b) and (c)

65. In which folk dances, dance is performed with misery songs to express one's plight?
(a) Jhumar (b) Sohrai
(c) Jharni (d) Karma

66. Which of the following dances is a dance depicting welcome to the guests?
(a) Kheeldin
(b) Pavadiya
(c) Nachaniya
(d) Dhotul

67. By which dance, worship of the Ganges is performed?
(a) Gangey
(b) Gangiya
(c) Gangachar
(d) Gangasutra

68. Which of the following dances is a dance related to 'Chhote-Chhote'?
(a) Khelni
(b) Chalni
(c) Dho-dho Rani
(d) Kho-Kho Rani

69. Which of the following dances is a farce committed by fisher women and customers?
(a) Gondin (b) Dhhotul
(c) Apartipi (d) Kaluta

70. Which folk dance is performed by a farmer with his animal herd while expressing different sentiments and singing and dancing?
(a) Lori (b) Lodiyari
(c) Kamaitha (d) Khochni

71. Bolbey dance is performed in which area?
(a) Bhagalpur
(b) Champaran
(c) Saran
(d) Buxar

72. In which of the following dances, women express such sentiments as when their husbands leave for another place?
(a) Khelni
(b) Janani Jhoomer
(c) Pavadiya
(d) Bolbey

73. Which folk song is an expression of sadness which is sung when an information reaches a poor sister about his brother reaching her house?
(a) Dhhotul (b) Dhhanto
(c) Sohar (d) Jugat

74. Inni Binni are the main folk dances of which place?
(a) Magadh (b) Bhagalpur
(c) Champaran (d) Angg

75. Which of the following dances is performed as representatives of the deity?
(a) Dehri (b) Devghar
(c) Galo (d) Kajri

76. Baglo is a folk dance of which area?
(a) North Bihar (b) South Bihar
(c) West Bihar (d) East Bihar

77. In which of the following folk dances, there is depiction of a woman arguing with another woman while she leaves her in laws house due to resentment?
(a) Deoghar (b) Kajri
(c) Dhhanto (d) Banglo

78. Which of the following is a dance drama sung and played in the month of 'Shravan'?
(a) Kajri (b) Sarhul
(c) Maranj (d) Dhhotul

FOLK PLAY

1. Which of the following folk plays is presented in the 'Shukla Paksha' of the months starting from 'Shravan' to 'Kartik'?
(a) Manjari (b) Kajri
(c) Jat-Jatin (d) Sama-Chakewa

2. Sama-Chakewa is celebrated in which month?
(a) Shravan (b) Baisakh
(c) Kartik (d) Jyeshtha

3. In Sama-Chakewa play, Sama and Chakewa are
(a) Bhai Behin
(b) Pati-Patni
(c) Chacha-Bhatiji
(d) Mama-Bhanji

4. Which of the following are not the characters in Sama Chakewa?
(a) Chugla (b) Ban Titar
(c) Gwela (d) Batdekhni

5. Which of the following are the characters in 'Domkutch'?
(a) Jalua
(b) Domin
(c) Anarkali
(d) All of the above

6. Who is the composer of 'Videshiya' play?
(a) Vidyapati
(b) Mandan Mishra
(c) Ram Kripal Shukla
(d) Bhikhari Thakur

7. In which of the following plays, Parbi, Gond and Pachda are the characters?
(a) Jat-Jatin (b) Sama-Chakewa
(c) Videshiya (d) Domkutch

8. Which of the following are devotional religious plays?
(a) Bhkuli-Banka
(b) Domkutch
(c) Gevali
(d) Kiratiyan

TRIBAL CULTURE

1. Gond Tribe is inhabitant of which place in Bihar?
(a) Chhapra
(b) Champaran
(c) Rohtas
(d) All of the above

2. What is the language of the Gond Tribe?
(a) Santhali (b) Mundari
(c) Khadiya (d) Kudukh

3. In which of the following tribes, people work as farm labourers?
(a) Khond (b) Gond
(c) Mahali (d) Bedia

4. What is the language of Khond tribe?
(a) Kudukh
(b) Mundari
(c) Sadani Santhali
(d) None of these

5. In which district does Bediya tribe reside?
(a) Munger (b) Bhagalpur
(c) Arrah (d) Betiya

6. Uraon Tribe is related to which family?
(a) Austroloid
(b) Proto-Austroloid
(c) Negro
(d) Dravid

7. Which of the following is a language of Uraon tribe?
(a) Santhali (b) Mundari
(c) Kudukh (d) Malto

8. In which district of Bihar does, Santhal tribe reside?
(a) Purnia
(b) Bhagalpur
(c) Sahrsa
(d) All of the above

9. Santhal tribe is related to which Homo Sapien?
(a) Dravid
(b) Austroloid
(c) Proto Austroloid
(d) Negro

10. Which of the following is a revered deity of Santhal tribe?
(a) Hatu Bonga (b) Dharmesh
(c) Singbonga (d) Both (a) and (b)

11. Gorait tribe resides in which area?
(a) Munger (b) Gaya
(c) Bhojpur (d) Both (b) and (c)

12. Godait Tribe is related to which group?
(a) Proto-Austroloid
(b) Negro
(c) Dravid
(d) Austroloid

13. Which of the following tribes live in Palamu area of Jharkhand?
(a) Kora (b) Godait
(c) Chero (d) Mahali

14. **Which tribe considers itself Rajpoots from kshatriya and Chauhan clan?**
(a) Chero (b) Gond
(c) Korva (d) Khairvar

15. **Which district in Bihar is a native place of the Korva tribal people?**
(a) Jamui
(b) Katihar
(c) Munger
(d) All of the above

16. **Which of the following is a language of Kora Tribe?**
(a) Malto (b) Mundari
(c) Kudukh (d) Khadiya

17. **In which district of Bihar Munda tribe resides?**
(a) Sasaram (b) Buxar
(c) Rohtas (d) Both (b) and (c)

18. **What is the language of the Munda tribe?**
(a) Malto (b) Magadhi
(c) Mundari (d) Mandiya

19. **Which of the following is the highest deity of Munda tribe?**
(a) Dharmesh
(b) Singbonga
(c) Murungburu
(d) Dhatu Bonga

20. **Singbonga's relation is considered to be with whom?**
(a) Hill (b) Earth
(c) Sky (d) Son

21. **'Anddi' song dance is performed on which occasion?**
(a) Marriage (b) Janeu
(c) Mundan (d) Birth

22. **'Jadur' song is sung in which season?**
(a) Winter (b) Spring
(c) Autumn (d) Summer

23. **'Herro' song is sung at what time?**
(a) At the time of sowing of rice
(b) Harvesting
(c) Spring season
(d) Birth

Answers

FOLK SONGS

1. (b)	**2.** (d)	**3.** (b)	**4.** (a)	**5.** (d)	**6.** (d)	**7.** (a)	**8.** (b)	**9.** (c)	**10.** (a)
11. (d)	**12.** (a)	**13.** (d)	**14.** (b)	**15.** (a)	**16.** (a)	**17.** (d)	**18.** (a)	**19.** (b)	**20.** (d)
21. (a)	**22.** (d)	**23.** (a)	**24.** (d)	**25.** (c)	**26.** (d)	**27.** (a)	**28.** (b)	**29.** (d)	**30.** (a)
31. (a)	**32.** (c)	**33.** (d)	**34.** (a)	**35.** (a)	**36.** (b)	**37.** (c)	**38.** (a)	**39.** (d)	**40.** (b)
41. (c)	**42.** (d)	**43.** (b)	**44.** (d)	**45.** (c)	**46.** (b)	**47.** (a)	**48.** (b)	**49.** (a)	**50.** (a)
51. (d)	**52.** (b)	**53.** (c)	**54.** (a)	**55.** (c)	**56.** (a)	**57.** (d)	**58.** (a)	**59.** (d)	**60.** (a)
61. (c)	**62.** (a)	**63.** (c)	**64.** (a)	**65.** (c)	**66.** (a)	**67.** (b)	**68.** (c)	**69.** (a)	**70.** (b)
71. (a)	**72.** (d)	**73.** (b)	**74.** (d)	**75.** (b)	**76.** (a)	**77.** (d)	**78.** (a)		

FOLK PLAY

1. (c)	**2.** (c)	**3.** (a)	**4.** (c)	**5.** (d)	**6.** (d)	**7.** (c)	**8.** (d)

TRIBAL CULTURE

1. (d)	**2.** (b)	**3.** (a)	**4.** (c)	**5.** (a)	**6.** (b)	**7.** (c)	**8.** (d)	**9.** (c)	**10.** (c)
11. (d)	**12.** (a)	**13.** (c)	**14.** (a)	**15.** (d)	**16.** (b)	**17.** (d)	**18.** (c)	**19.** (b)	**20.** (b)
21. (a)	**22.** (b)	**23.** (a)							

❑❑❑

9 Fairs and Festivals

FAIRS AND CEREMONIES

1. Which among the following is known as Asia's largest cattle fair, organized annually in Bihar on Kartik Purnima?
(a) Sonepur Cattle Fair
(b) Rajgir Mela
(c) Sitamarhi Fair
(d) Pitrapaksha Mela

2. In which month Sonepur fair is organized?
(a) Savan (b) Bhadrapada
(c) Kartik (d) Ashhad

3. Which of the following fairs is the Asia's biggest animal fair?
(a) Rampur ka Mela
(b) Jankipur ka Mela
(c) Sonepur ka Mela
(d) Vaishali ka Mela

4. Temple of which God is situated at the site of the Sonepur Fair?
(a) Ram (b) Vishnu
(c) Shiva (d) Both (b) and (c)

5. Sonepur Fair area is popularly known by which other name?
(a) Harihar Dham
(b) Vaikuntha Dham
(c) Manokamna Dham
(d) Baba Dham

6. During the Mughal period, which King gave an expanded view to Harihar Temple?
(a) Shivnarayan
(b) Ramnarayan
(c) Trilokinarayan
(d) Keshavnarayan

7. In Hariharnath Fair, common people take a bath at which ghat?
(a) Konhara Ghat
(b) Ram Ghat
(c) Sita Ghat
(d) Shiv Ghat

8. The Fair of Vaishali is held at the birthplace of which Jain 'Tirthankar'?
(a) 21st (b) 22nd
(c) 23rd (d) 24th

9. Vaishali Fair is held in which month?
(a) Chaitra (b) Baisakh
(c) Jyeshtha (d) Aashad

10. Deoghar Fair is organized in which month?
(a) Jyeshtha (b) Aashad
(c) Shravan (d) Kartik

11. How distant is Deoghar from Sultanganj (Bhagalpur)?
(a) 100 Km. (b) 105 km.
(c) 110 km. (d) 115 km.

12. From where is water brought by the devotees in Deoghar Fair?
(a) Sultanganj (b) Sultanpur
(c) Jamalpur (d) Raigarh

13. By which other name Baidyanath Dham is known?
(a) Savan Dham (b) Shiv Dham
(c) Baba Dham (d) Shanker Dham

14. Which of the following fairs is held a fortnight before the winter 'Navratras'?
(a) Sairath Fair (b) Navchandi Fair
(c) Kamna Fair (d) Pitrapaksha Fair

15. In Bihar where is the ritual of 'Pind-daan' performed?
(a) Mujaffarpur (b) Gaya
(c) Sitamarhi (d) Bhagalpur

16. Where does Baba Brahmeshwar-nath Fair take place?
(a) Buxar (b) Arrah
(c) Saran (d) Motihari

17. Baba Brahmeshwarnath Fair is held on the occasion of which festival?
(a) Holi (b) Durgapuja
(c) Shivratri (d) Teej

18. During which month Baba Brahmeshwarnath Fair is held?
(a) Savan (b) Kartik
(c) Bhadrapada (d) Vaishakh

19. On which occasion, Malmas Fair is held?
(a) Holi
(b) Durga Puja
(c) Makar Sankranti
(d) Ganesh Chaturthi

20. Where, on the occasion of Malmas, a fair is held?
(a) Rajgir (b) Nalanda
(c) Vaishali (d) Bihar Sharif

21. Betiya Fair is held every year on the occasion of which festival?
(a) Holi
(b) Makar Sankranti
(c) Ganesh Chaturthi
(d) Dusshera

22. Sairath Fair is held in which month?
(a) Jyeshtha (b) Savan
(c) Kartik (d) Bhadrapada

23. Where does Sairath Fair take place?
(a) Madhepura (b) Bhagalpur
(c) Munger (d) Madhubani

24. Simariya Fair is held in which month?
(a) Kartik (b) Savan
(c) Chaitra (d) Jyeshtha

25. Kosi Fair is held in which month?
(a) Magh (b) Pausha
(c) Jyeshtha (d) Savan

26. In which district Sabour Fair is held?
(a) Bhagalpur (b) Munger
(c) Motihari (d) Betiya

27. Madhi Fair is being organized since when?
(a) 1861 AD (b) 1871 AD
(c) 1881 AD (d) 1891 AD

28. Lauriya Nandangarh Fair is organized in which district?
(a) Munger (b) Bhagalpur
(c) Motihari (d) Purnia

29. Kakolat Fair is held every year on the occasion of__________.
(a) Makar Sankranti
(b) Pausha Sankranti
(c) Mesha Sankranti
(d) Bhadrapad Sankranti

30. Kakolat Fair is held in which district?
(a) Navada (b) Bihar Sharif
(c) Vaishali (d) Saran

31. Kakolat Waterfall is situated in which district?
(a) Buxar
(b) Arrah
(c) East Champaran
(d) Navada

32. Kakolat Waterfall has a height of __________feet.
(a) 160 (b) 150
(c) 140 (d) 130

33. In Bihar, a Book fair is organized every year since when?
(a) 1981 AD (b) 1983 AD
(c) 1985 AD (d) 1987 AD

34. Where in Bihar a Book Fair is held?
(a) Mujaffarpur
(b) Raxaul
(c) Patna
(d) Bihar Sharif

35. Where Papharni Pair is held?
(a) Bhagalpur (b) Munger
(c) Vaishali (d) Nalanda

36. Papharni Fair is organized on which occasion?
(a) Pausha Shukla
(b) Makar Sankranti
(c) Kartik Purnima
(d) Magh Purnima

37. In the foothills of which mountain, Papharni Fair of Bhagalpur is held?
(a) Barabar mountain
(b) Mandar Mountain
(c) Nagarjun Mountain
(d) Kartik Mountain

38. According to a folk-belief, a bath taken in Papharni pond frees a man from which disease?
(a) Chickenpox (b) Cholera
(c) Jaundice (d) Leprosy

39. Which of the following fairs is held in Bihar?
(a) Singheshwar Fair
(b) Bansi Fair
(c) Hardi Fair
(d) All of the above

40. When was Rajgir Festival organized for the first time?
(a) 1986 AD (b) 1984 AD
(c) 1982 AD (d) 1980 AD

41. When did Bakhtiyar Khilji destroy Vikramshila University suspecting it to be a fort?
(a) 1201 AD (b) 1203 AD
(c) 1205 AD (d) 1207 AD

42. Mandar Festival is held in which district?
(a) Banka (b) Arrah
(c) Arval (d) Jamui

43. On the Mandar Mountain, which Jain Tirthankar had achieved 'Kaivalya' (liberation)?
(a) Ajitnath (b) Vasupujya
(c) Rishabhdev (d) Mahavir Swami

44. Vasupujya was _________ Tirthankar of Jains?
(a) 12th (b) 13th
(c) 14th (d) 15th

45. In which district, an evidence is found of the Ashram of Ramayana period Maharishi Valmiki?
(a) Champaran (b) Munger
(c) Bhagalpur (d) Purnia

46. Where did Lord Buddha stay while going to Kushinagar?
(a) Vaishali (b) Kesariya
(c) Sugbauli (d) Betiya

47. In which district Vanavar festival is held?
(a) Bhagalpur (b) Munger
(c) Mujaffarpur (d) Jehanabad

48. In the famous Lomus Rishi Cave, an inscription engraved states Vanavar hill as_________.
(a) Gorakhgiri (b) Satwangiri
(c) Keshavgiri (d) Mandargiri

49. Where is 'Tapovan' festival held?
(a) Vaishali (b) Nalanda
(c) Bariyarpur (d) Rajgir

50. On which occasion 'Tapovan' festival is held?
(a) Pausha Purnima
(b) Chaitra Purnima
(c) Makar Sankranti
(d) Kartik Purnima

51. Along with 'Tapovan' festival, which other fair is held every third year?
(a) Sankranti Fair
(b) Shatabdi Fair
(c) Kajri Fair
(d) Malmaas Fair

52. It is said that the confluence place of Dharma, Desire and Moksha is_________.
(a) Hariharnath (b) Tapovan
(c) Ajgabinath (d) Trikut Dham

53. Who of the following has described the significance and age of Tapovan?
(a) Buchanan
(b) Jagdish Chandra Bose
(c) Ralph Fitch
(d) Both (a) and (b)

54. Who of the following Chinese travellers has described extensively the importance of 'Tapovan'?
(a) Huan Tsang (b) I Tsing
(c) Fa-Hien (d) Both (a) and (c)

55. In which of the following books, an interesting description of 'Tapovan' is made?
(a) Padmavat
(b) Ratnavali
(c) Swapnavasvattam
(d) Arthshastra

56. Who is the author of Swapnavadvadttam?
(a) Malik Mohd Jaycee
(b) Kabir Das
(c) Kautilya
(d) Bhas

57. In which ruler's period 'Tapobhumi Tapovan' was an 'Ashram'of Rishi Kashyap?
(a) Bimbisara (b) Ajatshatru
(c) Bimdusara (d) Ashoka

58. In Tapovan, son of Buddha, ______ had also practised penance?
(a) Kunal (b) Rahul
(c) Dasratha (d) Devdutt

59. When did 'Tapovan' festival start?
(a) 14 January 2015
(b) 26 January 2015
(c) 8 March 2015
(d) 16 June 2015

60. At which of the following places, seeds of Republic were sown for the first time?
(a) Vaishali (b) Patliputra
(c) Gaya (d) Sarnath

61. The organisation of Vaishali festival is mainly centered on promoter of Jain Religion______.
(a) Rishabhdev
(b) Ajitnath
(c) Mahavir Swami
(d) Both (a) and (c)

62. Mahavir Swami had spent how many years of his invaluable life in Vaishali itself?
(a) 24 (b) 26
(c) 28 (d) 30

63. Which festival is organized each year with the purpose of keeping alive the prosperous culture of Mithila and the painting of Madhubani?
(a) Vidyapati Festival
(b) Mithila Festival
(c) Kosi Festival
(d) Bihar Festival

FESTIVALS OF BIHAR

1. Which festival is celebrated in Bihar on the first day of first month of the Hindu calendar?
(a) Holi (b) Makar Sankranti
(c) Jitiya (d) Chhat Puja

2. The ancient Hindu Vedic festival, specially dedicated to the Sun God (Surya) and Chhathi Maiya, which is predominantly celebrated in Bihar is:
(a) Bihula
(b) Makar Sankranti
(c) Sama Chakeva
(d) Chhath Puja

3. Which festival is celebrated on the fourth day of 'Krishna paksha' of the month of Phagun?
(a) Ramnavami (b) Shivratri
(c) Dussehra (d) Makar Sankranti

4. Which festival has an acceptance as celebration of the marriage of Lord Shiva and goldess Parvati?

(a) Shivratri
(b) Shiv Charcha
(c) Shivmahotsava
(d) Shiva-Parvati Mahotsava

5. Which festival is celebrated on the nineth day of 'Shukla paksha' of Chaitra month?
(a) Ram Barat (b) Ram Navami
(c) Teej (d) Makar Sankranti

6. In Bihar, which festival is celebrated in happiness of arrival of new paddy crop?
(a) Teej
(b) Jitiya
(c) Makar Sankranti
(d) Basant Panchami

7. When is Makar Sankranti celebrated with pomp and show in the country?
(a) 14 January (b) 19 January
(c) 21 January (d) 29 January

8. Which are the main day time food items prepared on the occasion of Makar Sankranti?
(a) Chuda-dahi
(b) Khichdi
(c) Tilkut
(d) All of the above

9. Which of the following festivals is considered a festival to please the Godess of Learning, Saraswati?
(a) Basant Panchami
(b) Makar Sankranti
(c) Madhu Shravani
(d) Teej

10. When is Basant Panchami celebrated?
(a) Chaira (b) Vaishakh
(c) Magh (d) Kartik

11. Which of the following festivals is celebrated for 10 days?
(a) Durga Puja
(b) Shivratri
(c) Basant Panchami
(d) Makar Sankranti

12. Durga Puja is celebrated in which month?
(a) Kartik (b) Aashwin
(c) Magh (d) Chaitra

13. Which of the following festivals has another name as 'Navratras'?
(a) Basant Panchami
(b) Madhu Shravani
(c) Durga Puja
(d) Govardhan Puja

14. Which fast is kept by the newly married in the first year of marriage to wish for the long life of the husband?
(a) Madhu Shravani
(b) Teej
(c) Jitiya
(d) Basant Panchami

15. Which of the following festivals is celebrated on the 'amavasya' of the Kartik month?
(a) Ganesh Puja (b) Naag Panchami
(c) Deepawali (d) Durga Puja

16. On________day, Lord Rama had reached Ayodhya after the Lanka victory?
(a) Dussehra (b) Deepawali
(c) Teej (d) Govardhan Puja

17. On the night of Deepawali festival, which God is worshipped?
(a) Shri Krishna (b) Ganesha
(c) Lakshmi (d) Both (b) and (c)

18. Which Puja is performed on the next day of Diwali?
(a) Teej (b) Govardhan Puja
(c) Jitiya (d) Makar Sankranti

19. On the next day of which festival, the ladies and girls celebrate a festival called 'Bhaiyya-duj'?
(a) Madhu Shravani
(b) Teej
(c) Durga Puja
(d) Govardhan Puja

20. On the occasion of which Puja, cattle is given a bath?
(a) Govardhan Puja
(b) Makar Sankranti
(c) Teej
(d) Basant Panchami

21. Chitragupta puja is a famous festival of which society?
(a) Rajput (b) Brahmin
(c) Yadav (d) Kayastha

22. On the next day of 'Bhaiyya-duj' which puja is organized?
(a) Govardhan Puja
(b) Chitragupta Puja
(c) Teej Puja
(d) Indra Puja

23. On the occasion of which Puja, pen, inkpot and writing material is worshipped?
(a) Chitragupta Puja
(b) Indra Puja
(c) Govardhan Puja
(d) Durga Puja

24. Akshya Navami is a religious festival of which area?
(a) Magadh (b) Angg
(c) Champaran (d) Mithilanchal

25. On the occasion of which festival, 'Amla tree' is worshipped?
(a) Chitragupta Puja
(b) Akshya Navami
(c) Indra Puja
(d) Vishwakarma Puja

26. Akshay Navami is celebrated in which month?
(a) Savan (b) Kartik
(c) Ashhad (d) Magh

27. Indra Puja festival is celebrated in which month?
(a) Bhadrapada (b) Aashwin
(c) Baisakh (d) Chaitra

28. There is a belief that if Lord ________ is worshipped, rains befall in plenty.
(a) Vishnu (b) Shri Krishana
(c) Shiva (d) Indra

29. Kojgara is a festival of which place?
(a) Angg (b) Tirhut
(c) Mithila (d) Magadh

30. Kojgara festival is related to which community of Mithila area?
(a) Brahmin (b) Rajput
(c) Yadav (d) Kayastha

31. On the occasion of which festival, Lakshmi and Ganesha are formally worshipped?
(a) Makar Sankranti
(b) Kojgara
(c) Indra Puja
(d) Deepawali

32. 'Chauth Chandra' is celebrated in which area?
(a) Mithila (b) Angg
(c) Magadh (d) Tirhut

33. In which month 'Chauth Chandra' is celebrated?
(a) Chaitra (b) Baisakh
(c) Aashad (d) Bhadrapada

34. Which of the following festivals is a regional festival of Mithila area?
(a) Vat Savitri
(b) Vat Purnima
(c) Vat Sankranti
(d) Vat Chauth

35. Vat Savitri is celebrated by the women on 'Amavasya' of the month of ________.
(a) Kartik (b) Chaitra
(c) Jyeshtha (d) Fagun

36. Which of the following festivals is celebrated by married women?
(a) Vasant Panchami
(b) Naag Panchami
(c) Kojgara
(d) Teej

37. In which month, Teej festival is celebrated?
(a) Savan Bhadrapada
(b) Kartik
(c) Magh
(d) Aashad

38. When is Buddha Jayanti celebrated?
(a) Chaitra (b) Baisakh
(c) Jyeshtha (d) Savan

39. Mahavir Jayanti is celebrated in which month?
(a) Chaitra
(b) Baisakh
(c) Savan
(d) Bhadrapada

40. Guru Govind Singh birth centenary is celebrated in which month?
(a) Pausha (b) Aashwin
(c) Baisakh (d) Kartik

41. Guru Govind Singh birth centenary is celebrated on the birth day of _____ Guru of the Sikhs.
(a) 6th (b) 7th
(c) 9th (d) 10th

42. Who was the last Guru of Sikhs?
(a) Guru Nanak
(b) Guru Govind Singh
(c) Guru Ramdas
(d) Guru Teg Bahadur

43. Where was Guru Govind Singh born?
(a) Patna (b) Amritsar
(c) Alla (d) Ferozepur

44. When was Guru Govind Singh born?
(a) 1660 AD (b) 1662 AD
(c) 1664 AD (d) 1666 AD

45. Who of the following Sikh Gurus is also called 'Sarvasadani'?
(a) Guru Nanak
(b) Guru Angad
(c) Guru Govind Singh
(d) Guru Ramdas

46. What was the childhood name of Guru Govind Singh?
(a) Arvind (b) Kamal
(c) Suraj (d) Pritam

47. Guru Govind Singh was a saint who had the fortune of being called simultaneously a _____ and a Saint.
(a) Soldier (b) King
(c) Landlord (d) Peshwa

48. When did Guru Govind Singh become the Guru of the Sikhs?
(a) 1670 AD (b) 1672 AD
(c) 1674 AD (d) 1676 AD

49. Guru Govind Singh remained Guru of the Sikhs till when?
(a) 1708 AD (b) 1706 AD
(c) 1704 AD (d) 1702 AD

50. Who of the following is known for composition of 'Khalsa'?
(a) Guru Angad
(b) Guru Teg Bahadur
(c) Guru Nanak
(d) Guru Govind Singh

51. 'Harmandirji Patna Sahib' was constructed by whom?
(a) Raja Man Singh
(b) Kunwar Singh
(c) Ranjit Singh
(d) Amar Singh

52. Who of the following was the father of Guru Govind Singh?
(a) Guru Nanak
(b) Guru Ramdas
(c) Guru Amardas
(d) Guru Teg Bahadur

53. At the time of birth of Guru Govind Singh, Guru Teg Bahadur Singh had gone on a visit to which place?
(a) Meghalaya (b) Dhubri
(c) Guwahati (d) Shrirampur

54. Muharram is the name of _____ month of the Islamic calendar?
(a) First (b) Second
(c) Third (d) Fourth

55. On _________ day of Muharram, Hazrat Hussain was martyred?
(a) 8 (b) 9
(c) 10 (d) 11

56. What is the other name of 'Bakar–Id' Festival?
(a) Id-ul-fitr (b) Id-ul-Milad
(c) Id-ul-Ajha (d) Id-ul-Nabi

57. Bakar Id festival is celebrated in which month?
(a) Zilhiz (b) Safar
(c) Sabvan (d) Zilkad

58. Muslims observe 'Roza' for how many days?
(a) 30 days (b) 20 days
(c) 10 days (d) 15 days

59. On the occasion of which festival, Muslims sacrifice an animal?
(a) Bakar-Id
(b) Id
(c) Shabb-e-Barat
(d) Milaz-ul-Nabi

60. On the completion of which festival, the 'Haj' travel of the Muslims is over?
(a) Milad-ul-Nabi
(b) Id-ul-Fitr
(c) Shabb-e-Barat
(d) Id-ul-Ajha

61. The disciples of the Islam celebrate which festival after observing 'roza' for one month?
(a) Id-ul-Ajha
(b) Id-ul-Zuha
(c) Id-ul-Fitr
(d) Id-ul-Milad

62. Id festival is celebrated in which Arabian month?
(a) Ramzan (b) Shaival
(c) Sabvan (d) Muharram

63. Christmas is celebrated each year on which day?
(a) 26 January (b) 25 March
(c) 25 August (d) 25 December

64. People distribute gifts to the children by disguising as________ on the occasion of Christmas?
(a) Santa Claus (b) Santa Battum
(c) Santa Gift (d) Santa Cruz

65. Nagpanchami is a main festival celebrated in which area?
(a) Magadh (b) Angg
(c) Mithila (d) Both (b) and (c)

66. What is the other name of Nagpanchami festival?
(a) Vish Hara
(b) Nag Purnima
(c) Nag Chaturthi
(d) Nag Ekadashi

67. Nagpanchami festival is celebrated in which month?
(a) Chaitra (b) Fagun
(c) Kartik (d) Shrawan

68. Which of the following is a magnificent festival of Bihar?
(a) Nagpanchami
(b) Chhat Puja
(c) Dipawali
(d) Durga Puja

69. On the occasion of 'Chhat Puja', which deity is worshipped?
(a) Mountain (b) Water
(c) Sun (d) Tree

70. A fast begins one day before 'Chhat Puja' which is called ________.
(a) Kharna (b) Teej
(c) Jitiya (d) Sankranti

71. In which month, Chhat Puja is celebrated?
(a) Kartik (b) Ashhad
(c) Magh (d) Pausha

72. Krishnashtami is celebrated in which month?
(a) Chaitra (b) Bhadrapada
(c) Ashwin (d) Pausha

73. On the night of Krishnashtami, which drama is played?
(a) Jat-Jatini (b) Sarhul
(c) Chhau (d) Sama Chakewa

74. **On which festival, the sons bearing mothers observe a fast wishing for long life of their sons?**
(a) Indra Puja (b) Teej
(c) Jitiya (d) Vat Savitri

75. **Jitiya festival is celebrated in which month?**
(a) Ashwin
(b) Kartik
(c) Chaitra
(d) Fagun

76. **Which of the following folk dances is based on the love and affection of sister and brother?**
(a) Sama Chakewa
(b) Chhau
(c) Jat-Jatini
(d) Sarhaul

Answers

FAIRS AND CEREMONIES

1. (a)	**2.** (c)	**3.** (c)	**4.** (d)	**5.** (a)	**6.** (b)	**7.** (a)	**8.** (d)	**9.** (a)	**10.** (c)
11. (b)	**12.** (a)	**13.** (c)	**14.** (d)	**15.** (b)	**16.** (a)	**17.** (c)	**18.** (d)	**19.** (c)	**20.** (a)
21. (d)	**22.** (a)	**23.** (d)	**24.** (a)	**25.** (b)	**26.** (a)	**27.** (c)	**28.** (d)	**29.** (c)	**30.** (a)
31. (d)	**32.** (a)	**33.** (c)	**34.** (c)	**35.** (a)	**36.** (b)	**37.** (b)	**38.** (d)	**39.** (d)	**40.** (a)
41. (b)	**42.** (a)	**43.** (b)	**44.** (a)	**45.** (a)	**46.** (b)	**47.** (d)	**48.** (a)	**49.** (d)	**50.** (c)
51. (d)	**52.** (b)	**53.** (d)	**54.** (d)	**55.** (c)	**56.** (d)	**57.** (a)	**58.** (a)	**59.** (a)	**60.** (a)
61. (c)	**62.** (d)	**63.** (b)							

FESTIVALS OF BIHAR

1. (a)	**2.** (d)	**3.** (b)	**4.** (a)	**5.** (b)	**6.** (c)	**7.** (a)	**8.** (d)	**9.** (a)	**10.** (c)
11. (a)	**12.** (b)	**13.** (c)	**14.** (a)	**15.** (c)	**16.** (b)	**17.** (d)	**18.** (b)	**19.** (d)	**20.** (a)
21. (d)	**22.** (b)	**23.** (a)	**24.** (d)	**25.** (b)	**26.** (b)	**27.** (a)	**28.** (d)	**29.** (c)	**30.** (a)
31. (b)	**32.** (a)	**33.** (d)	**34.** (a)	**35.** (c)	**36.** (d)	**37.** (b)	**38.** (b)	**39.** (a)	**40.** (a)
41. (d)	**42.** (b)	**43.** (a)	**44.** (d)	**45.** (c)	**46.** (d)	**47.** (a)	**48.** (d)	**49.** (a)	**50.** (d)
51. (c)	**52.** (d)	**53.** (b)	**54.** (a)	**55.** (c)	**56.** (c)	**57.** (a)	**58.** (c)	**59.** (a)	**60.** (d)
61. (c)	**62.** (b)	**63.** (d)	**64.** (a)	**65.** (d)	**66.** (a)	**67.** (d)	**68.** (b)	**69.** (c)	**70.** (a)
71. (a)	**72.** (b)	**73.** (d)	**74.** (c)	**75.** (b)	**76.** (a)				

❑❑❑

10 Literature and Litterateur

1. **Which city in Bihar was selected to host the prestigious Sahitya Akademi Young Author Award 2025?**
(a) Patna (b) Bhagalpur
(c) Muzaffarpur (d) Gaya

2. **Who edited the book "English Poetry from Bihar" which was launched in New Delhi on December 1, 2024?**
(a) Dr Ramesh Kumar
(b) Prof. S.P. Singh
(c) Dr Anita Sinha
(d) Prof. Ram Bhagwan Singh

3. **Who is known as the "Shakespeare of Bhojpuri" for his significant contributions to Bhojpuri literature and creator of "Bidesiya"?**
(a) Mahendra Misir
(b) Kapil Pandy
(c) Bhikhari Thakur
(d) Viveki Rai

4. **Phanishwar Nath 'Renu', the author of the famous Hindi novel "Maila Anchal," was born in which district of Bihar?**
(a) Araria (b) Purnia
(c) Saharsa (d) Madhubani

5. **Which of the following is regarded as the most significant Hindi novel after Premchand's 'Godaan,' written by a Bihar-born author?**
(a) Parti Parikatha
(b) Maila Anchal
(c) Juloos
(d) Thumri

6. **Which language was given the title of 'Rajbhasha' in the 26th year of reign of Akbar?**
(a) Hindi
(b) Urdu
(c) Persian
(d) Afghani (Pashto)

7. **When did work in the courts of Bengal and Orissa started in Bangla and Oriya languages?**
(a) 1931 AD (b) 1933 AD
(c) 1935 AD (d) 1937 AD

8. **Which of the following newspapers, is the first one of Bihar?**
(a) The Bihar Samay
(b) The Patliputra
(c) The Bihar-Bandhu
(d) The Samrat Ashoka

9. **Who was the Editor of the newspaper the Bihar-Bandhu?**
(a) Keshav Bhatt
(b) Ram Krishna Pandey
(c) Ramdin Singh
(d) Hidaytullah Khan

10. **Since when the facility of Hindi language and submission of petitions in Devnagari script started alongwith the Urdu Language in the courts of Bihar?**
(a) 1871 AD (b) 1873 AD
(c) 1875 AD (d) 1878 AD

11. **'Kaithi' script was the script of the rural areas of which divisions of Bihar?**
(a) Saran
(b) Patna

(c) Bhagalpur
(d) Both (b) and (c)

12. Which Press in Bihar had first published a book in 'Kaithi' script?
(a) Geeta Press
(b) Mishra Press
(c) Khadag Vilas Press
(d) Nawab Press

13. When did 'Rajbhasha Movement' begin for the first time in Bihar?
(a) 1860 AD (b) 1858 AD
(c) 1856 AD (d) 1854 AD

14. When did Hindi language enter the schools of Bihar?
(a) 1864 AD (b) 1866 AD
(c) 1868 AD (d) 1870 AD

15. Which of the following books is the one written by Raja Shiv Prasad?
(a) Vidyankur
(b) Aalsiyon ka Koda
(c) Vir Singh Vratant
(d) All of the above

16. The book called 'Bhugol Hastamalak' was written by whom?
(a) Shiv Prasad
(b) Ram Ashray Singh
(c) Doman Sahoo
(d) Biullah Shah

17. Who of the following composed the book 'Varna-Vinod' for the primary classes?
(a) Munshi Ram Prakash Lal
(b) Bhudev Mukhopadhyay
(c) Mathura Nath Singh
(d) Chandi Prasad Singh

18. Who of the following collected Hindi Sahitya (Part-1)?
(a) Ramdin Singh
(b) Bachchandev Singh
(c) Naseem Khan
(d) Dev Dutt Shah

19. Who composed the Book called 'Sachitra Harishchandra'?
(a) Radha Krishan
(b) Ramdhari Dinkar
(c) Shivnandan Sahay
(d) Shivlal Shah

20. Who is the author of the book called 'Harishchandra ki Jeevni'?
(a) Raj Singh
(b) Ramavtar Singh
(c) Inayat Ali
(d) Radhakrishan Das

21. Which of the following is a work of Bankimchandra Chatterjee?
(a) Raja-Rani
(b) Durgesh Nandini
(c) Granthawali
(d) Geet Govind

22. Which of the following is a novel written by Bankimchandra Chatterjee?
(a) Indira
(b) Rajni
(c) Kapakkundla
(d) All of the above

23. What is the name of the first text on history of Bihar in Urdu language?
(a) Naksh-e-Paaydar
(b) Naksh-e-Bihar
(c) Biharnama
(d) Aain-e-Bihar

24. Who is the author of Nakshe Paaydar?
(a) Shad Ajmeri
(b) Shibli Nomani
(c) Maulana Shaukat Ali
(d) Ali Mohd. Shah

25. Who has first used the poem in English language called 'Shaili Sonnet'?
(a) Shah Mohammad
(b) Dr. Azimuddin Ahmad
(c) Shad Azimabad
(d) Gul Mohammad

26. Who composed Gul-e-Nagma?
(a) Peer Ali
(b) Shah Badrul Hasan
(c) Taz Khan
(d) Dr. Azimuddin Ahmad

27. Who is considered as the Chief propagandist of progressive Urdu ideology in Bihar?
(a) Shad Azimabadi
(b) Suhel Azimabadi
(c) Akbar Khan
(d) Shah Belal

28. Who has given scientific base in research of Urdu literature?
(a) Abdul Badid
(b) Abdul Qadir
(c) Abdul Wahab
(d) Suhel Shah

29. The collection of ghazals called 'Maikhana-e-Islam' belongs to whom?
(a) Mirza Ghalib
(b) Shad Azimabadi
(c) Ali Mohd. Shah
(d) Shibli Numani

30. The novel 'Do Gaz Zamin' belongs to whom?
(a) Abdul Kalim
(b) Abdul Shamad
(c) Shaukat Hayat
(d) Wafa Ashrafi

31. Whose composition among the following had won the Sahitya Akadami Award?
(a) Shafi Javed
(b) Rizvan Ahmad
(c) Abdul Shamad
(d) Kalim Ajiz

32. When did Urdu get the status of the second Rajbhasha in Bihar?
(a) 1984 AD (b) 1982 AD
(c) 1980 AD (d) 1978 AD

33. In which of the following countries, Bhojpuri language is the language commonly used for communication?
(a) Guyana
(b) Fiji
(c) Suriname
(d) All of the above

34. Who played a significant role in the development of Bhojpuri language?
(a) Gopal Das (b) Dharti Das
(c) Dariya Das (d) Both (b) and (c)

35. Which of the following is a sub-national language of Nepal?
(a) Maithili (b) Magadhi
(c) Pali (d) Bhojpuri

36. Where do we get the first evidence of Maithili Language?
(a) Mahabharat (b) Arthshastra
(c) Ramayan (d) Geet Govind

37. Who is the author of 'Varnratna-karan'?
(a) Vijay Tiwari
(b) Mandan Mitra
(c) Jyotishwar Thakur
(d) Vidyapati

38. When was Maithili included in the 8th schedule of the Indian Constitution?
(a) 2001 AD (b) 2003 AD
(c) 2005 AD (d) 2007 AD

39. When was Maithili granted the status of a literary language?
(a) 1959 AD (b) 1961 AD
(c) 1963 AD (d) 1965 AD

40. Who is called the father of the style of Magadhi dialect?
(a) Madan Pandey
(b) Suresh Dubey
(c) Mandan Mishra
(d) Gaurav Tiwari

41. Who of the following is a highly talked about litterateur in Magadhi?
(a) Mandan Mishra
(b) Ratneshwar Jha
(c) Yogeshwar Singh
(d) Zamin Qadri

42. Which of the following is a composition of Harinath Mishra?
(a) Lalit Katha
(b) Lalit Ramayan
(c) Lalit Bhagwat
(d) Both (b) and (c)

43. Who is the author of the epic called 'Loha Marad'?
(a) Charan Das
(b) Gopal Singh
(c) Ramprasad Singh
(d) Ratnesh Tiwari

44. Who composed the epic called 'Jarasandh'?
(a) Yogesh Pathak
(b) Ramanand Tiwari
(c) Gopal Mishra
(d) Chhotunarayan Sharma

45. Which of the following is a novel composed by Jaynathpati?
(a) Sumita
(b) Phoolbahar
(c) Gadahneet
(d) All of the above

46. Which of the following is a novel written by Chakradhar Sharma?
(a) Sangeet Katha
(b) Hay Re 3 Din
(c) Saklya
(d) Both (b) and (c)

47. Who is the author of the novel called 'Magahi ke do Phool'?
(a) Abdul Samad
(b) Chhotunarayan Sharma
(c) Lallan Tiwari
(d) Diwakar Mandal

48. Who is the author of the collection of one act plays 'Sona ki Seeta'?
(a) Baburam Singh
(b) Keshav Prasad Verma
(c) Jalaluddin Qureshi
(d) Gopal Rawat

49. Which of the following is untrue?

(a) Gopal Rawat Pipash	(i) Aadhi Raat ke Baad
(b) Raghubir Prasad Samdashi	(ii) Bhasmasur
(c) Baburam Singh	(iii) Lamgoda
(d) Ramesh Mehto	(iv) Ramatiya

50. The common man language in Bhagalpur and Munger districts is________.
(a) Magadhi (b) Soursaini
(c) Bundeli (d) Angika

51. Who wrote the history of the dialect 'Angika'?
(a) Madan Khurana
(b) Shahid Jamal Khan
(c) Tej Narayan Kushwaha
(d) Ratnesh Jha

52. The language 'Angika' is part of which group?
(a) Dravid (b) Arya
(c) Austroloid (d) Mandarin

53. Where in Bihar a printing press was installed for the first time?
(a) Buxar (b) Patna
(c) Bihar Sharif (d) Sasaram

54. Who had installed a printing press in Bihar for the first time?
(a) Shah Kabiruddin Ahmad
(b) Jamaluddin Asraf
(c) Jamal Obaid Khan
(d) Nurul Shah

55. What was the name of the first printing press installed in Bihar?
(a) Tohfa
(b) Muhasava
(c) Mutah-e-Kobra
(d) Shan-e-Bazm

56. When was the weekly Urdu Newspaper 'Akhbar-e-Bihar' published in Bihar?
(a) 1850 AD (b) 1852 AD
(c) 1854 AD (d) 1856 AD

57. Since when 'Akhbare-Akhiyar' has been getting published in Bihar?

(a) 1860 AD (b) 1858 AD
(c) 1856 AD (d) 1854 AD

58. Who had got published the Newspaper 'Akhbar-e-Akhiyar'?

(a) Chaman Lal Shah
(b) Rai Sohan Lal
(c) Munshi Surajmal
(d) Hazari Prasad

59. Since when is the newspaper 'The Chashm-e-Ilm' getting published?

(a) 1868 AD (b) 1867 AD
(c) 1865 AD (d) 1863 AD

60. Who got published the newspaper 'The Chashm-e-Ilm'?

(a) Rai Bahadur
(b) Jagat Seth
(c) Amirullah Shah
(d) Rai Sohan Lal

61. Who is the originator of Hindi journalism in Bihar?

(a) Munshi Suraj Mal
(b) Madan Mohan Bhatt
(c) Shamshad Khan
(d) Johar Qazmi

62. When was the 'The Bihar Bandhu' published?

(a) 1872 AD (b) 1870 AD
(c) 1868 AD (d) 1866 AD

63. The publication of 'The Bihar-Bandhu'began from which place?

(a) Bhagalpur (b) Calcutta
(c) Patna (d) Vaishali

64. Who was the author of the book, 'Vidya ki Neev'?

(a) Keshav Ram Bhatt
(b) Jugal Kishore
(c) Anand Mohan
(d) Nadeem Abbas

65. Which of the following dramas belong to Keshav Ram Bhatt?

(a) Aadmi Khilona Hai
(b) Sajjad Sambal
(c) Shamshad Shausan
(d) All of the above

66. Who of the following had installed the 'Kharagvilas Press'?

(a) Ramdin Singh
(b) Ramcharitra Singh
(c) Saheb Prasad Singh
(d) All of the above

67. When was 'Kharagvilas Press'installed?

(a) 1880 AD (b) 1878 AD
(c) 1876 AD (d) 1874 AD

68. Which is the first English Newspaper of Bihar?

(a) The Bihar
(b) The Bihar Herald
(c) The Bihar Times
(d) The Bihar Gazette

69. When was publication of the 'The Bihar Herald' started?

(a) 1871 AD (b) 1873 AD
(c) 1875 AD (d) 1877 AD

70. Who got started the publication of 'The Bihar Herald'?

(a) Guru Prasad Sen
(b) Saiyyad Ahmad
(c) Kunal Banerjee
(d) Tapan Chatterjee

71. When did the editing of the 'Indian Chronicle'began in Patna?

(a) 1878 AD (b) 1879 AD
(c) 1880 AD (d) 1881 AD

72. Who of the following had started publication of 'The Bihari'?

(a) Maheshwar Prasad
(b) Vipin Jha
(c) Shaukat Aziz
(d) Dilawar Khan

73. When did the editing of 'The Bihar Times' begin?
(a) 1890 AD (b) 1892 AD
(c) 1894 AD (d) 1896 AD

74. Who of the following had started editing 'The Bihar Times'?
(a) Mahesh Narayan
(b) Shri Krishna Sahay
(c) Dr. Sachidanand Singh
(d) All of the above

75. When did publication of 'The Search Light' begin?
(a) 1912 AD (b) 1914 AD
(c) 1916 AD (d) 1918 AD

76. Who had started publication of 'The Search Light'?
(a) Saiyyad Hussain
(b) Saiyyad Haider Hussain
(c) Najibganj
(d) Amanat Khalil

77. When did the publication of 'The Search Light' stop?
(a) 1981 AD (b) 1983 AD
(c) 1985 AD (d) 1985 AD

78. When did the Patna edition of 'The Hindustan Times' start?
(a) 1985 AD (b) 1983 AD
(c) 1981 AD (d) 1979 AD

79. Who was the Editor of 'The Patna Times'?
(a) Asgar Wajahat
(b) Kamil Haider
(c) Mohd. Yunus
(d) Ramzan Sheikh

80. 'The Patna Times' remained in circulation from which time to when?
(a) 1910-25 AD
(b) 1912-28 AD
(c) 1914-36 AD
(d) 1914-44 AD

81. Who got published 'The Indian Nation'?
(a) Kameshwar Singh
(b) Yogeshwar Singh
(c) Khurshid Alam
(d) Virendra Bhagat

82. When did the Patna edition of 'The Times of India' begin?
(a) 1980 AD (b) 1982 AD
(c) 1984 AD (d) 1986 AD

83. Where did the publication of 'The Aryavrit' started?
(a) Patna (b) Darbhanga
(c) Bihar Sharif (d) Katihar

84. When did the publication of 'The Aryavrit'begin?
(a) 1941 AD (b) 1943 AD
(c) 1945 AD (d) 1947 AD

85. What was the name of Hindi edition of 'The Search Light'?
(a) The Pratap (b) The Pradeep
(c) The Prakash (d) The Pratibimb

86. When did the publication of 'The Prakash'begin?
(a) 1939 AD (b) 1941 AD
(c) 1945 AD (d) 1947 AD

87. When did the publication of 'The Hindustan' in place of 'The Pradeep' start in Patna?
(a) 1980 AD (b) 1982 AD
(c) 1984 AD (d) 1986 AD

88. When did the publication of 'The Sarvahitaishi' begin?
(a) 1876 AD (b) 1878 AD
(c) 1880 AD (d) 1882 AD

89. When did the publication of 'The Naveen Bharat' begin?
(a) 1948 AD (b) 1946 AD
(c) 1944 AD (d) 1942 AD

90. When did publication of newspaper 'The Vishwamitra' begin?
(a) 1942 AD (b) 1944 AD
(c) 1946 AD (d) 1948 AD

91. When did the publication of newspaper 'The Jan Shakti'begin?

(a) 1952 AD (b) 1954 AD
(c) 1957 AD (d) 1960 AD

92. From where did the publication of newspaper 'The Atmakatha' begin?

(a) Patna (b) Bihar Sharif
(c) Akhal (d) Arrah

93. When did the publication of newspaper 'The Atmakatha' begin?

(a) 1966 AD (b) 1968 AD
(c) 1970 AD (d) 1972 AD

94. When did the publication of newspaper 'The Aaj' begin?

(a) 1977 AD (b) 1979 AD
(c) 1981 AD (d) 1983 AD

95. When did publication of the newspaper 'The Amrit Varsha' begin?

(a) 1981 AD (b) 1983 AD
(c) 1985 AD (d) 1987 AD

96. When did publication of 'The Dainik Jagran' begin?

(a) 1998 AD (b) 1999 AD
(c) 2000 AD (d) 2001 AD

97. When did publication of 'The Dainik Bhaskar' begin in Bihar?

(a) 2001 AD (b) 2005 AD
(c) 2009 AD (d) 2013 AD

98. From where did the publication of monthly magazine called 'Balak' start?

(a) Bihar Sharif (b) Patna
(c) Mujaffarpur (d) Vaishali

99. When did publication of the monthly magazine 'Balak'start?

(a) 1922 AD (b) 1924 AD
(c) 1926 AD (d) 1928 AD

100. From which place did the publication of the monthly magazine 'Kshatriya' start?

(a) Nalanda (b) Arrah
(c) Buxar (d) Patna

101. When did publication of the monthly magazine 'Kshatriya' begin?

(a) 1881 AD (b) 1883 AD
(c) 1885 AD (d) 1887 AD

102. When did publication of the monthly magazine 'Lakshmi'begin?

(a) 1901 AD (b) 1903 AD
(c) 1905 AD (d) 1907 AD

103. From which of the following places, publication of the monthly magazine 'Yuvak' began?

(a) Patna (b) Munger
(c) Motihari (d) Vaishali

104. When did publication of the monthly magazine 'Yuvak' begin?

(a) 1920 AD (b) 1922 AD
(c) 1924 AD (d) 1926 AD

105. From which place did the publication of the monthly magazine 'Bhookhey' start?

(a) Betiya (b) Patna
(c) Bhagalpur (d) Munger

106. When did publication of the monthly magazine 'Bhookey' begin?

(a) 1929 AD (b) 1931 AD
(c) 1933 AD (d) 1935 AD

107. From which place did the publication of the monthly magazine 'Aarti' start?

(a) Patna (b) Bihar Sharif
(c) Motihari (d) Bhagalpur

108. When did publication of the monthly magazine 'Aarti' start?

(a) 1936 AD (b) 1938 AD
(c) 1940 AD (d) 1942 AD

109. From which place did the publication of the monthly magazine 'Parijat' occurr?

(a) Patna (b) Mujaffarpur
(c) Ranchi (d) Jamshedpur

110. When did publication of the monthly magazine 'Parijat' begin?
(a) 1938 AD (b) 1940 AD
(c) 1943 AD (d) 1946 AD

111. Publication of which of the following magazines happened in Patna?
(a) Jyotsna (b) Avantika
(c) Patal (d) All of these

112. When did publication of the monthly magazine 'Janmat' begin?
(a) 1981 AD (b) 1982 AD
(c) 1983 AD (d) 1984 AD

113. When did publication of the magazine 'Shiksha Digest' begin?
(a) 1980 AD (b) 1982 AD
(c) 1984 AD (d) 1986 AD

114. From which place did publication of the magazine 'Shiksha Digest' begin?
(a) Patna (b) Gaya
(c) Munger (d) Bhagalpur

115. When did publication of the fortnightly magazine 'Avkash' begin?
(a) 1973 AD (b) 1975 AD
(c) 1977 AD (d) 1979 AD

116. From which place did publication of the fortnightly magazine 'Avkash' occur?
(a) Raxaul (b) Sugauli
(c) Patna (d) Gaya

117. Sadal Mishra was born at which place?
(a) Arrah
(b) Eastern Champaran
(c) Gaya
(d) Munger

118. Which of the following is a composition of Sadal Mishra?
(a) Nasiketopakhyan
(b) Sonam ke Thumb
(c) Bajne Laga
(d) All of the above

119. Who had founded the 'Bihar Art Theatre'?
(a) Anil Kumar Mukherjee
(b) Tapan Chatterjee
(c) Gautam Sen
(d) Rahim Sheikh

120. When was 'Bihar Art Theatre' founded?
(a) 1957 AD (b) 1959 AD
(c) 1961 AD (d) 1963 AD

121. Who was the writer of the play 'Biplavi'?
(a) Guru Prasad Sen
(b) Abbas Khan
(c) Amjad Hussain
(d) Anil Kumar Mukherjee

122. When was 'Bihar Natyakala Prikshanalaya' founded?
(a) 1968 AD (b) 1970 AD
(c) 1971 AD (d) 1972 AD

123. Who founded 'Bihar Natyakkala Prashikshanalaya'?
(a) Amit Mukt
(b) Shekhar Anand
(c) Nudain Kazmi
(d) Anil Kumar Mukherjee

124. Which of the following is a play which belongs to Anil Kumar Mukherjee?
(a) Palki
(b) Kanchan Rang
(c) Goron ke Intezar Mein
(d) All of the above

125. Who was the composer of the play called 'Trial of Sheikh Mujibur Rahman'?
(a) Anil Kumar Mukherjee
(b) Gyan Sudha Mishra
(c) Jagar Seth
(d) Irshad Adil

126. Anup Lal Mandal is called ______ of Bihar.
(a) Kalidas (b) Prem Chand
(c) Sur Das (d) Kabir Das

127. In which district of Bihar, Anup Lal Mandal was born?
(a) Kishanganj (b) Sahrasa
(c) Khagariya (d) Purnia

128. 'Garibon ke Din' is a memoir written by whom?
(a) Amit Dubey
(b) Devendra Goyal
(c) Jakir Musa
(d) Anup Lal Mandal

129. Which of the following is a novel composed by Anup Lal Mandal?
(a) Abhiyan ka Path
(b) Awaron ki Duniya
(c) Das Bigha Jamin
(d) All of the above

130. Which of the following is not a novel written by Anup Lal Mandal?
(a) Tufan aur Tinke
(b) Dard ki Tasviren
(c) Rakt aur Rang
(d) Sangeet aur Prem

131. Which film has been made based on Anup Lal Mandal's novel 'Mimansa'?
(a) Bahurani (b) Roti
(c) Gram Swaraj (d) Namak ka Karz

132. Who is the author of stories called 'Mann ki Ganthh'?
(a) Brajesh Mishra
(b) Lakshman Pandit
(c) Salam Niyaji
(d) Anup Lal Mandal

133. Arun Kamal was honoured by which of the following awards?
(a) Sahitya Akadami
(b) Shamsher Samman
(c) Nagarjun Puraskar
(d) All of the above

134. Where was Arun Kamal born?
(a) Arrah (b) Motihari
(c) Betiya (d) Rohtas

135. Which of the following is a collection of poems by Arun Kamal?
(a) Sabut
(b) Naye Ilake Mein
(c) Putli mein sansar
(d) All of the above

136. Which of the following is not a composition of Arun Kamal?
(a) Kavita aur Samay
(b) Sangeet aur Chetna
(c) Golmauz
(d) Kathopkathan

137. When was Arsi Prasad Singh born?
(a) Munger (b) Samastipur
(c) Bhagalpur (d) Rohtas

138. 'Aam Ka Ped', a poem written by Arsi Prasad Singh was published in which magazine?
(a) Balak (b) Deenbandhu
(c) Samay (d) Taal

139. Which of the following is a collection of poems by Arsi Prasad Singh?
(a) Arsi
(b) Do Kahani Sangrah
(c) Panchpallav
(d) All of the above

140. 'Khota Sikka' a collection of poems by Arsi Prasad Singh was published in which year?
(a) 1940 AD
(b) 1942 AD
(c) 1944 AD
(d) 1946 AD

141. Which of the following is a composition of Vachaspati Mishra?
(a) Sanghmitra
(b) Bhashya Bhamti
(c) Brahmsidhi Tikakar
(d) Both (b) and (c)

142. Which of the following is a composition of Kashi Prasad Jaiswal?
(a) Hindu Swaraj
(b) Hindi Polity
(c) Common Beel
(d) Second Citizen

143. Where was Kashi Prasad Jaiswal born?
(a) Midnapur (b) 24 Pargana
(c) Durgapur (d) Jhalda

144. Who is the author of the book called 'History of India'?
(a) Jitendra Lal
(b) Jagat Narayan Seth
(c) Kashi Prasad Jaiswal
(d) Jamil Akhtar

145. When was 'Bihar and Orissa Research Society' founded?
(a) 1911 AD (b) 1913 AD
(c) 1915 AD (d) 1917 AD

146. Who had prepared the present style of the Patna Museum?
(a) Bhagat Singh
(b) Vimal Kumar
(c) Arsi Prasad Singh
(d) Kashi Prasad Jaiswal

147. Which of the following was edited by Kashi Prasad Jaiswal?
(a) Sakhi (b) Balak
(c) Patliputra (d) Navyuvak

148. When did Kashi Prasad Jaiswal edit 'Patliputra'?
(a) 1917 AD (b) 1915 AD
(c) 1913 AD (d) 1911 AD

149. When was Kashi Prasad Jaiswal chosen the President of Indian Currency Committee?
(a) 1934 AD (b) 1935 AD
(c) 1936 AD (d) Both (a) and (c)

150. Who of the following was first called in London to give a lecture on the subject of Mauryan period coins?
(a) Ramdhari Singh Dinkar
(b) Prem Chand
(c) Kashi Prasad Jaiswal
(d) Abdul Hamid Shah

151. Where was Dr. Kumar Vimal born?
(a) Bhagalpur (b) Munger
(c) Patna (d) Gaya

152. When was the collection of poems by Kumar Vimal 'Angar' published?
(a) 1941 AD (b) 1944 AD
(c) 1947 AD (d) 1949 AD

153. Which of the following is a poetry collection by Kumar Vimal?
(a) Yug Manav Bapu
(b) Ek Rashtra hai - Ek Desh hai
(c) Srjana ke swar
(d) All of the above

154. Which of the following is an epic of criticism by Kumar Vimal?
(a) Ardhnarishwar Dinkar
(b) Mulya aur Mimansa
(c) Chintan
(d) All of the above

155. In which district was Kedarnath Mishra 'Prabhat'born?
(a) Arrah (b) Rohtas
(c) Gaya (d) Jamui

156. Which of the following is a poetry-collection of Kedarnath Mishra?
(a) Taptgrah (b) Karn
(c) Ritambar (d) All of these

157. Which of the following is not a composition of Kedar Nath Mishra Prabhat?
(a) Sangeet (b) Pravir
(c) Anand (d) Kaikeyi

158. Which of the following poetries is basically an epic of the greatness of humanity?
(a) Ritambara
(b) Pravir
(c) Karn
(d) Prabhash-Krishan

159. Which of the following prose-collection established Kedar Nath Mishra Prabhat as a skilled essay writer?
(a) Kheti aur Kisani
(b) Satyam Shivam Sundaram
(c) Pahiye ki Dhuri
(d) All of the above

160. Which poetry collection was honoured with an award by the Uttar Pradesh Government?
(a) Ritambara
(b) Baitho Mere Paas
(c) Setu Bandh
(d) Both (b) and (c)

161. Which weekly magazine was edited by Kedar Nath Mishra Prabhat?
(a) Yugantar (b) Navjivan
(c) Mahavir (d) Samarth

162. Where was Gopal Singh Nepali born?
(a) Motihari (b) Betiya
(c) Bihar Sharif (d) Navada

163. Which of the following is an initial composition of Gopal Singh Nepali?
(a) Ragini (b) Pakshi
(c) Umang (d) All of these

164. 'Himalaya ne Pukara'is a famous composition of whom?
(a) Gopal Das
(b) Gopal Singh Nepali
(c) Ram Avtar Chobey
(d) Choudhry Neshar Khan

165. Where was Dr. Chaturbhuj born?
(a) Bihar Sharif
(b) Vaishali
(c) Motihari
(d) Gaya

166. Which of the following is a famous play of Dr. Chaturbhuj?
(a) Nadi ka Pani
(b) Tipu Sultan
(c) Mir Qasim
(d) All of the above

167. Which of the following is not a play of Dr. Chaturbhuj?
(a) Sikandar-Porus
(b) Bahadur Shah
(c) Kailash Mansarovar
(d) Kalinga Vijay

168. Where was Janki Vallabh Shastri born?
(a) Gaya (b) Bhagalpur
(c) Vaishali (d) Betiya

169. Which of the following is the first poem of Janki Vallabh Shastri?
(a) Swadesh
(b) Prangan
(c) Jhansi ki Rani
(d) Roop-Arup

170. Which of the following is a composition of Janki Vallabh Shastri?
(a) Aparna
(b) Lila Kamal
(c) Vasanti
(d) All of the above

171. Which of the following is not a composition of Janki Vallabh Shastri?
(a) Ashwaghosh
(b) Kalidas
(c) Chosanth Yopgini
(d) Neelmohit

172. Who is the writer of the ghazal collection called 'Suno Kaun Nagma'?
(a) Mir Arshad Sheikh
(b) Jamshed Farooqi
(c) Nazam Kazmi
(d) Janki Vallabh Shastri

173. Where was great litterateur Devaki Nandam Khatri born?
(a) Mujaffarpur (b) Betiya
(c) Siwan (d) Patna

174. Which of the following is a composition of Devaki Nandan Khatri?
(a) Kusum Kumari
(b) Bhoot Nath
(c) Gupt Godan
(d) All of the above

175. Who is the author of the famous novel 'Chandrakanta'?
(a) Ram Kripal Sahay
(b) Narendra Nath
(c) Devaki Nandan Khatri
(d) Rajdeep Choudhry

176. Where did Devaki Nandan Khatri install 'Lehri Press'?
(a) Banaras (b) Allahabad
(c) Patna (d) Gorakhpur

177. In which district Devendra Nath Sharma was born?
(a) Balia (b) Gorakhpur
(c) Siwan (d) Gopalganj

178. Which of the following is a composition of Devendra Nath Sharma?
(a) Bhaktikaal
(b) Amar Bharti
(c) Brijbhasha ki Vibhutiyan
(d) All of the above

179. Where was the great story-teller Nalin Vilochan Sharma born?
(a) Patna (b) Motihari
(c) Mujaffarpur (d) Gaya

180. Which of the following is a famous story of Nalin Vilochan Sharma?
(a) Vish ke Daant
(b) Ye bimar log
(c) Barsane ki Radha
(d) All of the above

181. Which of the following story does not belong to Nalin Vilochan Sharma?
(a) Biscuit and Papad
(b) Lal Kothi
(c) Dukan ki Malkin
(d) Pados ki Koyal

182. Where was the famous poet Nagarjuna born?
(a) Darbhanga (b) Saharasa
(c) Arwal (d) Jamui

183. Which Maithili collection of Nagarjuna was awarded 'Sahitya Akadami' Award?
(a) Patra Hod
(b) Janm-jaat
(c) Patta Vihin Gachh
(d) Patrahin Nagn Gachh

184. Which of the following is a composition of Nagarjuna?
(a) Tumne Kaha Tha
(b) Pyasi Pathrai Ankhen
(c) Paka hai yeh Kathal
(d) All of the above

185. Which of the following is not a composition of Nagarjuna?
(a) Shikari
(b) Chandna
(c) Talab ki Machchliyan
(d) Satrange Pankho Wali

186. Who is the author of maithili novel 'Paro'?
(a) Vidyapati (b) Mandan Mishra
(c) Nagarjuna (d) Peer Ali

187. Which of the following poets had played a significant role in JP Movement?
(a) Paresh Sinha
(b) Zubair Shah
(c) Nagarjuna
(d) Shri Krishna Sahay

188. When was the first poem of Paresh Sinha "Sukhai'published?
(a) 1941 AD (b) 1943 AD
(c) 1945 AD (d) 1947 AD

189. Which of the following is a composition of Paresh Sinha?
(a) Teen Terah Log aur Nagphani ke Phool
(b) Uttar do Yaksha
(c) Purush Chhaya
(d) All of the above

190. Whose composition is this 'Gandhi Nahin Marega'?
(a) Gopal Singh Nepali
(b) Paresh Sinha
(c) Nagarjuna
(d) Abdul Mannan Khan

191. Where was Poddar Ramavtar Arun born?
(a) Samastipur (b) Siwan
(c) Motihari (d) Gaya

192. Which of the following is the first epic of Poddar Ramavtar Arun?
(a) Kalchakra (b) Arunima
(c) Kalidas (d) Vishwa-Manav

193. Which of the following are creations of Poddar Ramavtar Arun?
(a) Videh Amrapali
(b) Vidyapati Sursham
(c) Karl Marx
(d) All of the above

194. With which of the awards, Poddar Ramavtar Arun was honoured?
(a) Meera Samman
(b) Kalidas Samman
(c) Father Bulke
(d) All of the above

195. Where was the great regional novelist Phanishwar Nath Renu born?
(a) Saharasa (b) Arariya
(c) Arwal (d) Darbhanga

196. Battbab, Pahalwan ki Dholak and Gotranta are the initial composition of whom?
(a) Ramdhari Singh Dinkar
(b) Nagarjuna
(c) Gopal Singh Nepali
(d) Phanishwar Nath Renu

197. Phanishwar Nath Renu's famous composition 'Maila Anchal' was published in which year?
(a) 1950 AD (b) 1952 AD
(c) 1954 AD (d) 1956 AD

198. Which of the following is an important composition of Phanishwar Nath Renu?
(a) Teesri Kasam
(b) Paltu Babu Road
(c) Juloos
(d) All of the above

199. On which of the following novels, a film was made?
(a) Agnikher (b) Teesri Kasam
(c) Thumri (d) Juloos

200. Father Kamil Bulke was citizen of which country?
(a) England (b) Germany
(c) America (d) Belgium

201. When did Father Kamil Bulke compose English-Hindi dictionary?
(a) 1968 AD (b) 1966 AD
(c) 1964 AD (d) 1962 AD

202. Which of the following is a composition of Father Kamil Bulke?
(a) Neel Pakshi
(b) Prerit Charitra
(c) Path Sangrah
(d) All of the above

203. Whose composition is this-Ramkatha: Creation and Development?
(a) Ramdhari Singh Dinkar
(b) Phanishwar Nath Renu
(c) Ahmad Siraz
(d) Father Kamil Bulke

204. Where was Bhikhari Thakur born?
(a) Saran (b) Siwan
(c) Jehanabad (d) Arwal

205. Bihari Thakur is called ________ of Bhojpuri?
(a) Kalidas
(b) Prem Chand
(c) Shakespeare
(d) John Kitts

206. Which of the following is a play written by Bihari Thakur?
(a) Kaliyug Prem
(b) Bhai-Virodh
(c) Ganga Snan
(d) All of the above

207. Who is the writer of the play 'Videshiya'?
(a) Vidyapati
(b) Raghuvansh Sahay
(c) Raghubir Tyagi
(d) Bikhari Thakur

208. Which of the following is not a play written by Bhikhari Thakur?
(a) Bhai-Behen (b) Bhai Virodh
(c) Beti Viyog (d) Putravadhu

209. Madhukar Singh was born in Midnapore of Bengal while his 'karmbhumi' remained the ________ district of Bihar?
(a) Arwal (b) Saran
(c) Bhojpur (d) Purnia

210. Which of the following is a creation of Madhukar Singh?
(a) Brijlal Mehto
(b) Mandal Mishra
(c) Ramavtar Singh
(d) Madhukar Singh

211. 'Maxim Gorki' is creation of whom?
(a) Brijlal Mehto
(b) Mandan Mishra
(c) Ramavtar Singh
(d) Madhukar Singh

212. Which of the following is a story-collection of Madhukar Singh?
(a) Bhai Ka Zakhm
(b) Pehla Pathh
(c) Poora Sannata
(d) All of the above

213. Who is the writer of the story collection 'Michael Jackson ki Topi'?
(a) Raghubir Narain
(b) Madhukar Singh
(c) Bhikhari Thakur
(d) Irshad Ahmad

214. Madhukar Singh has been honored by Bihar Government by which of the following citations?
(a) Sarvochch Kalakar
(b) Phanishwar Nath Renu Samman
(c) Nai Dhara Rachna Samman
(d) All of the above

215. Where was Mohan Lal Mehto 'Vitogi' born?
(a) Gaya (b) Madhepura
(c) Arwal (d) Munger

216. Which of the following is a composition of Mohan Lal Mehto 'Viyogi'?
(a) Aryavart
(b) Ek Tara
(c) Nirmalya aur Kalpana
(d) All of the above

217. Famous Raja Radhika Raman Prasad Singh was born in which district of Bihar?
(a) Bhojpur (b) Munger
(c) Bhagalpur (d) Purnia

218. Which of the following is the famous creation of Raja Radhika Raman Prasad Singh?
(a) Chumban aur Chata
(b) Poorab aur Paschim
(c) Ram Rahim
(d) All of the above

219. Which of the following is not a composition of Raja Radhika Raman Prasad Singh?
(a) Toota ghar
(b) Maya mili na Ram
(c) Apni apni nazar
(d) Dev aur Danav

220. Who is the writer of the novels 'Modern' and 'Sundar'?
(a) Radhamohan Jha
(b) Mandan Mishra
(c) Raja Radhika Raman Prasad Singh
(d) Junaid Kadri

221. Raja Radhika Raman Prasad Singh got started publication of which magazine?
(a) Umang
(b) Nai Dhara
(c) Sarthak Pahal
(d) Navyuvak

222. When did the publication of 'Nai Dhara' started?
(a) 1971 AD (b) 1969 AD
(c) 1967 AD (d) 1965 AD

223. Where was Ramji Mishra Manohar born?
(a) Purnia (b) Munger
(c) Bhagalpur (d) Patna

224. Which of the following is the chief composition of Ramji Mishra Manohar?
(a) Dastan-e-Patliputra
(b) Guru Nanak
(c) Guru Govind Singh and his holy weapons
(d) All of the above

225. Who of the following keeps the status of a 'Rashtrakavi'?
(a) Phanishwar Nath Renu
(b) Gopal Singh Nepali
(c) Ramvriksha Benipuri
(d) Ramdhari Singh Dinkar

226. Where was Ramdhari Singh Dinkar born?
(a) Bihar Sharif (b) Begusarai
(c) Betiya (d) Motihari

227. Which of the following books is the first book of Ramdhari Singh Dinkar?
(a) Praman Patra
(b) Char Dham
(c) Hare ko Harinam
(d) Neelkusum

228. Which of the following is the main composition of Ramdhari Singh Dinkar?
(a) Rashmirathi
(b) Urvashi
(c) Kurukshetra
(d) All of the above

229. Who is the author of the novel 'Sanskriti ke Char Adhyay'?
(a) Ramdhari Singh Dinkar
(b) Ramvriksha Benipuri
(c) Phanishwar Nath Renu
(d) Ali Jan Sheikh

230. How many times Ramdhari Singh Dinkar was a member of Rajya Sabha?
(a) 1 (b) 2
(c) 3 (d) 4

231. Where was 'Kalam ke Sipahi' Ramvriksha Benipuri born?
(a) Mujaffarpur (b) Bhagalpur
(c) Munger (d) Patna

232. In which jail had Ramvriksha Benipuri composed his play 'Ambpali'?
(a) Ranchi (b) Patna
(c) Hajaribagh (d) Baliya

233. Which of the following is a composition of Ramvriksha Benipuri?
(a) Gehu aur Gulab
(b) Mati ki Moorat
(c) Sanghmitra
(d) All of the above

234. Who is the author of the book called 'Kaidi ki Patni'?
(a) Ramvriksha Benipuri
(b) Lal Singh
(c) Ramnaresh Tripathi
(d) Dilawar Khan

235. Which of the following is not a composition of Ramvriksha Benipuri?
(a) Shaktipunj
(b) Shakuntala
(c) Seeta ki Maa
(d) Amar Jyoti

236. Which of the following was edited by Ramvriksha Benipuri?
(a) Chunnu-Mubbu
(b) Kisan
(c) Himalaya
(d) All of the above

237. When was Ramvriksha Benipuri elected a member of the Bihar Legislative Assembly?
(a) 1952 AD (b) 1957 AD
(c) 1962 AD (d) 1967 AD

238. Who of the following was famous for being a Library Scientist apart from being a Storey teller and novelist?
(a) Ram Shobhit Prasad Singh
(b) Ramvriksha Benipuri
(c) Ramji Mishra Manohar
(d) Vinod Singh

239. In which district was Ram Shobhit Prasad Singh born?
(a) Vaishali (b) Munger
(c) Bhagalpur (d) Saran

240. Who had edited the monthly magazine 'Pustakalaya'?
(a) Ram Shobhit Prasad Singh
(b) Ramesh Singh
(c) Amjad Khan
(d) Mandan Mishra

241. Which of the following is a composition of Ram Shobhit Prasad Singh?
(a) Rashtriya ekta ka prateek
(b) Prem-Prasang
(c) Batohiya ke amar gayak
(d) All of the above

242. Where was Rameshwar Singh Kashyap alias Loha Singh born?
(a) Buxar (b) Rohtas
(c) Purnia (d) Bhagalpur

243. Which of the following is a composition of Ramvriksha Benipuri?
(a) Amrapali
(b) Mati ki moortat
(c) Chita ke phool
(d) All of the above

244. When was Rameshwar Singh Kashyap honoured with a 'Padam Shri'?
(a) 1987 AD (b) 1989 AD
(c) 1991 AD (d) 1993 AD

245. Which of the following is a main composition of Rameshwar Singh Kashyap?
(a) Aprajey Nirala
(b) Neelkanth Nirala
(c) Swarnrekha
(d) All of the above

246. In which district Lakshmi Narayam Sudhanshu was born?
(a) Purnia (b) Saharasa
(c) Khagadiya (d) Arwal

247. Which of the following is the first novel of Lakshmi Narayan Sudhanshu?
(a) Swadesh (b) Amar Prem
(c) Matra-Prem (d) Jagat-Prem

248. When was Lakshmi Narayan Sudhanshu elected unopposed as the Speaker of Bihar Legislative Assembly?
(a) 1962 AD (b) 1960 AD
(c) 1957 AD (d) 1952 AD

249. When was litterateur Shivpujan Sahay born?
(a) 1891 AD (b) 1893 AD
(c) 1895 AD (d) 1897 AD

250. Which of the following is the main composition of Shivpujan Sahay?
(a) Jagran
(b) Dehati Duniya
(c) Himay
(d) All of the above

251. 'Wahi din wahi log' is a composition of whom amongst the following?
(a) Vidyapati
(b) Bhikhari Thakur
(c) Shivpujan Sahai
(d) Ram Naresh Mishra

252. In which village of Darbhanga district, was Vidyapati born?
(a) Visafi (b) Damdama
(c) Kahalgaon (d) Bahurva

253. Which of the following is the main composition of Vidyapati?
(a) Purush Pariksha
(b) Kirti Lata
(c) Kirti Pataka
(d) All of the above

254. Whose composition is 'Durga Bhakti Tarangini'?
(a) Bhikhari Thakur
(b) Vidyapati
(c) Shashidhar Pandit
(d) Mandan Mishra

255. Which of the following is not a composition of Vidyapati?
(a) Begar Manushya
(b) Varsh Kritya
(c) Bhu parikrama
(d) Goraksha Vijay

256. Where was Udairaj Singh born?
(a) Buxar (b) Arrah
(c) Gaya (d) Rohtas

257. Which of the following is a composition of Udairaj Singh?
(a) Navtara
(b) Adhuri Nari
(c) Bhudani Soniya
(d) All of the above

258. Which magazine was edited by Udairaj Singh?
(a) Bhudan (b) Vikas
(c) Saurabh (d) Both (b) and (c)

259. In which district was Rajkamal Choudhary, a great litterateur, born?
(a) Saharasa (b) Gorakhpur
(c) Chhapra (d) Siwan

260. Which is the major composition of Rajkamal Choudhry?
(a) Agni Snan
(b) Nadi Bahati Thi
(c) Machhli mari hui
(d) All of the above

261. 'Bees Raniyon ke Bi-scope' is a composition of whom amongst the following?
(a) Rajkamal Choudhary
(b) Udairaj Singh
(c) Ramsewak Singh
(d) Ojair Anjum

262. Which of the following is a composition in Maithili by Rajkamal Choudhry?
(a) Patharphool
(b) Swargandha
(c) Vishhara
(d) All of the above

263. Famous critic Manager Pandey was born in which district of Bihar?
(a) Siwan (b) Gopalganj
(c) Arariya (d) Munger

264. Which of the following is a composition of Manager Pandey?
(a) Shabd aur Karma
(b) Sahitya evam Itihas
(c) Desh ki baat
(d) All of these

265. In which district was Robin Shaw born?
(a) Munger (b) Bhagalpur
(c) Khagariya (d) Saran

266. Which is the main composition of Robin Shaw?
(a) Anyay ko Kshama
(b) Dulhan Bazaar
(c) Agnikunda
(d) All of the above

267. Who is the author of the story collection called 'Ghar Kahan Bhag Gaya'?
(a) Ravindra Bhagat
(b) Ramavtar Singh
(c) Robin Shaw
(d) Prabhat Jha

268. In which district of Bihar was the famous litterateur Ravindra Prabhat born?
(a) Sitamarhi (b) Shivhar
(c) Siwan (d) Gopalganj

269. Which of the following is a composition of Ravindra Prabhat?
(a) Humsafar
(b) Smriti Shesh
(c) Prem na hat bikay
(d) All of the above

270. Who composed 'Hindi Blogging-Abhivyakti ki nai kranti'?
(a) Saraswati Devi
(b) Shailbala Devi
(c) Ravindra Bhagat
(d) Dileep Mandal

271. Which of the following is not a composition of Ravindra Bhagat?
(a) Mat Rona Ramjani Chacha
(b) Taki Bacha Rahe Loktantra
(c) Hindi Blogging ka Itihaas
(d) Jagte Raho

272. When was Ravindra Bhagat honoured with the citation 'Hindi Sahityashri Samman'?
(a) 2009 AD (b) 2010 AD
(c) 2011 AD (d) 2012 AD

273. In which district of Bihar, famous litterateur Saraswati Prasad was born?
(a) Arrah (b) Buxar
(c) Bhagalpur (d) Munger

274. Which of the following is a major composition of Saraswati Prasad?
(a) Nadi Pukare Sagar
(b) Ek thi Taru
(c) Nancy
(d) All of the above

275. In which district of Bihar, Rashmi Prabha was born?
(a) Sitamarhi
(b) Eastern Champaran
(c) Saran
(d) Bhagalpur

276. Which of the following is a composition of Rashmi Prabha?
(a) Anugoonj
(b) Anmol Sanchyan
(c) Anuttarit
(d) All of the above

277. Who composed 'Athens ka Satyarthi'?
(a) Saraswati Devi
(b) Rashmi Prabha
(c) Jagat Narayan
(d) Amarpratap Jha

278. Which of the following is a major composition of Ganganath Jha?
(a) Bhakti Kallolini
(b) Bhavbodhini
(c) Bela Mahatmyam
(d) All of the above

279. Who is the author of the book called 'Shankaracharya and his Work for the Upliftment of the Country'?
(a) Harimohan Jha
(b) Ganganath Jha
(c) Brijkishore Jha
(d) Lallan Jha

280. Where was famous litterateur Harimohan Jha born?
(a) Vaishali (b) Mujaffarpur
(c) Saran (d) Motihari

281. Which of the following is a major composition of Harimohan Jha?
(a) Kanyadan
(b) Pradamya Devta
(c) Rangshala
(d) All of the above

282. Which of the following is a major composition of Jagdish Chandra Mathur?
(a) Konark
(b) Pahla Raja
(c) Bhor ka Tara
(d) All of the above

283. Who composed the play called 'Dashrath Nandan aur Raghukul Reet'?

(a) Madan Mohan Jha
(b) Jagdish Mathur
(c) Harimohan Jha
(d) Mandan Mishra

284. Which of the following is a composition of Banbhatt?

(a) Yugantar
(b) Kadambari
(c) Harishcharitam
(d) Both (b) and (c)

285. Who of the following is the writer of 'Panchtantra'?

(a) Vishnu Dutt
(b) Vishnu Sharma
(c) Panini
(d) Amar Singh

286. Which of the following is a creation of Ashwaghosh?

(a) Mahayan Shradhhotpadna
(b) Buddhcharit
(c) Vajra Suchi
(d) All of the above

287. Who composed 'Kamasutram'?

(a) Mudrarakshas
(b) Vatsyanan
(c) Kautilya
(d) Aryabhatt

288. Which of the following is a composition of Mandan Mishra?

(a) Vidhi Vidhan
(b) Bhav Vivek
(c) Vidhi Vivek
(d) Both (b) and (c)

289. Which of the following is a composition of Mulla Dawood?

(a) Chandrayan
(b) Chandayan
(c) Mangalyan
(d) Prithviyan

290. Who of the following is the author of 'Darshanratnakar'?

(a) Mandan Mishra
(b) Bhikhari Thakur
(c) Jyotishwar Thakur
(d) Vidyapati

291. Which of the following is a composition of Phanishwar Nath Renu?

(a) Juloos
(b) Paltu Babu Road
(c) Deerghtap
(d) All of the above

292. Which of the following is not a composition of Ramdhari Singh Dinkar?

(a) Hunkar (b) Karamvir
(c) Rasvanti (d) Chakrawal

293. Which of the following is not a composition of Baba Nagarjuna?

(a) Dhup-chhaon
(b) Tumne kaha tha
(c) Hazar-hazar bahon wali
(d) Baba Bateshwarnath

294. Which of the following is a composition of Devaki Nandan Khatri?

(a) Bhootnath
(b) Kajal ki kothri
(c) Naulakha haar
(d) All of the above

295. Which of the following is not a composition of Rahul Sanskrityayan?

(a) Darshan-Digdarshan
(b) Suttpitaka
(c) Vinay Pitaka
(d) Dhammpad

296. Which of the following is a composition of Dr. Rajendra Prasad?

(a) India Divided
(b) Champaran mein Satyagrah

(c) Bapu ke kadmo mein

(d) All of the above

297. Who of the following composed 'Doob Janam Chhai'?

(a) Kedar Nath Mishra

(b) Shivsagar Mishra

(c) Mandan Mishra

(d) Mulla Dawood

Answers

1. (a)	**2.** (d)	**3.** (c)	**4.** (a)	**5.** (b)	**6.** (c)	**7.** (d)	**8.** (b)	**9.** (a)	**10.** (c)
11. (d)	**12.** (c)	**13.** (a)	**14.** (d)	**15.** (d)	**16.** (a)	**17.** (d)	**18.** (a)	**19.** (c)	**20.** (d)
21. (b)	**22.** (d)	**23.** (a)	**24.** (d)	**25.** (b)	**26.** (d)	**27.** (b)	**28.** (a)	**29.** (c)	**30.** (b)
31. (c)	**32.** (a)	**33.** (d)	**34.** (d)	**35.** (a)	**36.** (c)	**37.** (c)	**38.** (b)	**39.** (d)	**40.** (b)
41. (c)	**42.** (d)	**43.** (c)	**44.** (a)	**45.** (d)	**46.** (d)	**47.** (b)	**48.** (b)	**49.** (d)	**50.** (d)
51. (c)	**52.** (b)	**53.** (d)	**54.** (a)	**55.** (c)	**56.** (d)	**57.** (a)	**58.** (b)	**59.** (a)	**60.** (d)
61. (b)	**62.** (a)	**63.** (b)	**64.** (a)	**65.** (d)	**66.** (d)	**67.** (a)	**68.** (b)	**69.** (c)	**70.** (a)
71. (d)	**72.** (a)	**73.** (c)	**74.** (d)	**75.** (d)	**76.** (b)	**77.** (c)	**78.** (a)	**79.** (c)	**80.** (d)
81. (a)	**82.** (d)	**83.** (b)	**84.** (a)	**85.** (b)	**86.** (d)	**87.** (d)	**88.** (c)	**89.** (a)	**90.** (d)
91. (d)	**92.** (a)	**93.** (c)	**94.** (b)	**95.** (d)	**96.** (c)	**97.** (b)	**98.** (b)	**99.** (c)	**100.** (d)
101. (a)	**102.** (b)	**103.** (a)	**104.** (d)	**105.** (b)	**106.** (c)	**107.** (a)	**108.** (c)	**109.** (a)	**110.** (d)
111. (d)	**112.** (a)	**113.** (c)	**114.** (a)	**115.** (d)	**116.** (c)	**117.** (a)	**118.** (d)	**119.** (a)	**120.** (c)
121. (d)	**122.** (b)	**123.** (d)	**124.** (d)	**125.** (a)	**126.** (b)	**127.** (d)	**128.** (d)	**129.** (d)	**130.** (d)
131. (a)	**132.** (d)	**133.** (a)	**134.** (d)	**135.** (d)	**136.** (b)	**137.** (b)	**138.** (a)	**139.** (d)	**140.** (b)
141. (d)	**142.** (b)	**143.** (d)	**144.** (d)	**145.** (c)	**146.** (d)	**147.** (c)	**148.** (a)	**149.** (d)	**150.** (c)
151. (a)	**152.** (d)	**153.** (d)	**154.** (d)	**155.** (a)	**156.** (d)	**157.** (c)	**158.** (a)	**159.** (d)	**160.** (d)
161. (c)	**162.** (b)	**163.** (d)	**164.** (b)	**165.** (a)	**166.** (d)	**167.** (c)	**168.** (a)	**169.** (d)	**170.** (d)
171. (c)	**172.** (d)	**173.** (a)	**174.** (d)	**175.** (c)	**176.** (a)	**177.** (d)	**178.** (d)	**179.** (a)	**180.** (d)
181. (d)	**182.** (c)	**183.** (a)	**184.** (d)	**185.** (d)	**186.** (a)	**187.** (a)	**188.** (d)	**189.** (d)	**190.** (b)
191. (a)	**192.** (b)	**193.** (d)	**194.** (d)	**195.** (b)	**196.** (d)	**197.** (c)	**198.** (d)	**199.** (b)	**200.** (d)
201. (a)	**202.** (d)	**203.** (d)	**204.** (a)	**205.** (c)	**206.** (d)	**207.** (d)	**208.** (a)	**209.** (c)	**210.** (d)
211. (d)	**212.** (d)	**213.** (b)	**214.** (d)	**215.** (a)	**216.** (d)	**217.** (a)	**218.** (d)	**219.** (a)	**220.** (c)
221. (b)	**222.** (a)	**223.** (d)	**224.** (a)	**225.** (d)	**226.** (b)	**227.** (a)	**228.** (d)	**229.** (a)	**230.** (c)
231. (a)	**232.** (c)	**233.** (d)	**234.** (a)	**235.** (a)	**236.** (d)	**237.** (b)	**238.** (a)	**239.** (d)	**240.** (a)
241. (d)	**242.** (b)	**243.** (d)	**244.** (c)	**245.** (d)	**246.** (a)	**247.** (c)	**248.** (a)	**249.** (b)	**250.** (d)
251. (c)	**252.** (a)	**253.** (d)	**254.** (b)	**255.** (a)	**256.** (d)	**257.** (d)	**258.** (d)	**259.** (a)	**260.** (d)
261. (a)	**262.** (d)	**263.** (b)	**264.** (d)	**265.** (a)	**266.** (d)	**267.** (c)	**268.** (a)	**269.** (d)	**270.** (c)
271. (d)	**272.** (c)	**273.** (a)	**274.** (d)	**275.** (a)	**276.** (d)	**277.** (b)	**278.** (d)	**279.** (b)	**280.** (a)
281. (d)	**282.** (d)	**283.** (b)	**284.** (d)	**285.** (b)	**286.** (d)	**287.** (b)	**288.** (d)	**289.** (b)	**290.** (c)
291. (d)	**292.** (b)	**293.** (a)	**294.** (d)	**295.** (b)	**296.** (d)	**297.** (b)			

❑❑❑

11 The Personalities of Bihar

1. **When was Anugraha Narayan Singh elected as the President of Bihar Congress Committee?**
   (a) 1924 AD (b) 1926 AD
   (c) 1928 AD (d) 1930 AD
2. **Anugraha Narayan Singh was handed over the charge of which Ministry in the Government headed by Shri Krishna Singh from 1946 to 1952 AD?**
   (a) Home
   (b) Education
   (c) Public Welfare
   (d) Finance
3. **When did Abdul Karim Ansari become the President of Bihar Congress Committee?**
   (a) 1946 AD (b) 1944 AD
   (c) 1942 AD (d) 1940 AD
4. **Which of the following is the composition of Abdul Karim Ansari?**
   (a) Shaharnama (b) Naksh-e-Paedar
   (c) Masarvat (d) Masnui
5. **When was Ali Imam honoured with the title of 'Sir'?**
   (a) 1908 AD (b) 1910 AD
   (c) 1912 AD (d) 1914 AD
6. **Who of the following was nominated as the Judge of Patna High Court in the year 1917?**
   (a) Hasan Imam
   (b) Abdul Qayyum Ansari
   (c) Ali Imam
   (d) Rajendra Prasad
7. **Which of the following is an Organisation founded by Anand Kumar?**
   (a) Super 20 (b) Super 30
   (c) Super 40 (d) Super 50
8. **Which of the following is a famous composition of R. P. Sharma?**
   (a) Kaljayi Hanuman
   (b) Antaryatra
   (c) Adhyayan aur chintan
   (d) All of the above
9. **When did Karpuri Thakur become a legislator for the first time?**
   (a) 1952 AD (b) 1957 AD
   (c) 1960 AD (d) 1962 AD
10. **When did Karpuri Thakur become Deputy Chief Minister of Bihar?**
    (a) 1965 AD (b) 1966 AD
    (c) 1967 AD (d) 1968 AD
11. **When did Karpuri Thakur become the Chief Minister of Bihar for the first time?**
    (a) 1970 AD (b) 1969 AD
    (c) 1968 AD (d) 1967 AD
12. **When did Karpuri Thakur become the Chief Minister of Bihar again?**
    (a) 1971 AD (b) 1973 AD
    (c) 1975 AD (d) 1977 AD
13. **When did Karpuri Thakur resign from the post of Chief Minister?**
    (a) 16 January 1978
    (b) 21 April 1978
    (c) 11 May 1978
    (d) 13 June 1978

14. Kirti Azad was a member of which victorious World Cup team of India?
(a) 1983 AD (b) 1987 AD
(c) 1992 AD (d) 2011 AD

15. K. B. Sahay was the _______ Chief Minister of Bihar.
(a) Second (b) Third
(c) Fourth (d) Fifth

16. State the period during which Krishna Ballabh Sahay was the Chief Minister of Bihar.
(a) 1963-65 AD (b) 1963-66 AD
(c) 1963-67 AD (d) 1963-68 AD

17. Who gets the credit of establishing Oriental Public Library in Bihar?
(a) Krishna Ballabh Sahay
(b) Khuda Baksh Khan
(c) Jagjivan Ram
(d) Bhagwat Jha

18. Where in Bihar is Khudabaksh Library situated?
(a) Patna (b) Bihar Sharif
(c) Mujaffarpur (d) Vaishali

19. In which of the following films, Chitragupt Shrivastava had played a role?
(a) Bhabhi
(b) Bada Aadmi
(c) Aplam Chaplam
(d) All of the above

20. When was Babu Jagjivan Ram born?
(a) 3 January 1908
(b) 5 April 1908
(c) 8 May 1908
(d) 10 June 1908

21. When did Jagjivan Ram form the All India Ravidas Institute?
(a) 1923 AD
(b) 1925 AD
(c) 1927 AD
(d) 1929 AD

22. Which Ministry was granted to Jagjivan Ram in the interim government?
(a) Labour (b) Finance
(c) Railway (d) Tribal Affairs

23. When was Jagjivan Ram offered the post of Deputy Prime Minister?
(a) 1975 AD (b) 1976 AD
(c) 1977 AD (d) 1978 AD

24. Which Ministry was granted to Jaglal Choudhary in Congress Cabinet?
(a) Health (b) Labour
(c) Finance (d) Home

25. In which district was Jaiprakash Narayan born?
(a) Shivhar
(b) Sitamarhi
(c) Saran Bhagalpur

26. When was Jaiprakash Narayan born?
(a) 11 October 1902
(b) 15 August 1902
(c) 10 June 1902
(d) 11 May 1902

27. When did Jaiprakash Narayan accept membership of the Congress?
(a) 1928 AD (b) 1929 AD
(c) 1930 AD (d) 1931 AD

28. When was Jaiprakash Narayan honored with Magsaysay Award?
(a) 1963 AD (b) 1964 AD
(c) 1965 AD (d) 1966 AD

29. When did Jaiprakash Narayan announce a complete revolution?
(a) 1974 AD (b) 1975 AD
(c) 1976 AD (d) 1977 AD

30. Who of the following wrote the biography of Jaiprakash Narayan?
(a) Phanishwar Nath Renu
(b) Ramdhari Singh Dinkar
(c) Mandan Mishra
(d) Ramvriksh Benipuri

31. When was Jaiprakash Narayan honoured with 'Bharat Ratna'?
(a) 1997 AD (b) 1998 AD
(c) 1999 AD (d) 2000 AD

32. When did Jaiprakash Narayan die?
(a) 8 February 1979
(b) 12 March 1979
(c) 18 May 1979
(d) 8 October 1979

33. Who directed the film 'Manjhi-The Mountain Man'?
(a) Anurag Kashyap
(b) Abhinav Sinha
(c) Ketan Mehta
(d) Prakash Jha

34. In the film 'Manjhi-The Mountain Man' who played the role of Dashrath Manjhi?
(a) Irfan Khan
(b) Jishan Ayub
(c) Faisal Khan
(d) Nawazuddin Siddiqui

35. By which of the titles, Dukhan Ram was honoured?
(a) Rai Saheb (b) Sir
(c) Knighthood (d) Nawab Saheb

36. When was Dukhan Ram honoured with the title of Rai Saheb?
(a) 1943 AD (b) 1944 AD
(c) 1945 AD (d) 1946 AD

37. When was Dukhan Ram honoured with 'Padam Vibhushan'?
(a) 1962 AD (b) 1961 AD
(c) 1960 AD (d) 1959 AD

38. When was Dukhan Ram honoured with the title of 'Bihar Ratna'?
(a) 1985 AD (b) 1986 AD
(c) 1987 AD (d) 1988 AD

39. Pawan Kumar was the well known ________ of Bihar?
(a) Cartoonist (b) Politician
(c) Doctor (d) Journalist

40. Which of the following is a film directed by Prakash Jha?
(a) Hip Hip Hurray
(b) Katha Madhopur ki
(c) Parineeti
(d) All of the above

41. Which of the following is a serial directed by Prakash Jha?
(a) Sampadan
(b) Vidroh
(c) Mungeri Lal ke haseen sapne
(d) Both (b) and (c)

42. Who alongwith Bhagat Singh, threw a bomb in Assembly on 8 April 1929?
(a) Batukeshwar Dutt
(b) Khudiram Bose
(c) Prafull Chaki
(d) Sukhdev

43. In which district of Bihar was Babu Kunwar Singh born?
(a) Bhojpur (b) Saran
(c) Bhagalpur (d) Munger

44. When was Babu Kunwar Singh born?
(a) 18 February 1777
(b) 13 March 1777
(c) 23 April 1777
(d) 20 May 1777

45. Who started 'Sulabh Technique movement'?
(a) Pawan Kumar
(b) Bhagwat Jha
(c) Kirti Azad
(d) Bindeshwar Pathak

46. Where was Bismillah Khan born?
(a) Buxar (b) Bhagalpur
(c) Munger (d) Chhapra

47. When was Bismillah Khan born?
(a) 10 January 1916
(b) 21 March 1916
(c) 8 May 1916
(d) 10 June 1916

48. What was the real name of Bismillah Khan?
(a) Amjad Khan
(b) Ismail Khan
(c) Qamruddin Khan
(d) Jamaluddin Khan

49. When was Bismillah Khan honoured with 'Sangeet Natak Academy Award'?
(a) 1956 AD (b) 1954 AD
(c) 1952 AD (d) 1950 AD

50. On 15 August 1947, Bismillah Khan was given an opportunity to play _________ on the occasion of independence day celebrations in the Red Fort?
(a) Tabla
(b) Shehnai
(c) Harmonium
(d) Dhol

51. When was Bismillah Khan honoured with 'Bharat Ratna'?
(a) 1998 AD (b) 1999 AD
(c) 2000 AD (d) 2001 AD

52. When did Bismillah Khan die?
(a) 2006 AD (b) 2005 AD
(c) 2004 AD (d) 2003 AD

53. Moraraji Desai had constituted the Civil Rights Commission under whose leadership?
(a) Jagjivan Ram
(b) Jaiprakash Narayan
(c) Shri Krishna Singh
(d) B. P. Mandal

54. When did B. P. Mandal present its report relating to reservations?
(a) 1978 AD (b) 1979 AD
(c) 1980 AD (d) 1981 AD

55. When did B. P. Mandal become the Chief Minister of Bihar?
(a) 1968 AD (b) 1969 AD
(c) 1970 AD (d) 1971 AD

56. Who of the following had founded the Indian Orthopaedic Association?
(a) Dr. Ali Imam
(b) Mazhrul Haque
(c) B Mukhopadhyay
(d) Kartik Sen

57. When was Indian Orthopaedic Association established?
(a) 1955 AD
(b) 1954 AD
(c) 1953 AD
(d) 1952 AD

58. Who of the following was the first 'Dalit' chief Minister of Bihar?
(a) Jagjivan Ram
(b) Bhola Paswan Shastri
(c) Ram Vilas Paswan
(d) Jitan Manjhi

59. When did Bhola Paswan Shashtri become the Chief Minister for the first time?
(a) 1966 AD (b) 1967 AD
(c) 1968 AD (d) 1969 AD

60. For how many times did Bhola Paswan Shastri become the Chief Minister of Bihar?
(a) 1 (b) 2
(c) 3 (d) 4

61. Which Hindi weekly was edited by Bhola Paswan Shastri?
(a) Kaal
(b) Sandesh
(c) Rashtra Sandesh
(d) Honhaar

62. From which place Bhola Paswan Shastri had edited the Hindi weekly- Rashtra Sandesh?
(a) Bhagalpur (b) Kishanganj
(c) Saharasa (d) Purnia

63. In which of the following films did Manoj Bajpayee act?
(a) Road (b) Pinjar
(c) Satya (d) All of these

64. Who had started the 'Prithak Bihar Andolan' along with Sachchidanand Sinha?

(a) B. P. Mandal
(b) Bhola Paswan Shastri
(c) Mahesh Narayan
(d) Dr. Rajendra Prasad

65. Which of the following newspapers was edited by Mahesh Narayan?
(a) The Bihar Times
(b) The Bihari
(c) The Bihar Gazette
(d) The Bihar Samay

66. When was Dr. Rajendra Prasad born?
(a) 3 March 1884
(b) 3 May 1884
(c) 3 August 1884
(d) 3 December 1884

67. In which district was Rajendra Prasad born?
(a) Siwan (b) Saran
(c) Seetamarhi (d) Gopalganj

68. When did Dr. Rajendra Prasad become the President of Congress?
(a) 1930 AD (b) 1932 AD
(c) 1934 AD (d) 1936 AD

69. Which of Congress Sessions was presided over by Dr. Rajendra Prasad?
(a) 48th (b) 47th
(c) 46th (d) 45th

70. Under whose chairmanship amongst the following, the Constitutional Committee framed the Constitution of India?
(a) Subhash Chandra Bose
(b) Dr. Rajendra Prasad
(c) Jawaharlal Nehru
(d) Sachchidanand Sinha

71. When did Dr. Rajendra Prasad become the first President of India?
(a) 15 August 1947
(b) 28 October 1947
(c) 26 November 1949
(d) 26 January 1950

72. Till when did Dr. Rajendra Prasad remain the President of India?
(a) 1960 AD (b) 1961 AD
(c) 1962 AD (d) 1963 AD

73. For how many times did Dr. Rajendra Prasad become the President of India?
(a) 1 (b) 2
(c) 3 (d) 4

74. When was Dr. Rajendra Prasad honoured with 'Bharat Ratna'?
(a) 1962 AD (b) 1963 AD
(c) 1964 AD (d) 1965 AD

75. When did Dr. Rajendra Prasad die?
(a) 1962 AD (b) 1963 AD
(c) 1964 AD (d) 1965 AD

76. Ram Chatur Malik was given the 'Tansen Award' by which State Government?
(a) Uttar Pradesh (b) Bihar
(c) Rajasthan (d) Madhya Pradesh

77. When was Ram Chatur Malik honoured with 'Tansen Award'?
(a) 1978 AD (b) 1979 AD
(c) 1980 AD (d) 1981 AD

78. Who of the following is famous as 'Bihar Kokila'?
(a) Prabhavati Devi
(b) Shammi
(c) Vindhyavasini Devi
(d) Saraswati Devi

79. When did Vindhyavasini Devi found the 'Vindhya Kala Mandir'?
(a) 1948 AD (b) 1949 AD
(c) 1950 AD (d) 1951 AD

80. Which of the following texts of music was composed by Vindhyavasini Devi?
(a) Lok Sangeet Sagar
(b) Sohar Prakaran
(c) Vrihad Kosh
(d) All of the above

81. When was Vindhyavasini Devi honoured with Padma Shri'?
(a) 1974 AD (b) 1973 AD
(c) 1972 AD (d) 1971 AD

82. As Minister of which Department, Vir Chandra Patel had taken an oath of office in Vinodanand Jha Government?
(a) Labour (b) Health
(c) Home (d) Finance

83. Where was Shatrughan Sinha born?
(a) Patna (b) Ranchi
(c) Bhagalpur (d) Jamshedpur

84. Which of the following films belong to Shatrughan Sinha?
(a) Kala Paththar
(b) Khamosh
(c) Dostana
(d) All of the above

85. Where was Kedarnath Prasad born in the year 1926?
(a) Patna
(b) Saran
(c) East Champaran
(d) Munger

86. Which of the following is a major composition of Kedarnath Prasad?
(a) A case study of Bihar
(b) India's rural problems
(c) Lectures on Micro-economic Theory
(d) All of the above

87. Who composed the book called 'Á case study of Biharian relation to other States of India'?
(a) Maulana Mazhrul Haque
(b) Mandan Mishra
(c) Kedarnath Prasad
(d) K. B. Sahay

88. Which of the following is a composition by Kedarnath Prasad?
(a) Problems of Economy in the Third World
(b) History of Bihar
(c) Partition of Bihar
(d) Backwardness of Bihar

89. Which of the following is a serial in which Shekhar Suman acted?
(a) Pol Khol
(b) Reporter
(c) Dekh Bhai Dekh
(d) All of the above

90. To which area did Shrikant Thakur Vidya Alankar belong?
(a) Journalism (b) Politics
(c) Stage (d) Medical care

91. In which of the following Hindi literatures, Shrikant Thakur Vidya Alankar worked as an Assistant Editor?
(a) Mahatma (b) Mahavir
(c) Chintan (d) Karamvir

92. Which of the following magazines was edited by Shrikant Thakur Vidya Alankar?
(a) Anand (b) Chotarfa
(c) Sangharsh (d) Vishwamitra

93. In the year 1947, Shrikant Thakur Vidya Alankar had edited which magazine?
(a) Pratap (b) Prabhat
(c) Pradeep (d) Pratikriya

94. In which district of Bihar was Shri Krishna Singh born?
(a) Nawada (b) Vaishali
(c) Munger (d) Saran

95. When was Shri Krishna Singh born?
(a) 18 March 1887
(b) 14 May 1887
(c) 20 June 1887
(d) 21 October 1887

96. In the year 1937, under whose leadership in Bihar, a cabinet was formed?
(a) Jaiprakash Narayan
(b) Anugrah Narayan Sinha
(c) Shri Krishna Singh
(d) Prof. Abdul Bari

97. When did Shri Krishna Singh die?
(a) 1959 AD (b) 1960 AD
(c) 1961 AD (d) 1962 AD

98. Which of the following plays has been directed by Sanjay Upadhyay?
(a) Samaj (b) Bakri
(c) Videshiya (d) Both (b) and (c)

99. Which of the following plays belongs to Sanjay Upadhyay?
(a) Jasma Orhan
(b) Nal Damyanti
(c) Khadiya ka ghera
(d) All of the above

100. 'Dastan-e-hub' is a play which belongs to who of the following?
(a) Sanjay Upadhyay
(b) Mandan Mishra
(c) Ghulam Gaus
(d) Shaukat Aziz

101. Sachchidanand Sinha was born in which district of Bihar?
(a) Arwal (b) Vaishali
(c) Saran (d) Arrah

102. When did the second session of Bihar Provincial Conference take place?
(a) 1908 AD (b) 1909 AD
(c) 1910 AD (d) 1911 AD

103. Where did the second session of Bihar Provincial Conference take place?
(a) Motihari (b) Betiya
(c) Patna (d) Bhagalpur

104. Who presided over the second session of Bihar Provincial Conference?
(a) Jagatnarayan Seth
(b) Prof. Abdul Bari
(c) Rajendra Prasad
(d) Sachchidanand Sinha

105. When was 'Smt. Radhika Sinha and Sachchidanand Sinha Library' established?
(a) 1924 AD (b) 1925 AD
(c) 1926 AD (d) 1927 AD

106. When was Sachchidanand Sinha appointed the first non-government Vice Chancellor of Patna University?
(a) 1933 AD (b) 1934 AD
(c) 1935 AD (d) 1936 AD

107. In which district of Bihar, was Sir Ganesh Dutt born?
(a) Navada (b) Nalanda
(c) Saran (d) Vaishali

108. When was Sir Ganesha Dutt elected for Bihar Legislative Assembly?
(a) 1919 AD (b) 1920 AD
(c) 1921 AD (d) 1922 AD

109. Siyaram Tiwari was a famous singer of __________.
(a) Dhrupad (b) Thumri
(c) Khyal (d) All of these

110. When was Siyaram Tiwari honoured with a gold medal?
(a) 1954 AD (b) 1955 AD
(c) 1956 AD (d) 1957 AD

111. When was Siyaram Tiwari honoured by the Madhya Pradesh Government with 'Tansen' Award?
(a) 1996 AD (b) 1997 AD
(c) 1998 AD (d) 1999 AD

112. Dr. C. P. Thakur successfully discovered treatment of which disease?
(a) Measles (b) Cataract
(c) Jaundice (d) Black fever

113. Which of the following is a book composed by C. P. Thakur?
(a) Dynamics of Development
(b) World Trade Organisation
(c) Glimpses of Indian Technology
(d) All of the above

114. Who is the author of the Book called 'India under Atal Bihari Vajpayee'?
(a) Kedarnath Prasad
(b) C. P. Thakur
(c) Ravishankar Prasad
(d) Anurag Mishra

115. In which district of Bihar, was Jagdev Prasad born?
(a) Arwal (b) Jamui
(c) Jehanabad (d) Shivhar

116. Which magazine was edited by Jagdev Prasad?
(a) Satta (b) Uday
(c) Citizen (d) All of these

117. In which district of Bihar was Lalit Narayan Mishra born?
(a) Aurangabad (b) Saharasa
(c) Navada (d) Gaya

118. Where was Peer Ali hanged by the British?
(a) Bankipur
(b) Bihar Sharif
(c) Rajgir
(d) Pavapuri

119. From where did Peer Ali lead in the 1857 independence revolution?
(a) Arrah (b) Danapur
(c) Patna (d) Bhagalpur

120. Under whose leadership was 'Bihar Policemen Association' formed?
(a) Ramanand Tiwari
(b) Baikunth Shukla
(c) Haider Ali
(d) Jaglal Choudhry

121. When was 'Bihar Policemen Association' founded?
(a) 1944 AD (b) 1945 AD
(c) 1946 AD (d) 1947 AD

122. When is the birthday anniversary of Ramanand Tiwari celebrated each year?
(a) 25 March (b) 8 April
(c) 12 May (d) 14 June

123. In which district of Bihar was Suraj Narain Singh born?
(a) Shivhar (b) Mujaffarpur
(c) Arwal (d) Darbhanga

124. Who of the following became an active member of the Hindustan Socialist Republican Party at a young age of 22 only?
(a) Jaglal Choudhary
(b) Dhruv Gupta
(c) Suraj Narayan Singh
(d) Prof. Abdul Bari

125. When was Suraj Narayan Singh elected a legislator for the first time?
(a) 1952 (b) 1957
(c) 1960 (d) 1962

126. Who of the following was a disciple of the famous philosopher Kumaril Bhatt?
(a) Mandan Mishra
(b) Mandan Bharti
(c) Dhruv Narayan
(d) Sanjiv Jha

127. Acharya Kumaril Bhatt was counted amongst the great scholars of which place?
(a) Sitamarhi (b) Saharasa
(c) Shivhar (d) Darbhanga

128. Which ideology was propounded by Kumaril Bhatt?
(a) Nyaya (b) Mimansa
(c) Karma (d) All of these

129. In which district of Bihar was Udnacharya born?
(a) Darbhanga (b) Vaishali
(c) Munger (d) Chhapra

130. Udnacharya was a scholar of which ideology?
(a) Mimansa
(b) Nyaya
(c) Vaisheshik
(d) Both (b) and (c)

131. Which of the following was composed by Udnacharya?
(a) Kiranbali
(b) Lakshnavali
(c) Aatmatva Vivek
(d) All of the above

132. Aryabhatt was a mathematician and astronomer of which age?
(a) Mauryan Age
(b) Gupta Age
(c) Kanva Age
(d) Shunga Age

133. Which place in Bihar is considered to be the birthplace of Aryabhatt?
(a) Patliputra (b) Vaishali
(c) Nalanda (d) Pavapuri

134. Discovery of which of the following was made by Aryabhatt?
(a) Yoga (b) Zero
(c) Decimal (d) All of these

135. Who had first told that Sun and Moon eclipse occur due to the shadow of the moon on the earth?
(a) Chanakya (b) Amar Singh
(c) Aryabhatt (d) Udnacharya

136. From the ancient literary sources it is gathered that Aryabhatt was the Chancellor of which University?
(a) Takshshila (b) Nalanda
(c) Vikramshila (d) Odantpuri

137. What is the value of a Pi according to Aryabhatt?
(a) 3.1416 (b) 3.2416
(c) 3.34218 (d) 3.4114

138. Which of the following is a composition of Panini?
(a) Abhgyanshakuntalam
(b) Mimansa
(c) Ashtadhyayi
(d) Shunayavad

139. The knowledge of the administration of which dynasty is available in 'Ashtadhyayi'?
(a) Maurya (b) Gupta
(c) Shunga (d) Kanva

140. Yagyavalkya was a contemporary of which of the following kings?
(a) Dasrath
(b) Ashok
(c) Harshvardhan
(d) Janak

141. Who of the following Sikh Gurus, had made 'Panch Karaar' compulsory?
(a) Guru Nanak
(b) Guru Teg Bahadur
(c) Guru Ramdas
(d) Guru Govind Singh

142. Who of the following was there in the 'Panch Karaar'?
(a) Kangha (b) Kada
(c) Kachha (d) All of these

143. Which Guru had given the slogan of 'Sat Shri Akaal'?
(a) Gobind Singh
(b) Nanak
(c) Ramdas
(d) Teg Bahadur

144. Guru Gobind Singh had started which 'Panth'?
(a) Khalsa
(b) Singh
(c) Darbar Sahib
(d) Nanak

145. After which Guru, the tradition of Guru had seized to be in existence in Sikh religion?
(a) Ramdas
(b) Gobind Singh
(c) Teg Bahadur
(d) Nanak

146. When did death of Guru Gobind Singh had occurred?
(a) 1706 AD (b) 1707 AD
(c) 1708 AD (d) 1709 AD

147. Who of the following had made a national issue out of 'Bihar-Bihariyon ke liye'?
(a) Mahesh Narayan
(b) Ganesh Poddar
(c) Abhijit Mandal
(d) Prof. Abdul Bari

148. Which magazine was edited by Mahesh Narayan?
(a) Times of Bihar
(b) Bihar Times
(c) The Bihar
(d) Bihar Samay

149. When did Nand Kishore Lal become the main propagandist of Bihar Times?
(a) 1890 AD (b) 1892 AD
(c) 1894 AD (d) 1896 AD

150. In which district of Bihar was Maulana Mazhrul Haque born?
(a) Patna
(b) Gaya
(c) Bihar Sharif
(d) Mujaffarpur

151. Who of the following had formed 'Anjuman-e-Islamia'?
(a) Hakim Ajmal Khan
(b) Hasrat Mohani
(c) Maulana Mazhrul Haque
(d) Shoukat Ali

152. In the year 1896 Maulana Mazhrul Haque was elected the vice-chairman of the city council of which city?
(a) Chhapra (b) Gopalganj
(c) Darbhanga (d) Navada

153. Who of the following had established 'Sadaqat Ashram'?
(a) Sajjad Ali
(b) Hasrat Mohani
(c) Hasan Imam
(d) Maulana Mazhrul Haque

154. When did Maulana Mazhrul Haque die?
(a) 1926 AD (b) 1928 AD
(c) 1930 AD (d) 1932 AD

155. Kalawati Devi was born in which district of Bihar?
(a) Arariya (b) Arwal
(c) Jamui (d) Jehanabad

156. When was Kalawati Devi honoured with a 'Padma Shri'?
(a) 1972 AD (b) 1974 AD
(c) 1976 AD (d) 1978 AD

157. Which of the following is a distinct work of Nandlal Bose?
(a) Gauri (b) Yamuna
(c) Perumal (d) All of these

158. With which of the following awards Shobhna Narayan was honoured?
(a) Sangeet Natak Academy
(b) Indira Priyadarshini
(c) Rajiv Smriti
(d) All of the above

159. Which of the following is a famous book of Amarnath Jha?
(a) Vichardhara
(b) Occasional addresses
(c) Shakespearian Comedy
(d) All of the above

160. Pt. Indra Kishore Mishra 'Mallick' was a famous musician of which family?
(a) Betiya (b) Gaya
(c) Patna (d) Darbhanga

161. In which district of Bihar, Ishwar Chandra Gupta was born?
(a) Madhepura (b) Madhubani
(c) Saharasa (d) Arariya

162. Who of the following had enlightened name of Bihar in 'Chakshun Art'?

(a) Prashant Kishore
(b) Prabhat Bhushan
(c) Ishwar Chandra Gupta
(d) Mandan Mishra

163. Who of the following was a great sculptor?
(a) Ishwar Chandra Gupta
(b) Brij Kishore Sharma
(c) Amanat Sheikh
(d) Bulo Mandal

164. Which of the following is a sculpture made by Ishwar Chandra Gupta?
(a) Ram-Sita
(b) Sitamarhi ki Sita
(c) Ayodhya ke Ram
(d) Sita Ek Khoj

165. Ishwari Prasad Mishra was a painter of which style?
(a) Patna Kalam
(b) Madhubani Kala
(c) Manjusha Kala
(d) All of the above

166. The great actress Kumkum was born in which district of Bihar?
(a) Shivhar (b) Sitamarhi
(c) Arwal (d) Sheikhpura

167. What was the original name of the film actress Kumkum?
(a) Jebunnisa
(b) Jahan Arra
(c) Nusrat Arra
(d) Mehak Parveen

168. At which place in Bihar, Shad Aminabadi was born?
(a) Danapur
(b) Bihar Sharif
(c) Patna
(d) Mujaffarpur

169. Which was the first film of the actress Kumkum?
(a) Angare (b) Jhansi ki Rani
(c) Pyasa (d) Mirza Ghalib

170. Which of the following films belong to Kumkum?
(a) Kagaz ke Phool
(b) Mother India
(c) Geet
(d) All of the above

171. When was 'Jalte Badan,' the last film of actress Kumkum released?
(a) 1971 AD (b) 1972 AD
(c) 1973 AD (d) 1974 AD

172. Kumud Sharma started her art journey by copying Patna Kalam and ________.
(a) Madhubani Painting Art
(b) Pahadi Style
(c) Raja Ravi Verma
(d) Manjusha Style

173. Krishna Kumar Kashyap has written books on which painting style?
(a) Madhubani Painting Art
(b) Patna Kalam
(c) Mughal Art
(d) Manjusha Style

174. Which of the following books is written by Krishna Kumar Kashyap?
(a) Bahar (b) Aakhar
(c) Manmohak (d) Mithila

175. Where was Mithila Painting University established in honour of Krishna Kumar Kashyap?
(a) Bhagalpur (b) Darbhanga
(c) Madhubani (d) Saharasa

176. Which of the following is a composition of Gajendra Narayan Singh?
(a) Saptak
(b) Swarganga
(c) Bihar ka Sangeet
(d) All of the above

177. When was Gajendra Narayan Singh honoured with 'Bihar Ratna'?
(a) 2006 AD (b) 2008 AD
(c) 2010 AD (d) 2012 AD

178. Jagdamba Devi was born in which district of Bihar?
(a) Darbhanga (b) Saharasa
(c) Khagariya (d) Madhubani

179. Jagdamba Devi was a painter of which style?
(a) Manjusha (b) Madhubani
(c) Patna Kalam (d) Company Style

180. When was Jagdamba Devi given the national award for handicraft?
(a) 1966 AD (b) 1968 AD
(c) 1970 AD (d) 1972 AD

181. Who is the author of 'A History of Maithili Literature'?
(a) Jaikant Mishra
(b) Jagdamba Devi
(c) Mandan Mishra
(d) Umakant Jha

182. When was Jaikant Mishra given the honour of 'Bhasha Samman'by Sahitya Akadami?
(a) 1998 AD (b) 1999 AD
(c) 2000 AD (d) 2001 AD

183. In which district of Bihar, Pyare Mohan Sahay was born?
(a) Mujaffarpur
(b) Motihari
(c) Vaishali
(d) Madhepura

184. Who of the following had established Patliputra Art Temple?
(a) Anand Mohan Jha
(b) Raghuvansh Sahay
(c) Pyare Mohan Sahay
(d) Rajan Shrivastava

185. Mahasundari Devi was a painter of which style?
(a) Madhubani Painting Art
(b) Manjusha Style
(c) Patna Kalam
(d) Mughal Style

186. Yashoda Devi was related to which style of painting?
(a) Patna Kalam
(b) Pahadi Chitrakala
(c) Manjusha Style
(d) Madhubani Painting Art

187. When was Yashoda Devi honoured with 'Çhitragupta Samman'?
(a) 1981 AD (b) 1982 AD
(c) 1983 AD (d) 1984 AD

188. Which of the following is a book written by Yogendra Mishra?
(a) Ashok
(b) History of Videha
(c) Shwetpur ki Khoj
(d) All of the above

189. Who is the writer of 'The Hindu Shaheen of Afghanistan and Punjab'?
(a) Yogendra Mishra
(b) Ramvinay Singh
(c) Jagdamba Prasad
(d) Diwakar Sen

190. Which of the following is a composition of Yogendra Mishra?
(a) University of Vaishali
(b) University of Odantpuri
(c) Vaishali and its Remains
(d) Both (b) and (c)

191. Where was the famous historian Ramsharan Sharma born?
(a) Bihar Sharif (b) Vaishali
(c) Barauni (d) Motihari

192. When did Ramsharan Sharma become the Head of the Department of History in Patna University?
(a) 1958 AD (b) 1957 AD
(c) 1956 AD (d) 1955 AD

193. Which of the following is a book written by Ramsharan Sharma?
(a) Bhartiya Samantvad
(b) Prarambhik Bharat ka parichay
(c) Shudron ka pracheen itihas
(d) All of the above

194. Who wrote the book, 'Prachin Bharat mein rajneetik vichar evam sansthayen'?
(a) Ramsharan Sharma
(b) Devendra Mishra
(c) Umakant Jha
(d) Vinayak Sen

195. In which district of Bihar Dr Vishishttha Narayan Singh was born?
(a) Madhepura
(b) Saharasa
(c) Arariya
(d) Bhojpur

196. Dr. Vishishttha Narayan Singh was connected with which campaign of NASA?
(a) Mars Mission
(b) Apollo Campaign
(c) Peter Mission
(d) Pacific Mission

197. Which of the following is considered to be the father of Bhojpuri Cinema?
(a) Kunal
(b) Manoj Tiger
(c) Vishwanath Prasad Shahbadi
(d) Dinkar Mishra

198. When was the first Bhojpuri film produced in Bihar?
(a) 1962 AD
(b) 1964 AD
(c) 1966 AD
(d) 1968 AD

199. Which of the following is the first Bhojpuri film produced in Bihari?
(a) Kanyadan
(b) Vivah
(c) Gangapaar
(d) Ganga Maiyya Tohe Pihari Chadaibo

200. Which of the following films was produced by Vishwanath Prasad Shahabadi?
(a) Solhan singar kare dulhaniyan
(b) Rootha na karo
(c) Gangadham
(d) All of the above

201. Which of the following films is not a film produced by Vishwanath Prasad Shahabadi?
(a) Geetganga
(b) Ghayal
(c) Sasural
(d) Tulsi aur Ghar Jamai

202. Which of following is a dance and play created by Vishbandhu?
(a) Megh Malhar
(b) Ajhan ke bhor
(c) Hiran-Hirni
(d) All of the above

Answers

1. (c)	**2.** (d)	**3.** (a)	**4.** (c)	**5.** (b)	**6.** (c)	**7.** (b)	**8.** (d)	**9.** (a)	**10.** (c)
11. (a)	**12.** (d)	**13.** (b)	**14.** (a)	**15.** (b)	**16.** (c)	**17.** (b)	**18.** (a)	**19.** (d)	**20.** (b)
21. (d)	**22.** (a)	**23.** (c)	**24.** (a)	**25.** (c)	**26.** (a)	**27.** (c)	**28.** (c)	**29.** (a)	**30.** (d)
31. (c)	**32.** (d)	**33.** (c)	**34.** (d)	**35.** (a)	**36.** (c)	**37.** (a)	**38.** (d)	**39.** (a)	**40.** (d)
41. (d)	**42.** (a)	**43.** (a)	**44.** (c)	**45.** (d)	**46.** (a)	**47.** (b)	**48.** (c)	**49.** (a)	**50.** (b)
51. (d)	**52.** (a)	**53.** (d)	**54.** (c)	**55.** (a)	**56.** (c)	**57.** (a)	**58.** (b)	**59.** (c)	**60.** (c)
61. (c)	**62.** (d)	**63.** (d)	**64.** (c)	**65.** (a)	**66.** (d)	**67.** (a)	**68.** (c)	**69.** (a)	**70.** (b)

71. (d)	**72.** (c)	**73.** (c)	**74.** (a)	**75.** (c)	**76.** (d)	**77.** (d)	**78.** (c)	**79.** (b)	**80.** (d)
81. (a)	**82.** (d)	**83.** (a)	**84.** (d)	**85.** (c)	**86.** (d)	**87.** (c)	**88.** (a)	**89.** (d)	**90.** (a)
91. (b)	**92.** (d)	**93.** (c)	**94.** (a)	**95.** (d)	**96.** (c)	**97.** (c)	**98.** (d)	**99.** (d)	**100.** (a)
101. (d)	**102.** (b)	**103.** (d)	**104.** (d)	**105.** (a)	**106.** (d)	**107.** (b)	**108.** (c)	**109.** (a)	**110.** (b)
111. (c)	**112.** (d)	**113.** (d)	**114.** (b)	**115.** (a)	**116.** (d)	**117.** (b)	**118.** (a)	**119.** (c)	**120.** (a)
121. (c)	**122.** (a)	**123.** (c)	**124.** (d)	**125.** (c)	**126.** (b)	**127.** (d)	**128.** (d)	**129.** (a)	**130.** (d)
131. (d)	**132.** (b)	**133.** (a)	**134.** (d)	**135.** (c)	**136.** (b)	**137.** (a)	**138.** (c)	**139.** (a)	**140.** (d)
141. (d)	**142.** (d)	**143.** (a)	**144.** (a)	**145.** (b)	**146.** (c)	**147.** (a)	**148.** (b)	**149.** (c)	**150.** (a)
151. (c)	**152.** (a)	**153.** (c)	**154.** (a)	**155.** (a)	**156.** (c)	**157.** (d)	**158.** (d)	**159.** (d)	**160.** (a)
161. (b)	**162.** (c)	**163.** (a)	**164.** (d)	**165.** (a)	**166.** (d)	**167.** (a)	**168.** (c)	**169.** (d)	**170.** (d)
171. (c)	**172.** (c)	**173.** (a)	**174.** (b)	**175.** (c)	**176.** (d)	**177.** (b)	**178.** (d)	**179.** (b)	**180.** (c)
181. (a)	**182.** (c)	**183.** (a)	**184.** (c)	**185.** (a)	**186.** (d)	**187.** (c)	**188.** (d)	**189.** (a)	**190.** (d)
191. (c)	**192.** (a)	**193.** (d)	**194.** (a)	**195.** (d)	**196.** (b)	**197.** (c)	**198.** (a)	**199.** (d)	**200.** (d)
201. (b)	**202.** (d)								

❑❑❑

12 Education, Health and Sports

EDUCATION

1. Which of the following were the ancient Educational Institutions situated in Bihar?
(a) Odantipur University
(b) Nalanda University
(c) Vikramshila University
(d) All of the above

2. What was the literacy rate in Bihar according to 2011 census?
(a) 61.8% (b) 62.2%
(c) 63.5% (d) 64.1%

3. What was the male literacy rate in Bihar according to 2011 census?
(a) 67.3% (b) 68.4%
(c) 69.5% (d) 71.2%

4. What was the female literacy rate in Bihar according to 2011 census?
(a) 50.3% (b) 51.5%
(c) 52.2% (d) 53.1%

5. Bihar registered an increase of what percentage in literacy rate during 2001 to 2011?
(a) 14.2% (b) 15.6%
(c) 16.7% (d) 17.9%

6. What is the students-teacher ratio at primary level education in Bihar?
(a) 40:1 (b) 46:1
(c) 53:1 (d) 58:1

7. Which campaign was launched in Bihar to connect children of 6-14 years age group with Education?
(a) Sankalp
(b) Shikshaunnati
(c) Samiksha
(d) Anugrah

8. Which centre was started for emancipation of the Muslim children?
(a) Maktab (b) Talimi Markaj
(c) Markaj (d) Aalimi Markaj

9. Which centre was launched for emancipation of 'Dalit' children?
(a) Ambedkar Centre
(b) Unnati Centre
(c) Utthan Centre
(d) Jagriti Centre

10. 40000 rooms and ______ play grounds have been constructed in Bihar under the Chief Minsiter Integrated School Development Scheme.
(a) 10000 (b) 13000
(c) 17000 (d) 20000

11. Under which scheme, the school children in Bihar are getting an opportunity to travel outside?
(a) Mukhyamantri Darshan Yojna
(b) Mukhyamantri Protsahan Yojna
(c) Mukhyamantri Tirath Yojna
(d) Mukhyamantri Samaroh Yojna

12. Under which scheme in Bihar, girls from the minority communities are given vocational training?
(a) Hunar (b) Roshni
(c) Nai Manzil (d) Ustad

13. **Which vocational training programme has been launched to encourage girls education in 31 border blocks of Bihar?**
(a) Gyan Setu
(b) Gyan Sangam
(c) Gyan Jyoti
(d) Gyan Divya

14. **Under 'Mukhyamantri Balika and Balak Cycle yojna,' how much money per student is granted to the students studying in the 9th class?**
(a) 2000 (b) 2100
(c) 2250 (d) 2500

15. **When is Education Day observed in Bihar?**
(a) 22 March (b) 18 May
(c) 20 June (d) 11 November

16. **On birthday of which of the following political leaders, Education Day is observed in Bihar?**
(a) Maulana Abul Kalam Azad
(b) Rajendra Prasad
(c) Shri Krishna Singh
(d) Jaiprakash Narayan

17. **Where is Nagarjuna Museum situated in Bihar?**
(a) Patna (b) Jamui
(c) Navada (d) Jehanabad

18. **When was 'Bihar Shiksha Pariyojana Parishad' established?**
(a) 1989 AD (b) 1990 AD
(c) 1991 AD (d) 1992 AD

19. **Who had in Bihar advocated for free and compulsory education for the first time?**
(a) Maulana Mazharul Haque
(b) Shrikrishna
(c) Anugraha Narayan Singh
(d) Rajendra Prasad

20. **When did Shrikrishna Singh government in Bihar initiate the programme of elimination of illiteracy?**
(a) 1937 AD (b) 1938 AD
(c) 1939 AD (d) 1940 AD

21. **When did Government of India launch adult education programme?**
(a) 1975 AD (b) 1976 AD
(c) 1977 AD (d) 1978 AD

22. **When was in Bihar Literacy Mission launched with the support from Government of India?**
(a) 1986 AD (b) 1987 AD
(c) 1988 AD (d) 1989 AD

23. **In which district of Bihar, literacy mission was started for the first time?**
(a) Saran (b) Mujaffarpur
(c) Munger (d) Navada

24. **Which of the following is included under national literacy mission?**
(a) Total Literacy campaign
(b) Post Literacy programme
(c) Continuous Education Programme
(d) All of the above

25. **When was Total Literacy Campaign launched?**
(a) 1989 AD (b) 1990 AD
(c) 1991 AD (d) 1992 AD

26. **From which district of Bihar, Total Literacy Programme was launched?**
(a) Vaishali
(b) Eastern Champaran
(c) Madhepura
(d) Madhubani

27. **Which Forum was constituted in the schools of Bihar for girls empowerment?**
(a) Meena Forum
(b) Prabha Forum
(c) Jyoti Forum
(d) Vidya Forum

28. **When was 'Bihar Free Schooling and Education Board' constituted by the Government of Bihar?**
(a) 2009 AD (b) 2010 AD
(c) 2011 AD (d) 2012 AD

29. **When was the right to education declared as a fundamental right?**
(a) 1999 AD (b) 2000 AD
(c) 2001 AD (d) 2002 AD

30. **Under which constitutional amendment, the right to education was declared as a fundamental right?**
(a) 84th (b) 85th
(c) 86th (d) 87th

31. **Under which article of the Indian Constitution, right to education was announced as a fundamental right?**
(a) Article 21 (a)
(b) Article 22 (a)
(c) Article 23 (a)
(d) Article 24 (a)

32. **In Indian Constitution under fundamental duty, which article makes education compulsory?**
(a) Article 49 (a)
(b) Article 50 (a)
(c) Article 51 (a)
(d) Article 52 (a)

33. **Gross nomination rate at the national level for classes from 1 to 8 is the lowest in which of the states?**
(a) Bihar
(b) Uttar Pradesh
(c) Madhya Pradesh
(d) Orissa

34. **When was literacy programme launched by the Government of India?**
(a) 2006 AD (b) 2007 AD
(c) 2008 AD (d) 2009 AD

35. **Under Literate Bharat Campaign, what is the expense ratio of the Centre and the states?**
(a) 60:40 (b) 50:50
(c) 70:30 (d) 75:25

36. **The aim of Literate Bharat Campaign is to educate illiterates of the age of above________ years and increase literacy rate among the women?**
(a) 15 (b) 12
(c) 10 (d) 8

37. **When is Voters' Day celebrated every year?**
(a) 25 June (b) 18 May
(c) 13 March (d) 25 January

38. **Since when is 'Voters' Day' celebrated each year?**
(a) 2008 AD (b) 2009 AD
(c) 2010 AD (d) 2011 AD

39. **When was 'Sakshar Bharat' campaign launched in Bihar?**
(a) 2008 AD (b) 2009 AD
(c) 2010 AD (d) 2011 AD

40. **When was 'Akshar Aanchal' scheme launched to increase women literacy?**
(a) 2008 AD (b) 2009 AD
(c) 2010 AD (d) 2011 AD

41. **In which state of the country, lowest literacy rate prevails as per the 2011 census?**
(a) Jharkhand (b) Rajasthan
(c) Orissa (d) Bihar

42. **When was Patna University established?**
(a) 1915 AD (b) 1916 AD
(c) 1917 AD (d) 1918 AD

43. **Where was B. R. Ambedkar University founded?**
(a) Vaishali (b) Mujaffarpur
(c) Nalanda (d) Bhagalpur

44. **When B. R. Ambedkar University founded?**
(a) 1948 AD (b) 1950 AD
(c) 1952 AD (d) 1954 AD

45. Where was Tilka Manjhi University established?
(a) Bhagalpur (b) Arwal
(c) Jamui (d) Nalanda

46. When was Tilka Manjhi University founded?
(a) 1954 AD (b) 1956 AD
(c) 1958 AD (d) 1960 AD

47. Where is ASDS University situated?
(a) Madhubani (b) Navada
(c) Darbhanga (d) Bhagalpur

48. When was ASDS University founded?
(a) 1956 AD (b) 1958 AD
(c) 1960 AD (d) 1961 AD

49. Where is Magadh University is situated?
(a) Bodh Gaya (b) Nalanda
(c) Vaishali (d) Aurangabad

50. When was Magadh University founded?
(a) 1956 AD (b) 1958 AD
(c) 1960 AD (d) 1962 AD

51. Where is Rajendra Krishi University situated?
(a) Nalanda (b) Samastipur
(c) Vaishali (d) Patna

52. When was Rajendra Krishi University founded?
(a) 1966 AD (b) 1968 AD
(c) 1970 AD (d) 1972 AD

53. Where is Lalit Narayan Mishra University situated?
(a) Darbhanga (b) Saharasa
(c) Khagadiya (d) Jehanabad

54. When was Lalit Narayan University founded?
(a) 1966 AD (b) 1968 AD
(c) 1970 AD (d) 1972 AD

55. Where is Nalanda Open University situated?
(a) Buxar (b) Nalanda
(c) Patna (d) Mujaffarpur

56. When was Nalanda Open University founded?
(a) 1981 AD (b) 1983 AD
(c) 1985 AD (d) 1987 AD

57. Where is Veer Kunwar Singh University situated?
(a) Arrah (b) Buxar
(c) Vaishali (d) Patna

58. When was Veer Kunwar Singh University founded?
(a) 1980 AD (b) 1988 AD
(c) 1990 AD (d) 1992 AD

59. Where is Bhupendra Narayan Mandal University situated?
(a) Madhepura (b) Purnia
(c) Kishanganj (d) Saharasa

60. When was Bhupendra Narayan Mandal University founded?
(a) 1984 AD (b) 1986 AD
(c) 1988 AD (d) 1990 AD

61. Where is Jai Prakash Narayan University situated?
(a) Saran (b) Siwan
(c) Gopalganj (d) Patna

62. When was Jaiprakash Narayan University founded?
(a) 1996 AD (b) 1994 AD
(c) 1992 AD (d) 1990 AD

63. Where is Maulana Mazharul Haque Arabian-Persian University situated?
(a) Bihar Sharif
(b) Patna
(c) Rajgir
(d) Motihari

64. When was Maulana Mazharul Haque Arabian-Persian University founded?
(a) 1992 AD (b) 1994 AD
(c) 1996 AD (d) 1998 AD

65. Where is Bihar Agriculture University situated?
(a) Sabour (b) Pavapuri
(c) Motihari (d) Rajgir

66. When was Bihar Agriculture University founded?
(a) 2000 AD (b) 2002 AD
(c) 2004 AD (d) 2006 AD

67. Where in Bihar is Central University situated?
(a) Rajgir (b) Patna
(c) Hajipur (d) Gaya

68. When was Central University founded in Bihar?
(a) 2001 AD (b) 2003 AD
(c) 2005 AD (d) 2006 AD

69. Where in Bihar is Chanakya National University situated?
(a) Darbhanga (b) Motihari
(c) Mujaffarpur (d) Patna

70. When was Chanakya National Law University founded?
(a) 2007 AD (b) 2006 AD
(c) 2005 AD (d) 2004 AD

71. Where is Aryabhatt Technical University situated?
(a) Rajgir (b) Patna
(c) Betiya (d) Darbhanga

72. Where is Nalanda International University situated?
(a) Rajgir (b) Patna
(c) Betiya (d) Darbhanga

73. When was Nalanda International University founded?
(a) 2006 AD (b) 2007 AD
(c) 2008 AD (d) 2009 AD

74. Where is Bihar Yoga Bharti University situated?
(a) Bhagalpur (b) Rajgir
(c) Munger (d) Hajipur

75. In which of the following districts, Central University exists?
(a) East Champaran
(b) Vaishali
(c) Munger
(d) Bhagalpur

76. In which district of Bihar, a branch of Aligarh Muslim University is about to be launched?
(a) Purnia (b) Patna
(c) Kishanganj (d) Saharasa

77. When was Patna Medical College founded?
(a) 1919 AD (b) 1921 AD
(c) 1923 AD (d) 1925 AD

78. When was Darbhanga Medical College founded?
(a) 1947 AD (b) 1945 AD
(c) 1943 AD (d) 1941 AD

79. Where is A. N. Magadh Medical College situated?
(a) Darbhanga (b) Patna
(c) Gaya (d) Aurangabad

80. When was A. N. Magadh medical College founded?
(a) 1966 AD (b) 1967 AD
(c) 1968 AD (d) 1969 AD

81. Where is Nalanda Medical College situated?
(a) Navada (b) Rajgir
(c) Patna (d) Darbhanga

82. When was Nalanda medical College founded?
(a) 1969 AD (b) 1968 AD
(c) 1967 AD (d) 1966 AD

83. Where is S. K. Medical College situated?
(a) Darbhanga (b) Begusarai
(c) Rajgir (d) Mujaffarpur

84. When was S. K. Medical College established?
(a) 1969 AD (b) 1971 AD
(c) 1973 AD (d) 1975 AD

85. Where in Bihar is Jawaharlal Nehru Medical College situated?
(a) Munger (b) Madhepura
(c) Bhagalpur (d) Katihar

86. When was Jawaharlal Nehru medical College founded in Bhagalpur?
(a) 1970 AD (b) 1971 AD
(c) 1972 AD (d) 1973 AD

87. Where in Bihar is Indira Gandhi Ayurveda Institution situated?
(a) Mujaffarpur (b) Hajipur
(c) Patna (d) Begusarai

88. When was Indira Gandhi Ayurveda Institution founded in Patna?
(a) 1981 AD (b) 1983 AD
(c) 1985 AD (d) 1987 AD

89. Where is Jannayak Karpuri Thakur Medical College situated?
(a) Patna (b) Bhagalpur
(c) Munger (d) Madhepura

90. When was Jannayak Karpuri Thakur Medical College founded?
(a) 1998 AD (b) 1999 AD
(c) 2000 AD (d) 2001 AD

91. Where is Government Medical University situated?
(a) Darbhanga (b) Betiya
(c) Motihari (d) Hajipur

92. When was Government Medical University founded?
(a) 2006 AD (b) 2007 AD
(c) 2008 AD (d) 2009 AD

93. Where in Bihar is All India Institute of Medical Sciences situated?
(a) Patna (b) Hajipur
(c) Gaya (d) Mujaffarpur

94. When was Patna situated All India Institute of Medical Sciences founded?
(a) 2009 AD (b) 2010 AD
(c) 2011 AD (d) 2012 AD

95. Where is Mata Gurjari Memorial Medical College situated?
(a) Purnia (b) Begusarai
(c) Kishanganj (d) Darbhanga

96. When was Mata Gurjari Memorial Medical College founded?
(a) 2003 AD (b) 2001 AD
(c) 1999 AD (d) 1997 AD

97. When was Katihar Medical College founded?
(a) 1999 AD (b) 2000 AD
(c) 2001 AD (d) 2002 AD

98. Where in Bihar is Buddha Dental College situated?
(a) Patna (b) Gaya
(c) Hajipur (d) Barauni

99. When was Darbhanga Dental College founded?
(a) 1986 AD (b) 1988 AD
(c) 1990 AD (d) 1992 AD

100. Where is faculty of Veterinary Science and Animal Husbandry situated?
(a) Samastipur (b) Purnia
(c) Katihar (d) Bhagalpur

101. Where in Bihar is Rajendra Prasad Medical College founded?
(a) Chhapra (b) Siwan
(c) Gopalganj (d) Patna

102. Where in Bihar is Yatindra Narayan Ashtang Ayurvedic College situated?
(a) Hajipur (b) Rajgir
(c) Bhagalpur (d) Pavapuri

103. Where is Rajkiya Aarogya Shivkumari Ayurvedic College situated?
(a) Barauni (b) Begusarai
(c) Saharasa (d) Madhepura

104. Where is Government Tibbati-Yunani Medical University situated?
(a) Patna (b) Mujaffarpur
(c) Hajipur (d) Bihar Sharif

105. Where is Maharani Rameshwari Ayurvedic College situated?
(a) Hajipur (b) Rajgir
(c) Madhubani (d) Darbhanga

106. Where is Vardhman Mahavir Ayurvedic Sansthan situated?
(a) Nalanda
(b) Pavapuri
(c) Vaishali
(d) Bodh Gaya

107. Where is Faculty of Agriculture & Engineering College situated?
(a) Pusa (b) Rajgir
(c) Motihari (d) Betiya

108. Where in Bihar is Indian Institute of Technology situated?
(a) Patna (b) Mujaffarpur
(c) Hajipur (d) Rajgir

109. When was Faculty of Agriculture & Engineering founded?
(a) 1903 AD (b) 1904 AD
(c) 1905 AD (d) 1906 AD

110. When was Indian Institute of Technology founded?
(a) 2008 AD (b) 2006 AD
(c) 2004 AD (d) 2002 AD

111. When was Birla Institute of Technology established in Bihar?
(a) 2004 AD (b) 2005 AD
(c) 2006 AD (d) 2007 AD

112. Where in Bihar is Birla Institute of Technology situated?
(a) Rajgir (b) Patna
(c) Gaya (d) Motihari

113. When was Mujaffar Institute of Technology established?
(a) 1948 AD (b) 1950 AD
(c) 1952 AD (d) 1954 AD

114. When was Bhagalpur College of Engineering Sabaur established?
(a) 1960 AD (b) 1958 AD
(c) 1956 AD (d) 1954 AD

115. When was Loknayak Jaiprakash Narayan Institute of Technology established in Bihar?
(a) 2010 AD (b) 2011 AD
(c) 2012 AD (d) 2013 AD

116. Where has Loknayak Jaiprakash Narayan Institute of Technology been established?
(a) Motihari (b) Chhapra
(c) Siwan (d) Gopalganj

117. When was Bihar College of Engineering granted the status of a National Institute of Technology?
(a) 2002 AD (b) 2003 AD
(c) 2004 AD (d) 2005 AD

118. When was Bihar College of Engineering established?
(a) 1886 AD (b) 1888 AD
(c) 1890 AD (d) 1892 AD

119. Where is Bihar Institute of Silk and Textiles situated?
(a) Bihar Sharif (b) Munger
(c) Bhagalpur (d) Vaishali

120. When was Bihar Institute of Silk and Textiles established?
(a) 1988 AD (b) 1990 AD
(c) 1992 AD (d) 1994 AD

121. Where is Sanjay Gandhi Institute of Dairy Science and Technology situated?
(a) Patna (b) Mujaffarpur
(c) Hajipur (d) Motihari

122. When was Sanjay Gandhi Institute of Dairy Science and Technology established?
(a) 1980 AD (b) 1982 AD
(c) 1984 AD (d) 1986 AD

123. When was Darbhanga Engineering College established?
(a) 2002 AD (b) 2004 AD
(c) 2006 AD (d) 2008 AD

124. When was Nalanda Engineering College founded?
(a) 2008 AD (b) 2006 AD
(c) 2004 AD (d) 2002 AD

125. When was Gaya Engineering College founded?
(a) 2005 AD (b) 2006 AD
(c) 2007 AD (d) 2008 AD

126. Where in Bihar Maulana Azad College of Engineering and Technology situated?
(a) Gaya (b) Patna
(c) Mujaffarpur (d) Rajgir

127. Where in Bihar is R. P. Sharam Institute of Technology situated?
(a) Patna (b) Motihari
(c) Rajgir (d) Vaishali

128. Where is Women Institute of Technology situated?
(a) Hajipur (b) Patna
(c) Darbhanga (d) Rajgir

129. Where is Milia Institute of Technology situated?
(a) Begusarai (b) Purnia
(c) Katihar (d) Bihar Sharif

130. Where is L. N. Mishra College of Business Management situated?
(a) Patna (b) Rajgir
(c) Mujaffarpur (d) Darbhanga

131. When was L. N. Mishra College of Business Management established?
(a) 1969 AD (b) 1971 AD
(c) 1973 AD (d) 1975 AD

132. Where is Lalit Narayan Mishra Institute of Economic Development and Social Change situated?
(a) Darbhanga (b) Mujaffarpur
(c) Madhubani (d) Patna

133. When was Lalit Narayan Mishra Institute of Economic Development and Social Change established?
(a) 1971 AD (b) 1973 AD
(c) 1975 AD (d) 1977 AD

134. Where is Indian Institute of Business Management situated in Bihar?
(a) Hajipur (b) Mujaffarpur
(c) Rajgir (d) Patna

135. When was Indian Institute of Business Management established?
(a) 1970 AD (b) 1978 AD
(c) 1980 AD (d) 1982 AD

136. Where has Chandragupta Management Institute been established?
(a) Hajipur (b) Mujaffarpur
(c) Patna (d) Rajgir

137. When was Chandragupta Management Institute established?
(a) 2008 (b) 2006
(c) 2004 (d) 2002

138. Where in Bihar is Indian Institute of Management situated?
(a) Patna (b) Rajgir
(c) Gaya (d) Bihar Sharif

139. When was Indian Institute of Management established in Bihar?
(a) 2009 AD (b) 2011 AD
(c) 2013 AD (d) 2015 AD

140. Where is TNB Law University situated?
(a) Munger (b) Bhagalpur
(c) Hajipur (d) Motihari

141. Where is Tirhut College of Agriculture situated?
(a) Saran (b) Motihari
(c) Betiya (d) Mujaffarpur

142. Where in Bihar is Central Potato Research Institute located?
(a) Patna (b) Hajipur
(c) Sugauli (d) Vaishali

143. Where in Bihar is 'Lichi Anusandhan Kendra' located?
(a) Patna (b) Gaya
(c) Mujaffarpur (d) Rajgir

144. Where in Bihar is Pulses Research Centre located?
(a) Begusarai (b) Raxaul
(c) Madhubani (d) Mokama

145. Where in Bihar is Corn Research Centre located?
(a) Barauni (b) Begusarai
(c) Rajgir (d) Hajipur

146. Where in Bihar is Water Management Research Centre located?
(a) Patna (b) Rajgir
(c) Hajipur (d) Mujaffarpur

147. Where in Bihar is Potato Reseach Centre located?
(a) Nalanda (b) Navada
(c) Munger (d) Bhagalpur

148. Where in Bihar Government College of Art and Craft is located?
(a) Arrah (b) Buxar
(c) Patna (d) Gaya

149. Where in Bihar Faculty of Fine Arts and Crafts is located?
(a) Bhagalpur (b) Patna
(c) Munger (d) Hajipur

150. Where is TV Demonstration and Training Centre located?
(a) Gaya (b) Vaishali
(c) Bhagalpur (d) Patna

151. Where is Bihar Research Institution located?
(a) Patna (b) Gaya
(c) Bihar Sharif (d) Rajgir

152. Where is K. P. Jaiswal Research Institute located?
(a) Mokama (b) Begusarai
(c) Barauni (d) Patna

153. Where is Dr. A. N. Sinha Research Institute located?
(a) Munger (b) Patna
(c) Bhagalpur (d) Gaya

154. Where is A. N. Sinha Social Study Institute located?
(a) Rajgir (b) Gaya
(c) Patna (d) Munger

155. Where is Madarasa Islamic Shamshul Huda located?
(a) Patna (b) Rajgir
(c) Munger (d) Gaya

156. Where is Mandar Vidyapeeth located?
(a) Hajipur (b) Bhagalpur
(c) Gaya (d) Rajgir

157. Where is Sanskrit Vidyapeeth located?
(a) Patna (b) Gaya
(c) Hajipur (d) Rajgir

158. Where in Bihar, Deaf and Dumb School is situated?
(a) Patna (b) Gaya
(c) Rajgir (d) Hajipur

159. Where is Bihar Fire Safety Academy situated?
(a) Gaya (b) Hajipur
(c) Rajgir (d) Patna

160. Where is Bharatiya Nritya Kala Mandir situated?
(a) Hajipur (b) Gaya
(c) Jamui (d) Patna

161. Where is Government Joint Food and Drug Laboratory located?
(a) Patna (b) Barauni
(c) Begusarai (d) Gaya

162. Where is Fruit Research Institute located?
(a) Munger (b) Mokama
(c) Bhagalpur (d) Gaya

163. Where is Central Potato Research Institute located?
(a) Gaya (b) Patna
(c) Munger (d) Hajipur

164. Where is Shrinandan Library located?
(a) Haipur (b) Mokama
(c) Chhapra (d) Barauni

165. Where is Lakshmeshwar Public Library situated?
(a) Madhubani (b) Saran
(c) Saharasa (d) Darbhanga

166. Where is Gopal Narayan Library situated?
(a) Patna (b) Barauni
(c) Begusarai (d) Rajgir

167. Where is Shri Shardasadan Library situated?
(a) Gopalganj (b) Siwan
(c) Saharasa (d) Vaishali

168. Where is Mahant Ramsharan Das Library situated?
(a) Samastipur (b) Munger
(c) Bhagalpur (d) Hajipur

169. Where is 'Gyan Niketan' Library situated?
(a) Saharasa (b) Darbhanga
(c) Sitamarhi (d) Madhubani

170. Where is Prabhavati Library situated?
(a) Gaya (b) Patna
(c) Rajgir (d) Vaishali

171. Where are Smt. Radhika Sinha Institute and Sachchidanand Sinha Library situated?
(a) Mujaffarpur (b) Gaya
(c) Patna (d) Hajipur

172. Where is Bihar Urdu Academy situated?
(a) Arrah (b) Jehanabad
(c) Bihar Sharif (d) Patna

173. When was Bihar Urdu Academy established?
(a) 1971 AD (b) 1973 AD
(c) 1975 AD (d) 1977 AD

174. Where is Ancient Jain Research Institute located?
(a) Pavapuri (b) Nalanda
(c) Vaishali (d) Gaya

175. Where is Arabic and Persian Research Institute situated?
(a) Gaya (b) Patna
(c) Hajipur (d) Bhagalpur

176. When was Arabic and Persian Research Institute established?
(a) 1951 AD (b) 1953 AD
(c) 1955 AD (d) 1957 AD

177. Where is Mithila Sanskrit Vidyapeeth situated?
(a) Darbhanga (b) Madhubani
(c) Purnia (d) Saharasa

178. When was Mithila Sanskrit Vidyapeeth established?
(a) 1947 AD (b) 1946 AD
(c) 1951 AD (d) 1953 AD

179. Where is Bihar Rashtrabhasha Parishad located?
(a) Patna (b) Gaya
(c) Hajipur (d) Rajgir

180. When was Bihar Rashtrabhasha Parishad established?
(a) 1947 AD (b) 1948 AD
(c) 1949 AD (d) 1950 AD

181. When was Maithili Literature Council established?
(a) 1937 AD (b) 1939 AD
(c) 1941 AD (d) 1943 AD

182. When was Bodh Gaya Archaeological Museum established?
(a) 1956 AD (b) 1954 AD
(c) 1952 AD (d) 1950 AD

183. When was Bihar Hindi Literature Conference launched?
(a) 1919 AD (b) 1921 AD
(c) 1923 AD (d) 1925 AD

184. Where is Rajendra Memorial Museum located?
(a) Gaya (b) Patna
(c) Chhapra (d) Mujaffarpur

185. Where is Swami Sehjanand Saraswati Museum situated?
(a) Jehanabad (b) Arwal
(c) Madhepura (d) Kishanganj

186. When were Musuems started in India?
(a) 1810 AD (b) 1812 AD
(c) 1814 AD (d) 1816 AD

187. Where was the first museum of India-'India Museum' launched?
(a) Patna (b) Calcutta
(c) Mumbai (d) Delhi

188. When was the first museum launched in Bihar?
(a) 1851 AD (b) 1853 AD
(c) 1855 AD (d) 1857 AD

189. When was Patna Museum launched?
(a) 1913 AD (b) 1915 AD
(c) 1917 AD (d) 1919 AD

190. Who was the first President of Patna Museum?
(a) Gopal Rai
(b) Tapan Mishra
(c) Sharad Chandra Rai
(d) Smindra Singh

191. Where is Chandradhari Singh Museum located?
(a) Begusarai (b) Darbhanga
(c) Barauni (d) Patna

192. When was Chandradhari Singh Museum established?
(a) 1951 AD (b) 1953 AD
(c) 1955 AD (d) 1957 AD

193. When was Gaya Museum established?
(a) 1950 AD (b) 1952 AD
(c) 1954 AD (d) 1956 AD

194. Where is Narad Museum located?
(a) Navada (b) Nalanda
(c) Rajgir (d) Sitamarhi

195. When was Narad Museum established?
(a) 1970 AD (b) 1972 AD
(c) 1974 AD (d) 1976 AD

196. Where is Babu Kunwar Singh Museum located?
(a) Pratapgarh
(b) Jagdishpur
(c) Jagdish Nagar
(d) Jagdish Garh

197. When was Babu Kunwar Singh Museum established?
(a) 1968 AD (b) 1970 AD
(c) 1972 AD (d) 1974 AD

198. When was Bhagalpur Museum established?
(a) 1976 AD (b) 1974 AD
(c) 1972 AD (d) 1970 AD

199. Where is Maharaja Lakshishwar Singh Museum located?
(a) Betiya
(b) Vaishali
(c) Darbhanga
(d) Dumrao

200. When was Maharaja Lakshmishwar Singh Museum established?
(a) 1983 AD (b) 1985 AD
(c) 1987 AD (d) 1989 AD

201. Where is Ramchandra Shahi Museum located?
(a) Darbhanga (b) Mujaffarpur
(c) Khagariya (d) Nalanda

202. When was Ramchandra Shahi Museum established?
(a) 1973 AD (b) 1975 AD
(c) 1977 AD (d) 1979 AD

203. When was Begusarai Museum established?
(a) 1977 AD (b) 1979 AD
(c) 1981 AD (d) 1983 AD

204. Where is Mithila Lalit Museum located?
(a) Madhubani
(b) Darbhanga
(c) Purnia
(d) Saharasa

205. When was Mithila Lalit Museum established?
(a) 1979 AD (b) 1981 AD
(c) 1983 AD (d) 1985 AD

206. Where is Deep Narayan Singh Museum located?
(a) Navada (b) Vaishali
(c) Nalanda (d) Betiya

207. Where is Gandhi Memorial Museum located?
(a) Bhitrehava (b) Jagdishpur
(c) Rohini (d) Adampur

208. Where in Bihar Archaeological Museum has been established?
(a) Navada (b) Nalanda
(c) Vaishali (d) Mujaffarpur

209. When was Archaeological Museuam Nalanda established?
(a) 1913 AD (b) 1915 AD
(c) 1917 AD (d) 1919 AD

HEALTH

1. How many health institutions have been established in Bihar by January 2023 to increase health services in rural areas?

(a) 8,705 (b) 1,243
(c) 1,592 (d) 10,251

2. E-Sanjeevani telemedicine was launched in
(a) 2020 (b) 2021
(c) 2022 (d) 2023

3. How many people were given medical advice through e-Sanjeevani.in till September 2023?
(a) 70.45 lakh (b) 88.45 lakh
(c) 85.50 lakh (d) 87.50 lakh

4. What will be the working population of Bihar by 2026 (approx.)?
(a) 50% (b) 60.4%
(c) 55.9% (d) 65.3%

5. How much will be the population of children in the total population of Bihar by 2031 (approx.)?
(a) 29.2% (b) 31.0%
(c) 27.7% (d) 28.9%

6. What was the rural infant mortality rate in Bihar in the year 2020?
(a) 24 (b) 25
(c) 26 (d) 27

7. By the year 2036, the number of working population in Bihar will be (approx.)
(a) 60.2% (b) 61.4%
(c) 62% (d) 63.1%

8. How much budget provision was made for 'Special School-cum-Hostel Scheme' in 2023-24?
(a) ₹ 70.11 lakh
(b) ₹ 65.10 lakh
(c) ₹ 70.44 lakh
(d) ₹ 72.15 lakh

9. How many levels of health system are there in Bihar?
(a) Level-I (b) Level-II
(c) Level-IV (d) Level-III

10. What will be the percentage of elderly people in Bihar by the year 2036 (approx.)?
(a) 10% (b) 9.6%
(c) 8.5% (d) 11.0%

11. In Bihar when was the National Rural Health Mission launched?
(a) 2003 AD (b) 2004 AD
(c) 2005 AD (d) 2006 AD

12. When was 'Janani Suraksha Yojna' launched in Bihar?
(a) 2005 AD (b) 2006 AD
(c) 2007 AD (d) 2008 AD

13. How much money is given per woman under Janani Suraksha Yojna?
(a) 4000 (b) 5000
(c) 6000 (d) 7000

14. Which tablet is provided under National Deworming Programme?
(a) Cetrazine
(b) Almedazeel
(c) Chloroquine
(d) All of the above

15. An agreement has been reached for 5 years in the area of health, nutrition, hygiene, ICDS, Agriculture and rural development between the state government and which foundation?
(a) Bill and Milinda Gates
(b) Amazon
(c) Azeem Premji
(d) Ambani

16. Where is Tapovardhan Natural Cure centre located in Bihar?
(a) Munger (b) Bhagalpur
(c) Saharasa (d) Patna

17. When was the Integrated Child Development Scheme launched?
(a) 1970 AD (b) 1972 AD
(c) 1973 AD (d) 1974 AD

18. When was Rajiv Gandhi 'Kishori Sashaktikaran Yojna' launched?
(a) 2008 AD
(b) 2009 AD
(c) 2010 AD
(d) 2011 AD

19. What was the population of girls between age 11-18 in Bihar as per the 2011 census?
(a) 80 Lakh (b) 81 lakh
(c) 82 lakh (d) 83 lakh

20. Girls of which age are made the beneficiary under Rajiv Gandhi Kishori Sashaktikaran Scheme'?
(a) 6-10 years (b) 11-13 years
(c) 11-18 years (d) 12-18 years

21. In how many districts of Bihar, Rajiv Gandhi Kishori Sashaktikaran Scheme is in vogue?
(a) 10 (b) 11
(c) 12 (d) 13

22. What is the ratio of Scheme expenditure under Rajiv Gandhi Kishori Sashaktikaran Scheme?
(a) 50:50 (b) 60:40
(c) 70:30 (d) 75:25

23. When was Indira Gandhi Matratva Sahyog Yojna launched?
(a) 2008 AD (b) 2009 AD
(c) 2010 AD (d) 2011 AD

24. In which district of Bihar, Indira Gandhi Matratva Sahyog Yojna is in vogue?
(a) Saharasa (b) Vaishali
(c) Khagariya (d) Both (a) and (b)

25. Tap water is used in Bihar in ________ houses as per the 2011 census?
(a) 4% (b) 4.4%
(c) 5.2% (d) 5.8%

26. When was 'Clean India Mission' launched?
(a) 2013 AD (b) 2014 AD
(c) 2015 AD (d) 2016 AD

27. When was the aim of constructing toilets in all houses was set up under Clean India Mission?
(a) 2019 AD (b) 2020 AD
(c) 2021 AD (d) 2022 AD

28. Under 'Swachhta Abhiyaan', _____ campaign has been launched in the rural areas of Bihar?
(a) Jaiprakash Swachh
(b) Shrikrishna Swachh
(c) Lohia Swachh
(d) Anugrah Swachh

29. Under the National Rural Drinking Water Supply Programme, there was a plan to provide ...... liters of water per family per day to all the houses in the country by 2022?
(a) 60 (b) 70
(c) 80 (d) 90

SPORTS

1. When was Bihar State Sports Council constituted?
(a) 1957 AD (b) 1959 AD
(c) 1961 AD (d) 1963 AD

2. Who is the Ex-officio Chairman of Bihar State Sports Authority?
(a) Sports Minister
(b) Sports Secretary
(c) Governor
(d) Chief Minister

3. Football was started in Bihar in ________ with English Shield?
(a) 1897 AD (b) 1899 AD
(c) 1901 AD (d) 1903 AD

4. Where is Rajendra Stadium situated in Bihar?
(a) Bhagalpur (b) Chhapra
(c) Siwan (d) Gopalganj

5. Where in Bihar Secretariat, Indoor Stadium is situated?
(a) Patna
(b) Gaya
(c) Bhagalpur
(d) Jehanabad

6. Where is Sanjay Gandhi Mini Stadium situated?
(a) Hajipur (b) Vaishali
(c) Patna (d) Mujaffarpur

7. Where in Bihar is Khudiram Bose Stadium situated?
(a) Patna (b) Hajipur
(c) Vaishali (d) Mujaffarpur

8. Where in Bihar is Subrahmaniyam Stadium situated?
(a) Gaya (b) Hajipur
(c) Munger (d) Motihari

9. Where is Veer Kunwar Singh Police Stadium situated?
(a) Buxar (b) Arrah
(c) Gaya (d) Rohtas

10. Where is Moin-un-Haque stadium situated?
(a) Patna (b) Gaya
(c) Motihari (d) Betiya

11. Where is Jagjivan Ram Stadium situated?
(a) Khagol (b) Raxaul
(c) Rajgir (d) Bihta

12. Where in Bihar is Indira Gandhi Stadium situated?
(a) Gaya (b) Bhagalpur
(c) Purnia (d) Kishanganj

13. Where in Bihar is Mithilesh Stadium situated?
(a) Gaya (b) Patna
(c) Rohtash (d) Hajipur

14. Where are Post and Telegraph Entertainment and Indoor Stadium situated?
(a) Patna (b) Gaya
(c) Bhagalpur (d) Hajipur

15. Cousins' Cup and Jaipal Singh Cup are related to which sports?
(a) Football (b) Hockey
(c) Kabaddi (d) Chess

16. Which of the trophies is connected with football?
(a) Moin-ul-Haque Trophy
(b) Governor Gold Cup
(c) Ravi Neha Trophy
(d) All of the above

17. Anugrah Narayan Shield and Republic Shield are related to which sport?
(a) Hockey (b) Cricket
(c) Chess (d) Football

18. Which of the following is a shield connected with Cricket?
(a) Shrikrishan Singh Shield
(b) Hemant Trophy
(c) Randhir Verma Shield
(d) All of the above

19. Who of the following is a cricketer from Bihar?
(a) Saba Karim
(b) Kirti Azad
(c) Hari Kidwani
(d) All of the above

20. Who is a player of football from Bihar?
(a) P. K. Banerjee
(b) Subodh Kajiwal
(c) Ravi Ranjan
(d) All of the above

21. Who of the following is a hockey player from Bihar?
(a) L. K. Mitra
(b) James Karketa
(c) Gopal Nengra
(d) All of the above

22. Jaipal Singh and Amla Gudiya are related to which sport?
(a) Football (b) Hockey
(c) Cricket (d) Chess

23. Who of the following is related with Hockey?
(a) Amrit Lakra
(b) S Dungdung
(c) Sushila Topno
(d) All of the above

24. Who of the following players is connected with shooting?
(a) Jagarnam Singh
(b) Shekhar Bhagat
(c) Pranav Sinha
(d) All of the above

25. Who of the following players is related to Chess?
(a) Anjana Jha
(b) Barugese Kosi
(c) Vaishali Sharin
(d) All of the above

26. Dolan Champa Bose and Divyendu Barua are related to which sport?
(a) Hockey (b) Cricket
(c) Football (d) Chess

27. Bimude and Shailya Kumar are connected with which sport?
(a) Tennis (b) Chess
(c) Cricket (d) Volleyball

28. Ali Akbar, Kaveri Ghosh and Bagu Chatterjee are connected with which sport?
(a) Chess (b) Cricket
(c) Hockey (d) Badminton

29. Sita Paul, Ehsan Ahmad and Sudhanshu Shekhar are connected with which sport?
(a) Badminton (b) Hockey
(c) Baseball (d) Chess

30. Who of the following is related to Taekwondo?
(a) Sumil Singh
(b) Satyajit Shakt
(c) Shalini Shrivastava
(d) All of the above

31. Who of the following is connected with Billiards?
(a) Kumar Shyamanand Sinha
(b) Kumar Taranand Sinha
(c) Kumar Adhanand Sinha
(d) All of the above

32. Who of the following is connected with athletics?
(a) Saroj Lakra
(b) Sumitra Savaiyya
(c) Pushpa Ekka
(d) All of the above

33. Prachi Sharma is connected with which sport?
(a) Soft ball (b) Baseball
(c) Chess (d) Archery

34. Who of the following is connected with archery?
(a) Rajinder Guian
(b) Purnima Mehto
(c) Nirmal Singh
(d) All of the above

35. Who of the following is connected with basket ball?
(a) Prachi Sharma
(b) Rajesh Shrivastava
(c) Sunil Kumar Panda
(d) All of the above

36. Who of the following is connected with weight lifting?
(a) Budhwa Oraon
(b) Indrajit Singh
(c) Ratan Kumar Basat
(d) All of the above

37. Who of the following was a football referee?
(a) Tahir Hussain
(b) Yogendra Pandit
(c) Manik Sengupta
(d) All of the above

38. Who of the following is a cricket umpire?
(a) Gora Bose
(b) K. B. Rao
(c) S. B. Ramnik
(d) All of the above

39. Who of the following is a Hindi commentator?
(a) U. K. Sinha
(b) Dharambir Singh
(c) Badri Prasad
(d) All of the above

40. Who of the following is an English Commentator?
(a) Moin-ul-Haque
(b) Jayant Chatterjee
(c) Manik Sengupta
(d) All of the above

41. Where are the headquarters of Bihar State Sports Authority located?
(a) Patna (b) Munger
(c) Bhagalpur (d) Arrah

Answers

EDUCATION

1. (a)	**2.** (d)	**3.** (b)	**4.** (b)	**5.** (d)	**6.** (d)	**7.** (a)	**8.** (b)	**9.** (c)	**10.** (d)
11. (a)	**12.** (a)	**13.** (c)	**14.** (d)	**15.** (d)	**16.** (a)	**17.** (d)	**18.** (c)	**19.** (a)	**20.** (a)
21. (d)	**22.** (c)	**23.** (b)	**24.** (d)	**25.** (c)	**26.** (c)	**27.** (a)	**28.** (c)	**29.** (d)	**30.** (c)
31. (a)	**32.** (c)	**33.** (a)	**34.** (d)	**35.** (d)	**36.** (a)	**37.** (d)	**38.** (d)	**39.** (c)	**40.** (b)
41. (d)	**42.** (c)	**43.** (b)	**44.** (c)	**45.** (a)	**46.** (d)	**47.** (c)	**48.** (d)	**49.** (a)	**50.** (d)
51. (b)	**52.** (c)	**53.** (a)	**54.** (d)	**55.** (c)	**56.** (d)	**57.** (a)	**58.** (c)	**59.** (a)	**60.** (d)
61. (a)	**62.** (d)	**63.** (b)	**64.** (d)	**65.** (a)	**66.** (c)	**67.** (d)	**68.** (c)	**69.** (d)	**70.** (a)
71. (b)	**72.** (a)	**73.** (d)	**74.** (c)	**75.** (a)	**76.** (c)	**77.** (d)	**78.** (a)	**79.** (c)	**80.** (d)
81. (c)	**82.** (a)	**83.** (d)	**84.** (b)	**85.** (c)	**86.** (b)	**87.** (c)	**88.** (b)	**89.** (d)	**90.** (c)
91. (b)	**92.** (d)	**93.** (a)	**94.** (d)	**95.** (c)	**96.** (a)	**97.** (c)	**98.** (a)	**99.** (c)	**100.** (a)
101. (a)	**102.** (c)	**103.** (b)	**104.** (a)	**105.** (d)	**106.** (b)	**107.** (a)	**108.** (a)	**109.** (d)	**110.** (a)
111. (c)	**112.** (a)	**113.** (d)	**114.** (a)	**115.** (c)	**116.** (b)	**117.** (d)	**118.** (a)	**119.** (c)	**120.** (d)
121. (a)	**122.** (b)	**123.** (d)	**124.** (a)	**125.** (d)	**126.** (b)	**127.** (a)	**128.** (c)	**129.** (b)	**130.** (a)
131. (c)	**132.** (d)	**133.** (b)	**134.** (d)	**135.** (c)	**136.** (c)	**137.** (a)	**138.** (c)	**139.** (d)	**140.** (b)
141. (d)	**142.** (a)	**143.** (c)	**144.** (d)	**145.** (b)	**146.** (a)	**147.** (a)	**148.** (c)	**149.** (a)	**150.** (b)
151. (d)	**152.** (a)	**153.** (d)	**154.** (b)	**155.** (c)	**156.** (a)	**157.** (b)	**158.** (a)	**159.** (a)	**160.** (d)
161. (d)	**162.** (d)	**163.** (c)	**164.** (b)	**165.** (c)	**166.** (d)	**167.** (a)	**168.** (d)	**169.** (a)	**170.** (c)
171. (b)	**172.** (c)	**173.** (c)	**174.** (c)	**175.** (b)	**176.** (c)	**177.** (a)	**178.** (c)	**179.** (a)	**180.** (d)
181. (b)	**182.** (a)	**183.** (a)	**184.** (b)	**185.** (a)	**186.** (c)	**187.** (b)	**188.** (c)	**189.** (c)	**190.** (c)
191. (b)	**192.** (d)	**193.** (b)	**194.** (a)	**195.** (c)	**196.** (b)	**197.** (c)	**198.** (a)	**199.** (c)	**200.** (d)
201. (b)	**202.** (d)	**203.** (c)	**204.** (a)	**205.** (b)	**206.** (b)	**207.** (a)	**208.** (b)	**209.** (c)	

HEALTH

1. (d)	**2.** (b)	**3.** (b)	**4.** (b)	**5.** (a)	**6.** (d)	**7.** (b)	**8.** (a)	**9.** (d)	**10.** (d)
11. (c)	**12.** (a)	**13.** (c)	**14.** (b)	**15.** (a)	**16.** (b)	**17.** (b)	**18.** (c)	**19.** (d)	**20.** (c)
21. (c)	**22.** (b)	**23.** (c)	**24.** (d)	**25.** (b)	**26.** (b)	**27.** (a)	**28.** (c)	**29.** (b)	

SPORTS

1. (c)	**2.** (d)	**3.** (b)	**4.** (a)	**5.** (c)	**6.** (d)	**7.** (d)	**8.** (a)	**9.** (b)	**10.** (a)
11. (a)	**12.** (c)	**13.** (b)	**14.** (a)	**15.** (b)	**16.** (d)	**17.** (d)	**18.** (d)	**19.** (d)	**20.** (d)
21. (d)	**22.** (b)	**23.** (d)	**24.** (d)	**25.** (d)	**26.** (d)	**27.** (a)	**28.** (d)	**29.** (c)	**30.** (d)
31. (d)	**32.** (d)	**33.** (a)	**34.** (d)	**35.** (d)	**36.** (d)	**37.** (d)	**38.** (d)	**39.** (d)	**40.** (d)
41. (a)									

❑❑❑

13 Bihar Physical Features

LOCATION

1. Bihar is a state situated in the ganges plains of the middle India which is part of________India.

(a) Eastern (b) Western
(c) Northern (d) Southern

2. When was Jharkhand separated from Bihar?

(a) 1998 (b) 1999
(c) 2000 (d) 2001

3. What is the present shape of Bihar?

(a) Circular shape
(b) Rectangular Shape
(c) Triangular Shape
(d) Square Shape

4. The area of Bihar is of how many square kilometers?

(a) 90163 (b) 91770
(c) 92820 (d) 94163

5. The area of Bihar is of how many square miles?

(a) 36357 (b) 33120
(c) 32647 (d) 31740

6. How much area Bihar has in percentage terms as against the area of India?

(a) 2.64% (b) 2.7%
(c) 2.86% (d) 2.92%

7. Area-wise Bihar is the _________ biggest state of India.

(a) 12th (b) 13th
(c) 14th (d) 15th

8. Vaibhavgiri is situated ________ meters above the sea level.

(a) 350 (b) 360
(c) 370 (d) 380

9. The length of Bihar from north to south is________kms.

(a) 335 (b) 340
(c) 345 (d) 350

10. The width of Bihar from east to west is_________kms.

(a) 483 (b) 470
(c) 462 (d) 452

11. The northern border of Bihar touches the border of which country?

(a) Pakistan (b) Nepal
(c) Bhutan (d) Thailand

12. How many districts of Bihar touch Nepal?

(a) 4 (b) 5
(c) 6 (d) 7

13. Which of the following districts of Bihar touch Nepal?

(a) East Champaran
(b) West Champaran
(c) Madhubani
(d) All of the above

14. Which of the following districts do not touch Nepal?

(a) Supaul (b) Sitamarhi
(c) Arariya (d) Shivhar

15. The eastern border of Bihar touches which other state?

(a) Odisha
(b) Uttar Pradesh
(c) Bengal
(d) Assam

16. Which of the following districts do not touch Bengal?
(a) Kishanganj (b) Arariya
(c) Purnia (d) Katihar

17. On ______ border of Bihar, Jharkhand state is situated.
(a) Eastern (b) Western
(c) Northern (d) Southern

18. How many districts of Bihar touch the state of Jharkhand?
(a) 7 (b) 6
(c) 5 (d) 4

19. Which of the following district touches Jharkhand?
(a) Bhagalpur
(b) Banka
(c) Jamui
(d) All of these

20. Which of the following district does not touch Jharkhand State?
(a) Navada (b) Nalanda
(c) Gaya (d) Aurangabad

21. ________state is situated on the western border of Bihar.
(a) Madhya Pradesh
(b) Chhatisgarh
(c) Uttar Pradesh
(d) Jharkhand

22. How many districts of Bihar touch Uttar Pradesh?
(a) 6 (b) 7
(c) 8 (d) 9

23. Which of the following districts touches Uttar Pradesh?
(a) Rohtas
(b) Kaimur
(c) Buxar
(d) All of the above

24. Which of the following districts do not touch Uttar Pradesh?
(a) Gaya (b) Siwan
(c) Gopalganj (d) Arrah

25. In the changed Rajgir-oriented rocks, there is prominence of quartzite and _______.
(a) Slate (b) Granite
(c) Marble (d) Naseem

26. Which of the following rock areas is a part of Navada-Munger rock area?
(a) Khadagpur Hill
(b) Gidheshwar Hill
(c) Chakai Hill
(d) All of the above

27. Khadagpur Hill is extended from ________to Jamui.
(a) Navada (b) Nalanda
(c) Munger (d) Bhagalpur

28. Khadagpur Hill is of which shape out of the following?
(a) Rectangular (b) Triangular
(c) Circular (d) Square type

29. In Khadagpur hill, which of the following is prominent?
(a) Lime stone (b) Slate
(c) Granite (d) Quartzite

30. How many districts neither touch any international boundaries nor any other state's border?
(a) 10 (b) 11
(c) 12 (d) 13

31. How many districts are there in total in Bihar?
(a) 38 (b) 37
(c) 36 (d) 35

32. Which is the biggest district of Bihar area-wise?
(a) East Champaran
(b) West Champaran
(c) Saharasa
(d) Gaya

33. Which is the smallest district of Bihar area-wise?
(a) Shivhar (b) Jamui
(c) Jehanabad (d) Sheikhupura

34. Which district is located in the extreme southern part of the state?
(a) Saran (b) Gaya
(c) Jamui (d) Both (b) and (c)

35. Which of the following districts is the northern most district of the State?
(a) East Champaran
(b) West Champaran
(c) Sitamarhi
(d) Madhubani

36. Which is the most western district of the state?
(a) Buxar (b) Arrah
(c) Kaimur (d) Rohtash

37. Which of the following districts is the eastern most district of the state?
(a) Purnia (b) Kishanganj
(c) Katihar (d) Bhagalpur

38. Bihar state is situated in the north of_______line?
(a) Tropic of Cancer
(b) Tropic of Capricorn
(c) Equator
(d) Greenwich

39. From the point of view of structural built of Bihar, rocks for the period from_______to the fourth period are found.
(a) Cambrian (b) Pre-Cambrian
(c) Jurassic (d) Mesozoic

40. In which type, pre-Cambrian rocks are found in Bihar?
(a) Deccan
(b) Dharwad
(c) Vindhya
(d) All of the above

41. In which period, the middle area plains of the Ganges were formed?
(a) Mesozoic (b) Platonic
(c) Cambrian (d) Jurassic

42. Which of the following series of rocks are not found in Bihar?
(a) Deccan (b) Vindhyan
(c) Territory (d) Quartzsite

43. In which district of Bihar Dharwad period rocks are found?
(a) Munger (b) Jamui
(c) Navada (d) All of these

44. The mountain situated in the southern district of Bihar is a part of which place?
(a) Chhotanagpur Plateau
(b) Satpuda
(c) Aravali
(d) Dodabeta

45. Which of the following element is found in Dharwad series rocks?
(a) Slate (b) Quartzite
(c) Phi late (d) All of these

46. The rocks of Dharwad series are basically________.
(a) Igneous
(b) Sedimentary
(c) Peet
(d) Metamorphic

47. When were rocks of Vindhyan series formed?
(a) Pre-Cambrian
(b) Cambrian
(c) Plastocin
(d) Mesozoic

48. In which district of Bihar Vindhyan series rocks are found?
(a) Gaya
(b) Kaimur
(c) Rohtash
(d) Both (b) and (c)

49. In which river valley, an alluvial deposit is found on the Vindhyan series rocks?
(a) Sone (b) Ganga
(c) Kosi (d) Bagmati

50. Which mineral is found from Vindhyan series rocks?
(a) Gold (b) Asbestos
(c) Pyrite (d) Coal

51. What do we extract from pyrite mineral?
(a) Sulphur (b) Asbestos
(c) Sand (d) Tungsten

52. Which of the following is found from Vindhyan series rocks?
(a) Limestone (b) Dolomite
(c) Quartzite (d) All of these

53. In which district of southern Bihar, volcanic structures are found?
(a) Gaya (b) Aurangabad
(c) Banka (d) Navada

54. Territory rocks are found in southern ________ of Himalaya?
(a) Aravali series
(b) Middle Himalaya
(c) Shivalik Series
(d) Deccan Series

55. What type of rocks are found in Territory class I Bihar?
(a) Limestone
(b) Sandstone
(c) Boulder clay
(d) Both (b) and (c)

56. ________ is found from the tertiary rocks due to the depression of the tethys Ocean.
(a) Gold and silver
(b) Petroleum
(c) Natural Gas
(d) Both (b) and (c)

57. What type of rocks are found in the plains of the Ganges in Bihar?
(a) Tertiary rocks
(b) Vindhyan Rocks
(c) Quarternary Rocks
(d) All of the above

58. The average height of Bihar is _______ feet from the sea level?
(a) 162 (b) 166
(c) 169 (d) 173

59. What is the average height of Bihar in meters from the sea level?
(a) 48 (b) 53
(c) 58 (d) 62

60. Bihar has been divided in how many physical provinces according to its structure?
(a) 2 (b) 3
(c) 4 (d) 5

61. There is extension of the Himalayas' _________ series on the northern border of the Western Champaran district.
(a) Shivalik (b) Aravali
(c) Satpuda (d) Kaimur

62. In how many squre kms are Shivalik series rocks found in Bihar?
(a) 901 (b) 913
(c) 921 (d) 932

63. What is average height of Shivalik series hills in Bihar?
(a) 50-125 meters
(b) 75-205 meters
(c) 80-250 meters
(d) 90-275 meters

64. In how many sub divisions Shivalik Hills area has been divided in Bihar?
(a) 2 (b) 3
(c) 4 (d) 5

65. Which of the following is a part of sub-series of Shivalik series?
(a) Ramnagar Doon
(b) Harha Valley
(c) Someshwar class
(d) All of the above

66. Ramnagar Doon Hill situated in the south of Someshwar Class is 32 kms in length and ______ kms in width?
(a) 8 (b) 10
(c) 12 (d) 15

67. What is the width of Ramnagar Doon in meters?
(a) 230 (b) 236
(c) 242 (d) 245

68. How much is the length of Harha Valley in kms?
(a) 18 (b) 21
(c) 24 (d) 27

69. The area in sq. kms of Harha Valley is _________.
(a) 180 (b) 195
(c) 208 (d) 214

70. The total area of Someshwar series is how many square kms?
(a) 642 (b) 703
(c) 718 (d) 784

71. The top part of Someshwar series separates Bihar from which place?
(a) Nepal (b) Thailand
(c) Bhutan (d) China

72. The length of Someshwar series expanded from _______ canal to Bhikhnathori canyon is 70 kms.
(a) Triveni (b) Ganga
(c) Sone (d) Gandak

73. In Someshwar series, which canyon is built?
(a) Someshwar Canyon
(b) Bhikhnathori Canyon
(c) Makhat Canyon
(d) All of the above

74. In Someshwar Series itself, the highest point of Bihar, ______fort is situated?
(a) Mangla (b) Someshwar
(c) Bhikhna (d) Harha

75. What is the height in meters of the Someshwar Fort?
(a) 689 (b) 703
(c) 783 (d) 880

76. The Terai area in Bihar lies to the ______ of the Ganga and in the southern part parallel to Shivalik Series?
(a) North (b) South
(c) East (d) West

77. The Terai area is found in which area of th State?
(a) North-west (b) South-west
(c) North-east (d) Both (a) and (c)

78. The north-eastern Terai area is spread in which district?
(a) Purnia
(b) Arariya
(c) Kishanganj
(d) All of the above

79. In Bihar Terai land, up to how much rain occurs in cms?
(a) 80 (b) 120
(c) 160 (d) 200

80. In Bihar, the total area of the plains of Ganges is how much in sq. kms.?
(a) 90650 (b) 91112
(c) 91676 (d) 91920

81. The plains of the Ganges forms how much area in percentage of the total plain area of Bihar?
(a) 94.12 (b) 95.72
(c) 96.27 (d) 96.89

82. In Bihar the average height of the plains of the Ganges is up to _____ meters.
(a) 40-75 (b) 52-88
(c) 60-130 (d) 75-120

83. The area of the Northern Ganges is how many sq. kms.?
(a) 54120 (b) 54840
(c) 55740 (d) 56980

84. The built up of the northern plains of the Ganges occurred due to depression of which of the following rivers?
(a) Mahananda
(b) Kosi
(c) Ghaghra
(d) All of the above

85. The expansion of the northern plains of the Ganges has occurred in which of the following districts?
(a) Bhagalpur
(b) Mujaffarpur
(c) East Champaran
(d) All of the above

86. The abandoned and serpant type Gokhur lake and ________ were formed by the flow of rivers flowing through the northern plains of Bihar.
(a) Chaur
(b) Tand
(c) Sampraya
(d) Parvat (Mountain)

87. In sub terai or 'Bhabar' region of Bihar, which type of deposit is found?
(a) Limestone
(b) Pebble-sand
(c) Sandstone
(d) All of the above

88. In which district of Bihar there is expansion of 'Bhabar' region?
(a) Supaul
(b) Arariya
(c) Sitamarhi
(d) All of the above

89. 'Bangar' area is an area of old _______ deposits.
(a) Alluvium
(b) Sand
(c) Lime
(d) All of the above

90. In which area of Bihar there is expansion of 'Bangar'?
(a) North-East (b) North-west
(c) South-east (d) South-west

91. In Bihar there is expansion of 'Khadar' area from the river Gandak in the west to the river ________ in the east.
(a) Bagmati (b) Mahananda
(c) Kosi (d) Punpun

92. In northern plains of the Ganges, a natural underwater area is found which is known by the name of ________.
(a) Taand
(b) Chaur
(c) Sampray Plain
(d) Bhur

93. The total area of the southern plains of the Ganges is how many sq. kms?
(a) 31240 (b) 31890
(c) 32423 (d) 33670

94. Which of the following rivers flow in the Southern Bihar?
(a) Punpun (b) Bagmati
(c) Kiul (d) Falgu

95. The red area in Bihar starting from Patna to________ is an expansion in width of up to 25 Kms?
(a) Mokasa (b) Barauni
(c) Bhagalpur (d) Rajgir

96. Which of the following is an example of 'Tall' in Bihar?
(a) Badhiya Tall
(b) Sindhaul Tall
(c) Moll Tall
(d) All of the above

97. Which of the following examples of 'Mann' (chaur) is not situated in Bihar?
(a) Kesariya Mann
(b) Madhopur Mann
(c) Simri Mann
(d) Saraiyya Mann

98. The river flow system of the south Bihar is called the______.
(a) Aru (b) Shrung
(c) Peanut (d) Gorge

99. The southern plateau province is the end of the border of ________ plateau?

(a) Chhotanagpur
(b) Khadagpur
(c) Kaimur
(d) Mokama

100. In Southern Plateau area, there is abundance of igneous and metamorphic rocks of which types?
(a) Granite
(b) Nees
(c) Cyst
(d) Both (a) and (b)

101. In which district of Bihar, there is expansion of southern plateau area?
(a) Kaimur (b) Banka
(c) Munger (d) All of these

102. Which of the following plateaus is a part of Bihar's southern plateau area?
(a) Rohtash Plateau
(b) Giriyak Hill
(c) Munger Hill
(d) All of the above

103. The plateau Kaimur or Rohtash is the eastern part of ________ series.
(a) Vindhya (b) Aravali
(c) Satpuda (d) Mahadev

104. The expansion of Vindhya series is for 483 kms. in length and _______ kms. in width?
(a) 70 (b) 80
(c) 90 (d) 100

105. The expansion of Vindhya series starts from _______ and is up to Rohtash (Bihar).
(a) Jabalpur (b) Jalaun
(c) Khandwa (d) Bhopal

106. The average height of the Rohtash Plateau is between _________ meters.
(a) 100-200 (b) 150-250
(c) 200-250 (d) 300-450

107. The highest part of the Kaimur (Rohtash) plateau is _________.
(a) Rohtashgarh
(b) Bhairogarh
(c) Chambalgarh
(d) Devgarh

108. State the height of Rohtashgarh?
(a) 470 (b) 481
(c) 495 (d) 499

109. Kaimur plateau is separated from Chhotanagpur plateau by which river?
(a) Ganga (b) Sone
(c) Bagmati (d) Mahananda

110. In Kaimur plateau, there is abundance of ________.
(a) Sandstone (b) Volcano
(c) Granite (d) Nees

111. Which of the following is the highest hill?
(a) Sonegiri (b) Vaibhavgiri
(c) Vipulgiri (d) Udaigiri

112. Which area is the main part of hilly area of Gaya?
(a) Jethian
(b) Hindaz
(c) Haldia
(d) All of the above

113. Around the city of Gaya, which of the following hills is not situated?
(a) Karamshila
(b) Pretshila
(c) Bhootshila
(d) Brahmyoni

114. On the border of Jehanabad and Gaya districts are situated the hills of Barabar and______.
(a) Aravali (b) Nagarjuni
(c) Dasrath (d) Ashoka

115. Rajgir-Giriyak hilly area is mainly situated in which district?
(a) Bhagalpur (b) Nalanda
(c) Munger (d) Gaya

116. Which of the following places is a part of Rajgir-Giriyak hilly area?
(a) Vaibhavgiri
(b) Vipulgiri
(c) Peer
(d) All of the above

PHYSICAL REGION

1. Which of the following physical areas is not a part of Bihar?
(a) Shivalik Pradesh
(b) The plains of the Ganges
(c) The plateau area of the Aravali
(d) Chhota Nagpur border plateau area

2. In how many geographical areas Bihar has been divided by Prof Inayat Ahmad and Prof. Ram Pravesh Singh?
(a) 10 (b) 9
(c) 8 (d) 7

3. Which of the following places is a place distributed by Prof Inayat Ahmad and Prof Ram Pravesh Singh?
(a) Ghagra - Gandak Doab
(b) Gandak-Kosi Doab
(c) Ganga Diara area
(d) All of the above

4. Which of the following places is not the area distributed by Prof. Inayat Ahmad and Prof Ram Pravesh Singh?
(a) Abhrak province
(b) Gandak Diara province
(c) Kaimur Plateau
(d) Ganga Diara area

5. Which of the following areas is an area with highest rainfall in Bihar?
(a) North-east (b) North-west
(c) South-west (d) South-east

6. In North-east Bihar, rainfall up to ________ centimeters occur.
(a) 170 (b) 180
(c) 190 (d) 200

7. Which of the following districts is not situated in Bihar's north-east part?
(a) Purnia (b) Shivhar
(c) Arariya (d) Kishanganj

8. In which district of Bihar, there is an expansion of Ghagra-Gandak Doab?
(a) Saran
(b) Siwan
(c) Gopalganj
(d) All of the above

9. The development of which of the following industries has occurred to the maximum in Ghagra-Gandak Doab?
(a) Rice (b) Sugar
(c) Tea (d) Cotton cloth

10. Which of the following area in Bihar is famous for sugar production?
(a) Mirganj (b) Madau
(c) Chhapra (d) All of these

11. Which of the following districts fall under Gandak-Kosi Doab?
(a) East Champaran
(b) West Champaran
(c) Shivhar
(d) All of the above

12. Which of the following districts does not fall under the Gandak-Kosi Doab?
(a) Darbhanga (b) Banka
(c) Mujaffarpur (d) Vaishali

13. Which of the following pairs is not correct?
(a) Bhagalpur-Sharifa
(b) Darbhanga-Aam
(c) Mujaffarpur-Lichi
(d) Hajipur-kela

14. Which cash crop does not belong to Gandak-Kosi Doab area?
(a) Red Chilly (b) Tobacco
(c) Jute (d) Sugarcane

15. Which place is a place of sugar production in Gandak-Kosi Doab area?
(a) Chanpatiya
(b) Sugauli
(c) Bagha
(d) All of the above

16. Which city is most famous in Gandak-Kosi area?
(a) Begusarai (b) Motihari
(c) Barauni (d) Samastipur

17. Which of the following industries is not located in Barauni?
(a) Pulses Industry
(b) Fertilizers Industry
(c) Oil Refineries
(d) Electricity centres

18. Which of the following industries has developed in Mujaffarpur?
(a) Pulses Industry
(b) Rice Industry
(c) Sugar Industry
(d) Milk Industry

19. Which of the following districts fall under Kosi-Mahanadi Doab area?
(a) Madhepura
(b) Khagariya
(c) Saharasa
(d) All of the above

20. Which of the following Doab Areas is a backward area in agriculture, industry and transport due to excessive rains?
(a) Kosi-Mahananda
(b) Gandak-Ghagra
(c) Gandak-Kosi
(d) Gandak-Ganga

21. Which district comes under Karmnasha-Sone Doab?
(a) Bhojpur
(b) Rohtash
(c) Kaimur
(d) All of the above

22. From the point of view of climatic conditions which Doab area is the area with minimum rains?
(a) Karamnasha-Sone
(b) Gandak-Kosi
(c) Kosi-Mahananda
(d) Gandak-Ghagra

23. Which of the following has developed the most in Karamnasha-Sone Doab?
(a) Sugar Mill (b) Rice Mill
(c) Pulses Mill (d) Arra Mill

24. Which of the following districts comes under Sone-Kiul Doab area?
(a) Arwal
(b) Nalanda
(c) Lakhisarai
(d) All of the above

25. Which of the following districts does not come under Sone-Kiul Doab area?
(a) Aurangabad
(b) Darbhanga
(c) Patna
(d) Arwal

26. Which of the following is correct?
(a) Bihar Sharif and Obra-Silk clothes
(b) Manpur-Handicrafts and carpet
(c) Jehanabad-Rice
(d) Both (a) and (b)

27. In which of the following districts, cement and edible oil industries have been established?
(a) Aurangabad (b) Arwal
(c) Lakhisarai (d) Jehanabad

28. Which district comes under Bihar's plains area?
(a) Munger (b) Banka
(c) Bhagalpur (d) All of these

29. In Bihar's plains area, on which river a dam has been built to develop irrigation facility?

(a) Chandan (b) Kiul
(c) Barua (d) All of these

30. Which of the following industries has developed in Munger?
(a) Gun (b) Tobacco
(c) Milk (d) All of these

31. In which of the following districts, development of silk industry has taken place?
(a) Munger (b) Banka
(c) Bhagalpur (d) Jamui

32. Kaimur plateau is a part of which mountain?
(a) Aravali (b) Satpuda
(c) Vindhya (d) Mahadev

33. Which of the following industries has developed in Kaimur plateau area?
(a) Stone based (b) Sugar
(c) Rice (d) Saw Mill

34. Which of the following things is found in Kaimur Plateau?
(a) Pyrite
(b) Phosphate
(c) Slate
(d) Both (a) and (b)

35. In which districts of Bihar, asbestos is found?
(a) Gaya (b) Jamui
(c) Navada (d) All of these

Answers

LOCATION

1. (a)	**2.** (c)	**3.** (b)	**4.** (d)	**5.** (a)	**6.** (c)	**7.** (c)	**8.** (d)	**9.** (c)	**10.** (a)
11. (b)	**12.** (d)	**13.** (d)	**14.** (d)	**15.** (c)	**16.** (b)	**17.** (d)	**18.** (a)	**19.** (d)	**20.** (b)
21. (c)	**22.** (c)	**23.** (d)	**24.** (a)	**25.** (c)	**26.** (d)	**27.** (c)	**28.** (b)	**29.** (d)	**30.** (d)
31. (a)	**32.** (b)	**33.** (d)	**34.** (d)	**35.** (b)	**36.** (c)	**37.** (b)	**38.** (a)	**39.** (b)	**40.** (d)
41. (b)	**42.** (a)	**43.** (d)	**44.** (a)	**45.** (d)	**46.** (a)	**47.** (a)	**48.** (d)	**49.** (a)	**50.** (c)
51. (a)	**52.** (d)	**53.** (c)	**54.** (c)	**55.** (d)	**56.** (d)	**57.** (d)	**58.** (d)	**59.** (b)	**60.** (b)
61. (a)	**62.** (d)	**63.** (c)	**64.** (b)	**65.** (d)	**66.** (a)	**67.** (c)	**68.** (b)	**69.** (d)	**70.** (d)
71. (a)	**72.** (a)	**73.** (a)	**74.** (b)	**75.** (d)	**76.** (a)	**77.** (d)	**78.** (d)	**79.** (d)	**80.** (a)
81. (c)	**82.** (d)	**83.** (d)	**84.** (d)	**85.** (d)	**86.** (a)	**87.** (b)	**88.** (d)	**89.** (d)	**90.** (a)
91. (b)	**92.** (c)	**93.** (d)	**94.** (b)	**95.** (a)	**96.** (d)	**97.** (a)	**98.** (c)	**99.** (a)	**100.** (d)
101. (d)	**102.** (d)	**103.** (a)	**104.** (b)	**105.** (a)	**106.** (d)	**107.** (a)	**108.** (b)	**109.** (b)	**110.** (a)
111. (b)	**112.** (d)	**113.** (a)	**114.** (b)	**115.** (b)	**116.** (d)				

PHYSICAL REGION

1. (c)	**2.** (a)	**3.** (d)	**4.** (b)	**5.** (a)	**6.** (d)	**7.** (b)	**8.** (d)	**9.** (b)	**10.** (d)
11. (d)	**12.** (b)	**13.** (a)	**14.** (c)	**15.** (d)	**16.** (c)	**17.** (a)	**18.** (d)	**19.** (d)	**20.** (a)
21. (d)	**22.** (a)	**23.** (b)	**24.** (d)	**25.** (b)	**26.** (d)	**27.** (a)	**28.** (d)	**29.** (d)	**30.** (d)
31. (c)	**32.** (a)	**33.** (c)	**34.** (d)	**35.** (d)					

❑❑❑

14 The Drainage System

DRAINAGE SYSTEM

1. **The basis of river network system in Bihar is_______river.**
(a) Ganga (b) Sone
(c) Kosi (d) Mahananda

2. **_______of Bihar's surface development has occurred by the rivers' drainage system.**
(a) 70% (b) 80%
(c) 90% (d) 95%

3. **The average quantity of rainfall in Bihar is _______centimeters.**
(a) 106 (b) 109
(c) 114 (d) 118

4. **The most famous river for changing its route is______.**
(a) Bagmati (b) Gandak
(c) Kosi (d) Mahananda

5. **Keeping in view the geographical outlook, in how many river areas Bihar has been divided?**
(a) 4 (b) 5
(c) 6 (d) 7

6. **Which of the river area is present in Bihar?**
(a) Ghagra-Gandak
(b) Gandak-Bagmati
(c) Bagmati-Kosi
(d) All of the above

7. **Which river area does not exist in Bihar?**
(a) Sone-Punpun
(b) Sone-Mahanadi
(c) Kosi-Mahananda
(d) Punpun-Sakri

8. **Which river flows from west to east in the middle of Bihar?**
(a) Sone (b) Bagmati
(c) Ganga (d) Mahananda

9. **State the total length of the Ganga river in kms.**
(a) 2350 (b) 2400
(c) 2750 (d) 2500

10. **Ganga river flows through Bihar for how many kilometers?**
(a) 422 (b) 436
(c) 445 (d) 452

11. **How much is the flowing area of Ganga river in sq. kms in Bihar?**
(a) 15165 (b) 16120
(c) 16480 (d) 16920

12. **Where is the origin place of the river Ganga?**
(a) Uttar Pradesh
(b) Uttarakhand
(c) Himachal Pradesh
(d) West Bengal

13. **Ganga river enters in which district of Bihar from Uttar Pradesh?**
(a) Buxar
(b) Arrah
(c) Rohtash
(d) West Champaran

14. **Which of the following rivers decide the borders of Bihar and Uttar Pradesh?**
(a) Ganga (b) Gandak
(c) Karmnasha (d) All of these

15. Which river enters Ganga from the north side (left coast)?
(a) Balan
(b) Mahananda
(c) Ghaghra
(d) All of the above

16. Which of the following rivers enters Ganga from south side (right coast)?
(a) Karmnasha
(b) Punpun
(c) Kiul
(d) All of the above

17. Which river enters into Ganga 10 kms. away from Danapur near west Maner?
(a) Sone (b) Kiul
(c) Punpun (d) Sakri

18. The river Ganga forms the border of Bihar with which state?
(a) Bengal (b) Jharkhand
(c) Odisha (d) Chhattisgarh

19. Ganga river enters Bengal while forming border with which district of Bihar and Jharkhand?
(a) Sahebganj (b) Palamu
(c) Pakud (d) Garhwa

20. The river Ganga flows through how many districts of Bihar?
(a) 8 (b) 9
(c) 10 (d) 11

21. Through which of the following districts, river Ganga does not flow?
(a) Buxar (b) Arrah
(c) Jehandabad (d) Saran

22. Through which of the following districts, river Ganga flows?
(a) Samastipur
(b) Khagadiya
(c) Begusarai
(d) All of the above

23. The place of origin of the Ghaghra river is considered to be________.
(a) Nepal
(b) Uttar Pradesh
(c) Uttarakhand
(d) Himachal Pradesh

24. Which of the following rivers is known by the name of Saryu also?
(a) Karmnasha (b) Sakri
(c) Ghaghra (d) Punpun

25. What is the total length of the Ghaghra river in kms in Bihar?
(a) 76 (b) 83
(c) 87 (d) 93

26. Ghaghra river merges with Ganga river in which district of Bihar?
(a) Saran
(b) East Champaran
(c) West Champaran
(d) Arrah

27. Ghaghra river is known by which other name in the upper region?
(a) Lakhandei
(b) Karnali
(c) Teja
(d) All of the above

28. Which river is made up of mixing of the seven flows?
(a) Kosi (b) Gandak
(c) Karmnasha (d) Punpun

29. Which river is also known by the name of Narayani, Shaligrami and Sadaneera?
(a) Kosi (b) Mahananda
(c) Balan (d) Gandak

30. The origin of which river has occurred from the place in the middle of Manangmot and Kutang areas of Nepal under Annapurna series?
(a) Gandak (b) Kosi
(c) Punpun (d) Balan

31. What is the total length of Gandak river in kms in Bihar?
(a) 618 (b) 624
(c) 630 (d) 636

32. The river Gandak builds up ________ by cutting Annapurna series in Nepal?
(a) Gorge (b) Droni
(c) Kaimiyan (d) Visarp

33. The river Gandak enters which district of Bihar first?
(a) East Champaran
(b) West Champaran
(c) Bhojpur
(d) Buxar

34. In which district in Balmiki Nagar, a barrage has been built on the Gandak river?
(a) Saran
(b) Buxar
(c) Arrah
(d) West Champaran

35. Which world famous fair is held on the confluence of Gandak river?
(a) Shivnath Mela
(b) Babadham Mela
(c) Harihar kshetra Mela
(d) Makar Sankranti Mela

36. Which river flows in the eastern part parallel to the river Gandak?
(a) Karmnasha
(b) Saryu
(c) Boorhi Gandak
(d) Bagmati

37. Which river has its origin in Chautarva Chour near Vishambharpur under Someshwar series hills?
(a) Bagmati (b) Boorhi Gandak
(c) Kosi (d) Balan

38. Which of the following cities lie on riverside of Boorhi Gandak?
(a) Mujaffarpur
(b) Khagadiya
(c) Samastipur
(d) All of the above

39. Which of the following is a tributary of Boorhi Gandak river?
(a) Tilawe
(b) Dhanauti
(c) Kohra
(d) All of the above

40. Which of the following rivers has shifted 150 kms from east to west in the last 200 years?
(a) Kosi (b) Gandak
(c) Balan (d) Bagmati

41. Kosi river forms a delta near Kursaila before merging with which river?
(a) Ganga (b) Bagmati
(c) Kamla (d) Mahananda

42. Which of the following is a major tributary of the Boorhi Gandak?
(a) Bagmati (b) Gandak
(c) Karmnasha (d) Punpun

43. The origin of Bagmati has occurred in Nepal from _______ range?
(a) Aravali (b) Annpurna
(c) Mahabharat (d) Suleman

44. In which district Bagmati river flows?
(a) Darbhanga (b) Mujaffarpur
(c) Madhubani (d) All of these

45. Which of the following is the main tributary of Bagmati?
(a) Lal Vakaiyya
(b) Lakhan Dei
(c) Siptidhar
(d) All of the above

46. Which river enters in Terai area after passing through Mahabharat range in Nepal?
(a) Kamla (b) Punpun
(c) Gandak (d) Burhi Gandak

47. Kamla river enters in which district of Bihar?
(a) Darbhanga (b) Saharasa
(c) Khagariya (d) Madhubani

48. Which river is considered as holy as the Ganga in Mithila area?
(a) Kosi (b) Bagmati
(c) Kamla (d) Balan

49. Which of the following rivers is a tributary of Kamla river?
(a) Soni
(b) Dhori
(c) Bhutahi Balan
(d) All of the above

50. What is the total length in kms of river Kamla in Bihar?
(a) 100 (b) 110
(c) 120 (d) 130

51. Kamla has its major current from which river?
(a) Ganga (b) Kosi
(c) Mahananda (d) Sone

52. Kosi originates from _______ place in Nepal?
(a) Gosai (b) Manokamna
(c) Singhsthan (d) Vaikunth

53. What is the original name of the river Kosi?
(a) Kaushiki (b) Saptaprabha
(c) Keshaki (d) Kaushik

54. Which of the following is a current of the river Kosi?
(a) Indravati Nadi
(b) Arunkosi
(c) Tamrakosi
(d) All of the above

55. All the seven currents of Kosi merge at which place where its name forms as Kosi?
(a) Triveni (b) Balmiki Nagar
(c) Rajgir (d) Pavapuri

56. Which of the following rivers is called the 'Bihar ka shok'?
(a) Kosi (b) Bagmati
(c) Mahananda (d) Punpun

57. Kosi river flows through which district of Bihar?
(a) Supaul
(b) Saharasa
(c) Purnia
(d) All of the above

58. Which of the following rivers is a river of the east flowing through north Bihar?
(a) Mahananda (b) Kamla
(c) Balan (d) Bagmati

59. Which river determines the borders of Bengal and Bihar?
(a) Kamla (b) Kosi
(c) Gandak (d) Mahananda

60. Mahananda flows through which district of Bihar after emerging from the Himalayas?
(a) Kishanganj
(b) Purnia
(c) Katihar
(d) All of the above

61. Which of the following is a river of Bihar's plateau region?
(a) Fala
(b) Uttari Koyal
(c) Ajay
(d) All of the above

62. The origin of which of the following rivers lies in Amarkantak in Madhya Pradesh?
(a) Sone (b) Bagmati
(c) Ajay (d) Mahananda

63. The other name of which of the following rivers is 'Hiranyavah'?
(a) Kosi (b) Bagmati
(c) Sone (d) Fala

64. The origin of which of the following rivers lie near the origin of the Sone river?

(a) Mahanadi (b) Mahananda
(c) Narmada (d) Both (a) and (c)

65. The current of which of the following rivers builds up the 'Ariya' current system?
(a) Sone (b) Kosi
(c) Sakri (d) Gandak

66. Sone river flows in which state before entering into Bihar?
(a) Madhya Pradesh
(b) Uttar Pradesh
(c) Jharkhand
(d) All of the above

67. The total length of the river Sone is ________ kms.
(a) 752 (b) 766
(c) 784 (d) 796

68. For how many kms river Sone flows through the state of Bihar?
(a) 202 (b) 209
(c) 216 (d) 221

69. Which river is the longest flowing tributary of the Ganga in Southern Bihar?
(a) Karmnasha (b) Falgu
(c) Sone (d) Sakri

70. Sone river first enters in which district of Bihar?
(a) Buxar (b) Rohtash
(c) Arrah (d) Gaya

71. Which of the following is a tributary of the river Sone?
(a) Rihand
(b) Kanhar
(c) North Koyal
(d) All of the above

72. When was the first dam constructed on the river Sone?
(a) 1871-72 (b) 1872-73
(c) 1873-74 (d) 1874-75

73. Where was a dam constructed on the river Sone?
(a) Dehri (b) Rajgir
(c) Jamalpur (d) Sasaram

74. On which of the following rivers Indrapuri barrage has been constructed?
(a) Bagmati (b) Mahananda
(c) Sone (d) Kosi

75. When was was Indrapuri Barrage constructed?
(a) 1966 AD (b) 1968 AD
(c) 1970 AD (d) 1972 AD

76. When was a rail-cum road bridge of 1440 meters length was constructed on the river Sone in Koilavar?
(a) 1862 AD (b) 1864 AD
(c) 1866 AD (d) 1868 AD

77. The rail-cum-road bridge constructed in Koilavar is dedicated to which freedom fighter?
(a) Prof Abdul Bari
(b) Haszat Mohani
(c) Hasan Imam
(d) Maulana Mazhrul Haque

78. On which river in India, the longest railway bridge has been constructed?
(a) Ganga (b) Yamuna
(c) Godavari (d) Sone

79. Fala river emerges from which place?
(a) Chhota Nagpur plateau
(b) Kaimur plateau
(c) Kharagpur Hill
(d) Amarkantak plateau

80. What is the name of the main current of Fala?
(a) Ashoka (b) Nirjala
(c) Niranjana (d) Kshipra

81. Where does a river called Mohane merge with the river Fala?
(a) Patna
(b) Bodh Gaya
(c) Hajipur
(d) Vaishali

82. On riverbed of which of the following rivers, Gautam Buddha attained awakening?
(a) Falgu (b) Mahananda
(c) Karmnasha (d) Sakri

83. Where in Bihar 'Pitrapksha' fair is held?
(a) Patna (b) Gaya
(c) Sonepur (d) Pavapuri

84. In which of the following rivers, the ritual of 'Pind-dan'is performed?
(a) Karmnasha (b) Bagmati
(c) Falgu (d) Sakri

85. By which other name is the Falgu river is known?
(a) Karma
(b) Antah-Salila
(c) Lilijan
(d) All of the above

86. Which river gets divided in two parts in Jehanabad district near Barabar Hills?
(a) Shankh (b) Ajay
(c) Falgu (d) Karmnashak

87. Which of the following is a branch of Falgu?
(a) Bhutahi
(b) Karlua
(c) Lokayan
(d) All of the above

88. Which is the origin place of the river Punpun?
(a) Chauraha Pahadi
(b) Ranchi plateau
(c) Chhota Nagpur plateau
(d) Kaimur plateau

89. By which other name is the river Punpun known?
(a) Mohna (b) Kikat
(c) Magadhi (d) Both (b) and (c)

90. In which district, river Punpun flows parallel to river Ganga?
(a) Aurangabad
(b) Arwal
(c) Patna
(d) All of the above

91. At which place, Punpun river merges with Ganga river?
(a) Bihta (b) Fatuha
(c) Danapur (d) Sonepur

92. Which of the following is a tributary of Punpun river?
(a) Madar
(b) Bilaro
(c) Morhar
(d) All of the above

93. In which district, the origin of Ajay river takes place?
(a) Jamui (b) Jehanabad
(c) Navada (d) Arwal

94. Ajay river enters in which district of Jharkhand first from Bihar?
(a) Garhwa (b) Palamu
(c) Deoghar (d) Chhatra

95. Ajay river merges with which river after entering into Bengal?
(a) Ganga (b) Hughli
(c) Brahmputra (d) Gandak

96. Which is the place of origin of Sakri river?
(a) Kaimur plateau
(b) Chhota Nagpur plateau
(c) Amarkantak Hill
(d) Chidiya plateau

97. In which district of Bihar, Sakri river flows?
(a) Patna
(b) Navada
(c) Munger
(d) All of the above

98. Sakri river merges with which other river?
(a) Kosi (b) Gandak
(c) Karmnasha (d) Ganga

99. Which of the following rivers has another name 'Samagadhi'?
(a) Ajay (b) Sakri
(c) Falgu (d) Mohna

100. Which of the following rivers has developed by 5 currents?
(a) Chanan (b) Sakri
(c) Ajay (d) Karmnasha

101. What is the other name of Chanan river?
(a) Mohna (b) Karma
(c) Sakri (d) Panchane

102. Which of the following currents is a current belonging to Panchane?
(a) Paimar
(b) Tilega
(c) Dharanje
(d) All of the above

103. Where is the origin place of Karmnasha river?
(a) Vindhyachal hill
(b) Amarkantak Plateau
(c) Chhota Nagpur plateau
(d) Ranch plateau

104. Karmnasha river merges with which other river near Chausa?
(a) Bagmati (b) Sone
(c) Mahananda (d) Ganga

105. Which of the following rivers is considered unholy according to Hindu religious belief?
(a) Karmnasha (b) Sakri
(c) Mohna (d) Chanan

106. Kiul river has its origin in which plateau?
(a) Hazaribagh (b) Ranchi
(c) Amarkantak (d) Kaimur

107. Kiul river enters first in which district of Bihar?
(a) Arwal (b) Gaya
(c) Aurangabad (d) Jamui

108. Which of the following is a tributary of Kiul?
(a) Burner
(b) Anjan
(c) Halahal
(d) All of the above

109. Kiul river merges with which other river near Suryagarha of Lakhisarai district?
(a) Ganga (b) Gandak
(c) Sone (d) Karmnasha

HOT SPRINGS

1. Which of the following minerals is found in the hot water pond?
(a) Carbon sulphide
(b) Phosphate
(c) Sulphur
(d) Potash

2. Which of the following ponds is situated in Rajgir?
(a) Saptdhara
(b) Brahmkund
(c) Suryakund
(d) All of the above

3. Where are Makhdum kund, Nanak kund and Gomukh kund situated?
(a) Rajgir (b) Navada
(c) Munger (d) Pavapuri

4. The hot water located in Munger is basically situated in the hills of________.
(a) Barabar (b) Nagarjuni
(c) Khadagpur (d) Kaimur

5. Which of the following red Kunds is located in Munger?
(a) Sita Kund
(b) Rameshwar Kund
(c) Lakshman Kund
(d) All of the above

6. Rishi kund, Anya kund and Lakshmishwar kund are located in which district?
(a) East Champaran
(b) Gaya
(c) Munger
(d) Jamui

7. Which of the following hot water ponds is located in Munger?
(a) Shringarrishi kund
(b) Bharari kund
(c) Panchtar kund
(d) All of the above

8. Bhim Barrage is situated in which district?
(a) Munger (b) Bhagalpur
(c) Jamui (d) Arwal

9. Where is Agnikund hot water pond located?
(a) Bihar Sharif (b) Rajgir
(c) Gaya (d) Jamui

10. Which is the kund of Bihar with the highest hot water?
(a) Suryakund
(b) Brahmkund
(c) Makhdum Kund
(d) Rishi kund

11. The temperature of Brahmkund pond is how many centigrades high?
(a) 820 (b) 835
(c) 853 (d) 870

WATERFALLS

1. Waterfalls in Bihar are basically found in _______ district of border plateau area?
(a) Rohtash (b) Kaimur
(c) Gaya (d) All of these

2. Where is Kakolat water located?
(a) Navada (b) Nalanda
(c) Bihar Sharif (d) Rajgir

3. How much the height of Kakolat waterfall in meters?
(a) 30 (b) 47
(c) 58 (d) 60

4. What is the height of Kakolat waterfalls in feet?
(a) 140 (b) 150
(c) 160 (d) 170

5. Kakolat waterfalls has comprised of the seven currents receding from plateau?
(a) Hajaribagh (b) Koderma
(c) Ranchi (d) Chhota Nagpur

6. Sukhladri waterfall is located at which place?
(a) Jharkhand (b) Uttar Pradesh
(c) Bihar (d) Both (b) and (c)

7. Sukhladri waterfall was made of water from which river?
(a) Sakri (b) Kanhar
(c) Niranjana (d) Panchane

8. On which hill Dhuankund waterfall is situated?
(a) Kharagpur (b) Tarachandi
(c) Barabar (d) Nagarjuni

9. In which district Dhuankund waterfall is located?
(a) Rohtash (b) Buxar
(c) Arrah (d) Jamui

10. On which river Dhuankund waterfall is situated?
(a) Kaav (b) Muhane
(c) Tilaiyya (d) Sariswa

11. Durgawati waterfall is located at which place?
(a) Bhojpur (b) Buxar
(c) Rohtash (d) Gaya

12. What is the other name of Durgawati waterfall?
(a) Khadar Koh (b) Sangam
(c) Dhuandhar (d) Sita koh

13. What is the height of Durgawati waterfall in meters?
(a) 75 (b) 80
(c) 85 (d) 90

14. What is the height of Durgawati waterfall in feet?
(a) 300 (b) 290
(c) 280 (d) 270

15. Jiyarkund waterfall is situated in which district?
(a) Gaya (b) Aurangabad
(c) Munger (d) Bhojpur

16. **On which river Jiyarkund waterfall is situated?**
(a) Tilawe (b) Phulvariya
(c) Sariswa (d) Sikarhana

17. **Tamasin waterfall is situated on which river?**
(a) Niranjana (b) Mahane
(c) Sikarhana (d) Sakri

18. **Khuaridah waterfall is located in which district?**
(a) Rohtash (b) Navada
(c) Munger (d) Bhagalpur

19. **How much is the height of Khuaridah waterfall in meters?**
(a) 160 (b) 170
(c) 180 (d) 190

20. **Khuaridah waterfall is situated on which river?**
(a) Mahane (b) Sariswa
(c) Asane (d) Niranjana

21. **Rakim kund waterfall is located in which district?**
(a) Rohtash (b) Navada
(c) Nalanda (d) Buxar

22. **Rakimkund waterfall is situated on which river?**
(a) Mahane (b) Gayaghat
(c) Sariswa (d) Tilave

23. **Okharin kund waterfall is located in which district?**
(a) Rohtash (b) Buxar
(c) Arrah (d) Saharasa

24. **Okharin kund waterfall is located on which river?**
(a) Tilave (b) Sariswa
(c) Gopath (d) Sikarhana

25. **How much is the height of the Okharin kund waterfall in meters?**
(a) 60 (b) 70
(c) 80 (d) 90

26. **Suara waterfall is located in which district?**
(a) Rohtash (b) Bhojpur
(c) Navada (d) Nalanda

27. **How much is the height of Suara Waterfall in meters?**
(a) 120 (b) 110
(c) 100 (d) 90

28. **Devdari waterfall is situated in which district?**
(a) Munger (b) Bhagalpur
(c) Buxar (d) Rohtash

29. **Devdari waterfall is located on which river?**
(a) Karmnasha (b) Bagmati
(c) Gandak (d) Sakri

30. **What is the height of Devdari waterfall in meters?**
(a) 46 (b) 58
(c) 63 (d) 75

31. **Tel Harkund waterfall is located in which district?**
(a) Rohtash (b) Bhojpur
(c) Navada (d) Munger

32. **Telharkund waterfall is located on which river?**
(a) Karmnasha (b) Ajay
(c) West Suara (d) Sakri

33. **What is the height of Telharkund waterfall in meters?**
(a) 50 (b) 60
(c) 70 (d) 80

LAKES

1. **Which of the following rivers is building up Gokhur lake in Bihar?**
(a) Kosi
(b) Boorhi Gandak
(c) Mahananda
(d) All of the above

2. **A lake like submerged place in North Bihar is known by which name?**
(a) Chaur (b) Taal
(c) Mann (d) All of these

3. **Kanwar lake is situated in which district of Bihar?**
(a) Begusarai (b) Navada
(c) Nalanda (d) Darbhanga

4. **The area of Kanwar Lake is how much in sq. kms?**
   (a) 12 (b) 16
   (c) 20 (d) 24
5. **Which of the following lakes is Asia's biggest Gokhur lake?**
   (a) Domna lake
   (b) Anupam lake
   (c) Kanwar lake
   (d) Chilka lake
6. **Kanwar Lake was made by the glide of which river?**
   (a) Ganga (b) Gandak
   (c) Kosi (d) Bagmati
7. **Which of the following vegetation is found in the Kanwar lake?**
   (a) Potomongeton
   (b) Walesneria
   (c) Leplrals
   (d) All of the above
8. **Kusheshwar Sthan Lake is located in which district?**
   (a) Darbhanga (b) Madhubani
   (c) Nalanda (d) Navada
9. **Which river is the source of water for Kusheshwar Sthan Lake?**
   (a) Kamla (b) Balan
   (c) Kareh (d) Both (a) and (c)
10. **When was Kusheshwar Sthan Lake announced as bird sanctuary?**
    (a) 1970 (b) 1972
    (c) 1974 (d) 1976
11. **Dhodha Lake is situated in which district?**
    (a) Katihar (b) Purnia
    (c) Saharasa (d) Kishanganj
12. **Which river is the source of water for Dhodha Lake?**
    (a) Kosi (b) Gandak
    (c) Mahananda (d) Sakri
13. **Simri Bakhtiyarpur Lake is located in which district?**
    (a) Purnia (b) Saharasa
    (c) Kishanganj (d) Munger
14. **Which of the following lakes is the main lake of Simri Bakhtiyarpur Lake?**
    (a) Jamuniya
    (b) Saradiya
    (c) Gobra
    (d) All of the above

WETLAND REGIONS

1. **Which of the following conferences is related to wetland?**
   (a) Cartagena (b) Montreal
   (c) Ramsar (d) Vienna
2. **When was Ramsar Conference held?**
   (a) 1971 AD (b) 1972 AD
   (c) 1973 AD (d) 1974 AD
3. **The place called Ramsar is located in which country?**
   (a) China (b) Japan
   (c) France (d) Iran
4. **Which of the following is an example of a wetland?**
   (a) Chaur
   (b) Mann
   (c) Diyar
   (d) All of the above
5. **Which of the following is located in wetland of Bihar?**
   (a) Kanwar Lake
   (b) Barila
   (c) Kusheshwar Sthan
   (d) All of the above
6. **In which district of Bihar is Barila wetland situated?**
   (a) Vaishali (b) Nalanda
   (c) Navada (d) Munger
7. **What percentage out of the following represents private ownership of Bihar's total wetland?**
   (a) 28 (b) 26
   (c) 24 (d) 21

8. **In which district is Udaipur lake situated?**
   (a) West Champaran
   (b) Vaishali
   (c) Nalanda
   (d) Mujaffarpur
9. **Where is Bhusra Mann located?**
   (a) Motihari (b) Patna
   (c) Vaishali (d) Mujaffarpur
10. **Where is Brahmpura Mann located?**
   (a) Mujaffarpur (b) Katihar
   (c) Kishanganj (d) Purnia
11. **In which district Kesariya Chaur is located?**
   (a) Mujaffarpur
   (b) Vaishali
   (c) Navada
   (d) East Champaran
12. **Where is Chaita Chore located?**
   (a) West Champaran
   (b) East Champaran
   (c) Vaishali
   (d) Navada
13. **Where is Manasi Chaur located?**
   (a) Saharasa (b) Purnia
   (c) Khagariya (d) Kishanganj
14. **Bharthua Chaur is located in which district?**
   (a) Mujaffarpur (b) Vaishali
   (c) Arrah (d) Buxar
15. **Bhagwa Chaur is located in which district?**
   (a) Purnia (b) Khagariya
   (c) Saharasa (d) Katihar
16. **Where is Bora Chaur located?**
   (a) Saharasa (b) Saran
   (c) Siwan (d) Buxar
17. **Where is Parba Murli Chaur located?**
   (a) Gopalganj (b) Saharasa
   (c) Siwan (d) Arrah
18. **In which district is Muradpur Chaur located?**
   (a) Saharasa (b) Gopalganj
   (c) Siwan (d) Saran
19. **Haria Chaur is situated in which district?**
   (a) Saran
   (b) Siwan
   (c) East Champaran
   (d) Katihar
20. **Raghopur wetland area is located in which district?**
   (a) Mujaffarpur
   (b) Saharasa
   (c) Vaishali
   (d) Siwan

Answers

DRAINAGE SYSTEM

1. (a)	**2.** (c)	**3.** (b)	**4.** (c)	**5.** (d)	**6.** (d)	**7.** (b)	**8.** (c)	**9.** (d)	**10.** (c)
11. (a)	**12.** (b)	**13.** (a)	**14.** (d)	**15.** (d)	**16.** (d)	**17.** (a)	**18.** (b)	**19.** (a)	**20.** (d)
21. (c)	**22.** (d)	**23.** (a)	**24.** (c)	**25.** (b)	**26.** (a)	**27.** (d)	**28.** (b)	**29.** (d)	**30.** (a)
31. (c)	**32.** (a)	**33.** (b)	**34.** (d)	**35.** (c)	**36.** (c)	**37.** (b)	**38.** (d)	**39.** (d)	**40.** (a)
41. (a)	**42.** (a)	**43.** (c)	**44.** (d)	**45.** (d)	**46.** (a)	**47.** (d)	**48.** (c)	**49.** (d)	**50.** (c)
51. (b)	**52.** (b)	**53.** (a)	**54.** (d)	**55.** (a)	**56.** (a)	**57.** (d)	**58.** (a)	**59.** (d)	**60.** (d)
61. (d)	**62.** (a)	**63.** (c)	**64.** (d)	**65.** (a)	**66.** (d)	**67.** (c)	**68.** (a)	**69.** (c)	**70.** (b)
71. (d)	**72.** (c)	**73.** (a)	**74.** (c)	**75.** (b)	**76.** (a)	**77.** (a)	**78.** (d)	**79.** (a)	**80.** (c)
81. (b)	**82.** (a)	**83.** (b)	**84.** (c)	**85.** (d)	**86.** (c)	**87.** (d)	**88.** (a)	**89.** (d)	**90.** (d)
91. (b)	**92.** (d)	**93.** (a)	**94.** (c)	**95.** (a)	**96.** (b)	**97.** (d)	**98.** (d)	**99.** (b)	**100.** (a)
101. (d)	**102.** (d)	**103.** (a)	**104.** (d)	**105.** (a)	**106.** (a)	**107.** (d)	**108.** (d)	**109.** (a)	

HOT SPRINGS

1. (c) **2.** (d) **3.** (a) **4.** (c) **5.** (d) **6.** (c) **7.** (d) **8.** (a) **9.** (c) **10.** (b) **11.** (d)

WATERFALLS

1. (d) **2.** (a) **3.** (b) **4.** (c) **5.** (b) **6.** (d) **7.** (b) **8.** (b) **9.** (b) **10.** (a) **11.** (c) **12.** (a) **13.** (d) **14.** (a) **15.** (d) **16.** (b) **17.** (b) **18.** (a) **19.** (c) **20.** (c) **21.** (a) **22.** (b) **23.** (a) **24.** (c) **25.** (d) **26.** (a) **27.** (a) **28.** (d) **29.** (a) **30.** (b) **31.** (a) **32.** (c) **33.** (d)

LAKES

1. (d) **2.** (d) **3.** (a) **4.** (b) **5.** (c) **6.** (b) **7.** (d) **8.** (a) **9.** (d) **10.** (b) **11.** (a) **12.** (c) **13.** (b) **14.** (d)

WETLAND REGIONS

1. (c) **2.** (a) **3.** (d) **4.** (d) **5.** (d) **6.** (a) **7.** (d) **8.** (a) **9.** (d) **10.** (a) **11.** (d) **12.** (a) **13.** (c) **14.** (a) **15.** (c) **16.** (a) **17.** (b) **18.** (a) **19.** (a) **20.** (c)

❑❑❑

15 Climate and Soil

CLIMATE

1. **Bihar is a state situated in ______ zone.**
   (a) Tropical (b) Sub-tropical
   (c) Frigid (d) Temperate
2. **Bihar is a region with what type of climate?**
   (a) Monsoon type
   (b) Mediterranean type
   (c) Sahara like
   (d) Both (a) and (b)
3. **The effect of which of the following types of climate prevails most in Bihar?**
   (a) Cw (b) Cwa
   (c) T2 (d) Ta
4. **Which exerts its maximum effect on the climate of a place?**
   (a) Latitude (b) Longitude
   (c) Ocean (d) Coastal line
5. **Which of the following factors exert its influence on the climate of a place?**
   (a) The distance from the ocean
   (b) Forests
   (c) The quantity of rainfall
   (d) All of the above
6. **In Eastern part of Bihar viz. Arariya, Kishanganj, Purnia and Saharasa which type of climate prevails?**
   (a) Tropical (b) Sub-tropical
   (c) Humid (d) Dry
7. **In north-western Bihar, in Gopalganj, Siwan and Saran, which type of climate prevails?**
   (a) Dry (b) Dry and humid
   (c) Tropical (d) Sub-tropical
8. **The rainfall quantity gets reduced from east to ________in the State.**
   (a) West (b) North
   (c) South (d) Both (a) and (b)
9. **The cyclones in May-June and October-November emerging at which place have an impact over the climate of Bihar?**
   (a) The Arabian Sea
   (b) The Bay of Bengal
   (c) Southern China Sea
   (d) All of the above
10. **During the winter due to western depression, the impact of ________ cyclonic rain occurs on the State?**
    (a) Tropical
    (b) Sub-tropical
    (c) Frigid
    (d) Temperate
11. **Tiwartha has classified the climate of Bihar in which category?**
    (a) Tropical
    (b) Sub-tropical
    (c) Frigid
    (d) Sub-tropical humid
12. **Which is the hottest month in Bihar?**
    (a) April (b) May
    (c) June (d) July

13. **What do we call the hot and dry wind blowing through Bihar?**
(a) Lu (b) Kaal Baisakhi
(c) Mavat (d) Harmattan

14. **The tornades which hit Bihar in May-June are known by the name of what?**
(a) Cherry Blossom
(b) Norvester
(c) Torpedo
(d) Typhoon

15. **During summer, which is the hottest district in Bihar?**
(a) Gaya
(b) Aurangabad
(c) Jehanabad
(d) West Champaran

16. **In which district of Bihar, monsoon arrives first?**
(a) Katihar
(b) Kishanganj
(c) Purnia
(d) Saharasa

17. **Which is the most humid district of Bihar?**
(a) Saharasa
(b) Purnia
(c) Katihar
(d) Kishanganj

18. **In which district of Bihar, maximum rainfall occurs?**
(a) Saran
(b) Kishanganj
(c) Madhubani
(d) Purnia

19. **Rainfall up to how many cms. occurs in Kishanganj?**
(a) 160 (b) 170
(c) 180 (d) 190

20. **In North-east Bihar and Terai belt, the quantity of rainfall is up to _______ cms.**
(a) 170 (b) 180
(c) 190 (d) 200

SOIL

1. **Which of the following is found in soil?**
(a) Humus
(b) Air
(c) Micro-organism
(d) All of the above

2. **Which climatic factor has a main role in making of the soil?**
(a) Water
(b) Humidity
(c) Temperature
(d) All of the above

3. **On 90% of surface area of the state, _______ soil is found.**
(a) Jalaud (b) Chikni
(c) Balua (d) Lal-peeli

4. **Old Jalod or bangar soil is known by which other name?**
(a) Khadar (b) Balsundari
(c) Kagari (d) Balthar

5. **Balsundari soil is of which type?**
(a) Alkali
(b) Acidic
(c) Sandy
(d) All of the above

6. **What is prominent in Bangar soil?**
(a) Nitrogen (b) Potash
(c) Lime (d) All of these

7. **New Jalod soil is known by which other name?**
(a) Bangar (b) Baldhar
(c) Khadar (d) Kagari

8. **What is the colour of Khadar Soil?**
(a) Light Red
(b) Light Black
(c) Black
(d) Deep brown

9. **In which area, an expansion of Khadar soil is found?**
(a) Ganga Valley
(b) Boorhi Ganga Valley
(c) Kosi Valley
(d) All of the above

10. Khadar soil is best for which crop?
(a) Paddy
(b) Wheat
(c) Corn
(d) Millet and White Millet

11. In North-eastern Bihar, which crop is sown in Khadar soil because of high rainfall?
(a) Jute (b) Cotton
(c) Red Lentil (d) Millet

12. There is shortage of ________ in Khadar soil.
(a) Phosphate (b) Nitrogen
(c) Carbon (d) Potash

13. In south Bihar, Jalod soil was made by deposition of which river?
(a) Punpun
(b) Falgu
(c) Sone
(d) All of the above

14. The soil of the plains of south Bihar has been divided in how many sub-categories?
(a) 2 (b) 3
(c) 4 (d) 5

15. Which of the following soils is the soil from South Bihar?
(a) Kagari
(b) Tall
(c) Balthar
(d) All of the above

16. On the riverside of which river, kagari soil is found as an embank-ment?
(a) Sone
(b) Kiul
(c) Punpun
(d) All of the above

17. Which of the following is promi-nent in the Kagari Soil?
(a) Phosphate (b) Potash
(c) Lime (d) Nitrogen

18. During rainy season, what type of soil is found in water flushed areas?
(a) Balthat (b) Tall
(c) Kagari (d) Balsundari

19. Tall soil is famous for production of which crop?
(a) Oilseeds (b) Jute
(c) Cotton (d) Pulses

20. In which district Karail-keval soil is found?
(a) Bhojpur
(b) Jehanabad
(c) Nalanda
(d) All of the above

21. Which of the following soils has a colour ranging from deep brown to yellow?
(a) Balhat
(b) Balsundari
(c) Kagari
(d) Karail-keval

22. Which of the following is present in karail-keval soil?
(a) Balu
(b) Silt
(c) Chika
(d) All of the above

23. What type of soil is found in the congregation area of Chhota Nagpur plateau and the southern plains of the Ganges?
(a) Balthat
(b) Karail-keval
(c) Balsundari
(d) Kagari

24. In which district of Bihar 'red-yellow' soil is found?
(a) Jamui
(b) Banka
(c) Navada
(d) All of the above

25. By which of the following 'Red-Yellow' soil is made up?

(a) Granite

(b) Nees

(c) Chiate

(d) All of the above

26. Which crop is produced in 'red-yellow' soil?

(a) Coarse grains

(b) Pulses

(c) Jute

(d) All of the above

Answers

CLIMATE

1. (b) **2.** (d) **3.** (b) **4.** (a) **5.** (d) **6.** (c) **7.** (b) **8.** (a) **9.** (b) **10.** (d)

11. (b) **12.** (b) **13.** (a) **14.** (b) **15.** (a) **16.** (b) **17.** (d) **18.** (b) **19.** (c) **20.** (d)

SOIL

1. (d) **2.** (d) **3.** (a) **4.** (b) **5.** (d) **6.** (d) **7.** (c) **8.** (d) **9.** (d) **10.** (a)

11. (a) **12.** (b) **13.** (d) **14.** (c) **15.** (d) **16.** (d) **17.** (c) **18.** (b) **19.** (d) **20.** (d)

21. (d) **22.** (d) **23.** (a) **24.** (d) **25.** (d) **26.** (d)

❑❑❑

16 Forest and Wild Life

FOREST

1. **According to Forest Report 2023, the total forest area in Bihar is**
(a) 7,532.45 sq kms
(b) 6,594.47 sq kms
(c) 7,402.30 sq kms
(d) 6,945.47 sq kms

2. **According to the Forest Report 2023, what is the percentage of forest area in Bihar?**
(a) 8.50% (b) 9.50%
(c) 8.00% (d) 9.00%

3. **According to the Forest Report 2023, Bihar has the most dense forest:**
(a)387 sq km (b) 370 sq km
(c) 367 sq km (d) 360 sq km

4. **According to the Forest Report 2023, Bihar has medium dense forest:**
(a) 3,284.21 sq km
(b) 3,861.24 sq km
(c) 3,222.40 sq km
(d) None of the Above

5. **According to the Forest Report, Bihar has open forests in 2023:**
(a) 3,490.24 sq km
(b) 3,861.24 sq km
(c) 3,222.40 sq km
(d) 3,720.46 sq km

6. **According to the Forest Report 2023, the percentage of very dense forest in Bihar is:**
(a) 0.42% (b) 0.41%
(c) 0.43% (d) 0.44%

7. **According to the Forest Report 2023, the percentage of medium dense forests in Bihar is:**
(a) 2.70% (b) 2.94%
(c) 3.28% (d) 3.49%

8. **Keeping in view the rainfall quantity, the natural vegetation of Bihar has been divided in how many categories?**
(a) 2 (b) 3
(c) 4 (d) 5

9. **Which of the following types of forests is found in Bihar?**
(a) Humid Parnpati
(b) Dry Parnpati
(c) Sub-tropical Parnpati
(d) Both (b) and (c)

10. **By how many more centimeters of rain occurs in humid Parnpati forests?**
(a) 90 (b) 100
(c) 110 (d) 120

11. **How much less centimeters of rain occur in dry Parnpati forests?**
(a) 120 (b) 110
(c) 100 (d) 90

12. **Dry Parnpati forests are found in which district of Bihar?**
(a) Kaimur
(b) Rohtash
(c) Navada
(d) All of the above

13. **Which tree is found in dry Parnpati forests?**
(a) Sheesham

(b) Mahua
(c) Kamaltas
(d) All of the above

14. In how many categories forests have been divided in Bihar keeping in view their safety?
(a) 2 (b) 3
(c) 4 (d) 5

15. In which type of forests, permission to graze animals and wood cutting is not granted?
(a) Protected
(b) Reserved
(c) Classified
(d) Unclassified

16. In which type of forests, Government grants permission to graze animals, cut wood and take it away?
(a) Unclassified (b) Classified
(c) Protected (d) Reserved

17. In which type of forests there is no bar on animal grazing and wood cutting but for this a tax is levied?
(a) Classified (b) Unclassified
(c) Reserved (d) Protescted

18. According to Forest Report 2023, the percentage of open forests in Bihar is:
(a) 4.10% (b) 4.09%
(c) 4.36% (d) 4.55%

19. According to Forest Report 2023, what is the area of bushes in Bihar?
(a) 260.80 sq km
(b) 260.90 sq km
(c) 260.50 sq km
(d) 2260.40 sq km

20. According to the Forest Report 2023, which district in Bihar has the most dense forest?
(a) Jamui
(b) Lakhisarai
(c) Munger
(d) West Champaran

21. According to the Forest Report 2023, in which district of Bihar the most medium dense forests are found?
(a) West Champaran
(b) Nalanda
(c) Rohtas
(d) Saran

22. According to Forest Report 2023, which district in Bihar has the highest total open forest?
(a) Buxar (b) Bhaujpur
(c) Gaya (d) Kaimur

23. What is the area of very dense forest in Jamui district?
(a) 38.78 sq km
(b) 35.32 sq km
(c) 30.44 sq km
(d) 27.78 sq km

24. According to the Forest Report 2023, what is the area of medium dense forest in Patna, the capital of Bihar?
(a) 20.3 sq km (b) 19.4 sq km
(c) 19.90 sq km (d) 19.70 sq km

25. According to Forest Report 2023, what is the area of open forest in Bihar?
(a) 3,861.24 sq km
(b) 3,502.20 sq km
(c) 3,701.34 sq km
(d) 3,465.80 sq km

26. According to Forest Report 2023, what is the area of medium dense forest in Bihar?
(a) 3,861.24 sq km
(b) 3,260.21 sq km
(c) 3,877.05 sq km
(d) 3,284.21 sq km

27. According to Forest Report 2023, what is the area of dense forest in Bihar?
(a) 330.00 (b) 387.00
(c) 350.00 (d) 349.00

28. According to Forest Report 2023, Siwan district in Bihar has open forests:

(a) 6.80 sq km
(b) 6.50 sq km
(c) 6.90 sq km
(d) 6.30 sq km

29. Which of the following trees is mainly found in hilly slopes and terai belts?
(a) Semal (b) Sheesham
(c) Sal (d) Toon

30. Which of the following types of wood is used for making boxes and in Toy Industry?
(a) Semal (b) Sal
(c) Sheesham (d) Mango

31. Tussar (a type of silk) is produced mainly in ________district.
(a) Munger (b) Bhagalpur
(c) Gaya (d) Navada

32. In ________district 'setsar'- the silk worms reared on the 'Arjun' trees are produced.
(a) Navada (b) Nalanda
(c) Munger (d) Bhagalpur

33. 'Lah' is produced by rearing of which worm?
(a) Bonex (b) Lesifer
(c) Legim (d) Kogem

34. The 'Lah' worm is reared on which tree?
(a) Semal (b) Kusum
(c) Palash (d) Both (b) and (c)

35. 'Lah' is used in which industry?
(a) Toys (b) Bangles
(c) Lehethi (d) Both (b) and (c)

36. In which district, 'Sabai' grass is produced?
(a) Bhagalpur (b) Munger
(c) Navada (d) Jamui

37. 'Sabai' grass is used to manufacture________.
(a) Toys (b) Glue
(c) String (d) Bangles

38. In which district, 'sijiming' and cardboard industry has developed?
(a) Saharasa
(b) Samastipur
(c) Darbhanga
(d) Both (b) and (c)

39. In which district of Bihar, plywood industry has developed?
(a) Hajipur
(b) Mujaffarpur
(c) Betia
(d) All of the above

40. In which district catholic (kaththa) industry has developed?
(a) East Champaran
(b) West Champaran
(c) Sara
(d) Siwan

41. In which district in Bihar silk industry is centered?
(a) Bhagalpur
(b) Jamui
(c) Jehanabad
(d) Saharasa

42. When was the first forest policy of the independent India formulated?
(a) 1949 (b) 1950
(c) 1951 (d) 1952

43. In which of the following year, the new Forest policy was announced?
(a) 1988 (b) 1986
(c) 1984 (d) 1982

44. According to National Forest policy, how much area in percentage should bear forests?
(a) 30.30% (b) 31.31%
(c) 32.32% (d) 33.31%

45. According to National Forest Policy, how much area in percentage is fixed where forests are compulsory in Bihar for the purpose of safeguarding environment?
(a) 20 (b) 22
(c) 25 (d) 28

46. The aim of Hariyali Mission was to increase the coverage area of forests in Bihar to upto 15% by which year?
(a) 2017 (b) 2019
(c) 2020 (d) 2022

47. Under Hariyali Mission, uptil 2012-17, tree plantation on how many lakhs of hectares of land in Bihar was to be done?
(a) 2.50 (b) 3.15
(c) 3.95 (d) 4.60

48. Which scheme is being operated to make Hariyali Mission a success?
(a) Krishi Vaniki
(b) Krishi Vikas
(c) Krishi Madad
(d) Krishi Samaj

49. Under Krishi Vaniki Scheme, plantation of which of the following is done?
(a) Semal (b) Ashok
(c) Poplar (d) Goolar

50. Which of the following schemes are run by the Government of Bihar to encourage tree plantation and to safeguard environment?
(a) Mukhyamantri Chhatra Vriksharopan Yojna
(b) Mukhyamantri kisan vriksharopan Yojna
(c) Mukhyamantri Niji Poudhshala Yojna
(d) Both (a) and (c)

51. Which class of students have been included under the Mukhyamantri Chhatra Vriksharopan Yojna?
(a) 5th (b) 6th
(c) 7th (d) 8th

52. Which of the following works is done under Hariyali Mission Scheme?
(a) Beej sangrahan
(b) Mrada janch
(c) Identification of good trees
(d) All of these

53. 'Har Parisar-Hara Parisar' scheme has been launched by which State Government?
(a) Bihar
(b) Jharkhand
(c) Uttar Pradesh
(d) Odisha

54. How many districts have been selected under the Green Mission Scheme?
(a) 2 (b) 3
(c) 4 (d) 5

55. Which of the following pairs is not a selected place under Green India Mission?
(a) Adhyor-Kaimur
(b) Imamganj-Gaya
(c) Raxaul-Eastern Champaran
(d) Dharhara-Munger

56. When is World Humid Land day is celebrated?
(a) 26 January (b) 2 February
(c) 8 March (d) 5 June

57. When is World Forestry Day celebrated?
(a) 15 January (b) 28 February
(c) 21 March (d) 18 April

58. When is World Migratory Birds day celebrated?
(a) First week of January
(b) Second week of May
(c) Third week of August
(d) Fourth week of December

59. When is World Organism Diversity Day celebrated?
(a) 21 March
(b) 22 May
(c) 18 June
(d) 16 August

60. When is World Environment Day celebrated?
(a) 4 February (b) 22 March
(c) 18 May (d) 5 June

61. When is Bihar Prithvi Diwas celebrated?
(a) 9 August (b) 12 June
(c) 18 May (d) 13 March

62. When is World Ozone day celebrated?
(a) 18 March
(b) 16 June
(c) 16 September
(d) 8 October

63. **When is Forest Fauna Day celebrated?**
(a) 2-9 March
(b) 9-16 May
(c) 1-7 August
(d) 2-9 October

64. **When is World Animal Welfare Day celebrated?**
(a) 4 October
(b) 5 August
(c) 13 May
(d) 4 June

65. **When is Dolphin Day celebrated?**
(a) 16 March
(b) 18 May
(c) 14 August
(d) 5 October

66. **When is Earth Day celebrated?**
(a) 14 February
(b) 21 March
(c) 22 April
(d) 14 June

67. **When is World Water Day celebrated?**
(a) 22 March (b) 18 May
(c) 14 June (d) 18 August

WILD LIFE & ITS CONSERVATION

1. **When was Forest Animal Protection Act Passed?**
(a) 1970 (b) 1972
(c) 1974 (d) 1976

2. **Who is the Chairman of Forest Animal Board?**
(a) The President
(b) The Environment Minister
(c) The Environment Secretary
(d) The Prime Minister

3. **How many National Parks are there at present in Bihar?**
(a) 1 (b) 2
(c) 3 (d) 4

4. **How many Forest Animal Sanctuaries are there at present in Bihar?**
(a) 10 (b) 11
(c) 12 (d) 13

5. **In which district, Valmiki National Park is situated?**
(a) East Champaran
(b) West Champaran
(c) Navada
(d) Vaishali

6. **When was Valmiki National Park founded?**
(a) 1983 (b) 1985
(c) 1987 (d) 1989

7. **Where is Gautam Buddha Forest Animals Sanctuary situated?**
(a) Gaya
(b) Nalanda
(c) Munger
(d) Bhagalpur

8. **In which district Nagi Bandh Bird Sanctuary is located?**
(a) Jehanabad
(b) Jamui
(c) Navada
(d) Buxar

9. **In which district, Nakti Bandh Bird Sanctuary is located?**
(a) Jamui
(b) Aurangabad
(c) Gaya
(d) Arrah

10. **In which district Valmilki Tiger Reserve is situated?**
(a) Saran
(b) Siwan
(c) West Champaran
(d) Buxar

11. **In which district Kusheshwar Sthan Bird Sanctuary is situated?**
(a) Darbhanga (b) Begusarai
(c) Shivhar (d) Sheikhupura

12. In which district Bhimbandh Forest Animal Sanctuary is located?

(a) Buxor (b) Arrah
(c) Madhubani (d) Munger

13. In which district Vikramshila Gangey Dolphin Aashrayeni is located?

(a) Bhagalpur
(b) Buxar
(c) Arrah
(d) Jehanabad

14. In which district Udaipur Forest Animal Sanctuary is located?

(a) East Champaran
(b) West Champaran
(c) Navada
(d) Madhubani

15. In which district Pant Forest Animal Sanctuary is located?

(a) Nalanda
(b) Navada
(c) Madhubani
(d) Jamui

16. In which district Barela Lake Bird Sanctuary is located?

(a) Mujaffarpur
(b) Samastipur
(c) Gaya
(d) Vaishali

17. In which district Kaimur Forest Animal Sanctuary is located?

(a) Madhubani
(b) Kaimur
(c) Rohtash
(d) Both (b) and (c)

18. Where is Indian Forest Animal Institute located?

(a) Chennai
(b) Dehradun
(c) Patna
(d) Asansol

19. Where is Ganga Dolphin Research Centre situated?

(a) Patna (b) Dhanbad
(c) Bhopal (d) Lucknow

20. The total area in sq. kms of Valmiki Tiger Reserve is________.

(a) 864 (b) 878
(c) 889 (d) 899

21. How many tigers were there in Valmiki Tiger Reserve area in the year 2018-19 according to the data released by Government of India?

(a) 36 (b) 38
(c) 40 (d) 42

22. Where is Sanjay Gandhi Zoologocal Garden located?

(a) Patna (b) Bhagalpur
(c) Mujaffarpur (d) Samastipur

23. In which Park of Bihar, Asia's biggest Rhinoceros Reproduction Centre is located?

(a) Valmiki National Garden
(b) Gautam Buddha Sanctuary
(c) Sanjay Gandhi Zoological Garden
(d) Nakti Bandh Bird Sanctuary

24. How much compensation amount is paid to the family of a victim of forest animal attack by the State Government?

(a) 1 lakh (b) 1.5 lakh
(c) 2 lakh (d) 2.5 lakh

25. How much money is paid by the State Government to the critically injured person on account of attack by forest animals?

(a) 60 thousand
(b) 70 thousand
(c) 80 thousand
(d) 90 thousand

26. Who has been authorized to give permission to kill a 'Neel Gaay'?

(a) District officer
(b) Sub-Division Officer
(c) Zonal Officer
(d) Both (a) and (b)

Answers

FOREST

1. (a)	**2.** (c)	**3.** (a)	**4.** (a)	**5.** (b)	**6.** (b)	**7.** (d)	**8.** (a)	**9.** (d)	**10.** (d)
11. (a)	**12.** (d)	**13.** (d)	**14.** (b)	**15.** (a)	**16.** (d)	**17.** (b)	**18.** (a)	**19.** (a)	**20.** (d)
21. (a)	**22.** (d)	**23.** (d)	**24.** (c)	**25.** (a)	**26.** (d)	**27.** (b)	**28.** (c)	**29.** (c)	**30.** (a)
31. (b)	**32.** (d)	**33.** (b)	**34.** (d)	**35.** (d)	**36.** (a)	**37.** (c)	**38.** (d)	**39.** (d)	**40.** (b)
41. (a)	**42.** (d)	**43.** (a)	**44.** (d)	**45.** (b)	**46.** (a)	**47.** (d)	**48.** (a)	**49.** (c)	**50.** (d)
51. (b)	**52.** (d)	**53.** (a)	**54.** (c)	**55.** (c)	**56.** (b)	**57.** (c)	**58.** (b)	**59.** (b)	**60.** (d)
61. (a)	**62.** (c)	**63.** (d)	**64.** (a)	**65.** (d)	**66.** (c)	**67.** (a)			

WILD LIFE & ITS CONSERVATION

1. (b)	**2.** (d)	**3.** (a)	**4.** (c)	**5.** (b)	**6.** (d)	**7.** (a)	**8.** (b)	**9.** (a)	**10.** (c)
11. (a)	**12.** (d)	**13.** (a)	**14.** (b)	**15.** (a)	**16.** (d)	**17.** (d)	**18.** (b)	**19.** (a)	**20.** (d)
21. (c)	**22.** (a)	**23.** (c)	**24.** (c)	**25.** (a)	**26.** (d)				

❑❑❑

17 Agriculture

AGRICULTURE

1. **Bihar is predominantly an agricultural State where ________ percent population is dependent on Agriculture.**
(a) 80 (b) 82
(c) 84 (d) 86

2. **Out of the total food grain production of the country what percentage is produced by Bihar A what percentage?**
(a) 4.2 (b) 5.4
(c) 6.6 (d) 7.2

3. **Of the total gross produce of the State how much is obtained from agriculture sector is percentage?**
(a) 22.9 (b) 21.5
(c) 20.9 (d) 19.8

4. **Of the total working population of Bihar, what percentage is engaged in agriculture activity only?**
(a) 75 (b) 77
(c) 79 (d) 81

5. **The basic fundamental of Bihar's economy is________.**
(a) Industry
(b) Agriculture
(c) Mineral resources
(d) Construction

6. **Which of the following natural calamities affect Bihar every year and make it suffer?**
(a) Tsunami (b) Flood
(c) Drought (d) Both (b) and (c)

7. **Most of Bihar's land area is ________.**
(a) Plains (b) Plateau
(c) Marshy (d) All of these

8. **Which of the following factors leave an effect on the development of land use model in Bihar?**
(a) Terrain (b) Climate
(c) Rains (d) All of these

9. **In ________ Bihar, development of agricultural land is minimum because of plateau areas, hilly areas and uneven land belts.**
(a) Northern (b) Southern
(c) Western (d) Eastern

10. **In which part of Bihar, the maximum number of forests and grazing areas are situated?**
(a) Eastern (b) Western
(c) Northern (d) Southern

11. **In which district of Bihar in particular, there is plenty of barren land?**
(a) Aurangabad
(b) Navada
(c) Gaya
(d) All of the above

12. **In South-Western Bihar, due to expansion of________canal irrigation system, the area under cultivation has increased.**
(a) Sone
(b) Gandak
(c) Mahananda
(d) Bagmati

13. In which district, Barela, Saleem Ali and Jubba Sahni forest animals sanctuaries are located?
(a) Munger (b) Bhagalpur
(c) Vaishali (d) Navada

14. In which district, Rajgir Forest Animal Santuary is situated?
(a) Navada (b) Nalanda
(c) Munger (d) Gaya

15. What is the net sowing area in percentage terms of the State?
(a) 52.1 (b) 53.8
(c) 55.3 (d) 56.1

16. In how many districts of the State, net sowing area is more than 60 percent?
(a) 3 (b) 4
(c) 5 (d) 6

17. The maximum net sowing area in percentage is in which district of the state?
(a) Buxar (b) Arrah
(c) Bhagalpur (d) Siwan

18. What is the net sowing area in percentage in Buxar?
(a) 81 (b) 83
(c) 85 (d) 87

19. The minimum net sowing area in percentage is in which district of Bihar?
(a) Gaya (b) Vaishali
(c) Jamui (d) Navada

20. What is the net sowing area in percentage in Jamui?
(a) 15 (b) 17
(c) 19 (d) 21

21. The ratio of the Gross sown area to the net sown area is called what?
(a) Agricultura Ratio
(b) Crop density
(c) The agricultural area (per sq. meter)
(d) Net sowing area

22. The study of crop density is always made in _______.
(a) Acre (b) Percentage
(c) Beegha (d) Hectare

23. In how many agricultural density areas India has been divided?
(a) 2 (b) 3
(c) 4 (d) 5

24. In which of the following agricultural density areas, Bihar has been categorized?
(a) Low
(b) Middle
(c) Low-middle
(d) High

25. Out of the following, what figure represents the actual agriculture density of Bihar?
(a) 138 (b) 132
(c) 126 (d) 120

26. What is the main reason of increase in Bihar's agricultural density?
(a) Use of high quality seeds
(b) Expansion of irrigation facility
(c) Increased mechanization of agriculture
(d) Increased use of fertilizers

27. The gross crop area of Bihar is how many hectares?
(a) 75.75 (b) 76.12
(c) 77.89 (d) 78.82

28. Which district in Bihar gives the maximum crop density?
(a) Saharasa
(b) Shivhar
(c) Arariya
(d) All of the above

29. Which district of Bihar gives the minimum crop density?
(a) Sheikhpura
(b) Arwal
(c) Munger
(d) All of the above

30. A study of agriculture crop model makes it clear that in Bihar there is abundance of ______ crop.
(a) Cash
(b) Pulses
(c) Food grains
(d) All of the above

31. In how much area in percentage of the total agricultural land in Bihar, production of food grains happens?
(a) 60 (b) 70
(c) 80 (d) 90

32. ______ means that group of crop which is produced in a particular region in one particular year.
(a) Gross sowing area
(b) Crop combination
(c) Crop density
(d) Crop irrigation area

33. The American scholar ______ has first used the statistical method to determine the area for crop combination.
(a) James Edmus
(b) Chris Jacks
(c) Vibhar
(d) Michael Holmes

34. The determination of crop combination area in Bihar has been done on the basis of how many crops?
(a) 6 (b) 8
(c) 10 (d) 12

35. Which vegetable has been included for determination of crop combination?
(a) Tomatoes (b) Potatoes
(c) Cauliflower (d) Spinach

36. Which of the following pulse crops has not been included in crop combination?
(a) Soyabean (b) Red Lentil
(c) Tur (d) All of these

37. Which of the following pulse crops has been included in crop combination?
(a) Khesari
(b) Moong
(c) Chana
(d) All of the above

38. Which of the following foodgrain crops has not been included in crop combination?
(a) Paddy (b) Millet
(c) Wheat (d) Corn

39. Which of the following cash crops has been included in crop combination?
(a) Cotton
(b) Jute
(c) Sugarcane
(d) Both (b) and (c)

40. India has been divided into how many crop combination areas?
(a) 4 (b) 5
(c) 6 (d) 7

41. Largest part of Bihar has been divided in how many cash combination areas?
(a) 2 (b) 3
(c) 4 (d) 5

42. Who of the following has used the procedure based on experience to determine the agricultural region of Bihar?
(a) Hazari Prasad
(b) Parmeshwar Dayal
(c) Ayodhya Prasad
(d) Both (b) and (c)

43. Prof. Parmeshwar Dayal has divided Bihar into how many agricultural regions based on his method based on experience?
(a) 51 (b) 53
(c) 55 (d) 57

44. In how many agricultural regions Ayodhya Prasad has divided Bihar?
(a) 3 (b) 4
(c) 5 (d) 6

45. Who has divided Bihar into 12 agricultural regions by using statistical method?
(a) Prof Inayat Ahmad
(b) Prof Imtiaz Ahmad
(c) Prof Khalil Ahmad
(d) Avdhesh Singh

46. Prof. Inayat Ahmad has divided Bihar into how many agricultural regions?
(a) 8 (b) 10
(c) 12 (d) 14

47. R. L. Singh has divided Bihar into how many agricultural regions?
(a) 4 (b) 5
(c) 6 (d) 7

48. Which district of the State has been kept in single crop region?
(a) Munger (b) Madhubani
(c) Saran (d) Gaya

49. Which of the following districts has been kept under two crops region?
(a) Purnia (b) Katihar
(c) Kishanganj (d) Saharasa

50. In how many agricultural climate areas, the entire India has been divided?
(a) 9 (b) 11
(c) 13 (d) 15

51. Bihar comes under which Agricultural Climate Zone of India?
(a) Zone 4 (b) Zone 3
(c) Zone 2 (d) Zone 1

52. Which area of Bihar comes under agriculture climatic Zone-4?
(a) Terai Province
(b) The northern plain of the Ganges
(c) The intermediate province of the Ganges
(d) Southern Bihar

53. In how many sub-agriculture climatic zones Bihar has been divided into?
(a) 2 (b) 3
(c) 4 (d) 5

54. In north-western 'jalod' plains of Bihar, how many districts have been included?
(a) 9 (b) 11
(c) 13 (d) 15

55. What type of climate prevails in the north-western 'jalod' plains province?
(a) Tropical
(b) Dry
(c) Sub humid
(d) Both (b) and (c)

56. On what percentage of the north-western 'jalod' plains province of the State, agricultural activities are being undertaken?
(a) 60 (b) 65
(c) 70 (d) 75

57. How much area of the state's north-western 'jalod' plains province is irrigated (in percentage)?
(a) 38 (b) 40
(c) 42 (d) 44

58. How many districts of the state have been included in the north-western 'jalod' plains region?
(a) 8 (b) 9
(c) 10 (d) 11

59. Which of the following areas is a flood area of Bihar?
(a) North-west
(b) North-east
(c) South-east
(d) South-west

60. What percentage of area, agriculture activities take place in north-eastern 'jalod' plains region of the State?
(a) 56 (b) 58
(c) 60 (d) 62

61. What percentage of land in north-eastern 'jalod' plains region is irrigated?
(a) 42 (b) 44
(c) 46 (d) 48

62. In which area of Bihar, highest irrigation facilities have developed?
(a) North-east
(b) North-west
(c) South-west
(d) South

63. What percentage of land of South Bihar is irrigated?
(a) 71 (b) 73
(c) 75 (d) 77

64. Which of the following districts come under north-western jalod plains region?
(a) East Champaran
(b) West Champaran
(c) Saran
(d) All of the above

65. Which district comes under north-western jalod plains region?
(a) Siwan (b) Sitamarhi
(c) Shivhar (d) All of these

66. Which district does not come under north-western jalod plains region?
(a) Samastipur
(b) Gaya
(c) Mujaffarpur
(d) Begusarai

67. Which district comes under norteastern jalod plains region?
(a) Saharasa (b) Katihar
(c) Supaul (d) All of these

68. Which of the following districts does not come under north-eastern jalod plains region?
(a) Madhepura (b) Gopalganj
(c) Khagariya (d) Arariya

69. Which district come under south Bihar jalod plains region?
(a) Sheikhpura
(b) Munger
(c) Jamui
(d) All of the above

70. Which district does not come under south Bihar jalod plains region?
(a) Banka
(b) Kishanganj
(c) Buxar
(d) Patna

71. Which district comes under South Bihar jalod plains region?
(a) Arwal
(b) Aurangabad
(c) Kaimur
(d) All of the above

72. Which district does not come under South Bihar jalod plains region?
(a) Rohtash (b) Saran
(c) Navada (d) Lakhisarai

73. Which type of soil is found in Southern region?
(a) Domat
(b) Balui Domat
(c) Clay
(d) All of the above

74. Which crop is produced in Bihar?
(a) Fibrous
(b) Oil-seeds
(c) Sugarcane
(d) All of the above

75. Land reforms come under which class of reforms?
(a) Structural
(b) Institutional
(c) Fundamental
(d) Both (a) and (b)

76. Which of the following comes under structural reforms?
(a) Use of advanced seeds
(b) Use of chemical fertilizer
(c) Agriculture mechanization
(d) All of the above

77. After division of the State in the year 2000, mineral resources and the industries based on minerals went to which State?
(a) Bengal (b) Odisha
(c) Jharkhand (d) Chhattisgarh

78. How many types of crops are mainly produced in Bihar?
(a) 2 (b) 3
(c) 4 (d) 5

79. Which of the following crops is produced in Bihar?
(a) Kharif (b) Rabi
(c) Jayad (d) All of these

80. Bhadai and Aghani type of crops are produced in which crop season?
(a) Jayad (b) Kharif
(c) Rabi (d) All of these

81. Which of the following crops are produced during Kharif season?
(a) Paddy (b) Corn
(c) Millet (d) All of these

82. Which crop does not come under Kharif season?
(a) Pearl millet
(b) Chickpeas
(c) Arhar
(d) Moong

83. When does sowing of Kharif season crop takes place?
(a) January-February
(b) March-April
(c) June-July
(d) August-Septemebr

84. When does harvesting of the kharif season crop takes place?
(a) October-November
(b) September-October
(c) March-April
(d) January-February

85. Which of the following Kharif season crops is produced annually?
(a) Sugarcane
(b) Cotton
(c) Jute
(d) Both (a) and (c)

86. Which of the following crops come under Rabi crop season?
(a) Wheat (b) Jo
(c) Chickpeas (d) All of these

87. Which crop does not come under Rabi season?
(a) Peas
(b) Mustard
(c) Moong
(d) Potatoes

88. When does sowing of the Rabi season crops takes place?
(a) January-February
(b) March-April
(c) May-June
(d) October-November

89. When does harvesting of the Rabi season crops takes place?
(a) January-February
(b) March-April
(c) May-June
(d) August-September

90. Jayad crop is produced in between _______in regular irrigated areas.
(a) January-February
(b) March-June
(c) May-July
(d) August-September

91. Which of the following is the main crop of Bihar?
(a) Paddy (b) Wheat
(c) Corn (d) Pearl Millets

92. Which of the following is an example of cash crop?
(a) Tobacco
(b) Jute
(c) Red Chilly
(d) All of the above

93. In Bihar which crop is cultivated in the maximum area?
(a) Wheat (b) Paddy
(c) Corn (d) Sugarcane

94. __________is a crop cultivated in tropical and humid air conditions?
(a) Paddy (b) Wheat
(c) Corn (d) Pearl millet

95. In which district of Bihar, 'Boro' paddy is cultivated?
(a) Purnia
(b) East Champaran
(c) West Champaran
(d) All of the above

96. When is 'Boro' paddy sown?
(a) April-May
(b) June-July
(c) August-September
(d) November-December

97. Which of the following are rice producing districts of Bihar?
(a) Rohtash (b) Mujaffarpur
(c) Sitamarhi (d) All of these

98. Which of the following is a major variety of paddy?
(a) Prabhat (b) Saket
(c) Sita (d) All of these

99. Which of the following is not a major variety of paddy?
(a) Kanak
(b) Sonalika
(c) Swarga sab-1
(d) All of the above

100. IR-36 is a species of which crop?
(a) Paddy (b) Wheat
(c) Corn (d) Sugarcane

101. Which crop is Bihar's second major food grains crop?
(a) Corn (b) Sugarcane
(c) Wheat (d) Barley (Jau)

102. Jalod domat soil, temperature from 140 to 180 degree centigrade and rains of 50-100 centimetres are the geographical conditions for which of the following crops?
(a) Wheat (b) Paddy
(c) Corn (d) Mustard

103. Which of the following is a wheat producing district?
(a) Darbhanga
(b) Saran
(c) Aurangabad
(d) All of the above

104. Which is highest producing district in respect of wheat production?
(a) Rohtash (b) Saran
(c) Siwan (d) Gopalganj

105. Which district has the highest production density in respect of wheat crop?
(a) Kishanganj (b) Katihar
(c) Purnia (d) Saharasa

106. On what percentage of total cultivated area in Bihar, wheat is produced?
(a) 23 (b) 25
(c) 27 (d) 29

107. What place does Bihar occupy in respect of wheat production?
(a) 5th (b) 7th
(c) 9th (d) 11th

108. Which of the following is a variety of wheat?
(a) C-306 (b) K-9107
(c) PBW-343 (d) All of these

109. HD-2824 is a species of which crop?
(a) Wheat (b) Paddy
(c) Corn (d) Mustard

110. Which type of insects are seen predominantly in wheat?
(a) Mahu
(b) Bhoora Harda
(c) Peela Harda
(d) All of the above

111. Which of the following diseases is the one which afflicts wheat?
(a) Jhulsa Disease
(b) Kalika disease
(c) Akdi disease
(d) All of the above

112. Which is the third major crop cultivated in Bihar?
(a) Sugarcane
(b) Corn
(c) Mustard
(d) Soya bean

113. Which of the following crops is cultivated in Bihar during Kharif, Rabi and summer seasons?
(a) Sugarcane
(b) Corn
(c) Millet
(d) Pearl Millet

114. Domat and Baloi soil, temperature 180-270 degree celcius and rains 60-110 centimetres are the geographical conditions for which of the following crops?
(a) Wheat (b) Corn
(c) Sugarcane (d) Cotton

115. Which is the major corn producing district?
(a) Katihar
(b) Madhepura
(c) Khagariya
(d) All of the above

116. Which district holds the first position in respect of corn production?
(a) Bhagalpur (b) Katihar
(c) Khagariya (d) Purnia

117. During Rabi season, which crop is cultivated along with corn?
(a) Potatoes
(b) Peas
(c) Raddish
(d) All of the above

118. During Kharif season, which crop is cultivated along with corn?
(a) Urad (b) Arhar
(c) Lobia (d) All of these

119. 'Shaktiman' is a seed belonging to which crop?
(a) Corn (b) Sugarcane
(c) Paddy (d) Arhar

120. In corn which quality protein is found high quantity?
(a) Laikodin
(b) Licin
(c) Triptofen
(d) All of the above

121. Which of the following insects is found in corn?
(a) Kajra
(b) Dhad Chhedak
(c) Bhutta Chhidrak
(d) All of the above

122. Which disease is found in corn?
(a) Jhulsa
(b) Harda
(c) Mahu
(d) Both (a) and (b)

123. Which of the following crops is mainly cultivated in un-irrigated area?
(a) Corn (b) Barley (Jau)
(c) Wheat (d) Paddy

124. Which is the major Jo producing district of Bihar?
(a) Western Champaran
(b) Kaimur
(c) Aurangabad
(d) All of the above

125. Which of the following is a major variety of Jo?
(a) Ratna (b) Azad
(c) Jyoti (d) All of these

126. K-125 is a species of which crop?
(a) Jau (b) Wheat
(c) Corn (d) Sugarcane

127. Madua (ragi) is a crop which comes up in which type of climate?
(a) Tropical (b) Subtropical
(c) Dry (d) Temperate

128. Which place does Bihar occupy in the country in production of Ragi?
(a) First (b) Second
(c) Third (d) Fourth

129. In which district of Bihar, highest production of Ragi is achieved?
(a) Begusarai
(b) Gaya
(c) Rohtash
(d) Darbhanga

130. Which pulse crop is cultivated in Bihar?
(a) Arhar (b) Moong
(c) Chana (d) All of these

131. In which district of Bihar, chickpeas is produced to the maximum?
(a) Patna
(b) Gaya
(c) Aurangabad
(d) Kaimur

132. By which of the following crops nitrogen is stabilized?
(a) Barley
(b) Cotton Chickpeas
(c) Jute
(d) All of the above

133. Which of the following is a species of chickpeas?
(a) Rajendra
(b) Pusa-256
(c) BR-72
(d) All of the above

134. RAU-52 is the species of which crop?
(a) Arhar (b) Wheat
(c) Chickpeas (d) Sugarcane

135. Which crop is jointly cultivated along with chickpeas in the State?
(a) Rai (b) Sarson
(c) Shrisee (d) All of these

136. Which of the following insects is found in chickpeas?
(a) Fali Chhedak keet
(b) Kajra keet
(c) Semilooper
(d) All of the above

137. Which of the following diseases is found in chickpeas?
(a) Ukhda (b) Jemophil
(c) Stemfilium (d) Both (a) and (c)

138. Which crop bears the other name - 'Tuar'?
(a) Barley (b) Arhar
(c) Moong (d) Fali

139. Which is the highest producing district of Arhar?
(a) Gaya (b) Navada
(c) Munger (d) Jamui

140. Which is the district with highest Arhar producing area?
(a) Nalanda (b) Sheikhpura
(c) Kaimur (d) Supaul

141. Which is the low quality pulse crop?
(a) Arhar (b) Masur
(c) Khesari (d) Moong

142. In which district, maximum production of Khesari is obtained?
(a) Bhagalpur (b) Navada
(c) Gaya (d) Patna

143. In which district, maximum Khesari production area is there?
(a) Gaya (b) Aurangabad
(c) Bhagalpur (d) Saran

144. For Khesari production, which type of soil is suitable?
(a) Domat (b) Black
(c) Red (d) Laterite

145. Which is the highest masoor producing district?
(a) East Champaran
(b) Samastipur
(c) Begusarai
(d) Patna

146. Which of the following is a Moong producing district?
(a) Mujaffarpur
(b) Saharasa
(c) Darbhanga
(d) All of the above

147. Which is the major oilseeds crop of Bihar?
(a) Soyabean (b) Mustard
(c) Rai (d) Both (b) and (c)

148. Which district has the highest cultivated area of mustard?
(a) Samastipur (b) Navada
(c) Supaul (d) Munger

149. Which is the highest mustard producing district?
(a) East Champaran
(b) Mujaffarpur
(c) Begusarai
(d) Navada

150. Bihar occupies which position in production of tobacco in the country?
(a) 1st (b) 3rd
(c) 5th (d) 6th

151. In Bihar tobacco is mainly produced in the ______ river valley area?
(a) Sone (b) Gandak
(c) Bagmati (d) Kosi

152. Which of the following is a tobacco producing district?
(a) Vaishali (b) Sitamarhi
(c) Begusarai (d) All of these

153. Which of the following is an 'aghani' (which is produced in the month of Aghan) crop?
(a) Chilly (b) Tobacco
(c) Jute (d) Cotton

154. Which soil is most suitable for chilly production?
(a) Black (b) Jalod
(c) Laterite (d) Balsundari

155. Which district of Bihar is chilly producing one?
(a) Darbhanga (b) Samastipur
(c) Vaishali (d) All of these

156. In which district of Bihar, tea production takes place?
(a) Katihar
(b) Kishanganj
(c) Purnia
(d) Both (b) and (c)

157. Which of the following is a fibrous crop?
(a) Mesta (b) Arandi
(c) Barley (d) Moong

158. In which district of Bihar, mesta is produced?
(a) Purnia
(b) Saharasa
(c) Darbhanga
(d) All of the above

159. Which of the following has been included in the technology for 'Harit'Revolution?
(a) Advanced seed
(b) Fertilizers
(c) Expansion of irrigation facilities
(d) All of the above

160. In Bihar, how much fertilizer in kilograms is used per hectare of kharif cultivation?
(a) 160 (b) 172
(c) 181 (d) 192

161. In Bihar, how much fertilizer in kilograms is used per hectare of rabi cultivation?
(a) 214 (b) 226
(c) 238 (d) 240

162. How much is the average consumption of fertilizer in kilograms per hectare in Bihar?
(a) 201 (b) 192
(c) 183 (d) 174

163. Under Agriculture Roadmap-II, on which of the following emphasis has been laid by the Bihar Government?
(a) Availability of fertilizers
(b) Mechanization in agriculture
(c) Advanced seeds
(d) All of the above

164. _________camps are organized in order to ensure that farmers get advanced seeds.
(a) Kisan Beej
(b) Kisan Vikas
(c) Kisan Madad
(d) Kisan Protsahan

165. In which district of Bihar, nursery of Artimesia Annua is located?
(a) Banka
(b) Saran
(c) Siwan
(d) All of the above

166. Which is the district with maximum land under mustard production?
(a) Samastipur (b) Gaya
(c) Aurangabad (d) Saran

167. Which is the highest mustard producing district?
(a) Navada (b) Nalanda
(c) Begusarai (d) Samastipur

168. Arandi is a _________crop.
(a) Dalhan (b) Tilhan
(c) Jayad (d) Oshdhiya

169. _________is produced in areas with excess rainfall and good irrigation facilities.
(a) Corn (b) Arhar
(c) Sugercane (d) Jo

170. Lime containing domat soil, average temperature 260 degree centigrade and average rainfall of 140 centimetres are the ideal pre-requisites for cultivation of which crop?
(a) Sugarcane (b) Corn
(c) Arhar (d) Mustard

171. Which of the following is a sugarcane producing district?
(a) East Champaran
(b) West Champaran
(c) Mujaffarpur
(d) All of the above

172. On how many lakhs of hectares, sugarcane is cultivated in the State?
(a) 2 lakh (b) 3 lakh
(c) 4 lakh (d) 5 lakh

173. In which district of Bihar, maximum land is under sugarcane production?
(a) West Chmparan
(b) Navada
(c) Nalanda
(d) Munger

174. In which district of Bihar, maximum sugarcane production is achieved?
(a) Gopalganj (b) Siwan
(c) Saharasa (d) West Champaran

175. In which district of Bihar, maximum sugarcane production per hectare is obtained?
(a) Nalanda
(b) Munger
(c) Bhagalpur
(d) Saran

176. _______is produced in areas with excessive rains, high temperature and fertile jalod soil.
(a) Arhar (b) Jute
(c) Jo (d) Moong

177. In which district of Bihar, maximum jute production is achieved?
(a) Purnia
(b) Katihar
(c) Kishanganj
(d) Both (a) and (b) both

178. Bihar occupies which place in the country for jute production?
(a) First (b) Second
(c) Third (d) Fourth

179. In which State maximum quantity of jute is produced?
(a) West Bengal
(b) Assam
(c) Gujarat
(d) Odisha

180. Which of the following items is used in packing industry, and for making carpet and strings?
(a) Arandi (b) Borley
(c) Cotton (d) Jute

181. Artimisia Annua is used to make medicine for which disease?
(a) Maleria (b) Cholera
(c) Polio (d) Dysentry

182. The state government is encouraging cultivation of_________to limit the use of chemical fertilizers?
(a) Sanai (b) Dhaicha
(c) Kaithi (d) All of these

183. Which of the following is a major source of green fertilizer?
(a) Dhaicha (b) Kaithi
(c) Palak (d) Methi

184. The green fertilizer made of Daicha is more useful for cultivation of _____.
(a) Wheat (b) Jo
(c) Paddy (d) Cotton

185. To encourage medicinal agriculture in the state, National Mission on Medical Hand Year is celebrated since which year?
(a) 2004-05 (b) 2006-07
(c) 2008-09 (d) 2010-11

186. Which medicinal plant is cultivated in the State?
(a) Khas (b) Kalmegh
(c) Sarpgandha (d) All of these

187. Which plant is not cultivated as a medicinal plant in the State?
(a) Tulsi (b) Dhaicha
(c) Jamarosa (d) Jatropa

188. There is provision for providing 50 % subsidy to a commercial unit producing tonnes of wormy compost annually under Bihar's agricultural roadmap-2?
(a) 700 (b) 800
(c) 900 (d) 1000

189. _______soil is useful in Bihar for cultivation of fruits plants.
(a) Jalod
(b) Balsundari
(c) Balthar
(d) Kagari

190. Which of the following fruits is not cultivated in Bihar?
(a) Banana (b) Pineapple
(c) Orange (d) Guava

191. Which State in India contributes to half of the total production of litchi?

(a) Uttarakhand
(b) Bihar
(c) Madhya Pradesh
(d) Himachal Pradesh

192. What type of climate is suitable for litchi cultivation?

(a) Tropical (b) Sub-tropical
(c) Humid (d) Cold

193. In which district of Bihar, litchi is cultivated?

(a) Mujaffarpur
(b) Samastipur
(c) Bhagalpur
(d) All of the above

194. There are litchi gardens in the State covering around _______ hectares of land.

(a) 32000
(b) 30000
(c) 28000
(d) 26000

195. Which district is a major mango producing area?

(a) Darbhanga
(b) Samastipur
(c) East Champaran
(d) All of the above

196. Litchi production rate is_______ tons per hectare.

(a) 4.6 (b) 5.7
(c) 8.2 (d) 10.8

197. Which is the main species of litchi?

(a) Shahi
(b) Mandraji (Chinese)
(c) Kaswa
(d) All of the above

198. Arlibedana is a species of which fruit?

(a) Mango
(b) Litchi
(c) Papaya
(d) Apple

199. Which of the following is a species of Mango?

(a) Maldah (b) Aamrapali
(c) Ratna (d) All of these

200. Which of the following is not a species of mango?

(a) Manjira (b) Piyush
(c) Langda (d) Dashahari

201. Which of the following is a species of mango?

(a) Sukul (b) Sipiya
(c) Jardalu (d) All of these

202. Shahad Gulab is a species of which fruit?

(a) Mango (b) Litchi
(c) Papaya (d) Jamun

203. Which state occupies the first place in production of vegetables in India?

(a) Uttar Pradesh
(b) Himachal Pradesh
(c) Bihar
(d) Bengal

204. Potatoes cultivation is done in ________season in the winter.

(a) Rabi (b) Kharif
(c) Jayad (d) Both (a) and (b)

205. Which of the following is a species of potatoes?

(a) Kufri Jyoti
(b) Kufri Badshah
(c) Kufri Pokhraj
(d) All of the above

206. Rajendra-3 is a species of which crop?

(a) Potatoes (b) Tomatoes
(c) Onion (d) Cauliflower

207. Which district in Bihar is the highest potatoes producing one?

(a) Navada
(b) Nalanda
(c) Gaya
(d) Jehanabad

208. Which district in Bihar is the highest onion producing one?
(a) Patna
(b) Aurangabad
(c) Nalanda
(d) Darbhanga

209. Which district in Bihar is the highest cauliflower producing one?
(a) Vaishali
(b) Banka
(c) Supaul
(d) Sheikhpura

210. What is the productivity of rice in kilograms per hectare in Bihar?
(a) 2115 (b) 2114
(c) 2386 (d) 2415

211. What is the productivity of wheat in kilograms per hectare in Bihar?
(a) 2156 (b) 2234
(c) 2365 (d) 2436

212. What is the productivity of corn in kilograms per hectare in Bihar?
(a) 3816 (b) 3611
(c) 3415 (d) 3256

213. When was the first roadmap for agriculture issued by Bihar Government?
(a) 2006 (b) 2007
(c) 2008 (d) 2009

214. When was the second roadmap for agriculture issued by Bihar Government?
(a) 2009 (b) 2010
(c) 2011 (d) 2012

215. Whe was the third roadmap for agriculture issued by Bihar Government?
(a) 2017 (b) 2016
(c) 2015 (d) 2014

216. The duration of the third agriculture roadmap starts from 2017 till which year?
(a) 2019 (b) 2020
(c) 2021 (d) 2022

217. Seed spread scheme was launched during which roadmap?
(a) First
(b) Second
(c) Third
(d) Both (a) and (b)

218. What is the budget provision for agriculture and allied activities under the third roadmap?
(a) 1.54 lakh crore
(b) 1.60 lakh crore
(c) 1.70 lakh crore
(d) 1.85 lakh crore

219. Under which agricultural roadmap organic corridor is envisaged?
(a) First
(b) Second
(c) Third
(d) Both (a) and (b)

LIVESTOCK AND FISHERY

1. Animal husbandry contributes to around ________ part of rural income.
(a) Second (b) Third
(c) Fourth (d) Fifth

2. No. of cattle heads in Bihar according to 2012 animal census was around ______ lakhs.
(a) 329 (b) 327
(c) 325 (d) 323

3. How many crore eggs were produced in Bihar in 2022-23?
(a) 325.44 (b) 327.43
(c) 320.56 (d) 328.40

4. How many lakh kg of wool was produced in Bihar in 2022-23?
(a) 1.46 lakh kg
(b) 1.55 lakh kg
(c) 1.75 lakh kg
(d) 1.60 lakh kg

5. ______ is the main source of income for poor people in Bihar.
(a) Goat (b) Buffalo
(c) Cow (d) Bull

6. **Which of the following is called the cow of the poor?**
(a) Goat (b) Buffaloes
(c) Camel (d) Sheep

7. **In which district of the State, maximum number of cows and buffaloes are found?**
(a) Bhagalpur (b) Navada
(c) Arrah (d) Patna

8. **In which district of the State, maximum number of goats are found?**
(a) West Champaran
(b) East Champaran
(c) Madhubani
(d) Darbhanga

9. **How many lakh tonnes of meat was produced in Bihar in 2022-23?**
(a) 1.94 lakh tonnes
(b) 1.93 lakh tonnes
(c) 1.96 lakh tonnes
(d) 1.90 lakh tonnes

10. **How many lakh tonnes of fish was produced in Bihar in 2022-23?**
(a) 7.55 lakh tonnes
(b) 6.83 lakh tonnes
(c) 8.46 lakh tonnes
(d) 7.62 lakh tonnes

11. **The only breed of cow originating from Bihar state is**
(a) Bachaur (b) Sahiwal
(c) Malvi (d) Murrah

12. **The number of organized cooperative societies under various milk unions in Bihar was 26,504 in 2021-22, which increased to ______ in 2022-23.**
(a) 27,109 (b) 28,108
(c) 28,110 (d) 29,108

13. **According to Bihar Economic Survey, 2023-24, an increase was recorded in the daily milk collection figures which is in 2022-23.**
(a) 1762.0 thousand kg
(b) 1555.4 thousand kg
(c) 1662.0 thousand kg
(d) 1655.5 thousand kg

14. **Which of the following suitable conditions are available in the State for milk production?**
(a) Suitable climate
(b) Water
(c) Fodder in sufficient quantity
(d) All of the above

15. **Which of the following is used as animal fodder?**
(a) Corn (b) Jinora
(c) Berseem (d) All of these

16. **When was the Bihar State Cooperative Milk Producers Confederation established?**
(a) 1981 (b) 1983
(c) 1985 (d) 1987

17. **Milk production in Bihar is distributed by the name of ______ dairy?**
(a) Sudha (b) Amul
(c) Kapila (d) Ananda

18. **How many milk producers confederations are operative in the State?**
(a) 4 (b) 5
(c) 6 (d) 7

19. **Where is Vaishali-Patliputra Milk Confederation located ?**
(a) Nalanda (b) Patna
(c) Begusarai (d) Mujaffarpur

20. **Where is 'Deshratan' Dr. Rajendra Prasad Milk Confederation located?**
(a) Barauni (b) Bihar Sharif
(c) Chhapra (d) Gaya

21. **Where is Mithila Milk Confederation located?**
(a) Darbhanga (b) Madhubani
(c) Samastipur (d) Saran

22. **Where is Tirhut Milk Confederation located?**
(a) Samastipur
(b) Muzaffarpur
(c) Saran
(d) Motihari

23. Where is Shahbad Milk Confederation located?
(a) Kaimur (b) Buxar
(c) Rohtash (d) Arrah

24. Where is Vikramshila Milk Confederation located?
(a) Munger (b) Bhagalpur
(c) Purnia (d) Khagariya

25. Where is Magadh Milk Project located?
(a) Patna (b) Aurangabad
(c) Saran (d) Gaya

26. Where is Kosi Milk Scheme located?
(a) Kishanganj
(b) Purnia
(c) Saharasa
(d) Katihar

27. In which district of Bihar, liquid nitrogen collection centre has been established for artificial insemination?
(a) Patna (b) Munger
(c) Saharasa (d) All of these

28. In which district of the state, no storage centre for artificial insemination has been set up?
(a) Purnia (b) Katihar
(c) Darbhanga (d) Banka

29. Under which project, milk purchase expansion is undertaken in the state to the maximum extent?
(a) Kosi Dairy Project
(b) Magadh Dairy Project
(c) Tirhut Milk Confederation
(d) Mithila Milk Confederation

30. Which of the following are species of cow?
(a) Jarsi
(b) Dogli
(c) Australian
(d) All of the above

31. Which of the following is not a breed of cow?
(a) Sahiwal
(b) Gorkha
(c) Sindhi
(d) Gir

32. Which of the following is the breed of cow?
(a) Tharparkar (b) Devani
(c) Punjabi (d) All of these

33. Which of the following are species of buffalo?
(a) Mathurahi
(b) Murrah
(c) Bhadavari
(d) All of the above

34. Which of the following are not species of buffalo?
(a) Jafrabadi
(b) Faijabadi
(c) Soorti
(d) Rohtak

35. Mehsana and Nagpuri are species of which animal?
(a) Sheep
(b) Goat
(c) Buffalo
(d) Camel

36. In Bihar, total area submerged under water is ______ thousand hectares.
(a) 270 (b) 273
(c) 276 (d) 279

37. What percentage of total area of the state comes under submerged category?
(a) 3.3 (b) 3.5
(c) 3.7 (d) 3.9

38. Which district in the state is fish producing one?
(a) Darbhanga
(b) Madhubani
(c) Samastipur
(d) All of the above

39. Where, in the state, it is proposed to establish a Fishing Research centre?

(a) Patna (b) Darbhanga
(c) Madhubani (d) Kishanganj

40. Since when is the state Government providing facility of ambulance loaded with modern technology, drugs and equipments to encourage the sector of animal husbandry?

(a) 2008-09 (b) 2010-11
(c) 2012-13 (d) 2014-15

41. _____ is the first state in the country enacting land reform acts?

(a) Bihar (b) Madhya Pradesh
(c) Karnataka (d) Kerala

42. What percentage of land holdings in Bihar are of less than 1 hectare?

(a) 55 (b) 64
(c) 72 (d) 80

43. When was permanent settlement system implemented in Bengal-Bihar area?

(a) 1791 AD (b) 1793 AD
(c) 1795 AD (d) 1797 AD

44. In the period of which Governor General, permanent settlement system was implemented?

(a) Lord Cornwallis
(b) Lord Dalhousie
(c) Lord Irvin
(d) Lord Canning

45. When was Agricultural Income Tax Act implemented in Bihar?

(a) 1934 AD (b) 1936 AD
(c) 1938 AD (d) 1940 AD

46. When was Land Reformation Act passed in Bihar?

(a) 1950 AD (b) 1953 AD
(c) 1955 AD (d) 1957 AD

47. When was ownership of the State established over the entire land of Bihar?

(a) 1951 AD (b) 1953 AD
(c) 1955 AD (d) 1957 AD

48. When was 'Bataidari' (Leasing) Act implemented in Bihar?

(a) 1951 AD (b) 1953 AD
(c) 1955 AD (d) 1957 AD

49. Under 'Bataidari'Act 1957, land owner having less than how much land was entitled to the right of getting a permanent lease?

(a) 1 acre (b) 2 acre
(c) 3 acre (d) 4 acre

50. When was in Bihar Land Ceiling Act implemented?

(a) 1957 (b) 1959
(c) 1961 (d) 1963

51. Under the Land Ceiling Act 1961, arrangement for how much canal irrigated land a person can own was made?

(a) 14 (b) 16
(c) 18 (d) 20

52. Under the Land Ceiling Act 1961, arrangement for how much un-irrigated land a person can own was made?

(a) 40 (b) 52
(c) 60 (d) 72

53. When was 'Kashtkari' Act implemented in Bihar?

(a) 1980 AD (b) 1982 AD
(c) 1984 AD (d) 1986 AD

54. When was Land Reform Commission constituted by the State goverment?

(a) 1956 AD (b) 1976 AD
(c) 1996 AD (d) 2006 AD

55. Under whose leadership Land Reform Commission was constituted?

(a) Shekhar Bandopadhyaya
(b) D Bandopadhyaya
(c) Aamir Subahali
(d) Lallan Jha

56. From where in Bihar, the pilot project of digitalization of the land record was started?

(a) Musahari (b) Ramgarhwa
(c) Sugauli (d) Raxaul

Answers

AGRICULTURE

1. (d)	**2.** (c)	**3.** (a)	**4.** (b)	**5.** (b)	**6.** (d)	**7.** (a)	**8.** (d)	**9.** (b)	**10.** (d)
11. (d)	**12.** (a)	**13.** (c)	**14.** (b)	**15.** (d)	**16.** (c)	**17.** (a)	**18.** (b)	**19.** (c)	**20.** (a)
21. (b)	**22.** (b)	**23.** (d)	**24.** (d)	**25.** (a)	**26.** (b)	**27.** (d)	**28.** (d)	**29.** (d)	**30.** (c)
31. (d)	**32.** (b)	**33.** (c)	**34.** (c)	**35.** (b)	**36.** (d)	**37.** (d)	**38.** (b)	**39.** (d)	**40.** (c)
41. (b)	**42.** (d)	**43.** (d)	**44.** (c)	**45.** (a)	**46.** (c)	**47.** (d)	**48.** (b)	**49.** (a)	**50.** (d)
51. (a)	**52.** (c)	**53.** (b)	**54.** (c)	**55.** (d)	**56.** (c)	**57.** (c)	**58.** (a)	**59.** (b)	**60.** (c)
61. (b)	**62.** (d)	**63.** (c)	**64.** (d)	**65.** (d)	**66.** (b)	**67.** (d)	**68.** (b)	**69.** (d)	**70.** (b)
71. (d)	**72.** (b)	**73.** (d)	**74.** (d)	**75.** (d)	**76.** (d)	**77.** (c)	**78.** (b)	**79.** (d)	**80.** (b)
81. (b)	**82.** (b)	**83.** (d)	**84.** (a)	**85.** (d)	**86.** (d)	**87.** (c)	**88.** (d)	**89.** (b)	**90.** (b)
91. (a)	**92.** (d)	**93.** (b)	**94.** (a)	**95.** (d)	**96.** (d)	**97.** (d)	**98.** (d)	**99.** (d)	**100.** (a)
101. (c)	**102.** (b)	**103.** (d)	**104.** (a)	**105.** (c)	**106.** (d)	**107.** (b)	**108.** (d)	**109.** (a)	**110.** (d)
111. (d)	**112.** (b)	**113.** (b)	**114.** (b)	**115.** (d)	**116.** (b)	**117.** (d)	**118.** (d)	**119.** (a)	**120.** (d)
121. (d)	**122.** (d)	**123.** (b)	**124.** (d)	**125.** (d)	**126.** (a)	**127.** (c)	**128.** (a)	**129.** (d)	**130.** (d)
131. (a)	**132.** (c)	**133.** (d)	**134.** (c)	**135.** (d)	**136.** (d)	**137.** (d)	**138.** (b)	**139.** (a)	**140.** (c)
141. (c)	**142.** (d)	**143.** (b)	**144.** (a)	**145.** (d)	**146.** (d)	**147.** (d)	**148.** (a)	**149.** (c)	**150.** (d)
151. (b)	**152.** (d)	**153.** (a)	**154.** (b)	**155.** (d)	**156.** (d)	**157.** (a)	**158.** (d)	**159.** (d)	**160.** (a)
161. (d)	**162.** (a)	**163.** (c)	**164.** (b)	**165.** (d)	**166.** (a)	**167.** (c)	**168.** (b)	**169.** (c)	**170.** (a)
171. (d)	**172.** (b)	**173.** (a)	**174.** (d)	**175.** (a)	**176.** (b)	**177.** (d)	**178.** (b)	**179.** (a)	**180.** (d)
181. (a)	**182.** (b)	**183.** (a)	**184.** (c)	**185.** (c)	**186.** (d)	**187.** (b)	**188.** (d)	**189.** (a)	**190.** (c)
191. (b)	**192.** (c)	**193.** (d)	**194.** (a)	**195.** (d)	**196.** (c)	**197.** (d)	**198.** (b)	**199.** (d)	**200.** (b)
201. (d)	**202.** (a)	**203.** (c)	**204.** (a)	**205.** (d)	**206.** (a)	**207.** (b)	**208.** (c)	**209.** (a)	**210.** (c)
211. (d)	**212.** (a)	**213.** (c)	**214.** (d)	**215.** (a)	**216.** (d)	**217.** (a)	**218.** (a)	**219.** (c)	

LIVESTOCK AND FISHERY

1. (d)	**2.** (a)	**3.** (a)	**4.** (b)	**5.** (b)	**6.** (a)	**7.** (d)	**8.** (b)	**9.** (b)	**10.** (d)
11. (d)	**12.** (a)	**13.** (c)	**14.** (d)	**15.** (d)	**16.** (b)	**17.** (a)	**18.** (c)	**19.** (b)	**20.** (a)
21. (c)	**22.** (b)	**23.** (d)	**24.** (b)	**25.** (d)	**26.** (b)	**27.** (d)	**28.** (b)	**29.** (a)	**30**(d)
31. (b)	**32.** (d)	**33.** (d)	**34.** (b)	**35.** (c)	**36.** (c)	**37.** (d)	**38.** (d)	**39.** (a)	**40.** (b)
41. (a)	**42.** (d)	**43.** (b)	**44.** (a)	**45.** (c)	**46.** (a)	**47.** (b)	**48.** (d)	**49.** (a)	**50.** (c)
51. (d)	**52.** (c)	**53.** (d)	**54.** (d)	**55.** (b)	**56.** (a)				

❑❑❑

18 Sources of Irrigation

1. **The agriculture in Bihar is dependent on ________.**
(a) Monsoon
(b) Tornado
(c) Tsunami
(d) Artificial irrigation
2. **Which of the following is a special feature of the monsoon rains?**
(a) Arrival in time
(b) Uncertainty
(c) Uneven distribution
(d) All of the above
3. **In Bihar, what is the average monsoon rain in millimetres?**
(a) 1009 (b) 1045
(c) 1075 (d) 1085
4. **What approximate percentage of rain Bihar gets uptil June-September from South-Western monsoon?**
(a) 70% (b) 75%
(c) 80% (d) 85%
5. **There is need for irrigation of crops and the other agricultural activities in the state because of ________weather.**
(a) Tropical (b) Dry
(c) Sub-tropical (d) Temperate
6. **Which of the following are requirements for agriculture?**
(a) Advanced seeds
(b) Fertilizers
(c) Use of pesticides
(d) All of the above
7. **What was the capacity created from major and medium irrigation projects in Bihar in 2022-23?**
(a) 37.38 lakh hectares
(b) 37.40 lakh hectares
(c) 36.50 lakh hectares
(d) 4.50 lakh hectares
8. **'Dagmara' hydroelectric project is a project of which district?**
(a) Rohtas (b) Arwal
(c) Patna (d) Supaul
9. **The states benefiting from the Bansagar project are**
(a) Bihar, Rajasthan, Uttar Pradesh
(b) Tamil Nadu, Gujarat, Maharashtra
(c) Punjab, Uttar Pradesh, Haryana
(d) Bihar, Uttar Pradesh, Madhya Pradesh
10. **The states/countries benefiting from the Gandak project are**
(a) Bihar, Uttar Pradesh, Nepal
(b) Rajasthan, Pakistan, China
(c) Uttar Pradesh, China, Nepal
(d) Bihar, Bangladesh, Manipur
11. **In how many districts of Bihar is the 'Bihar Shatabdi Private Tubewell Scheme' running?**
(a) 20 districts (b) 25 districts
(c) 30 districts (d) All 38 districts
12. **How many lakh hectares of irrigation capacity was created in Bihar till March 2023?**
(a) 35.36 (b) 37.38
(c) 37.39 (d) 38.42

13. How much cultivable area is included under major irrigation project?
(a) More than 10 thousand hectares
(b) Less than 10 thousand hectares
(c) 5 thousand hectares area
(d) Less than 5 thousand area

14. How much cultivable area is included in minor irrigation project?
(a) Up to 5 thousand hectares
(b) Up to 3 thousand hectares
(c) Up to 2 thousand hectares
(d) Up to 1 thousand hectares

15. 'Teur Canal' is related to which district?
(a) East Champaran
(b) West Champaran
(c) Munger
(d) Jehanabad

16. Which of the following are the means of irrigation in Bihar?
(a) Tubewell
(b) Canal
(c) Well
(d) All of the above

17. Which of the following are the means of irrigation especially in the plains of Southern Bihar?
(a) Tapkan (b) Aher
(c) Pain (d) Both (b) and (c)

18. 'Sebari' hydroelectric project is related to which district?
(a) Arwal (b) Gaya
(c) Supaul (d) Rohtas

19. When was 'Jal Jeevan Hariyali Abhiyan Mission' launched?
(a) 2017 (b) 2018
(c) 2019 (d) 2020

20. Which of the following is the main means of irrigation in Bihar?
(a) Canals (b) Wells
(c) Tubewells (d) Aaher

21. In Bihar, there are ______ main canals and its sub-sections?
(a) 10 (b) 11
(c) 12 (d) 13

22. The canals which keep a storage of water for the full year, are called________.
(a) Sampray (b) Nityavahi
(c) Sadgami (d) Anugami

23. Most of the canals in ______Bihar are 'Nityavadi' canals which have carved out from the rivers directly or from the artificial ponds made on the dams constructed on the rivers.
(a) Northern (b) Southern
(c) Eastern (d) Western

24. Which is the second major means of irrigation in Bihar?
(a) Tubewells (b) Pain
(c) Ponds (d) Wells

25. The geographical structure of the plains of______river in Bihar is like an abyss breaking well.
(a) Bagmati (b) Mahananda
(c) Ganga (d) Kosi

26. Due to electricity development in the State,______irrigation has expanded rapidly.
(a) Canal (b) Tubewell
(c) River (d) Pond

27. In which district of the state, irrigation is done mostly by ponds?
(a) Gopalganj (b) Siwan
(c) Saharasa (d) Saran

28. In which of the sources of irrigation, water is extracted by the use of 'Dhekuli'or 'Rahat'?
(a) Pond (b) Well
(c) Canal (d) River

29. In which district of the State, irrigation is done mostly by wells?
(a) Saran
(b) Siwan
(c) Gopalganj
(d) All of the above

30. Which district is most irrigated by use of tubewells in the state?
(a) Gaya (b) Patna
(c) Supaul (d) Shivhar

31. Which is the most irrigated district in the state by canals?
(a) Rohtash (b) Kishanganj
(c) Purnia (d) Bhagalpur

32. Which is the most irrigated district in the State by ponds?
(a) East Champaran
(b) Madhubani
(c) Purnia
(d) Chhapra

33. Which is the most irrigated district of the State?
(a) Arwal Jamui
(b) Jehanabad
(c) Darbhanga
(d) All of the above

34. Which of the following districts is irrigated for more than 70%?
(a) Rohtash
(b) Buxar
(c) Jamui
(d) All of the above

35. Which district is irrigated by up to 50-70 percent?
(a) Patna (b) Gaya
(c) Aurangabad (d) All of these

36. Which of the following districts is irrigated by more than 50%?
(a) Supaul
(b) Arariya
(c) Kishanganj
(d) All of the above

37. Arwal district is irrigated up to what percentage?
(a) 86.85 (b) 83.18
(c) 80.78 (d) 77.52

38. Which of the following is Bihar's multipurpose river valley project?
(a) Kosi
(b) Gandak
(c) Sone
(d) All of the above

39. Kosi Project is a joint project of the Government of India and which other country?
(a) Nepal (b) Tibet
(c) Bangladesh (d) Bhutan

40. When did construction work of Kosi Project start?
(a) 1953 AD (b) 1955 AD
(c) 1957 AD (d) 1959 AD

41. When was an agreement signed between Government of India and Nepal for Kosi Project?
(a) 1952 AD (b) 1953 AD
(c) 1954 AD (d) 1955 AD

42. When did Kosi Project get completed after construction?
(a) 1963 AD (b) 1961 AD
(c) 1959 AD (d) 1957 AD

43. Which of the following purposes were set to be achieved from Kosi Project?
(a) Flood control
(b) Irrigation
(c) Water Electricity generation
(d) All of the above

44. Which of the following was the purpose of constructing Kosi Project?
(a) Elimination of Malaria
(b) Land conservation
(c) Fishery
(d) Both (a) and (b)

45. Kosi river cuts the mountain near which gorge and enters into the plains?
(a) Chatra (b) Mehar
(c) Godavari (d) Kailash

46. In Hanuman Nagar (Nepal), a dam of the length of how many meters has been made?
(a) 1050 (b) 1090
(c) 1110 (d) 1140

47. In east Kosi canal system, the length of the main canal is _______ kms.
(a) 40 (b) 42
(c) 44 (d) 46

48. How many branches are there of the east Kosi canal system?
(a) 2 (b) 3
(c) 4 (d) 5

49. Which of the following is a branch of east Kosi canal system?
(a) Murliganj Canal
(b) Janaki Nagar Canal
(c) Purnia (Banmankhi) canal
(d) All of the above

50. Irrigation in which district does not take place by east Kosi canal system?
(a) Purnia (b) Madhubani
(c) Madhepura (d) Katihar

51. On the east Kosi canal system in Kataiyya, an electricity generation centre of how many megawatt power is located?
(a) 10 (b) 15
(c) 20 (d) 25

52. How many lakh hectares of land is irrigated by east Kosi canal system?
(a) 5 (b) 4
(c) 3 (d) 2

53. What is the total length of the western Kosi canal system?
(a) 110 (b) 115
(c) 120 (d) 125

54. In which district irrigation takes place from Western Kosi Canal System?
(a) Madhubani
(b) Darbhanga
(c) Mujaffarpur
(d) All of the above

55. How many lakh hectares of land is irrigated by western Kosi canal system?
(a) 3.25 (b) 4.10
(c) 5.15 (d) 6.25

56. With cooperation from Government of India, Gandak project is a joint project of Bihar with which other State?
(a) Uttar Pradesh
(b) Jharkhand
(c) Bengal
(d) Odisha

57. When was an agreement signed between government of India and Nepal in respect of Gandhak Project?
(a) 1957 AD (b) 1958 AD
(c) 1959 AD (d) 1960 AD

58. Under which of the following projects a dam was constructed in Valmiki Nagar (Bihar) ?
(a) Kosi (b) Gandak
(c) Sone (d) Ganga

59. Under Gandak Project, a dam called ________Ghat has been built.
(a) Triveni (b) Lakshman
(c) Sita-Ram (d) Krishna

60. When was construction of Triveni Ghat Project started?
(a) 1969-70 (b) 1971-72
(c) 1973-74 (d) 1975-76

61. What is the other name of the Eastern Triveni canal?
(a) Champaran Canal
(b) Tirhut Canal
(c) Bihar Canal
(d) Valmiki Canal

62. What is the total length of Tirhut canal in kilometres?
(a) 280 (b) 287
(c) 293 (d) 297

63. ______lakh hectares of land is irrigated by the east Triveni canal system.
(a) 2.3 (b) 3.8
(c) 4.7 (d) 6.6

64. Irrigation in which district takes place by east Triveni canal system?
(a) East Champaran
(b) West Champaran
(c) Vaishali
(d) All of the above

65. What is the total length in kms. of western Triveni canal system?
(a) 200 (b) 205
(c) 209 (d) 215

66. Western Triveni canal is also known as ______canal?
(a) Siwan (b) Sangam
(c) Saran (d) Bihar

67. Irrigation in which districts takes place by west Triveni canal system?
(a) Saran (b) Siwan
(c) Gopalganj (d) All of these

68. Irrigation of ______lakh hectares of land takes place by the west Triveni canal system.
(a) 3.85 (b) 4.14
(c) 4.36 (d) 4.84

69. On which of the following canals, a Hydel Electricity centre is located in Surajpura?
(a) Eastern Triveni
(b) Western Triveni
(c) Western Nepal
(d) Eastern Nepal

70. A hydel power centre of how many megawatt capacity is located on western Nepal canal system?
(a) 10 (b) 15
(c) 20 (d) 25

71. In Valmiki Nagar, a hydel power centre of how many megawatt is located?
(a) 25 (b) 20
(c) 15 (d) 10

72. Which of the following is Bihar's first irrigation project?
(a) Sone Project
(b) Gandak Project
(c) Kosi Project
(d) Ganga Project

73. When was Sone Project constructed?
(a) 1870 (b) 1872
(c) 1874 (d) 1876

74. The length of the dam built on Sone Project is______meter?
(a) 3412 (b) 3572
(c) 3688 (d) 3801

75. When was a barrage constructed in Indrapuri?
(a) 1966 (b) 1967
(c) 1968 (d) 1969

76. The total length of the east Sone canal is how many kilometres?
(a) 120 (b) 130
(c) 140 (d) 150

77. Around how many lakh hectares of land is irrigated by east Sone canal system?
(a) 2.5 (b) 3
(c) 3.5 (d) 24

78. In which district irrigation takes place by east Sone canal system?
(a) Aurangabad
(b) Gaya
(c) Jehanabad
(d) All of the above

79. Western Sone canal passes through ______.
(a) Rajgir (b) Dehri
(c) Bihta (d) Maner

80. Around ______ lakh hectares of land is irrigated by the Western Sone canal system.
(a) 5 (b) 4
(c) 3 (d) 2

81. In which district, irrigation is done by western Sone canal system?
(a) Rohtash
(b) Kaimur
(c) Buxar
(d) All of the above

82. In Dehri, a hydel power centre of how many megawatt capacity is established on the Sone canal system?
(a) 4.2 (b) 5.3
(c) 6.6. (d) 7.4

83. In Barun, a hydel power centre of how many megawatt capacity is established on the Sone canal system?
(a) 2.6 (b) 3.3
(c) 4.7 (d) 5.2

84. Bansagar water dispute is between Bihar and which other state?
(a) Uttar Pradesh
(b) Jharkhand
(c) West Bengal
(d) Odisha

85. Bansagar water agreement occurred between Uttar Pradesh, Bihar and which other State?
(a) Rajasthan
(b) Madhya Pradesh
(c) Jharkhand
(d) Chhattisgarh

86. When was an agreement signed between Madhya Pradesh, Bihar and Uttar Pradesh in connection with water distribution of Sone river?
(a) 1971 AD (b) 1973 AD
(c) 1975 AD (d) 1977 AD

87. Bansagar Water Pond was constructed in which district of Madhya Pradesh?
(a) Shahdol (b) Umariya
(c) Gwalior (d) Murena

88. Bansagar water pond is constructed on which river?
(a) Kosi (b) Saryu
(c) Sone (d) Bagmati

89. When was construction work on Bansagar water pond started?
(a) 1972 AD
(b) 1974 AD
(c) 1976 AD
(d) 1978 AD

90. When was construction of Bansagar water pond completed?
(a) 2000 AD
(b) 2003 AD
(c) 2006 AD
(d) 2009 AD

91. In which ratio, water of Sone river has been agreed to be distributed between Madhya Pradesh, Bihar and Uttar Pradesh?
(a) 1:1:1 (b) 2:1:1
(c) 2:1:2 (d) 1:1:2

92. Electricity of how many megawatt units is produced under Bansagar pond project?
(a) 390 (b) 425
(c) 456 (d) 502

93. The electricity generated by Bansagar pond project is used by which State?
(a) Bihar
(b) Uttar Pradesh
(c) Madhya Pradesh
(d) All of the above

94. Which river commission was constituted in the year 1980?
(a) Sone (b) Ganga
(c) Gandak (d) Kosi

95. Sone River Commission was dismissed in which year?
(a) 1984 AD (b) 1985 AD
(c) 1986 AD (d) 1987 AD

96. In which district does the flow of Dhaka canal exist?
(a) Saran
(b) East Champaran
(c) Siwan
(d) Gaya

97. In which district, there exists flow of Tehar canal?
(a) Mujaffarpur
(b) West Champaran
(c) Bhagalpur
(d) East Champaran

98. In which district, there exists the flow of Kamla canal?
(a) Madhubani
(b) Darbhanga
(c) Both (a) and (b)
(d) Saharasa

99. In which district, there exists the flow of Sakri canal?
(a) Bhagalpur (b) Gaya
(c) Munger (d) Both (b) and (c)

100. In which district there exists the flow of Yamuna canal?
(a) Jamui (b) Jehanabad
(c) Arrah (d) Buxar

101. In the plains of Bihar, when did irrigation by tubewells start?
(a) 1926 AD (b) 1928 AD
(c) 1930 AD (d) 1932 AD

102. In which district, maximum irrigation is done by tubewells?
(a) Arwal (b) Jamui
(c) Navada (d) Supaul

103. The minimum irrigation is done by tubewells in ________ district.
(a) Jehanabad (b) Rohtash
(c) Buxar (d) Arrah

104. Which state government had started the centenary private tubewell scheme?
(a) Bihar
(b) Jharkhand
(c) Uttar Pradesh
(d) Madhya Pradesh

105. What was the standard for mapping the depth of a shallow tube well under the Bihar Centenary Private Tubewells Scheme?
(a) 60 meter (b) 70 meter
(c) 80 meter (d) 90 meter

106. Subsidy of maximum up to which amount shall be given for a shallow tube well under the Bihar Centenary Private Tubewells Scheme?
(a) 10000 (b) 15000
(c) 20000 (d) 25000

107. Subsidy of maximum up to what-amount shall be given for a deep tube well under the Bihar Centenary Private Tubewells Scheme?
(a) 25000 (b) 30000
(c) 35000 (d) 40000

108. Which Scheme has been initiated to encourage construction of private tubewells?
(a) Lohia Irrigation Scheme
(b) Million Shallow Tubewells Programme
(c) Bihar Surface Water Irrigation Scheme
(d) All of the above

109. In which district, use of 'Ahar' and 'Pain' like sources of irrigation is made?
(a) Patna (b) Munger
(c) Darbhanga (d) All of these

110. The maximum use of irrigation capacity viz. around 80% is made in the State for which crop?
(a) Paddy (b) Wheat
(c) Sugarcane (d) Both (a) and (b)

111. In which district irrigation is done by Durgawati Pond Scheme?
(a) Bhojpur (b) Kaimur
(c) Rohtash (d) Both (b) and (c)

112. What is the origin of Durgawati river?
(a) Kaimur Hill
(b) Khadagpur Hill
(c) Jhanjha Hill
(d) Someshwar Hill

113. Durgawati River merges with which of the following rivers?
(a) Bagmati (b) Karmnasha
(c) Kosi (d) Gandak

114. In which district irrigation is done by Kiul Pond Project?
(a) Navada (b) Munger
(c) Lakhusarai (d) Both (b) and (c)

115. There is inter-connection between Boorhi Ganga and Noon via ______ River?
(a) Ganga
(b) Kosi
(c) Bagmati
(d) Mahananda

116. Due to inter-connection of Boorhi Ganga-Noon with Ganga river, which district shall get benefitted?
(a) Samastipur (b) Begusarai
(c) Khagadiya (d) All of these

117. Which district will get benefitted from the inter-connection of Sakri-Nata Rivers?
(a) Navada (b) Nalanda
(c) Sheikhpura (d) All of these

118. Which district will get benefitted from the inter-connection of Kosi-Metchi rivers?
(a) Arariya
(b) Saharasa
(c) Supaul
(d) All of the above

119. When was the Water Policy of the State of Bihar announced?
(a) 2013 (b) 2015
(c) 2017 (d) 2019

120. ______percent central assistance is provided for the schemes for Uttar Bihar under the prompt irrigation benefit programme?
(a) 75 (b) 80
(c) 85 (d) 90

121. ______percent central assistance is provided for the schemes for rest of Bihar under the prompt irrigation benefit programme?
(a) 70 (b) 75
(c) 80 (d) 85

122. Which canal system has been included under the prompt irrigation benefit programme?
(a) Western Kosi Canal Scheme
(b) Kosi Barrage Scheme
(c) Durgawati Pond Scheme
(d) All of the above

123. ______revolution has been initiated in Bihar under Krishi Roadmap for the development of agriculture.
(a) Sadabahari
(b) Harit
(c) Indradhanushi
(d) Khadyanna

124. In which area in Bihar, electricity is needed?
(a) Domestic use
(b) Business uses
(c) Agriculture irrigation
(d) All of the above

125. ______ percent only of the total energy consumption is used for agricultural irrigation in the country at present.

(a) 8.14 (b) 7.24
(c) 6.42 (d) 5.83

126. In which State at present, maximum electricity consumption occurs for the purpose of agricultural irrigation?

(a) Haryana
(b) Rajasthan
(c) Chhattisgarh
(d) Kerala

127. How many units of electricity consumption occur per capita in Bihar?

(a) 590 (b) 596
(c) 603 (d) 610

128. How much is per capita electricity consumption in India?

(a) 1081 (b) 1102
(c) 1144 (d) 1181

129. On which river Barnal Pond Scheme is located?

(a) Sakri (b) Karmnasha
(c) Barnal (d) Durgawati

130. In which district Barnal Pond system is located?

(a) Jamui
(b) Arwal
(c) Jehanabad
(d) Nalanda

131. In which district Chandan Pond System is located?

(a) Supaul (b) Shivhar
(c) Navada (d) Bhagalpur

132. When was Chandan Pond established?

(a) 1970 AD (b) 1972 AD
(c) 1974 AD (d) 1976 AD

133. In which district Badua Pond is situated?

(a) Bhagalpur (b) Supaul
(c) Saharasa (d) Kishanganj

134. When was Badua Pond established?

(a) 1961 AD (b) 1963 AD
(c) 1965 AD (d) 1967 AD

135. In which district Bagmati Irrigation Project is located?

(a) Sitamarhi (b) Sahrasa
(c) Shivhar (d) Navada

136. In which district Sammat Morhar Irrigation System is located?

(a) Jamui (b) Navada
(c) Nalanda (d) Jehanabad

137. In which district Kachnama Irrigation System is located?

(a) Jamui (b) Jehanabad
(c) Navada (d) Supaul

138. In which district Navgarh Irrigation system is located?

(a) East Champaran
(b) Madhubani
(c) Saharasa
(d) Jehanabad

139. In which district Seswa Irrigation system is located?

(a) Munger (b) Bhagalpur
(c) Jehanabad (d) Darbhnaga

140. Where is Rubber Check Dam located?

(a) Supaul (b) Saharasa
(c) Gaya (d) Madhubani

141. In which district Bhataura Dam is located?

(a) Jamui (b) Gaya
(c) Vaishali (d) Arrah

142. In which district Kadhar Irrigation system is located?

(a) Gaya (b) Madhubani
(c) Navada (d) Nalanda

143. In which district Bachhraja Irrigation system is located?

(a) Vaishali (b) Gaya
(c) Madhubani (d) Darbhanga

144. What is the demand for electricity in Bihar for agricultural sector is in Megawatt?
(a) 3990 (b) 3490
(c) 3200 (d) 3852

145. What is the total demand of electricitiy in Bihar in Megawatt?
(a) 10760 (b) 7601
(c) 6515 (d) 6324

146. How many megawatt of electricity is estimated to be available in Bihar?
(a) 5014 (b) 6144
(c) 8280 (d) 9314

147. The demand for electricity in Bihar in 2022-23 was 7495 MW, which increased to _____ 2024-25.
(a) 9112 MW
(b) 8908 MW
(c) 8848 MW
(d) 7908 MW

148. Aganur Hydroelectric Project is related to which district?
(a) Rohtas (b) Patna
(c) Saharsa (d) Arwal

149. Under which five years scheme, a research centre of the Indian Agriculture Research Councial was set up for the eastern region?
(a) 8th (b) 9th
(c) 10th (d) 11th

150. When was the research centre of the Indian Agriculture Research Council established for the eastern region?
(a) 2000 AD (b) 2001 AD
(c) 2002 AD (d) 2003 AD

151. Where was the research centre of the Indian Agriculture Research Council was set up for the eastern region?
(a) Patna (b) Bhagalpur
(c) Ranchi (d) Calcutta

152. Where in Bihar 'Makhana' Research Centre is located?
(a) Madhubani (b) Sahrasa
(c) Darbhanga (d) Purnia

Answers

1. (a)	**2.** (d)	**3.** (a)	**4.** (d)	**5.** (b)	**6.** (d)	**7.** (a)	**8.** (d)	**9.** (d)	**10.** (a)
11. (d)	**12.** (b)	**13.** (a)	**14.** (c)	**15.** (a)	**16.** (d)	**17.** (d)	**18.** (d)	**19.** (c)	**20.** (a)
21. (b)	**22.** (b)	**23.** (a)	**24.** (a)	**25.** (c)	**26.** (b)	**27.** (a)	**28.** (b)	**29.** (d)	**30.** (c)
31. (a)	**32.** (b)	**33.** (a)	**34.** (d)	**35.** (d)	**36.** (d)	**37.** (a)	**38.** (d)	**39.** (a)	**40.** (b)
41. (c)	**42.** (a)	**43.** (d)	**44.** (d)	**45.** (a)	**46.** (d)	**47.** (c)	**48.** (c)	**49.** (d)	**50.** (b)
51. (c)	**52.** (a)	**53.** (b)	**54.** (d)	**55.** (a)	**56.** (a)	**57.** (c)	**58.** (b)	**59.** (a)	**60.** (a)
61. (b)	**62.** (c)	**63.** (d)	**64.** (d)	**65.** (a)	**66.** (c)	**67.** (d)	**68.** (d)	**69.** (c)	**70.** (b)
71. (c)	**72.** (a)	**73.** (c)	**74.** (d)	**75.** (c)	**76.** (b)	**77.** (a)	**78.** (d)	**79.** (b)	**80.** (c)
81. (d)	**82.** (c)	**83.** (b)	**84.** (a)	**85.** (b)	**86.** (b)	**87.** (a)	**88.** (c)	**89.** (d)	**90.** (c)
91. (b)	**92.** (b)	**93.** (c)	**94.** (a)	**95.** (d)	**96.** (b)	**97.** (d)	**98.** (c)	**99.** (d)	**100.** (b)
101. (c)	**102.** (a)	**103.** (b)	**104.** (a)	**105.** (b)	**106.** (b)	**107.** (c)	**108.** (d)	**109.** (d)	**110.** (d)
111. (d)	**112.** (a)	**113.** (b)	**114.** (d)	**115.** (a)	**116.** (d)	**117.** (d)	**118.** (d)	**119.** (b)	**120.** (d)
121. (b)	**122.** (d)	**123.** (c)	**124.** (d)	**125.** (d)	**126.** (a)	**127.** (b)	**128.** (d)	**129.** (c)	**130.** (a)
131. (d)	**132.** (b)	**133.** (a)	**134.** (c)	**135.** (a)	**136.** (d)	**137.** (b)	**138.** (d)	**139.** (c)	**140.** (c)
141. (b)	**142.** (a)	**143.** (c)	**144.** (b)	**145.** (a)	**146.** (d)	**147.** (b)	**148.** (d)	**149.** (d)	**150.** (b)
151. (a)	**152.** (c)								

□□□

19 Minerals and Industries

MINERALS

1. Which of the following minerals are available in Bihar at present?
(a) Pyrite
(b) Manganese
(c) Asbestos
(d) All of the above

2. Which mineral is not found in Bihar?
(a) Thorium
(b) Porcelain
(c) Asbestos
(d) Igneous soil

3. In which area of Bihar, stones of archaic period are found?
(a) North-east
(b) South-west
(c) South-east
(d) All of the above

4. In which district archaic period rocks are found?
(a) Gaya
(b) Navada
(c) Jamui
(d) All of the above

5. _______stone groups are found in the State's southern-western parts?
(a) Vindhyan
(b) Kudappa
(c) Deccan
(d) All of the above

6. _______mineral is basically found in archaic period rocks.
(a) Energy
(b) Metallic
(c) Non-metallic
(d) Construction material

7. What contribution minerals' sector has in the State's Gross Domestic Product?
(a) 1 (b) 2
(c) 3 (d) 4

8. Deposit of non-metallic minerals has taken place in_______group of rocks.
(a) Kudappa (b) Vindhyan
(c) Dharwad (d) Archaean

9. Manganese is found in depressive cells of which of the following rocks?
(a) Kudappa (b) Dharwad
(c) Vindhyan (d) All of these

10. Which of the following are ingredients of manganese?
(a) Trynite (b) Bronite
(c) Cylomolon (d) Both (a) and (c)

11. In which of the following industries manganese is used?
(a) Cement
(b) Atomic Energy
(c) Steel
(d) Leather

12. In which district of Bihar Manganese is found?
(a) Gaya
(b) Patna
(c) Munger
(d) All of the above

13. Which of the following minerals has an expanse from eastern part of Navada district to Jharkhand?
(a) Petroleum (b) Coal
(c) Asbestos (d) Limestone

14. Which mineral is found in granules in many districts of Bihar with arthoe cloth and terceline?
(a) Asbestos (b) Pyrite
(c) Uranium (d) Sulphur

15. In which district asbestos is found?
(a) Gaya
(b) Munger
(c) Bhagalpur
(d) All of the above

16. Which mineral is used in equipments which are bad conductors of electricity and temperature?
(a) Bronite (b) Asbestos
(c) Beryl (d) Dolomite

17. In which of the following industries asbestos is used?
(a) Rubber
(b) Paint
(c) Electronic
(d) All of the above

18. Which mineral has the maximum collective deposition and production in Bihar?
(a) Pyrite
(b) Nickel
(c) Bronite
(d) Dolomite

19. What percentage of pyrite deposit of India is in Bihar?
(a) 65 (b) 75
(c) 85 (d) 95

20. Pyrite is a mineral found in which stone group?
(a) Kudappa (b) Vindhyan
(c) Archaic (d) Dharwad

21. In which district of Bihar, pyrite mineral is found?
(a) Rohtash (b) Gaya
(c) Navada (d) Munger

22. In which of the following areas, deposit of 40 crore tons of pyrite is there?
(a) Manda
(b) Kuriyari
(c) Karariya
(d) All of the above

23. Which of the following is a source of sulphur mineral?
(a) Pyrite (b) Bronite
(c) Thorium (d) Gypsum

24. In which of the following pyrite is used?
(a) Petroleum refinement
(b) Solidification of rubber
(c) Sugar making
(d) All of the above

25. Which mineral is used for super phosphate, sulphur acid and rayon?
(a) Asbestos (b) Dolomite
(c) Pyrite (d) Kynite

26. In Bihar where has Pyrite Phosphate and Chemical Limited been established?
(a) Barahi (b) Amjhor
(c) Bihiya (d) Satuha

27. Which mineral is made by the decline of Phelspar mineral of granite?
(a) Dolomite (b) Bromite
(c) Porcelain (d) Asbestos

28. Porcelain is bad conductor of fire because of lack of which of the following things?
(a) Sulphur
(b) Potash
(c) Soda
(d) Both (a) and (c)

29. In which of the following industries, porcelain is used?
(a) Ceramic items
(b) Temperature furnaces
(c) Cloth Industry
(d) All of the above

30. In which of the following industries, porcelain is not used?
(a) Fertilizers (b) Paint
(c) Bricks (d) Medicines

31. In which district of Bihar, porcelain is found?
(a) Vaishali
(b) Munger
(c) Bhagalpur
(d) All of the above

32. Fire bearing soil is made of______ shells?
(a) Granite
(b) Sedimentary
(c) Shape-changing
(d) Sandy

33. Fire bearing soil is used in which of the following?
(a) High temperature furnaces
(b) Boilers
(c) Cement
(d) Both (a) and (b)

34. In which district of Bihar fire bearing soil is found?
(a) Purnia
(b) Bhagalpur
(c) Munger
(d) All of the above

35. Lime stone is a mineral found in ______ shells.
(a) Vindhyan (b) Kadappa
(c) Dharwad (d) Archaic

36. Which of the following minerals is used in cement steel industry?
(a) Dolomite (b) Asbestos
(c) Limestone (d) Bronite

37. In______, porcelain is required in purification process.
(a) Sugar (b) Cotton
(c) Leather (d) Pesticide

38. From where is high quality lime stone obtained in the state?
(a) Munger
(b) Kaimur Plateau
(c) Hills of Rohtash
(d) All of the above

39. Ramdihra, Bauliya and Banjari in Rohtash are famous for which mineral?
(a) Coal (b) Asbestos
(c) Limestone (d) Petroleum

40. Which of the following mineral is made of mixture of magnesium, celia and water?
(a) Porcelain
(b) Limestone
(c) Fire bearing soil
(d) Asbestos

41. Which of the following are the types of asbestos?
(a) Bronite (b) Amphibole
(c) Caisolyte (d) Both (b) and (c)

42. In making of which of the following, asbestos is used?
(a) Railway coaches
(b) Ships
(c) Boilers
(d) All of the above

43. In fire diffusion works, clothes made of which of the following things are used?
(a) Asbestos (b) Polymer
(c) Rayon (d) Rubber

44. Where are asbestos mines located in the State?
(a) Gaya (b) Navada
(c) Munger (d) Aurangabad

45. Which mineral is found in the shape of sodium nitrate and potassium?
(a) Asbestos (b) Salt petre
(c) Bronite (d) Dolomite

46. In which of the following industry salt petre is used?
(a) Paint
(b) Explosive making
(c) Glass industry
(d) Both (a) and (c)

47. Which mineral is used to make steel elastic?
(a) Asbestos (b) Salt petre
(c) Dolomite (d) Bromite

48. In which district of the State, salt petre is found?
(a) Mujaffarpur
(b) Darbhanga
(c) Saran
(d) All of the above

49. Which mineral is found from pegmatite rocks?
(a) Dolomite (b) Cawsolite
(c) Monazite (d) Amphibole

50. Monazite is mixture of which of the following minerals?
(a) Thorium
(b) Uranium
(c) Cerium
(d) All of the above

51. In which district of Bihar monazite is found?
(a) Navada (b) Gaya
(c) Munger (d) Both (b) and (c)

52. Beryllium is made of which of the shells below?
(a) Igneous
(b) Sedimentary
(c) Shape-changing
(d) All of the above

53. Which mineral is made up of mixed metal?
(a) Dolomite (b) Beryllium
(c) Crisolite (d) Amphibole

54. Which of the following is made up of beryllium?
(a) Bulb
(b) Neon Sign
(c) Cyclotroll
(d) All of the above

55. In which of the following industries, beryllium is used?
(a) Spring Industry
(b) Explosive material
(c) Florescent lamps
(d) All of the above

56. Beryllium is found in which district of Bihar?
(a) Gaya
(b) Jamui
(c) West Champaran
(d) Shivhar

57. Atomic mineral is found from which of the following rocks?
(a) Sedimentary
(b) Shape changing
(c) Igneous
(d) All of the above

58. Which of the following is an atomic mineral?
(a) Beryllium (b) Uranium
(c) Amphibole (d) Chromonite

59. Which of the following mineral is found as a mixture of Pegmatite and pitch bland?
(a) Asbestos (b) Salt petre
(c) Uranium (d) Beryllium

60. Pegmatite type of uranium is found in which district of the State?
(a) Munger (b) Gaya
(c) Navada (d) Both (b) and (c)

61. A large mine of which mineral is located in Sungari of Dhalbhum?
(a) Asbestos (b) Abhrak
(c) Uranium (d) Salt petre

62. Awareness about a huge stock of which mineral's availability in boundary fault of Magadh region was made?
(a) Gold (b) Uranium
(c) Salt petre (d) Asbestos

63. In which district of the State, gold is found?
(a) Siwan
(b) Jamui
(c) Navada
(d) East Champaran

64. Which region is popular in the State for its gold stock?
(a) Karmatiya
(b) Rani Pahadi
(c) Badmariya
(d) All of the above

65. Marahi Hill is popular in the State for having a deposited stock of which mineral?
(a) Asbestos (b) Gold
(c) Salt petre (d) Beryllium

66. GSI has confirmed about availability of gold stock in Kabutara and Nakiya hilly areas of which region?
(a) Rajgir (b) Begusarai
(c) Lakhisarai (d) Hajipur

67. In which district of Bihar, coal is found?
(a) Aurangabad
(b) Bhagalpur
(c) Munger
(d) Both (b) and (c)

68. Quartz and Silica sand is found in which district of the State?
(a) Bhagalpur (b) Navada
(c) Jamui (d) All of these

69. Quartzite mineral is found in which district of the State?
(a) Lakhisarai
(b) Nalanda
(c) Munger
(d) All of the above

70. Which mineral is found in Gelena minerals bed?
(a) Asbestos (b) Lead and Zinc
(c) Gold (d) Uranium

71. Lead and Zinc are found in small quantity in which districts of the State?
(a) Bhagalpur (b) Gaya
(c) Navada (d) Sitamarhi

72. Granite mineral is found from which district of the State?
(a) Jehanabad
(b) Jamui
(c) Bhagalpur
(d) All of the above

73. Iron Ore is found in which district of the State?
(a) Bhagalpur
(b) Gaya
(c) Jamui
(d) All of the above

74. Which type of iron ore is found from Jamui?
(a) Hematite (b) Magnetite
(c) Siderite (d) Limonite

75. In which district of Bihar, Hematite iron ore is found?
(a) Navada (b) Jamui
(c) Munger (d) Bhagalpur

76. Talc or soap stone is found in which district of the State?
(a) Munger (b) Jamui
(c) Jehanabad (d) Bhagalpur

77. Bauxite mineral is found in which district of the State?
(a) Navada
(b) Rohtash
(c) Munger
(d) All of the above

78. Feldspar mineral is found in which district of the State?
(a) Gaya
(b) Munger
(c) Jamui
(d) All of the above

79. Indian Geology Survey Department has affirmed availability of gold at which place?
(a) Valmiki Nagar
(b) Senduar
(c) Nakiya Hill
(d) All of the above

80. GSI has discovered availability of silver in which district of the State?
(a) Arrah (b) Gaya
(c) Rohtash (d) Navada

81. GSI has affirmed availability of which mineral in Khadagpur in Munger district?
(a) Salt petre (b) Celica
(c) Bauxite (d) Both (b) and (c)

82. GSI has affirmed availability of deposited stock of which mineral at Dhanras Chakbanda in Aurangabad district?
(a) Tin
(b) Copper
(c) Tungsten
(d) All of the above

83. GSI has discovered the stock of magnetite at Majos block of which district?
(a) Jamui (b) Jehanabad
(c) Gaya (d) Navada

84. Amjhor and Banjari are mineral rich areas of which district?
(a) Gaya (b) Bhagalpur
(c) Rohtash (d) Buxar

85. Devraj and Kurkkhand areas are mineral rich places of which district?
(a) Mujaffarpur (b) Gaya
(c) Vaishali (d) Arrah

86. Which area in Bihar is famous for tin production?
(a) Bihiya (b) Devraj
(c) Kurkkhand (d) Both (b) and (c)

87. Which area in Bihar is famous for graphite?
(a) Bihar Sharif (b) Sonar Hill
(c) Simultalla (d) Banjari

88. Simultalla graphite area comes in which district of Bihar?
(a) Saran (b) Jamui
(c) Siwan (d) Gaya

89. Selkhadi is found at which place in Bihar?
(a) Munger
(b) Navada
(c) Gaya
(d) All of the above

90. Dolomite is found in which district of Bihar?
(a) Rohtash (b) Munger
(c) Gaya (d) Bhagalpur

91. In which district of Bihar, petroleum is found?
(a) West Champaran
(b) Purnia
(c) Kishanganj
(d) All of the above

INDUSTRIES

1. Industry is considered the_______ area of economy.
(a) First (b) Second
(c) Third (d) Fourth

2. Bihar is basically an economy based on_________.
(a) Agriculture
(b) Construction
(c) Industry
(d) Both (a) and (b)

3. Keeping in view the number of industrial workers, Bihar's contribution on an All India level is just________per cent.

(a) 4.6 (b) 5.2
(c) 5.9 (d) 6.4

4. In State's GSDP, the contribution of the second most important area was just______per cent.

(a) 12.2 (b) 14.6
(c) 16.3 (d) 18.5

5. What percentage contribution is made by the second most important area in India's GDP?

(a) 15% (b) 23%
(c) 30% (d) 42%

6. In which of the following states, the second most important area contributes the highest percentage in the State's GDP?

(a) Gujarat (b) Odisha
(c) Karnataka (d) Jharkhand

7. Where are the large and middle sized industrial units located in maximum number?

(a) Begusarai (b) Arrah
(c) Patna (d) Bhagalpur

8. In which of the following sub-divisions, not even one industrial unit is established?

(a) Kosi (b) Tirhut
(c) Saran (d) Magadh

9. Out of the total 38 districts in the state, how many districts are not having even a single industrial unit located in them at present?

(a) 8 (b) 10
(c) 12 (d) 14

10. After division of the State, maximum large industries went to _________ State.

(a) Odisha (b) Jharkhand
(c) Bengal (d) Uttar Pradesh

11. Which of the following large industries of Bihar are afflicted with problems?

(a) Cement
(b) Sugar
(c) Jute
(d) All of the above

12. ________industries are labour oriented.

(a) Large
(b) Medium
(c) Micro and Cottage
(d) Both (a) and (b)

13. ________Industrial Centres were established with the purpose of developing small industries.

(a) District
(b) Block
(c) Regional
(d) Village

14. In Bihar which of the agriculture based industries are established?

(a) Rice Mills
(b) Cloth Industry
(c) Pulses mills
(d) All of the above

15. Which of the following is an industry based on impure raw material i.e. loss of weight ?

(a) Sugar (b) Cloth
(c) Jute (d) Rice

16. In Bihar, how many tons of sugar is produced out of 100 tons of sugarcane?

(a) 20 (b) 15
(c) 12 (d) 10

17. In which area of Bihar sugarcane is predominantly cultivated?

(a) North-Western
(b) South-Western
(c) North-East
(d) South-East

18. On how many lakh hectares area in the state, sugarcane is cultivated?
(a) 1 (b) 2
(c) 3 (d) 4

19. What percentage of agricultural land is used for sugarcane cultivation in the state?
(a) 4 (b) 6
(c) 8 (d) 10

20. How many sugar mills are there in total in Bihar?
(a) 23 (b) 25
(c) 27 (d) 29

21. How many sugar mills are operative in Bihar at present?
(a) 9 (b) 11
(c) 13 (d) 15

22. Bihar State Sugar Corporation has leased out its own sugar mill to which company?
(a) Reliance (b) ONDC
(c) HPCL (d) BPCL

23. When was a sugar mill leased to HPCL?
(a) 2010 AD (b) 2011 AD
(c) 2012 AD (d) 2013 AD

24. Which of the following peoples' company had first attempted to set up a sugar mill in Bihar?
(a) Dutch (b) French
(c) British (d) Spanish

25. When had a dutch company first tried to set up a sugar mill in Bihar?
(a) 1839 AD (b) 1841 AD
(c) 1843 AD (d) 1845 AD

26. When was the first sugar mill set up in Bihar?
(a) 1903 AD (b) 1905 AD
(c) 1907 AD (d) 1909 AD

27. Where was the first sugar mill set up in Bihar?
(a) Bihiya (b) Fatuha
(c) Madoura (d) Shahabad

28. In which district of Bihar the first sugar mill was set up?
(a) Saran (b) Madhubani
(c) Shivhar (d) Gaya

29. Which of the following areas in Bihar are famous for sugar industry?
(a) Sugauli
(b) Chanpatiya
(c) Gerol
(d) All of the above

30. At the time of independence in the year 1947, Bihar occupied ______ place in sugar production in the country.
(a) First (b) Second
(c) Third (d) Fourth

31. In 1947 what percentage of sugar in India was produced by Bihar?
(a) 20.1 (b) 21.7
(c) 22.7 (d) 23.4

32. Bihar is at present producing what percentage of India's sugar production?
(a) 2 (b) 4
(c) 6 (d) 8

33. At the time of independence, how many sugar mills were there in the country?
(a) 60 (b) 62
(c) 64 (d) 66

34. At the time of independence, how many sugar mills were there in Bihar?
(a) 31 (b) 32
(c) 33 (d) 34

35. At present how many sugar mills exist in total in India?
(a) 351 (b) 362
(c) 374 (d) 386

36. At present how many sugar mills exist in Bihar?
(a) 29 (b) 27
(c) 25 (d) 23

37. When was Bihar State Sugar Corporation established?
(a) 1970 AD (b) 1972 AD
(c) 1974 AD (d) 1976 AD

38. When were the seven sick sugar mills of Bihar nationalized?
(a) 1976 (b) 1974
(c) 1972 (d) 1970

39. Which sugar mill was nationalized in the year 1976?
(a) Banmanakhi (b) Raiyyam
(c) Goroul (d) All of these

40. When was Motipur sugar mill nationalized?
(a) 1980 AD (b) 1978 AD
(c) 1976 AD (d) 1974 AD

41. Which of the following industries is based on Sugar Industry?
(a) Paper
(b) Ethanol-alcohol
(c) Medicines
(d) All of the above

42. Which of the following places does not have a sugar mill?
(a) Raxaul (b) Sugouli
(c) Reega (d) Hasanpur

43. How many Basic Weavers Cooperative Committees are operative in the State?
(a) 991 (b) 1003
(c) 1054 (d) 1089

44. Which of the following organizations are active in the State?
(a) Bihar Silk Co-operative Union
(b) Bihar Handicrafts Co-operative Union
(c) Bihar State Wool and Sheep Union
(d) Both (b) and (c)

45. At which of the following places, Regional Handicrafts Union is located?
(a) Nalanda
(b) Siwan
(c) Sitamarhi
(d) All of the above

46. How many institutions have been established in the State by the State Government for imparting training to handicrafts weavers and enhancing their capacity?
(a) 6 (b) 8
(c) 10 (d) 12

47. Where, in Bihar, a Handicraft 'Mahasankul' (large complex) has been set up?
(a) Bhagalpur (b) Munger
(c) Gaya (d) Navada

48. When did Chief Minister's Integrated Handicrafts Development Scheme start?
(a) 2010-11 (b) 2011-12
(c) 2012-13 (d) 2013-14

49. How much money in total is made available to each weaver under the Chief Minister's Integrated Handicrafts Scheme?
(a) 40 thousand (b) 50 thousand
(c) 60 thousand (d) 70 thousand

50. How many power looms are operative in the state at places Bhagalpur, Gaya and Banka?
(a) 8 thousand (b) 10 thousand
(c) 12 thousand (d) 14 thousand

51. Where has a training center been established by the ministry of cloth Govt. of India?
(a) Bhagalpur
(b) Munger
(c) Gaya
(d) Darbhanga

52. Which area is a main center for silk production in Bihar?
(a) Gaya (b) Madhubani
(c) Bhagalpur (d) Darbhanga

53. In Bihar, how many mulberry centers have been established for cloth development?
(a) 9 (b) 10
(c) 11 (d) 12

54. How many provincial offices have been opened to encourage silk industry in the entire state?
(a) 3 (b) 4
(c) 5 (d) 6

55. Which place does not have a provincial office for encouraging silk industry?
(a) Patna (b) Gaya
(c) Mujaffarpur (d) Darbhanga

56. Where in Bihar a Silk and Textiles Institute is being established?
(a) Gaya (b) Bhagalpur
(c) Patna (d) Darbhanga

57. What was the period of the Chief Minister's Tussar Development Scheme?
(a) 2014-16 (b) 2014-17
(c) 2014-18 (d) 2014-19

58. In which district, the Chief Minister's Tussar Development Scheme is being implemented?
(a) Banka
(b) Kaimur
(c) Jamui
(d) All of the above

59. Which tree is being planted under the CM Tussar Development Scheme?
(a) Shahtoot
(b) Arjun
(c) Aasan
(d) Both (b) and (c)

60. In which districts of the state, Arjuna and Aasan trees are planned to be sown under the CM Tussar Development Scheme?
(a) Munger
(b) Navada
(c) Gaya
(d) All of the above

61. Which of the following trees is suitable for rearing of silk worm?
(a) Aasan (b) Ashoka
(c) Arjuna (d) Both (a) and (c)

62. Under which five year plan, the government had made a provision of spending 17090.12 lakhs to encourage silk industry?
(a) 12th (b) 11th
(c) 10th (d) 9th

63. When did the CM Kosi Mulberry Scheme start?
(a) 2012-13 (b) 2014-15
(c) 2016-17 (d) 2018-19

64. Which district is not included under the CM Kosi Mulberry Scheme?
(a) Supaul (b) Gaya
(c) Arariya (d) Katihar

65. What is the budget provision under CM Kosi mulberry Scheme?
(a) 110 crore (b) 113 crore
(c) 118 crore (d) 120 crore

66. What name has been given to the brand of thread produced under the CM Kosi Mulberry Scheme?
(a) Ketaki
(b) Koshiki
(c) Kesari
(d) Seemanchal

67. Which species of silk (of the following) is produced to the maximum in Bihar?
(a) Menga (b) Mulberry
(c) Arandi (d) Tussar

68. Which is the only district in Bihar where andi (Arandi) Silk is produced?
(a) Gaya (b) Lakhisarai
(c) Begusarai (d) Jehanabad

69. When was the Bihar Silk and Textile Institute established?
(a) 1922 AD (b) 1930 AD
(c) 1942 AD (d) 1958 AD

70. Where is Bihar Silk and Textiles Institute located?
(a) Gaya (b) Bhagalpur
(c) Patna (d) Darbhanga

71. Where in Bihar mulberry reeling center is located?
(a) Katihar (b) Kishanganj
(c) Bhagalpur (d) Both (b) and (c)

72. When was Bihar State Textile Corporation established?
(a) 1968 (b) 1970
(c) 1972 (d) 1974

73. Which of the following districts is the main center of cotton clothes in the State?
(a) Vaishali (b) Gaya
(c) Bhagalpur (d) Both (b) and (c)

74. _______ area of the Gaya City is the main center of cotton clothes?
(a) Hasanpur (b) Imamganj
(c) Manpur (d) Shiv Nagar

75. Which of the following industries is mainly based upon jute?
(a) Silk (b) Cotton textiles
(c) Jute (d) Glass

76. In which of the following districts, jute is produced?
(a) Purnia
(b) Katihar
(c) Kishanganj
(d) All of the above

77. At the time of independence where was a jute factory established in Bihar?
(a) Samastipur
(b) Katihar
(c) Purnia
(d) All of the above

78. How many Jute factories are operative in the State at present?
(a) 2 (b) 3
(c) 4 (d) 5

79. Where jute factories are located in Bihar?
(a) Katihar
(b) Purnia
(c) Darbhanga
(d) All of the above

80. In which district of the State, a jute Park is being established?
(a) Saharasa
(b) Purnia
(c) Katihar
(d) Kishanganj

81. At which of the following places, a jute Park is being established?
(a) Bihiya (b) Saidpur
(c) Kehalgaon (d) Maranga

MINERAL BASED INDUSTRIES

1. In which region of Bihar, there are unlimited possibilities of cement industry development?
(a) North-east (b) North-west
(c) South-west (d) South-east

2. In which of the following places cement industry is established?
(a) Banjari
(b) Amjhor
(c) Dalmiya Nagar
(d) Both (a) and (c)

3. Dalmiya Nagar Industrial area comes under which district?
(a) Rohtash (b) Kaimur
(c) Arrah (d) Buxar

4. When was Kalyanpur Cement Ltd. established in Bihar?
(a) 1935 AD (b) 1937 AD
(c) 1939 AD (d) 1941 AD

5. Where was Kalyanpur Cement Ltd established in Bihar in 1937?
(a) Banjari (b) Maranga
(c) Amjhor (d) Dalmiya Nagar

6. Where has Shri Cement been established?
(a) Navada (b) Gaya
(c) Aurangabad (d) Rohtash

7. Where has Eco cement been established?
(a) Bhabhua (b) Bihar Sharif
(c) Rajgir (d) Danapur

8. In which of the following areas, crusher industry has developed due to availability of granite, nees and shiest etc.?
(a) Eastern Bihar
(b) Western Bihar
(c) Northern Bihar
(d) Southern Bihar

9. In which district of Bihar crusher industry has developed on a large scale?
(a) Jamui
(b) Munger
(c) Aurangabad
(d) All of the above

10. Despite lack of mineral material in Bihar,_______has developed as a place based on Mineral chain?
(a) Barauni (b) Kahalgaon
(c) Hajipur (d) Mokama

11. Which of the following is located in Barauni?
(a) Oil Refinery
(b) Heat Energy Plant
(c) Fertilizer Factory
(d) All of the above

12. When was Barauni Oil Refinery established?
(a) 1960 AD (b) 1962 AD
(c) 1964 AD (d) 1966 AD

13. Under which five year plan, Barauni Oil Refinery was established?
(a) Fourth (b) Third
(c) Second (d) First

14. Which of the following countries had cooperated in establishing Barauni Oil Refinery?
(a) Romania
(b) Japan
(c) Soviet Sangh
(d) Both (a) and (c)

15. From where is from the raw oil supplied to Barauni Oil Refinery?
(a) Assam (b) Nigeria
(c) Iraq (d) All of these

16. Baruani is connected to _______ port through oil pipeline?
(a) Chennai (b) Paradweep
(c) Haldia (d) Both (b) and (c)

17. When was Barauni Thermal Power Plant established?
(a) 1960 AD (b) 1962 AD
(c) 1964 AD (d) 1966 AD

18. What is the megawatt capacity of Barauni Thermal power plant?
(a) 380 (b) 360
(c) 340 (d) 320

19. Where in Bihar is Hindustan Fertilizer Industries factory established?
(a) Mokama (b) Begusarai
(c) Barauni (d) Fatuha

20. _______ fertlizer based Hindustan Fertilizer Factory is established in Barauni?
(a) Nitrogen
(b) Phosphate
(c) Potash
(d) All of the above

21. Which of the following items is used as a raw material in Hindustan Fertilizers Factory?
(a) Limestone (b) Gypsum
(c) Naphtha (d) Both (b) and (c)

22. Where in Bihar is sulphur and phosphate fertilizer manufactured?
(a) Amjhor (b) Bihiya
(c) Danapur (d) Hajipur

23. In which district of Bihar, Pyrite, phosphates and Chemical Ltd. factory is located?
(a) Rohtash (b) Gaya
(c) Arrah (d) Begusarai

24. When was Bihar Insecticide established?
(a) 1980 (b) 1982
(c) 1984 (d) 1986

25. Where was Bihar Insecticide Ltd. established?
(a) Patna (b) Gaya
(c) Purnia (d) Munger

26. Where in Bihar industry related to railways is established?
(a) Mokama (b) Jamalpur
(c) Betiya (d) Both (a) and (b)

27. Where is Bharat Wagon and Engineering Ltd Company located?
(a) Manakpur (b) Mokama
(c) Maronga (d) Amjhor

28. Where in Bihar Railway Workshop is located?
(a) Gaya (b) Hajipur
(c) Raxaul (d) Jamalpur

29. Jamalpur Railway Workshop is situated in which district?
(a) Munger (b) Bhagalpur
(c) Katihar (d) Kishanganj

30. Bharat Wagon and Engineering Co. Ltd. is certified by which of the following?
(a) ISO 9000: 2008
(b) ISO11000: 2008
(c) ISO14000: 2008
(d) All of the above

31. When was Bharat Wagon and Engineering Ltd. handed over to the Railway Ministry?
(a) 2006 AD (b) 2007 AD
(c) 2008 AD (d) 2009 AD

32. When was Bharat Wagon and Engineering Ltd. company established?
(a) 1978 AD (b) 1976 AD
(c) 1974 AD (d) 1972 AD

33. When was Jamalpur Locomotive Workshop established?
(a) 1860 AD (b) 1862 AD
(c) 1864 AD (d) 1866 AD

34. Permission for setting up of Rajgir, Nalanda situated weapon Factory was obtained in which year?
(a) 2001 AD (b) 2002 AD
(c) 2003 AD (d) 2004 AD

35. Rajgir Weapon Factory is a modern factory ________ in Asia manufacturing ultra model BNCS (Bi-modular Change System).
(a) First (b) Second
(c) Third (d) Fourth

36. BMCD increases the capability of the ball of________to kill.
(a) AK 47 (b) Rifle
(c) Cannon (d) Missile

37. Where among the following places a Railway factory is being established?
(a) Harnaut
(b) Marhaura
(c) Madhepur
(d) All of the above

38. Which of the following is not correct?
(a) Jamalpur-Munger
(b) Mokama-Gaya
(c) Madhaura-Sal
(d) Harnaut-Nalanda

39. When was a rail Wheel factory established in Bela (Saran)?
(a) 2002 AD (b) 2003 AD
(c) 2004 AD (d) 2005 AD

40. Where are the headquarters of Bela Rail Wheel Factory?
(a) New Delhi
(b) Calcutta
(c) Chennai
(d) Vishakhapatnam

41. When did production start from Bela Rail Wheel Factory?
(a) 2012 AD (b) 2013 AD
(c) 2014 AD (d) 2015 AD

42. Where in Bihar a Railway Electric Engines Factory is being established?
(a) Vaishali (b) Madhepura
(c) Barauni (d) Mujaffarpur

43. Which of the following Companies is coordinating as a joint venture of Indian Railways in establishing a railway electric engines factory?
(a) Hitachi (b) Ikea
(c) Alstom SA (d) Tata

44. Alstom SA is a company belonging to which country?
(a) France (b) Spain
(c) Germany (d) Britain

45. In the next 11 years time, engine of what high capacity should be manufactured in Madhepura Electricity rail engines factory?
(a) 650 (b) 700
(c) 750 (d) 800

46. Where in Bihar, Carriage Repair Workshop has been established?
(a) Madhaura (b) Harnaut
(c) Bela (d) Mokama

47. When was Carriage Repair Workshop established in Harnaut?
(a) 2001 (b) 2002
(c) 2003 (d) 2004

48. Where in the State a Diesel Engine Factory is being established?
(a) Madhaura (b) Madhepura
(c) Barauni (d) Mokama

49. In which area of Bihar, glass industry has developed?
(a) Northern (b) Southern
(c) Eastern (d) Western

50. Which of the following things constitute a raw material for the glass industry?
(a) Sodium sulphate
(b) Silica
(c) Potassium Carbonate
(d) All of the above

51. Which of the following places is a main center of glass industry?
(a) Patna
(b) Bhagalpur
(c) Darbhanga
(d) All of the above

52. In which area of Bihar, tobacco is produced?
(a) North (b) South
(c) East (d) West

53. In which of the following districts, cigarette and bidi industry has developed?
(a) Begusarai
(b) Bihar Sharif
(c) Buxar
(d) All of the above

54. In which district, tobacco based cigarette factory is located?
(a) Arrah
(b) Jamui
(c) Munger
(d) Bhagalpur

55. Which of the following was India's oldest Tobacco restructuring unit?
(a) Raj Enterprises
(b) Mehta Tobacco Ltd
(c) Indian Tobacco Co.
(d) Classic Enterprises

56. When was Raj Enterprises Company established?
(a) 1901 AD (b) 1903 AD
(c) 1905 AD (d) 1907 AD

57. In which district Raj Enterprises was established?
(a) Saran (b) Munger
(c) Gaya (d) Patna

58. Which company had acquired Raj Enterprises?
(a) ITC (b) Reliance
(c) Tata (d) Bajaj

59. When was Indian Tobaco Company established?
(a) 1906 AD (b) 1908 AD
(c) 1910 AD (d) 1912 AD

60. Where are the headquarters of Indian Tobacco Company situated?
(a) New Delhi (b) Calcutta
(c) Chennai (d) Ahmedabad

61. Where is Indian Tobacco Company establishing a dairy plant?
(a) Munger (b) Gaya
(c) Kishanganj (d) Vaishali

62. The milk processing center in Munger has a capacity of _____ litres per day.
(a) 1 lakh (b) 1.5 lakh
(c) 2 lakh (d) 2.5 lakh

FOREST BASED INDUSTRY

1. In which of the following districts, development of saw mills took place?
(a) East Champaran
(b) West Champaran
(c) Arariya
(d) All of the above

2. Which of the following is called the wood of the poor?
(a) Sheesham (b) Arjuna
(c) Bamboo (d) Semal

3. Which of the following items is a raw material in the state for paper industry?
(a) Bamboo (b) Sawai Grass
(c) Jute (d) Both (a) and (b)

4. Where among the following places paper mill is situated?
(a) Samastipur
(b) Motihari
(c) Dalmiya Nagar
(d) Valmiki Nagar

5. Where is Thakur Paper Mill situated?
(a) Samastipur
(b) Motihari
(c) Dalmiya Nagar
(d) Valmilki Nagar

6. Where is Ashok Paper Mill situated?
(a) Motihari (b) Darbhanga
(c) Katihar (d) Supoul

7. Where in Bihar catechu based industry is located?
(a) Gaya (b) Betia
(c) Shivhar (d) Both (a) and (b)

FOOD PROCESSING INDUSTRY

1. Where in the State fox nut cultivation is done on commercial level?
(a) Darbhanga
(b) Madhubani
(c) Sitamarhi
(d) All of the above

2. Fox nut is a source of which of the following?
(a) Vitamin
(b) Protein
(c) Carbohydrate
(d) Both (b) and (c)

3. Where in the state a fox nut Research Institute is located?
(a) Darbhanga (b) Madhubani
(c) Patna (d) Mujaffarpur

4. In which place, an unlimited scope for litchi based food processing industry is available?
(a) Vaishali
(b) Patna
(c) Mujaffarpur
(d) Both (a) and (c)

5. In which district, an unlimited scope for banana based food processing industry is available?
(a) Vaishali (b) Darbhanga
(c) Shivhar (d) Nalanda

6. In which district, an unlimited scope for mango based food processing industry is available?
(a) Lakhisarai (b) Darbhanga
(c) Bhagalpur (d) Both (b) and (c)

7. In which of the following district, an unlimited scope for guava based food processing industry is available?
(a) Rohtash
(b) Buxar
(c) Kaimur
(d) Both (a) and (c)

8. Under integrated development scheme, subsidy up to what percentage is being provided by the Government for developing food processing industry?
(a) 30% (b) 35%
(c) 40% (d) 45%

9. Interest subsidy up to what percentage of cost of project is being given by the government for setting up of Food Park in the State?
(a) 30% (b) 35%
(c) 40% (d) 45%

10. Where is a mega Food Park being established by JVL Company?
(a) Rohtash
(b) Patna
(c) East Champaran
(d) Navada

11. In which district, a Food Park is being developed by the Pristine Company?
(a) Arariya (b) Supoul
(c) Khagariya (d) Saharasa

12. Where in the State Amrapali Group is developing a Food Park?
(a) Buxar (b) Arrah
(c) Navada (d) Nalanda

13. What percentage of subsidy has been granted by the Govt. of India under National Food Processing Mission for modernization of the rice mills?
(a) 20 (b) 25
(c) 30 (d) 35

14. What percentage of subsidy is being given in the state for setting up cold storage up to 5-10 tons capacity under the Cold Storage Scheme?
(a) 30 (b) 25
(c) 20 (d) 15

15. On how many acres of land, tea plantation is being done at present in Bihar?
(a) 30000 (b) 40000
(c) 50000 (d) 60000

16. In which district in the state, highest production of tea is being achieved?
(a) Kishanganj (b) Katihar
(c) Supoul (d) Arariya

17. Which of the following areas in Kishanganj are the main centers of tea production?

(a) Imamganj (b) Thakurganj
(c) Pothia (d) Both (b) and (c)

18. How many tea processing centers are established in Kishanganj?
(a) 5 (b) 6
(c) 7 (d) 8

19. What percentage of India's tea Production is achieved in Bihar?
(a) 5 (b) 8
(c) 10 (d) 12

20. Where is Central Leather Research Institute located?
(a) Lucknow (b) Patna
(c) Ranchi (d) Chennai

21. Where of the following is the main center for leather?
(a) Patna
(b) Arrah
(c) Aurangabad
(d) All of the above

SIXTH ECONOMIC CENSUS, 2013

1. How many economic units are located in the state according to the sixth economic census?
(a) 10 lakh (b) 13.7 lakh
(c) 17.7 lakh (d) 20.4 lakh

2. When was the fifth economic census held in the State?
(a) 2002 (b) 2003
(c) 2004 (d) 2005

3. What percentage of progress has been achieved in the sixth economic census as compared to the fifth economic census?
(a) 39.4 (b) 36.1
(c) 34.8 (d) 29.9

4. Which of the following schemes has been launched to encourage rural industry?
(a) MGNREGA
(b) CM Industry Development
(c) Pradhan Mantri Rozgar Srijan Karyakram
(d) All of the above

5. When was 'Udhyogmitra' established?
(a) 2004 (b) 2003
(c) 2002 (d) 2001

6. Under which Act 'Udhyogmitra' has been constituted?
(a) Factory Act, 1948
(b) Factory Act, 1956
(c) Society Act, 1860
(d) Bihar Factory Act, 1964

7. When was Industrial Data Bank established?
(a) 1980 (b) 1982
(c) 1984 (d) 1986

8. When was Single Window System launched in the state?
(a) 1982 (b) 1984
(c) 1986 (d) 1988

9. When was Bihar Industrial Area Act passed?
(a) 1972 (b) 1974
(c) 1976 (d) 1978

10. How many units were in operative state upto October 2019 under Bihar Industrial Area Development Act (BIYADA)?
(a) 1471 (b) 1582
(c) 1673 (d) 1775

11. Where are the headquarters of BIYADA located?
(a) New Delhi (b) Patna
(c) Calcutta (d) Ranchi

12. At which of the following places, the regional office of BIYADA is not located?
(a) Hajipur
(b) Bhagalpur
(c) Mujaffarpur
(d) Darbhanga

13. Before partition, how many industrial area development authorities were established in Bihar?
(a) 4 (b) 6
(c) 8 (d) 10

14. Where is the Court of Bihar Industrial Commissioner functioning?
(a) Patna (b) Bhagalpur
(c) Mujaffarpur (d) Darbhanga

15. Where in Bihar Indian Oil Corporation Ltd. undertaking is located?
(a) Mokama (b) Hajipur
(c) Barouni (d) Bhagalpur

16. Where in the State Gun Industry has developed?
(a) Munger (b) Bhagalpur
(c) Saharasa (d) Supoul

17. Where among the following places, leather industry has developed?
(a) Raxaul (b) Munger
(c) Mokama (d) Motihari

18. Where among the following places sugar mills are located?
(a) Guraru (b) Nath Nagar
(c) Kehalgaon (d) Bihiya

19. Which of the following is a main center of rice mills?
(a) Narkatiyaganj
(b) Jogbani
(c) Raxaul
(d) All of the above

Answers

MINERALS

1. (a)	**2.** (a)	**3.** (a)	**4.** (a)	**5.** (a)	**6.** (b)	**7.** (b)	**8.** (b)	**9.** (b)	**10.** (a)
11. (c)	**12.** (a)	**13.** (c)	**14.** (a)	**15.** (a)	**16.** (b)	**17.** (a)	**18.** (a)	**19.** (a)	**20.** (b)
21. (a)	**22.** (a)	**23.** (a)	**24.** (a)	**25.** (c)	**26.** (b)	**27.** (c)	**28.** (a)	**29.** (a)	**30.** (c)
31. (a)	**32.** (b)	**33.** (a)	**34.** (a)	**35.** (a)	**36.** (c)	**37.** (a)	**38.** (a)	**39.** (c)	**40.** (a)
41. (a)	**42.** (a)	**43.** (a)	**44.** (c)	**45.** (b)	**46.** (a)	**47.** (b)	**48.** (a)	**49.** (c)	**50.** (a)
51. (a)	**52.** (a)	**53.** (b)	**54.** (a)	**55.** (a)	**56.** (a)	**57.** (c)	**58.** (b)	**59.** (c)	**60.** (a)
61. (c)	**62.** (b)	**63.** (b)	**64.** (a)	**65.** (b)	**66.** (a)	**67.** (a)	**68.** (a)	**69.** (a)	**70.** (b)
71. (a)	**72.** (a)	**73.** (a)	**74.** (b)	**75.** (a)	**76.** (a)	**77.** (a)	**78.** (a)	**79.** (a)	**80.** (c)
81. (a)	**82.** (a)	**83.** (a)	**84.** (c)	**85.** (b)	**86.** (a)	**87.** (c)	**88.** (b)	**89.** (a)	**90.** (a)
91. (a)									

INDUSTRIES

1. (b)	**2.** (a)	**3.** (b)	**4.** (a)	**5.** (c)	**6.** (a)	**7.** (c)	**8.** (a)	**9.** (b)	**10.** (b)
11. (a)	**12.** (c)	**13.** (a)	**14.** (a)	**15.** (a)	**16.** (a)	**17.** (a)	**18.** (c)	**19.** (b)	**20.** (a)
21. (b)	**22.** (c)	**23.** (b)	**24.** (a)	**25.** (b)	**26.** (a)	**27.** (c)	**28.** (a)	**29.** (a)	**30.** (b)
31. (c)	**32.** (a)	**33.** (a)	**34.** (c)	**35.** (a)	**36.** (a)	**37.** (c)	**38.** (a)	**39.** (a)	**40.** (a)
41. (a)	**42.** (a)	**43.** (a)	**44.** (a)	**45.** (a)	**46.** (b)	**47.** (a)	**48.** (c)	**49.** (c)	**50.** (a)
51. (a)	**52.** (b)	**53.** (c)	**54.** (b)	**55.** (a)	**56.** (b)	**57.** (b)	**58.** (a)	**59.** (a)	**60.** (a)
61. (a)	**62.** (a)	**63.** (c)	**64.** (b)	**65.** (c)	**66.** (b)	**67.** (a)	**68.** (c)	**69.** (a)	**70.** (b)
71. (a)	**72.** (b)	**73.** (a)	**74.** (c)	**75.** (c)	**76.** (a)	**77.** (a)	**78.** (b)	**79.** (a)	**80.** (b)
81. (a)									

MINERAL BASED INDUSTRIES

1. (c)	**2.** (a)	**3.** (a)	**4.** (b)	**5.** (a)	**6.** (c)	**7.** (a)	**8.** (a)	**9.** (a)	**10.** (a)
11. (a)	**12.** (c)	**13.** (b)	**14.** (a)	**15.** (a)	**16.** (a)	**17.** (b)	**18.** (a)	**19.** (c)	**20.** (a)
21. (a)	**22.** (a)	**23.** (a)	**24.** (b)	**25.** (c)	**26.** (a)	**27.** (b)	**28.** (a)	**29.** (a)	**30.** (a)
31. (c)	**32.** (a)	**33.** (b)	**34.** (a)	**35.** (a)	**36.** (c)	**37.** (a)	**38.** (b)	**39.** (c)	**40.** (a)
41. (c)	**42.** (b)	**43.** (c)	**44.** (a)	**45.** (a)	**46.** (b)	**47.** (c)	**48.** (a)	**49.** (b)	**50.** (a)
51. (a)	**52.** (a)	**53.** (a)	**54.** (c)	**55.** (a)	**56.** (c)	**57.** (b)	**58.** (a)	**59.** (c)	**60.** (b)
61. (a)	**62.** (c)								

FOREST BASED INDUSTRIES

1. (a)	**2.** (c)	**3.** (a)	**4.** (c)	**5.** (a)	**6.** (b)	**7.** (a)

FOOD PROCESSING INDUSTRIES

1. (a)	**2.** (a)	**3.** (a)	**4.** (a)	**5.** (a)	**6.** (a)	**7.** (a)	**8.** (c)	**9.** (b)	**10.** (a)
11. (c)	**12.** (a)	**13.** (b)	**14.** (a)	**15.** (c)	**16.** (a)	**17.** (a)	**18.** (c)	**19.** (b)	**20.** (a)
21. (a)									

SIXTH ECONOMIC CENSUS 2013

1. (c)	**2.** (a)	**3.** (a)	**4.** (c)	**5.** (a)	**6.** (c)	**7.** (a)	**8.** (c)	**9.** (b)	**10.** (c)
11. (b)	**12.** (a)	**13.** (b)	**14.** (a)	**15.** (c)	**16.** (a)	**17.** (b)	**18.** (a)	**19.** (a)	

❑❑❑

20 Basic Infrastructure Development

1. Which of the following are the main ingredients of the fundamental structure?
(a) Transport
(b) Communication
(c) Power
(d) All of the above

2. At the time of independence, what was the total length in kms of the paved road in Bihar?
(a) 1840 (b) 1971
(c) 2086 (d) 2104

3. How many types of roads have been developed in the State on the basis of width?
(a) 5 (b) 4
(c) 3 (d) 2

4. According to Bihar Economic Survey, 2023-24, what was the total length of National Highway in Bihar by 2023?
(a) 5969 km (b) 5550 km
(c) 5960 km (d) 5650 km

5. 'Bharatmala Project' is related to?
(a) Banking sector
(b) Education sector
(c) National Highway Network
(d) None of these

6. What is the total available capacity of electricity likely to be in the year 2025-26?
(a) 12862 MW (b) 12650 MW
(c) 11780 MW (d) 11950 MW

7. How many crore units will be the estimated energy demand of all the consumers of the state by the year 2025-26?
(a) 3810 (b) 4940
(c) 3950 (d) 4660

8. How many crore rupees did the Bihar government spend on the construction of the state's road network during the year 2020 to 2024?
(a) ₹ 17,844 crore
(b) ₹ 17,880 crore
(c) ₹ 17,550 crore
(d) ₹ 17,250 crore

9. According to Bihar Economic Survey 2023-24, what was the total road density per 1000 square km geographical area in Bihar?
(a) 3267 km (b) 3167 km
(c) 3360 km (d) 3250 km

10. The top three districts in terms of length of national highways as of September 2023 are
(a) Patna, Madhubani, Muzaffarpur
(b) Patna, Nalanda, Begusarai
(c) Rohtas, Patna, Munger
(d) Patna, Gaya, Saharsa

11. What was the total length of state highways in Bihar as of September 2023?
(a) 3538 km (b) 3638 km
(c) 3450 km (d) 3350 km

12. In which district is the 'Raghunathpur' small hydropower project located?
(a) West Champaran
(b) East Champaran
(c) Saharsa
(d) Munger

13. In which district is the 'Bagaha' hydroelectric project located?
(a) West Champaran
(b) East Pancharan
(c) Rohtas
(d) Kishanganj

14. In which district is the 'Basantpur' small hydroelectric project located?
(a) Purnia (b) Gaya
(c) Araria (d) Rohtas

15. In which district is the 'Sonapur' Small Hydroelectric Project located?
(a) West Champaran
(b) Shivhar
(c) Arwal
(d) Purnia

16. In which district is the 'Dalkhola' Small Hydroelectric Project located?
(a) Supaul (b) Aurangabad
(c) Rohtas (d) Kishanganj

17. In which district is the 'Rupadhar' Small Hydroelectric Project located?
(a) Kishanganj (b) Purnia
(c) Araria (d) East Champaran

18. Where is the 'Bada Govindpur' Small Hydroelectric Project located?
(a) Mahananda River Basin
(b) Budhi Gandak River Basin
(c) Gandak River Basin
(d) None of these

19. In which river basin is the 'Bagaha' Hydroelectric Project located?
(a) Mahananda River Basin
(b) Gandak River Basin
(c) Budhi Gandak River Basin
(d) None of these

20. Which of the following pairs is not correctly matched?
(a) Dhelabag Project - Rohtas
(b) Triveni Project - West Champaran
(c) Sebari Project - Rohtas
(d) Belsar Project - Munger

21. According to Bihar Economic Survey 2023-24, how many crores of rupees did the Bihar government spend on roads and bridges and rural road network during the period from 2005 to 2024?
(a) 1,54,208 (b) 1,50,254
(c) 1,30,330 (d) 1,60,220

22. The estimated total expenditure on roads and bridges in Bihar during the period 2020 to 2024 is
(a) ₹ 34738 crore
(b) ₹ 34740 crore
(c) ₹ 33550 crore
(d) ₹ 33480 crore

23. How much revenue was estimated to be spent by the Bihar government on roads and bridges during the period 2020-24?
(a) ₹ 17340 crore
(b) ₹ 15390 crore
(c) ₹ 16960 crore
(d) ₹ 16894 crore

24. Under PM Sadak Yojana, villages and group habitations of population up to what number are to be connected with the roads?
(a) 200 (b) 250
(c) 300 (d) 350

25. When was the Chief Minister Gram Sadak Yojana started?
(a) 2010-11 (b) 2011-12
(c) 2012-13 (d) 2013-14

26. Bihar Highway Project-2 in the State is financed by which of the following Institutions?
(a) World Bank
(b) IMF
(c) Japan Bank
(d) Asian Development Bank

27. What is the estimated capital expenditure incurred by the Bihar government on roads and bridges during the period 2020-24?
(a) ₹ 16894 crore
(b) ₹ 21903 crore
(c) ₹ 17844 crore
(d) ₹ 34738 crore

28. What is the estimated capital expenditure incurred by the Bihar government on rural roads during the period 2020-24?
(a) ₹ 21903 crore
(b) ₹ 21960 crore
(c) ₹ 21903 crore
(d) ₹ 21340 crore

29. By which of the following Institutions, a support is being extended to construct 8 huge bridges by providing debts under the Bihar Rural Infrastructure Development Fund?
(a) RBI (b) SBI
(c) IFCI (d) NABARD

30. Which of the following is not correctly matched?
(a) Sebari Hydroelectric Project - 1.0 MW
(b) Jaynagar Hydroelectric Project - 1.0 MW
(c) Sirkhinda Hydroelectric Project - 0.7 MW
(d) Belsar Hydroelectric Project - 1.5 MW

31. What is the MW capacity of Walidad Small Hydroelectric Project?
(a) 1.0 MW (b) 0.7 MW
(c) 0.8 MW (d) 1.2 MW

32. Under CM Bridge Construction Scheme, a district collector can administer schemes up to what amount in lakhs?
(a) 15 lakh (b) 20 lakh
(c) 25 lakh (d) 30 lakh

33. In which district is Sipaha Small Hydroelectric Project located?
(a) Rohtas (b) Supaul
(c)Aurangabad (d) Purnia

34. The administration of schemes of rupees in excess of how much amount in lakhs in the State is done by the Bihar State Bridge Corporation Ltd?
(a) 20 (b) 25
(c) 30 (d) 35

35. When was the Bihar State Bridge Corporation Limited established?
(a) 1973 (b) 1974
(c) 1975 (d) 1976

36. What is the total share capital of the Bihar State Bridge Corporation Limited?
(a) 175 lakh (b) 236 lakh
(c) 375 lakh (d) 500 lakh

37. When was the Bihar State Road Transport Corporation established?
(a) 1957 (b) 1959
(c) 1961 (d) 1963

38. When was public-private partnership (PPP) started by the Bihar Road Transport Corporation?
(a) 2008-09 (b) 2009-10
(c) 2010-11 (d) 2011-12

39. How many types of rail lines have been developed in India?
(a) 2 (b) 3
(c) 4 (d) 5

40. What is the length of Broad Gauge is meters?
(a) 1.32 meter (b) 1.44 meter
(c) 1.50 meter (d) 1.67 meter

41. What is the length of Meters Gauge in meters.
(a) 0.66 meter (b) 0.76 meter
(c) 1.0 meter (d) 1.20 meter

42. What is the length of Narrow Gauge in meters?
(a) 0.41 meter
(b) 0.52 meter
(c) 0.63 meter
(d) 0.76 meter

43. What is the percentage share of the broad gauge railway in Bihar in total rail line?
(a) 76 (b) 81
(c) 84 (d) 86

44. What is the percentage share of broad gauge in total rail line in India?
(a) 81 (b) 83
(c) 85 (d) 87

45. How many MW is Rampur Small Hydroelectric Project?
(a) 0.30 MW
(b) 0.25 MW
(c) 0.20 MW
(d) 0.15 MW

46. Mathauli Hydroelectric Project is located in
(a) Munger (b) Patna
(c) Gaya (d) West Champaran

47. How many MW is Natwar Hydroelectric Project?
(a) 1.35 MW (b) 1.15 MW
(c) 0.25 MW (d) 1.20 MW

48. Patna is the top district in terms of length of National Highways as of September 2023, the total length of National Highways there is
(a) 612 km (b) 590 km
(c) 506 km (d) 492 km

49. Which district in Bihar has the shortest length of national highways?
(a) Sheohar (b) Sheikhpura
(c) Lakhisarai (d) Arwal

50. In how many zones the entire India has been divided from the point of view of administration?
(a) 14 (b) 15
(c) 16 (d) 17

51. Which of the following is a lone railway zone is Bihar?
(a) South-east Railway
(b) East-central railway
(c) Northern railway
(d) North-East railway

52. Where are the headquarters of east-central railway located?
(a) Hajipur (b) Sonepur
(c) Patna (d) Mujaffarpur

53. When was the east-central railway established?
(a) 2000 (b) 2002
(c) 2004 (d) 2006

54. In Bihar how many railway divisions exist?
(a) 2 (b) 3
(c) 4 (d) 5

55. In which of the following places a railway division has been established?
(a) Sonepur (b) Katihar
(c) Samastipur (d) All of these

56. When was Sonepur railway division constituted?
(a) 1951 (b) 1953
(c) 1955 (d) 1957

57. When was Samastipur railway division constituted?
(a) 1963 (b) 1965
(c) 1967 (d) 1969

58. When was Katihar division of railway constituted?
(a) 1958 (b) 1956
(c) 1954 (d) 1952

59. When was Kolkata-Mughalsarai rail road passing through Bihar constructed?
(a) 1858-60 (b) 1860-62
(c) 1864-66 (d) 1868-70

60. Where is Jaiprakash Narayan Airport situated?
(a) Patna (b) Gaya
(c) Mujaffarpur (d) Bhagalpur

61. In which of the following cities an airport exists?
(a) Jogbani
(b) Raxoul
(c) Mujaffarpur
(d) All of the above

62. Which of the following companies provides air service to Bihar?
(a) Go Air
(b) Indigo
(c) Jet Airways
(d) All of the above

63. Which has the maximum number of flights operating from Bihar?
(a) Indigo (b) Go Air
(c) Air India (d) Jet Airways

64. Air Asia belongs to which country's air travel companies?
(a) Japan (b) Indonesia
(c) Malaysia (d) Sri Lanka

65. In which district Chunapur airport is located?
(a) Katihar (b) Purnia
(c) Gaya (d) Kishanganj

66. On the river Ganges, which number National Waterway Transport is situated?
(a) 1 (b) 2
(c) 3 (d) 4

67. The national waterway situated on the river Ganges starts from Allahabad and ends which place?
(a) Banaras (b) Bhagalpur
(c) Patna (d) Haldiya

68. What is the total length in kilometres of the National Waterway Number-1?
(a) 1540 (b) 1620
(c) 1650 (d) 1682

69. When was National Waterway No. 1 established?
(a) 1982 (b) 1984
(c) 1986 (d) 1988

70. When was the Indian International Waterway Transport established?
(a) 1986 (b) 1984
(c) 1982 (d) 1980

71. Where are the headquarters of the Indian International Waterway Transport established?
(a) Patna (b) Noida
(c) Lucknow (d) Allahabad

72. Where is the Regional Office of the Indian International Waterway Transport situated?
(a) Patna
(b) Calcutta
(c) Guwahati
(d) All of the above

73. Where has 'Rajju Marg' in Bihar been constructed?
(a) Rajgir
(b) Bihar Sharif
(c) Bhagalpur
(d) Darbhanga

74. Which place does India occupy in World Communication Field?
(a) First (b) Second
(c) Third (d) Fourth

75. Which country occupies the number one position in the world in communication field?
(a) China (b) America
(c) Japan (d) Britain

76. What was the total length of state highways in Bihar till September 2023?
(a) 3638 km (b) 3600 km
(c) 3490 km (d) 3200 km

77. What percentage of post-offices of the country exist in Bihar?
(a) 5.8% (b) 6.6%
(c) 7.3% (d) 8.9%

78. What was the length of National Waterways in Madhubani district as of September 2023?
(a) 325 km (b) 322 km
(c) 320 km (d) 310 km

79. What is the length of National Waterways in Muzaffarpur district as of September 2023?
(a) 297 km (b) 290 km
(c) 295 km (d) 260 km

80. The top three districts with main district road network as of 2022 were-
(a) Patna, Gaya, Munger
(b) Gaya, Nalanda, Arwal
(c) Arwal, Sheohar, Patna
(d) Patna, Gaya, Darbhanga

81. What is the MW capacity of Triveni Link Canal Hydroelectric Project?
(a) 3.0 MW (b) 3.12 MW
(c) 2.90 MW (d) 2.50 MW

82. What place does Bihar occupy in the country in respect of availability, transmission capacity and consumption of electricity?
(a) Second (b) Fourth
(c) Sixth (d) Eighth

83. When was Bihar State Electricity Board constituted?
(a) 1958 (b) 1956
(c) 1954 (d) 1952

84. When was Bihar State Electricity Reformation Transfer Scheme launched?
(a) 2010 (b) 2011
(c) 2012 (d) 2013

85. When was integrated Electricity Development Scheme launched?
(a) 2012 (b) 2013
(c) 2014 (d) 2015

86. Under which five year plan, was the integrated Electricity Scheme launched?
(a) 9th (b) 10th
(c) 11th (d) 12th

87. When was Deen Dayal Upadhyaya Gram Jyoti Yojana launched?
(a) 2012 (b) 2013
(c) 2014 (d) 2015

88. In which district is Kehalgaon Super Thermal Power Station located?
(a) Munger (b) Bhagalpur
(c) Gaya (d) Vaishali

89. When was Kehalgaon Super Thermal Power Station established?
(a) 1988 (b) 1990
(c) 1992 (d) 1994

90. What is the production capacity in megawatt of the Kehalgaon Super Thermal Power Station?
(a) 2140 (b) 2246
(c) 2340 (d) 2412

91. In which district Barh Super Thermal Power Station is located?
(a) Patna (b) Gaya
(c) Bhagalpur (d) Nalanda

92. When did construction of Barh Super Thermal Power Station begin?
(a) 1996 (b) 1997
(c) 1998 (d) 1999

93. What is the production capacity in megawatt of Barh Super Thermal Power Station?
(a) 3100 (b) 3200
(c) 3300 (d) 3400

94. What is the production capacity in megawatt of Barauni Thermal Power center?
(a) 220 (b) 280
(c) 310 (d) 370

95. In which district Kanti Electricity Production Corporation Limited is located?
(a) Vaishali
(b) Darbhanga
(c) Mujaffarpur
(d) Gaya

96. What is the production capacity in megawatt of the Kanti Electricity Production Corporation Ltd?
(a) 200 (b) 220
(c) 240 (d) 260

97. What is the share capital ratio between the Centre and the State of Kanti Electricity Production Corporation Ltd. ?
(a) 50:50 (b) 60:40
(c) 65:35 (d) 70:30

98. When was Kosi Water Power centre merged with Bihar State Water Power Corporation?
(a) 2001 (b) 2002
(c) 2003 (d) 2004

99. In which district is Navinagar Thermal Power Project located?
(a) Aurangabad (b) Arrah
(c) Buxar (d) Navada

100. What is the production capacity in megawatt of the Navinagar Thermal Power Project?
(a) 1860 (b) 1910
(c) 1980 (d) 2040

101. In which district is Super Power Project located?
(a) Banka
(b) Nalanda
(c) Gaya
(d) East Champaran

102. What is the production capacity in megawatt of the Super Power Project?
(a) 1000 (b) 2000
(c) 3000 (d) 4000

103. Under Super Power Project, how many megawatt units of electricity will be given to Bihar?
(a) 2000 (b) 1800
(c) 1600 (d) 1400

104. In which district Peerpanti Thermal Power Project is located?
(a) Navada (b) Banka
(c) Supoul (d) Bhagalpur

105. What is the production capacity in megawatt of the Peerpanti Thermal Power Project?
(a) 1300 (b) 1320
(c) 1350 (d) 1380

106. In which district Kajra Thermal Power Project is located?
(a) Lakhisarai (b) Jamui
(c) Arrah (d) Shivhar

107. What is the production capacity in megawatt of the Kajra Thermal Power Project?
(a) 1320 (b) 1350
(c) 1380 (d) 1410

108. In which district East Gandak Water Electricity Centre is located?
(a) Sitamarhi
(b) West Champaran
(c) East Champaran
(d) Gaya

109. Where is West Sone Water Electricity Centre located?
(a) Imamganj
(b) Nay Nagar
(c) Dehri-o-Sone
(d) Navinagar

110. Where is East Water Electricity Centre located?
(a) Barun
(b) Motipur
(c) Narkatiya Ganj
(d) Bhabhua

111. Where is Kosi Water Electricity Centre located?
(a) Fatuha (b) Imamganj
(c) Refiganj (d) Katiya

112. In which district Agnoor Water Electricity Centre located?
(a) Arwal (b) Supoul
(c) Saharasa (d) Saran

113. What percentage of renewable energy in total is produced in Bihar?

(a) 2.3 (b) 2.9

(c) 3.1 (d) 3.5

114. When was conservation policy in respect of the new and renewable energy sources implemented in Bihar?

(a) 2011 (b) 2012

(c) 2013 (d) 2014

115. The new and renewable energy conservation policy in Bihar remained effective until when?

(a) 2015

(b) 2016

(c) 2017

(d) 2018

Answers

1. (d)	**2.** (d)	**3.** (b)	**4.** (a)	**5.** (c)	**6.** (a)	**7.** (b)	**8.** (a)	**9.** (b)	**10.** (a)
11. (b)	**12.** (b)	**13.** (a)	**14.** (c)	**15.** (d)	**16.** (d)	**17.** (a)	**18.** (b)	**19.** (b)	**20.** (d)
21. (a)	**22.** (a)	**23.** (d)	**24.** (b)	**25.** (d)	**26.** (d)	**27.** (c)	**28.** (a)	**29.** (d)	**30.** (d)
31. (b)	**32.** (c)	**33.** (c)	**34.** (b)	**35.** (c)	**36.** (d)	**37.** (b)	**38.** (b)	**39.** (b)	**40.** (d)
41. (c)	**42.** (d)	**43.** (c)	**44.** (d)	**45.** (b)	**46.** (d)	**47.** (c)	**48.** (c)	**49.** (a)	**50.** (d)
51. (b)	**52.** (a)	**53.** (b)	**54.** (c)	**55.** (d)	**56.** (a)	**57.** (d)	**58.** (a)	**59.** (b)	**60.** (a)
61. (d)	**62.** (d)	**63.** (a)	**64.** (c)	**65.** (b)	**66.** (a)	**67.** (d)	**68.** (b)	**69.** (c)	**70.** (a)
71. (b)	**72.** (d)	**73.** (a)	**74.** (b)	**75.** (a)	**76.** (a)	**77.** (a)	**78.** (b)	**79.** (a)	**80.** (d)
81. (a)	**82.** (c)	**83.** (a)	**84.** (c)	**85.** (c)	**86.** (d)	**87.** (d)	**88.** (b)	**89.** (c)	**90.** (c)
91. (a)	**92.** (d)	**93.** (c)	**94.** (a)	**95.** (c)	**96.** (b)	**97.** (c)	**98.** (c)	**99.** (a)	**100.** (c)
101. (a)	**102.** (c)	**103.** (a)	**104.** (d)	**105.** (b)	**106.** (a)	**107.** (c)	**108.** (b)	**109.** (c)	**110.** (a)
111. (d)	**112.** (a)	**113.** (a)	**114.** (a)	**115.** (b)					

❑❑❑

21 Population and Habitat

POPULATION

1. Who of the following is father of sources of geography?

(a) Imanuel Kant
(b) Adam Smith
(c) Jeerman
(d) To Pen

2. What is the total area of Bihar in square kilometres?

(a) 91163 (b) 92460
(c) 93120 (d) 94163

3. What is Bihar's total area in square kilometres of India's total area in square kilometres in percentage?

(a) 2.56 (b) 2.67
(c) 2.86 (d) 2.97

4. What was the total population of Bihar according to the 2011 census?

(a) 10.10 crore (b) 10.20 crore
(c) 10.30 crore (d) 10.40 crore

5. What percentage was Bihar's total population to the total population of India according to the 2011 census?

(a) 6.11 (b) 7.32
(c) 8.56 (d) 9.38

6. Which place does Bihar occupy in respect to population in the country according to the 2011 census?

(a) Fourth (b) Third
(c) Second (d) First

7. Which of the following states has population more than that of Bihar?

(a) Rajasthan
(b) Madhya Pradesh
(c) Maharashtra
(d) Tamilnadu

8. Which place does Bihar occupy in India in respect to density of population?

(a) First (b) Second
(c) Third (d) Fourth

9. The density of Bihar is how many persons per square kilometre?

(a) 1102 (b) 1104
(c) 1106 (d) 1108

10. How many districts are there in Bihar at present?

(a) 38 (b) 37
(c) 36 (d) 35

11. Which district in Bihar has the maximum population?

(a) East Champaran
(b) Patna
(c) Bhagalpur
(d) Buxar

12. Which district in Bihar has the minimum population?

(a) Shivhar (b) Arwal
(c) Sheikpura (d) Jamui

13. Which district in the State has a maximum density of population?

(a) Patna (b) Shivhar
(c) Arwal (d) Sheikhpura

14. Shivhar has a density of population of how many persons per square kilometre?

(a) 1850 (b) 1860
(c) 1870 (d) 1882

15. Which district of Bihar has the minimum density of population?

(a) Kaimur
(b) Gaya
(c) West Champaran
(d) Saharasa

16. The density of population in Kaimur district is how many persons per square kilometre?

(a) 432 (b) 488
(c) 491 (d) 530

17. Which district in the State has a highest sex ratio?

(a) Siwan (b) Saran
(c) Gopalganj (d) Patna

18. What is the sex ratio of Gopalganj district?

(a) 1008 (b) 1014
(c) 1019 (d) 1021

19. Which district in the State has a minimum sex ratio?

(a) Gaya (b) Munger
(c) Arrah (d) Kaimur

20. What is the sex ratio of Munger?

(a) 842 (b) 853
(c) 864 (d) 876

21. Which district is the most literate district of Bihar keeping in view literacy ratio?

(a) Patna (b) Rohtash
(c) Arrah (d) Buxar

22. What percentage of literacy does Rohtash district have?

(a) 71.42 (b) 72.84
(c) 73.37 (d) 74.42

23. Which is the least literate district of Bihar from the point of view of literacy?

(a) Purnia (b) Siwan
(c) Madhepura (d) Supoul

24. What is the literacy rate of Purnia district?

(a) 50.82 (b) 51.08
(c) 52.42 (d) 53.82

25. When did census in India start?

(a) 1861 AD (b) 1866 AD
(c) 1870 AD (d) 1872 AD

26. In whose period census in India had started?

(a) Lord Mayo
(b) Lord Litton
(c) Lord Dalhousie
(d) Lord McAlley

27. When did 10 yearly and an organized census start in India?

(a) 1877 AD (b) 1879 AD
(c) 1881 AD (d) 1883 AD

28. In whose period did 10 yearly and an organized census was start in India?

(a) Lord Ripon (b) Lord Litton
(c) Lord Curzon (d) Lord Canning

29. When was Population Act implemented after independence for population census?

(a) 1947 (b) 1948
(c) 1949 (d) 1950

30. What was the decadal growth rate of population in Bihar according to the 2011 census?

(a) 21.42 (b) 22.84
(c) 24.12 (d) 25.07

31. In which of the following decades, there was negative population growth rate?

(a) 1891-1900 (b) 1900-11
(c) 1911-21 (d) 1921-31

32. What was the rate of growth of population during the decade 1911-21?

(a) 0.97 (b) (-)1.41
(c) (-)1.81 (d) (-)1.92

33. What was the decadal growth rate of population according to the 2011 census?
(a) 15.41 (b) 16.82
(c) 17.71 (d) 18.25

34. What was the decadal growth rate of population in Bihar during 1941-1950?
(a) 10.58 (b) 12.10
(c) 15.28 (d) 16.44

35. What is the target for achieving a total fertility rate in India by the year 2045?
(a) 2.1 (b) 2.2
(c) 2.3 (d) 2.4

36. Which district registered the highest decadal growth rate in population during 2001-11?
(a) Madhepura (b) Arariya
(c) Supoul (d) Kishanganj

37. What was the decadal growth rate of population in Madhepura district?
(a) 28.14 (b) 29.52
(c) 30.65 (d) 31.14

38. Which district registered a minimum growth rate of population in the decade 2001-11?
(a) Munger (b) Gopalganj
(c) Siwan (d) Patna

39. What percentage of total area in square kilometre Patna district has to the total are of Bihar in square kilometre?
(a) 2.95 (b) 3.14
(c) 3.40 (d) 3.67

40. What percentage of Bihar's total population resides in Patna district?
(a) 5.14 (b) 5.29
(c) 5.42 (d) 5.56

41. What was the density of population of India per square kilometre according to 2011 census ?
(a) 372 (b) 377
(c) 382 (d) 387

42. The density of population of how many districts in Bihar is more than the average density of population in Bihar?
(a) 16 (b) 18
(c) 20 (d) 22

43. What was the sex ratio of Bihar in the year 1901?
(a) 1022 (b) 1034
(c) 1048 (d) 1068

44. What was the sex ratio in Bihar according to the 2011 census?
(a) 911 (b) 916
(c) 923 (d) 931

45. What was the national average for sex ratio according to the 2011 census?
(a) 943 (b) 947
(c) 952 (d) 957

46. What was the sex ratio in Bihar's rural areas according to the 2011 census?
(a) 916 (b) 927
(c) 931 (d) 937

47. What was the sex ratio in urban areas of Bihar according to the 2011 census?
(a) 863 (b) 865
(c) 867 (d) 869

48. What was the sex ratio prevailing in rural areas of India according to the 2011 census?
(a) 942 (b) 944
(c) 946 (d) 948

49. What was the sex ratio prevailing in urban areas of India according to the 2011 census?

(a) 900 (b) 905
(c) 909 (d) 914

50. A person of above what age is included for literacy according to the population census department of Government of India?
(a) 5 (b) 7
(c) 9 (d) 11

51. What was the literacy rate of Bihar according to the 2011 census?
(a) 61.32 (b) 62.44
(c) 63.82 (d) 64.51

52. What was the literacy percentage in India according to the 2011 census?
(a) 71.82 (b) 72.44
(c) 73.18 (d) 74.04

53. In which State there is maximum literacy according to the 2011 census?
(a) Goa (b) Kerala
(c) Mizoram (d) Tamilnadu

54. What was the male literacy percentage in Bihar according to the 2011 census?
(a) 71.14 (b) 72.12
(c) 73.39 (d) 74.28

55. What was the female literacy percentage in Bihar according to the 2011 census?
(a) 50.62 (b) 51.89
(c) 52.44 (d) 53.33

56. What was the rural literacy percentage in Bihar according to the 2011 census?
(a) 60.12 (b) 61.83
(c) 62.44 (d) 63.35

57. What was the urban literacy percentage in Bihar according to the 2011 census?
(a) 72.85 (b) 74.14
(c) 76.28 (d) 78.75

58. What percentage of population lives in cities in Bihar according to the 2011 census?
(a) 11.30 (b) 12.85
(c) 13.14 (d) 14.25

59. What percentage of population lives in villages in Bihar according to the 2011 census?
(a) 86.14 (b) 87.82
(c) 88.70 (d) 89.40

60. Which district in Bihar has the highest rural population?
(a) Samastipur (b) Supoul
(c) Saharasa (d) Khagariya

61. What percentage of population of Samastipur district lives in villages?
(a) 92.14 (b) 93.54
(c) 94.96 (d) 96.54

62. In which district of the State, minimum population is living in cities?
(a) Patna (b) Bhagalpur
(c) Samastipur (d) Vaishali

63. Which district of Bihar has a minimum rural population?
(a) Patna (b) Bhagalpur
(c) Munger (d) Vaishali

64. What percentage of inhabitants of Patna district live in villages?
(a) 50.84 (b) 51.14
(c) 53.82 (d) 56.52

65. In which district of Bihar, maximum inhabitants live in cities?
(a) Vaishali (b) Patna
(c) Munger (d) Bhagalpur

66. In which district, more than 95% population with in villages?
(a) Banka
(b) Sitamarhi
(c) Supoul
(d) All of the above

67. What is the percentage of urban population of Patna district?
(a) 41.42 (b) 42.83
(c) 43.48 (d) 44.81

68. In how many categories cities have been divided by the Census Department?
(a) 4 (b) 5
(c) 6 (d) 7

69. What was the percentage of children in age group 0-14 years in Bihar according to the 2011 census?
(a) 12.42 (b) 13.24
(c) 13.98 (d) 14.21

70. What was the percentage of children of less than 6 years of age in Bihar according to the 2011 census?
(a) 14.14 (b) 15.20
(c) 16.48 (d) 17.90

71. What was the percentage of children of less than 6 years of age in the country according to the 2011 census?
(a) 11.44 (b) 12.66
(c) 13.12 (d) 14.89

72. What percentage were of boys in age group 0-6 years ăccording to the 2011 census?
(a) 16.42 (b) 17.74
(c) 18.06 (d) 19.21

73. What percentage were of girls in age group 0-6 years according to the 2011 census?
(a) 15.12 (b) 16.24
(c) 17.28 (d) 18.07

74. What was the sex ratio of children of 0-6 years age group according to the 2011 census?
(a) 931 (b) 933
(c) 935 (d) 937

75. In which district, maximum sex ratio of 0-6 years age group children is found?
(a) Kishanganj (b) Gopalganj
(c) Siwan (d) Gaya

76. What is the sex ratio of children of age group 0-6 years in Kishanganj district?
(a) 967 (b) 969
(c) 971 (d) 973

77. In which district lowest sex ratio of children of age group 0-6 years is found?
(a) Vaishali (b) Munger
(c) Navada (d) Patna

78. What is the sex ratio of children of 0-6 years age group in Vaishali district?
(a) 902 (b) 904
(c) 906 (d) 908

79. In which district maximum number of children in age group 0-6 years years is found?
(a) Saharasa (b) Sasaram
(c) Khagariya (d) Gaya

80. What percentage of rural population is among children of 0-6 years age group?
(a) 14.31 (b) 15.37
(c) 16.89 (d) 18.55

81. What percentage of urban population is among children of 0-6 years age group?
(a) 12.51 (b) 13.44
(c) 14.35 (d) 15.06

82. What percentage of population Bihar has of Scheduled Caste according to the 2011 census?
(a) 11.21 (b) 12.43
(c) 13.46 (d) 14.56

83. In which district the highest percentage of population of Scheduled Caste was registered according to the 2011 census?
(a) Kaimur
(b) Gaya
(c) Banka
(d) West Champaran

84. What was the percentage of Scheduled Caste population in 2011 in Gaya District?
(a) 26.14 (b) 27.42
(c) 28.19 (d) 29.6

85. In which district the lowest percentage of Scheduled Caste population was registered according to the 2011 census?
(a) Vaishali (b) Kishanganj
(c) Saharasa (d) Arrah

86. What percentage Scheduled Caste population formed in 2011 in Kishanganj district?
(a) 6.6 (b) 7.1
(c) 8.2 (d) 9.4

87. What was the sex ratio of Scheduled Caste population in 2011?
(a) 918 (b) 923
(c) 928 (d) 933

88. What was the literacy percentage of Scheduled Caste population according to the 2011 census?
(a) 23.4 (b) 25.4
(c) 28.5 (d) 30.1

89. The maximum sex ratio of Scheduled Caste population was registered in which district as per the 2011 census?
(a) Siwan (b) Gaya
(c) Saharasa (d) Navada

90. In which district the lowest sex ratio of Scheduled Caste population was registered as per the 2011 census?
(a) Shivhar (b) Banka
(c) Bhagalpur (d) Patna

91. What percentage Scheduled Tribe population had in Bihar according to the 2011 census?
(a) 0.9 (b) 1.2
(c) 1.5 (d) 1.9

92. In which district maximum population of Scheduled Tribes were registered according to the 2011 census?
(a) Saran (b) Gaya
(c) Katihar (d) Aurangabad

93. What percentage of Scheduled tribe population lives in Katihar district?
(a) 5.9 (b) 6.4
(c) 7.2 (d) 8.4

94. In which of the following districts, population of Scheduled Tribes is not found?
(a) Shivhar
(b) Sheikhpura
(c) Nalanda
(d) All of the above

95. What was the sex ratio of Scheduled tribe population in Bihar according to the 2011 census?
(a) 929 (b) 927
(c) 925 (d) 923

96. What was the literacy rate among the Scheduled tribe population according to the 2011 census?
(a) 27.31 (b) 28.20
(c) 29.1 (d) 30.6

97. In which district sex ratio of Scheduled Caste population was the maximum according to the 2011 census?
(a) Siwan (b) Saran
(c) Gopalganj (d) Munger

98. In which district sex ratio of Scheduled Caste population was the lowest according to the 2011 census?
(a) Patna (b) Arrah
(c) Gaya (d) Buxar

99. In which district highest literacy rate was observed in Seheduled Caste according to 2011 census?
(a) Arrah (b) Begusarai
(c) Navada (d) Buxar

100. What percentage of population in Bihar was follower of Hindu religion according to the 2011 census?
(a) 81.4 (b) 82.7
(c) 83.2 (d) 84.6

101. What percentage of population in Bihar was the follower of Islam Religion in 2011?
(a) 17.8 (b) 16.5
(c) 15.9 (d) 14.3

102. What was the annual growth rate of population of Bihar according to the 2011 census?
(a) 2.11 (b) 2.31
(c) 2.43 (d) 2.57

103. When was family planning programme launched?
(a) 1948 AD (b) 1951 AD
(c) 1953 AD (d) 1956 AD

104. When was the National Population Commission constituted?
(a) 1972 (b) 1974
(c) 1976 (d) 1978

105. When was Swaminathan Committee constituted?
(a) 1982 (b) 1984
(c) 1986 (d) 1987

106. When was the National Population Policy announced?
(a) 1996 (b) 1997
(c) 1998 (d) 1999

107. By which time a target for achieving stability in population is set out?
(a) 2020 (b) 2032
(c) 2040 (d) 2045

RURAL AND URBAN SETTLEMENT

1. From which district in Bihar evidence of rehabilitation of new stoneage period is found?
(a) Saharasa
(b) Gaya
(c) Saran
(d) Nalanda

2. Which new stone-age colony is situated in Saran district of Bihar?
(a) Chirand
(b) Guha
(c) Balrampur
(d) Navgarhi

3. In how many square kilometres area in Bihar rural colonies exist?
(a) 90163 (b) 91440
(c) 92358 (d) 93415

4. In how many square kilometres area in Bihar urban colonies are found?
(a) 1804 (b) 1776
(c) 1640 (d) 1589

5. A colony with less than _______ persons is called a rural colony.
(a) 2000 (b) 3000
(c) 4000 (d) 5000

6. Colonies with population exceeding are called urban colonies?
(a) 5000 (b) 4000
(c) 3000 (d) 2000

7. What percentage of rural population is engaged in agricultural activities?
(a) 71% (b) 73%
(c) 75% (d) 77%

8. A colony is called an urban area when population in excess of_____ per cent is engaged in non-agricultural activities?

(a) 71 (b) 73
(c) 75 (d) 77

9. Which group of population is termed as the working population?

(a) 15-45 (b) 14-52
(c) 14-60 (d) 14-62

10. A human inhabitation with population exceeding how many persons is termed as a city colony?

(a) 200 (b) 350
(c) 400 (d) 450

11. A human inhabitation with population less than how many persons is termed as a rural colony?

(a) 400 (b) 350
(c) 300 (d) 250

12. Which of the following is a type of rural inhabitation?

(a) Saghan (b) Viral
(c) Chauras (d) Both (a) and (b)

13. In flood hit areas of Kosi, Kamla, Gandak and Ganga rivers, which of the following type of colony is mainly found?

(a) Saghan
(b) Viral
(c) Rekhiya
(d) All of the above

14. On which type of colonies from the following colonies, there was more influence of the social life and landlord system?

(a) Saghan (b) Ardh Saghan
(c) Viral (d) Rekhiya Saghan

15. Which type of colonies have developed on the brink of road, canal and river etc.?

(a) Viral
(b) Saghan
(c) Ardh-Saghan
(d) Rekhiya saghan

16. Which type of colony has developed around 'Diyara' area of the river Ganges?

(a) Viral
(b) Rekhiy Saghan
(c) Ardh-Saghan
(d) Saghan

17. In which district, dilapidated colonies have developed?

(a) Purnia (b) Katihar
(c) Darbhanga (d) All of these

18. Which of the following type of colonies have developed around difficult plateau areas and on the pavements in forest areas?

(a) Dilapidated colocy
(b) Rekhiya viral
(c) Ardh viral
(d) Rekhiya saghan

19. Since which period, evidence of urbanisation in Bihar are found?

(a) Vaidik
(b) Post Vaidik
(c) Mahajan Pad
(d) Both (b) and (c)

20. Who had established Patliputra on the bank of Ganga?

(a) Ajatshatru
(b) Udayin
(c) Kalashok
(d) Chandragupta Maurya

21. Who of the following had established Patna city?

(a) Shershah
(b) Islam Shah
(c) Bakhtiyar Khilji
(d) Aurangzeb

22. Who of the following mughal emperors had established a city called Aminabad in Patna?
(a) Akbar (b) Jehangir
(c) Shahjahan (d) Aurangzeb

23. What percentage of Bihar's population used to live in cities in the year 1901?
(a) 4.7 (b) 5.1
(c) 6.3 (d) 7.2

24. What was the decadal growth rate in urban population of Bihar according to the 2011 census?
(a) 31.80 (b) 32.91
(c) 33.61 (d) 35.11

25. When was the highest decadal growth rate in urban population found in Bihar?
(a) 1971-81 (b) 1961-71
(c) 1951-61 (d) 1941-51

26. What was the percentage of decadal growth rate in urban population in Bihar during period 1971-81?
(a) 41.63 (b) 43.40
(c) 47.61 (d) 53.63

27. In Bihar, in rural-urban population when was the highest urban population ratio observed?
(a) 2001 (b) 1991
(c) 1981 (d) 1971

28. What was the ratio of rural-urban population in Bihar in percentage according to the 2011 census?
(a) 10.21 (b) 10.96
(c) 11.30 (d) 11.92

29. In which district of Bihar maximum urban population growth was observed according to the 2011 census?
(a) Saran (b) Begusarai
(c) Jamui (d) Patna

30. What percentage of growth in urban population was registered in Begusarai according to the 2011 census?
(a) 151.12 (b) 241.20
(c) 344.21 (d) 426.89

31. What is the population of Patna city according to the 2011 census?
(a) 1840120 (b) 1952460
(c) 2046652 (d) 2148411

32. Which of the following cities is the second most populated city of Bihar after Patna?
(a) Gaya (b) Hajipur
(c) Bhagalpur (d) Mujaffarpur

Answers

POPULATION

1. (c)	**2.** (d)	**3.** (c)	**4.** (d)	**5.** (c)	**6.** (b)	**7.** (c)	**8.** (a)	**9.** (c)	**10.** (a)
11. (b)	**12.** (c)	**13.** (b)	**14.** (d)	**15.** (a)	**16.** (b)	**17.** (c)	**18.** (d)	**19.** (b)	**20.** (d)
21. (b)	**22.** (c)	**23.** (a)	**24.** (b)	**25.** (d)	**26.** (a)	**27.** (c)	**28.** (a)	**29.** (b)	**30.** (d)
31. (c)	**32.** (a)	**33.** (c)	**34.** (a)	**35.** (a)	**36.** (a)	**37.** (c)	**38.** (b)	**39.** (c)	**40.** (d)
41. (c)	**42.** (c)	**43.** (d)	**44.** (b)	**45.** (a)	**46.** (b)	**47.** (d)	**48.** (c)	**49.** (a)	**50.** (b)
51. (c)	**52.** (d)	**53.** (b)	**54.** (c)	**55.** (d)	**56.** (b)	**57.** (d)	**58.** (a)	**59.** (c)	**60.** (a)
61. (d)	**62.** (c)	**63.** (a)	**64.** (d)	**65.** (b)	**66.** (d)	**67.** (c)	**68.** (c)	**69.** (b)	**70.** (d)
71. (c)	**72.** (b)	**73.** (d)	**74.** (c)	**75.** (a)	**76.** (c)	**77.** (a)	**78.** (b)	**79.** (c)	**80.** (d)
81. (c)	**82.** (d)	**83.** (b)	**84.** (d)	**85.** (b)	**86.** (a)	**87.** (b)	**88.** (c)	**89.** (a)	**90.** (c)

91. (a) **92.** (c) **93.** (a) **94.** (d) **95.** (a) **96.** (b) **97.** (c) **98.** (a) **99.** (b) **100.** (c)
101. (b) **102.** (d) **103.** (a) **104.** (d) **105.** (b) **106.** (d) **107.** (d)

RURAL AND URBAN SETTLEMENT

1. (c) **2.** (a) **3.** (c) **4.** (a) **5.** (d) **6.** (a) **7.** (c) **8.** (c) **9.** (c) **10.** (c)
11. (a) **12.** (d) **13.** (a) **14.** (b) **15.** (d) **16.** (a) **17.** (d) **18.** (b) **19.** (d) **20.** (b)
21. (a) **22.** (d) **23.** (a) **24.** (d) **25.** (a) **26.** (d) **27.** (b) **28.** (c) **29.** (b) **30.** (d)
31. (c) **32.** (a)

❑❑❑

22 Tourism and Tourist Places

TOURISM

1. Tourism is a word originated from which language?

(a) Latin (b) Spanish
(c) Roman (d) Yunani

2. When was the word tourism first used?

(a) 1640 AD (b) 1643 AD
(c) 1647 AD (d) 1650 AD

3. Which of the following is a tourist place of international level?

(a) Rajgir (b) Bodh Gaya
(c) Vikramshila (d) Both (a) and (b)

4. Which of the following is a symbol of Bihar Tourism?

(a) Peepal Tree
(b) Ashoka Tree
(c) Ganga Dolphin
(d) Stupa of Rajgir

5. Which of the following is a tag line of Bihar tourism?

(a) Padharo Bihar
(b) Blissful Bihar
(c) Clean Bihar, Beautiful Bihar
(d) Expanding Bihar, Changing Bihar

6. By which name a map has been devised to encourage tourism?

(a) A journey to Bihar
(b) Progressive Bihar
(c) Growth and Beautiful Bihar
(d) Travel across Bihar

7. How many tourist circuits have been marked by Bihar Government?

(a) 6 (b) 7
(c) 8 (d) 9

8. At which of the following places, Buddha circuit is located?

(a) Gaya
(b) Rajgir
(c) Lauriya Nandangarh
(d) All of the above

9. In which district Lauriya Nandangarh tourist place is situated?

(a) East Champaran
(b) West Champaran
(c) Saran
(d) Siwan

10. In which district, Kesariya tourist place is located?

(a) Saran
(b) Mujaffarpur
(c) Gaya
(d) East Champaran

11. In which district Vikramshila tourist place is located?

(a) Munger (b) Bhagalpur
(c) Patna (d) Gopalganj

12. At which of the following places, Sufi circuit is located?

(a) Maner Sharif
(b) Mittan Ghat
(c) Hajipur Karbala
(d) All of the above

13. In which district Maner Sharif Dargah is situated?

(a) Patna (b) Vaishali
(c) Bihar Sharif (d) Hajipur

14. In which district Mittan Ghat is located?
(a) Gaya (b) Bhagalpur
(c) Patna (d) Munger

15. Where is the tomb of Bibi Kamal Saheb located?
(a) Jehanabad (b) Begusarai
(c) Bihar Sharif (d) Rajgir

16. At which of the places Jain circuit is located?
(a) Nathnagar
(b) Pavapuri
(c) Mandar Hill
(d) All of the above

17. In which district Pavapuri is situated?
(a) Nalanda (b) Navada
(c) Munger (d) Gaya

18. In which district Mandar Hill is located?
(a) Bhagalpur (b) Banka
(c) Aurangabad (d) Gaya

19. At which place Champanagar Jain circuit is situated?
(a) Vaishali (b) Gaya
(c) Bhagalpur (d) Buxar

20. In which district Kundalgram Jain circuit is situated?
(a) East Champaran
(b) Siwan
(c) Lakhisarai
(d) Nalanda

21. In which district Samosaran Jain circuit is situated?
(a) Nalanda (b) Bhagalpur
(c) Arrah (d) Kaimur

22. In which district Lachhaur Jain circuit is located?
(a) Gaya (b) Jamui
(c) Jehanabad (d) Vaishali

23. At which places Ramayan circuit is located?
(a) Valmiki Nagar
(b) Sitapur
(c) Giddheshwar
(d) All of the above

24. In which district Valmiki Nagar Ramayan circuit is situated?
(a) West Champaran
(b) East Champaran
(c) Vaishali
(d) Gaya

25. In which district Pretshila Ramayan circuit is located?
(a) Vaishali (b) Gaya
(c) Munger (d) Bhagalpur

26. In which district Ahilyasthan Ramayan circuit is located?
(a) Darbhanga (b) Madhubani
(c) Saharasa (d) Gaya

27. In which district Kako Ramayan circuit is located?
(a) Madhubani
(b) Gaya
(c) Jehanabad
(d) Patna

28. In which district Sitakund Ramayan Circuit is situated?
(a) Sitamarhi (b) Shivhar
(c) Saharasa (d) Arrah

29. In which district Singheshwar Ramayan Circuit is located?
(a) Aurangabad (b) Arrah
(c) Buxar (d) Madhepura

30. In which district Ramshila Ramayan Circuit is located?
(a) Gaya
(b) Buxar
(c) Saran
(d) East Champaran

31. In which district Giddheshwar Ramayan Circuit is located?
(a) Jehanabad (b) Munger
(c) Banka (d) Jamui

32. In which district Shivshakti Circuit is located?
(a) Saran (b) Gopalganj
(c) Rohtash (d) All of these

33. In which district Mundeshawari Sthan Shivshakti Circuit is located?
(a) Kaimur (b) Rohtash
(c) Arrah (d) Buxar

34. In which district Chandi Sthan Shivshakti circuit is located?
(a) Gaya (b) Munger
(c) Bhagalpur (d) Siwan

35. In which district Ugratara Sthan Shivshakti Circuit is located?
(a) Saharasa (b) Gaya
(c) Katihar (d) Saran

36. In which district Thave Shivshakti Circuit is located?
(a) Gaya (b) Siwan
(c) Gopalganj (d) Saran

37. In which district Tarachandi Sthan Shivshakti circuit is located?
(a) Rohtash (b) Arrah
(c) Kaimur (d) Gaya

38. In which district Shyamakali Shivshakti circuit is located?
(a) Bhagalpur (b) Rohtash
(c) Darbhanga (d) Banka

39. In which district Matsyagandha Raktkali Mandir Shivshakti circuit is located?
(a) Darbhanga (b) Banka
(c) Saharasa (d) Gopalganj

40. In which district Koteshwar Dham Shivshakti circuit is located?
(a) Gaya (b) Bhagalpur
(c) Munger (d) Patna

41. In which district Kusheshwar Dham Shivshakti Peeth is located?
(a) Navada (b) Begusarai
(c) Darbhanga (d) Saharasa

42. In which district Ajgaivinath Shivshakti circuit is located?
(a) Bhagalpur (b) Munger
(c) Shivhar (d) Saharasa

43. In which district Ashok Dham Shivshakti circuit is situated?
(a) Jamui (b) Jehanabad
(c) Lakhisarai (d) Gaya

44. In which district Garibnath Shivshakti circuit is located?
(a) Mujaffarpur (b) Vaishali
(c) Gaya (d) Navada

45. In which district Mahendranath Shivshakti circuit is located?
(a) Jehanabad (b) Saran
(c) Siwan (d) Gopalganj

46. In which district Brahmeshwarnath Shivshakti circuit is located?
(a) Darbhanga (b) Arrah
(c) Kaimur (d) Buxar

47. In which district, sikh circuit has been constructed?
(a) Patna Saheb
(b) Rajgir
(c) Betiya
(d) All of the above

48. In which district Bal Leela Saheb Sikh circuit is located?
(a) Patna (b) Gaya
(c) Bhagalpur (d) Munger

49. Where is Guru Teg Bahadur Gurudwara Sikh circuit located?
(a) Motihari Patna
(b) Mujaffarpur
(c) Hajipur
(d) All of the above

50. Where is Guru Nank Kund Sikh circuit located?
(a) Gaya
(b) Bhabhua
(c) Rajgir
(d) Bihar Sharif

51. In which district Gurudwara Pakki Sangat Sikh Circuit is located?
(a) Munger (b) Bhagalpur
(c) Gaya (d) Patna

52. Where is Gurudwara Harmander Saheb Sikh Circuit located?
(a) Begusarai (b) Barauni
(c) Danapur (d) Gaya

53. In which district Gandhi Circuit has been constructed?
(a) East Champaran
(b) West Champaran
(c) Patna
(d) All of the above

54. In which district Motihari Gandhi Circuit is located?
(a) East Champaran
(b) Gaya
(c) Bhagalpur
(d) Aurangabad

55. In which district Betiya Gandhi circuit is located?
(a) East Champaran
(b) Saran
(c) West Champaran
(d) Gopalganj

56. In which district Mitiherva Ashram Gandhi Circuit is located?
(a) East Champaran
(b) West Champaran
(c) Saran
(d) Siwan

57. In which district Vrandavan Gandhi Circuit is located?
(a) West Champaran
(b) Gopalganj
(c) Saran
(d) Munger

58. In which district Sadaqat Ashram Gandhi Circuit is located?
(a) Vaishali (b) Patna
(c) Munger (d) Bhagalpur

59. Where is Bihar Museum located?
(a) Patna (b) Gaya
(c) Munger (d) Bhagalpur

60. In which district Rajgir tourist place is located?
(a) Jehanabad (b) Patna
(c) Nalanda (d) Madhubani

61. In which district Bhim Dam Sanctuary is located?
(a) Munger (b) Bhagalpur
(c) Gaya (d) Navada

62. In which district Gautam Buddha Sanctuary is located?
(a) Bhagalpur (b) Munger
(c) Gaya (d) Navada

63. In which district Naktidham is located?
(a) Jehanabad (b) Jamui
(c) Munger (d) Bhagalpur

64. In which district Gogabeel Sanctuary is situated?
(a) Bhagalpur (b) Gaya
(c) Navada (d) Buxar

65. In which district Kanwar Lake is situated?
(a) Gaya (b) Begusarai
(c) Lakhisarai (d) Supoul

66. In which district Ghodkatora Lake is situated?
(a) Nalanda (b) Gaya
(c) Khagariya (d) Saharasa

67. In which district Kakolat waterfall is located?
(a) Supoul (b) Shivhar
(c) Navada (d) Arrah

68. In which district Telhara Waterfall is located?
(a) Rohtash (b) Arrah
(c) Buxar (d) Kaimur

69. In which district Gangatic Dolphin Sanctuary is located?
(a) Munger (b) Gaya
(c) Patna (d) Bhagalpur

70. In which district Valmiki Nagar National Park is located?

(a) East Champaran
(b) West Champaran
(c) Saran
(d) Siwan

71. Keeping tourism in view, Bihar occupies which place at present?

(a) 3 (b) 5
(c) 7 (d) 9

72. Which of the following has been included in UNESCO's World Heritage List?

(a) Nalanda Mahavihar
(b) Vikramshila Mahavihar
(c) Gautam Buddha Sanctuary
(d) Golghar

73. Where is Jan-nayak Karpoori Thakur Memorial Museum located?

(a) Gaya (b) Patna
(c) Saran (d) Betiya

74. Where in Bihar proposal to establish a film city has been initiated?

(a) Gaya (b) Patna
(c) Rajgir (d) Begusarai

75. Where has Buddha Memorial Park been constructed?

(a) Mujaffarpur (b) Hajipur
(c) Patna (d) Bhagalpur

76. In which of the following districts, permission to set up a Buddha Memory-cum-Thorough Philosophy Museum has been given?

(a) Vaishali (b) Gaya
(c) Munger (d) Supoul

77. In which district Jamaluddin Chak Archaeological place is located?

(a) Vaishali (b) Patna
(c) Nalanda (d) Bhagalpur

78. In which district Eksara Archaeological Place is located?

(a) Patna (b) Navada
(c) Nalanda (d) Supoul

79. In which district Lorikdih Archaeological place is situated?

(a) Darbhanga (b) Saharasa
(c) Supoul (d) Buxar

80. In which district Rajnagar Archaeological place is located?

(a) Supoul (b) Siwan
(c) Madhubani (d) Gaya

81. In which district Kalimandir Archaelogical place is situated?

(a) Patna (b) Gaya
(c) Bhagalpur (d) Munger

82. In which district Chak Archaeological place is located?

(a) Supoul (b) Madhubani
(c) Darbhanga (d) Saharasa

TOURIST PLACES

1. Nalanda University has been a major centre of _______ education?

(a) Bodh (b) Jain
(c) Islamic (d) Both (a) and (b)

2. Which of the following Gupta period rulers, had established Nalanda University?

(a) Chandragupt Maurya
(b) Ashok
(c) Kumargupt
(d) Brahmgupt

3. The downfall of Nalanda University occurred due to a struggle between Pal dynasty and ______ dynasty?

(a) Gupta (b) Maurya
(c) Sen (d) Kanva

4. Nalanda University is being reconstructed at present with cooperation from which country?

(a) China (b) Indonesia
(c) Japan (d) Thailand

5. Which of the following dynasties had its capital 'Rajagriha'?
(a) Gupta (b) Haryak
(c) Kanva (d) Pal

6. An evidence of the most ancient architectural art has been found from ______?
(a) Patliputra (b) Vaishali
(c) Rajagriha (d) Chirand

7. Where was the first Both Sangiti was organized?
(a) Rajagriha (b) Vaishali
(c) Patliputra (d) Kundalvan

8. In which cave of Rajagriha, the first Both Sangiti was organized?
(a) Barabar (b) Nagarjuni
(c) Saptparini (d) Lomash Rishi

9. On which of the following hills, the World's highest Peace Stupa has been got built?
(a) Barabar (b) Ratnagiri
(c) Kaimur (d) Sonegiri

10. World's highest World Peace 'Stupa' is built at which place?
(a) Rajagriha (b) Vaishali
(c) Kesariya (d) Pavapuri

11. The World Peace 'Stupa' has been built with support from which country?
(a) China (b) Japan
(c) Srilanka (d) Thailand

12. Which of the following tourist places is situated in Rajgir?
(a) Jeevika Bhraman
(b) Sone Bhandar
(c) Amra Van
(d) All of the above

13. Where tourist place called Venuvan is situated?
(a) Rajgir (b) Gaya
(c) Bihar Sharif (d) Pavapuri

14. In which district Ramshila Mountain is located?
(a) Bhagalpur (b) Supoul
(c) Arrah (d) Gaya

15. In which district Pavapuri is located?
(a) Navada (b) Gaya
(c) Vaishali (d) Nalanda

16. The salvation place of who of the following is Pavapuri?
(a) Rishabhdev
(b) Ajitnath
(c) Mahavir Jain
(d) Gautam Buddha

17. Where is 'Jal Mandir' located?
(a) Rajgir (b) Pavapuri
(c) Gaya (d) Bhagalpur

18. Which of the following cities had its ancient name as 'Up-puri'?
(a) Ayodhya (b) Patliputra
(c) Pavapuri (d) Gaya

19. In which of the following districts, does tomb of Sheikh Makhdoom Shah Sharfuddin exist?
(a) Nalanda (b) Vaishali
(c) Gaya (d) Patna

20. Where is Makhdoom Kund located?
(a) Bihar Sharif (b) Rajgir
(c) Gaya (d) Patna

21. Where is the tomb of Malik Ibrahim Bayan situated?
(a) Patna (b) Rajgir
(c) Bihar Sharif (d) Hajipur

22. When was World Peace 'Stupa' situated in Rajgir constructed?
(a) 1963 AD (b) 1965 AD
(c) 1967 AD (d) 1969 AD

23. Who had given to Venuvan as a gift to Mahatma Buddha?
(a) Ajatshatru (b) Bimbisara
(c) Ashok (d) Kalashok

24. Which of the following is the birth-place of Mahavir Jain?
(a) Kundgram (b) Rajagriha
(c) Pavapuri (d) Gaya

25. In which district Kundgram is located?
(a) Navada (b) Gaya
(c) Nalanda (d) Munger

26. Kundgram is a holy pilgrimage to people of which religion?
(a) Jains (b) Bodh
(c) Shaiva (d) Sikh

27. Where are Maniarmath and Sone Bhandar situated?
(a) Rajgir (b) Gaya
(c) Pavapuri (d) Barauni

28. In which district Pretshila Mountain is situated?
(a) Gaya
(b) Saharasa
(c) East Champaran
(d) Saran

29. On the banks of which river Gaya city is located?
(a) Falgu (b) Sone
(c) Kosi (d) Ajay

30. Where is Vishnupad Mandir located?
(a) Munger (b) Gaya
(c) Rajgir (d) Mujaffarpur

31. Who got Vishnupad Mandir reconstructed?
(a) Lakshmi Bai
(b) Jija Bai
(c) Ahilya Bai
(d) Rani Maheshwari

32. Ahilya Bai Holkar was the queen of which place?
(a) Indore (b) Puna
(c) Mewal (d) Bundelkhand

33. Brahmyoni Hill and Ramshila Hill are located in which district?
(a) Vaishali (b) Munger
(c) Gaya (d) Bhagalpur

34. Where is Mangla Gauri Temple located?
(a) Gaya (b) Mujaffarpur
(c) Patna (d) Munger

35. In Bodh Gaya, a Stupa constructed by whom had existed?
(a) Chandragupt Maurya
(b) Bindusara
(c) Ashok
(d) Kumaragupt

36. Huvishaka belonging to which dynasty got Bodh Gaya a glorious and huge temple built in Bodh Gaya?
(a) Maurya (b) Kushan
(c) Kanva (d) Shung

37. In Mahabodhi Temple located at Bodh Gaya, an idol of Mahatma Buddha is situated in which position?
(a) Padmasan
(b) Dharti-Sparsha
(c) Chakrasan
(d) All of the above

38. A huge______ tree is located near the Mahabodhi Temple.
(a) Bargad (b) Peepal
(c) Arjuna (d) Mango

39. As per a legend, Mahatma Buddha had achieved salvation under which tree?
(a) Peepal
(b) Bargad
(c) Ashok
(d) Arjun

40. The 'Bodhi Vriksha' existing today is of which generation?
(a) Third (b) Fourth
(c) Fifth (d) Sixth

41. Who had sat for 'Attarsadhna' near the Vajrasan platform?
(a) Mahatma Buddha
(b) Mahavir Jain
(c) Rishabhdev
(d) Ajitnath

42. Who of the following had destroyed 'Bodhi-vraksha'?
(a) Kalashok
(b) Shashank
(c) Tishyarakshita
(d) Both (b) and (c)

43. Who had 'Tishyarakshita' as his wife?
(a) Ghananand (b) Ashok
(c) Shashank (d) Kumargupt

44. Shashank was a disciple of which religion?
(a) Shaiva (b) Vaishnav
(c) Ajivika (d) Jain

45. Which country has got built a glorious temple at Bodh Gaya?
(a) Srilanka
(b) China
(c) Thailand
(d) All of the above

46. In which district Chovar ka Shiv-mandir is located?
(a) Gaya (b) Bhagalpur
(c) Siwan (d) Vaishali

47. On Brahmyoni Hill, whose temple under the huge banyan tree is located?
(a) Vishnu (b) Shiva
(c) Krishna (d) Ganesha

48. In which district of Bihar famous 'Surya Mandir' is located?
(a) Vaishali (b) Munger
(c) Gaya (d) Aurangabad

49. Who had got built the famous 'Surya Mandir' situated at Aurangabad?
(a) Bhairo Singh
(b) Chandradev Singh
(c) Bhairvendra Singh
(d) Arjun Singh

50. Who of the following had his birth-place as Vaishali?
(a) Mahatma Buddha
(b) Rishabhdev
(c) Mahavir
(d) Panini

51. Where among the following places, the first republic of the world was established around 2500 years ago?
(a) Patliputra (b) Vaishali
(c) Nalanda (d) Bodh Gaya

52. Who of the following rulers had established a republic in Vaishali?
(a) Lichhavi (b) Pal
(c) Maurya (d) Gupta

53. Where had Ashoka established a 'Singh-Stambha'?
(a) Bodh Gaya (b) Nalanda
(c) Vaishali (d) Rajgir

54. What is the height of India's highest 'World Peace Stupa' situated in Vaishali in meters?
(a) 120 (b) 125
(c) 130 (d) 135

55. Which of the following is located in Vaishali?
(a) Bavan Pokhar Temple
(b) Hari Katora Temple
(c) Bodh Stupa
(d) All of the above

56. In which of the following district, 'Ashoka's Latt' (Pillar) exists?
(a) Gaya (b) Vaishali
(c) Bhagalpur (d) Munger

57. In which district is Choumukhi Mahadev Temple situated?
(a) East Champaran
(b) Gaya
(c) Vaishali
(d) Mujaffarpur

58. Where is 'Harihar-kshetra' temple located?
(a) Sonepur (b) Gaya
(c) Aurangabad (d) Motihari

59. Harihar-Kshetra Temple is located on the banks of which river?
(a) Sone (b) Kosi
(c) Gandak (d) Niranjana

60. Where is Nepali Temple situated?
(a) Hajipur
(b) Sultanpur
(c) Bakhtiyarpur
(d) Sonepur

61. Nepali Temple is situated on the banks of which river?
(a) Ganga (b) Kosi
(c) Gandak (d) Both (a) and (c)

62. Who discovered stone age place known as 'Chechar'?
(a) Brahmdutt Tiwari
(b) Munir Khan
(c) Dr. Jogendra Mishra
(d) Kumud Sharma

63. When had Dr. Jogendra Mishra discovered the stone age place Chechar?
(a) 1972 (b) 1974
(c) 1976 (d) 1978

64. Which of the following is not another name of Chechar?
(a) Baikunth Dham
(b) Kotigram
(c) Shwetpur
(d) Kushpallav

65. Which of the following is not an ancient name of Patna City?
(a) Patliputra
(b) Phoolpur
(c) Pushpur
(d) Ajimabad

66. Who has called Patliputra as Palibothra in his book?
(a) Udayin (b) Megasthanese
(c) Koutilya (d) Amar Singh

67. Which of the following books was written by Megasthanese?
(a) Patnav (b) Indigo
(c) Indica (d) Swetson

68. Megasthanese was a traveller from which country?
(a) Iran (b) Yunnan
(c) Syria (d) Rome

69. Who of the medieval period ruler had changed name of Patliputra to Patna?
(a) Allauddin Khilji
(b) Balban
(c) Shershah Suri
(d) Aurangzeb

70. Which Sikh Guru was born in Patna Sahib?
(a) The second (b) The fourth
(c) The seventh (d) The tenth

71. Who of the following sikh gurus was born in Patna Sahib?
(a) Guru Angad
(b) Guru Tegh Bahadur
(c) Guru Gobind Singh
(d) Guru Arjun Dev

72. When was Guru Gobind Singh born?
(a) 1666 AD (b) 1668 AD
(c) 1670 AD (d) 1672 AD

73. The remains of Patliputra are found at _______.
(a) Adam Kuan (b) Kumharar
(c) Bankipur (d) Phulwari Sharif

74. The remains of ________ period have been found from Kumharar?
(a) Mauryan (b) Gupta
(c) Pal (d) Sen

75. According to a legend, who had killed his 99 brothers to become a ruler and put their bodies in to 'AgamKuan'?

(a) Ajatshatru
(b) Udayin
(c) Chandragupt Maurya
(d) Ashok

76. Where is Sheetla Devi Temple located?
(a) Patna
(b) Mujaffarpur
(c) Valmiki Nagar
(d) Munger

77. Who had got built a mosque at Dhavalpur?
(a) Balban
(b) Ferozshah Tughlak
(c) Shershah Suri
(d) Shah Mohd. II

78. Where had Saif Khan got built temples and mosques?
(a) Patna (b) Hajipur
(c) Bakhtiyarpur (d) Bihar Sharif

79. Where is 'Padri ki haveli' situated?
(a) Betiya (b) Dehri-O-Sone
(c) Patna (d) Mujaffarpur

80. When was 'Padri ki haveli' built in Patna?
(a) 1749 AD (b) 1751 AD
(c) 1753 AD (d) 1755 AD

81. Who got built 'Padri ki haveli' in Patna?
(a) Father Peter
(b) Father Richard Mixon
(c) Father Kapuchin
(d) Father Rand

82. Where is Khudabaksh Library located?
(a) Patna (b) Hajipur
(c) Bihar Sharif (d) Darbhanga

83. Khudabaksh Library is an example of the Mughal period and _______ architecture?
(a) Pahadi (b) Rajput
(c) British (d) Gothick

84. In Khudabaksh Library, apart from the main building, a reading room known as______ is there?
(a) Curzon (b) Rippon
(c) Litten (d) Mountbatten

85. When was Khudabaksha Library established?
(a) 1889 AD (b) 1890 AD
(c) 1891 AD (d) 1892 AD

86. Which Mughal ruler had got built mosque made of stones?
(a) Shah Alam II
(b) Raj Kumar Parvez
(c) Aurangzeb
(d) Shershah

87. Where was the famous Stone Mosque built in Bihar?
(a) Bihar Sharif
(b) Hajipur
(c) Patna
(d) Mujaffarpur

88. When was a mosque made of stones built in Patna?
(a) 1619 AD (b) 1621 AD
(c) 1623 AD (d) 1625 AD

89. Where is Hazari Old Dharamshala located?
(a) Patna (b) Mujaffarpur
(c) Betiya (d) Motihari

90. After which revolution, a Martyr Memorial was built in Patna?
(a) Swadeshi
(b) Quit India
(c) Non co-operation
(d) Champaran

91. When was Patna Museum built?
(a) 1917 AD (b) 1919 AD
(c) 1921 AD (d) 1923 AD

92. Where in Bihar is 'Golghar' located?
(a) Gaya (b) Hajipur
(c) Patna (d) Bhagalpur

93. Who had got built Patna situated 'Golghar'?
(a) Captain John Jarsittan
(b) Lord Curzon
(c) Lord Mayo
(d) Captain Cook

94. When was Patna situated 'Golghar' built?
(a) 1780 AD (b) 1782 AD
(c) 1784 AD (d) 1786 AD

95. Who was India's Viceroy in the year 1786?
(a) Lord Canning
(b) Warren Hastings
(c) Lord Curzon
(d) Lord Mayo

96. Where is Peer Ali Park located?
(a) Patna (b) Bhagalpur
(c) Mujaffarpur (d) Munger

97. Where is Sanjay Gandhi Park located?
(a) Gaya (b) Sonepur
(c) Patna (d) Bihar Sharif

98. Where is Shrikrishna Science Centre located?
(a) Patna (b) Munger
(c) Bhagalpur (d) Rajgir

99. Where is Chhajjubagh Kothi situated?
(a) Motihari (b) Betiya
(c) Saharasa (d) Patna

100. When was Patna College established?
(a) 1861 AD (b) 1863 AD
(c) 1865 AD (d) 1867 AD

101. Patma College Building was built by _______ East India Company as a godown?
(a) Dutch (b) British
(c) Portuguese (d) French

102. Where is the tomb of Shah Daulat located?
(a) Bihar Sharif (b) Patna
(c) Hajipur (d) Bakhtiyarpur

103. In which century Mahavir Temple of Jalle was built?
(a) 15th (b) 16th
(c) 17th (d) 18th

104. In which area of Patna, Chaitanya Mahaprabhu Temple is located?
(a) Gardanibagh (b) Kumharar
(c) Danapur (d) Gaighat

105. When was Patna situated Birla Temple built?
(a) 1940 (b) 1942
(c) 1944 (d) 1946

106. Who had got built Patna situated Birla temple?
(a) Rajbaldev Birla
(b) Rajendra Prasad
(c) Shrikrishna Singh
(d) Ghanshyam das Birla

107. Where is Umanath Temple situated?
(a) Gaya (b) Patna
(c) Buxar (d) Arrah

108. In which century Khankah Fulwari Sharif was got built?
(a) 13th (b) 14th
(c) 15th (d) 16th

109. In which month a 'Urs' (Mela) is organized at Khankah Fulwari Sharif?
(a) Ramzan
(b) Razab
(c) Rabi-ul-avval
(d) Rabi-ul-aakhir

110. When did Guru Nanak stay at Gurudwara Gaighat?
(a) 1509 AD
(b) 1511 AD
(c) 1513 AD
(d) 1515 AD

111. Where is Gurudwara Hadri Sahib located?
(a) Fulwari Sharif
(b) Patna Sahib
(c) Bankipur
(d) Danapur

112. Where is Guru ka Bagh situated?
(a) Nalanda (b) Patna
(c) Vaishali (d) Bhagalpur

113. A religious place is situated at Kamaldah which relates to which religion?
(a) Sikh (b) Bodh
(c) Jain (d) Shaiva

114. Where is St. Joseph Church located?
(a) Patna (b) Rajgir
(c) Gaya (d) Bhagalpur

115. Which city of Bihar is called 'Silk Nagar'?
(a) Hajipur (b) Patna
(c) Bhagalpur (d) Munger

116. In which district the ancient Vikramshila University is situated?
(a) Bhagalpur (b) Navada
(c) Nalanda (d) Gaya

117. Champa (Bhagalpur) was the capital of which ancient 'Mahajanpad'?
(a) Magadh
(b) Angg
(c) Vajji
(d) All of the above

118. On the banks of which river, Sultanganj situated Ajgaibinath Temple is located?
(a) Ganga (b) Gandak
(c) Kosi (d) Bagmati

119. According to a legend, which mountain was used at the time of churning of ocean?
(a) Kaimur (b) Vindhyan
(c) Mandar Giri (d) Sone Giri

120. Ajgaibinath Temple is dedicated to which God?
(a) Shiva (b) Krishna
(c) Vishnu (d) Ganesha

121. Who had got established the capital of the ancient 'Mahajanpad' Angg, Chamba?
(a) Ajatshatru
(b) Mahagobind
(c) Dhananand
(d) Chandragupt Maurya

122. Who of the following foreign travellers had travelled to Chamba?
(a) Megasthenese
(b) Fa Hien
(c) Huen-Tsang
(d) Both (b) and (c)

123. Munger is a city situated on the banks of which river?
(a) Ganga (b) Kosi
(c) Ajay (d) Niranjana

124. Which ruler had developed Munger as a capital?
(a) Mir Jaffar (b) Mir Qasim
(c) Mir Sadiq (d) Mir Usman

125. Where is Bihar Yog Bharti Ganga Darshan Vishwa Yogpeeth located?
(a) Munger (b) Bhagalpur
(c) Gaya (d) Arrah

126. Who had established Bihar School of Yoga?
(a) Swami Sehjanand Saraswati
(b) Swami Satyanand Saraswati
(c) Swami Parmanand Maharaj
(d) Swami Shivanand Saraswati

127. When was Bihar School of Yoga established?
(a) 1961 (b) 1963
(c) 1965 (d) 1967

128. Who had established Bihar Yog Bharti?
(a) Niranjananand Saraswati
(b) Parmanand Saraswati
(c) Sehjanand Saraswati
(d) All of the above

129. When was Bihar Yog Bharti established?
(a) 1990 (b) 1992
(c) 1994 (d) 1996

130. In which district of Bihar, Bihar Yog Bharti was established?
(a) Gaya (b) Patna
(c) Buxar (d) Munger

131. In which district famous Chandikadevi Temple is situated?
(a) Munger (b) Buxar
(c) Saharasa (d) Supoul

132. Against which Governor General, White Mutiny had occurred?
(a) Lord Curzon (b) Lord Rippon
(c) Lord Litten (d) Lord Clive

133. When did White Mutiny occur?
(a) 1762 AD (b) 1764 AD
(c) 1766 AD (d) 1768 AD

134. In which district Tarachandi Maa Temple is located?
(a) Rohtash (b) Arrah
(c) Kaimur (d) Saran

135. Where is the tomb of Shershah Suri located?
(a) Hajipur (b) Maner
(c) Sasaram (d) Bihar Sharif

136. Where is the tomb of Hasan Khan Soor located?
(a) Gaya (b) Sasaram
(c) Navada (d) Patna

137. In which of the following styles Sher Shah Suri's tomb is constructed?
(a) Mughal (b) Rajput
(c) Afghan (d) Iranian

138. In which district Mata Mundeshwari Devi Temple is situated?
(a) Kaimur (b) Rohtash
(c) Arrah (d) Buxar

139. In which of the following temples, does 'Ek Panchmukhi Shivling' exist?
(a) Maa Chandeshwari Temple
(b) Maa Tara Chandi Temple
(c) Manokamna Temple
(d) Mundeshwari Temple

140. In which district of Bihar Girijasthan Temple is situated?
(a) Sasaram (b) Madhubani
(c) Gaya (d) Arrah

141. In which of the following temples, the virgin girls worship Mata Parvati to seek good husband for them?
(a) Chandika Devi Temple
(b) Maa Tara Chandi Temple
(c) Manokamna Devi Temple
(d) Girijasthan Temple

142. Where is Somnath Temple located?
(a) Darbhanga (b) Madhubani
(c) Saharasa (d) Arrah

143. In which of the following temples, marriages of Maithili Brahmins are decided?
(a) Guptdham Temple
(b) Somnath Temple
(c) Tara Chandi Devi Temple
(d) Somnath Temple

144. In which district Chhinmastika Temple is located?
(a) Gaya (b) Madhubani
(c) Saharasa (d) Aurangabad

145. Chhinnmastika Temple is dedicated to which female deity?
(a) Durga (b) Lakshmi
(c) Saraswati (d) Parvati

146. In Chhinnmastika Temple, the great poet_______used to worship Mahakali.
(a) Soor Das
(b) Kabir Das
(c) Kali Das
(d) Ramdhari Singh Dinkar

147. Where in Bihar is famous Ram-Janki Temple situated?
(a) Sitamarhi (b) Shivhar
(c) Aurangabad (d) Thave

148. In which district Ahiroli Temple is situated?
(a) Supoul (b) Buxar
(c) Navada (d) Saran

149. In which district Ugratara Temple is situated?
(a) Saharasa (b) Katihar
(c) Nalanda (d) Gaya

150. In which district of the State Kapileshwarsthan is situated?
(a) Saharasa (b) Khagadiya
(c) Madhepura (d) Supoul

151. In which district Kesariya Tourism place is situated?
(a) East Champaran
(b) West Champaran
(c) Mujaffarpur
(d) Siwan

152. The height of Kesariya located Bodh 'Stupa'is ________ft.
(a) 1011 (b) 1021
(c) 1032 (d) 1042

153. Stupa' located at which of following places is called 'Raja Ben Ka Devra'?
(a) Vaishali (b) Kesariya
(c) Patna (d) Rajgir

154. In which of the following places, Ashoka period pillar inscriptions have been found?
(a) Betiya (b) Motihari
(c) Rampurva (d) Sugouli

155. The place called Rampurva is related to which district?
(a) Gaya
(b) West Champaran
(c) Madhubani
(d) Arrah

156. Who discovered Rampurva pillar inscription?
(a) Carlleyle
(b) James Cunningham
(c) Tom Cook
(d) Norman Lesley

157. When did carlleyle discover Rampurva pillar inscription?
(a) 1895 AD (b) 1897 AD
(c) 1899 AD (d) 1901 AD

158. A picture of who of the following is inscripted on Rampurva pillar inscription?
(a) Lion (b) Cow
(c) Bullock (d) Both (a) and (c)

159. Thave situated Temple is dedicated to which female deity?
(a) Lakshmi (b) Parvati
(c) Durga (d) Saraswati

160. Where is Ambika Bhavani Temple located?
(a) Chhapra (b) Gopalganj
(c) Siwan (d) Arrah

161. In which district Deklu Dham Temple is located?
(a) Arrah (b) Buxar
(c) Darbhanga (d) Madhubani

162. Dekludham Temple is dedicated to which God?
(a) Shiva (b) Vishnu
(c) Krishna (d) Brahma

163. On banks of which river Koteshwarnath Temple is situated?
(a) Ajay (b) Gumani
(c) Morhar (d) Sarisava

164. In which district Shaktipeeth Chamunda Devi Temple is located?
(a) Arrah (b) Buxar
(c) Kaimur (d) Navada

165. According to a legend, which body part of the 'Sati' has fallen in Chamunda Devi Temple premise?
(a) Hand (b) Head
(c) Ear (d) Eye

166. In which district Dhimeshwarsthan Temple is located?
(a) Purnia (b) Munger
(c) Bhagalpur (d) Gaya

167. Which body part of Mata Sati had fallen on Dhimeshwarsthan Temple?
(a) Hand (b) Foot
(c) Heart (d) Head

168. In which district Navlakha Temple is situated?
(a) Begusarai (b) Gaya
(c) Buxar (d) Arrah

169. When was construction of Navlakha Temple got done by Mahant Mahavir Das?
(a) 1951 (b) 1953
(c) 1955 (d) 1957

170. Where is the St. Thomas the Apostle Church is located?
(a) Gaya (b) Patna
(c) Betiya (d) Mujaffarpur

171. Where is St. Francis Assisi Church located?
(a) Bhagalpur (b) Gaya
(c) Mujaffarpur (d) Motihari

172. Where is Our Lady of Soroz Church located?
(a) Arrah (b) Patna
(c) Kaimur (d) Buxar

173. In which district Patalpuri cave is situated?
(a) Buxar (b) Arrah
(c) Bhagalpur (d) Kaimur

174. In which district Shilamurti Samuh is located?
(a) Bhagalpur (b) Supoul
(c) Khagadiya (d) Saharasa

175. In which district ancient hillock of Somnath Hill is located?
(a) Madhubani (b) Gaya
(c) Arrah (d) Aurangabad

176. In which district Saptagufa Samuh is located?
(a) Jamui (b) Supoul
(c) Jehanabad (d) Gaya

177. Where is the tomb of Shamsher Khan located?
(a) Aurangabad
(b) East Champaran
(c) Patna
(d) Munger

178. In which district, a pillar inscription of Ashoka has been found?
(a) Arrah (b) Buxar
(c) Rohtash (d) Munger

179. Where is the tomb of Bakhtiyar Khan located?
(a) Patna (b) Bhabhua
(c) Hajipur (d) Bihar Sharif

180. In which district, the paternal house of Dr. Rajendra Prasad is located?
(a) Siwan (b) Saran
(c) Munger (d) Gaya

181. Where is the mosque of Begu Hajjam located?
(a) Hajipur (b) Patna
(c) Bihar Sharif (d) Navada

182. Where is the tomb of Alawal Khan situated?
(a) Patna
(b) Munger
(c) Bhagalpur
(d) Sasaram

183. In which district Katragarh is located?
(a) Mujaffarpur (b) Gaya
(c) Munger (d) Bhagalpur

184. In which district Kheri Archaeological place is situated?
(a) Aurangabad (b) Gaya
(c) Supoul (d) Bhagalpur

185. In which district Jalalgarh Fort is located?
(a) Katihar (b) Purnia
(c) Kishanganj (d) Saharasa

186. Where is Chausagarh situated?
(a) Arrah (b) Kaimur
(c) Buxar (d) Saran

187. Where is the fort of Dawood Khan situated?
(a) Aurangabad (b) Gaya
(c) Munger (d) Arrah

Answers

TOURISM

1. (a)	**2.** (b)	**3.** (d)	**4.** (a)	**5.** (b)	**6.** (a)	**7.** (c)	**8.** (d)	**9.** (a)	**10.** (d)
11. (b)	**12.** (d)	**13.** (a)	**14.** (c)	**15.** (a)	**16.** (d)	**17.** (a)	**18.** (b)	**19.** (c)	**20.** (d)
21. (a)	**22.** (b)	**23.** (d)	**24.** (a)	**25.** (b)	**26.** (a)	**27.** (c)	**28.** (a)	**29.** (d)	**30.** (a)
31. (d)	**32.** (d)	**33.** (a)	**34.** (b)	**35.** (a)	**36.** (c)	**37.** (a)	**38.** (c)	**39.** (c)	**40.** (a)
41. (c)	**42.** (a)	**43.** (c)	**44.** (a)	**45.** (b)	**46.** (d)	**47.** (d)	**48.** (a)	**49.** (b)	**50.** (c)
51. (a)	**52.** (c)	**53.** (d)	**54.** (a)	**55.** (c)	**56.** (b)	**57.** (a)	**58.** (b)	**59.** (a)	**60.** (c)
61. (a)	**62.** (c)	**63.** (b)	**64.** (a)	**65.** (b)	**66.** (a)	**67.** (c)	**68.** (a)	**69.** (d)	**70.** (b)
71. (c)	**72.** (a)	**73.** (b)	**74.** (c)	**75.** (c)	**76.** (a)	**77.** (b)	**78.** (c)	**79.** (a)	**80.** (c)
81. (b)	**82.** (c)								

TOURIST PLACES

1. (a)	**2.** (c)	**3.** (c)	**4.** (a)	**5.** (b)	**6.** (c)	**7.** (a)	**8.** (c)	**9.** (b)	**10.** (a)
11. (b)	**12.** (d)	**13.** (a)	**14.** (d)	**15.** (d)	**16.** (c)	**17.** (b)	**18.** (c)	**19.** (a)	**20.** (b)
21. (c)	**22.** (d)	**23.** (b)	**24.** (a)	**25.** (c)	**26.** (a)	**27.** (a)	**28.** (a)	**29.** (a)	**30.** (b)
31. (c)	**32.** (a)	**33.** (c)	**34.** (a)	**35.** (c)	**36.** (b)	**37.** (a)	**38.** (b)	**39.** (a)	**40.** (c)
41. (a)	**42.** (d)	**43.** (b)	**44.** (a)	**45.** (d)	**46.** (a)	**47.** (b)	**48.** (d)	**49.** (c)	**50.** (c)
51. (b)	**52.** (a)	**53.** (c)	**54.** (b)	**55.** (d)	**56.** (b)	**57.** (c)	**58.** (a)	**59.** (c)	**60.** (a)
61. (d)	**62.** (c)	**63.** (d)	**64.** (a)	**65.** (b)	**66.** (b)	**67.** (c)	**68.** (b)	**69.** (c)	**70.** (d)
71. (c)	**72.** (a)	**73.** (b)	**74.** (a)	**75.** (d)	**76.** (a)	**77.** (c)	**78.** (a)	**79.** (c)	**80.** (b)
81. (c)	**82.** (a)	**83.** (b)	**84.** (a)	**85.** (c)	**86.** (b)	**87.** (c)	**88.** (b)	**89.** (c)	**90.** (b)
91. (a)	**92.** (c)	**93.** (a)	**94.** (d)	**95.** (b)	**96.** (a)	**97.** (c)	**98.** (a)	**99.** (d)	**100.** (b)
101. (a)	**102.** (b)	**103.** (b)	**104.** (d)	**105.** (b)	**106.** (a)	**107.** (b)	**108.** (a)	**109.** (c)	**110.** (a)
111. (d)	**112.** (b)	**113.** (c)	**114.** (a)	**115.** (c)	**116.** (a)	**117.** (b)	**118.** (a)	**119.** (c)	**120.** (a)
121. (b)	**122.** (d)	**123.** (a)	**124.** (b)	**125.** (a)	**126.** (b)	**127.** (b)	**128.** (a)	**129.** (b)	**130.** (d)
131. (a)	**132.** (d)	**133.** (c)	**134.** (a)	**135.** (c)	**136.** (b)	**137.** (c)	**138.** (a)	**139.** (d)	**140.** (b)
141. (d)	**142.** (b)	**143.** (b)	**144.** (b)	**145.** (a)	**146.** (c)	**147.** (a)	**148.** (b)	**149.** (a)	**150.** (d)
151. (a)	**152.** (d)	**153.** (c)	**154.** (c)	**155.** (b)	**156.** (a)	**157.** (c)	**158.** (d)	**159.** (c)	**160.** (a)
161. (c)	**162.** (a)	**163.** (c)	**164.** (d)	**165.** (b)	**166.** (a)	**167.** (c)	**168.** (a)	**169.** (b)	**170.** (a)
171. (c)	**172.** (a)	**173.** (c)	**174.** (a)	**175.** (b)	**176.** (c)	**177.** (a)	**178.** (c)	**179.** (b)	**180.** (a)
181. (b)	**182.** (d)	**183.** (a)	**184.** (d)	**185.** (b)	**186.** (c)	**187.** (a)			

❑❑❑

23 Disaster Management

1. What percentage of India's total geographical area is prone to normal to high density earthquakes?

(a) 56.1 (b) 58.6
(c) 60.3 (d) 62.4

2. What percentage of India's geographical area is affected each year by floods?

(a) 10 (b) 12
(c) 14 (d) 16

3. In India how many lakh hectares of land is affected each year by floods?

(a) 40 lakh (b) 38 lakh
(c) 36 lakh (d) 34 lakh

4. What is India's coastal area in square kilometetres ?

(a) 7424 (b) 7516
(c) 7654 (d) 7740

5. What percentage of India's geographical area is drought prone?

(a) 64 (b) 66
(c) 68 (d) 70

6. What percentage of Bihar's geographical area is affected by floods?

(a) 70 (b) 68
(c) 66 (d) 64

7. What percentage of Bihar's geographical area is drought prone?

(a) 26 (b) 28
(c) 30 (d) 32

8. When was the National Flood Commission constituted?

(a) 1980 (b) 1982
(c) 1984 (d) 1986

9. How many hectares of land is drought prone in the State?

(a) 20 lakh (b) 18 lakh
(c) 16 lakh (d) 14 lakh

10. According to the water report (1993-94) of Bihar Government, what percentage of area in North Bihar is affected by floods?

(a) 70 (b) 72
(c) 74 (d) 76

11. How many districts of the State are affected by floods at present?

(a) 28 (b) 26
(c) 24 (d) 22

12. Which district is not highly affected district by floods?

(a) Sitamarhi (b) Madhubani
(c) Buxar (d) Vaishali

13. Bihar occupies _______ position in India in respect of areas most affected by floods?

(a) First (b) Second
(c) Third (d) Fourth

14. Which State in India gets affected for the longest period each year by floods?

(a) Assam
(b) Uttar Pradesh
(c) Gujarat
(d) Odisha

15. Due to which project, a lot of low lying land of Bihar has submerged in water?

(a) Sone (b) Kosi
(c) Gandak (d) Both (b) and (c)

16. Which river is called 'Bihar ka Shok'?

(a) Bagmati (b) Ganga
(c) Kosi (d) Mahananda

17. Under which of the following five year plans, priority was accorded to the multipurpose river valley projects?

(a) First (b) Second
(c) Third (d) Both (a) and (c)

18. Under which of the following five year plans, coastal area construction was accorded priority?

(a) Fourth (b) Third
(c) Second (d) First

19. Under which five year plan, drainage system was arranged?

(a) Sixth (b) Fifth
(c) Fourth (d) Third

20. How many flood information centres are established in India?

(a) 8 (b) 7
(c) 6 (d) 5

21. Where is flood information centre located in Bihar?

(a) Patna (b) Betia
(c) Motihari (d) Saharasa

22. In which district, Koilover embankment is built on the bank of Ganga river?

(a) Arrah (b) Buxar
(c) Kaimur (d) Patna

23. Badlaghat-Nagarpada embankment is situated in which district?

(a) Saharasa (b) Madhubani
(c) Khagariya (d) Supoul

24. In which district Teenmohani-Kursela embankment is built?

(a) Khagariya (b) Darbhanga
(c) Jamui (d) Jehanabad

25. Teenmohani-Kursela embankment is built on which river?

(a) Bagmati (b) Kosi
(c) Gandak (d) Saryu

26. In which district Bhutahi Balan embankment is built?

(a) Darbhanga (b) Madhubani
(c) Arrah (d) Siwan

27. In which district Bajipur embankment is built?

(a) Saharasa (b) Supoul
(c) Vaishali (d) Gaya

28. Under which five year plan, drainage area development programme was launched?

(a) 8th (b) 7th
(c) 6th (d) 5th

29. Which of the following should be given priority in flood affected areas?

(a) Fishery
(b) Fox nut cultivation
(c) Water chestnut cultivation
(d) All of the above

30. Definite drought prone areas are termed by geographers where less than __________ cm of rain occurs.

(a) 30 (b) 40
(c) 50 (d) 60

31. In what percentage of land in Bihar possibility of drought remains according to the book authored by Prof Inayat Ahmad and D. K. Singh?

(a) 30 (b) 35
(c) 40 (d) 45

32. Who is the author of the book 'Regional Planning in India'?
(a) Brij Kishore Prasad
(b) D K Singh
(c) Prof Inayat Ahmad
(d) Both (b) and (c)

33. What is the area of forests in Bihar in square kilometres?
(a) 7 (b) 7.21
(c) 7.62 (d) 7.91

34. Which of the following is a drought affected district of the State?
(a) Jamui
(b) Lakhisarai
(c) Bhagalpur
(d) All of the above

35. Which of the following problems people face at the time of drought?
(a) Lack of fodder
(b) Lack of drinking water
(c) Food security
(d) All of the above

36. When was Sone Command Area Project constructed?
(a) 1870 AD (b) 1874 AD
(c) 1878 AD (d) 1882 AD

37. Which of the following is the most ancient project of the State?
(a) Gandak Project
(b) Kosi Project
(c) Sone Project
(d) Ganga Project

38. Which district is not the beneficiary of the Sone Project?
(a) Gaya (b) Arwal
(c) Bhojpur (d) Kaimur

39. Koel Karo Project is a joint project of Bihar and which other State?
(a) West Bengal (b) Uttar Pradesh
(c) Jharkhand (d) Both (a) and (c)

40. Which district of Bihar will get the maximum benefit under Koel Karo Project?
(a) Bhagalpur (b) Aurangabad
(c) Munger (d) Jehanabad

41. Which district will get the benefit of Chandan-Barua-Kiel Command Area Project?
(a) Munger
(b) Banka
(c) Sheikhpura
(d) All of the above

42. The Irrigation projects with less than how many hectares of capacity are termed as Small Irrigation Projects?
(a) 2000 (b) 1500
(c) 1000 (d) 500

43. When was Small Irrigation Department constituted by the Government of Bihar?
(a) 1961 (b) 1963
(c) 1965 (d) 1967

44. In which of the following years, National Water Policy was formulated?
(a) 1987 (b) 1984
(c) 1981 (d) 1978

45. The water standing on the railway lines or in the pits along side roads can be used for protection of the standing crops – this was declared under which policy?
(a) National Flood Control Policy
(b) National Water Policy
(c) National Irrigation Policy
(d) All of the above

46. Since when is drough affected development programme being operated?
(a) 1973 (b) 1971
(c) 1969 (d) 1967

47. With support of which International Institution, the Plateau Area Development Programme is being operated?
(a) World Environment Fund
(b) IMF
(c) World Bank
(d) Asian Development Bank

48. Which of the following irrigation projects have been completed to eliminate the problem of droughts?
(a) Bachhraja Ware Yojana
(b) Kachnama Ware Yojana
(c) Sammat Bigha Ware Yojana
(d) All of the above

49. What percentage of the total geographical area of Bihar comes under earthquake zone -V?
(a) 8.2 (b) 11.4
(c) 15.2 (d) 19.6

50. Which district in Bihar comes under Earthquake Zone -V?
(a) Shivhar
(b) Sitamarhi
(c) Kishanganj
(d) All of the above

51. In which district of Bihar, effect of tropical tornado persists?
(a) North-East
(b) North-West
(c) South-East
(d) All of the above

52. Which of the following district is affected by tropical cyclone?
(a) Madhubani (b) Purnia
(c) Kishanganj (d) Both (b) and (c)

53. Which main crop gets developed in October-November?
(a) Paddy (b) Wheat
(c) Mustard (d) Masoor

54. Because of cold wave conditions in Bihar, which crop gets adversely affected?
(a) Kharif
(b) Jayad
(c) Rabi
(d) All of the above

55. Which of the following phases is the main phase of disaster management?
(a) Pre-disaster phase
(b) Disaster Time phase
(c) Post disaster phase
(d) All of the above

56. When was the National Disaster Management Act implemented?
(a) 2001 (b) 2003
(c) 2005 (d) 2007

57. How many chapters are there in National Disaster Management Act 2005?
(a) 5 (b) 7
(c) 9 (d) 11

58. How many sections are there in National Disaster Management Act 2005?
(a) 79 (b) 77
(c) 75 (d) 73

59. When was the National Disaster Management Authority constituted?
(a) 2004 (b) 2005
(c) 2006 (d) 2007

60. Under which Ministry, National Disaster Management Authority works?
(a) Agriculture Ministry
(b) Home Ministry
(c) Information and Technology Ministry
(d) Panchayati Raj Ministry

61. How many members are there in the National Disaster Management Authority?
(a) 9 (b) 11
(c) 13 (d) 15

62. Who is the Chairman of the National Disaster Management Authority?
(a) President
(b) Prime Minister
(c) Home Minister
(d) Defence Minister

63. National Executive Committee was constituted under which section of the National Disaster Management Act 2005?
(a) Section - 4 (b) Section - 6
(c) Section - 8 (d) Section - 10

64. Bihar State Disaster Management Authority has been established under section________of National Disaster Management Act-2005?
(a) 1 (1) (b) 12 (1)
(c) 13 (1) (d) 14 (1)

65. Who is the Chairman of the State Disaster Management Authority?
(a) Governor
(b) Chief Minister
(c) Home Minister
(d) Secretary to the Governor

66. Which of the following has been constituted under Section 30 (2) (xvi) of Disaster Management Act -2005?
(a) State Disaster Management Authority
(b) Divisional Disaster Management Authority
(c) District Disaster Management Authority
(d) Block Disaster Management Authority

67. State Disaster Management Scheme is mentioned under which section of the National Disaster Management Act?
(a) 19 (2) (b) 21 (4)
(c) 23 (1) (d) 25 (2)

68. When was Bihar State Disaster Management Scheme was launched?
(a) 2008 (b) 2010
(c) 2012 (d) 2014

69. Upto which time periods, Bihar State Disaster Risk minimisation roadmap is there?
(a) 2015-35 (b) 2015-30
(c) 2015-25 (d) 2015-20

70. When was the Third World Disaster Risk Minimisation Conference organized?
(a) 2012 (b) 2013
(c) 2014 (d) 2015

71. Where was the Third World Disaster Risk Minimisation Conference organised?
(a) Tokyo (b) Nicoya
(c) Nagasaki (d) Cedai

72. How many country had participated in the Third World Disaster Risk Minimization Conference?
(a) 190 (b) 185
(c) 180 (d) 175

73. Which State of India had first accepted the CEDAI framework?
(a) Bihar (b) Odisha
(c) Bengal (d) Gujarat

74. When was the Bihar Disaster Risk Minimization structure adopted under the Patna Declaration?
(a) 2013
(b) 2014
(c) 2015
(d) 2016

75. How many targets have been set for the period 2015-30 under Bihar Disaster Risk Minimization roadmap?
(a) 6 (b) 5
(c) 4 (d) 3

Answers

1. (b)	**2.** (b)	**3.** (a)	**4.** (b)	**5.** (c)	**6.** (a)	**7.** (c)	**8.** (d)	**9.** (a)	**10.** (d)
11. (a)	**12.** (c)	**13.** (b)	**14.** (a)	**15.** (d)	**16.** (c)	**17.** (d)	**18.** (a)	**19.** (a)	**20.** (b)
21. (a)	**22.** (b)	**23.** (c)	**24.** (a)	**25.** (b)	**26.** (a)	**27.** (c)	**28.** (a)	**29.** (d)	**30.** (c)
31. (d)	**32.** (d)	**33.** (b)	**34.** (d)	**35.** (d)	**36.** (b)	**37.** (c)	**38.** (a)	**39.** (c)	**40.** (b)
41. (d)	**42.** (a)	**43.** (d)	**44.** (a)	**45.** (b)	**46.** (a)	**47.** (c)	**48.** (d)	**49.** (c)	**50.** (d)
51. (a)	**52.** (d)	**53.** (a)	**54.** (c)	**55.** (d)	**56.** (c)	**57.** (d)	**58.** (a)	**59.** (c)	**60.** (b)
61. (a)	**62.** (b)	**63.** (c)	**64.** (d)	**65.** (b)	**66.** (c)	**67.** (c)	**68.** (d)	**69.** (b)	**70.** (d)
71. (d)	**72.** (a)	**73.** (a)	**74.** (c)	**75.** (c)					

❑❑❑

24 Political Structure of Bihar

ADMINISTRATIVE STRUCTURE

1. **When were new States in the name of Bihar and Odisha established?**
   (a) 1910 (b) 1912
   (c) 1914 (d) 1916
2. **Who had taken charge of first Governor of Bihar?**
   (a) Sir Ali Imam
   (b) Satish Chandra Jha
   (c) Satyendra Prasanna Sinha
   (d) Mandan Mishra
3. **Under Government of India Act ______, dual administration was implemented at the Centre?**
   (a) 1920 (b) 1925
   (c) 1930 (d) 1935
4. **How many seats were arranged for in Bihar Legislative Assembly and Bihar Legislative Council respectively under the 1935 Act?**
   (a) 160-38 (b) 156-34
   (c) 152-30 (d) 146-26
5. **Two separate states were created in the name of Bihar and Odisha on 1 April_______.**
   (a) 1930 (b) 1932
   (c) 1934 (d) 1936
6. **When were the first Assembly elections held in Bihar?**
   (a) 1937 AD (b) 1935 AD
   (c) 1933 AD (d) 1931 AD
7. **How many seats were reserved for women in the first Bihar assembly elections?**
   (a) 15 (b) 13
   (c) 7 (d) 4
8. **How many seats were reserved for the general category in the first Bihar assembly elections?**
   (a) 64 (b) 66
   (c) 68 (d) 70
9. **How many seats were reserved for the Muslims in the first Bihar assembly elections?**
   (a) 33 (b) 35
   (c) 37 (d) 39
10. **How many seats were reserved for the Scheduled Castes in the first Bihar assembly elections?**
    (a) 11 (b) 13
    (c) 15 (d) 17
11. **How many seats were reserved for the Scheduled Tribes in the first Bihar assembly elections?**
    (a) 5 (b) 7
    (c) 9 (d) 11
12. **How many seats were reserved for the Anglo Indians and European community respectively in the first Bihar assembly elections?**
    (a) 2-2 (b) 3-5
    (c) 4-6 (d) 3-2
13. **In the first assembly elections, how many seats were won by the Congress?**
    (a) 92 (b) 94
    (c) 96 (d) 98

14. In the first assembly elections, how many seats were won by the Muslim League?
(a) 16 (b) 18
(c) 20 (d) 22

15. After the first Bihar Assembly elections, who was chosen as the first leader of the Congress?
(a) Shrikrishna Singh
(b) Anugrah Narayan Singh
(c) Maulana Mazhrul Haque
(d) Mohd. Yunus

16. After Bihar Assembly elections, who of the following was chosen as the Chief Minister?
(a) Maulana Mazhrul Haque
(b) Mohd. Yunus
(c) Hasan Imam
(d) Prof. Abdul Bari

17. Under whose leadership in Bihar on 20 July 1937, Congress government was established?
(a) Anugrah Narayan Singh
(b) Mohd. Yunus
(c) Jaiprakash Narayan
(d) Shrikrishna Singh

18. Who was elected as the pro-tem speaker of the Bihar assembly?
(a) Satyendra Mishra
(b) Sachchidanand Sinha
(c) Anugrah Narayan Singh
(d) Mohd. Juber

19. Who was elected the first Speaker of the Bihar Assembly?
(a) Mandan Mishra
(b) Daroga Rai
(c) Prof. Abdul Bari
(d) Ram Dayalu Singh

20. Who was elected the first deputy Speaker of the Bihar Assembly?
(a) Prof. Abdul Bari
(b) Hasan Imam
(c) Jaiprakash Narayan
(d) Gopal Rai

21. When did Shrikrishna Government tender resignation?
(a) 31 July 1939
(b) 14 August 1939
(c) 20 September 1939
(d) 31 October 1939

22. Who became the Chief Minister after the 1946 Assembly Elections in Bihar?
(a) Shrikrishna Singh
(b) Rajendra Prasad
(c) Jaiprakash Narayan
(d) Anugrah Narayan Singh

23. How many members of the Bihar Assembly after the 1946 assembly elections were nominated as members in the Constitutional Committee?
(a) 33 (b) 35
(c) 37 (d) 39

24. Who was chosen from Bihar a member of the Constitutional Committee?
(a) Sarojini Naidu
(b) Dr. Rajendra Prasad
(c) Tajul Hussain
(d) All of the above

25. When did the first election in Bihar complete according to the Constitution of Independent India?
(a) 1948 AD (b) 1950 AD
(c) 1952 AD (d) 1954 AD

26. What number is determined for members of Bihar Assembly according to the Constitution of Independent India?
(a) 331 (b) 333
(c) 335 (d) 337

27. Who became the Chief Minister of Bihar after the general elections of Independent India?

(a) Mohd. Yunus
(b) Shrikrishna Singh
(c) Anugrah Narayan Singh
(d) Jagjivan Ram

28. When was Jharkhand separated from Bihar?

(a) 2000 (b) 2001
(c) 2002 (d) 2003

29. At the time of division, how many districts in total were there in Bihar?

(a) 52 (b) 54
(c) 56 (d) 58

30. How many districts in total were separated to create the State of Jharkhand?

(a) 18 (b) 19
(c) 20 (d) 21

31. After division of Bihar, how many districts remained with Bihar?

(a) 36 (b) 37
(c) 38 (d) 39

32. What was the number of Lok Sabha Members in the undivided Bihar?

(a) 48 (b) 50
(c) 52 (d) 54

33. What was the number of Rajya Sabha members in the undivided Bihar?

(a) 20 (b) 22
(c) 24 (d) 26

34. What was the number of State Assembly members in total in the undivided Bihar?

(a) 320 (b) 322
(c) 324 (d) 326

35. What was the number of members of State Legislative Council in the undivided Bihar?

(a) 96 (b) 94
(c) 92 (d) 90

36. At present, how many seats are there in total in the State Legislative Council in Bihar?

(a) 241 (b) 243
(c) 245 (d) 247

37. At present, how many seats are there in total in Bihar Legislative Council?

(a) 75 (b) 73
(c) 71 (d) 69

38. At present, how many seats are there in Lok Sabha from Bihar?

(a) 36 (b) 38
(c) 40 (d) 42

39. At present, how many seats are there in Rajya Sabha from Bihar?

(a) 16 (b) 15
(c) 14 (d) 13

40. Which of the following is a part of the Government?

(a) Legislative
(b) Executive
(c) Judiciary
(d) All of the above

THE GOVERNOR

1. Who of the following is the head of the State?

(a) Governor
(b) President
(c) Chief Minister
(d) Both (a) and (b)

2. Under which article one person can be made Governor of two States?

(a) 151 (b) 153
(c) 155 (d) 157

3. **Under which Article the rights of the Governors have been mentioned?**
(a) Article 162-165
(b) Article 160-163
(c) Article 153-162
(d) Article 165-167

4. **Under which article of the Constitution, the eligibility criteria for the post of Governor have been determined?**
(a) Article 153 (b) Article 155
(c) Article 157 (d) Article 159

5. **What is the minimum age required to become Governor of a State?**
(a) 31 (b) 33
(c) 35 (d) 37

6. **Who of the following appoints a Governor?**
(a) President
(b) Prime Minister
(c) Vice-President
(d) Chief Minister

7. **Under Article ________ of the Constitution, the term Governor is as per the President?**
(a) 154 (b) 156
(c) 158 (d) 160

8. **Under which article of the Constitution, salary and allowances of the Governor cannot be reduced?**
(a) Article 155
(b) Article 156
(c) Article 157
(d) Article 158

9. **Which of the following rights are not available to the Governor?**
(a) Executive related
(b) Military related
(c) Finance related
(d) Judiciary related

10. **How many members are nominated by the Governor to the Legislative Council?**
(a) 1/3 (b) 1/4
(c) 1/5 (d) 1/6

11. **Who of the following is appointed by the Governor?**
(a) Solicitor-General
(b) The Chairman of the State Public Service Commission
(c) The Chairman of the State Finance Commission
(d) All of the above

12. **Who of the following posesses a right to call session of the Legislative Assembly, end the session or announce its dissolution?**
(a) Chief Minister
(b) Governor
(c) Speaker of the Legislative Assembly
(d) Parliamentary Affairs Minister

13. **Who presents the Annual Financial Report before the Legislative Assembly?**
(a) Governor
(b) Chief Minister
(c) Finance Minister
(d) Parliamentary Affairs Minister

14. **Under which article of the Constitution of India, Govenor issues an ordinance?**
(a) Article 123 (b) Article 163
(c) Article 193 (d) Article 213

15. **The State Public Service Commission sends its annual report to whom?**
(a) Governor
(b) Chief Minister
(c) Speaker of the Legislative Assembly
(d) Parliamentary Affairs Minister

16. Under which article of the Constitution, Provision for invoking national emergency is made?
(a) Article 350 (b) Article 352
(c) Article 354 (d) Article 356

17. Under which article of the Constitution, Governor makes recommendations for imposing President Rule?
(a) Article 352 (b) Article 356
(c) Article 360 (d) Article 364

18. Under which Article of the Constitution, financial emergency can be declared?
(a) Article 356
(b) Article 358
(c) Article 358
(d) Article 360

19. Under which article of the Constitution, Governor can keep an ordinance reserved for the President?
(a) Article 201 (b) Article 203
(c) Article 205 (d) Article 207

STATE LEGISLATURE

1. Under which Article of the Indian Constitution each State will have its own Legislative Assembly?
(a) Article 162 (b) Article 164
(c) Article 166 (d) Article 168

2. Under which of the following articles, Legislative Council is formed?
(a) Article 169
(b) Article 170
(c) Article 171
(d) Article 172

3. In how many States of the country, Legislative Council exists at present?
(a) 6 (b) 7
(c) 8 (d) 9

4. In which of the following states, legislative council exists?
(a) Bihar
(b) Uttar Pradesh
(c) Maharashtra
(d) All of the above

5. In which of the following states, legislative council does not exist?
(a) Andhra Pradesh
(b) Telangana
(c) Tamil Nadu
(d) Karnataka

6. When did legislative councils of Bihar-Odisha come into existence?
(a) 1919 AD (b) 1921 AD
(c) 1923 AD (d) 1925 AD

7. Who of the following was the Chairman of Bihar-Odisha Legislative Council?
(a) Lord David
(b) James Cook
(c) Sir Walter Mande
(d) Kevin Cooper

8. When was a separate Legislative Council from Odisha constituted for Bihar?
(a) 1934 AD (b) 1936 AD
(c) 1938 AD (d) 1940 AD

9. How many minimum members are compulsorily required for a Legislative council?
(a) 40 (b) 42
(c) 44 (d) 45

10. What is term of office of the members of Legislative Council?
(a) 3 (b) 4
(c) 5 (d) 6

11. How many members of the Legislative Council retire after every 2 years?
(a) 1/2 (b) 1/3
(c) 1/4 (d) 1/5

12. How many members of the legislative council are elected by the members of the local bodies, city municipalities, district councils etc.?

(a) 1/3 (b) 1/4
(c) 1/5 (d) 1/6

13. How many members of the legislative council are elected by the teachers of the Higher Secondary Schools?

(a) 1/10 (b) 1/11
(c) 1/12 (d) 1/13

14. What is the quoram of the Legislative Council?

(a) 1/10 (b) 1/11
(c) 1/12 (d) 1/13

15. After a session begins for the Legislative council, its members cannot be arrested for civil matters for_______days and after the session ends, they cannot be arrested within 40 days?

(a) 35 (b) 40
(c) 45 (d) 50

16. What is minimum age requirement for becoming a member of the legislative council?

(a) 30 (b) 32
(c) 34 (d) 36

17. A finance bill can be stopped by the legislative council for how many days?

(a) 10 (b) 12
(c) 14 (d) 16

18. With a prior notice of minimum how many days a proposal for removal of the Chairman or Deputy Chairman can be brought and they can be removed with a majority decision?

(a) 14 (b) 12
(c) 10 (d) 8

19. Under which article of the Constitution, a Legislative Assembly can be formed?

(a) Article 168 (b) Article 169
(c) Article 170 (d) Article 171

20. What can be the maximum number of members of any State Legislative Assembly?

(a) 500 (b) 475
(c) 450 (d) 425

21. What can be the minimum number of members of any State Legislative Assembly?

(a) 40 (b) 45
(c) 50 (d) 60

22. Which of following State's Legislative Assembly has the minimum number of members?

(a) Goa (b) Sikkim
(c) Manipur (d) Mizoram

23. What is the number of members in Sikkim State Legislative Assembly?

(a) 32 (b) 35
(c) 38 (d) 41

24. Which of the following State's Legislative Assembly has 40 members?

(a) Mizoram
(b) Arunchal Pradesh
(c) Goa
(d) All of the above

25. How many seats are reserved for the Scheduled Castes in Bihar Legislative Assembly?

(a) 36 (b) 38
(c) 40 (d) 42

26. How many seats are reserved for the Scheduled Tribes in Bihar Legislative Assembly?

(a) 2 (b) 4
(c) 6 (d) 8

27. **How many seats are reserved for the general category in Bihar Legislative Assembly?**
(a) 201 (b) 202
(c) 203 (d) 204

28. **Under which Article of the Constitution, the term of a State Legislative Assembly can be increased beyond a period of 5 years?**
(a) Article 172 (1)
(b) Article 173 (2)
(c) Article 174 (3)
(d) Article 175 (4)

29. **What minimum age is required to become a member of the Legislative Assembly?**
(a) 21 (b) 23
(c) 25 (d) 27

30. **Under which article the speaker of the Legislative Assembly is elected?**
(a) Article 172 (b) Article 174
(c) Article 176 (d) Article 178

31. **Under which article of the Constitution, a cabinet of Ministers is required to advise the Governor?**
(a) Article 163
(b) Article 165
(c) Article 167
(d) Article 169

32. **Under which article of the Constitution, a Chief Minister is elected?**
(a) Article 162
(b) Article 164
(c) Article 166
(d) Article 168

33. **One who is appointed a Chief Minister is required to become a member of either house of State Legislature within how many months?**
(a) 2 (b) 4
(c) 6 (d) 8

34. **Under which act of Constitutional Amendment, the number of Ministers including the Chief Minister cannot be more than 15%?**
(a) 90th (b) 91st
(c) 92nd (d) 93rd

35. **When was the 91st Constitutional amendment passed?**
(a) 2001 (b) 2002
(c) 2003 (d) 2004

36. **Under the 91st Constitutional amendment, what can be the minimum number of Ministers?**
(a) 10 (b) 12
(c) 14 (d) 16

37. **Under Article______of the Constitution, the term of the Council of Ministers is 5 years.**
(a) 164 (1)
(b) 165 (2)
(c) 167 (3)
(d) 169 (4)

38. **Who of the following is the State's Law Officer?**
(a) Attorney General
(b) Advocate General
(c) Solicitor General
(d) Both (b) and (c)

39. **Under which article of the Constitution, Advocate General is appointed?**
(a) Article 161 (b) Article 163
(c) Article 165 (d) Article 167

40. **Under which article of the Constitution, Attorney General is appointed?**
(a) Article 70 (b) Article 72
(c) Article 74 (d) Article 76

41. **Under article______of the Constitution, the State Election Commission conducts elections for the Panchayats?**

(a) Article 243 (t)
(b) Article 242 (c)
(c) Article 240 (b)
(d) Article 238 (c)

42. When was Human Rights Commission established in Bihar?
(a) 1998 (b) 2000
(c) 2002 (d) 2004

43. Who of the following was elected the President of Bihar Human Rights Commission?
(a) S. N. Jha
(b) Wajahat Habibullah
(c) Vikram Chandra
(d) Gyan Sudha Mishra

44. When was Human Rights Protection Act passed by the Government of India?
(a) 1991 (b) 1993
(c) 1995 (d) 1997

45. What can be the maximum term of the State Women Commission?
(a) 2 (b) 3
(c) 4 (d) 5

46. Under which article of the Constitution, there is a provision for constituting State Public Service Commission?
(a) Article 30 (b) Article 311
(c) Article 313 (d) Article 315

47. When did Bihar Public Service Commission started functioning?
(a) 1948 (b) 1949
(c) 1950 (d) 1951

48. Who was the first Chairman of the Bihar Public Service Commission?
(a) Rajdhari Sinha
(b) Madan Jha
(c) Pramod Mishra
(d) Asgar Wazahat

49. What is the term of office of the members of Bihar Public Service Commission?
(a) 4 (b) 5
(c) 6 (d) 7

Answers

ADMINISTRATIVE STRUCTURE

1. (b)	**2.** (c)	**3.** (d)	**4.** (c)	**5.** (d)	**6.** (a)	**7.** (d)	**8.** (d)	**9.** (d)	**10.** (c)
11. (b)	**12.** (a)	**13.** (d)	**14.** (c)	**15.** (a)	**16.** (b)	**17.** (d)	**18.** (b)	**19.** (d)	**20.** (a)
21. (d)	**22.** (a)	**23.** (d)	**24.** (d)	**25.** (c)	**26.** (a)	**27.** (b)	**28.** (a)	**29.** (c)	**30.** (a)
31. (c)	**32.** (d)	**33.** (b)	**34.** (c)	**35.** (a)	**36.** (b)	**37.** (a)	**38.** (c)	**39.** (a)	**40.** (d)

THE GOVERNOR

1. (a)	**2.** (b)	**3.** (c)	**4.** (c)	**5.** (c)	**6.** (a)	**7.** (b)	**8.** (d)	**9.** (b)	**10.** (d)
11. (d)	**12.** (b)	**13.** (a)	**14.** (d)	**15.** (a)	**16.** (b)	**17.** (b)	**18.** (c)	**19.** (a)	

STATE LEGISLATURE

1. (d)	**2.** (a)	**3.** (a)	**4.** (d)	**5.** (c)	**6.** (b)	**7.** (c)	**8.** (b)	**9.** (a)	**10.** (d)
11. (b)	**12.** (a)	**13.** (c)	**14.** (a)	**15.** (b)	**16.** (a)	**17.** (c)	**18.** (a)	**19.** (d)	**20.** (a)
21. (d)	**22.** (b)	**23.** (a)	**24.** (d)	**25.** (b)	**26.** (a)	**27.** (c)	**28.** (a)	**29.** (c)	**30.** (d)
31. (a)	**32.** (b)	**33.** (c)	**34.** (b)	**35.** (c)	**36.** (b)	**37.** (a)	**38.** (b)	**39.** (c)	**40.** (d)
41. (a)	**42.** (b)	**43.** (a)	**44.** (b)	**45.** (b)	**46.** (d)	**47.** (b)	**48.** (a)	**49.** (c)	

❑❑❑

25 Administrative Structure

1. In which of the following years, Bihar was divided?
(a) 1912 AD
(b) 1936 AD
(c) 2000 AD
(d) All of the above

2. Which is the largest district of Bihar (in terms of area)?
(a) East Champaran
(b) West Champaran
(c) Patna
(d) Gaya

3. Which of the following is not a division of Bihar?
(a) Darbhanga
(b) Tirhut
(c) Saran
(d) Sahebganj

4. How many divisions are there in the state?
(a) 6 (b) 7
(c) 8 (d) 9

5. How many districts are there in Bihar at present?
(a) 36 (b) 37
(c) 38 (d) 39

6. How many sub-divisions are there in Bihar?
(a) 100 (b) 101
(c) 104 (d) 106

7. How many blocks are there in total in Bihar?
(a) 530 (b) 532
(c) 534 (d) 536

8. Which of the following is a division in Bihar?
(a) Magadh
(b) Kosi
(c) Tirhut
(d) All of the above

9. Which of the following is not a division of Bihar?
(a) Patna (b) Saran
(c) Madhepura (d) Munger

10. East Champaran district comes under which division?
(a) Darbhanga (b) Saran
(c) Munger (d) Tirhut

11. At which of the following places headquarters of Tirhut division are located?
(a) Mujaffarpur (b) Hajipur
(c) Sonepur (d) Motihari

12. At which place, headquarters of Kosi division are located?
(a) Supoul (b) Saharasa
(c) Madhepura (d) Arariya

13. In how many divisions of Bihar 6 districts come?
(a) 3 (b) 5
(c) 6 (d) 7

14. Which district does not fall under Patna Division?
(a) Nalanda
(b) Gaya
(c) Rohtash
(d) Kaimur

15. Which district comes under Magadh division?
(a) Arwal
(b) Jehanabad
(c) Aurangabad
(d) All of the above

16. Which district does not fall under Saran division?
(a) Chhapra (b) Siwan
(c) Gaya (d) Gopalganj

17. Which district does not fall under Tirhut division?
(a) Shivhar (b) Madhubani
(c) Sitamarhi (d) Mujaffarpur

18. Which district comes under Darbhanga division?
(a) Madhubani
(b) Darbhanga
(c) Samastipur
(d) All of the above

19. Which district does not fall under Purnia division?
(a) Madhepura (b) Katihar
(c) Kishanganj (d) Arariya

20. In which division, lowest number of districts fall?
(a) Munger (b) Bhagalpur
(c) Saran (d) Kosi

21. Banka district comes under which Division?
(a) Munger (b) Purnia
(c) Magadh (d) Bhagalpur

22. Which of the following districts does not fall under Munger division?
(a) Khagariya (b) Supoul
(c) Sheikhpura (d) Jamui

23. Begusarai and Jamui fall under which division?
(a) Munger (b) Bhagalpur
(c) Magadh (d) Patna

24. What is the area in square kilometres of Patna district?
(a) 3012 (b) 3140
(c) 3202 (d) 3314

25. Which of the following river does not pass along Patna?
(a) Ganga
(b) Sone
(c) Punpun
(d) Niranjana

26. What is the population density of Patna per square kilometre?
(a) 1812 (b) 1818
(c) 1823 (d) 1828

27. Which of the following districts does not touch the border of Patna?
(a) Saran (b) Mujaffarpur
(c) Vaishali (d) Arwal

28. What percentage of literacy does Patna district possess?
(a) 70.7 (b) 71.8
(c) 72.4 (d) 73.9

29. What is sex-ratio of Patna district?
(a) 889 (b) 893
(c) 897 (d) 902

Answers

1. (d) **2.** (b) **3.** (d) **4.** (d) **5.** (c) **6.** (b) **7.** (c) **8.** (d) **9.** (c) **10.** (d)
11. (a) **12.** (b) **13.** (a) **14.** (b) **15.** (d) **16.** (c) **17.** (b) **18.** (d) **19.** (a) **20.** (b)
21. (d) **22.** (b) **23.** (a) **24.** (c) **25.** (d) **26.** (c) **27.** (b) **28.** (a) **29.** (c)

❑❑❑

26 Judiciary

1. Under which article of the Constitution, a High Court has been provided for in each State?

(a) Article 210 (b) Article 212

(c) Article 214 (d) Article 216

2. Who appoints the Chief Justice of the High Courts and their other judges?

(a) President

(b) Governor

(c) Chief Minister

(d) Legislative Assembly

3. Which High Court in the country has maximum number (sanctioned posts) of the judges?

(a) Mumbai (b) Allahabad

(c) Kolkata (d) Delhi

4. What is the strength of sanctioned posts of judges in Allahabad High Court?

(a) 160 (b) 165

(c) 170 (d) 175

5. What is the total number of judges including the Chief Justice in Patna High Court?

(a) 25 (b) 30

(c) 35 (d) 40

6. When was Patna High Court established?

(a) 1916 AD (b) 1918 AD

(c) 1920 AD (d) 1922 AD

7. What is the minimum period for a judge to undergo before becoming eligible to be chosen as Judge of a High Court?

(a) 8 (b) 9

(c) 10 (d) 11

8. At what age, the judges of the High courts retire from service?

(a) 60 (b) 62

(c) 64 (d) 65

9. Which house does not participate in impeachment proceedings of a judge of a High Court?

(a) State Legislative Assembly

(b) Lok Sabha

(c) Rajya Sabha

(d) Both (a) and (b)

10. Under which article of the Constitution, any fundamental rights related case is brought for hearing before a High Court?

(a) 220 (b) 222

(c) 224 (d) 226

11. A high Court can issue how many writs in order to get fundamental rights enforced?

(a) 3 (b) 4

(c) 5 (d) 6

12. Which of the following writs can be issued by a High Court?

(a) The Supreme Order

(b) Judicial Review

(c) Quo-warranto

(d) All of the above

13. **Which of the following issues fall under the initial rights regime of the High Court?**
(a) Divorce
(b) Water
(c) Will
(d) All of the above

14. **Which of the following has a right to elaborate on the Constitution?**
(a) The Supreme Court
(b) The High Courts
(c) The Subordinate Courts
(d) All of the above

15. **There is a mention of the Subordinate courts in the Constitution under which of its articles?**
(a) 12-15 (b) 23-26
(c) 233-236 (d) 242-245

16. **Who appoints district judges and judges of the Subordinate courts?**
(a) The President
(b) The Governor
(c) The Chief Minister
(d) The Chief Justice of a High Court

17. **For being eligible to become a District Judge, it is compulsory that a person had been in Central or State Judicial service or, to have practised as an advocate for a minimum duration of ______ years?**
(a) 4 (b) 5
(c) 6 (d) 7

Answers

1. (c) **2.** (a) **3.** (b) **4.** (a) **5.** (b) **6.** (a) **7.** (c) **8.** (b) **9.** (a) **10.** (d)
11. (c) **12.** (d) **13.** (d) **14.** (d) **15.** (c) **16.** (b) **17.** (d)

❑❑❑

27 The Local Administration

1. **Panchayati Raj System was implemented in India under recommendations of which Committee?**
(a) Balwant Mehta
(b) Balwant Singh
(c) Arjun Sen
(d) Dinesh Goswami

2. **When was Balwant Rai Mehta Committee constituted?**
(a) 1953 (b) 1955
(c) 1957 (d) 1959

3. **In which year was Panchayati Raj System implemented in India?**
(a) 1956 (b) 1957
(c) 1958 (d) 1959

4. **In which State of India, Panchayati Raj System was first implemented?**
(a) Madhya Pradesh
(b) Rajasthan
(c) Bihar
(d) Himachal Pradesh

5. **On 2nd October 1959, from which district in Rajasthan, Panchayati Raj System was introduced in the country?**
(a) Bikaner (b) Jodhpur
(c) Nagour (d) Jaipur

6. **Which of the following is not a participant in threefold system of Panchayati Raj?**
(a) Gram Panchayat
(b) Nagar Parishad
(c) Panchyat Samiti
(d) Zila Parishad

7. **Which of the following Committees is related to Panchayati Raj System?**
(a) Ashok Kumar
(b) Ashok Mehta
(c) Ashok Singh
(d) Ashok Shrivastava

8. **When was Ashok Mehta committee constituted?**
(a) 1974 (b) 1976
(c) 1978 (d) 1986

9. **Which of the following Committees had recommended to make Panchayati Raj System a two level system?**
(a) Balwant Rai Mehta
(b) Ramesh Mehta
(c) Ashok Mehta
(d) Jai Shah

10. **When was GVK Rao Committee constituted?**
(a) 1984
(b) 1986
(c) 1988
(d) 1990

11. **Which committee had recommended to enliven the Panchayati Raj System?**
(a) GVK Rao
(b) Ashok Mehta
(c) Lakshmimal Singhvi
(d) Fazal Ali

12. When was Lakshmimal Singhvi Committee constituted?
(a) 1986 (b) 1984
(c) 1982 (d) 1980

13. Which Committee had recommended that Panchayats be given a statutory status?
(a) P. K. Thungan
(b) Ashok Mehta
(c) Balwant Rai Mehta
(d) Dinesh Goswami

14. When was Bihar Panchayat Committee and District Council Act passed?
(a) 1960 (b) 1961
(c) 1962 (d) 1963

15. Under which amendment of the Constitution, the present Panchayati Raj System has been implemented?
(a) 71st (b) 72nd
(c) 73rd (d) 74th

16. Under which schedule of the Constitution Panchayati Raj System is mentioned?
(a) 8th (b) 9th
(c) 10th (d) 11th

17. How many District Councils in exist in Bihar?
(a) 36 (b) 37
(c) 38 (d) 39

18. The article related to the formation of Panchayats is
(a) Article-243 (D)
(b) Article-243 (F)
(c) Article-243 (I)
(d) Article-243 (B)

19. What is described in Article 243(E)?
(a) Gram Sabha
(b) Formation of Panchayats
(c) Structure of Panchayats
(d) Tenure of Panchayats

20. When was the 73rd constitutional amendment Act passed by the Indian Parliament?
(a) 1990 (b) 1992
(c) 1994 (d) 1996

21. Under the 73rd Constitutional Amendment Act, when was Bihar State Panchyati Raj Act passed?
(a) 1999 (b) 2001
(c) 2004 (d) 2006

22. How many segments of Gram Panchayats are there in Bihar?
(a) 6 (b) 5
(c) 4 (d) 3

23. Which of the following is a part of the Gram Panchyat?
(a) Mukhiya
(b) Gram Sevak
(c) Gram Kachehri
(d) All of the above

24. Each Panchayat works for how many years starting from its session?
(a) 3 (b) 4
(c) 5 (d) 6

25. If a Panchayat, for any reason, has been dissolved, provision for getting fresh elections done is there during how many months of dissolution?
(a) 3 months
(b) 4 months
(c) 5 months
(d) 6 months

26. What is the minimum age criterion for a person to take part in Panchayat elections?
(a) 21 (b) 22
(c) 25 (d) 28

27. What percentage of reservation is provided for women in panchayat elections in Bihar?
(a) 30 (b) 33
(c) 40 (d) 50

28. Under which schedule of the Constitution, there is a provision for providing proportionate reservation to the people of Scheduled Castes and Scheduled Tribes in accordance with their population, in each Gram Panchayat?

(a) 243 A (b) 243 B
(c) 243 C (d) 243 D

29. The main unit at the block level is

(a) Gram Sabha
(b) Gram Panchayat
(c) Both a and b
(d) Panchayat Samiti

30. What is the starting age for a person to become a member of Gram Panchayat?

(a) 12 (b) 14
(c) 16 (d) 18

31. What minimum number of sittings of Gram Sabha are required to be held in a year?

(a) 2 (b) 3
(c) 4 (d) 5

32. Who is the Head of the Executive Committee in a Gram Panchayat?

(a) District Council
(b) Block Head
(c) Mukhiya
(d) Sarpanch

33. How many members are there in an Executive Committee apart from the Mukhiya?

(a) 5 (b) 6
(c) 7 (d) 8

34. In absence of the Mukhiya, Up-Mukhiya can handle the work of Mukhiya for how many months?

(a) 4 (b) 5
(c) 6 (d) 7

35. In the 11th schedule to the Constitution, how many subjects have been talked about?

(a) 29 (b) 27
(c) 25 (d) 23

36. Which subject comes under 11th Schedule of the Constitution?

(a) Land Reform
(b) Small irrigation
(c) Fishery
(d) All of the above

37. Under which schedule of the Constitution, powers have been divided between State Legislative assemblies and Panchayats?

(a) 8th (b) 9th
(c) 10th (d) 11th

38. Under which schedule of the Constitution, powers have been divided between the Centre and the State Legislative Assemblies?

(a) 4th (b) 5th
(c) 6th (d) 7th

39. A state by law can authorize a Panchayat to recover, collect and appropriate which of the following?

(a) Taxes
(b) Levy
(c) Road Tax
(d) All of the above

40. A State Government constitutes a Finance Commission after how many years?

(a) 5 (b) 4
(c) 3 (d) 2

41. Which of the following is a unit of local administration at the block level

(a) Gram Panchayat
(b) Panchayat Committee
(c) District Council
(d) City Panchayat

42. A member of Panchayat Committe is elected per __________ of population?

(a) 2000 (b) 3000
(c) 4000 (d) 5000

43. A member of District Council is elected at how much population?
(a) 50000 (b) 45000
(c) 40000 (d) 35000

44. Under which amendment to the Constitution, city administration was introduced?
(a) 72nd (b) 73rd
(c) 74th (d) 75th

45. When was the 74th amendment to the Constitution passed?
(a) 1992 (b) 1993
(c) 1994 (d) 1995

46. In which part of the Constitution, city administration is talked about?
(a) 9 (b) 9(a)
(c) 10 (d) 10(a)

47. What could be the maximum number of ward counsellors in a city with population exceeding 10 lakhs?
(a) 75 (b) 73
(c) 71 (d) 69

48. What could be the maximum number of ward counsellors in a city with population of more than 5 lakhs and less than 10 lakhs?
(a) 67 (b) 65
(c) 63 (d) 61

49. For a City Panchayat area, provision of maximum how many counsellors is made?
(a) 21 (b) 23
(c) 25 (d) 27

50. What should be the minimum age for getting elected ward counsellor of a city municipality?
(a) 18 years
(b) 21 years
(c) 24 years ·
(d) 27 years

51. The number of municipal corporations in Bihar is
(a) 12 (b) 15
(c) 17 (d) 19

52. In which of the following cities, a municipal corporation exists?
(a) Bhojpur
(b) Katihar
(c) Gaya
(d) All of the above

53. In which city, municipal corporation does not exist?
(a) Begusarai (b) Purnia
(c) Munger (d) Betiya

54. When was Bihar City Municipality Act passed?
(a) 2005 (b) 2007
(c) 2009 (d) 2011

55. On what percentage of population one member of Panchayat Samiti is elected?
(a) 5,000 (b) 4,000
(c) 3,0000 (d) 2,000

56. In which article the structure of Panchayats is mentioned?
(a) 243 (O)
(b) 243 (K)
(c) 243 (J)
(d) 243 (C)

57. In which of the following municipal corporations, the post of the Chief Counsellor is reserved for women?
(a) Patna
(b) Arrah
(c) Bhagalpur
(d) All of the above

58. In which municipal corporation, the post of Chief Counsellor is reserved for the Schedule Caste?
(a) Mujaffarpur
(b) Gaya
(c) Katihar
(d) Purnia

59. When was Patna Municipal Corporation established?
(a) 1948 (b) 1950
(c) 1952 (d) 1954

60. How many meetings of the Gram Sabha are required to be held in a year?
(a) 4 (b) 3
(c) 2 (d) 1

61. When was the 'e-Gram Panchayat Bihar Portal' launched in Bihar?
(a) 2020 (b) 2021
(c) 2022 (d) 2023

62. The Chief Counsellor of a Municipal Corporation is called what?
(a) Mahapour
(b) Nagar Sabhapati
(c) Adhyakshay
(d) Upaukta

63. The Chief Counsellor of a city council is called what?
(a) Adhyakshay
(b) Aayukta
(c) Pramukh
(d) Sabhapati

64. The Chief Counsellor of a city Panchayat is called what?
(a) Aayukta
(b) Adhyakshya
(c) Pramukh
(d) Up-Mayor

65. When was Chhapra given the status of a Municipal Corporation?
(a) 2010 (b) 2012
(c) 2014 (d) 2016

66. When were Begusarai, Purnia, Munger and Katihar given the status of a municipal corporation?
(a) 2009 (b) 2008
(c) 2007 (d) 2006

67. In which municipal corporation, the number of wards is the lowest?
(a) Bihar Sharif (b) Chhapra
(c) Begusarai (d) Gaya

68. In which municipal corporation, the post of Chief Counselor has been kept reserved?
(a) Munger
(b) Purnia
(c) Chhapra
(d) All of the above

69. In which municipal corporation, the post of Chief Counsellor is reserved for backward class candidate?
(a) Mujaffarpur (b) Bhagalpur
(c) Katihar (d) Darbhanga

70. How many oceans are there in Bihar?
(a) 1 (b) 2
(c) 3 (d) 4

Answers

1. (a)	**2.** (c)	**3.** (d)	**4.** (b)	**5.** (c)	**6.** (b)	**7.** (b)	**8.** (c)	**9.** (c)	**10.** (b)
11. (c)	**12.** (a)	**13.** (a)	**14.** (b)	**15.** (c)	**16.** (d)	**17.** (c)	**18.** (d)	**19.** (d)	**20.** (b)
21. (d)	**22.** (a)	**23.** (d)	**24.** (c)	**25.** (d)	**26.** (a)	**27.** (d)	**28.** (d)	**29.** (d)	**30.** (d)
31. (a)	**32.** (c)	**33.** (d)	**34.** (c)	**35.** (a)	**36.** (d)	**37.** (d)	**38.** (d)	**39.** (d)	**40.** (a)
41. (b)	**42.** (d)	**43.** (a)	**44.** (c)	**45.** (a)	**46.** (b)	**47.** (a)	**48.** (a)	**49.** (c)	**50.** (b)
51. (d)	**52.** (d)	**53.** (d)	**54.** (b)	**55.** (a)	**56.** (d)	**57.** (d)	**58.** (b)	**59.** (c)	**60.** (c)
61. (d)	**62.** (a)	**63.** (d)	**64.** (b)	**65.** (d)	**66.** (a)	**67.** (a)	**68.** (d)	**69.** (a)	**70.** (a)

❑❑❑

28 Major Economic Indicators

1. **By whom was the Bihar Budget for the Financial Year 2026-27 presented?**
   (a) Samrat Chaudhary
   (b) Vijay Kumar Chaudhary
   (c) Munna Yadav
   (d) Bijendra Prasad Yadav
2. **What is the total outlay of the Bihar Budget 2026-27?**
   (a) ₹ 2,17,589.76 crore
   (b) ₹ 3,17,589.16 crore
   (c) ₹ 3,47,589.76 crore
   (d) ₹ 2,91,300.50 crore
3. **How much is the total "Revenue & Committed Expenditure" estimated in the Bihar Budget 2026-27?**
   (a) ₹ 2,52,361.55 crore
   (b) ₹ 2,25,434.00 crore
   (c) ₹ 3,15,155.45 crore
   (d) ₹ 3,25,300.10 crore
4. **How much is the total "Annual Scheme Outlay" estimated in the Bihar Budget 2026-27?**
   (a) ₹ 1,22,155.00 crore
   (b) ₹ 1,00,563.15 crore
   (c) ₹ 1,50,600.10 crore
   (d) ₹ 1,56,750.05 crore
5. **Bihar's Population was what percentage of total population of the country according to 2011 census?**
   (a) 8.4% (b) 8.6%
   (c) 8.8% (d) 9.1%
6. **What percentage of decadal growth was registered in population in Bihar during the period from 2001 to 2011?**
   (a) 25.1 (b) 25.6
   (c) 25.8 (d) 26.1
7. **According to Bihar Budget 2026-27, the state's Fiscal Deficit is estimated to be what percentage of the Gross State Domestic Product (GSDP)?**
   (a) 2.08% (b) 2.18%
   (c) 2.99% (d) 3.05%
8. **What was the density of population per square kilometre in Bihar according to 2011 census?**
   (a) 1102 (b) 1104
   (c) 1106 (d) 1108
9. **The urbanisation level in Bihar increased by merely ______ during the period 2001 to 2011.**
   (a) 0.8% (b) 1.1%
   (c) 1.2% (d) 1.3%
10. **What was the growth in percentage terms in urbanisation level of India during the period from 2001 to 2011?**
    (a) 3% (b) 3.2%
    (c) 3.4% (d) 3.6%
11. **What was the children's sex ratio in Bihar according to the census 2011?**
    (a) 938 (b) 940
    (c) 942 (d) 944
12. **What was the sex ratio in India according to the 2011 census?**
    (a) 913 (b) 915
    (c) 917 (d) 919

13. On the basis of which of the following, human development index is prepared?
(a) Life Expectancy
(b) Education
(c) Per capita income
(d) All of the above

14. Who had conceived and presented the human development index?
(a) Amartya Sen
(b) Mehboob-Ul-Haque
(c) Kaushik Basu
(d) David Heir

15. Which of the following institutions had first developed the human development index?
(a) World Bank (b) UNDP
(c) UNESCO (d) IMF

16. When was Human Development Index first developed?
(a) 1988 (b) 1990
(c) 1992 (d) 1994

17. When was inequality reconciliation human development index included in Human Development Index?
(a) 2006 (b) 2008
(c) 2010 (d) 2012

18. What is the total estimated Fiscal Deficit of Bihar for the Financial Year 2026-27 in terms of rupees?
(a) ₹ 39,111.86 crore
(b) ₹ 35,152.15 crore
(c) ₹ 39,250.55 crore
(d) ₹ 39,750.60 crore

19. According to Bihar Budget 2026-27, by which year is the target set to provide jobs and employment opportunities to 1 crore youth under the "Saat Nishchay-3" scheme?
(a) By 2030 (b) By 2028
(c) By 2032 (d) By 2034

20. In which district of Bihar, per capita income is the highest?
(a) Patna (b) Shivhar
(c) Munger (d) Bhagalpur

21. In which district of Bihar, per capita income is the lowest?
(a) Shivhar (b) Sitamarhi
(c) Gaya (d) Arwal

22. The estimated expenditure on education in Bihar Budget 2025-26 is
(a) 5.19% (b) 13.52%
(c) 15.44% (d) 19.44%

23. Around 21% cultivable land of the state is owned by merely______ percent people.
(a) 5 (b) 4
(c) 3 (d) 2

24. Under the 'Mukhyamantri Mahila Rojgar Yojana' announced in Bihar Budget 2026-27, how much financial assistance will be provided to one woman from each eligible family for self-employment?
(a) Upto ₹ 1 lakh
(b) Upto ₹ 1.5 lakh
(c) Upto ₹ 2 lakh
(d) Upto ₹ 3 lakh

25. In the Bihar Budget 2026-27, the combined allocation for Education and Higher Education is approximately what percentage of the total budget estimate?
(a) 19.63% (b) 15.75%
(c) 18.60% (d) 10.50%

26. How much land in Bihar in lakh hectares is affected by water-logging?
(a) 2.5 (b) 2
(c) 1.5 (d) 1

27. What percentage of flood-affected land of the country falls in Bihar?
(a) 16.8 (b) 17.0
(c) 17.2 (d) 17.4

28. What percentage of the total population of the country which is affected by floods resides in Bihar?

(a) 19 (b) 21
(c) 23 (d) 25

29. According to Bihar Budget 2026-27, what is the total amount allocated for the Education sector?
(a) ₹ 68,216.95 crore
(b) ₹ 62,300.00 crore
(c) ₹ 55,215.15 crore
(d) ₹ 54,320.10 crore

30. In how many districts of Bihar, not even a single industry exists?
(a) 4 (b) 5
(c) 6 (d) 7

31. Bihar is ranked ______ among the fastest developing states in the country.
(a) First (b) Second
(c) Third (d) Fourth

32. The contribution of the industry sector in Bihar's GSDP in 2024-25 is
(a) 31.5% (b) 25.2%
(c) 24.5% (d) 21.5%

33. The contribution of the agriculture sector in Bihar's GSDP in 2024-25 is
(a) 19.9% (b) 18.8%
(c) 20.2% (d) 17.9%

34. According to Bihar Budget 2026-27, how much receipt is estimated from 'Public Debt' for the state government to bridge its Own Tax Revenue and Fiscal Deficit?
(a) Own Tax Revenue ₹ 65,800 crore; Fiscal Deficit ₹ 39,111 crore
(b) Own Tax Revenue ₹ 60,500 crore; Fiscal Deficit ₹ 25,058 crore
(c) Own Tax Revenue ₹ 55,950 crore; Fiscal Deficit ₹ 35,650 crore
(d) Own Tax Revenue ₹ 90,600 crore; Fiscal Deficit ₹ 85,000 crore

35. The top district of Bihar in electricity consumption is
(a) Rohtas (b) Vaishali
(c) Patna (d) Nalanda

36. What is the length of rural paved roads in Bihar from 2005 to 2025?
(a) 1.17 lakh km (b) 1.02 lakh km
(c) 0.20 lakh km (d) 1.32 lakh km

37. When was Bihar Industrial Incentives Scheme announced?
(a) 2012 (b) 2014
(c) 2016 (d) 2018

38. When was State Administrative Reforms Commission constituted?
(a) 2003 (b) 2005
(c) 2007 (d) 2009

39. In which district mango and fox nut based industry is based?
(a) Darbhanga (b) Mujaffarpur
(c) Begusarai (d) Patna

40. When was the first official effort made by the Planning Commission in India to determine the poverty line?
(a) 1961 (b) 1963
(c) 1965 (d) 1967

41. Which of the following Finance Commissions had propounded the concept of an expanded poverty line?
(a) 5th (b) 6th
(c) 7th (d) 8th

42. When was Prof. D. T. Lakadwala Committee constituted?
(a) 1983 (b) 1985
(c) 1987 (d) 1989

43. How many fundamental needs were made the base for determining poverty line by Suresh Tendulkar Committee?
(a) 4 (b) 5
(c) 6 (d) 7

44. How much money in rupees per person per month was determined by Tendulkar Committee for the rural areas?
(a) 816 (b) 826
(c) 836 (d) 846

45. How much money in rupees per person per month was determined

by Tendulkar Committee for the urban areas?

(a) 950 (b) 1000
(c) 1050 (d) 1100

46. The population of slum areas in Bihar was ______ lakhs according to the 2011 census?

(a) 12.4 (b) 12.8
(c) 13.2 (d) 13.6

47. When did Economist Keynes propound the principle of employment in his book 'General Theory of Employment, Interest and Money'?

(a) 1932 (b) 1934
(c) 1936 (d) 1938

48. With eight hours of daily work, how many days are called as a 'Standard Year'?

(a) 270 (b) 273
(c) 276 (d) 279

49. Who of the following had first propounded the concept of disguised unemployment?

(a) Keynes
(b) John Robinson
(c) Amartya Sen
(d) Kuntz

50. When was Bhagwati Committee constituted?

(a) 1973 (b) 1975
(c) 1977 (d) 1979

51. Which Commission was constituted to measure the extent of unemployment?

(a) Bohra Commission
(b) Dhar Commission
(c) Bhagwati Commission
(d) Fazal Ali Commission

52. How many theories were propounded by Bhagwati Committee for measurement of unemployment?

(a) 2 (b) 3
(c) 4 (d) 5

53. When was Mahatma Gandhi Rashtriya Gramin Rojgar Guarantee Act imeplemented?

(a) 2004 (b) 2005
(c) 2006 (d) 2007

54. In 12th Five Year Plan, creation of how many employment opportunities was the target?

(a) 50 million (b) 40 million
(c) 30 million (d) 20 million

55. According to Bihar Budget 2026-27, what percentage is the economic growth rate of Bihar estimated to be in the upcoming financial year?

(a) 14.9% (b) 10.5%
(c) 12.1% (d) 15.09%

Answers

1. (d)	**2.** (c)	**3.** (b)	**4.** (a)	**5.** (b)	**6.** (a)	**7.** (c)	**8.** (c)	**9.** (a)	**10.** (c)
11. (c)	**12.** (d)	**13.** (d)	**14.** (b)	**15.** (b)	**16.** (b)	**17.** (c)	**18.** (a)	**19.** (a)	**20.** (c)
21. (a)	**22.** (d)	**23.** (d)	**24.** (c)	**25.** (a)	**26.** (a)	**27.** (c)	**28.** (b)	**29.** (a)	**30.** (d)
31. (b)	**32.** (d)	**33.** (a)	**34.** (a)	**35.** (c)	**36.** (a)	**37.** (c)	**38.** (b)	**39.** (a)	**40.** (b)
41. (c)	**42.** (d)	**43.** (c)	**44.** (a)	**45.** (b)	**46.** (a)	**47.** (c)	**48.** (b)	**49.** (b)	**50.** (a)
51. (c)	**52.** (b)	**53.** (c)	**54.** (a)	**55.** (a)					

❑❑❑

29 Central and State Sponsored Schemes

CENTRAL-SPONSORED SCHEMES

1. When was 'Ayushman Bharat Yojna' started?
(a) 2016 (b) 2017
(c) 2018 (d) 2019

2. When was 'Ayushman Bharat Yojna' launched in Bihar?
(a) 15th August 2018
(b) 2nd October 2018
(c) 14th November 2018
(d) 13th September 2018

3. Under Ayushman Scheme, health insurance of up to Rs. _____ lakh is made available.
(a) 3 (b) 4
(c) 5 (d) 6

4. How many families will be provided with health insurance under the Ayushman Bharat Scheme?
(a) 10 crore (b) 8 crore
(c) 6 crore (d) 4 crore

5. How many people will be provided with health insurance under the Ayushman Bharat Scheme?
(a) 40 crore (b) 45 crore
(c) 50 crore (d) 54 crore

6. When was 'Gramin Jeevika Mission' of Bihar Government launched?
(a) 2011 (b) 2013
(c) 2015 (d) 2017

7. When did the Parliament pass the National Rural Employment Guarantee Act?
(a) 2004 (b) 2005
(c) 2006 (d) 2007

8. When was the National Rural Employment Scheme launched?
(a) 2005 (b) 2006
(c) 2007 (d) 2008

9. When was 'NREGA' converted into 'MNREGA'?
(a) 2006 (b) 2007
(c) 2008 (d) 2009

10. In how many districts of the country was NREGA implemented in the year 2006?
(a) 100 (b) 150
(c) 200 (d) 250

11. Under MGNREGA, work for how many days is ensured?
(a) 25 (b) 50
(c) 75 (d) 100

12. Under MGNREGA, what percentage of employment is reserved for the women?
(a) 33 (b) 31
(c) 29 (d) 27

13. In how many days of making an application for employment under MGNREGA, it is compulsory to provide employment?
(a) 9 (b) 11
(c) 13 (d) 15

14. When was 'Indira Aawas Yojna' launched?
(a) 1981 (b) 1983
(c) 1985 (d) 1987

15. When was the name of the scheme 'Indira Aawas Yojna' changed to 'Prime Minister Aawas Yojna'?

(a) 2016 (b) 2015
(c) 2014 (d) 2013

16. The PM Aawas Scheme is a flagship programme of which ministry?

(a) Finance Ministry
(b) Home Ministry
(c) Rural Development Ministry
(d) All of the above

17. Under PM Aawas Scheme all people in rural areas shall be given a residence facility till when?

(a) 2018 (b) 2020
(c) 2022 (d) 2024

18. Under PM Aawas Scheme, what percentage of total fund has been reserved for the handicapped people?

(a) 1 (b) 2
(c) 2.5 (d) 3

19. Under PM Aawas Scheme, how much amount is being granted to at present?

(a) 1.20 lakh (b) 1.25 lakh
(c) 1.30 lakh (d) 1.35 lakh

20. Which of the following is a programme under 'Seven Resolves' Scheme?

(a) Shochalaya Nirman Ghar Ka Samman
(b) Har Ghar Nal ka Jal
(c) Aarakshit Rozgar-Mahilaon ka Adhikar
(d) All of the above

21. When was the 'Seven Resolves' Scheme launched in Bihar?

(a) 2014 (b) 2015
(c) 2016 (d) 2017

22. Under 'Shochalaya Nirman Ghar Ka Samman' programme, what is the target of providing toilet to those houses without having one?

(a) 1.40 crore (b) 1.48 crore
(c) 1.54 crore (d) 1.68 crore

23. Under which of the following programmes, toilets are being built in Bihar?

(a) Clean Bihar Campaign
(b) Lohia Clean Bihar Campaign
(c) Jai Prakash Narayan Clean Bihar Campaign
(d) Gandhi Clean Bihar Campaign

24. When was Atal Mission for Rejuvenation and Urban Transformation (Amrut) launched?

(a) 2014 (b) 2015
(c) 2016 (d) 2017

25. Under the 'Amrut' Scheme, cities with what minimum population should be selected?

(a) 1 lakh (b) 3 lakh
(c) 5 lakh (d) 7 lakh

26. Under 'Amrut' Yojna, how many cities of Bihar have been selected?

(a) 25 (b) 23
(c) 21 (d) 19

27. Which urban body has been selected under the Amrut Scheme?

(a) Danapur
(b) Saharasa
(c) Dehri
(d) All of the above

28. Which urban body has not been selected under the Amrut Scheme?

(a) Motihari (b) Munger
(c) Buxar (d) Jamalpur

29. In which proportion, finance shall be made available by the Centre and the States under Amrut Scheme?

(a) 80:20 (b) 70:30
(c) 60:40 (d) 50:50

30. When was the Smart City Scheme launched?
(a) 2014 (b) 2015
(c) 2016 (d) 2017

31. Under the Smart City Scheme, how many cities are to be developed into smart cities in the next 5 years duration?
(a) 70 (b) 80
(c) 90 (d) 100

32. Under Smart City Scheme, each selected city has to be provided what amount for development?
(a) 100 crore (b) 75 crore
(c) 50 crore (d) 25 crore

33. How many cities of Bihar have been selected under the Smart City Scheme?
(a) 2 (b) 3
(c) 4 (d) 5

34. Which of the following cities has been selected under the Smart City Scheme?
(a) Bihar Sharif
(b) Mujaffarpur
(c) Bhagalpur
(d) All of the above

35. The Clean India Campaign was launched on 2nd October ________.
(a) 2014
(b) 2015
(c) 2016
(d) 2017

36. The aim of the Clean India Mission was to make the entire India clean by the 150th birth anniversary of Mahatma Gandhi i.e. 2nd October ________.
(a) 2018 (b) 2019
(c) 2020 (d) 2021

37. Under Clean India Campaign how much amount as subsidy is provided to each family to construct a toilet?
(a) 10000 (b) 11000
(c) 12000 (d) 13000

38. When was 'Namami Gange' Scheme launched?
(a) 2014 (b) 2015
(c) 2016 (d) 2017

39. Under Namami Gange Scheme, what amount has to be spent in the next 5 years duration on protection and cleanliness of the Ganga River?
(a) 20 thousand crore
(b) 15 thousand crore
(c) 10 thousand crore
(d) 5 thousand crore

40. How many cities of Bihar have been marked under the Namami Gange Scheme?
(a) 30 (b) 32
(c) 35 (d) 38

41. When did the Central Government give approval to 4 sewerage and water disposal projects in Bihar?
(a) 2010 (b) 2013
(c) 2016 (d) 2019

42. In which cities of Bihar, sewerage and water disposal projects have been set up?
(a) Hajipur
(b) Begusarai
(c) Munger
(d) All of the above

43. Rajiv Gandhi Aawas Yojna is related to the urban poor which was launched in the year____.
(a) 2010 (b) 2011
(c) 2012 (d) 2013

44. How many district headquarters of Bihar were selected under the Rajiv Gandhi Aawas Scheme?

(a) 32 (b) 34
(c) 36 (d) 38

45. When was Rajiv Gandhi Scheme for Empowerment of Adolescent Girls (SABLA) launched?
(a) 2008 (b) 2009
(c) 2010 (d) 2011

46. 'Sabla' Scheme service is available for how many days in a year?
(a) 300 (b) 250
(c) 100 (d) 150

47. In how many districts of Bihar 'Sabla' Scheme is being operated?
(a) 10 (b) 11
(c) 12 (d) 13

48. In which of the following districts, 'Sabla' Scheme is being operated?
(a) Gaya
(b) West Champaran
(c) Vaishali
(d) All of the above

49. In which of the following districts, 'Sabla' scheme is not being operated?
(a) Saharasa (b) Arwal
(c) Katihar (d) Banka

50. When was 'Indira Gandhi Matratva Sahyog Yojna' launched on a pilot basis?
(a) 2008 (b) 2009
(c) 2010 (d) 2011

51. In how many districts of the country, Indira Gandhi Matratva Sahyog Yojna is being operated?
(a) 53 (b) 60
(c) 91 (d) 115

52. How much money is paid to each beneficiary under Indira Gandhi Matratva Sahyog Yojna?
(a) 5000 (b) 6000
(c) 7000 (d) 8000

53. When was 'Integrated Child Development Scheme (ICDS) launched?
(a) 1975 (b) 1980
(c) 1985 (d) 1990

54. Which of the following services are offered under ICDS?
(a) Supplementary nutrition to mothers
(b) Health Check-up
(c) Referral Services
(d) All of the above

55. When was 'Sarv Shiksha Abhiyan' launched?
(a) 2001 (b) 2003
(c) 2005 (d) 2007

56. The main objective of the 'Sarv Shiksha Abhiyan' is to provide a satisfactory, quality and free education to children up to which class?
(a) 5th (b) 6th
(c) 7th (d) 8th

57. Under which amendment to the Constitution, education was made a fundamental right?
(a) 86th (b) 84th
(c) 82nd (d) 80th

58. When was mid-day meal programme launched for schools?
(a) 1993 (b) 1995
(c) 1997 (d) 1999

59. When was 'Smart Ganga City Yojna' launched?
(a) 2014 (b) 2015
(c) 2016 (d) 2017

60. In how many cities of the country, Smart Ganga City Yojna was launched?
(a) 8 (b) 10
(c) 12 (d) 15

61. How many cities of Bihar were chosen for benefit under the Smart Ganga City Yojna?

(a) 1 (b) 2
(c) 3 (d) 4

62. Which citiy of Bihar was chosen under the Smart Ganga City Yojna?

(a) Madhubani (b) Bhagalpur
(c) Chhapra (d) Patna

63. Which city has been chosen under the Smart Ganga City Yojna?

(a) Allahabad
(b) Kanpur
(c) Bairakpur
(d) All of the above

64. Which of the following cities has not been selected under the Smart Ganga City Project?

(a) Delhi (b) Sahebganj
(c) Lucknow (d) Banaras

65. When was 'Indira Gandhi Rashtriya Vidhwa Pension Scheme' launched?

(a) 2005-06 (b) 2006-07
(c) 2008-09 (d) 2009-10

66. Under Indira Gandhi National Widow Pension Scheme, how much money is paid to each beneficiary?

(a) 600 (b) 800
(c) 1000 (d) 1200

67. Under Indira Gandhi National Widow Pension Scheme, in which ratio the financing of the scheme is shared between the Centre and the States?

(a) 80:20 (b) 70:30
(c) 60:40 (d) 50:50

68. When was the National Family Benefit Scheme launched?

(a) 1995 (b) 1997
(c) 1999 (d) 2001

69. Under the National Family Benefit Scheme, if the head of the family dies in an accident, how much money is paid to his/her dependants?

(a) 10000 (b) 15000
(c) 20000 (d) 25000

70. When was 'Rashtriya Baghbani Yojna' launched?

(a) 2005-06 (b) 2006-07
(c) 2007-08 (d) 2008-09

71. How many districts of Bihar have been marked under the 'Rashtriya Baghbani Yojna'?

(a) 20 (b) 21
(c) 22 (d) 23

72. Which district has not been selected under the 'Rashtriya Baghbani Yojna'?

(a) Buxar (b) Rohtash
(c) Jamui (d) Banka

73. Which district has been chosen under the Rashtriya Baghbani Mission?

(a) Gaya
(b) Vaishali
(c) East Champaran
(d) All of the above

74. When was National Agriculture Insurance Scheme launched?

(a) 1995 (b) 1997
(c) 1999 (d) 2001

75. Under Season Based Crop Insurance Scheme, how many districts of Bihar have been selected?

(a) 10 (b) 11
(c) 12 (d) 13

76. Which district of the State has not been selected under the Season Based Crop Insurance Scheme?

(a) Banka (b) Kaimur
(c) Katihar (d) Khagariya

77. Which district has been selected under the Season Based Crop Insurance Scheme?
(a) Jamui
(b) Jahanabad
(c) Madhepura
(d) All of the above

78. Since when is 'Mahila Samakhya Programme' being operated in Bihar?
(a) 1990 (b) 1992
(c) 1994 (d) 1996

79. In how many districts of the State 'Mahila Samakhya Programme' is being operated?
(a) 10 (b) 12
(c) 14 (d) 16

80. ______Project is being launched for the initial level education of girls under the national programme by Bihar Education Project Council .
(a) Hunar (b) Nai Manzil
(c) Nai Roshni (d) Ustad

81. When was the 'Janani and Bal Suraksha Yojna' launched in Bihar?
(a) 2004 (b) 2005
(c) 2006 (d) 2007

82. When was 'Mahila Smriddhi Yojna' launched?
(a) 2004-05 (b) 2005-06
(c) 2007-08 (d) 2008-09

83. Under the Mahila Smriddhi Yojna, how much money is provided as credit to the women belonging to the Scheduled Castes?
(a) 50000 (b) 60000
(c) 70000 (d) 80000

84. Since when in Bihar, Mahila Svadhara Yojna is being operated?
(a) 2001 (b) 2003
(c) 2005 (d) 2007

85. Since when the "Lakshmibai Samajik Suraksha Pension Yojna' is being operated by the State Government?
(a) 2009 (b) 2010
(c) 2011 (d) 2012

86. Under the 'Lakshmibai Samajik Suraksha Pension Yojna', how much money is provided to pay pension to all the widows of all categories from age 18 to 39 years for their entire life?
(a) 400 (b) 500
(c) 600 (d) 700

87. When was the 'Patrakar Kalyan Nidhi Yojna' launched by the Central Government?
(a) 1999-2000 (b) 2000-01
(c) 2001-02 (d) 2002-03

88. When was 'Annapurna Yojna' launched in Bihar?
(a) 2000 (b) 2001
(c) 2002 (d) 2003

89. When was the 'Deendayal Upadhyay a Gramin Jyoti Yojna' launched?
(a) 2015 (b) 2016
(c) 2017 (d) 2018

STATE-SPONSORED SCHEMES

1. When was the 'Mukhyamantri Kanya Utthan Yojna' launched?
(a) 2016 (b) 2017
(c) 2018 (d) 2019

2. Which initiative did the Bihar government launch in January 2026 to strengthen rural infrastructure, including the construction of 909 bridges?
(a) Aapda Setu Yojana
(b) CM Gramin Setu Yojana
(c) CM Gramin Vikas Yojana
(d) CM Gramin Sadak Yojana

3. **Under the Mukhyamantri Kanya Utthan Yojna, how much money will be given to the girls from birth till they become graduate?**
(a) 51100 (b) 52100
(c) 53300 (d) 54100
4. **When was the Mukhyamantri Scheduled Caste and Scheduled Tribes Entrepreneurs Scheme launched?**
(a) 2016 (b) 2017
(c) 2018 (d) 2019
5. **Since when is the Bihar 'Mukhyamantri Vridh Jan Pension Yojna' in operation?**
(a) 2019 (b) 2010
(c) 2006 (d) 2001
6. **As per the latest reports (Sept 2025), which scheme focuses on providing health insurance coverage to rural households associated with self-help groups (SHGs) under the Jeevika programme?**
(a) Jeevika Health Insurance Scheme
(b) Ayushman Bharat Bihar
(c) Bihar State Health Security Scheme
(d) Mukhyamantri Parivarik Labh Yojana
7. **Under Bihar Patrakar Samman Yojna, journalist will be given an amount of ₹ ________ per month.**
(a) 4000 (b) 5000
(c) 6000 (d) 7000
8. **When was Bihar Students' Credit Card Scheme launched?**
(a) 2014 (b) 2015
(c) 2016 (d) 2017
9. **When was the 'Mukhyamantri Nishchay Swayam Sahayata Bhatta Yojna' launched?**
(a) 2015 (b) 2016
(c) 2017 (d) 2018
10. **Under the Mukhyamantri Nishchay Swayam Sahayata Bhatta Yojna, how much money per month is given?**
(a) 500 (b) 1000
(c) 1500 (d) 2000
11. **Under the Mukhyamantri Nishchay Swayam Sahayata Bhatta Yojna, the benefit shall be extended for what period?**
(a) 1 Year (b) 2 years
(c) 2.5 years (d) 3 years
12. **When was the 'Kushal Yuva Yojna' launched?**
(a) 2014 (b) 2015
(c) 2016 (d) 2017
13. **When was the 'Mukhyamantri Vidyut Sambandh Nishchay Yojna' launched?**
(a) 2017 (b) 2016
(c) 2015 (d) 2014
14. **When was Child Marriage Prevention Act passed?**
(a) 2002 (b) 2004
(c) 2006 (d) 2008
15. **When was 'Kabir Antyeshti Anudan Yojna' launched?**
(a) 2001 (b) 2003
(c) 2005 (d) 2007
16. **Under the 'Kabir Antyeshti Anudan Yojna', how much money is given as subsidy to the BPL families for last rites?**
(a) 1500 (b) 2000
(c) 2500 (d) 3000
17. **Under the Mukhyamantri Setu Nirman Yojna, bridges and culverts requiring construction cost from ₹ 10 lakhs to ________ crores will be built up.**
(a) 10 (b) 8
(c) 6 (d) 4
18. **When was 'Mukhyamantri Kshetra Vikas Yojna' launched?**

(a) 2009-10 (b) 2010-11
(c) 2011-12 (d) 2012-13

19. Under Mukhyamantri Kshetra Vikas Yojna, how much money will be made available each year for each legislative assembly area?
(a) 1 Crore (b) 1.5 crore
(c) 2 crore (d) 2.5 crore

20. Under the 'Shatabdi Ann Kalash Yojna', there is a provision that an adult can have ______of food grains per week.
(a) 6 kilogram (b) 8 kilogram
(c) 10 kilogram (d) 12 kilogram

21. When was the 'Mukhyamantri Tivra Beej Vistar Yojna' launched?
(a) 2006-07 (b) 2007-08
(c) 2008-09 (d) 2009-10

22. When was the 'Beej Gram Yojna' launched in Bihar?
(a) 2007-08 (b) 2008-09
(c) 2009-10 (d) 2011-12

23. When was the 'Mukhyamantri Niji Podhshala Yojna' launched?
(a) 2011 (b) 2012
(c) 2013 (d) 2014

24. When was the work for sugarcane development started by the Government of Bihar?
(a) 2007-08 (b) 2009-10
(c) 2010-11 (d) 2012-13

25. When was the 'Mission Indradhanusha' started in Bihar?
(a) 2014 (b) 2015
(c) 2016 (d) 2017

26. When was the 'Yukti Yojna' launched by the Government of Bihar?
(a) 2009 (b) 2010
(c) 2011 (d) 2012

27. When was the 'Jaiprabha Janani Shishu Aarogya Express Yojna' launched?
(a) 2012 (b) 2010
(c) 2008 (d) 2006

28. When was the 'Parvarish Yojna' launched by Bihar Government?
(a) 2011 (b) 2012
(c) 2013 (d) 2014

29. When was the 'Mukhyamantri Kanya Suraksha Yojna' launched?
(a) 2002 (b) 2004
(c) 2006 (d) 2008

30. Under the 'Mukhyamantri Kanya Suraksha Yojna', how much money is invested on birth of a girl child?
(a) 2000 (b) 5000
(c) 8000 (d) 10000

31. When was the 'Mukhyamantri Kanya Vivah Yojna' launched?
(a) 2005 (b) 2007
(c) 2009 (d) 2011

32. Under the Mukhyamantri Kanya Vivah Yojna, how much money is given to the girl at the time of her marriage?
(a) 8000 (b) 10000
(c) 12000 (d) 15000

33. In October 2023, the Art and Culture Minister of Bihar launched which of the following to nurture the talent of sportspersons?
(a) Non-Residential Sports Training Scheme
(b) Khel Protsahan Scheme
(c) Bihar Sports Policy
(d) Rural Sports Academy

34. Where has the Integrated Tharuhar Development Authority been established?
(a) Betiya (b) Motihari
(c) Patna (d) Gaya

35. When was the Students' Guidance Center Scheme launched by the State Government?
(a) 2006-07 (b) 2007-08
(c) 2008-09 (d) 2009-10

36. When was the Mukhyamantri Mahadalit Yojna launched?

(a) 2010-11 (b) 2011-12
(c) 2012-13 (d) 2013-14

37. When was the Mukhyamantri Mahadali Poshak Yojna launched?
(a) 2007-08 (b) 2008-09
(c) 2009-10 (d) 2010-11

38. When was the 'Dashrath Manjhi Kaushal Vikas Yojna' launched?
(a) 2010 (b) 2011
(c) 2012 (d) 2013

39. When was the 'Mukhyamantri Shramshakti Yojna' launched?
(a) 2007-08 (b) 2008-09
(c) 2009-10 (d) 2010-11

40. Where is the Central Institute of Plastic Engineering Technology situated?
(a) Patna
(b) Hajipur
(c) Mujaffarpur
(d) Bhagalpur

41. When was the 'Bihar Grahsthal Yojna' launched?
(a) 2008-09 (b) 2009-10
(c) 2010-11 (d) 2011-12

42. Under the Bihar Grahsthal Yojna, Rs.20000 per family aid is given for purchasing how many dismil of land?
(a) 1 (b) 2
(c) 3 (d) 4

43. When was the 'Kerosene Tel Coupon Yojna' launched in Bihar?
(a) 2005 (b) 2006
(c) 2007 (d) 2008

44. The owners of how many acres of land can approach a district collector with details of the land to get themselves registered under the 'Aao Bihar Yojna'?
(a) 1 (b) 2
(c) 3 (d) 4

45. When was the first Five Year Plan launched in Bihar?
(a) 1950 (b) 1951
(c) 1952 (d) 1953

46. When was the Small Industry Development Organisation established?
(a) 1952 (b) 1953
(c) 1954 (d) 1955

47. When was the differential rate of interest scheme launched?
(a) 1970 (b) 1972
(c) 19740 (d) 1976

48. When was the '20 point Programme' launched?
(a) 1971 (b) 1973
(c) 1975 (d) 1977

49. When was the Integrated Rural Development Programme launched?
(a) 1974 (b) 1976
(c) 1978 (d) 1980

50. When was the Women and Child Development Programme launched in the rural areas?
(a) 1980 (b) 1982
(c) 1984 (d) 1986

51. When was the Rural Landless Employment Guarantee Programme launched?
(a) 1979 (b) 1981
(c) 1983 (d) 1985

52. When was the Public Programme and Rural Technology Development Council (CAPART) launched?
(a) 1980 (b) 1982
(c) 1984 (d) 1986

53. When was the 'Sangam Yojna' launched?
(a) 1996 (b) 1994
(c) 1992 (d) 1990

54. When was the Kasturba Gandhi Education Scheme launched?
(a) 1993 (b) 1995
(c) 1997 (d) 1999

55. When was the Golden Jubilee Village Self employment Scheme launched?
(a) 1993 (b) 1995
(c) 1997 (d) 1999

56. When was the Prime Minister Gramodaya Yojna launched?
(a) 2000 (b) 1999
(c) 1997 (d) 1996

57. When was the Balmiki Ambedkar Aawas Yojna launched?
(a) 1999 (b) 2000
(c) 2001 (d) 2002

58. When was the 'Nirmal Bharat Yojna' launched?
(a) 2000 (b) 2002
(c) 2004 (d) 2006

59. When was the 'PM Gram Sadak Yojna' launched?
(a) 1998 (b) 1999
(c) 2000 (d) 2001

60. When was the availability of urban facilities in the rural areas programme (PURA) launched?
(a) 2000 (b) 2001
(c) 2002 (d) 2003

61. When was Jawaharlal Nehru National Urban Renewal Mission started?
(a) 2001 (b) 2003
(c) 2005 (d) 2007

62. When was the National Rural Health Mission launched?
(a) 2005 (b) 2003
(c) 2001 (d) 1999

63. When was India Nirman Yojna launched?
(a) 2002 (b) 2003
(c) 2004 (d) 2005

64. When was General Public Insurance Scheme launched?
(a) 2007 (b) 2008
(c) 2009 (d) 2010

65. When was 'Beti Bachao, Beti Padao Programme' launched?
(a) 2011 (b) 2013
(c) 2015 (d) 2017

66. When was 'PM Jan-Dhan Yojna' launched?
(a) 2014 (b) 2015
(c) 2016 (d) 2017

67. When was the 'PM Insurance Scheme' launched?
(a) 2011 (b) 2013
(c) 2015 (d) 2017

68. When was 'Atal Pension Yojna' launched?
(a) 2014 (b) 2015
(c) 2016 (d) 2017

69. When was the 'Sansad Adarsh Gram Yojna' launched?
(a) 2017 (b) 2016
(c) 2015 (d) 2014

70. When was the 'PM Ujjavala Yojna' launched?
(a) 2014 (b) 2015
(c) 2016 (d) 2017

Answers

CENTRAL-SPONSORED SCHEMES

1. (c)	**2.** (d)	**3.** (c)	**4.** (a)	**5.** (c)	**6.** (b)	**7.** (b)	**8.** (b)	**9.** (d)	**10.** (c)
11. (d)	**12.** (a)	**13.** (d)	**14.** (c)	**15.** (a)	**16.** (c)	**17.** (c)	**18.** (d)	**19.** (c)	**20.** (d)
21. (c)	**22.** (d)	**23.** (b)	**24.** (c)	**25.** (a)	**26.** (a)	**27.** (d)	**28.** (a)	**29.** (d)	**30.** (b)
31. (d)	**32.** (a)	**33.** (c)	**34.** (d)	**35.** (a)	**36.** (b)	**37.** (c)	**38.** (c)	**39.** (a)	**40.** (b)

41. (a)	**42.** (d)	**43.** (b)	**44.** (d)	**45.** (c)	**46.** (a)	**47.** (c)	**48.** (d)	**49.** (b)	**50.** (c)
51. (a)	**52.** (b)	**53.** (a)	**54.** (d)	**55.** (a)	**56.** (d)	**57.** (a)	**58.** (b)	**59.** (c)	**60.** (b)
61. (a)	**62.** (d)	**63.** (d)	**64.** (a)	**65.** (d)	**66.** (a)	**67.** (d)	**68.** (a)	**69.** (c)	**70.** (a)
71. (d)	**72.** (a)	**73.** (d)	**74.** (c)	**75.** (d)	**76.** (a)	**77.** (d)	**78.** (b)	**79.** (c)	**80.** (a)
81. (c)	**82.** (d)	**83.** (b)	**84.** (a)	**85.** (c)	**86.** (a)	**87.** (b)	**88.** (b)	**89.** (a)	

STATE-SPONSORED SCHEMES

1. (c)	**2.** (a)	**3.** (d)	**4.** (c)	**5.** (a)	**6.** (a)	**7.** (c)	**8.** (c)	**9.** (b)	**10.** (b)
11. (a)	**12.** (c)	**13.** (b)	**14.** (c)	**15.** (d)	**16.** (d)	**17.** (a)	**18.** (c)	**19.** (a)	**20.** (c)
21. (c)	**22.** (b)	**23.** (c)	**24.** (d)	**25.** (b)	**26.** (c)	**27.** (a)	**28.** (d)	**29.** (d)	**30.** (a)
31. (b)	**32.** (b)	**33.** (a)	**34.** (a)	**35.** (d)	**36.** (c)	**37.** (c)	**38.** (d)	**39.** (b)	**40.** (b)
41. (c)	**42.** (c)	**43.** (d)	**44.** (b)	**45.** (b)	**46.** (c)	**47.** (b)	**48.** (c)	**49.** (d)	**50.** (b)
51. (c)	**52.** (c)	**53.** (a)	**54.** (c)	**55.** (d)	**56.** (a)	**57.** (c)	**58.** (b)	**59.** (c)	**60.** (d)
61. (c)	**62.** (a)	**63.** (d)	**64.** (a)	**65.** (c)	**66.** (a)	**67.** (c)	**68.** (a)	**69.** (d)	**70.** (c)

❑❑❑

30 Fiscal System

1. **How many major parts does Indian Financial System have?**
   (a) 2 (b) 3
   (c) 4 (d) 5
2. **Which of the following is a major organ of the Indian Financial System?**
   (a) Loan Market
   (b) Capital Market
   (c) Currency Market
   (d) Both (b) and (c)
3. **Which market means a market where financial instruments are purchased and sold?**
   (a) Capital Market
   (b) Loan Market
   (c) Currency market
   (d) Cash Market
4. **By which of the following Institutions, currency Bank is controlled?**
   (a) SBI (b) RBI
   (c) LIC (d) SEBI
5. **Since when banks are considered to have been developed in India?**
   (a) 1786 (b) 1805
   (c) 1829 (d) 1844
6. **When was Bank of Hindustan established?**
   (a) 1866 (b) 1868
   (c) 1870 (d) 1872
7. **When was the Bank of Bengal established?**
   (a) 1830 (b) 1840
   (c) 1850 (d) 1860
8. **When was Bank of Mumbai established?**
   (a) 1840 (b) 1841
   (c) 1842 (d) 1843
9. **When was Allahabad Bank established?**
   (a) 1845 (b) 1855
   (c) 1865 (d) 1875
10. **When was Punjab National Bank established?**
    (a) 1864 (b) 1874
    (c) 1884 (d) 1894
11. **When was Imperial Bank established?**
    (a) 1919 (b) 1921
    (c) 1923 (d) 1925
12. **When was Reserve Bank of India established?**
    (a) 1931 (b) 1933
    (c) 1935 (d) 1937
13. **Where were the Headquarters of Punjab National Bank in the beginning?**
    (a) Lahore (b) Amritsar
    (c) Karachi (d) Delhi
14. **In India, ______ percent of the total assets of the banking system are controlled by the Public Sector banks.**
    (a) 50 (b) 60
    (c) 70 (d) 80
15. **Which of the following is not a type of a Scheduled Bank?**
    (a) Public Sector Bank
    (b) Cooperative Bank

(c) Foreign Bank
(d) Private Bank

16. What is the approximately Credit-Deposit ratio of banks in Bihar as of 2025?
(a) 53-57% (b) 45-49%
(c) 35-40% (d) 55-60%

17. The number of scheduled commercial bank branches in Bihar as on 31st March 2025 is
(a) 8,304 (b) 7,150
(c) 9,150 (d) 10,050

18. According to Bihar Economic Survey 2025-26, what is the growth rate of Bihar recorded at Current Prices for the financial year 2024-25?
(a) 13.1% (b) 14.25%
(c) 14.75% (d) 14.85%

19. Which sector had the largest network of banks in Bihar (as on 2023)?
(a) Public (b) Private
(c) Rural (d) Urban

20. The period of new tourism policy in Bihar is
(a) 2023-28 (b) 2024-29
(c) 2025-30 (d) 2022-27

21. According to Bihar Economic Survey 2025-26, what is the economic growth rate of Bihar recorded at Constant Prices based on Base Year (2011-12)?
(a) 8.6% (b) 9.5
(c) 3.7% (d) 9.7%

22. On the recommendations of which committee, regional rural banks in India were established?
(a) Goswami Committee
(b) Abid Ali Committee
(c) Narsimha Samiti
(d) Verma Committee

23. When were regional rural banks established in India?
(a) 1971 (b) 1973
(c) 1975 (d) 1977

24. When was the Regional Rural Bank Act passed?
(a) 1975 (b) 1976
(c) 1977 (d) 1978

25. What is the share holding of the central government in regional rural banks?
(a) 50% (b) 60%
(c) 70% (d) 80%

26. What is the share holding of the State Government in regional rural banks?
(a) 10% (b) 15%
(c) 20% (d) 25%

27. What is the share holding of the promoter bank in regional rural banks?
(a) 25% (b) 30%
(c) 35% (d) 40%

28. According to Bihar Economic Survey 2025-26, what is the Gross State Domestic Product (GSDP) of Bihar recorded at Current Prices for the financial year 2024-25?
(a) ₹ 9,91,997 core
(b) ₹ 8,50,054 crore
(c) ₹ 8,75,000 crore
(d) ₹ 9,50,150 crore

29. What is the increase in the length of rural paved roads during 2005-25?
(a) 1.17 lakh km
(b) 1.18 lakh km
(c) 2.18 lakh km
(d) 2.10 lakh km

30. Which Regional Rural bank is not functioning in Bihar?
(a) West Bihar Regional Rural Bank
(b) Bihar Regional Rural Bank
(c) Central Bihar Regional Rural Bank
(d) North Bihar Regional Rural Bank

31. Bihar Regional Rural Bank is sponsored by which bank?

(a) SBI
(b) PNB
(c) ICICI
(d) United Commercial Bank

32. Central Bihar Regional Rural Bank is sponsored by which Bank?
(a) PNB
(b) Allahabad Bank
(c) Dena Bank
(d) Central Bank of India

33. North Bihar Regional Rural bank is sponsored by which bank?
(a) SBI
(b) Central Bank of India
(c) PNB
(d) Allahabad Bank

34. When was the National Agriculture and Rural Development Bank (NABARD) established?
(a) 1978 (b) 1980
(c) 1982 (d) 1984

35. On which committee's recommendations, NABARD was established?
(a) Narsimha Committee
(b) Verma Committee
(c) Fazal Ali Committee
(d) Shivraman Committee

36. For which of the following projects, NABARD makes credit available to the state governments?
(a) Irrigation
(b) Soil Conservation
(c) Water Filtration Management
(d) All of the above

37. When was Rural Infrastructure Development Fund (RIDP) established?
(a) 1994-95 (b) 1995-96
(c) 1996-97 (d) 1997-98

38. The Rural Infrastructure Development Fund makes available to all the State Governments ____ percent of project cost relating to agriculture and allied areas as credit?
(a) 80 (b) 85
(c) 90 (d) 95

39. According to Bihar Economic Survey 2025-26, which is the correct ascending order of districts with lowest Per Capita Income in Bihar?
(a) Sheohar < Araria < Sitamarhi
(b) Sheohar < Sitamarhi < Araria
(c) Araria < Sheohar < Sitamarhi
(d) Sitamarhi < Araria < Sheohar

40. According to Bihar Economic Survey 2025-26, what is the percentage contribution of Primary, Secondary and Tertiary sectors respectively in Bihar's GSVA at Current Prices?
(a) 18.3%, 26.8%, 54.8%
(b) 19.5%, 21.3%, 25.3%
(c) 20.1%, 26.5%, 27.4%
(d) 30.1%, 32.5%, 33.6%

Answers

1. (a)	**2.** (d)	**3.** (a)	**4.** (b)	**5.** (a)	**6.** (c)	**7.** (b)	**8.** (d)	**9.** (c)	**10.** (d)
11. (b)	**12.** (c)	**13.** (a)	**14.** (c)	**15.** (b)	**16.** (a)	**17.** (a)	**18.** (a)	**19.** (a)	**20.** (a)
21. (a)	**22.** (c)	**23.** (c)	**24.** (b)	**25.** (a)	**26.** (b)	**27.** (c)	**28.** (a)	**29.** (a)	**30.** (a)
31. (d)	**32.** (a)	**33.** (b)	**34.** (c)	**35.** (d)	**36.** (d)	**37.** (b)	**38.** (d)	**39.** (a)	**40.** (a)

❑❑❑

31 Major Schemes and Policies

1. **When was Industrial Promotion Policy announced by the Bihar Government?**
(a) 2002 (b) 2004
(c) 2006 (d) 2008

2. **When was Bihar Single Window Clearance Act passed?**
(a) 2000 (b) 2002
(c) 2004 (d) 2006

3. **When was Bihar Fundamental Structure Development Capability Act implemented?**
(a) 2004 (b) 2005
(c) 2006 (d) 2007

4. **Under the Industrial Promotion Policy 2006, what percentage of stamp duty is exempted on registration of micro, small, medium and large industries?**
(a) 25% (b) 50%
(c) 75% (d) 100%

5. **The products made by small and medium units registered in Bihar will attract only _____ of the central sales tax.**
(a) 1% (b) 2%
(c) 3% (d) 4%

6. **In which of the following years, industrial promotion policy in the State was implemented?**
(a) 2009 (b) 2010
(c) 2011 (d) 2012

7. **Which of the following was structured under the Industrial Promotion Policy 2011?**
(a) Land Bank
(b) IT Park
(c) Industrial Park
(d) Both (a) and (c)

8. **Under the Industrial promotion policy 2011, what percentage of project cost as prepared by the Industrial units with minimum of ₹ 2 lakh shall be compensated with?**
(a) 40% (b) 50%
(c) 60% (d) 70%

9. **Under the industrial promotion policy 2011, what percentage of the cost of plant and machinery to the units engaged in production of power through unconventional sources is available to the industries as subsidy?**
(a) 40 (b) 50
(c) 60 (d) 70

10. **Under the industrial promotion policy 2011, industries shall be given duty exemption by the Electricity Regulation Commission for how many years?**
(a) 3 (b) 4
(c) 5 (d) 6

11. **Under the industrial promotion policy 2011, ____ percent capital related subsidy will be payable on the capital cost of the plant and machinery incurred by industrialists under the micro, small and medium category?**

(a) 10 (b) 20
(c) 25 (d) 30

12. Under the industrial promotion policy 2011, what percentage of the expenditure incurred on obtaining ISO Standard Certification will be compensated with by the state government?
(a) 60 (b) 65
(c) 70 (d) 75

13. When was the new industrial policy implemented in the State?
(a) 2015 (b) 2016
(c) 2017 (d) 2018

14. Under the industrial promotion policy 2016, what percentage of annual industrial growth is targeted to be achieved?
(a) 10 (b) 15
(c) 20 (d) 25

15. Under the industrial promotion policy 2016, how many employment opportunities are to be created in all the areas taken together?
(a) 3 lakh (b) 4 lakh
(c) 5 lakh (d) 6 lakh

16. Under the industrial policy 2016, how much real investment has to be attracted?
(a) 10 thousand crore
(b) 15 thousand crore
(c) 20 thousand crore
(d) 25 thousand crore

17. Which of the following districts of Bihar has been a cent for making silk threads?
(a) Bhagalpur (b) Gaya
(c) Patna (d) Begusarai

18. In which district of the state, power looms are mainly installed?
(a) Gaya
(b) Bhagalpur
(c) Banka
(d) All of the above

19. What is the electricity consumption in units per capita in the state?
(a) 261 (b) 272
(c) 280 (d) 292

20. What is the child death rate per one thousand in the state?
(a) 22 (b) 33
(c) 42 (d) 51

21. When was Bihar Industrial Area Development Authority Act passed?
(a) 1968 (b) 1970
(c) 1972 (d) 1974

22. When was the Bihar Right to Public Service Act passed?
(a) 2009 (b) 2010
(c) 2011 (d) 2012

23. When was the Bihar Public Grievances Redressal Right Act passed?
(a) 2012 (b) 2013
(c) 2014 (d) 2015

24. What percentage of the State's total land area is used for agriculture?
(a) 52 (b) 57
(c) 62 (d) 65

25. In which district Pristine Mega Food Park is being established?
(a) Bhagalpur (b) Khagariya
(c) Gaya (d) Jehanabad

26. In which district, proposal for installing Mathouli Power Project is there?
(a) Patna
(b) Gaya
(c) West Champaran
(d) Katihar

27. The main pipe line of GAIL will pass through which district?
(a) Gaya
(b) Aurangabad
(c) Rohtash
(d) All of the above

28. When was 'Private Industrial Park Policy' implemented in Bihar?
(a) 2011 (b) 2013
(c) 2015 (d) 2017

29. What will be the minimum area of Private Industrial Park in Bihar?
(a) 15 acre
(b) 20 acre
(c) 25 acre
(d) 30 acre

30. With cooperation of which organization, a corpus fund to rehabilitate sick industries in Bihar shall be constituted?
(a) Commercial Banks
(b) State Government
(c) Industrial Union
(d) All of the above

31. When was Bihar start-up policy announced?
(a) 2016 (b) 2017
(c) 2018 (d) 2019

32. Under Bihar Start-up policy, how many new social promoters, in support of their views, shall be provided with subsidy through Entrepreneurs Development Fund?
(a) 10 (b) 15
(c) 20 (d) 25

33. The Government-approved state dedicated private incubators shall be compensated with at a maximum rate of ₹ _____lakh for start-up.
(a) 1 (b) 2
(c) 3 (d) 4

34. When was information and communication technology policy implemented by Bihar Government?
(a) 2007 (b) 2009
(c) 2011 (d) 2013

35. When did Bihar Government present information technology vision?
(a) 2009 (b) 2011
(c) 2013 (d) 2015

36. Under the information and communication technology act 2011, 100% exemption in luxury tax shall be given for how many years?
(a) 3 (b) 5
(c) 7 (d) 9

37. When was the State Information Technology Department constituted?
(a) 2005 (b) 2007
(c) 2009 (d) 2011

38. When was Bihar Advertisement Policy announced?
(a) 2010 (b) 2012
(c) 2014 (d) 2016

39. When was Bihar Agricultural Land (Acquisition for non-agricultural purposes) Act passed?
(a) 2006 (b) 2008
(c) 2010 (d) 2012

40. When was Indian Stamp Act implemented?
(a) 1899 (b) 1905
(c) 1910 (d) 1921

41. When was Bihar Public Grievances Redressal Rights Act implemented?
(a) 2010 (b) 2012
(c) 2014 (d) 2016

42. When was Bihar Prohibition and Excise Act implemented?
(a) 2014
(b) 2015
(c) 2016
(d) 2017

Answers

1. (c)	**2.** (d)	**3.** (c)	**4.** (d)	**5.** (a)	**6.** (c)	**7.** (d)	**8.** (b)	**9.** (c)	**10.** (c)
11. (b)	**12.** (d)	**13.** (b)	**14.** (b)	**15.** (c)	**16.** (b)	**17.** (a)	**18.** (d)	**19.** (c)	**20.** (c)
21. (d)	**22.** (c)	**23.** (d)	**24.** (b)	**25.** (b)	**26.** (c)	**27.** (d)	**28.** (b)	**29.** (c)	**30.** (d)
31. (b)	**32.** (c)	**33.** (b)	**34.** (c)	**35.** (d)	**36.** (c)	**37.** (b)	**38.** (d)	**39.** (c)	**40.** (a)
41. (d)	**42.** (c)								

❑❑❑

32 The Division of the State

1. **When was Bihar separated from Bengal?**
   (a) 1910 (b) 1912
   (c) 1914 (d) 1916
2. **When was Bihar separated from Odisha?**
   (a) 1910 (b) 1932
   (c) 1934 (d) 1936
3. **When was Jharkhand separated from Bihar?**
   (a) 1999 (b) 2000
   (c) 2001 (d) 2002
4. **At the time of independence which class of state was Bihar classified into?**
   (a) A (b) B
   (c) C (d) D
5. **When was State Reconstitution Commission formed under leadership of Fazal Ali?**
   (a) 1951 (b) 1953
   (c) 1955 (d) 1957
6. **When was Fazal Ali Committee's report submitted?**
   (a) 1954 (b) 1955
   (c) 1956 (d) 1957
7. **On the basis of which of the following committee's report, Bihar's political boundaries were reconstituted?**
   (a) Fazal Ali Committee
   (b) Goswami Committee
   (c) B. K. Pandey Committee
   (d) Shashidhar Committee
8. **When was Jharkhand self administration Area Council constituted?**
   (a) 1991 (b) 1993
   (c) 1995 (d) 1997
9. **How much was the area in square kilometers of the undivided Bihar in the year 2000?**
   (a) 170411 (b) 171219
   (c) 172829 (d) 173476
10. **How much is the total area in square kilometers of Bihar at present?**
    (a) 94163 (b) 95840
    (c) 96113 (d) 97930
11. **What percentage of land was given to Jharkhand by dividing Bihar?**
    (a) 42 (b) 44
    (c) 46 (d) 48
12. **After division, what percentage of population remained in Bihar?**
    (a) 71 (b) 73
    (c) 75 (d) 77
13. **Before the division, how many districts in total were there in Bihar?**
    (a) 50 (b) 52
    (c) 54 (d) 56
14. **With how many districts taken together, Jharkhand was formed?**
    (a) 16 (b) 18
    (c) 20 (d) 22
15. **How many Legislative Assembly seats were there in the undivided Bihar?**
    (a) 314 (b) 318
    (c) 324 (d) 330

16. How many Lok Sabha seats were there in the undivided Bihar?
(a) 51 (b) 52
(c) 53 (d) 54

17. How many Legislative Council seats were there in the undivided Bihar?
(a) 96 (b) 94
(c) 92 (d) 90

18. Which of the following area rich in mineral resources went to Jharkhand state after the division?
(a) Bokaro
(b) Dhanbad
(c) Palamu
(d) All of the above

19. Which of the following industrial area is at present in Bihar?
(a) Barauni (b) Hazaribagh
(c) Adityapur (d) Dhanbad

20. Out of the total installed power capacity of undivided Bihar, what percentage went to Bihar?
(a) 30 (b) 32
(c) 34 (d) 36

21. What percentage of total mineral assets went to Bihar after the division?
(a) 10 (b) 8
(c) 6 (d) 4

22. The urbanization in Bihar reduced to what percentage as a result of division?
(a) 10.76 (b) 11.28
(c) 12.44 (d) 13.51

23. When did Bihar Assembly pass unanimously the proposal relating to the status of a special state?
(a) 2004 (b) 2005
(c) 2006 (d) 2007

24. Special assistance is provided to a state having special status by the Central Government on the basis of formula suggested by which Committee?
(a) Fazal Ali Committee
(b) Gadgil-Mukherjee Committee
(c) Gujral Committee
(d) Avdhesh Mishra Committee

25. Normal status states get the assistance from the central government at the rate of 70% of debt whereas states with special status get ______ percent assistance in the shape of subsidy.
(a) 70 (b) 80
(c) 90 (d) 100

26. How many states in the country have special status at present?
(a) 8 (b) 9
(c) 10 (d) 11

27. Which committee was formulated to determine the criteria for allowing special status to the backward states?
(a) Vimal Jalan Committee
(b) Raghuram Rajan Committee
(c) Vivek Devroy Committee
(d) Urijit Patel Committee

28. When was name of the Agriculture Ministry changed to Agriculture and Farmers' Welfare Ministry?
(a) 2014
(b) 2015
(c) 2016
(d) 2017

Answers

1. (b)	**2.** (d)	**3.** (b)	**4.** (a)	**5.** (b)	**6.** (d)	**7.** (a)	**8.** (c)	**9.** (d)	**10.** (a)
11. (c)	**12.** (c)	**13.** (d)	**14.** (b)	**15.** (c)	**16.** (d)	**17.** (a)	**18.** (d)	**19.** (a)	**20.** (d)
21. (c)	**22.** (a)	**23.** (c)	**24.** (b)	**25.** (c)	**26.** (d)	**27.** (b)	**28.** (b)		

❑❑❑

33 Naxalism

1. **Naxalism is inspired by the ideology of which of the following persons?**
(a) Marx
(b) Lenin
(c) Mao-Tse-Tung
(d) All of the above
2. **When did naxalism start in India?**
(a) 1967 (b) 1965
(c) 1963 (d) 1961
3. **Who is considered the Father of Naxalism in India?**
(a) Dipankar Manjhi
(b) Charu Majumdar
(c) Shibu Sanyal
(d) All of the above
4. **In which state of India, naxalism started first?**
(a) West Bengal (b) Bihar
(c) Odisha (d) Maharashtra
5. **How many districts of Bihar are affected by Naxalism?**
(a) 11 (b) 13
(c) 15 (d) 17
6. **Which of the following districts is affected by naxalism?**
(a) Sitamarhi
(b) Jehandabad
(c) Navada
(d) All of the above
7. **Which of the following districts is not affected by naxalism?**
(a) Mujaffarpur
(b) East Champaran
(c) Shivhar
(d) Bhagalpur
8. **In which district of Bihar, incident of mass murder had taken place?**
(a) Purnia (b) Munger
(c) Arrah (d) Jehanabad
9. **In which district of the State, there is expansion of the Marxist Communist centre related to the peoples' war group of Andhra Pradesh?**
(a) Jehanabad
(b) Gaya
(c) Aurangabad
(d) All of the above
10. **Which of the following is correct (Establishment and its year)?**
(a) Ranvir Sena-1992
(b) Sunlight Sena-1989
(c) Lorik Sena-1985
(d) Bhumi Sena-1979
11. **When was Kunwar Sena constituted?**
(a) 1974 (b) 1976
(c) 1978 (d) 1980
12. **In which area of Bihar a Marxist organization called 'The Peoples' Liberation Gorilla Army' is active?**
(a) Kaimur (b) Rohtash
(c) Purnia (d) Both (a) and (b)
13. **Which force has been constituted to tackle the problem of naxalism?**
(a) Chetak (b) Mosad
(c) Kobra (d) Prahari

14. When did the State Government launch the programme 'Aapki Sarkar Aapke Dwar'?
(a) 2004 (b) 2006
(c) 2008 (d) 2010

15. In which district the programme called 'Aapki Sarkar Aapke Dwar' was started?
(a) Jehanabad (b) Jamui
(c) Lakhisarai (d) Gaya

16. In how many districts of the State at present, the programme 'Aapki Sarkar Apke Dwar' is being operated?
(a) 4 (b) 6
(c) 8 (d) 10

17. When was SAP (Special Auxiliary Police) constituted?
(a) 2004 (b) 2006
(c) 2008 (d) 2010

18. When was Special Task Force (STF) constituted to tackle the problem of naxalism?
(a) 1998 (b) 2000
(c) 2001 (d) 2004

19. How many 'Cheetah' units of STF are operating in the State?
(a) 30 (b) 31
(c) 32 (d) 33

20. Where, in the State, STF Training School is being established?
(a) Patna
(b) Gaya
(c) Bhagalpur
(d) Hajipur

21. A provision for giving how much as an instant assistance amount is made by the State Government to high category communist extremists on their surrender?
(a) 1 lakh (b) 1.5 lakh
(c) 2 lakh (d) 2.5 lakh

22. A provision for giving how much money as a special assistance has been made by the State Government to the dependants of family heads killed in terrorism violence or in violent activities?
(a) 7 lakh (b) 8 lakh
(c) 9 lakh (d) 10 lakh

Answers

1. (d) **2.** (a) **3.** (b) **4.** (a) **5.** (c) **6.** (d) **7.** (d) **8.** (a) **9.** (d) **10.** (a)
11. (c) **12.** (d) **13.** (c) **14.** (b) **15.** (a) **16.** (c) **17.** (b) **18.** (b) **19.** (d) **20.** (b)
21. (d) **22.** (d)

❑❑❑

34 Good Governance and Seven Resolution

1. **When was arrangement for fast track courts made to deliver instant justice in the State?**
(a) 2000 (b) 2001
(c) 2002 (d) 2003
2. **Bihar is the________state of the country where a fully computerized planning system has been developed for strengthening of administration and its progress?**
(a) First (b) Second
(c) Third (d) Fourth
3. **In how many districts of the State, women police stations have been set up?**
(a) 35 (b) 36
(c) 37 (d) 38
4. **When was mobile application called 'Disha' launched in the state?**
(a) 2014 (b) 2015
(c) 2016 (d) 2017
5. **Which scheme is being operated in the state to make women literate?**
(a) Janani Shiksha Abhiyan
(b) Akshar Anchal Yojna
(c) Shikshit Lado Yojna
(d) Atmanirbhar Kanya Yojna
6. **When was the women empowerment policy implemented in the state?**
(a) 2011 (b) 2013
(c) 2015 (d) 2017
7. **Bihar Government has made a provision of _______ percent reservation for women in panchayat level elections.**
(a) 30 (b) 40
(c) 50 (d) 60
8. **Since when in Bihar a reservation of 35 percent has been made for women in all the state government's jobs?**
(a) 2013 (b) 2014
(c) 2015 (d) 2016
9. **When was Right to Information Act implemented in Bihar?**
(a) 2004 (b) 2005
(c) 2006 (d) 2007
10. **When was Public Grievances Redressal Act implemented in Bihar?**
(a) 2013 (b) 2014
(c) 2015 (d) 2016
11. **When was the Prohibition Act made operative in the state?**
(a) 1 January 2016
(b) 1 April 2016
(c) 1 August 2016
(d) 1 December 2016
12. **Until when the duration of the Seven Resolves programme remains in the state?**
(a) 2015-17 (b) 2015-18
(c) 2015-19 (d) 2015-20
13. **Which of the following is an element of the Seven Resolve Programme?**
(a) Har Ghar Nal Ka Jal
(b) Avsar Baden Aage Paden
(c) Har Ghar Bijli Lagataar
(d) All of the above

14. Which of the following is not an element of the Seven Resolve Programme?
(a) Har Khet Jal
(b) Aarthik Hal Yuvaon Ka Bal
(c) Aarakshit Rozgar Mahilayon ka Adhikar
(d) Shochalaya Nirman Ghar Ka Samman

15. When was students' credit cards scheme launched under the 'Aarthik Hal Yuvaon Ka Bal' Resolve?
(a) 1 April 2016
(b) 10 May 2016
(c) 15 June 2016
(d) 2 October 2016

16. Since when in Bihar a programme to ensure electricity 24×7 in each home has been launched?
(a) 1 April 2016
(b) 15 May 2016
(c) 15 August 2016
(d) 15 November 2016

17. When was the scheme 'Har Ghar Nal Ka Jal' launched?
(a) 21 January 2016
(b) 1 May 2016
(c) 27 September 2016
(d) 15 November 2016

18. When was the 'Gramin Total Sampark Nishchay Yojna' launched?
(a) 15 March 2016
(b) 10 June 2016
(c) 28 October 2016
(d) 31 December 2016

19. When was 'Lohia Swachch Bihar' programme launched?
(a) 22 March 2016
(b) 1 May 2016
(c) 22 July 2016
(d) 27 September 2016

20. What percentage of reservation of women in government jobs has been provided for in the state under the 'Aarakshit Rozgar Mahilaon ka Adhikar' Scheme?
(a) 30 (b) 35
(c) 40 (d) 45

21. When is Bihar Establishment Day celebrated each year?
(a) 1 January (b) 22 March
(c) 30 June (d) 11 October

22. When was the convention of celebrating Bihar Day started?
(a) 2006 (b) 2008
(c) 2010 (d) 2012

23. Who was appointed the first Governor of the newly constituted Bihar in 1912?
(a) Charles Stuart Bailey
(b) Edward Great
(c) Lee Grand
(d) Norman Lesley

24. Who of the following holds the honour of becoming the first Indian Governor of Bihar?
(a) Fazal Ali
(b) Kedarnath Tripathi
(c) Satyendra Prasann Sinha
(d) Baikunth Shukla

Answers

1. (a) **2.** (a) **3.** (d) **4.** (b) **5.** (b) **6.** (c) **7.** (c) **8.** (d) **9.** (c) **10.** (d)
11. (b) **12.** (d) **13.** (d) **14.** (a) **15.** (d) **16.** (d) **17.** (c) **18.** (c) **19.** (d) **20.** (b)
21. (b) **22.** (c) **23.** (a) **24.** (c)

❑❑❑

Part–II
Practice Questionnaire

Practice Questionnaire

SET-1

1. **Which famous German researcher has done research work on Mithila painting?**
   (a) Buchanan
   (b) Eric Smith
   (c) George Orwell
   (d) Lord Cooper
2. **Which site of Bihar has been included in UNESCO's World Heritage List?**
   (a) Golghar
   (b) Mahabodhi Temple
   (c) Nalanda Mahavihara
   (d) (b) and (c)
3. **Ghodakatora Lake is located in which district?**
   (a) Supaul (b) Gaya
   (c) Nalanda (d) Bhagalpur
4. **On which tree is a worm called lecipher lakka found?**
   (a) Banyan (b) Laquer
   (c) Kadamba (d) Arjuna
5. **The image of a lion in Mithila style is a symbol of -**
   (a) power
   (b) prosperity
   (c) lineage growth
   (d) wealth
6. **Where is the 400 year-old Chaitanya Mahaprabhu Temple located?**
   (a) Gaya (b) Aurangabad
   (c) Patna (d) Munger
7. **One of the 51 Shaktipeeths is the famous Big Patandevi Temple of Mother Durga. Where is it located?**
   (a) Patna (b) Vaishali
   (c) Bhagalpur (d) Ara
8. **Where has Buddha Smriti Park been built?**
   (a) Gaya (b) Nalanda
   (c) Patna (d) Hajipur
9. **When was the Bihar Right to Public Grievances Redressal Act, 2015 constituted?**
   (a) 2015 AD (b) 2016 AD
   (c) 2017 AD (d) 2018 AD
10. **In which year were Begusarai, Munger, Purnia and Katihar granted municipal status?**
    (a) 2005 AD (b) 2007 AD
    (c) 2009 AD (d) 2011 AD
11. **Which temple is named after Ahilya, wife of Gautama Rishi?**
    (a) Ahiroli Temple
    (b) Alodi Temple
    (c) Lahlaura Dham
    (d) Anjani Dham
12. **When did the Bihar Public Service Commission come into existence?**
    (a) 1947 AD (b) 1948 AD
    (c) 1949 AD (d) 1950 AD
13. **Where is the Shiva temple of Koteshwar Nath located?**
    (a) Supaul (b) Arwal
    (c) Jamui (d) Jehanabad

14. Kesaria, where the stupa of Lord Buddha was found after excavation, is located at which of these places?
(a) East Champaran
(b) Katihar
(c) Purnia
(d) Arwal

15. Where is Katra Garh located?
(a) Sitamarhi (b) Shivhar
(c) Saharsa (d) Muzaffarpur

16. Where is the tomb of Malik Ibrahim Bayan located?
(a) Patna (b) Bihar Sharif
(c) Hajipur (d) Muzaffarpur

17. Who was the destroyer of the Mahabodhi tree?
(a) Shashank (b) Pushyagupta
(c) Maitrayani (d) Anantsen

18. In which area was the red sandstone used in the construction of Mauryan palace?
(a) Makrana Coast
(b) Chunar
(c) Takshashila
(d) Katni

19. At the time of which Karnat ruler did the 'register management' develop?
(a) Nanya Dev (b) Gangdev
(c) Harisingh (d) Surya Singh

20. Where is Mundeshwari temple located?
(a) Kaimur (b) Bhojpur
(c) Rohtas (d) Buxar

Answers

1. (b)	2. (d)	3. (c)	4. (b)
5. (a)	6. (c)	7. (a)	8. (c)
9. (a)	10. (c)	11. (a)	12. (c)
13. (d)	14. (a)	15. (d)	16. (b)
17. (a)	18. (b)	19. (c)	20. (a)

SET-2

1. 'Gehu and Gulab' is the work of which litterateur?
(a) Gopal Singh Neeraj
(b) Vidyapati
(c) Nagarjuna
(d) Ramvriksha Benipuri

2. Which of these is known as silk city of Bihar?
(a) Bhagalpur (b) Gaya
(c) Saharsa (d) Madhubani

3. Nakti Lake is located in which district of Bihar?
(a) Munger (b) Patna
(c) Jamui (d) Arwal

4. Who founded the Bihar School of Yoga (Munger)?
(a) Swami Agnivesh
(b) Swami Shraddhananda
(c) Swami Panchanan
(d) Swami Satyananda Saraswati

5. Where is Khanqah established by Hazrat Makhdoomshah in the 13th century located?
(a) Phulwari Sharif
(b) Bihar Sharif
(c) Maner
(d) Hajipur

6. How many national parks are there in Bihar?
(a) 4 (b) 3
(c) 2 (d) 1

7. When was the Student Plantation Scheme launched in Bihar?
(a) 2004 AD (b) 2005 AD
(c) 2006 AD (d) 2007 AD

8. In which financial year was the Bihar Grihasthal Yojana launched by the Government of Bihar?
(a) 2008 AD (b) 2010 AD
(c) 2012 AD (d) 2014 AD

9. Where was the Buddha Smriti Stupa-cum-Samyak Darshan Museum established?

(a) Gaya (b) Vaishali
(c) Munger (d) Arwal

10. The shape of an elephant and a horse in Mithila style is a symbol of?
(a) Opulence (b) Power
(c) Wealth (d) Dynasty Growth

11. Who was the first Chairman of Bihar Public Service Commission?
(a) Talat Azim
(b) Rakesh Upadhyay
(c) Rajdhari Singh
(d) Maheshwar Jha

12. Kakolat Waterfall is located in which district?
(a) Nawada (b) Nalanda
(c) Gaya (d) Vaishali

13. Under whose leadership was the Bihar Yuva Sangh established at the Bihari Students' Conference?
(a) Naveen Kumar
(b) Gayatri Mani Tripathi
(c) Gyan Saha
(d) Abbas Sheikh

14. Birla Temple, Patna was built by?
(a) Mangal Birla
(b) Rajbal Dev Birla
(c) Rahul Birla
(d) Mahendra Birla

15. Which silk worm is reared on the leaves of arjuna tree?
(a) Tasar (b) Lakh
(c) Malabri (d) Cocoon

16. Under which scheme will sewerage treatment plants and improved drainage network be set up in Bihar?
(a) Namami Gange
(b) Saat Nirbhaya Yojana
(c) Swachh Bharat Abhiyan
(d) Smart Ganga City Scheme

17. After which war was the treaty between Lord Clive and Mughal Emperor Shah Alam II signed in Allahabad on 12th August, 1765 AD?
(a) Plassey War (b) Chausa War
(c) Buxar War (d) Chanderi War

18. Which mineral produces Sulphur?
(a) Pyrite (b) Bellenite
(c) Asbestos (d) Ilmenite

19. Which Buddhist stupa is also known as The Deora of King Ben?
(a) Kesaria (b) Rampurwa
(c) Nandangarh (d) Gaya

20. Where is the Ahiroli Temple located?
(a) Kaimur (b) Bhojpur
(c) Buxar (d) Gaya

Answers

1. (d)	**2.** (a)	**3.** (c)	**4.** (d)
5. (a)	**6.** (d)	**7.** (c)	**8.** (c)
9. (b)	**10.** (a)	**11.** (c)	**12.** (a)
13. (c)	**14.** (b)	**15.** (a)	**16.** (d)
17. (d)	**18.** (a)	**19.** (a)	**20.** (c)

SET-3

1. Padma Shri Siya Devi, Kaushalya Devi, Ganga Devi, Jagadamba Devi, Bhagwati Devi, Maina Devi, Lal Baba and Shashikala Devi are prominent artists of which art?
(a) Patna Kalam
(b) Manjusha style
(c) Madhubani Painting
(d) (a), (b) and (c)

2. Which artist from Bihar has been exhibited in Japan?
(a) Kaushalya Devi
(b) Shashikala Devi
(c) Jagadamba Devi
(d) Maina Devi

3. Which fish has been declared as the state fish of Bihar?
(a) Mriga (b) Rohu
(c) Katla (d) Mangur

4. Which Muslim ruler abolished the pilgrimage tax?
(a) Sher Shah
(b) Akbar
(c) Mohd Bin Tughlaq
(d) Shah Alam-II

5. What is the name of the Maithili writer who won the Sahitya Akademi Award for the year 2000 for his first book?
(a) Ratanesh Jha
(b) Saket Upadhyay
(c) Saket Nandan
(d) Chandrabhan Mishra

6. In which soil is the excess of iron found?
(a) Alluvial (b) Black
(c) Balther (d) Red Yellow

7. In which inscription does Ashoka mention the casualties of Kalinga war?
(a) Vanshila Rajadesh
(b) Paramadesh
(c) Adhikaar Prichcha
(d) Rajpatra Sankalp

8. The name of the state is represented on the nameplate of vehicles of Bihar in which letters?
(a) BA (b) BH
(c) BR (d) BI

9. According to which scholar, the main reason for the Kalinga war was to capture the elephant area?
(a) Ashwasen (b) Kautilya
(c) Kalhan (d) Aryabhata

10. Udaipur Lake is located in which of the following districts?
(a) West Champaran
(b) Gaya
(c) Arwal
(d) Jamui

11. Which rebellion is called 'Ganga-narayana's Hungama'?
(a) Chero Rebellion
(b) Bhumij Rebellion
(c) Santhal Rebellion
(d) Munda Rebellion

12. In which financial year was the Bihar Veterinary University Bill, 2016 notified?
(a) 2015–16 AD
(b) 2016–17 AD
(c) 2017–18 AD
(d) 2018–19 AD

13. In which year did the Prince of Wales come to Patna?
(a) 1917 AD (b) 1919 AD
(c) 1921 AD (d) 1920 AD

14. When was Santhal Pargana district established?
(a) 1855 AD (b) 1856 AD
(c) 1857 AD (d) 1858 AD

15. Which Indian was appointed by Robert Clive as Naib Diwan of Bihar?
(a) Sitab Roy
(b) Jaglal Chaudhary
(c) Mir Jafar
(d) Pir Ali

16. For which project was an agreement signed between Nepal and India in 1959 AD?
(a) Kosi (b) Gandak
(c) Bagmati (d) Ghaghra

17. Under which project has Hanuman Nagar Barrier Dam been constructed?
(a) Son (b) Gandak
(c) Kosi (d) Kamala

18. Which stone site is known as Shwetpur, Kotigram, Kushpallava, Vishalanagari etc.
(a) Chechar (b) Hastinapur
(c) Kumharar (d) Lauria Areraj

19. When is Bihar Prithvi Diwas celebrated?
(a) 8th March (b) 9th June
(c) 9th August (d) 11th September

20. **Which Pal ruler donated 200 villages to Nalanda Mahavihara?**
(a) Devpal (b) Dharmapal
(c) Anantpal (d) Mihir Pal

Answers

1. (c)	**2.** (b)	**3.** (d)	**4.** (b)
5. (c)	**6.** (d)	**7.** (a)	**8.** (c)
9. (b)	**10.** (a)	**11.** (b)	**12.** (b)
13. (c)	**14.** (b)	**15.** (a)	**16.** (b)
17. (c)	**18.** (a)	**19.** (c)	**20.** (b)

SET-4

1. **Which pal ruler is called the second founder of pal dynasty?**
(a) Dharampal (b) Devpal
(c) Mahipal (d) Anantpal

2. **What was the name of the Pal ruler who defeated Vatsaraj, the anti-hara ruler, and the Rashtrakuta ruler Dhruv?**
(a) Anantpal (b) Mahipal
(c) Dharampal (d) Devpal

3. **Which book has the early history of the arrival of Turks in India?**
(a) Tabkate-Nasiri
(b) Tabkate-Hind
(c) Chachanama
(d) Badshahnama

4. **Which practice was prohibited by enacting a law in Akbar's time?**
(a) Caste System
(b) Sati System
(c) Purdah System
(d) (a), (b) and (c)

5. **Which famous Iranian traveler visited Saif Khan's Madrasa (Patna) in 1807 AD?**
(a) Mullah Takiya
(b) Mullah Bahbahani
(c) Ahmed Bahani
(d) Abdul Razzaq

6. **Which famous German researcher has done research work on Mithila painting?**
(a) Eric Smith
(b) James Motis
(c) David Moon
(d) George Cunningham

7. **Which king is called 'Kali's ka ansh,' Sarvakshatrantak,' the second incarnation of Parshuram, Bhargava, Ekrat, etc.**
(a) Ghanananda
(b) Kalashok
(c) Ajatshatru
(d) Mahapadamananda

8. **Name the kind who shifted the capital of Magadha from Vaishali to Patliputra.**
(a) Shishunag (b) Ajatshatru
(c) Kalashok (d) Brihadratha

9. **Which king first made Pataliputra the capital of Magadha?**
(a) Ajatshatru (b) Kalashok
(c) Udayeen (d) Ashoka

10. **Which king established Pataliputra?**
(a) Udayeen
(b) Bimbisara
(c) Ajatshatru
(d) Chandragupta Maurya

11. **Bhagva chaur is located in which district of Bihar?**
(a) Supaul (b) Arwal
(c) Saharsa (d) Nalanda

12. **Which ruler is known as the founder of the Second Afghan Empire?**
(a) Ahmed Shah
(b) Sher Shah
(c) Gufran Afghani
(d) Bakhtiyar Khijali

13. **Which ruler is called the forerunner of Akbar?**
(a) Sher Shah
(b) Balaban

(c) Qutubuddin Aibak
(d) Mahmud Ghaznavi

14. Nalanda University was established through the efforts of which ruler?
(a) Samudragupta
(b) Chandragupta II
(c) Kumargupta
(d) Kunal Gupta

15. During whose reign, did the 12 years of severe famine occur in Magadha?
(a) Ajatshatru
(b) Bimbisara
(c) Chandragupta Maurya
(d) Ashoka

16. What was the name of the ruler who gave the kingdom of Magadha the glory of an empire?
(a) Bimbisara
(b) Chandragupta Maurya
(c) Ashoka
(d) Ajatshatru

17. Pataliputra was named after which ruler of Patna?
(a) Akbar (b) Aurangzeb
(c) Sher Shah (d) Jahangir

18. Which ruler reinstalled Pataliputra as the capital and Pataliputra remained the capital of the Magadha Empire?
(a) Shashank (b) Shishunag
(c) Brihadratha (d) Kalashok

19. Sher Shah's tomb at Sasaram is the best specimen of which style?
(a) Greek Style
(b) Iranian Style
(c) Afghani style
(d) Italian style

20. Which sect developed charvaka philosophy?
(a) Lokayat (b) Ajeevak
(c) Shaiva (d) Vaishnava

Answers

1. (c)	**2.** (c)	**3.** (a)	**4.** (b)
5. (c)	**6.** (a)	**7.** (d)	**8.** (a)
9. (c)	**10.** (a)	**11.** (c)	**12.** (b)
13. (a)	**14.** (c)	**15.** (c)	**16.** (a)
17. (c)	**18.** (d)	**19.** (c)	**20.** (a)

SET-5

1. Graphite is found in which district in Bihar?
(a) Gaya (b) Jamui
(c) Munger (d) Buxar

2. Which Mughal emperor was formally crowned in Patna?
(a) Parvez
(b) Shah Alam-II
(c) Farukkhkhasiyar
(d) Bahadur Shah Zafar

3. Which litterateur is called Premchand of Bihar?
(a) Mandan Mishra
(b) Vidyapati
(c) Bhikhari Thakur
(d) Anuplal Mandal

4. Where is the Gupta dham located?
(a) Bhojpur (b) Rohtas
(c) Gaya (d) Aurangabad

5. Bihar Students' Council was organized by which freedom fighter?
(a) Rajendra Prasad
(b) Majhrul Haque
(c) Shri Krishna Singh
(d) Anugrah Narayan Singh

6. Which column article is called 'Rani ka Abhilekh'?
(a) Bairath Articles
(b) Areraj Articles
(c) Allahabad Articles
(d) Junagadh Articles

7. Which park has been made the first plastic prohibited area of the state?

(a) Sanjay Gandhi Organic Park
(b) Buddha Organic Garden
(c) Chanakya Organic Garden
(d) (a), (b) and (c)

8. In which park is Asia's largest center of rhino breeding and the second largest Centre in the world established?
(a) Indira Gandhi Organic Park
(b) Mahatma Gandhi Organic Park
(c) Jawaharlal Nehru Organic Park
(d) Sanjay Gandhi Organic Park

9. In which decade was the population growth rate of the State negative (-0.97 percent)?
(a) 1901–11 AD
(b) 1911–21 AD
(c) 1921–31 AD
(d) 1931–41 AD

10. Which country's border is connected to the State of Bihar?
(a) Nepal (b) Bangladesh
(c) Bhutan (d) Myanmar

11. In which year did mahila samakhya get autonomy in the name of Bihar Mahila Samakhya Society?
(a) 2002 AD (b) 2004 AD
(c) 2006 AD (d) 2008 AD

12. In which year was the State Directorate of Archaeology established?
(a) 1956 AD (b) 1958 AD
(c) 1960 AD (d) 1962 AD

13. Jarasandha was the most famous king of which dynasty?
(a) Brihadratha (b) Hariyank
(c) Kanva (d) Shunga

14. The golden age of Mithila is called the reign of which dynasty?
(a) Sen dynasty
(b) Karnat dynasty
(c) Pala Dynasty
(d) Gupta Dynasty

15. Kaushiki is the brand name of which item?
(a) silk thread
(b) jute products
(c) Mangoes of Bihar
(d) Litchi of Muzaffarpur

16. What kind of forest is kept under government protection?
(a) Reserved Forest
(b) Safe Forest
(c) Protected Forest
(d) Mixed Forest

17. In which Jain Literature, the 16 'mahajanapadas' were described for the first time?
(a) Shatpath Brahmin
(b) Aranyaka
(c) Bodh Charitra
(d) Bhagwati Sutra

18. The naked strike (1930 AD) was conducted by the prisoners of which jail?
(a) Patna Jail (b) Chhapra Jail
(c) Ranchi Jail (d) Hazaribagh Jail

19. Bhikhari Thakur, the famous folk poet of Bihar, is the author of which play?
(a) Desh Pardesh
(b) Chhaila Bihari
(c) Videshiya
(d) Samman

20. How many Shaktipeeths are there in Bihar?
(a) 7 (b) 8
(c) 9 (d) 10

Answers

1. (b)	**2.** (c)	**3.** (d)	**4.** (b)
5. (a)	**6.** (c)	**7.** (a)	**8.** (d)
9. (b)	**10.** (a)	**11.** (c)	**12.** (d)
13. (a)	**14.** (b)	**15.** (a)	**16.** (b)
17. (d)	**18.** (b)	**19.** (c)	**20.** (d)

SET-6

1. **Which river is known as Sum-agadhi?**
(a) Niranjana (b) Kosi
(c) Sakri (d) Sone
2. **Which river is known as Lakhandei and Karanali?**
(a) Ghaghra (b) Sone
(c) Gandak (d) Sakri
3. **Indrapuri Barrage was constructed in 1968 AD on which river?**
(a) Ganga (b) Bagmati
(c) Kosi (d) Sone
4. **Which city was called 'siraj of India'?**
(a) Jaunpur (b) Hyderabad
(c) Ahmednagar (d) Bihar Sharif
5. **The shape of fish in Mithila style is a symbol of**
(a) Opulence (b) Orgasm
(c) Strength (d) Descent Growth
6. **Actress Sonakshi Sinha is the daughter of which actor from Bihar?**
(a) Shekhar Suman
(b) Kunal
(c) Shatrughan Sinha
(d) Prakash Sinha
7. **In which record are the various achievements of Rudradaman - I mentioned?**
(a) Bhabru (b) Kalinga
(c) Jaunpur (d) Junagadh
8. **In which record is Ashoka called Buddha Shakya?**
(a) Warat (b) Junagadh
(c) Maski (d) Amravati
9. **Ashoka is called 'Priyadarshi' in which record?**
(a) Bhabru (b) Lauria Areraj
(c) Maski (d) Gurjara
10. **At what age did Parsvanatha leave home?**
(a) 26 years (b) 28 years
(c) 30 years (d) 32 years
11. **Under which article does the Governor recommend president's rule in a state to the President?**
(a) Article-350 (b) Article-352
(c) Article-354 (d) Article-356
12. **National Emergency is declared by the President of India under which article?**
(a) Article-352 (b) Article-354
(c) Article-356 (d) Article-358
13. **In which book was compiled Tritiya Buddhist music?**
(a) Sutta Pitak
(b) Vinay Pitak
(c) Abhidhamma Pitak
(d) (a), (b) and (c)
14. **In which book is the law of Buddhism described?**
(a) Vinay Pitak
(b) Bhagwati Sutra
(c) Khuddak Sanstha
(d) Jataka Katha
15. **In which book is the philosophical interpretation of Buddhism given?**
(a) Sutta Pitak
(b) Abhidhamma Pitak
(c) Vinay Pitak
(d) Bhagwati Sutra
16. **In which book mahajanapadas were known for the first time?**
(a) Jataka Katha
(b) Angutar Sanstha
(c) Bhagwati Sutra
(d) (b) and (c)
17. **Which folk poet is known as Kalidasa of Bihar?**
(a) Vidyapati
(b) Bhikhari Thakur
(c) Mandan Mishra
(d) Ramdhari Singh Dinkar

18. During which Lodhi ruler's tenure did Subedar Daria Khan Nouhani of Bihar revolt?
(a) Bahlol Lodhi
(b) Sikander Lodhi
(c) Ibrahim Lodhi
(d) Ahmed Lodhi

19. Which article shows that Ashoka had set up separate hospitals for humans and animals?
(a) Junagadh Article
(b) Lauria Areraj Article
(c) Vairat Article
(d) Girnar Article

20. On whose advice does the Governor appoint other members of the Council of Ministers?
(a) Chief Minister
(b) Council of Ministers
(c) Speaker of the Legislative Assembly
(d) All of the above

Answers

1. (c)	**2.** (a)	**3.** (d)	**4.** (a)
5. (b)	**6.** (c)	**7.** (d)	**8.** (c)
9. (a)	**10.** (c)	**11.** (d)	**12.** (a)
13. (c)	**14.** (a)	**15.** (b)	**16.** (d)
17. (b)	**18.** (c)	**19.** (d)	**20.** (a)

SET-7

1. Which ruler also called Sinhasen?
(a) Ajatshatru (b) Bimbisara
(c) Ashoka (d) Bindusar

2. Which queen has other names like Bimba, Gopa, Bhadrakcha etc.
(a) Trishala (b) Sanghmitra
(c) Yashodhara (d) Chelna

3. The shape of bamboo in Mithila style is a symbol of
(a) Progeny (b) Orgasm
(c) Power (d) Wealth

4. The second session of Bihar provincial congress was held by whose efforts?
(a) Rajendra Prasad
(b) Deepnarayan Singh
(c) Shri Krishna Singh
(d) Hasan Imam

5. In which agricultural sub-zone does the monsoon first fall in the state?
(a) Zone-I (b) Zone-II
(c) Zone-III (d) Zone-IV.

6. Jayprakash Narayan International Airport is located in which district?
(a) Patna (b) Saran
(c) Gaya (d) Bhagalpur

7. Kaushal was finally merged in Magadha during whose reign?
(a) Bimbisara (b) Ajatshatru
(c) Ghanananda (d) Ashoka

8. Chandragupta Maurya is said to be the liberator of India for liberation from whom?
(a) Greeks (b) Aryans
(c) Turks (d) Iranians

9. Which type of airport is Chunapur Airport of Purnia?
(a) Defence (b) Trade
(c) Tourism (d) All of these

10. When did Bihar Bandhu, the first Hindi newspaper of Bihar, start?
(a) 1870 AD (b) 1872 AD
(c) 1874 AD (d) 1876 AD

11. Who was the first to give information about Bodhi temple and granite railing stated to be built in Bodh Gaya?
(a) Buchanan (b) Cunningham
(c) Eric Smith (d) Lee Grand

12. The important historical book 'Khulast-Ut-Tawarikh' is the creation of
(a) Khudabakhsh Khan
(b) Kalyan Singh
(c) Mir Baki
(d) Shah Alam-II

13. Which ruler held the title of Hazrat-e-Ala after becoming the ruler of Bihar?
(a) Shah Alam-II
(b) Farukkhasier
(c) Sher Shah
(d) Rajkumar Parvez

14. Who founded the Singh Pillar at Vaishali?
(a) Ajatshatru (b) Ashoka
(c) Kalashok (d) Shishunag

15. Who burnt Nalanda university and destroyed it?
(a) Shashank
(b) Balaban
(c) Bakhtiyar Khilji
(d) Iltutmish

16. How many environmentally sensitive areas have been earmarked by the State Government to protect wildlife, water birds and environment?
(a) 11 (b) 12
(c) 13 (d) 14

17. After how many years of rigorous penance did Mahavir attain knowledge?
(a) 10 (b) 12
(c) 14 (d) 16

18. Which British ruler wrote a comment on the situation in India during British rule?
(a) Catherine Mayo
(b) Eldus Huxley
(c) Charles Andrews
(d) (a), (b) and (c)

19. Who is called the father of Indian archaeology?
(a) Eric Smith
(b) George Mason
(c) Cunningham
(d) John Cooper

20. Who built the Fort-e-Kuhn Masjid and where?
(a) Sher Shah-Delhi
(b) Parvez-Patna
(c) Aurangzeb-Delhi
(d) Balaban-Hisar

Answers

1. (d)	**2.** (c)	**3.** (a)	**4.** (b)
5. (b)	**6.** (a)	**7.** (b)	**8.** (a)
9. (a)	**10.** (c)	**11.** (b)	**12.** (b)
13. (c)	**14.** (b)	**15.** (c)	**16.** (c)
17. (b)	**18.** (d)	**19.** (c)	**20.** (a)

SET-8

1. Which is the caste festival of the Brahmin community of Mithila?
(a) Sahodra (b) Kojgara
(c) Mohgra (d) Jogra

2. Purnia district falls in which earthquake affected zone?
(a) Zone-2 (b) Zone-3
(c) Zone-4 (d) Zone-5

3. Which king is known by the names sandrocoats, androcoats, sandrocopus etc.
(a) Ajatshatru
(b) Ashoka
(c) Chandragupta Maurya
(d) Kumargupta

4. The shape of banana in Mithila style is a symbol of
(a) fleshliness (b) opulence
(c) orgasm (d) power

5. Which city in the state was granted municipal status in August 2016?
(a) Sivan (b) Chhapra
(c) Gopalganj (d) Shivhar

6. How many times did Rabri Devi become the Chief Minister of Bihar?
(a) 1 (b) 2
(c) 3 (d) 4

7. Shiva Temple, Bekatpur was built by

(a) Man Singh
(b) Hari Singh
(c) Kalyan Singh
(d) Surya Singh

8. Which model was selected as 'MTV India's Next Model' of Bihar in 2016?
(a) Bhudev Dutt
(b) Pranti Rai
(c) Adila Ali
(d) Reshma Jha

9. Who became the first Governor of Bihar in independent India?
(a) Ramaiah Patnaik
(b) Jairam Das Daulat Ram
(c) Shubhendu Chatterjee
(d) Shafi Ahmed

10. What was the name of Vidyapati's mother?
(a) Hasini Devi
(b) Prabhavati Devi
(c) Jagmati Devi
(d) Madhurani Devi

11. When was Mithila Sanskrit Vidyapeeth established?
(a) 1949 AD (b) 1951 AD
(c) 1953 AD (d) 1955 AD

12. In which district was the first sugar mill of Bihar established?
(a) East Champaran
(b) West Champaran
(c) Supaul
(d) Katihar

13. In how many districts of the State of Bihar has Mission Indra Dhanush been launched?
(a) 13 (b) 14
(c) 15 (d) 16

14. In which district of Bihar is the highest cultivation of barley?
(a) Patna
(b) Gaya
(c) East Champaran
(d) Vaishali

15. Where is the Mangala Gauri temple, the main shaktipeeth of Hindus, located?
(a) Aurangabad
(b) Gaya
(c) Kaimur
(d) Dandy

16. Which river is known as Hiranyawah and Sonbhadra?
(a) Kosi (b) Sone
(c) Gandak (d) Ganga

17. What is meaning of Bihar in Hindi language?
(a) Chaitra
(b) Buddhist Monastery
(c) Shaktipeeth
(d) University

18. Which river is considered impure or inauspicious according to Hindu religious belief?
(a) Karmanasha
(b) Niranjana
(c) Sakri
(d) Sariswan

19. In which city has the industry been set up under the name of Hindustan Fertilizers Limited?
(a) Begusarai
(b) Aurangabad
(c) Barauni
(d) Muzaffarpur

20. When and where was Bhikhari Thakur born?
(a) 1887 AD Saran
(b) 1885 AD Sivan
(c) 1883 AD Gopalganj
(d) 1881 AD Supaul

Answers

1. (b)	**2.** (d)	**3.** (c)	**4.** (a)
5. (b)	**6.** (a)	**7.** (a)	**8.** (d)
9. (b)	**10.** (a)	**11.** (b)	**12.** (a)
13. (b)	**14.** (c)	**15.** (b)	**16.** (b)
17. (b)	**18.** (a)	**19.** (c)	**20.** (a)

SET-9

1. **At which place does a grand and huge fair take place during Pitru Paksha?**
(a) Aurangabad (b) Supaul
(c) Madhubani (d) Gaya

2. **Where was the Delhi-Meerut column article earlier?**
(a) Meerut (b) Lahore
(c) Allahabad (d) Amravati

3. **The Princely State Tenancy Act is known as which other Act?**
(a) mahalwadi law
(b) ryotwadi law
(c) bataydari law
(d) bhu-sudhar law

4. **When was the Reserve Bank established?**
(a) 1931 AD (b) 1933 AD
(c) 1935 AD (d) 1937 AD

5. **109 paintings of Thangka painting style are preserved in which museum in the state of Bihar?**
(a) Patna (b) Gaya
(c) Vaishali (d) Darbhanga

6. **What type of style is called thangka style?**
(a) Rajput style (b) Tibetan style
(c) Greek style (d) Mughal style

7. **Shishunag was 'Amatya' of which district?**
(a) Kashi (b) Ujjain
(c) Amravati (d) Mathura

8. **Who was the best ruler of the Shishunag dynasty?**
(a) Ajatshatru (b) Bimbisara
(c) Kalashok (d) Udayan

9. **The figure of swan and peacock in Mithila style is a symbol of**
(a) Wealth (b) Peace
(c) Meditation (d) Life style

10. **Who was his charioteer at the time of Siddhartha's renunciation?**
(a) Bhatri (b) Upali
(c) Chhandak d) Kushan

11. **What was the name of the horse that was with Siddhartha at the time of his renunciation?**
(a) Kanthak (b) Chetak
(c) Apran (d) Grahan

12. **Where was Sidhu and Kanhu hanged?**
(a) Khuti (b) Berhet
(c) Chutu Pali (d) Dhurwa

13. **Which festival is celebrated on the occasion of the birth anniversary of Guru Govind Singh, the 10th Guru of Sikhs?**
(a) Prakash Parv (b) Gyan Parv
(c) Teej Parv (d) Satya Parv

14. **Which crop does the farmer produce with paddy in irrigated areas?**
(a) Mustard (b) Sugarcane
(c) wheat (d) Barley

15. **Where is Simaria Mela held in Bihar?**
(a) Gaya (b) Barauni
(c) Madhubani (d) Saharsa

16. **What was the name of Vidyapati's father?**
(a) Ganesh Thakur
(b) Shiva Shankar Thakur
(c) Ganpati Thakur
(d) Laxman Thakur

17. **What is the purpose of Akshara Aanchal Scheme starting from 17th September, 2009 AD?**
(a) Increase in female literacy
(b) Making women self-reliant
(c) Free legal aid to women
(d) All three of them (a), (b) and (c)

18. **Where is Chinnamastika Temple, Ucchaith located?**
(a) Aurangabad (b) Gaya
(c) Madhubani (d) Buxar

19. **Who was the first ruler of Bihar to sit on the throne of Delhi?**
(a) Ibrahim Shah
(b) Islam Shah
(c) Sheikh Ismat Khan
(d) Sher Shah

20. **How many times has President's rule been imposed in Bihar so far?**
(a) 6 times (b) 7 times
(c) 8 times (d) 9 times

Answers

1. (d)	**2.** (a)	**3.** (c)	**4.** (c)
5. (a)	**6.** (b)	**7.** (a)	**8.** (c)
9. (b)	**10.** (c)	**11.** (a)	**12.** (b)
13. (a)	**14.** (c)	**15.** (b)	**16.** (c)
17. (a)	**18.** (c)	**19.** (d)	**20.** (c)

SET-10

1. **Delhi-Meerut Column article was brought to Delhi by**
(a) Sher Shah
(b) Balaban
(c) Akbar
(d) Feroz Shah Tughlaq

2. **Azad Squad was formed by whom in Bihar?**
(a) Rajendra Prasad
(b) Rajendra Singh
(c) Jai Prakash Narayan
(d) Amar Singh

3. **Where is Vishnupad temple located?**
(a) Sivan (b) Gaya
(c) Banka (d) Kaimur

4. **Where was the world's first republic established?**
(a) Greece (b) Italy
(c) Bihar (d) Andhra Pradesh

5. **Where is the world's tallest World Peace Stupa located in Bihar?**
(a) Rajgir (b) Kesaria
(c) Vaishali (d) Patna

6. **Where is the Paddy Bill introduced after it is passed in the Bihar Legislative Assembly?**
(a) Legislative Council
(b) Rajya Sabha
(c) Lok Sabha
(d) (b) and (c)

7. **Where was the world's first democratic republic established?**
(a) Anga (b) Kashi
(c) Magadha (d) Vajji

8. **Where is Chandragupta Basadi temple located?**
(a) Amravati
(b) Gaya
(c) Allahabad
(d) Shravanabelagola

9. **Who can dissolve the Assembly?**
(a) Governor
(b) President
(c) Chief Minister
(d) Prime Minister

10. **Where is Vikramshila Mahotsav held in Bihar?**
(a) Supaul (b) Vaishali
(c) Bhagalpur (d) Bhojpur

11. **After at least how many days of prior notice of passing of no-confidence motion can the Speaker and the Deputy Speaker be removed from office?**
(a) 12 days (b) 14 days
(c) 16 days (d) 18 days

12. **In which language are the famous works of Vidyapati composed?**
(a) Maghi (b) Bhojpuri
(c) Angika (d) Maithili

13. **When does the Sonpur Mela take place at the confluence of river Ganga and Gandak in north Bihar?**
(a) Chaitra (b) Vaisakh
(c) Sawan (d) Karthik

14. Who did the work of educating Vidyapati?
(a) Mandan Mishra
(b) Hari Mishra
(c) Devdutt Mishra
(d) Kailash Jha

15. The shape of sun and moon in Mithila style is a symbol of
(a) Peace (b) Progress
(c) Courage (d) Life

16. When did the Battle of Plassey between Sirajuddaula and the British occur?
(a) 1753 AD (b) 1755 AD
(c) 1757 AD (d) 1759 AD

17. Which one State and which one country benefit from Kosi project?
(a) Bihar-Nepal
(b) Uttar Pradesh-Nepal
(c) West Bengal -Bangladesh
(d) Sikkim-Nepal

18. When has the Madhyanan Bhojan Yojana been launched for schools?
(a) 1991 AD (b) 1993 AD
(c) 1995 AD (d) 1997 AD

19. After the partition of the state, the area of Bihar has reduced to how many square kilometer?
(a) 90,414 (b) 91,840
(c) 93,011 (d) 94,163

20. What was dar-ul-safa established by Feroz Tughlaq?
(a) hospital
(b) restaurant
(c) orphanage
(d) employment office

Answers

1. (d)	**2.** (a)	**3.** (b)	**4.** (c)
5. (a)	**6.** (a)	**7.** (d)	**8.** (d)
9. (a)	**10.** (c)	**11.** (b)	**12.** (d)
13. (d)	**14.** (c)	**15.** (a)	**16.** (c)
17. (a)	**18.** (c)	**19.** (d)	**20.** (a)

SET-11

1. Increase in posts in administrative departments takes place with the consent of which department?
(a) Home department
(b) Finance department
(c) Chief Minister's office
(d) Both (a) and (b)

2. In the court of which king of Videha did Yagyavalkya and his wife Maitreyi live?
(a) Janaka (b) Siddhartha
(c) Dasharatha (d) Lakshman

3. The world's first republic was established in Vaishali by
(a) pal (b) sen
(c) lichchavi (d) gupt

4. Who is the Chairman of District Disaster Management Authority?
(a) deputy commissioner
(b) district magistrate
(c) district collector
(d) police captain

5. Vishnupad temple was newly constructed by
(a) Ahilya Bai (b) Lakshmi Bai
(c) Karnavati (d) Durgavati

6. Mahatma Gandhi Setu, one of the longest road bridges in the world, is located in which state of India?
(a) Bihar
(b) Assam
(c) Goa
(d) Arunachal Pradesh

7. Annual Finance Report of the Legislature is submitted by
(a) Governor
(b) Chief Minister
(c) Finance Minister
(d) Chief Election Commissioner

8. Where was the great mathematician Aryabhata born?

(a) Shravasti (b) Kusumpur
(b) Pavapuri (d) Gaya

9. Vikramshila Mahavihara was founded by which Pal ruler?
(a) Dharmapala (b) Devpal
(b) Gopal (d) Mahipal

10. A nominated member of the Assembly is nominated by
(a) President
(b) Prime Minister
(c) Chief Minister
(d) Governor

11. Which state is located to the east of Bihar?
(a) Jharkhand (b) West Bengal
(c) Odisha (d) Chhattisgarh

12. Where is Vikramshila Ganga Dolphin Sanctuary located?
(a) Patna (b) Munger
(c) Buxar (d) Bhagalpur

13. Which river divides the northern plains of Bihar into two parts?
(a) Kosi (b) Bagmati
(c) Kamla (d) Balaan

14. What is the conqueror called in Jainism?
(a) Bhratra (b) Vairagya
(c) Vitarag (d) Sampath

15. Vinay Pitak has been compiled by
(a) Upali (b) Jamali
(c) Anand (d) Ajitam

16. Which river in Bihar often changes its path?
(a) Bagmati (b) Ganga
(c) Kosi (d) Son

17. In which year was Chirand excavated?
(a) 1960 AD (b) 1962 AD
(c) 1964 AD (d) 1966 AD

18. In which year was the Chakbandi Act passed in Bihar?
(a) 1950 AD (b) 1952 AD
(c) 1954 AD (d) 1956 AD

19. Chirand is situated on the banks of which river 11km southeast of Chhapra?
(a) Ganga (b) Balan
(c) Niranjana (d) Ghaghara

20. At what level the target of setting up e-Kisan Bhawan is set out in Bihar?
(a) village level
(b) block level
(c) Divisional Level
(d) District Level

Answers

1. (b)	**2.** (a)	**3.** (c)	**4.** (c)
5. (a)	**6.** (a)	**7.** (a)	**8.** (b)
9. (a)	**10.** (d)	**11.** (b)	**12.** (d)
13. (b)	**14.** (c)	**15.** (a)	**16.** (c)
17. (b)	**18.** (d)	**19.** (a)	**20.** (b)

SET-12

1. According to Tibetan historian Tara Nath, Gopal belonged to which clan?
(a) Kshatriya (b) Brahmin
(c) Vaishya (d) Shudra

2. Which is the river formed by seven streams?
(a) Sone (b) Bagmati
(c) Kosi (d) Niranjana

3. Who is the Head of District Planning and Development Council?
(a) district collector
(b) police captain
(c) district councilor
(d) district development officer

4. In which year was the Land Reforms Act passed in the State?
(a) 1948 AD (b) 1949 AD
(c) 1950 AD (d) 1951 AD

5. Who is the head of district administration?
(a) police captain
(b) district development officer
(c) district collector
(d) deputy commissioner

6. Where is the evidence of the hegemony of the gahadwalas on Bihar?
(a) Maner (b) Sasaram
(c) Buxar (d) Aurangabad

7. Which district has the highest irrigation by tube wells in Bihar?
(a) Gaya (b) Bhojpur
(c) Sivan (d) Patna

8. Which river originates from the hills of Someshwar?
(a) Gandak (b) old Gandak
(c) Bagmati (d) Kosi

9. Which traveller coming to Bihar was the Ambassador of Seleucus?
(a) Hawkins (b) Megasthenes .
(c) Tomas Roe (d) Rolf Fitch .

10. Which state is located on the southern border of the State of Bihar?
(a) Jharkhand
(b) Odisha
(c) West Bengal
(d) Uttar Pradesh

11. When was Vikramshila Ganga Dolphin Sanctuary established?
(a) 1986 AD (b) 1988 AD
(c) 1990 AD (d) 1992 AD

12. Which river is the second name of The river Karanali?
(a) Ghaghara (b) Falgu
(c) Punpun (d) Niranjana

13. Which National Highway is known as Grand Trunk Road?
(a) NH-7 (b) NH-5
(c) NH-4 (d) NH-2

14. Which district has the highest irrigation area from canals in Bihar?
(a) Rohtas (b) Gaya
(c) Buxar (d) Bhojpur

15. When was the literacy campaign launched in Bihar?
(a)1973 AD (b) 1975 AD
(c)1977 AD (d) 1979 AD

16. Which university has the distinction of being the first university of Bihar?
(a) Bihar University
(b) Magadh University
(c) Patna University
(d) Gaya University

17. What is the level in the proposed structure of the Panchayat State in the Bihar Panchayat State Act, 1993?
(a) Two tier (b) Three tier
(c) Four Tier (d) Five Tier

18. After which ruler's name, is Chirand named?
(a) Cher ruler (b) Sen ruler
(c) Gupta Ruler (d) Mauryan Ruler

19. Who is the creator of the 'Gita Mystery'?
(a) Rajendra Prasad
(b) Hassan Imam
(c) Shri Krishna Singh
(d) Bal Gangadhar Tilak

20. The Lagui dance style is mainly associated with which state?
(a) Jharkhand
(b) Bihar
(c) Uttar Pradesh
(d) Bengal

Answers

1. (a)	**2.** (c)	**3.** (d)	**4.** (c)
5. (c)	**6.** (a)	**7.** (d)	**8.** (b)
9. (b)	**10.** (a)	**11.** (c)	**12.** (a)
13. (d)	**14.** (a)	**15.** (c)	**16.** (c)
17. (b)	**18.** (a)	**19.** (d)	**20.** (b)

SET-13

1. Lothal was a port of which civilization?
(a) Harappan
(b) Egupt
(c) China
(d) Mesopotamia

2. Which king of Magadha was a contemporary of Alexander the Great?
(a) Ajatshatru (b) Bimbisara
(c) Ghanananda (d) Ashoka

3. Anand Kumar is the founder of which coaching institute?
(a) Super-20 (b) Super-30
(c) Super-40 (d) Super-50

4. Kautilya belonged to which university?
(a) Nalanda (b) Vikramshila
(c) Takshashila (d) Odantpuri

5. How many States is Bihar surrounded by?
(a) 3 (b) 4
(c) 5 (d) 6

6. What is the meaning of nigranthi?
(a) sin free (b) to do virtue
(c) bondage Free (d) Sainthood

7. Which is the position of Bihar in the country according to sex ratio?
(a) 22nd (b) 23rd
(c) 24th (d) 25th

8. Which Gupta ruler is called Lichchavi Douhitra?
(a) Chandragupta II
(b) Samudragupta
(c) Kumargupta
(d) Kunalgupta

9. Bimbisara or Shrenik of the Haryak dynasty was the founder of which empire?
(a) Magadha Empire
(b) Lichchavi Empire
(c) Ang Empire
(d) Vajji Empire

10. The great astrologer of India, Aryabhata has a close relationship with which city of Bihar?
(a) Gaya (b) Pavapuri
(c) Nalanda (d) Pataliputra

11. Basatin-al-uns is a valuable source in respect of which region of Bihar?
(a) Tirhut (b) Patna
(c) Kosi (d) Bhagalpur

12. Shuddhodhana was the king of which kingdom?
(a) Vajji (b) Ang
(c) Kapilavastu (d) Magadha

13. Which dynasty ruled the Magadha Empire after the Haryak dynasty?
(a) kanva (b) shishunag
(c) Maurya (d) Shunga

14. Who was the famous physician of Ayurveda in the Gupta period?
(a) Jeevak (b) Charak
(c) Dhanwantari (d) Lilavati

15. Who killed Nagdashak, the last ruler of the Haryak dynasty?
(a) Brihadratha (b) Shishunag
(c) Pushyamitra (d) Udayan

16. Which waterfall is located on the Kanhar river?
(a) Jonha (b) Gautamdhara
(c) Sukhaldari (d) Hundru

17. Dhunkund Falls is located on which river?
(a) Kav (b) Sakri
(c) Tilave (d) Sariswa

18. Who was the friend, philosopher and guide of Chandragupta Maurya?
(a) Aryabhata (b) Dhanwantari
(c) Charak (d) Vishnugupta

19. Hemchandra was a scholar living in the court of the ruler of which dynasty of Gujarat?
(a) Gurjar Pratihara
(b) Chalukya
(c) Solanki
(d) Rao

20. Where is the big dargah of Hazrat Malik and Sheikh Makhdoom shah Sharfuddin located?
(a) Nalanda (b) Patna
(c) Bihar Sharif (d) Hajipur

Answers

1. (a)	**2.** (c)	**3.** (b)	**4.** (c)
5. (a)	**6.** (c)	**7.** (d)	**8.** (b)
9. (a)	**10.** (d)	**11.** (a)	**12.** (c)
13. (b)	**14.** (c)	**15.** (b)	**16.** (d)
17. (a)	**18.** (d)	**19.** (b)	**20.** (a)

SET-14

1. According to which scholar, the cause of Kalinga war was to get a beach for trade commerce?
(a) Plato
(b) Aristotle
(c) Pliny
(d) Socrates

2. Bhimbandh Sanctuary is located in which district?
(a) Munger (b) Gaya
(c) Aurangabad (d) Vaishali

3. In which state was Aryabhatta, the world's first mathematician born?
(a) Uttar Pradesh
(b) Assam
(c) Bihar
(d) Rajasthan

4. How many kilometers does Ganga, India's longest river, flow in Bihar?
(a) 445 kms (b) 450 kms
(c) 455 kms (d) 460 kms

5. Which is the first empire of India?
(a) Lichchavi (b) Kapilvastu
(c) Magadha (d) Kashi

6. India's largest railway bridge Abdul Bari Bridge is on which river in Bihar?
(a) Sone (b) Kosi
(c) Ganga (d) Bagmati

7. Where is Mithila Sanskrit Vidyapeeth located?
(a) Darbhanga (b) Madhubani
(c) Saran (d) Sivan

8. When was Mission Indra Dhanush launched in Bihar?
(a) 2014 AD (b) 2015 AD
(c) 2016 AD (d) 2017 AD

9. Which is the fastest flowing river in Bihar?
(a) Kosi (b) Gandak
(c) Ganga (d) Old Gandak

10. Who was the second ruler of the Haryak dynasty?
(a) Jarasandha (b) Ajatshatru
(c) Kalashok (d) Ashoka

11. When and where was country's gem Dr. Rajendra Prasad born?
(a) 1880 AD Patna
(b) 1882 AD Motihari
(c) 1884 AD Sivan
(d) 1886 AD Darbhanga

12. Under which article of the Constitution of India will the Chief Minister of a State along with Council of Ministers be appointed by the Governor?
(a) Article-162 (b) Article-164
(c) Article-166 (d) Article-168

13. Which article of the Constitution provides for a Assembly state?
(a) Article-166 (b) Article-168
(c) Article-170 (d) Article-172

14. In which year did taekwondo player Neetu Chandra represent India at the World Taekwondo Championship in Hong Kong?
(a) 1995 AD (b) 1997 AD
(c) 1999 AD (d) 2001 AD

15. The first bilingual record obtained from Bihar belongs to which medieval ruler?
(a) Sher Shah
(b) Akbar
(c) Bakhtiyar Khilji
(d) Iltutmish

16. Film director Imtiaz Ali was born in which city of Bihar?

(a) Vaishali (b) Gaya
(c) Patna (d) Bhagalpur

17. Which is the first composition of Persian language in India?
(a) Tabkate-Hind
(b) Rehla
(c) Ajwaje-Futuhat
(d) Tabkate-Nasiri

18. When was the first census conducted in India?
(a) 1870 AD (b) 1872 AD
(c) 1874 AD (d) 1876 AD

19. Who was the leader of the Wahabi movement?
(a) Syed Ahmed Barelvi
(b) Shibli Nomani
(c) Vilayat Ali
(d) Pir Ali

20. Census in India started during the time of which Viceroy?
(a) Lord Liton
(b) Lord Curzon
(c) Lord Dalhousie
(d) Lord Mayo

Answers

1. (c)	**2.** (a)	**3.** (c)	**4.** (a)
5. (c)	**6.** (a)	**7.** (a)	**8.** (b)
9. (d)	**10.** (b)	**11.** (c)	**12.** (b)
13. (c)	**14.** (b)	**15.** (a)	**16.** (c)
17. (d)	**18.** (b)	**19.** (a)	**20.** (d)

SET-15

1. In which district of Bihar is there highest production of litchi?
(a) Muzaffarpur (b) Darbhanga
(c) Patna (d) East Champaran

2. When was Bharat Nirman yojana launched?
(a) 2001 AD (b) 2003 AD
(c) 2005 AD (d) 2007 AD

3. When was the provisions of the Government of India Act, 1919 introduced in Bihar?
(a) 1919 AD (b) 1920 AD
(b) 1921 AD (d)1922 AD

4. Which dynasty in history is known as pitruhanta dynasty?
(a) Haryak (b) Maurya
(b) Gupt (d) Pal

5. Who was made secretary of The Bhartiya Congress Samajwadi Party?
(a) Meenu Masani
(b) Mo- Zubair
(b) Jayaprakash Narayan
(d) Narendra Dev

6. When was the Land Delimitation Act enacted?
(a) 1960 (b) 1961
(b) 1962 (d) 1963

7. How many delegates participated in the first session of the Indian National Congress?
(a) 68 (b) 70
(c) 72 (d) 74

8. Where is Bhupendra Narayan Mandal University located?
(a) Darbhanga (b) Madhepura
(c) Kishanganj (d) Saharsa

9. When did the Railways celebrate its 150th anniversary?
(a) 2003 AD (b) 2004 AD
(c) 2005 AD (d) 2006 AD

10. Who did the work of decorating the original copy of the Constitution?
(a) MF Hussain
(b) Syed Haider Rizvi
(c) Nandalal Bose
(d) Soumitra Das

11. In which article of the Constitution has the post of one Speaker and one Vice-President prescribed for each State Assembly?
(a) Article-172 (b) Article-174
(c) Article-176 (d) Article-178

12. Where is the origin of river Sone?
(a) Kaimur
(b) Amarkantak

(c) Chhotanagpur
(d) Himalayas

13. Under which article of the Constitution of India the qualifications have been prescribed for the post of Governor?
(a) Article-153 (b) Article-155
(c) Article157 (d) Article-159

14. The concept of which has been introduced under Article 169 of the Indian Constitution?
(a) Legislative Assembly
(b) Legislative Council
(c) Chief Minister
(d) Governor

15. What is the maximum number of members of the Assembly under Article 170 of the Indian Constitution?
(a) 470 (b) 480
(c) 490 (d) 500

16. When was the State Bank of India nationalized?
(a) 1951 AD (b) 1953 AD
(c) 1955 AD (d) 1957 AD

17. By what other names the materialistic sects are known?
(a) Ajeevak (b) Lokayat
(c) Jain (d) Vaishnava

18. Who was the founder of the materialistic community?
(a) Charvak
(b) Panini
(c) Chaitanya Mahaprabhu
(d) Ajit Keskambli

19. Which regional language of Bihar is spoken in Mauritius?
(a) Maghi (b) Bhojpuri
(c) Maithili (d) Angika

20. In which area is the deposit of Balther soil found in Bihar?
(a) Kaimur (b) Sivan
(c) Shivhar (d) Madhubani

Answers

1. (a)	**2.** (c)	**3.** (b)	**4.** (a)
5. (c)	**6.** (b)	**7.** (c)	**8.** (b)
9. (a)	**10.** (c)	**11.** (d)	**12.** (b)
13. (c)	**14.** (a)	**15.** (d)	**16.** (c)
17. (b)	**18.** (d)	**19.** (b)	**20.** (a)

SET-16

1. Which Mauryan king conquered the Deccan?
(a) Chandragupta Maurya
(b) Bindusara
(c) Ashoka
(d) Kunal

2. Which is the 28th State of the Indian Union?
(a) Uttarakhand (b) Chhattisgarh
(c) Jharkhand (d) Telangana

3. Which important industry is established in Bhagalpur?
(a) Cotton Clothes
(b) Silk Industry
(c) Sugar Mills
(d) Dairy Industry

4. Where is the pyrite-based Sulphur industry established?
(a) Bihta (b) Nautan
(c) Nabinagar (d) Amzor

5. Bhulani Dham is located in which district?
(a) Rohtas (b) Kaimur
(c) Saharsa (d) Supaul

6. Who was made the President of The Bhartiya Congress Samajwadi Party?
(a) Jai Prakash Narayan
(b) Meenu Masani
(c) Narendra Dev
(d) Mo- Zubair

7. When was the Land Army formed?
(a) 1973 AD (b) 1975 AD
(b) 1977 AD (d) 1979 AD

8. Which soil is found to be deficient in lime and alkali?

(a) bangar (b) khadar
(c) balther (d) kaskari

9. Which state has described Kalhana in Rajatarangini?
(a) Tamil Nadu (b) Karnataka
(c) Bihar (d) Kashmir

10. On which river did Lord Buddha attain enlightenment?
(a) Niranjana (b) Saryu
(c) Ganga (d) Mahanadi

11. Which soil is useful for paddy and wheat crops?
(a) domat (b) kali
(c) laterite (d) daldali

12. Which king got repaired the Grand Trunk Road?
(a) Balaban (b) Sher Shah
(c) Akbar (d) Aurangzeb

13. What were the followers of Parsvanatha called?
(a) polytheist (b) non -violent
(c) truthful (d) dormant

14. How many forest days are declared every year by the Publicity and Public Relations Division of the Department of Environment and Forests?
(a) 11 (b) 13
(c) 15 (d) 17

15. What is the name of the map prepared by the Department of Tourism, Bihar to promote tourism?
(a) Con & C Bihar
(b) Incredible Bihar
(c) Legacy Weeth Vihar
(d) A Journey Through Bihar

16. What is mango rainfall?
(a) January-February Rains
(b) March-April Rains
(c) June-July Rains
(d) August-September Rains

17. Who takes the decision to hold panchayat elections?
(a) Central Government
(b) State Government
(c) District Administration
(d) Divisional Administration

18. Which is the highest institution of the district in the Panchayati Raj system?
(a) gram panchayat
(b) panchayat samiti
(c) zilla parishad
(d) sarpanch

19. Parishisht-Parvan was composed by
(a) Hemchandra
(b) Madhav Lal
(c) Vidyapati
(d) Naval Kishore Singh

20. Who discovered Rampurwa situated in West Champaran?
(a) Cunningham
(b) Eric Smith
(c) Clyle
(d) John Marshall

Answers

1. (a)	**2.** (c)	**3.** (b)	**4.** (d)
5. (a)	**6.** (c)	**7.** (d)	**8.** (b)
9. (d)	**10.** (a)	**11.** (a)	**12.** (b)
13. (d)	**14.** (c)	**15.** (d)	**16.** (b)
17. (b)	**18.** (c)	**19.** (a)	**20.** (c)

SET-17

1. At which place was the first Bihar Day organized on 22nd March, 2010?
(a) Legislative Assembly
(b) Gandhi Maidan
(c) Raj Bhawan
(d) Champaran

2. In which year was the Parvarish Yojana launched by the Government of Bihar?
(a) 2012 AD (b) 2013 AD
(c) 2014 AD (d) 2015 AD

3. Who was the Pargana chief, an administrative officer at the time of Sher Shah?

(a) Jagirdar (b) Shikdar
(c) Musharraf (d) Mir Bahri

4. Sone river is a tributary of which river?
(a) Ganga (b) Kosi
(c) Gandak (d) Bagmati

5. Where is Papaharani Mela held in Bihar?
(a) Munger (b) Shivhar
(c) Bhagalpur (d) Sitamarhi

6. Which Gupta emperor defeated the Huns?
(a) Samudragupta
(b) Chandragupta II
(c) Kumargupta
(d) Skandagupta

7. Where is the priest's mansion located?
(a) Patna (b) Gaya
(c) Muzaffarpur (d) Bettiah

8. When was Patna College established?
(a) 1861 AD (b) 1863 AD
(c) 1865 AD (d) 1867 AD

9. Kundgram, the birth place of Lord Mahavir, is located in which district?
(a) Nalanda (b) Gaya
(c) Vaishali (d) Nawada

10. What was the ancient name of Pavapuri?
(a) Uppur (b) Kusmeri .
(c) Harnaut (d) Singh Sthal

11. Whose two records have been found from Basadhar in Vaishali district?
(a) Ajatshatru
(b) Ashoka
(c) Kanishka
(d) Mahadevi Prabhudaya

12. Who were the main disciples of Parsvanatha?
(a) Keshi (b) Upali
(c) Jamali (d) Anand

13. The objective of the Mandal Commission was to identify the social and economic backwardness of which category?
(a) scheduled caste
(b) scheduled tribe
(c) backward class
(d) extremely backward class

14. Patna Nagar was the center of which movement in the 1830s?
(a) Wahabi Movement
(b) Bareilly Movement
(c) Aligarh Movement
(d) land movement

15. Who founded Pataliputra?
(a) Ajatshatru
(b) Kalashok
(c) Udayan
(d) Ashoka

16. The Golghar in Patna was built during the time of which Governor General?
(a) Warren Hastings
(b) Lord Mayo
(c) Lord Curzon
(d) Lord Ripon

17. Triveni Canal is part of which river project of Bihar?
(a) Kosi (b) Ganga
(c) Gandak (d) Sone

18. Which ruler built the fort of Pataliputra?
(a) Ajatshatru (c) Bimbisara
(c) Ashoka (d) Kumargupta

19. Who built the Vishnupad temple in Gaya?
(a) Lakshmibai (b) Durgavati
(c) Ahilyabai (d) Karnavati

20. Which Indian was appointed by Robert Clive as Naib Diwan of Bihar?
(a) Raja Hussain
(b) Shitab Rai
(c) Muzaffar Ali
(d) Nandalal Chatterjee

Answers

1. (b)	**2.** (c)	**3.** (b)	**4.** (a)
5. (c)	**6.** (d)	**7.** (a)	**8.** (b)
9. (c)	**10.** (a)	**11.** (d)	**12.** (a)
13. (c)	**14.** (a)	**15.** (c)	**16.** (a)
17. (c)	**18.** (a)	**19.** (c)	**20.** (b)

SET-18

1. Which ruler of the Pala dynasty was elected by the feudal and general public of Bengal?
(a) Gopal (b) Devpal
(c) Dharmapala (d) Mahipal

2. Which dynasty was founded by Pushyamitra Shunga?
(a) Kanva dynasty
(b) Shun dynasty
(c) Kushan dynasty
(d) Gupta dynasty

3. Which is the dance performed by men in the costume of a woman?
(a) Itsi Dance
(b) Panjara Dance
(c) Pavandia dance
(d) Jat-jatin dance

4. Punpun river meets River Ganga near which place?
(a) Patna (b) Gaya
(c) Bhagalpur (d) Buxar

5. What is the other name of old alluvial soil?
(a) khadar (b) bangar
(c) balther (d) kaskari

6. On what percentage of the area of Bihar did the State of Jharkhand become?
(a) 40% (b) 41%
(c) 42 % (d) 43%

7. Which national highways passing through Bihar fall under eastern-western corridor?
(a) NH-2 (b) NH–27
(c) NH-85 (d) NH-527D

8. When and by whom was the 'stone Mosque' built?
(a) 1540 AD Sher Shah
(b) 1572 AD Akbar
(c) 1621 AD Parvez
(d) 1658 AD Aurangzeb

9. At the age of 35, Buddha attained enlightenment under Peepal tree after eating 'kheer' from the hand of which girl on the 49th day of penance?
(a) Sumitra (b) Sujata
(c) Suchitra (d) Sangh Mitra

10. Bihar is connected by which waterway with sea?
(a) Ganga-Hooghly
(b) Swarn Rekha
(c) Godavari
(d) Krishna

11. When and by whom was the 'Priest's Mansion' built?
(a) 1750 AD Father Hoffman
(b) 1751 AD Kapuchin Fathers
(c) 1752 AD Father David
(d) 1753 AD Father Smith

12. Who was the leader of the 1857 freedom struggle in Patna?
(a) Amar Singh (b) Mohd Zubair
(c) Vilayat Ali (d) Pir Ali

13. In how many parts is Bihar divided on the basis of high and low surface?
(a) 2 (b) 3
(c) 4 (d) 5

14. What is the name of the idol of Stree Ratna or Yakshini obtained from Didar Ganj (Patna)?
(a) Raj Dancer (b) Chamaragrahini
(c) Devi (d) (a), (b) and (c)

15. Gautam Buddha Sanctuary is located in which district of Bihar?
(a) Gaya (b) Munger
(c) Bhagalpur (d) Buxar

16. Who was the first Vice Chancellor of Nalanda International University?
(a) Krishnakanta
(b) Dr. APJ Abdul Kalam
(c) Dr. Manmohan Singh
(d) Amartya Sen

17. Golghar was built by
(a) David lemon
(b) Eric Smith
(c) Cunningham
(d) John Garstin

18. Patna kalam or Patna style is known as
(a) Mughal style
(b) Bihar style
(c) Kampani Style
(d) Mixed Style

19. Who was the last important painter of Patna kalam?
(a) Ishwari Prasad Verma
(b) Havalidari Ram
(c) Hulas Ram
(d) Mahadev Lal

20. Who was the father of Parsvanatha?
(a) King of Ujjain
(b) King of Kashi
(c) King of Videha
(d) King of Lichchavi

Answers

1. (a)	**2.** (b)	**3.** (c)	**4.** (a)
5. (b)	**6.** (c)	**7.** (d)	**8.** (c)
9. (b)	**10.** (a)	**11.** (b)	**12.** (d)
13. (b)	**14.** (b)	**15.** (a)	**16.** (b)
17. (d)	**18.** (c)	**19.** (a)	**20.** (b)

SET-19

1. How many wards are there in Patna Municipal Corporation?
(a) 71 (b) 73
(c) 75 (d) 77

2. What is the part made of trembling soil and sand in the northern plains of ganga called?
(a) diyara (b) taal
(c) don (d) bill

3. When was Deendayal Upadhyay Grameen Jyoti yojana launched from Patna district in the state?
(a) 2014 AD (b) 2015 AD
(c) 2016 AD (d) 2017 AD

4. Who led the Wahabi movement in Patna?
(a) Pir Ali (b) Vilayat Ali
(c) Inayat Ali (d) (b) and (c)

5. Golghar is located in which city?
(a) Patna (b) Hajipur
(c) Bihar Sharif (d) Muzaffarpur

6. Whose seals are recovered from Basadhar?
(a) Laxman Sen
(b) Mahipal
(c) Mahadevi Dhruv Swami
(d) Hari Singh

7. Who is the creator of Rashmirthi?
(a) Ramdhari Singh Dinkar
(b) Ramvriksha Benipuri
(c) Nagarjuna
(d) Bhikhari Thakur

8. Who was the first Vice Chancellor of Patna University?
(a) Eric Smith (b) Scott Morris
(c) JG Jwings (d) David Coleman

9. What is the height of Someshwar Hill?
(a) 860 meter (b) 870 meter
(c) 880 meter (d) 890 meter

10. Patna Book Fair is organized by
(a) State Government
(b) C.R.D
(c) NGO
(d) Central Government

11. Which Patna-style connoisseur is called the acharya of 'Portrait of Sarjana'?

(a) Radha Mohan Babu
(b) Ishwari Prasad Verma
(c) Ram Balaka Mahato
(d) Kedar Mishra

12. The idol of Yakshini from Didar Ganj dates back to which period?
(a) Hariyank period
(b) Mauryan period
(c) Gupta Period
(d) Pal Kaal

13. Which Gupta ruler's stone record has been found from Afshad village near Nawada?
(a) Kumar Gupta
(b) Kunal Gupta
(c) Aditya Sen
(d) Laxman Sen

14. Who was appointed as the first Vice-Chairman of Bihar Legislative Assembly?
(a) Abdul Bari
(b) Anugrah Narayan Singh
(c) Mohd Zubair
(d) Kedarnath Mishra

15. Who formed the Hindu Boys Association?
(a) Vivekananda
(b) Bankim Chandra
(c) Raj Krishna
(d) Ramakrishna Paramahamsa

16. Which leaders of Bihar were elected permanent presidents of the Constituent Assembly?
(a) Sachchidanand Sinha
(b) Rajendra Prasad
(c) Pro. Abdul Bari
(d) Vinod Anand Jha

17. Plywood factory is in which district of Bihar?
(a) Hajipur (b) Muzaffarpur
(c) Patna (d) Bhagalpur

18. Which is the first full-fledged Indian bank?
(a) Allahabad Bank
(b) PNB
(c) SBI
(d) Bank of India

19. What is the length of East to West Bihar?
(a) 483 Kms (b) 485 kms
(c) 487 Kms (d) 489 kms

20. What is the length of the main canal in the Eastern Kosi Canal system?
(a) 40 Kms (b) 42 kms
(c) 44 Kms (a) 46 km

Answers

1. (c)	**2.** (a)	**3.** (b)	**4.** (d)
5. (a)	**6.** (c)	**7.** (a)	**8.** (c)
9. (c)	**10.** (b)	**11.** (a)	**12.** (b)
13. (c)	**14.** (a)	**15.** (b)	**16.** (a)
17. (b)	**18.** (b)	**19.** (a)	**20.** (c)

SET-20

1. What is the total length of eastern Triveni canal?
(a) 290 Kms (b) 293 kms
(c) 296 Kms (d) 299 kms

2. Who was the first Chief Justice of Patna High Court?
(a) Fazal Ali
(b) Surendra Singh
(c) Gopal Diwakar
(d) Narasimha Mehta

3. Which ruler placed the Prayag columnist in the fort of Allahabad?
(a) Akbar (b) Sher Shah
(b) Aurangzeb (d) Jahangir

4. Where was the Prayag columnist located earlier?
(a) Shravasti (b) Kaushambi
(c) Mathura (d) Bodh Gaya

5. Who is the head of block administration?
(a) Main
(b) Zilla Parishad President

(c) Block Development Officer
(d) Zone Officer

6. Who is the head of the divisional administration?
(a) Commissioner
(b) Secretary
(c) District Collector
(d) District Development Officer

7. The first Buddhist music was presided over by
(a) Moglipat Tiss
(b) Mahakashyap
(c) Sthulbhadr
(d) Ajatshatru

8. In which State of India was the First Minority Commission given statutory powers?
(a) Bihar (b) Madhya Pradesh
(c) Haryan (d) Goa

9. When was the formal announcement of the formation of Kisan Sabha in Bihar made?
(a) 1926 AD (b) 1928 AD
(c) 1930 AD (d) 1932 AD

10. Before assuming office, every Minister takes oath of office and secrecy in front of whom?
(a) Chief Minister
(b) Governor
(c) Chief Justice of the High Court
(d) President

11. There are 12 chakras in Buddhism, what is it called?
(a) dvadash nadan
(b) ashtanga
(c) pratiyodayamutpada
(d) agam nadan

12. In which century did the Magadha Empire first flourish?
(a) 4th Century AD
(b) 5th Century BC
(c) 6th Century AD
(d) 7th Century BC

13. Who was appointed as the first Protem Speaker of Bihar Legislative Assembly?
(a) Rajkumar Shukla
(b) Abdul Bari
(c) Jai Ramdas Daulat Ram
(d) Sachchidanand Sinha

14. Who was appointed as the first Museum President of Patna Museum?
(a) Sharad Chandra Rai
(b) Khudabakhsh Khan
(c) Kumar Sarvesh
(d) Bhola Shastri

15. Who was appointed as the first Speaker of Bihar legislative assembly?
(a) Abdul Bari
(b) Ramdayalu Singh
(c) Anugrah Narayan
(d) Ram Narayan Singh

16. Smt. Chakraborty Devi is a prominent painter of which style?
(a) Manjusha Style
(b) Madhubani Style
(c) Patna Pen
(d) (a), (b) and (c)

17. Where is Srihari Mandir Sahib Gurudwara located?
(a) Gaya (b) Muzaffarpur
(c) Patna (d) Aurangabad

18. Who was the first ruler who brought into practice the pure silver currency?
(a) Sher Shah (b) Akbar
(c) Aurangzeb (d) Jahangir

19. Who presided over the first Jain Council?
(a) Mahakashyap
(b) Mogliputta Tiss
(c) Sathibhadra
(d) Anand Tisya

20. Where was the first Jain council held?

(a) Pataliputra
(b) Ballabhi
(c) Shravanabelagola
(d) Pavapuri

Answers

1. (b)	**2.** (a)	**3.** (a)	**4.** (b)
5. (c)	**6.** (a)	**7.** (b)	**8.** (a)
9. (b)	**10.** (b)	**11.** (a)	**12.** (c)
13. (d)	**14.** (a)	**15.** (b)	**16.** (a)
17. (c)	**18.** (a)	**19.** (c)	**20.** (a)

SET-21

1. The first Jain council was organized during whose reign?
(a) Ajatshatru
(b) Kalashok
(c) Ghanananda
(d) Chandragupta Maurya

2. The publication of the first English newspaper 'The Bihar Herald' was started by
(a) Guruprasad Sen
(b) Maheshwar Singh
(c) Mohd Yunus
(d) Jagapati Sahay

3. Where was the famous Buddhist scholar Sariputra born?
(a) Gaya (b) Nawada
(c) Nalanda (d) Buxar

4. Maithili poet Vidyapati was in the court of which Darbhanga king?
(a) Hari Singh
(b) Kriti Singh
(c) Shiv Singh
(d) (b) and (c)

5. What did Chinese traveller Fahi-yan say to the palace of Magadha Emperor Chandragupta Maurya?
(a) Buddhist Monastery
(b) Chaitya Vihar
(c) Dev Nirmit Mahal
(d) University

6. What was the language of magadha empire in ancient times?
(a) Maghi (b) Bhojpuri
(c) Maithili (d) Angika

7. Who is credited with the beginning and development of the empire in India?
(a) Ashoka
(b) Ajatshatru
(c) Chandragupta Maurya
(d) Chandragupta II

8. After marrying which daughter of Prasenjeet did Ajatshatru end the struggle?
(a) Chelna (b) Trishala
(c) Sanghmitra (d) Wajira

9. Where did Prasenjeet take refuge when he was defeated?
(a) Sarnath (b) Shravasti
(c) Mathura (d) Kurukshetra

10. On the basis of the recommendation of which report in Bihar, the municipal administration was separated from the district administration?
(a) Campwell Report
(b) Marley-Minto Report
(c) Ekworth report
(d) Mantegu Chelmsford Report

11. In which year did panchayat elections were held in Bihar after a gap of 23 years?
(a) 2000 AD (b) 2001 AD
(c) 2002 AD (d) 2003 AD

12. When was the National Rural Employment Guarantee Scheme implemented all over the country?
(a) 2002 AD (b) 2004 AD
(c) 2006 AD (d) 2008 AD

13. According to Mahipal's Nalanda Stone Article, which mahavihara was burnt by Baladitya?
(a) Nalanda (b) Sompur
(c) Odantpuri (d) Vikramshila

14. Ramesh Saxena is related to which sport?
(a) Cricket (b) Football
(c) Shooting (d) Kabaddi

15. Ravi Mehta Shield is related to which sport?
(a) Volleyball (b) Chess
(c) Hockey (d) Lawn Tennis

16. How many seats did the Congress get in the first Bihar Assembly elections?
(a) 94 (b) 96
(c) 98 (d) 100

17. How many seats did the Muslim League get in the first Bihar Assembly elections?
(a) 20 (b) 22
(c) 24 (d) 26

18. Who was the first person from Bihar to become the Director of Shriram Centre, New Delhi?
(a) Ajit Anjum
(b) Sanjay Upadhyay
(c) Kishore Singh
(d) Nair Hasnain Khan

19. According to Sri Lanka literature, where was Ashoka a governor before becoming ruler?
(a) Ujjain (b) Vallabhi
(c) Shravasti (d) Prayag

20. When and where was national poet Ramdhari Singh Dinkar born?
(a) 1906 AD Arrah
(b) 1907 AD Banka
(c) 1908 AD Begusarai
(d) 1909 AD Gaya

Answers

1. (d)	**2.** (a)	**3.** (c)	**4.** (d)
5. (c)	**6.** (a)	**7.** (c)	**8.** (d)
9. (b)	**10.** (d)	**11.** (b)	**12.** (d)
13. (a)	**14.** (c)	**15.** (a)	**16.** (c)
17. (a)	**18.** (b)	**19.** (a)	**20.** (c)

SET-22

1. In which year was the management of Valmiki Tiger Sanctuary evaluated by the National Tiger Authority?
(a) 2010 AD (b) 2012 AD
(c) 2014 AD (d) 2016 AD

2. Who is the Head of District Planning and Development Council in Bihar?
(a) Deputy Commissioner
(b) District Collector
(c) Zilla Parishad President
(d) District Development Officer

3. The northern plain of Ganga is spread in how much area of Bihar?
(a) 52,140 sq. km
(b) 53,149 sq. km
(c) 54,986 sq. km
(d) 56,980 sq. km

4. Which two places does NH 2 connect?
(a) Delhi-Mumbai
(b) Delhi-Lucknow
(c) Delhi-Kolkata
(d) Patna-Ranchi

5. Who is the author of Tareekh-e-Shershahi?
(a) Abul Fazal
(b) Mullah Bahbahani
(c) Nusrat Khan
(d) Abbas Khan Sharwani

6. As per the survey conducted by National Tiger Conservation Authority in 2014 through camera trap system, how many tigers were there in Valmiki Tiger Sanctuary, West Champaran?
(a) 20 (b) 22
(c) 25 (d) 28

7. As per the National Forest Policy, 1988, what percentage of the total area of a region should be forested?

(a) 30% (b) 33%
(c) 35% (d) 38%

8. Who burnt Nalanda university and destroyed it?
(a) Balban
(b) Shashank
(c) Bakhtiyar Khilji
(d) Iltutmish

9. According to National Wildlife Council, where are zoo safaris being planned to be set up?
(a) Patna (b) Rajgir
(c) Gaya (d) Aurangabad

10. When was the National Population Commission constituted?
(a) 1974 AD (b) 1976 AD
(c) 1978 AD (d) 1980 AD

11. Which film has been made on the life of famous mathematician Anand Kumar?
(a) Super-20 (b) Super-30
(c) Super-40 (d) Super-50

12. Randhir Verma Shield is related to which sport?
(a) Cricket (b) Hockey
(c) Football (d) Chess

13. Old alluvial soil in the southern part of Ganga is known as
(a) Kagari (b) Karel-Kewal
(c) Balther (d) Balsundari

14. At which place Khudiram Bose was arrested due to Muzaffarpur bomb incident?
(a) Samastipur (b) Ara
(c) Saran (d) Muzaffarpur

15. Who was the first Dalit Speaker of Bihar Assembly?
(a) Jitan Ram Manjhi
(b) Ramai Ram
(c) Purnawasi Ram
(d) Udaynarayan Chaudhary

16. Ram Janaki Temple is located in which district?
(a) Sitamarhi (b) Patna
(c) Kaimur (d) Aurangabad

17. Who was the first woman Chairman of Bihar Legislative Council?
(a) Kahkasha Parveen
(b) Naima Khatun
(c) Sarojini Devi
(d) Bima Devi

18. Ramsharan Sharma belongs to which area?
(a) historian (b) doctor
(c) journalist (d) litterateur

19. Who presided over the Ramgarh Congress Session?
(a) Subhash Chandra Bose
(b) Maulana Abdul Kalam Azad
(c) Shri Krishna Singh
(d) Dr. Rajendra Prasad

20. Pictures based on Ragini Todi are made by which artist?
(a) Madholal
(b) Yamuna Prasad
(c) Ishwari Prasad Verma
(d) Hulas Ram

Answers

1. (c)	**2.** (b)	**3.** (d)	**4.** (c)
5. (d)	**6.** (d)	**7.** (b)	**8.** (c)
9. (b)	**10.** (c)	**11.** (b)	**12.** (a)
13. (b)	**14.** (a)	**15.** (d)	**16.** (a)
17. (b)	**18.** (a)	**19.** (b)	**20.** (a)

SET-23

1. Ragini Gandhari paintings are made by which artist?
(a) Yamuna Prasad
(b) Mahadev Lal
(c) Hulas Ram
(d) Sevak Ram

2. Rahul Sankrityayan was active in which field in the non-cooperation movement of 1920?
(a) Chhapra (b) Munger
(c) Ara (d) Darbhanga

3. In which district of Bihar is the 'Thawe' pilgrimage site located?
(a) West Champaran
(b) Gopalganj
(c) Kaimur
(d) Jamui

4. How many Anglo-Indian members can the Governor nominate in the Assembly?
(a) 4 (b) 3
(c) 2 (d) 1

5. Which service has been launched in the State for medical counselling and grievance redressal of the patient?
(a) Dial-1911 (b) Dial-1941
(c) Dial-1969 (d) Dial-1981

6. Which is the smallest unit of state administration?
(a) ward
(b) gram panchayat
(c) panchayat samiti
(d) zilla parishad

7. The executive powers of the State are vested in the Governor, but in reality these powers are vested with the Council of Ministers under whose chairmanship?
(a) Speaker of legislative assembly
(b) Deputy Speaker of Legislative Assembly
(c) Chief Minister
(d) Chief Secretary

8. Which Chief Minister of Bihar is called 'Dhoti Kurta Se I.A.S.' because of his strong administrative image?
(a) Chandrashekhar Singh
(b) Mohd Yunus
(c) Shri Krishna Singh
(d) Kapuri Thakur

9. Who was the first Muslim Chief Minister of Bihar?
(a) Mohd Zubair
(b) Majhrul Haque
(c) Abdul Ghafoor
(d) Abdul Bari

10. In whose consultation does the Governor make all the important appointments of the State?
(a) Chief Minister
(b) Chief Secretary
(c) The Cabinet
(d) (a), (b) and (c)

11. What is the total area of Valmiki Tiger Sanctuary, West Champaran, the only tiger sanctuary in Bihar?
(a) 871.2 sq km
(b) 883.8 sq km
(c) 898.34 sq km
(d) 912.7 sq km

12. What percentage of the total agricultural area of Bihar produces foodgrains crop?
(a) 60% (b) 72%
(c) 84% (d) 90%

13. Advocate General is appointed by whom in the State?
(a) Governor (b) Chief Minister
(c) Cabinet (d) Chief Secretary

14. What percentage of the area of Bihar is irrigated from the canal?
(a) 23.14% (b) 28.41%
(c) 33.49% (d) 39.14%

15. Who is responsible for implementing any law made by the Legislature in the State?
(a) Governor
(b) Chief Minister
(c) Chief Secretary
(d) State Council of Ministers

16. By whom are the members of the State Public Service Commission appointed?
(a) State Council of Ministers
(b) Governor

(c) Chief Minister
(d) Chief Secretary

17. To whom is the State Council of Ministers responsible?
(a) Governor
(b) Legislative Assembly
(c) Legislative Council
(d) (a), (b) and (c)

18. Bihar State Sugar Corporation Limited is located in which district?
(a) Patna (b) Sivan
(c) Gopalganj (d) East Champaran

19. In which year was the Bihar State Minority Financial Corporation established?
(a) 1981 AD
(b) 1983 AD
(c) 1985 AD
(d) 1987 AD

20. Which scheme has been implemented in the State for vocational orientation and economic self-reliance of Muslim girls?
(a) Hunar
(b) Nayi Roshni
(c) Nayi Manzil
(d) (a), (b) and (c)

Answers

1. (b)	**2.** (a)	**3.** (b)	**4.** (d)
5. (a)	**6.** (b)	**7.** (c)	**8.** (a)
9. (c)	**10.** (c)	**11.** (c)	**12.** (d)
13. (a)	**14.** (b)	**15.** (d)	**16.** (b)
17. (b)	**18.** (a)	**19.** (b)	**20.** (a)

SET-24

1. Which is the tribe found in Chhapra, Champaran and Rohtas districts?
(a) Chero (b) Gond
(c) Mahli (d) Godait

2. Which is the main occupation of the Kond tribe?
(a) agriculture
(b) animal husbandry
(c) lift the tuber root from the forest
(d) basket

3. Which district has the lowest Scheduled Caste population in Bihar?
(a) Shivhar (b) Bhojpur
(c) Kishanganj (d) Katihar

4. What is the residence of Birhor tribe of Bihar called?
(a) Don (b) Tanda
(c) Sabor (d) Diyara

5. What is the percentage of scheduled tribes population in Gaya district?
(a) 29.6% (b) 31.4%
(c) 33.5% (d) 37.9%

6. Governor presents the Annual Budget of the State in the State Legislative Assembly through which Minister of the Council of Ministers?
(a) Chief Minister
(b) Finance Minister
(c) Chief Secretary
(d) Finance Secretary

7. When did Rajkumar Shukla die?
(a) 1923 AD (b) 1925 AD
(c) 1927 AD (d) 1929 AD

8. Where is The Sheetala Mata Temple located?
(a) Patna (b) Bhojpur
(c) Banka (d) Jamui

9. What is the phenomenon of enlightenment called in Buddhism?
(a) moksha (b) conversion
(c) Nirvana (d) Kaivalya

10. Where did Chanakya, the one who taught the world the lessons of politics and diplomacy, Live?
(a) Bihar (b) Bengal
(c) Assam (d) Kashmir

11. Which district of the state ranks first in terms of Scheduled Caste literacy?
(a) Gaya (b) Buxar
(c) Rohtas (d) Munger

12. Which is the most backward district in terms of literacy in scheduled castes in the State?
(a) Shivhar (b) Gaya
(c) Jamui (d) Banka

13. Which district in Bihar has the highest sex ratio among Scheduled Castes?
(a) Gopalganj (b) Sivan
(c) Saran (d) Patna

14. Which district has the minimum sex ratio in Scheduled Castes in the State?
(a) Bhagalpur (b) Munger
(c) Vaishali (d) Gaya

15. What is the sex ratio rate in the Scheduled Tribes in the State?
(a) 923 (b) 928
(c) 933 (d) 938

16. What is the percentage of literacy rate in the Scheduled Tribes in the State?
(a) 25.4% (b) 28.5%
(c) 33.9% (d) 38.6%

17. Who is the leader of the State Legislature?
(a) Governor
(b) Speaker of Legislative Assembly
(c) Chief Minister
(d) Finance Minister

18. By whom is the State Election Commissioner appointed?
(a) Governor
(b) President
(c) Chief Minister
(d) Prime Minister

19. When was rajgir mahotsav organized for the first time?
(a) 1984 AD (b) 1986 AD
(c) 1988 AD (d) 1990 AD

20. Which ruler of Magadha established the fort and stupa in Rajgir?
(a) Ajatshatru (b) Bimbisara
(c) Ashoka (a) Jarasandha

Answers

1. (b)	**2.** (a)	**3.** (c)	**4.** (b)
5. (a)	**6.** (b)	**7.** (d)	**8.** (a)
9. (c)	**10.** (a)	**11.** (d)	**12.** (a)
13. (b)	**14.** (a)	**15.** (a)	**16.** (b)
17. (c)	**18.** (a)	**19.** (b)	**20.** (a)

SET-25

1. Which areas/sites have been decided to be developed in the first phase by the State Government in an agreement with the Archaeological Survey of India?
(a) Kesariya stupa
(b) Maner's Tomb
(c) Sher Shah's Tomb
(d) (a), (b) and (c)

2. Who is the constitutional head of the State Government?
(a) Governor
(b) Chief Minister
(c) Chief Secretary
(d) Advocate General

3. Which is the first State in the country which gave legal powers to the State Commission for Minorities?
(a) Madhya Pradesh
(b) Karnataka
(c) Bihar
(d) Kerala

4. Where is Lord Narasimha Avatar Pillar located in Bihar?
(a) Purnia (b) Gaya
(c) Shivhar (d) Bhagalpur

5. In which article of the Constitution, the powers of the Governor described are?

(a) Articl 151 (b) Articl 153
(c) Article 155 (d) Articl 157

6. Which district has registered the highest increase in urban population in the state?
(a) Patna (b) Darbhanga
(c) Begusarai (a) Vaishali

7. Which is the district with the highest Scheduled Caste population in Bihar?
(a) Kishanganj
(b) Gaya
(c) West Champaran
(d) Araria

8. When was the Khudabakhsh Oriental Library declared by Parliament as an institution of national importance?
(a) 1963 AD (b) 1965 AD
(c) 1967 AD (d) 1969 AD

9. Who is the author of the oldest and greatest Brahmin book 'shatpath Brahmin'?
(a) Tulsidas (b) Yagyavalvaya
(c) Valmiki (d) Tasi August

10. Prince Azim renamed Patna as what?
(a) Azimabad (b) Azimpur
(c) Azimgarh (d) Azimnagar

11. Saint Francis Aussie Church is located in which district?
(a) Patna (b) Gaya
(c) Muzaffarpur (d) Bhagalpur

12. Rajendra Agricultural University, Pusa is located in which district?
(a) Vaishali (b) Samastipur
(c) Sivan (d) Saaran

13. Who constituted the Bihar Students' Council?
(a) Rajendra Prasad
(b) Sri Krishna Singh
(c) Majhrul Haque
(d) Jai Prakash Narayan

14. On which hill of Rajgrah the world's tallest World Peace Stupa has been constructed by the Government of Japan?
(a) Parasnath (b) Sonagiri
(c) Ratnagiri (d) Someshwar

15. Where is the State Council of Education Research and Training located in Bihar?
(a) Patna (b) Hajipur
(c) Darbhanga (d) Gaya

16. Which architect planned the palace?
(a) Vallabhacharya
(b) Upali
(c) Mahagovind
(d) Sambhuti

17. Rajendra Bridge is located on which river?
(a) Ganga (b) Sone
(c) Bagmati (d) Kosi

18. How many levels of structure have been advised by the Ashok Mehta Committee to be set up under the Panchayati Raj system?
(a) 2 Level (b) 3 levels
(b) 4 Level (d) 5 levels

19. Under whose control the state administration completely is?
(a) Governor
(b) Chief Minister
(c) Council of ministers
(d) Speaker of Legislative Assembly

20. What is the prime goal of Panchayati Raj?
(a) Abolition of caste system
(b) decentralization of power
(c) Reservation for women
(d) (a), (b) and (c)

Answers

1. (d)	**2.** (a)	**3.** (c)	**4.** (a)
5. (b)	**6.** (c)	**7.** (b)	**8.** (d)
9. (b)	**10.** (a)	**11.** (c)	**12.** (b)
13. (a)	**14.** (c)	**15.** (a)	**16.** (c)
17. (a)	**18.** (a)	**19.** (b)	**20.** (b)

Set-26

1. **Which place Bihar in India occupies in the production of Ragi?**
   (a) 1st (b) 2nd
   (c) 3rd (d) 4th
2. **Shruti Jaiswal is related to which sport?**
   (a) Cricket (b) Football
   (c) Hockey (d) Tennis
3. **When was the Regulating Act passed?**
   (a) 1771 AD (b) 1773 AD
   (c) 1775 AD (d) 1777 AD
4. **Who recognizes a political party as a national party or a regional party?**
   (a) President
   (b) Governor
   (c) Election Commission
   (d) Speaker of Lok Sabha
5. **According to 'Shatpath Brahmin', who extended arya culture to north Bihar?**
   (a) Aditya Sen
   (b) Madhav Videh
   (c) Ratnakar Videh
   (d) Ajatshatru
6. **Who was the last ruler of the Shunga dynasty?**
   (a) Nagdashak (b) Kunal
   (c) Devabhuti (d) Brihadratha
7. **Who killed the last ruler of the Shunga dynasty?**
   (a) Ajatshatru (b) Kalashok
   (c) Pushyamitra (d) Vasumitra
8. **What was the name of Siddhartha's horse at the time of his renunciation?**
   (a) Kanthak (b) Chetak
   (c) Ajitam (d) Ghatwar
9. **What was the name of Siddhartha's charioteer at the time of his renunciation?**
   (a) Chetak
   (b) Ghtok
   (c) Kharag Singh
   (d) Chandak
10. **What measurement did Sher Shah use to measure the land?**
    (a) Shershahi Gaj
    (b) Sikandri Gaj
    (c) Suri Gaj
    (d) Afghani Yards
11. **What was Mahavira called after attaining emancipation?**
    (a) Kaivalya (b) Nirmani
    (c) Jain (d) Tapasvi
12. **Who published the newspaper 'The Motherland'?**
    (a) Rajendra Prasad
    (b) Mohd Yunus
    (c) Sri Krishna Singh
    (d) Maulana Majhrul Haque
13. **Who was the first Indian President of Bihar Legislative Council?**
    (a) Abdul Bari
    (b) Ramdayalu Singh
    (c) Sachchidanand Sinha
    (d) Hassan Imam
14. **Who was the first Indian Governor of Bihar?**
    (a) Satyendra Prasad Sinha
    (b) Ramdayalu Singh
    (c) Manohar Jha
    (d) Dilip Pandey
15. **When and who established the Shunga dynasty?**
    (a) 181 AD Vasumitra
    (b) 183 AD nagdashak
    (c) 185 AD Pushyamitra
    (d) 187 AD Brihadratha
16. **Mauryan Dynasty was established after killing which Last ruler of Shunga Dynasty?**

(a) Brihadratha
(b) Nagdashak
(c) Pushyagupta
(d) Amoghvarman

17. Jayaprakash Narayan along with his colleagues escaped from which jail on 9th November,1942 AD?
(a) Bankipur (b) Ambala
(c) Hazaribagh (d) Calcutta

18. Where was Anga Mahajanadpada located?
(a) Uttar Pradesh
(b) Bihar
(c) Madhya Pradesh
(d) Maharashtra

19. When and where was Loknayak Jai Prakash Narayan born?
(a) 1902 AD Saran
(b) 1903 AD Sivan
(c) 1904 AD Saharsa
(d) 1905 AD Darbhanga

20. What was the real name of Sher Shah?
(a) Farid Khan
(b) Majid Khan
(c) Dilawar Khan
(d) Ibrahim Khan

Answers

1. (a)	**2.** (d)	**3.** (b)	**4.** (c)
5. (b)	**6.** (c)	**7.** (d)	**8.** (a)
9. (d)	**10.** (b)	**11.** (a)	**12.** (a)
13. (c)	**14.** (a)	**15.** (c)	**16.** (a)
17. (c)	**18.** (b)	**19.** (a)	**20.** (a)

SET-27

1. Who was known as 'sher-e-Punjab'?
(a) Bhagat Singh
(b) Lala Lajpat Rai
(c) Sukhdev
(d) Udham Singh

2. When was the octagonal tomb of Sher Shah built?
(a) 1541 AD (b) 1543 AD
(c) 1545 AD (d) 1547 AD

3. What is Buddha called after attaining knowledge?
(a) Kaivalya (b) Bodhisattva
(c) Bodhitattva (d) Boddh Bhikshu

4. Sher Shah died while running which firearm?
(a) ukka (b) turgil
(c) khanjar (d) rathmusal

5. Where did Mahavira give his first sermon after attaining knowledge?
(a) Pavapuri (b) Vallabhpuri
(c) Sarnath (d) Rajagraha

6. Where was Sher Shah born?
(a) Hisar (b) Bajwara
(c) Jaunpur (d) Sasaram

7. At whose behest did Buddha admit women to the Buddhist Union?
(a) Upali (b) Anand
(c) Sariputra (d) Devdutt

8. Sher Shah was the grandson of which Afghan chieftain?
(a) Shaista Khan Sur
(b) Ibrahim Khan Sur
(c) Zafar Khan Sur
(d) Mansoor Khan Sur

9. Who is the first person from Bihar to receive jnanpith award?
(a) Nagarjuna
(b) Bhikhari Thakur
(c) Vidyapati
(d) Ramdhari Singh Dinkar

10. Who was 'muhasilana' in Sher Shah's administration?
(a) city head
(b) village head
(c) tax collection fee
(d) kaji

11. Which department used to look after foreign affairs during the Sher Shah administration?

(a) Diwan-e-Sadar
(b) Diwan-e-Wajarat
(c) Diwan- e-Qaum
(d) Diwan- e-Rasalat

12. When was the Chhotanagpur Tenancy Act enacted?
(a) 1906 AD (b) 1908 AD
(c) 1910 AD (d) 1912 AD

13. Cleveland was assassinated in 1784 AD by
(a) Tilka Manjhi (b) Sidhu
(c) Kanhu (d) Birsa Munda

14. What was 'Zaribana' in the Sher Shah administration?
(a) new-revenue (b) home fees
(c) Survey Fee (d) Trade Fee

15. What was the name of the department related to 'lagaan' and economy in the administration of Sher Shah?
(a) Diwan-e-Wajarat
(b) Diwan- e-Kohi
(c) Diwan-e-Bandgan
(d) Diwan-e-Mass

16. Who was appointed subedar of Malwa by Sher Shah?
(a) Suarez Khan (b) Dilawar Khan
(c) Mesur Khan (d) Shujaat Khan

17. What does 'Syadvad' mean?
(a) Must (b) Possibly
(c) Moksha (d) Nirvana

18. Syadvad is also known as
(a) Saptabhaninya
(b) Jamwat
(c) Aguhar
(d) Karman

19. Who was made the first District Collector of Santhal Pargana district?
(a) Eric Smith
(b) Lee Grand
(c) George Mason
(d) Ashley Aden

20. Under which article of the Constitution does the Governor have the right to promulgate an Ordinance?
(a) Articl 211 (b) Articl 213
(c) Article 215 (d) Article 217

Answers

1. (b)	**2.** (c)	**3.** (c)	**4.** (a)
5. (d)	**6.** (b)	**7.** (b)	**8.** (b)
9. (d)	**10.** (c)	**11.** (d)	**12.** (b)
13. (a)	**14.** (c)	**15.** (a)	**16.** (d)
17. (b)	**18.** (a)	**19.** (d)	**20.** (b)

SET-28

1. Under which article of the Constitution can the Governor issue an Ordinance if the Assembly session is not operational?
(a) Article 213 (b) Article 215
(c) Article 217 (d) Article 219

2. Under which article of the Constitution will the Governor have a Council of Ministers to assist and advise him in his actions?
(a) Article 161 (b) Article 162
(c) Article 163 (d) Article 164

3. What was the name of the Department of Government Orders and Correspondence in the administration of Sher Shah?
(a) Diwan-e-Insha
(b) Diwan-e-Mohtasim
(c) Diwan-e-Narm
(d) Diwan-e-Rasad

4. For how many months does the Ordinance issued by the Governor as per Article 213 of the Constitution remain effective?
(a) 2 Month (b) 4 months
(c) 6 Month (d) 8 months

5. Under which article of the Constitution the tenure of the Council of Ministers is for 5 years?

(a) Article 164 (1)
(b) Article 166 (2)
(c) Article163
(d) Article 164

6. What is the name of Vidyapati in the mixed languages of Sanskrit, Prakrit and Maithili?
(a) Aprahat (b) Avhatta
(c) Samangi (d) Bhatri

7. Where was the residence of Saint Makhdoomshah Sheikh Sharfud-din located?
(a) Rajgir (b) Bihar Sharif
(c) Aurangabad (d) Patna

8. Sanjay Gandhi Organic Park, Patna is spread over a total of how many acres of land?
(a) 151 Acres (b) 153 acres
(c) 155 Acres (d) 157 acres

9. Which district has the lowest sex ratio in the state?
(a) Munger (b) Saharsa
(c) Sivan (d) Madhepura

10. What was the name of the intelligence department in Sher Shah's administration?
(a) Diwan-e-Wajarat
(b) Diwan-e-Barid
(c) Diwan-e-Insha
(d) Diwan-e-Intelligence

11. Which language of Bihar is included in the Eighth Schedule of the Constitution?
(a) Bhojpuri (b) Maithili
(c) Angika (d) Maghi

12. Who was the head of the military system in the administration of Sher Shah?
(a) Diwan-e-Wazir
(b) Diwan-e-Nadd
(c) Diwan-e-Ariz
(d) Diwan-e-Jung

13. Who is the author of the oldest and greatest Brahmin book 'shatpath Brahmin'?
(a) Taasi Agastya
(b) Yagyavalkya
(c) Sakya Muni
(d) Bhartruhari

14. When was Bhagalpur district of Bihar covered under Smart City Mission Scheme?
(a) 2014 AD (b) 2015 AD
(c) 2016 AD (d) 2017 AD

15. What is the average height of Bihar from sea level?
(a) 51 m (b) 53 m
(c) 55 m (d) 57 m

16. When did Emperor Shah Alam II provide civil aid to the East India Company from Bengal, Bihar and Orissa?
(a) 1761 AD (b) 1763 AD
(c) 1765 AD (d) 1767 AD

17. Who was the originator of the Sthavir community?
(a) Charvaka
(b) Mahakachyana
(c) Mahakashyap
(d) Rishi August

18. With whom was the 'sthayi bandobast' done?
(a) zamindars
(b) batayidaars
(c) bhumiheens
(d) (a), (b) and (c)

19. When and where was Satchi-dananda Sinha born?
(a) 1869 AD Nalanda
(b) 1871 AD Ara
(c) 1873 AD Jamui
(d) 1875 AD Munger

20. What type of forest belt (trees) is found in the northern frontier areas of Saharsa and Purnia?
(a) sal tree (b) mahua tree
(c) Ashoka Tree (d) Arjuna Tree

Answers

1. (a)	2. (c)	3. (a)	4. (c)
5. (a)	6. (b)	7. (a)	8. (b)
9. (a)	10. (b)	11. (b)	12. (c)
13. (b)	14. (c)	15. (b)	16. (c)
17. (b)	18. (a)	19. (b)	20. (a)

SET-29

1. **Who has created 'Siyar-ul-Mutakharayin'?**
   (a) Shad Azimabadi
   (b) Ghulam Hussain Tabai
   (c) Meen Hassan
   (d) Mullah Bahbahani
2. **Chairman or Deputy Chairman can be removed by the members by majority with a motion frought by giving a priod notice of minimum how many days?**
   (a) 10 days (b) 12 days
   (c) 14 days (d) 16 days
3. **When and where was Sir Ganesh Dutt born?**
   (a) 1866 AD Gaya
   (b) 1868 AD Nalanda
   (c) 1870 AD Munger
   (d) 1872 AD Kishanganj
4. **From which year has the 'saakshar Bharat Abhiyan' been implemented across the state?**
   (a) 2007 AD (b) 2009 AD
   (c) 2011 AD (d) 2013 AD
5. **Which is the most literate district in the state from the point of view of literacy?**
   (a) Rohtas (b) Patna
   (c) Buxar (d) Bhojpur
6. **Sanjhi style is the painting style of which area?**
   (a) Jharkhand (b) Bihar
   (c) Assam (d) Uttar Pradesh
7. **Using the statistical method, Prof. Inayat Ahmed divided Bihar into a total of how many agricultural regions in 1959 AD?**
   (a) 10 (b) 12
   (c) 14 (d) 16
8. **In which year was the statistical method first used by American scholar Vibhar?**
   (a) 1950 AD (b) 1952 AD
   (c) 1954 AD (d) 1956 AD
9. **Who built the great stupa of Sanchi?**
   (a) Ashoka (b) Ajatshatru
   (c) Kunal (d) Kalashok
10. **Where is Sabor Mela held in Bihar?**
    (a) Gaya (b) Munger
    (c) Bhagalpur (d) Banka
11. **When was the litterateur Shiv Pujan Sahai born?**
    (a)1891 AD (b) 1893 AD
    (c)1895 AD (d)1897 AD
12. **The remains of which era have been found in Chirand of Saran and Chechar in Vaishali?**
    (a) stone age
    (b) neolithic age
    (c) middle stone age
    (d) post-stone age
13. **What kind of pillar is the state symbol of India at Sarnath?**
    (a) Shaurya Stambh
    (b) Peace Pillar
    (c) Pragati Stambh
    (d) Leo Pillar
14. **On which hill is Someshwar Pass, Bhikhana Thori Pass and Marat Pass located?**
    (a) Kaimur (b) Parasnath
    (c) Someshwar (d) Ratnagiri
15. **Somnath Temple is located in which district of Bihar?**
    (a) Madhubani (b) Gaya
    (c) Banka (d) Jamui

16. Where is the Sourath Mela held in Bihar?
(a) Darbhanga (b) Jehanabad
(c) Arwal (d) Madhubani

17. When was the Sone Command Area Project constructed?
(a) 1870 AD (b) 1872 AD
(c) 1874 AD (d) 1876 AD

18. Which is the least literate district in the state?
(a) Purnia (b) Saharsa
(c) Supaul (d) Gaya

19. Sonpur Animal Fair is held in which district?
(a) Patna (b) Saran
(c) Gaya (d) Banka

20. Which district has the lowest population?
(a) Sheikhpura (b) Shivhar
(c) Jamui (d) Arwal

Answers

1. (b)	**2.** (c)	**3.** (b)	**4.** (c)
5. (a)	**6.** (d)	**7.** (b)	**8.** (c)
9. (a)	**10.** (c)	**11.** (b)	**12.** (b)
13. (b)	**14.** (c)	**15.** (a)	**16.** (d)
17. (c)	**18.** (a)	**19.** (b)	**20.** (a)

SET-30

1. Sonpur Nagar is situated on the banks of which river?
(a) Gandak (b) Ganga
(c) Kosi (d) Bagmati

2. Which of the 16 Mahajanapadas was located in Bihar?
(a) Magadha (b) Ang
(c) Vajji (d) all three

3. Which is the district with the lowest population density?
(a) Kaimur (b) Jehanabad
(c) Arwal (d) Gaya

4. Who was Married to Gautam Buddha at the age of 16?
(a) Yashodhara (b) Trishala
(c) Chelna (d) Karuvaki

5. Sadakat Ashram belongs to which politician?
(a) Sri Krishna Singh
(b) Rajendra Prasad
(c) Baldev Sahay
(d) Anugrah Narayan Singh

6. When was the Bihar Cricket Association formed?
(a) 1931 AD (b) 1933 AD
(c) 1935 AD (d) 1937 AD

7. Which house was formed by Swami Sahajananda Saraswati in 1930 AD?
(a) Bihar Kisan Sangh
(b) Bihar Kisan Sabha
(c) Bharat Kisan Sabha
(d) Akhil Bharatiya Sanyukt Kisan Sabha

8. Chirand is situated on the banks of which river?
(a) Ganga (b) Kosi
(c) Gandak (d) Son

9. Yogeshwar Singh as the most famous litterateur, is a litterateur of which language?
(a) Bhojpuri (b) Maghi
(c) Maithili (d) Angika

10. Which district has the highest population density in the State?
(a) Shivhar (b) Madhepura
(c) Gaya (d) Arrah

11. Which district has the highest population in the State?
(a) East Champaran
(b) Bhagalpur
(c) Patna
(d) Gaya

12. Where is Lauria Nandan Garh Mela held in Bihar?
(a) Purnia (b) Gaya
(c) Jehanabad (d) Arwal

13. Which district has the highest Scheduled Caste population?

(a) Gaya (b) West Champaran
(c) Supaul (d) Arwal

14. Which district has the highest number of Scheduled Tribes in terms of population in the State?

(a) Vaishali (b) Arwal
(c) Jamui (d) Katihar

15. In which year was the first forest policy of independent India formulated?

(a) 1950 AD (b) 1952 AD
(c) 1954 AD (d) 1956 AD

16. When was the first general election of Bihar held as per the Constitution of India?

(a) 1948 AD (b) 1950 AD
(c) 1952 AD (d) 1954 AD

17. Who was the first Chief Justice of Patna high court of independent India?

(a) Manmohan Agarwal
(b) Fazal Ali
(c) Bhupendra Chaudhary
(d) Santosh Yadav

18. When was the Department of Ancient Indian History and Archaeology established in Patna University?

(a) 1948 AD (b) 1949 AD
(c) 1950 AD (d) 1951 AD

19. What were the means of saving the political power of big zamindars in pre independence Bihar?

(a) economic situation
(b) social status
(c) religious status
(d) cultural status

20. Where is the origin of river Sone?

(a) Parasnath
(b) Aravalli
(c) Amarkantak
(d) Mahendragiri

Answers

1. (a)	**2.** (d)	**3.** (a)	**4.** (a)
5. (b)	**6.** (d)	**7.** (d)	**8.** (a)
9. (c)	**10.** (a)	**11.** (c)	**12.** (a)
13. (a)	**14.** (d)	**15.** (b)	**16.** (c)
17. (a)	**18.** (b)	**19.** (a)	**20.** (c)

SET-31

1. Who was the first Chief Minister of independent Bihar?

(a) Shri Krishna Singh
(b) Anagram Narayan Singh
(c) Rajendra Prasad
(d) Mohd Ghafoor

2. Who was given the title of 'Desh-bhushan' by Gandhiji?

(a) Rajendra Prasad
(b) Majhrul Haque
(c) Shri Krishna Singh
(d) Jai Prakash Narayan

3. Dinkarji was distinguished as a national poet by which of his works?

(a) Urvashi (b) Sandesh
(c) Renuka (d) Maila Aanchal

4. When was the Sarva Shiksha Abhiyan launched in the country?

(a) 2000 AD (b) 2001 AD
(c) 2002 AD (d) 2003 AD

5. Which ruler of Magadha made Vaishali also his capital in addition to Girivraj (Rajagraha)?

(a) Ajatshatru (b) Ghanananda
(c) Ashoka (d) Shishunag

6. Who first explained the meaning of Ashoka's inscriptions and when?

(a) John Morschel-1835 AD
(b) Cunningham-1836 AD
(c) James Prinsep-1837 AD
(d) Qual-1838 AD

7. Where is the famous Surya Kund located?

(a) Rajgir (b) Gaya
(c) Munger (d) Aurangabad

8. When and where was the well-known critic Manager Pandey born?
(a) 1940 AD Sivan
(b) 1941 AD Gopal Ganj
(c) 1942 AD Patna
(d) 1943 AD Shivhar

9. In which year was Sudama, a cave was built after Ashoka's accession?
(a) 10th year (b) 11th year
(c) 12th year (d) 13th year

10. What is the second name of Sudama Cave?
(a) Karnachaupada
(b) Lomash Rishi
(c) Barabar
(d) Nyagrodh

11. Sutta Pitak is compiled by
(a) Anand (b) Upali
(c) Buddha (d) Ajitabh

12. What had the Arab traveller Suleiman said about the Pala dynasty?
(a) palibrotha (b) ruhaila
(c) ruhaiya (d) kantkushil

13. Who has identified Chandragupta Maurya from Sandrokotus?
(a) William jones
(b) James Pricep
(c) Cunningham
(d) John Marshall

14. When and where was Syed Ahmed Bareli born?
(a) 1776 AD Rae Bareli
(b) 1777 AD Banda
(c) 1778 AD Allahabad
(d) 1779 AD Agra

15. In which year did Syed Ahmed Bareli visit Patna?
(a) 1817 AD (b) 1819 AD
(c) 1821 AD (d) 1823 AD

16. St. Joseph's Church, Bankipur is located in
(a) Patna (b) Gaya
(c) Muzaffarpur (d) Bhagalpur

17. Famous servants Ram and Hulas Lal are painters of which style?
(a) Madhubani Style
(b) Patna Kalam
(c) Manjusha Style
(d) (a), (b) and (c)

18. Who founded the Sen dynasty?
(a) Laxman Sen
(b) Rajendra Sen
(c) Gopal Sen
(d) Mihir Sen

19. Which mathematician first invented the decimal system?
(a) Kautilya (b) Charak
(c) Aryabhata (d) Lilavati

20. Which daughter of Seleucus was married to Chandragupta Maurya?
(a) Helena (b) Rexona
(c) Brigenja (d) Dolly

Answers

1. (a)	**2.** (b)	**3.** (c)	**4.** (b)
5. (d)	**6.** (c)	**7.** (a)	**8.** (b)
9. (c)	**10.** (d)	**11.** (a)	**12.** (c)
13. (a)	**14.** (a)	**15.** (c)	**16.** (a)
17. (b)	**18.** (a)	**19.** (c)	**20.** (a)

SET-32

1. Which ambassador was sent by Seleucus to the court of Chandragupta Maurya?
(a) Antioccus
(b) Megasthenes
(c) Veem Kadaphisus
(d) Rolf Fitch

2. Which province did Seleucus give to Chandragupta Maurya as dowry?

(a) Herat
(b) Kandahar
(c) Makran Coast
(d) All of the above

3. Who led Bihar in the revolution of 1857?
(a) Amar Singh (b) Kunwar Singh
(c) Pir Ali (d) Tantya Tope

4. Where was Sanyasi Baikunth Shukla born?
(a) Vaishali (b) Gaya
(c) Arrah (d) Buxar

5. Who was the President of the Indian National Congress of Gaya session in 1922?
(a) Maulana Abdul Kalam Azad
(b) Chittaranjan Das
(c) Mahatma Gandhi
(d) Shri Krishna Singh

6. What is Lorik Maniyar?
(a) large lyricist (b) scripture
(c) social law (d) deva granth

7. Who was the first Governor of independent Bihar?
(a) J.B. Kripalani
(b) Ramdayalu Singh
(c) Asaf Ali
(d) Jairam Das Daulat Ram

8. Who was the last ruler of the Sen dynasty?
(a) Kunal Sen (b) Samant Sen
(c) Gopal Sen (d) Surya Sen

9. When was the Sunlight Army formed?
(a) 1983 AD (b) 1985 AD
(c) 1987 AD (d) 1889 AD

10. As per the State Forest Report 2015, what percentage of the total forest cover found in Bihar is very dense forest?
(a) 0.26% (b) 0.32%
(c) 0.41% (d) 0.52%

11. In which financial year was the Students Guidance Centre scheme launched in Bihar?
(a) 2007 AD (b) 2009 AD
(c) 2011 AD (d) 2013 AD

12. When and where was the popular poet, singer and playwright Bhikhari Thakur born?
(a) 1887 AD Saran
(b) 1888 AD Sivan
(c) 1889 AD Gaya
(d) 1890 AD Jamui

13. Shyama Kali Temple in Darbhanga is built on whose pyre?
(a) Maheshwar Singh
(b) Rameshwar Singh
(c) Dineshwar Singh
(d) Rajeshwar Singh

14. Sun Temple, Aurangabad was built by which ruler?
(a) Hari Singh
(b) Man Singh
(c) Ahilyabai
(d) Bhairavendra Singh

15. Sukhaldari Falls has been constructed on which river?
(a) Kanhar (b) Sarisava
(c) Tilave (d) Narayani

16. In which jail was Dr. Rajendra Prasad housed on 9th August, 1942?
(a) Ranchi (b) Ambala
(c) Poona (d) Bankipur

17. Dr. Sachchidanand Sinha Award is given for which subject?
(a) Literature (b) Method
(c) Journalism (d) Medicine

18. The law of renunciation of the body by fasting exists in Jainism, this is called?
(a) Kaivalya (b) Sanlekhna
(c) Jeevtrapt (d) Amodyatrapt

19. Which region was declared their state by the Santhals in (1855-56) AD?

(a) Raajmahal (b) Manbhum
(c) Dhalbhum (d) Veerbhum

20. Who was the first Indian Governor General of independent India?

(a) J.B. Kripalani
(b) Rajendra Prasad
(c) Arfana Asaf Ali
(d) Rajagopalachari

Answers

1. (b)	**2.** (d)	**3.** (b)	**4.** (a)
5. (b)	**6.** (a)	**7.** (d)	**8.** (b)
9. (d)	**10.** (a)	**11.** (b)	**12.** (a)
13. (b)	**14.** (d)	**15.** (a)	**16.** (d)
17. (b)	**18.** (b)	**19.** (a)	**20.** (d)

SET-33

1. Who was the first Chairman of Odisha-Bihar legislative council?

(a) Walter Mande
(b) James Mill
(c) Kevid Baro
(d) Lee Grand

2. Who has first used the absolute pattern for measurement of direction?

(a) Amartya Sen
(b) Mahbul-ul-Haq
(c) R. Wayed
(d) James Mill

3. Where is Udaipur Wildlife Sanctuary located?

(a) West Chamaparan
(b) Gaya
(c) Banka
(d) Shivhar

4. What are the two methods of measuring relative poverty?

(a) Son curve
(b) Larang curve
(c) Gini Coefficient
(d) (b) and (c)

5. Who propounded the Gini coefficient method?

(a) James Ganini
(b) David Gini
(c) Koredo Gini
(d) William Gini

6. Udayan was governor of which place during the reign of his father Ajatshatru?

(a) Champa (b) Ujjain
(c) Kashi (d) Takshashila

7. When and where was Shah Azimabadi, who made Bihar famous for Urdu Shayari, born?

(a) 1845 AD Nalanda
(b) 1846 AD Patna
(c) 1847 AD Gaya
(d) 1848 AD Vaishali

8. When was Patna College established as a godown by Dutch East India Company?

(a) 1859 AD (b) 1861 AD
(c) 1863 AD (d) 1865 AD

9. In which article is the High Court of Records called as 'Court of Records'?

(a) Article 211 (b) Article 213
(c) Article 215 (d) Article 217

10. When did the Orissa-Bihar Legislative Council come into existence?

(a) 1920 AD (b) 1921 AD
(c) 1922 AD (d) 1923 AD

11. What is the length of North to South Bihar?

(a) 345 Kms (b) 350 kms
(c) 355 Kms (d) 360 kms

12. Who is the author of the book 'Jayaprakash' based on the biography of Loknayak Jayaprakash Narayan?

(a) Nagarjuna
(b) Ramvriksha Benipuri

(c) Ramdhari Singh Dinkar
(d) Suryakant Tripathi Nirala

13. Material related to North Neolithic period is found from which place of Bihar?
(a) Gaya (b) Aurangabad
(c) Pataliputra (d) Chirand

14. What is the low land area naturally submerged in the northern Ganga plain called?
(a) diyara (b) mana
(c) chaur (d) (b) and (c)

15. Which technique is called improved seeds, food and water?
(a) green revolution
(b) farming revolution
(c) machine revolution
(d) evergreen revolution

16. Where is the Ugrastara Temple located?
(a) Saran (b) Sivan
(c) Purnia (d) Saharsa

17. When was the first official attempt made by the Planning Commission to determine the poverty line in India?
(a) 1960 AD (b) 1962 AD
(c) 1964 AD (d) 1966 AD

18. By whom was the 'The Bihar Herald' published?
(a) Guruprasad Sen
(b) Maheshwar Singh
(c) Majhrul Haque
(d) Mohd Yunus

19. Which metal was found stocked in Magadha in the sixth century BC?
(a) copper (b) pyrite
(c) iron (d) mica

20. When was an Expert Team constituted by the Planning Commission under the Chairmanship of Prof. D.T. Lakdawala to measure poverty in the country?
(a) 1988 AD (b) 1989 AD
(c) 1990 AD (d)1991 AD

Answers

1. (a)	**2.** (c)	**3.** (a)	**4.** (d)
5. (c)	**6.** (a)	**7.** (b)	**8.** (c)
9. (c)	**10.** (b)	**11.** (a)	**12.** (b)
13. (d)	**14.** (d)	**15.** (a)	**16.** (d)
17. (b)	**18.** (a)	**19.** (c)	**20.** (b)

SET-34

1. Which is the longest tributary of Ganga flowing in South Bihar?
(a) Sone (b) Ghaghara
(c) Kosi (d) Gandak

2. In which direction is the slope of the plain of the Southern Ganga?
(a) South (b) North
(c) West (d) East

3. What was the head of Diwan-e-Wajarat called?
(a) Munsif (b) Rai Bahadur
(c) Chaudhary (d) Wazir

4. Which leader of Bihar participated with Gandhiji in Dandi March?
(a) Mahjorule Haque
(b) Girivardhari Chaudhary
(c) Rajendra Prasad
(d) Rajkumar Shukla

5. Which is the script written from right to left?
(a) Brahmi (b) Armic
(c) Greek (d) Kharosthi

6. When was Dashrath Manjhi skill development scheme launched in Bihar?
(a) 2009 AD (b) 2011 AD
(c) 2013 AD (d) 2015 AD

7. When was the Chhotanagpur Tenancy Act passed?
(a) 1906 AD (b) 1908 AD
(c) 1910 AD (d)1912 AD

8. What is the name of the soil found in the meeting area of

Chhotanagpur Plateau and the south plain of Ganga?

(a) Kagari (b) Kewal
(c) Balther (d) Balsundari

9. Suresh Tendulkar Committee is related to

(a) poverty line fixation
(b) unemployment
(c) economic growth
(d) border security

10. Where was Smriti Jha, the heroine of the serial Kumkum Bhagya, born in Bihar?

(a) Gaya (b) Begusarai
(c) Patna (d) Nalanda

11. Which is the state tree of Bihar?

(a) Peepal (b) banyan
(c) Mango (d) Arjuna

12. Where is Durgavati Falls located?

(a) Bhojpur (b) Gaya
(c) Kaimur (d) Patna

13. What is Chhatri Chauhan?

(a) folk saga
(b) folk dance
(c) Painting
(d) Religious Rituals

14. In which state is the country's largest animal fair held?

(a) Uttar Pradesh
(b) Rajasthan
(c) Bihar
(d) Punjab

15. Renowned shehnai player Ustad Bismillah Khan was a resident of which district of Bihar?

(a) Buxar (b) Siwan
(c) Patna (d) Nalanda

16. Who was the Vibhuti of Bihar to become the Deputy Prime Minister of the country?

(a) Asaf Ali
(b) Rajendra Prasad
(c) Mahamaya Prasad
(d) Babu Jagjivan Ram

17. Where was the great clarinet player Bismillah Khan born?

(a) Dumraon (b) Bihar Sharif
(c) Hajipur (d) Maner

18. At whose time and when did the regular 10-year census in the country begin?

(a) Lord Mayo, 1852 AD
(b) Lord Litton, 1862 AD
(c) Lord Ripnai 1881 AD
(d) Lord Curzon, 1834 AD

19. When was the family planning programme implemented in the country?

(a) 1947 AD (b) 1948 AD
(c) 1949 AD (d)1950 AD

20. Which animal is the state animal of Bihar?

(a) Bull (b) Elephant
(c) Horse (d) Lion

Answers

1. (a)	**2.** (a)	**3.** (d)	**4.** (b)
5. (d)	**6.** (c)	**7.** (b)	**8.** (c)
9. (a)	**10.** (b)	**11.** (a)	**12.** (c)
13. (a)	**14.** (c)	**15.** (a)	**16.** (d)
17. (a)	**18.** (c)	**19.** (b)	**20.** (a)

SET-35

1. Which were the two provinces in the country whose provincial conference had already called for non-cooperation before the Calcutta session?

(a) Gujarat
(b) Bihar
(c) Tamil Nadu
(d) (a) and (b)

2. Which fruits are desi, arlybedana, shahi, mandraji (china), kaswa etc.

(a) mango (b) litchi
(c) Guava (d) Banana

3. Who has been given the title of 'Deshratna'?
(a) Rajendra Prasad
(b) Majhrul Haque
(c) Jayaprakash Narayan
(d) vinova bhave

4. Which Commission was constituted by the Planning Commission in 1973 AD to measure unemployment?
(a) lakadwala commission
(b) Sen Commission
(c) Abid Ali Commission
(d) Bhagwati Commission

5. At which place was the dam constructed at Valmiki Nagar under Gandak project in (1969–70) AD?
(a) Hanuman Ghat
(b) Gandak Ghat
(c) Triveni Ghat
(d) Pyawarja Ghat

6. The general unemployment rate is known as
(a) disguised unemployment
(b) gradual unemployment
(c) cyclic unemployment
(d) educated unemployment

7. What was the population of Bihar as per census 2011?
(a) 10.30 crores (b) 10.35 crores
(c) 10.41 crores (d) 10.47 crores

8. What is the average height of Bihar from the sea-level?
(a) 53 meter (b) 55 meter
(c) 57 meter (d) 59 meter

9. Who created 'Nachari Raag' and 'Lagni Raag'?
(a) Bhikhari Thakur
(b) Naval Kishore Singh
(c) Vidyapati
(d) Sukhdev Roy

10. Ramdhari Singh 'Dinkar' was awarded the Jnanpith Award for the creation of which epic?
(a) Urvashi
(b) Renuka
(c) Maila Aanchal
(d) Sanskriti ke char adhyay

11. Who is the author of 'India Divided'?
(a) Indira Gandhi
(b) Mahatma Gandhi
(c) Hasan Imam
(d) Rajendra Prasad

12. Where was the first meeting of the Congress Socialist Party held?
(a) Patna (b) Ranchi
(c) Hazaribagh (d) Dhanbad

13. Who played the role of the mastermind of the formation of Nana Sena in Nepal?
(a) Pir Ali
(b) Amar Singh
(c) Jagdev Sahay
(d) Sachindranath Sanyal

14. What was the name of the last ruler of the Brihadratha dynasty?
(a) Kapalijaya (b) Amarjay
(c) Dipjaya (d) Ripunjaya

15. Who was the capital of the Vajji Sangha?
(a) Vaishali (b) Champa
(c) Mall (d) Ujjain

16. Who was the ruler of Magadha who defeated the Lichchavis of the Vajji Sangha?
(a) Bimbi Sara (b) Ajatshatru
(c) Ghanananda (d) Ashoka

17. Who wrote the book Revolutionary Quest?
(a) Jai Prakash Narayan
(b) Hassan Imam
(c) Rajendra Prasad
(d) Shri Krishna Singh

18. Who was the first commander to lead the English army in Arrah against Kunwar Singh?
(a) Captain Lee Grand
(b) Captain Dunver
(c) Major Baro
(d) Major Lee

19. Who has composed the book 'Bapu's Footsteps'?
(a) Majhrul Haque
(b) Jawaharlal Nehru
(c) Shri Krishna Singh
(d) Rajendra Prasad

20. What is the sect that believes in the pure religious doctrine of Buddha?
(a) Hinayana (b) Vajrayana
(c) Mahayana (d) Shuddhayana

Answers

1. (d)	**2.** (b)	**3.** (a)	**4.** (d)
5. (c)	**6.** (b)	**7.** (c)	**8.** (a)
9. (c)	**10.** (b)	**11.** (d)	**12.** (a)
13. (b)	**14.** (d)	**15.** (a)	**16.** (b)
17. (a)	**18.** (b)	**19.** (d)	**20.** (a)

SET-36

1. Who was the first Mughal ruler whose inscriptions have been found in Bihar?
(a) Humayun (b) Akbar
(c) Jahangir (d) Aurangzeb

2. Who was the first Indian to get membership of the House of Lords and the Privy Council?
(a) Sachchidanand Sinha
(b) Dada Bhai Naoroji
(c) Arfana Asaf Ali
(d) Krishna sahay

3. Prabodh Sahitya Samman is the highest literary award of which language?
(a) Bhojpari (b) Maghi
(c) Maithili (d) Angika

4. How many seats are reserved for Scheduled Tribes in Bihar Assembly?
(a) 2 (b) 3
(c) 4 (d) 5

5. When was Veer Kunwar Singh University established?
(a) 1992 AD (b) 1994 AD
(c) 1996 AD (d) 1998 AD

6. Who is addressed by 'Bihar Kesari'?
(a) Rajendra Prasad
(b) Majhrul Haque
(c) Jagjivan Ram
(d) Shri Krishna Singh

7. Architect Mahagovinda was in the court of which ruler?
(a) Bimbisara (b) Ajatshatru
(c) Udayan (d) Ashoka

8. When was Loknayak Jayaprakash Narayan awarded Bharat Ratna?
(a) 1999 AD (b) 2000 AD
(c) 2001 AD (d) 2002 AD

9. Which is the first state in the country to launch the mobile service of Bharat Sanchar Nigam Limited?
(a) Jharkhand (b) West Bengal
(c) Assam (d) Bihar

10. Valmiki National Park is located in which district?
(a) West Chamaparan
(b) Gaya
(c) Aurangabad
(d) Munger

11. When was the 'Sampurn Kranti' declared by Jayaprakash Narayan in Patna?
(a) 1970 AD (b) 1972 AD
(c) 1974 AD (d) 1976 AD

12. Which ruler started the practice of confession and lease?
(a) Sher Shah
(b) Akbar

(c) Ibrahim Lodi
(d) Aurangzeb

13. Navnalanda Mahavihara is famous for
(a) Buddhist monastery
(b) Pali research
(c) University
(d) (a), (b) and (c)

14. How many departments are there in Bihar Secretariat?
(a) 40 (b) 42
(c) 44 (d) 46

15. Which university is being renovated in collaboration with China?
(a) Nalanda University
(b) Vikramshila University
(c) Odantpuri
(d) (a), (b) and (c)

16. The present Bodhi tree belongs to which generation?
(a) 4th (b) 5th
(c) 6th (d) 7th

17. Bindusara was a follower of which sect?
(a) Ajivak (b) Jain
(c) Buddhist (d) Shaiva

18. Which Afghan subedar of Bihar revolted during the time of Lodi ruler Ibrahim Khan Lodi?
(a) Aamir Khan Nouhani
(b) Dare khan Nuhani
(c) Mir Zafar
(d) Bakhtiyar Khan

19. How many national parks are there in Bihar?
(a) 1 (b) 2
(c) 3 (d) 4

20. How many wildlife sanctuaries are there in Bihar at present?
(a) 10 (b) 11
(c) 12 (d) 13

Answers

1. (b)	**2.** (a)	**3.** (c)	**4.** (a)
5. (a)	**6.** (d)	**7.** (a)	**8.** (a)
9. (d)	**10.** (a)	**11.** (c)	**12.** (a)
13. (b)	**14.** (c)	**15.** (a)	**16.** (b)
17. (a)	**18.** (b)	**19.** (a)	**20.** (c)

SET-37

1. In which year did Lord Cornwallis implement zamindari system under permanent settlement in Bihar-Bengal region?
(a) 1791 AD
(b) 1793 AD
(c) 1795 AD
(d) 1797 AD

2. Under which scheme is the State Road being developed in Bihar?
(a) National Even Development Scheme
(b) Mukhyamantri Sadak Yojana
(c) Pradhan Mantri Sadak Yojana
(d) National Road Scheme

3. A compilation of letters of which Sufi saint is known as 'Maktubate Sadi?
(a) Sant Daulat Shah
(b) Sant Mehrab Ali
(c) Sant Makhdoom Shah
(d) Sant Karam Shah

4. Who presided over the Bombay Convention of the Muslim League (1915)?
(a) Majhrul Haque
(b) Rajendra Prasad
(c) Jayaprakash Narayan
(d) Hassan Imam

5. Which main weapon was used by Ajatshatru in the war?
(a) trench
(b) thorn rock
(c) Rathmusal
(d) Both (b) and (c)

6. When was the Archaeological Museum established in Vaishali?
(a) 1945 AD (b) 1946 AD
(c) 1947 AD (d) 1948 AD

7. Two inseriptions of whose have been recovered from Basadhar (Vaishali)?
(a) Ajatshatru
(b) Ghanananda
(c) Ashoka
(d) Mahadevi Prabhudaya

8. In which Vedic book the evidence of the arrival and settlement of the Aryans in the Videha state of Bihar is found?
(a) Tatgveda
(b) Shatpath Brahmin
(c) Aranyaka
(d) Atharvaveda

9. Where did Mir Qasim build his capital?
(a) Munger
(b) Bhagalpur
(c) Hajipur
(d) Bihar Sharif

10. At whose level, compensation is paid on crop loss, loss of life, loss of home and loss of life of human beings, disability etc. caused by Wild animals?
(a) District Collector
(b) Forest Division Officer
(c) Zone Officer
(d) Deputy Commissioner

11. The Wildlife (Protection) Act, 1972 is applicable in states other than which State of the country?
(a) Andhra Pradesh
(b) J&K
(c) Karnataka
(d) West Bengal

12. Who created the 'Precision Diary'?
(a) Jai Prakash Narayan
(b) Mahatma Gandhi
(c) Asaf Ali
(d) Rajendra Prasad

13. What is the area of Bihar?
(a) 91,120 sq km
(b) 92,480 sq km
(c) 93,840 sq km
(d) 94,163 sq km

14. What percentage of total area of India is occupied by Bihar?
(a) 262% (b) 2.69%
(c) 273% (d) 2.86%

15. Who was the Prime Minister of Chandragupta Maurya?
(a) Chanakya (b) Ghanananda
(c) Upgupta (d) Nagdashak

16. Who was the first English traveller to travel to Bihar?
(a) Tomas roe
(b) James mill
(c) John Marshall
(d) Rolf Fitch

17. Who was the ruler who sent Megasthenes to the court of Chandragupta Maurya?
(a) Cellucus (b) Antioccus
(c) George V (d) Alexander

18. At which place was the first Jain conference held?
(a) Pavapuri (b) Vaishali
(c) Pataliputra (d) Vallabhpuri

19. Who built Champa (Bhagalpur)?
(a) Nagdashak (b) Pushyamitra
(c) Ashwasen (d) Mahagovind

20. Who was the national leader of Champaran neel movement?
(a) Mahatma Gandhi
(b) Brajkishore Prasad
(c) Jawaharlal Nehru
(d) Rajkumar Shukla

Answers

1. (b)	**2.** (a)	**3.** (c)	**4.** (a)
5. (d)	**6.** (a)	**7.** (d)	**8.** (b)
9. (a)	**10.** (b)	**11.** (b)	**12.** (a)
13. (d)	**14.** (d)	**15.** (a)	**16.** (d)
17. (a)	**18.** (c)	**19.** (d)	**20.** (a)

SET-38

1. **From which place was the Neolithic relic first found in Bihar?**
(a) Chirand (b) Gaya
(c) Kesaria (d) Areraj
2. **In which century did Chinese traveller Shisingsh visit Bihar?**
(a) 5th century (b) 6th century
(c) 7th century (d) 8th century
3. **During whose reign did Hnesang go all over Bihar?**
(a) Harshvardhan
(b) Mahipal
(c) Laxman Sen
(d) Kumargupta
4. **Who was the first resident of Bihar to become the Chief Justice of the Supreme Court?**
(a) Fazal Ali
(b) Bhubaneswar Prasad Sinha
(c) Gyan Sudha Mishra
(d) Dipak Misra
5. **Chanakya Award is given in which field?**
(a) Politics (b) journalism
(c) Medical (d) Diplomacy
6. **Which is the first electronic city in India?**
(a) New Delhi (b) Pune
(c) Bengaluru (d) Hajipur
7. **Which district of the state produces the highest production of tea?**
(a) Araria (b) Kishanganj
(c) Katihar (d) Bhagalpur
8. **The statue of Chamargrahini Yakshini is the best symbol of Mauryan folk art, from which place was this idol obtained?**
(a) Didarganj (b) Bihar Sharif
(c) Nalanda (d) Bodh Gaya
9. **Which is the first state in the country to give legal powers to the Minority Commission?**
(a) Assam (b) Kerala
(c) Maharashtra (d) Bihar
10. **What is the position of Bihar in the country in rice production?**
(a) Third (b) Fourth
(c) Fifth (d) Sixth
11. **When was the Right to Public Grievances Act implemented?**
(a) 2010 AD (b) 2012 AD
(c) 2014 AD (d) 2016 AD
12. **Which is the first yoga school in the world?**
(a) Patanjali Yoga Vidyalaya, Haridwar
(b) Munger Yoga Vidyalaya
(c) New Delhi Yoga Vidyalaya
(d) Ambala Yoga Vidyalaya
13. **When was the Battle of Chausa fought?**
(a) 1536 AD (b) 1537 AD
(c) 1538 AD (d) 1539 AD
14. **Which bhishti saved Humayun's life after his defeat in the Battle of Chausa?**
(a) Nizam (b) Safdar Khan
(c) Mir Baki (d) Shujaat Khan
15. **14 Purvas is the only literature of which Jain sect?**
(a) Shwetambar Jain
(b) Digambar Jain
(c) Mahavir Jain
(d) Both (a), (b)
16. **When was smallpox discovered?**
(a) 1974 AD (b) 1976 AD
(c) 1978 AD (d) 1980 AD
17. **Where is Chaitanya Mahaprabhu temple located?**
(a) Patna (b) Aurangabad
(c) Gaya (d) Shivhar
18. **Where is Chandragupta basadi temple located?**
(a) Vallabhi
(b) Vaishali
(c) Shravanabelagola
(d) Pavapuri

19. Which ruler issued the first coin of rupee in India?
(a) Sher Shah
(b) Akbar
(c) Iltutmish
(d) Mohd bin Tughlaq .

20. Chandragupta Maurya was a follower of which religion?
(a) Ajivak (b) Jain
(c) Buddhist (d) Shaiva

Answers

1. (a)	**2.** (c)	**3.** (a)	**4.** (b)
5. (a)	**6.** (d)	**7.** (b)	**8.** (a)
9. (d)	**10.** (c)	**11.** (d)	**12.** (b)
13. (d)	**14.** (a)	**15.** (b)	**16.** (c)
17. (a)	**18.** (c)	**19.** (a)	**20.** (b)

SET-39

1. Chanakya, the famous guru of Chandragupta Maurya, belonged to which vidya Kendra?
(a) Takshashila (b) Nalanda
(c) Odantpuri (d) Somapuri

2. When did Chandragupta Maurya fight seleucus?
(a) 301 AD (b) 303 AD
(c) 305 AD (d) 307 AD

3. Who was the first person from the State of Bihar to receive the Ashoka Chakra?
(a) Randhir Verma
(b) Chandrabhan Singh
(c) Shahid Khan
(d) Arjun Singh

4. Where is the limestone-based cement industry established?
(a) amzor (b) banjari
(c) Gaya (d) Aurangabad

5. Who was the first Chairman of Bihar State Commission for Women?
(a) Manju Prakash
(b) Jayanti Yadav
(c) Ejya Singh
(d) Nahid Parveen

6. Who was Phaneeswarnath Renu?
(a) Poet (b) Litterateur
(c) playwright (d) historian

7. When and where was Father Kamil Bulke born?
(a) 1909 AD Belgium
(b) 1910 AD London
(c) 1911 AD Lahore
(d) 1912 AD Ranchi

8. Which city is situated on the banks of river Falgu?
(a) Aurangabad
(b) Gaya
(c) Bhagalpur
(d) Munger

9. Where was the third Buddhist conference held?
(a) Rajagraha (b) Vaishali
(c) Pataliputra (d)Gaya

10. What is the name of the stupa built by Ashoka at Takshashila?
(a) Raj Prasad
(b) Dharmarajika Stupa
(c) Dhamma Stupa
(d) Shanti Stupa

11. When was the third Round Table Conference held?
(a) 1930 AD (b) 1931 AD
(c) 1932 AD (d) 1933 AD

12. What kind of settlements are more common in Terai region due to rough land?
(a) scattered settlements
(b) fragmented settlements
(c) Square Settlements
(d) (b) and (c)

13. Who is the author of 'Tareekh-e-Shershahi'?
(a) Abdul Hamid Lahori
(b) Mullah Bahbahani
(c) Abbas Khan Sharwani
(d) Abul Fazal

14. Tasar is produced mainly in which district of the state?

(a) Bhagalpur (b) Gaya
(c) Munger (d) Banka

15. From which literary source does the Turk invasion come to light?

(a) Shahnama
(b) Tabkat-e-Hind
(b) Tabkate Nasiri
(d) Dat -e-Shershahi

16. Which place was the capital of Bihar during the Tughlaq period?

(a) Patna (b) Darbhanga
(c) Bihar Sharif (d) Hajipur

17. From which river is the Teur Canal drawn?

(a) Son (b) kosi .
(c) Bagmati (d) Gandak

18. Telhar Waterfall is located in which district?

(a) Rohtas (b) West Champaran
(c) Sivan (d) Gopalganj

19. When and where was Jayaprakash Narayan born?

(a) 1901 AD Sivan
(b) 1902 AD Saran
(c) 1903 AD Patna
(d) 1904 AD Munger

20. Jayaprakash Narayan was known by what another name?

(a) Loknayak (b) Jannayak
(c) Deshratna (d) Deshbhushan

Answers

1. (a)	**2.** (b)	**3.** (a)	**4.** (b)
5. (a)	**6.** (b)	**7.** (a)	**8.** (b)
9. (c)	**10.** (b)	**11.** (c)	**12.** (a)
13. (c)	**14.** (a)	**15.** (a)	**16.** (c)
17. (d)	**18.** (a)	**19.** (b)	**20.** (a)

SET-40

1. When is the birth anniversary of Jayaprakash Narayan celebrated?

(a) 12 May (b) March 28
(c) 11 October (d) 21 January

2. Which party was founded by Jayaprakash Narayan?

(a) Bihar Socialist Party
(b) Bihar People's Party
(c) Bihar Ekta Party
(d) Bihar Congress Party

3. When was Jayaprabha Janani shishu Arogya express scheme launched in Bihar?

(a) 2008 AD (b) 2010 AD
(c) 2012 AD (d) 2014 AD

4. When was the law on abolition of zamindari and termination of middleman enacted?

(a) 1949 AD (b) 1950 AD
(c) 1951 AD (d) 1952 AD

5. Which prince was appointed governor of Bihar by Jahangir in 1621 AD?

(a) Azim
(b) Shah Alam-II
(c) Parvez
(d) Bahadur Shah Zafar

6. What was the name of Jarasandha's father?

(a) bridraha (b) brihadratha
(c) Nagadas (d) Pushyamitra

7. In which city of Japan has the Mithila Museum been built in collaboration with Hasegawa?

(a) Tokama (b) Nagoya
(c) Tokyo (d) Nagasaki

8. What causes rainfall in Bihar during winters?

(a) Monsoon
(b) Pachuva Disturbance
(c) Eastern Disturbances
(d) Commercial Wind

9. When and where was Jawaharlal Nehru Medical College established in Bihar?

(a) Bhagalpur 1971
(b) Gaya 1972

(c) Patna 1973
(d) Munger 1974

10. When was the Jawaharlal Nehru Nagar Renewal Mission (Shra-chanda) launched?
(a) 2004 AD (b) 2005 AD
(c) 2006 AD (d) 2007 AD

11. What justice have the Jains imagined to explain the ultimate element?
(a) kavalya (b) moksha
(c) Saptakarma (d) Saptabhan

12. Jain and Buddhist texts consider Chandragupta Maurya to be related to which Kshatriya dynasty?
(a) Maurya (b) Aprait
(c) Gyatak (d) Kareva

13. Which is the first irrigation project of Bihar?
(a) Gandak (b) Ganga
(c) Sone (d) Kosi

14. Where is the birthplace of Vasupujya, the 12th Tirthankara of Jainism?
(a) Munger (b) Pavapuri
(c) Pataliputra (d) Bhagalpur

15. Where was Mahavir Swami, the 24th Tirthankara of Jainism, born?
(a) Kundgram (b) Kundlavan
(c) Pavapuri (d) Gaya

16. Which rule did Mahavir Swami add to the five rules of Jainism?
(a) Truth (b) Non-violence
(c) Asteya (d) Celibacy

17. Who was the first Tirthankara of Jainism who is considered to be the founder of Jainism?
(a) Rishabhdev
(b) Ajitnath
(c) Parsvanatha
(d) Mahavir Swami

18. Where was the first municipality established in Bihar?
(a) Patna (b) Arrah
(c) Buxar (d) Chhapra

19. Who is called the first great poet of Bihar?
(a) Vidyapati
(b) Mandan Mishra
(c) Bhikhari Thakur
(d) Ramdhari Singh Dinkar

20. How many Tirthankaras have there been in Jainism?
(a) 21 (b) 22
(c) 23 (d) 24

Answers

1. (c)	**2.** (a)	**3.** (c)	**4.** (b)
5. (c)	**6.** (b)	**7.** (a)	**8.** (b)
9. (a)	**10.** (b)	**11.** (d)	**12.** (a)
13. (a)	**14.** (d)	**15.** (a)	**16.** (d)
17. (a)	**18.** (b)	**19.** (a)	**20.** (d)

SET-41

1. In which city of Bihar was the first centre of All India Radio established?
(a) Patna (b) Muzaffarpur
(c) Gaya (d) Hajipur

2. Who created 12 angas of Jain literature?
(a) Rishabhdev (b) Mahavir Swami
(c) Jamali (d) Sathlbhadra

3. Agam granth belongs to which sect?
(a) Jain (b) Shaiva
(c) Ajivak (d) Vaishnava

4. The birth place of Gautam Buddha is recorded by which article?
(a) Bairath
(b) Amravati
(c) Lauria-Areraj
(d) Rummindei

5. According to Jain anushruti, where did Chandragupta Maurya die?

(a) Vallabhi
(b) Shravanabelagola
(c) Pataliputra
(d) Pavapuri

6. Where is kamaldah, the ancient and famous temple of Jainism, located?
(a) Patna (b) Gaya
(c) Vaishali (d) Pavapuri

7. From the point of view of population density, what is the position of Bihar in the country?
(a) 1st (b) 2nd
(c) 3rd (d) 4th

8. Which place does Bihar have in the country in terms of population?
(a) 1st (b) 2nd
(c) 3rd (d) 4th

9. In which year was the Bihar State Pollution Prevention Council constituted?
(a) 1947 AD (b) 1948 AD
(c) 1949 AD (d) 1950 AD

10. Since when was Janani and Bal suraksha yojana implemented in Bihar?
(a) 2004 AD (b) 2006 AD
(c) 2008 AD (d) 2010 AD

11. In which year was the Jayaprakash Employment Guarantee Scheme launched?
(a) 2002 AD (b) 2004 AD
(c) 2006 AD (d) 2008 AD

12. Where is Jagjivan Stadium located?
(a) Purnia (b) Dihata
(c) Khagol (d) Bihar Sharif

13. Where is Lalgarh Fort located?
(a) Kishanganj (b) Katihar
(c) Purnia (d) Araria

14. Khadar mitti is known as
(a) loam soil
(b) laterite soil
(c) Balther Soil
(d) New Alluvial Soil

15. Which district has minimum population density?
(a) Kaimur (b) Gaya
(c) Buxar (d) Rohtas

16. Where is Indira Gandhi medical centre located in Bihar?
(a) Bhagalpur (b) Munger
(c) Hajipur (a) Patna

17. Which is the district with minimum population?
(a) Sheikhupura
(b) Banka
(c) Shivhar
(d) Jamui

18. Who was the founder of Nanda dynasty?
(a) Ghanananda
(b) Mahapadmananda
(c) Gopananda
(d) Navananda

19. Under which Act was the Bihar State Pollution Prevention Council constituted?
(a) Environment Protection Act-1986
(b) The Water Pollution (Prevention and Control) Act,1974
(c) Forest Conservation Act-1980
(d) (a), (b) and (c)

20. At what rate compensation is paid to the farmers if a crop is damaged by antelopes?
(a) 10,000 (b) 15,000
(c) 20,000 (d) 25,000

Answers

1. (a)	**2.** (d)	**3.** (a)	**4.** (d)
5. (b)	**6.** (a)	**7.** (a)	**8.** (c)
9. (a)	**10.** (b)	**11.** (a)	**12.** (c)
13. (c)	**14.** (d)	**15.** (a)	**16.** (d)
17. (a)	**18.** (b)	**19.** (b)	**20.** (c)

SET-42

1. **Which language was named 'Chhikachiki' by Dr. Gearson?**
(a) angika (b) maghi
(c) Maithili (d) Bhojpuri

2. **Where did Nanyadeva build the capital of Karnat?**
(a) Rajgarh (b) Vallabhgarh
(c) Rohtasgarh (d) Simraogarh

3. **What is 'Nagdashak' called in the Puranas?**
(a) Darshak (b) Shatak
(c) Ahaan (d) Jamita

4. **The ancient university of Nalanda was built during the reign of which dynasty?**
(a) Mauryan dynasty
(b) Gupta dynasty
(c) Pal dynasty
(d) Shun dynasty

5. **In which year was Urdu given the status of second official language in Bihar?**
(a) 1980 AD (b) 1982 AD
(c) 1984 AD (d)1986 AD

6. **Which pratihara king's coins have been found in Nalanda?**
(a) Bhoj (b) Rudradaman
(c) Ahichatra (d) Nagdashak

7. **Which litterateur from Bihar is called the Shakespeare of Bhojpuri?**
(a) Vidyapati
(b) Bhikhari Thakur
(c) Kanhaiya Dubey
(d) Chaman Yadav

8. **Nalanda University was established by which Gupta ruler?**
(a) Kumargupta (b) Samudragupta
(c) Varungupta (d) Chandragupta II

9. **Which litterateur is called the style of Magahi?**
(a) Sharad Jha (b) Suresh Dubey
(c) Vidyapati (d) Anjani Jha

10. **Who was the famous Vice Chancellor of Nalanda University?**
(a) Sheelbhadra (b) Dipankar
(c) Vridrath (d) Ashwaghosh

11. **When was the Maithili Literary Council established in Bihar?**
(a) 1933 AD (b) 1935 AD
(c) 1937 AD (d) 1939 AD

12. **When was Navnalanda Mahavihara given the status of a deemed university?**
(a) 2002 AD (b) 2004 AD
(c) 2006 AD (d) 2008 AD

13. **Where is Navrang Kala Manch located?**
(a) buxar (b) saw
(c) Rohtas (d) Saran

14. **In which shaktipeeth of Bihar can a man perform his 'shradh-karma' in his lifetime?**
(a) Madhubani (b) Gaya
(c) Aurangabad (d) Jamui

15. **Which British engineer built a Golghar for storage of food grains?**
(a) George Orwell
(b) James Prinsep
(c) Kevin Lugard
(d) John Garston

16. **When was the integrated child development project first launched in three blocks of Bihar?**
(a) 1971 AD (b) 1973 AD
(c) 1975 AD (d) 1977 AD

17. **Where is the Super thermal Power Project located?**
(a) Dandy (b) Supaul
(c) Chhapra (d) Jehanabad

18. **At the confluence of which two rivers is the Nepali temple located in Hajipur?**
(a) Kosi (b) Ganga
(c) Gandak (d) (b) and (c)

19. According to Nepali literature, Ashoka was the governor of which place before he became a ruler?
(a) Takshashila (b) Ujjain
(c) Champa (d) Kashi

20. When was the National Council of Education established?
(a) 1901 AD (b) 1903 AD
(c) 1905 AD (d) 1907 AD

Answers

1. (a)	**2.** (d)	**3.** (a)	**4.** (b)
5. (c)	**6.** (a)	**7.** (b)	**8.** (a)
9. (b)	**10.** (a)	**11.** (d)	**12.** (c)
13. (a)	**14.** (b)	**15.** (d)	**16.** (c)
17. (a)	**18.** (d)	**19.** (a)	**20.** (c)

SET-43

1. In which period were the metal coins first made?
(a) Vedic period
(b) Post-Vedic Period
(c) Buddha Period
(d) Gupta period

2. At which place in Bihar has the Indian Institute of Handloom Technology been established?
(a) Kishanganj (b) Purnia
(c) Katihar (d) Begusarai

3. Under whose leadership did afghan power was revived after the fall of the Noohinis?
(a) saiyad bandhu
(b) Ibrahim Lodi
(c) Sher Shah
(d) Bahlol Lodi

4. From latitude angle, Bihar is located on which side of the Tropic of Cancer?
(a) North (b) South
(c) East (d) West

5. Where is Ambika Temple located?
(a) Munger (b) Kaimur
(c) Buxar (d) Chhapra

6. Where was anga, the capital of Mahajanapada?
(a) Ujjain (b) Champa
(c) videh (d) vajji

7. Where is the only cigarette factory located in Bihar?
(a) Patna (b) Bhagalpur
(c) Gaya (d) Munger

8. Who was the President of the Congress at the time of transfer of power by the British to Indians in 1947?
(a) J.P. Kripalani
(b) Rajendra Prasad
(c) C.R. Das
(d) Maulana Abul Kalam Azad

9. What was the tax charged by the British from the farmers at the rate of ₹ 3 per annum for ploughing?
(a) Takavi (b) Somdhar
(c) Usar (d) Betmaaf

10. What was the tax levied by the British on the successor for transfer of property after the raiyyat had died?
(a) bapahiputahi
(b) likhiputahi
(c) basimat putahi
(d) khet khalihan Putahi

11. What was the tax levied in lieu of irrigation from canal water in the British period?
(a) Irrigation Expenses
(b) Water Expenditure
(c) Pan Expenses
(d) Canal Expenses

12. According to the beliefs, who built the Singheshwar temple at Madhopura?
(a) Lord Shiva
(b) Lord Vishnu
(c) Lord Ganesha
(d) Lord Indra

13. **In Buddhism, bull is related to which event of Buddha's life?**
(a) renunciation
(b) Home leaving
(c) Enlightenment
(d) Youth

14. **Who was entrusted with the responsibility of killing Fanindra Ghosh, who became a government witness in the Lahore conspiracy case?**
(a) Baikunth Shukla
(b) Kheti Naag
(c) Sachindranath Sanyal
(d) Bhagwati Bohra

15. **Which metal had a huge stock in Magadha in the sixth century AD?**
(a) coal (b) iron
(c) Copper (d) tin

16. **Akbar defeated the Rajput king of Mithila in 1574 AD and gave the right to which Maithili Brahmin to collect revenue in that area?**
(a) Mahesh Thakur
(b) Ramesh Thakur
(c) Kunal Thakur
(d) Suraj Thakur

17. **Which of his generals was sent by Akbar against King Veerashal of Chhotanagpur?**
(a) Shaista Khan
(b) Zafar Khan
(c) Shahbaz Khan
(d) Shujaat Khan

18. **Umpire Gora Bose is related to which sport?**
(a) Football (b) Cricket
(c) Hockey (d) Chess

19. **The first session of the All-India Kisan Sabha was presided over by**
(a) Swami Sahajananda Saraswati
(b) Swami Vidyananda
(c) M.G. Ranga
(d) Mahatma Gandhi

20. **Which conference of All India Trade Union Congress was attended and presided over by Pandit Jawaharlal Nehru?**
(a) Ranchi (b) Deogarh
(c) Jharia (d) Aurangabad

Answers

1. (c)	**2.** (a)	**3.** (c)	**4.** (a)
5. (d)	**6.** (b)	**7.** (d)	**8.** (a)
9. (d)	**10.** (a)	**11.** (c)	**12.** (b)
13. (a)	**14.** (a)	**15.** (b)	**16.** (a)
17. (c)	**18.** (b)	**19.** (a)	**20.** (c)

SET-44

1. **Where is The Ahiroli Temple Located?**
(a) Buxar (b) Gaya
(c) Nawada (d) Supaul

2. **In which year of the kingdom anointing The Lumbini yatra was undertaken by Ashoka and the land there was reduced to 1/8th?**
(a) 16th (b) 18th
(c) 20th (d) 22nd

3. **Abhidhamma Pitak is compiled by**
(a) Anand
(b) Upali
(c) Ajitam
(d) Mowgliputis

4. **Who is known as 'Abhinav Jayadev'?**
(a) Vidyapati
(b) Bhikhari Thakur
(c) Rajendra Prasad
(d) Ramdhari Singh Dinkar

5. **In Atharvaveda the word 'vratya' is used for the people of which state?**
(a) anga (b) vajji
(c) Magadha (d) Kashi

6. **What the land that is being added by the tribes is called in 'Airthshastra'?**

(a) Sita Bhoomi (b) Aprahat
(c) kanujo (d) Bhratra

7. Which crop is described as inferior in 'Airthshastra'?
(a) paddy (b) wheat
(c) Maize (d) Sugarcane

8. At which place is Veer Kunwar Singh Stadium located in Bihar?
(a) Aara (b) chhapra
(c) Buxar (d) Patna

9. How many pilgrimages are mentioned in 'Airthshastra'?
(a) 12 (b) 14
(c) 16 (d) 18

10. What is the Chairman of the Pilgrimage called in 'Airthshastra'?
(a) Mahamata
(b) Rajjak
(c) The Head of The Forest
(d) The Head of The Tax

11. In which year was the Bihar State Sports Council constituted?
(a) 1959 AD (b) 1961 AD
(c) 1963 AD (d) 1965 AD

12. What is the total number of members of legislative council in Bihar?
(a) 71 (b) 73
(c) 75 (d) 77

13. What is the total number of members of legislative assembly in the State?
(a) 237 (b) 239
(c) 241 (d) 243

14. What is the total number of Rajya Sabha members in Bihar?
(a) 12 (b) 14.
(c) 16 (d) 18

15. What was the total number of Lok Sabha members in undivided Bihar?
(a) 50 (b) 52
(c) 54 (d) 56

16. Who was the founder of the indecisive community?
(a) Charvaka
(b) Amoghvarman
(c) Sanjay Tisya
(d) Sanjay Velthaputra

17. Who was the last Mauryan emperor?
(a) Brihadratha (b) Kunal
(c) Samprati (d) Dasharatha

18. After the death of his father, Mahavira left home at the age of 30 at the behest of whom?
(a) wife
(b) elder brother
(c) Younger Brother
(d) Guru

19. Who was the prime accused in the Muzaffarpur bomb case of April 19, 1908?
(a) Baikunth Shukla
(b) Prafulla Chaki
(c) Khudiram Bose
(d) (b) and (c)

20. Where is the Shiva temple of Areraj located?
(a) Motihari (b) Bettiah
(c) Patna (d) Muzaffarpur

Answers

1. (a)	**2.** (c)	**3.** (d)	**4.** (a)
5. (c)	**6.** (a)	**7.** (d)	**8.** (a)
9. (d)	**10.** (a)	**11.** (b)	**12.** (c)
13. (d)	**14.** (c)	**15.** (c)	**16.** (d)
17. (a)	**18.** (b)	**19.** (d)	**20.** (a)

SET-45

1. Aryabhata Award is given for which subject?
(a) Science
(b) Mathematics
(c) Medical
(d) (a), (b) and (c)

2. **Where has Aryabhata Gyan University been established?**
(a) Gaya (b) Bhagalpur
(c) Patna (d) Munger

3. **According to Ain-e-Akbari, how many governments (districts) were divided into Bihar provinces?**
(a) 4 (b) 5
(c) 6 (d) 7

4. **In the light of which section of the Disaster Management Act, 2005 has Bihar State Disaster Management Authority (BSDMA) been constituted?**
(a) Section-12(2)
(b) Section-14(1)
(c) Section-16(3)
(d) Section-18(2)

5. **A stone idol of which ruler has been found near Arrah from Deva-Varunaq, which contains the genealogy of the northern Gupta rulers?**
(a) Kumar Gupta
(b) Aditya Gupta
(c) Madhav Gupta
(d) Jeevatgupta II

6. **In which region there was unrest during Bindusara's rule?**
(a) Ujjain (b) Champa
(c) Kashi (d) Takshashila

7. **What was Ashoka's initial name?**
(a) Lankashok
(b) Chandasok
(c) Kamashok
(d) (b) and (c)

8. **Which is Ashoka's shortest pillar inscription?**
(a) Rummindei (b) Junagadh
(c) Kalinga (d) Bhabru

9. **At which place of Bihar is the Fruit Development and Research Institute located?**
(a) Pusa (b) Bankipur
(c) Rubour (d) Bihar Sharif

10. **Who first read Ashoka's Brahmi inscriptions?**
(a) Prinsep (b) Smith
(c) Legrand (d) Marshal

11. **Which large inscription of Ashoka reveals the Kalinga war?**
(a) 11th (b) 12th
(c) 13th (d) 14th

12. **Which is the inscription of Ashoka written in Brahmi script (right to left)?**
(a) Bhabru (b) Yerargudi
(c) Sarainahar (d) Damdama

13. **In which pillar of Ashoka is taxation discussed?**
(a) Junagadh
(b) Warat
(c) Lauria-Areraj
(d) Rummindei

14. **At which place of Bihar is the Rice Development and Research Institute located?**
(a) Arrah (b) Rohtas
(c) Buxar (d) Sivan

15. **Who was the Greek Governor of Avanti at the time of Ashoka?**
(a) Upratha (b) Kundak
(c) Jambarin (d) Tushasapa

16. **Ashoka was influenced by which Buddhist monk and converted to Buddhism?**
(a) Upagupta
(b) Jeevagupta
(c) Ashwagupta
(d) Mehirgupta

17. **In which four inscriptions Ashoka's name is mentioned?**
(a) Maski (b) Gurjara
(c) Netur (d) (a), (b) and (c)

18. **Srinagar was established by which ruler?**
(a) Ashoka (b) Ajatshatru
(c) Bindusar (d) Kanishka

19. Which city was established by Ashoka in Nepal?
(a) Nepatan (b) Lalitpatan
(c) Paharpatan (d) Buddhapatan

20. Which is the only war Ashoka fought in his life?
(a) Sanchi (b) Sarnath
(c) Amravati (d) Kalinga

Answers

1. (a)	**2.** (c)	**3.** (d)	**4.** (b)
5. (d)	**6.** (d)	**7.** (d)	**8.** (a)
9. (c)	**10.** (a)	**11.** (c)	**12.** (b)
13. (d)	**14.** (a)	**15.** (d)	**16.** (a)
17. (d)	**18.** (a)	**19.** (b)	**20.** (d)

SET-46

1. Where was the International Conference on Wetlands held in 1971 AD?
(a) Ramsar (b) Montreal
(c) Bali (d) Madrid

2. Who built the Sun Temple at Aurangabad?
(a) Ahilyabai
(b) Mansingh
(c) Kunwar Singh
(d) Bhervedra Singh

3. Which of his grandsons was appointed subedar of Bihar by Aurangzeb in 1702 AD?
(a) Parvez
(b) Azim
(c) Shah Alam
(d) Bahadur Shah Zafar

4. Which Pal ruler is credited with the establishment of Odantpuri, Nalanda, Vikramshila and Sompura Viharas?
(a) Mahipal (b) Dharmapala
(c) Devpal (d) (b) and (c)

5. Who was the founder of the ajeevika community?
(a) makhali gosal
(b) charvak
(c) Panini
(d) Kapilmuni

6. Which is the highest producer of potato in the State?
(a) Nawada (b) Patna
(c) Sivan (d) Nalanda

7. In which year did Buddha die at the age of 80 years?
(a) 481 AD (b) 483 AD
(c) 485 AD (d) 487 AD

8. Who declared Bihar an independent state after the death of Afghan Darya Khan Nouhani in 1523 AD?
(a) Bahar Khan
(b) Darya Khan
(c) Shahbaz Khan
(d) Shujaat Khan

9. In which year was tourism recognized as an industry by the Government of Bihar?
(a) 1981 AD (b) 1983 AD
(c) 1985 AD (d) 1987 AD

10. What was the surname of Ajatshatru?
(a) Kunik (b) Priyadarshi
(c) Devaputra (d) Upagupta

11. Ajatshatru was a follower of which religion?
(a) Buddhism (b) Jain
(c) Shaiva (d) Ajeevak

12. Who became the ruler of the Magadha Empire by killing the ruler Ajatshatru?
(a) Udayan (b) Ghanananda
(c) Kalashok (d) Ashoka

13. Amrapali, a dancer known for her love affair with Ajatshatru, belonged to which place?
(a) Anga (b) Champa
(c) Vaishali (d) Kashi

14. Lord Narasimha Avatar Stambh (Banamankhi) is located in which district of Bihar?

(a) Purnia (b) Gaya
(c) Buxar (d) Champaran

15. Which tribe of Bihar is called a fighter tribe?
(a) Chero (b) Gond
(c) Kharvar (d) Munda

16. With which state did Ajatshatru use weapons called 'Rathmusal' and 'Mahashilakantak' for the first time in the war?
(a) Lichchavi (b) Kashi
(c) Anga (d) Kalinga

17. In which year of his rule did Ajatshatru construct a stupa in rajagraha on the remains of Gautam Buddha after his mahaparinirvan?
(a) 7th (b) 8th
(c) 9th (d) 10th

18. Where is the temple of Ajgabinath located?
(a) Bhagalpur (b) Patna
(c) Sasaram (d) Jamui

19. Who is the head of the divisional administration?
(a) Head
(b) Sub-divisional Officer
(c) Zone Officer
(d) DSP

20. Which bird sanctuary in Bihar is the largest bird sanctuary in North India?
(a) Gogal Beal
(b) Udaipur
(c) Kusheshwarsthan
(d) Kanwar

Answers

1. (a)	**2.** (d)	**3.** (b)	**4.** (d)
5. (a)	**6.** (d)	**7.** (b)	**8.** (a)
9. (d)	**10.** (a)	**11.** (b)	**12.** (a)
13. (c)	**14.** (a)	**15.** (c)	**16.** (a)
17. (d)	**18.** (a)	**19.** (b)	**20.** (c)

SET-47

1. What is the sex ratio of Scheduled Tribes in the State?
(a) 923 (b) 925
(c) 927 (d) 929

2. Which is the district with the lowest sex ratio among Scheduled Tribes?
(a) Patna (b) Arrah
(c) Buxar (d) Munger

3. Gandak river is known as
(a) Vipasha (b) Chandrabhaga
(c) Sadanira (d) Tilave

4. What is the area of Ganga plain?
(a) 87,430 sq. km
(b) 88,120 sq. km
(c) 89,870 sq. km
(d) 90, 650 sq. km

5. Where did Gautam Buddha find Kondinya and 5 Brahmins?
(a) Veerbhum (b) Uruvela
(c) Pavapuri (d) Sarnath

6. Where did Gautama Buddha attain emaucipation?
(a) Sarnath (b) Shravasti
(c) Bodh Gaya (d) Amravati

7. When was the Antyodaya Yojana launched?
(a) 1998 AD (b) 2000 AD
(c) 2002 AD (d) 2004 AD

8. When was Annapurna scheme launched in the state of Bihar?
(a) 1999 AD (b) 2000 AD
(c) 2001 AD (d) 2002 AD

9. Where is Annapurna Temple located?
(a) Patna (b) Gaya
(c) Shivhar (d) Saharsa

10. When was the Atal Rejuvenation and Urban Transformation Mission (AMRUT) scheme launched?
(a) 2014 AD (b) 2015 AD
(c) 2016 AD (d) 2017 AD

11. Which city was was recognized as the 12th Municipal Corporation in August, 2016?
(a) Chhapra (b) Madhubani
(c) Shivhar (d) Supaul

12. Bihar Education Project is mainly related to
(a) Primary Education
(b) Higher Education
(c) Adult Education
(d) (a) and (c)

13. Alarkalam was a scholar of which philosophy?
(a) numeric (b) special
(c) materialism (d) biology

14. Who was the ruler of Devagiri at the time of Alauddin Khilji's invasion?
(a) Devchandra
(b) Ramachandra deva
(c) Suryadeva
(d) Mahendradev

15. Where has it been decided to open the branch of Aligarh Muslim University in Bihar?
(a) Patna (b) Purnia
(c) Katihar (d) Kishanganj

16. What narrative scenes are inscribed on the walls of the ruins of a temple found in the abyss of Gaya?
(a) Ramayana (b) Mahabharata
(c) Gita (d) Rigveda

17. Which district is famous for 'Langra' mangoes in Bihar?
(a) Darbhanga (b) Madhubani
(c) Muzaffarpur (d) Shivhar

18. When did the airport at Gaya get the status of international airport?
(a) 2000 AD (b) 2002 AD
(c) 2004 AD (d) 2006 AD

19. Who was the President of Gaya session of Indian National Congress?
(a) CR Das
(b) Maulana Abul Kalam Azad
(c) Rajendra Prasad
(d) RS Swami

20. Who was the ruler of Tirhut during the Bengal campaign of Gyasudin Tughlaq?
(a) Laxman Sen
(b) Chandradev Singh
(c) Harisingh Dev
(d) Bhurendra Singh

Answers

1. (d)	**2.** (a)	**3.** (c)	**4.** (d)
5. (b)	**6.** (c)	**7.** (b)	**8.** (c)
9. (a)	**10.** (c)	**11.** (a)	**12.** (d)
13. (a)	**14.** (b)	**15.** (d)	**16.** (a)
17. (c)	**18.** (b)	**19.** (a)	**20.** (c)

SET-48

1. How long after he left home, Mahavira gave up his clothes?
(a) 10 Month (b) 11 months
(c) 12 Month (d) 13 months

2. Gandak is a tributary of which river?
(a) Kosi (b) Kamla
(c) Ganga (d) Bagmati

3. Which is the district with the lowest literacy rate among Scheduled Tribes?
(a) Banka (b) Lakhisarai
(c) Gaya (d) Jamui

4. What is the percentage of literacy rate among Scheduled Tribes?
(a) 28.2% (b) 30.4%
(c) 32.6% (d) 34.8%

5. What percentage of the total area of Bihar is accounted for by Ganga plain?
(a) 90.16% (b) 92.28%
(c) 94.35% (d) 96.27%

6. The plains of Ganga are the remains of which sea?

(a) Tethis sea
(b) Atlantic sea
(c) Pacific Ocean
(d) Arabian Sea

7. Who was the first ruler to become a Buddhist in Bihar?
(a) Brihadratha (b) Bimbisara
(c) Ajatshatru (d) Ashoka

8. Where is the deepest alluvial deposit found in the Ganga plain?
(a) Patna
(b) Bhagalpur
(c) Barauni
(d) Buxar

9. Which famous ruler is called the father of inscriptions?
(a) Ajatshatru
(b) Ghanananda
(c) Ashoka
(d) Chandragupta Maurya

10. What was the name of Gautam Buddha's father?
(a) Shuddhodhan
(b) Janak
(c) Ramdev
(d) Lakshyadev

11. In which book are the teachings of Gautam Buddha compiled?
(a) Abhidhamma Pitak
(b) Sutta Pitak
(c) Vinay Pitak
(d) Jataka Katha

12. Which place in Bihar is a historical site famous for hot water sources?
(a) Rajgir (b) Gaya
(c) Munger (d) Aurangabad

13. What tax is discussed in the maner copper plate of Govind Chandra, the ruler of the Gahadwal dynasty?
(a) ramdanda (b) turuskadanda
(c) sondanda (d) takavidanda

14. In whose court Jaydev, the author of the song Govind, lived?
(a) Samant Sen (b) Ashwa Sen
(c) Laxman Sen (d) Kumar Sen

15. Where is Gautam Buddha Wildlife Sanctuary located?
(a) Gaya (b) Munger
(c) Saharsa (d) Aurangabad

16. Gandhiji's Champaran Satyagraha was associated with
(a) Do Bigha
(b) Tinkathia
(c) Char Katta
(d) (a), (b) and (c)

17. Where did Gandhiji first visit Champaran on April 16, 1917?
(a) Jasauli Patti (b) Motihari
(c) Sugauli (d) Ramgarhwa

18. Who became the ruler of Pal dynasty after Gopal?
(a) Gopal (b) Dharmapala
(c) Mihir Pal (d) Mahipal

19. Film actor Sushant Singh Rajput was born in which district of Bihar?
(a) Patna (b) Gaya
(c) Muzaffarpur (d) Vaishali

20. Gautam Buddha's mother belonged to which clan?
(a) Kshatriya (b) Kolya
(c) Suryavanshi (d) Chandravanshi

Answers

1. (d)	**2.** (c)	**3.** (b)	**4.** (a)
5. (d)	**6.** (a)	**7.** (b)	**8.** (a)
9. (c)	**10.** (a)	**11.** (b)	**12.** (a)
13. (b)	**14.** (c)	**15.** (a)	**16.** (b)
17. (a)	**18.** (b)	**19.** (a)	**20.** (b)

SET-49

1. Gautam Buddha was brought up by
(a) Prajapati Gautami
(b) Lakshmipati Gautami

(c) Durgapati Gautami
(d) Kalipati Gautami

2. In which clan was Gautam Buddha born?
(a) Kshatriya (b) Brahmin
(c) Sakya (d) Shudra

3. Which Gupta emperor defeated the Huns?
(a) Samudragupta
(b) Skandagupta
(c) Jeevgupta
(d) Amargupta

4. Where is the Gupta Dham located?
(a) Rohtas (b) Buxar
(c) Ara (d) gaya

5. Which is the district with the highest sex ratio of Scheduled Tribes?
(a) Gaya (b) Buxar
(c) Gopalganj (d) Supaul

6. Which is the district with the highest literacy rate of Scheduled Tribes?
(a) Begusarai (b) Buxar
(c) Supaul (d) Saharsa

7. Gautam Buddha attained knowledge on the banks of which river?
(a) Ganga (b) Niranjana
(c) Saryu (d) Kosi

8. What was Gautam Buddha's childhood name?
(a) Siddharth (b) Rahul
(c) Kapil (d) Utpal

9. What was the name of Gautam Buddha's mother?
(a) Maitreyani
(b) Prajapati Gautami
(c) Yashodhara
(d) Mahamaya Devi

10. Which is the origin of river Ganga?
(a) Gangotri (b) Bandarpoonch
(c) Haridwar (d) Rishikesh

11. River Ganga enters which district of Bihar from Uttar Pradesh?
(a) Kaimur
(b) Buxar
(c) West Champaran
(d) Saran

12. Where did Gandhiji first launch the Satyagraha movement in India?
(a) Champaran (b) Patna
(c) Chanpatia (d) Muzaffarpur

13. What is the incident of Gautam buddha's renunciation called?
(a) Mahaabhinirman
(b) Nirvana
(c) Dharma chakra parivartan
(d) Mahaparinirvan

14. Who was the Sultan of Delhi who imposed jazia tax on Brahmins?
(a) Iltutmish
(b) Balaban
(c) Ferozshah Tughlaq
(d) Ibrahim Lodi

15. Where is Lakshman Kund located?
(a) Munger (b) Rajgir
(c) Gaya (d) Aurangabad

16. Dadabhai Naoroji made which person from Bihar vice-president while he was the president of London Indian Society?
(a) Santosh Yadav
(b) Chandragupta Singh
(c) Parameswarlal
(d) Mandan Jha

17. Gogabil Sanctuary is located in which district?
(a) Bhagalpur (b) Katihar
(c) Gaya (d) Aurangabad

18. When was Golghar constructed?
(a) 1780 AD (b) 1782 AD
(b) 1784 AD (d) 1786 AD

19. **Kalyani Lake is located in which district?**
(a) Katihar (b) Gaya
(c) Purnia (d) Jehanabad
20. **When was Guru Gobind Singh born?**
(a) 1662 AD (b) 1664 AD
(c) 1666 AD (d) 1668 AD

Answers

1. (a)	**2.** (c)	**3.** (b)	**4.** (a)
5. (c)	**6.** (a)	**7.** (b)	**8.** (a)
9. (d)	**10.** (a)	**11.** (b)	**12.** (a)
13. (a)	**14.** (c)	**15.** (a)	**16.** (c)
17. (a)	**18.** (d)	**19.** (a)	**20.** (c)

SET-50

1. **Who is called the Prophet of New India?**
(a) Raja Ram Mohan Roy
(b) Swami Dayanandsaraswati
(c) Vivekananda
(d) Ramakrishna Paramahamsa
2. **Gurudwara Handri Sahib is located in**
(a) Bihta (b) Bankipur
(c) Gaighat (d) Danapur
3. **Where is Kala Bhawan located in Bihar?**
(a) Purnia
(b) Chhapra
(c) Sivan
(d) Buxar
4. **Gautam Buddha was blessed with a son at the age of 29, what was his name?**
(a) Sankalp (b) Kunal
(c) Rahul (d) Dasharatha
5. **What is the language and script of the Gupta record?**
(a) Sanskrit-Brahmi
(b) Sanskrit-Kharosthi
(c) Prakrit-Brahmi
(d) Prakrit-Kharosthi
6. **In which of his works the poet Sodhal of Gujarat was called Dharmapala, the lord of the north in the 11th century?**
(a) Jayasundari
(b) Udaysundari
(c) Brahmasundari
(d) Karmasundari
7. **Who was the first ruler of the slave dynasty?**
(a) Qutbuddin Aibak
(b) Iltutmish
(c) Balaban
(d) Razia Sultan
8. **Gangatic Dolphin Sanctuary is located in which district?**
(a) Gaya (b) Buxar
(c) Saran (d) Bhagalpur
9. **In which financial year was the Sugarcane Development Programme launched by the Government of Bihar?**
(a) 2010-11 AD
(b) 2011–12 AD
(c) 2012-13 AD
(d) 2013-14 AD
10. **Which district of Bihar remains the hottest in summer?**
(a) Gaya (b) Kishanganj
(c) Jamui (d) Banka
11. **Which city of Bihar remains the hottest in summer?**
(a) Jehanabad (b) Patna
(c) Vaishali (d) Gaya
12. **The hot winds in summer are called what?**
(a) loo (b) garma
(c) Kalvaisakhi (d) Harmatton
13. **Where is Mata Bhagwati Durga temple, Mandargiri, made of granite rocks located?**
(a) Aurangabad (b) Sitamarhi
(c) Gaya (d) Bhagalpur

14. **When was the Great Public Library established?**
(a) 1912 AD (b) 1914 AD
(c) 1916 AD (d) 1918 AD

15. **When was Gautam Buddha born?**
(a) 561 AD (b) 563 AD
(c) 565 AD (d) 567 AD

16. **What is the position of Bihar in the country in the production of litchi?**
(a) 1st (b) 2nd
(c) 3rd (d) 4th

17. **Where is Litchi Research Centre located in Bihar?**
(a) Bhagalpur (b) Patna
(c) Motihari (d) Muzaffarpur

18. **Which insect produces Lakh?**
(a) lakka
(b) mulberry insects
(c) Ointment insects
(d) (a), (b) and (c)

19. **Where did Kunkunth Shukla murder Fanindra Ghosh, who had become an official witness in the Lahore conspiracy case?**
(a) Motihari (b) Bettiah
(c) Raxaul (d) Muzaffarpur

20. **The capital of Mauryan empire was?**
(a) Vaishali
(b) Ujjain
(c) Pataliputra
(d) Takshashila

Answers

1. (a)	**2.** (d)	**3.** (a)	**4.** (c)
5. (a)	**6.** (b)	**7.** (a)	**8.** (d)
9. (c)	**10.** (a)	**11.** (d)	**12.** (a)
13. (d)	**14.** (c)	**15.** (b)	**16.** (a)
17. (d)	**18.** (a)	**19.** (b)	**20.** (c)

SET-51

1. **When was Bihar separated from Bengal as a province?**
(a) 1910 AD (b) 1912 AD
(c) 1914 AD (d) 1916 AD

2. **Where is ekpira chaur located?**
(a) Kishanpur (b) Darbhanga
(c) Hajipur (d) Maner

3. **Which place does Bihar have in the country in terms of area?**
(a) 11th (b) 12th
(c) 13th (d) 14th

4. **Which is the largest fresh water gokhur lake in Asia?**
(a) Chilka Lake
(b) Kanwar Lake
(c) Loktak Lake
(d) Anupam Lake

5. **Which person is mentioned in the stone record of Dharampala obtained from Bodh Gaya who built a Shiva temple in Bodh Gaya?**
(a) Mahendra (b) Shursen
(c) Keshav (d) Dharmasena

6. **When and at which place is Asia's largest animal fair held?**
(a) Karthik, Sonpur
(b) Sawan, Sonepur
(c) Baisakh, Sonepur
(d) Chaitra, Sonepur

7. **At which place is the rail wheel factory located in Bihar?**
(a) Sivan (b) Saran
(c) Madhepura (a) Munger

8. **Pala period artist Dhiman and his son Bithpal were a resident of**
(a) Gaya (b) Nawada
(c) Nalanda (d) Patna

9. **Who left Patna College before the examination during the non-cooperation movement?**
(a) Rajendra Prasad
(b) Maulana Majhrul Haque

(c) Jayaprakash Narayan
(d) Shri Krishna Singh

10. In Bihar, coins made of metal pertaining to which period have been found first?
(a) Vedic period
(b) Post-Vedic Period
(c) Buddha Period
(d) Gupt period

11. On which mountain Sudarshan Lake was constructed according to Junagadh record of Rudradaman?
(a) Girnar Mountain
(b) Urjayant Mountain
(c) Kaimur Mountain
(d) Aravalli Mountain

12. Which element is found to be deficient in the Khadar (jalod) soil?
(a) nitrogen
(b) potash
(c) Phosphate
(d) (a), (b) and (c)

13. What is the total number of Rajya Sabha members in Bihar after the formation of Jharkhand?
(a) 12 (b) 14
(c) 16 (d) 18

14. When was the 'Yukti Yojana' launched by the Government of Bihar?
(a) 2005 AD (b) 2007 AD
(c) 2009 AD (d) 2011 AD

15. Nav Nalanda Mahavihara is famous for
(a) Ashoka Pillar
(b) Buddha's Statue
(c) Mahavihara
(d) Pali research institute

16. Who have the Greeks called 'unfriendly' which means, the destroyer of enemies?
(a) Ajatshatru
(b) Bimbisara
(c) Bindusara
(d) Ashoka

17. The Greek Ambassador and author of 'Indica' Megasthenes came to whose court in Pataliputra?
(a) Kalashok
(b) Kautilya
(c) Ghanananda
(d) Chandragupta Maurya

18. Where is Ghogha Lake located?
(a) Katihar (d) Kishanganj
(c) Begusarai (d) Gaya

19. Who led the Kharwar movement?
(a) Birsa Shaved
(b) Bhagirath Manjhi
(c) Tilka Manjhi
(d) Sidhu-Kanhu

20. Who built Sudarshan Lake?
(a) Pushyagupta
(b) Amodhvarman
(c) Rudradaman
(d) Ajatshatru

Answers

1. (b)	**2.** (a)	**3.** (c)	**4.** (b)
5. (c)	**6.** (a)	**7.** (b)	**8.** (c)
9. (c)	**10.** (c)	**11.** (b)	**12.** (a)
13. (c)	**14.** (d)	**15.** (d)	**16.** (c)
17. (d)	**18.** (a)	**19.** (b)	**20.** (a)

SET-52

1. In which area of Bihar does the Kond tribe live?
(a) East Champaran
(b) Bhojpur
(c) Sivan
(d) Saaran

2. When was Khudabakhsh Library established?
(a) 1887 AD (b) 1889 AD
(c) 1891 AD (d) 1893 AD

3. What is the total number of Lok Sabha members in Bihar?
(a) 38 (b) 40
(c) 42 (d) 44

4. Which actor is known as 'Bihari Babu'?

(a) Shatrughan Sinha
(b) Shekhar Suman
(c) Prakash Jha
(d) Kunal

5. Where was the 12th session of Bihar provincial conference held on 18-29 August 1920?

(a) Gaya (b) Patna
(b) Bhagalpur (d) Gopalganj

6. Which ruler said that all human beings were his children?

(a) Ajatshatru
(b) Bindusara
(c) Chandragupta Maurya
(d) Ashoka

7. Who wrote the book 'Chandogya Dasasystem'?

(a) Mandan Alloy
(b) Veereshwar Thakur
(c) Nagarjuna
(d) Vidyapati

8. The 'stone Mosque' in Patna is known as

(a) Parvez Masjid
(b) Shahi Masjid
(c) Sangi Masjid
(d) Jama Masjid

9. Where is Bharat Wagon and Engineering Company Limited located in Bihar?

(a) Mokama (b) Begusarai
(c) Madhepura (a) Munger

10. Which Gupta king assumed the title of 'Vikramaditya'?

(a) Chandragupta I
(b) Chandragupta II
(c) Samudragupta
(b) Kumargupta

11. Which of the following divisions of Rigveda mentions the caste system for the first time?

(a)7th (b) 8th
(c) 9th (d) 10th

12. Who became the ruler of the Pala dynasty after Dharmapala?

(a) Devpal (b) Anantpal
(c) Mihirpal (d) Rudrapal

13. Who was appointed by Dharmapala as the ruler of Kannauj?

(a) Pushyamitra (b) Chakrayudh
(c) Nagarjuna (d) Ashwasen

14. SPUR project in Bihar is related to

(a) eradication of poverty
(b) vaccination
(c) Urban Management Reforms
(d) self-employment loan

15. What was the literacy rate of Bihar as per 2011 census?

(a) 60.9% (b) 61.4%
(c) 62.6% (d) 63.8%

16. Which city was the main center of Islam religion and culture in the 15th century?

(a) Jaunpur
(b) Hisar
(c) Ahmednagar
(d) Ajmer

17. Who led the revolt of 1857 AD in Bihar?

(a) Amar Singh (b) Kunwar Singh
(c) Pir Ali (d) Nana Saheb

18. Which district of Bihar will get the highest benefit from the koelkars project under construction in Jharkhand?

(a) Aurangabad (b) Gaya
(c) Munger (d) Bhagalpur

19. When was the Planning Commission constituted in India?

(a) 1948 AD (b) 1949 AD
(c) 1950 AD (d) 1951 AD

20. When was the Bihar State Khadi Village Industries established?

(a) 1953 AD (b) 1954 AD
(c) 1955 AD (d) 1956 AD

Answers

1. (b)	**2.** (c)	**3.** (b)	**4.** (a)
5. (c)	**6.** (d)	**7.** (b)	**8.** (c)
9. (a)	**10.** (b)	**11.** (d)	**12.** (a)
13. (b)	**14.** (c)	**15.** (d)	**16.** (a)
17. (b)	**18.** (a)	**19.** (c)	**20.** (d)

SET-53

1. **Around 1050 BC, from which place in the Ganga Valley evidences of iron being found are available?**
(a) Atranjikheda (b) Chirand
(c) Chechar (d) Mahdah

2. **Where was the 3rd World Disaster Risk Reduction Conference held on 14-18 March, 2015?**
(a) USA (b) Brazil
(c) India (d) Japan

3. **What is the total number of members of Bihar Legislative Council after the formation of Jharkhand?**
(a) 71 (b) 73
(c) 75 (d) 77

4. **Which place in Patna was chosen to break the Salt Act on April 16, 1930?**
(a) Phulwari Sharif
(b) Bihta
(c) Agamakuna
(d) Nail

5. **In 1758 AD, which company acquired a monopoly on the trade of shorey in Bihar?**
(a) English East India Company
(b) Portuguese East India Company
(c) Dutch East India Company
(d) French East India Company

6. **Where is it described that 'the king of Videha gifted nishka or Suvarna or shatman'?**
(a) Tagveda
(b) Samaveda
(c) Brihadaranyaka
(d) Upanishads

7. **Who presided over the 12th session of Bihar provincial conference on 18-29 August 1920?**
(a) Rajendra Prasad
(b) Hassan Imam
(c) Shri Krishna Singh
(d) Mohd Zubair

8. **Patna Nagar was the center of which religious movement in the 1830s?**
(a) Nakshbandi (b) Chishthi
(c) Wahabi (d) Firdausi

9. **What percentage of population lives in cities in Bihar as per 2011 census?**
(a) 10.86% (b) 11.30%
(c) 11.96% (d) 12.30%

10. **Who led the revolt of 1857 AD in Bihar after the death of Kunwar Singh?**
(a) Amar Singh (b) Tatya Tope
(c) Pir Ali (d) Nana Saheb

11. **In 1857 AD, where did the Maharajas and their fellow zamindars help the British with man and money?**
(a) Dumraon
(b) Hathua
(c) Darbhanga
(d) (a), (b) and (c)

12. **Barauni Oil Refinery has been connected by pipeline to which oil field?**
(a) Assam
(b) Bombay High
(c) Gujarat
(d) (a), (b) and (c)

13. **What is the total number of members of Bihar Legislative**

Assembly after the formation of Jharkhand?

(a) 241 (b) 243

(c) 245 (d) 247

14. Dhiman and his son Bithpal were contemporaries of which Pala ruler?

(a) Gopal (b) Dharmapala

(c) Devpal (d) (b) and (c)

15. Who was the Governor General of India at the time of revolt of 1857 AD?

(a) Lord Curzon (b) Lord caning .

(c) Lord Mayo (d) Lord Ripon

16. Bihar has a monopoly in the production of which mineral resources?

(a) Sulphur (b) asbestos

(c) pyrite (d) mica

17. By which Act was the land rights in Bengal and Bihar given to the tenants?

(a) Bengal Tenancy Act-1881

(b) Bengal Act-1883

(c) Bengal Tenancy Act-1885

(d) Bengal Tenancy Act-1887

18. Who was the leader of munda movement in 1899. 1900?

(a) Gaya Munda

(b) Birsa Munda

(c) Sugana Munda

(d) Ramnath Munda

19. Which practice was banned by the Chhotanagpur Kasht Act of 1908 AD?

(a) khutaktti (b) jhumkrishi

(c) Bhuihari (d) (a), (b) and (c)

20. Who attended the Congress session in Lucknow in 1916 AD as a representative of Bihar?

(a) Mohd Zubair

(b) Rajkumar Shukla

(c) Braj Kishore Prasad

(d) (b) and (c)

Answers

1. (a)	**2.** (d)	**3.** (c)	**4.** (d)
5. (a)	**6.** (c)	**7.** (a)	**8.** (c)
9. (b)	**10.** (a)	**11.** (d)	**12.** (a)
13. (b)	**14.** (d)	**15.** (b)	**16.** (c)
17. (c)	**18.** (b)	**19.** (a)	**20.** (d)

SET-54

1. Which University was established by Gandhiji in Patna in 1921 AD?

(a) Patna University

(b) Gandhi University

(c) Bihar University

(d) Buddha University

2. In 1922 AD, the 37th Session of the Congress under the Chairmanship of Chitranjan Das was held in which city of Bihar?

(a) Gaya (b) Ramgarh

(c) Patna (d) Muzaffarpur

3. Kahalgaon Thermal Power Plant under the control of NTPC is located in which district of Bihar State?

(a) Munger (b) Madhepura

(c) Bhagalpur (d) Saran

4. Which party was formally announced at Anjuman Islamia Hall in Patna in 1934 AD?

(a) Indian Congress Samajwadi Party

(b) Peace Party

(c) People's Party

(d) Bihar Ekta Party

5. How many seats were provided for legislative Council and legislative Assembly in Bihar under the Act of 1935 respectively?

(a) 30-150 (b) 30-152

(c) 28-150 (d) 28-152

6. Beryllium is found in which district of Bihar?

(a) Gaya (b) Jamui

(c) Shivhar (d) Kaimur

7. Who was appointed as the first Private Vice Chancellor of Patna University?
(a) Rajendra Prasad
(b) Majhrul Haque
(c) Sachidanand Sinha
(d) Shri Krishna Singh

8. In 1940 AD, at which place was the 53rd session of the Indian National Congress held?
(a) Ramgarh (b) Ranchi
(c) Dhanbad (d) Patna

9. In which jail was Dr. Rajendra Prasad lodged during the Quit India Movement?
(a) Kanpur (b) Ranchi
(c) Hazaribagh (d) Bankipur

10. Where did the Secretariat shooting in Bihar on 11th August, 1942 happen?
(a) Gaya (b) Patna
(c) Vaishali (d) Ranchi

11. Which leader was appointed chief minister of Bihar in 1946 AD?
(a) Shri Krishna Singh
(b) Anugrah Narayan Singh
(c) Rajendra Prasad
(d) Mohd Zubair

12. Dr. Rajendra Prasad was the Minister of which department in the interim government?
(a) information broadcasting
(b) finance
(c) Food & Agriculture
(d) rail

13. Who was appointed president of the Indian National Congress in November 1947 AD?
(a) Dr. Rajendra Prasad
(b) Maulana Abul Kalam Azad
(c) Subhash Chandra Bose
(d) Shri Krishna Singh

14. What was the number of Members of Bihar Legislative Assembly in 1952 AD?
(a) 329 (b) 331
(c) 333 (d) 335

15. In which decade did Bihar have the highest population growth rate?
(a) 1951-61 (b) 1971-81
(c) 1991-2001 (d) 2001-11

16. Who was elected as the Speaker of Bihar assembly on 20 July1937?
(a) Pro. Abdul Bari
(b) Hassan Imam
(c) Mohd Zubair
(d) majhrul haque

17. Which district had the lowest population growth rate in Bihar in the decade 2001 to 2011?
(a) Sivan (b) Patna
(c) Bhagalpur (d) Gopalganj

18. Which district had the highest population growth rate in Bihar in the decade 2001 to 2011?
(a) Madhepura (b) Gaya
(c) Jamui (d) Katihar

19. Where did the revolt of 1857 AD first start in Bihar?
(a) Hajipur (b) Gaya
(c) Danapur (d) Bhagalpur

20. Barauni Thermal Power Station receives coal from which state?
(a) Jharkhand (b) Odisha
(c) Bengal (d) Chhattisgarh

Answers

1. (c)	**2.** (a)	**3.** (c)	**4.** (a)
5. (b)	**6.** (a)	**7.** (c)	**8.** (a)
9. (d)	**10.** (b)	**11.** (a)	**12.** (c)
13. (a)	**14.** (b)	**15.** (c)	**16.** (a)
17. (d)	**18.** (a)	**19.** (c)	**20.** (a)

SET-55

1. **Kataiya (Supaul) Hydro Power Station is part of which river project?**
(a) Bagmati (b) Gandak
(c) kosi (d) Niranjana

2. **In which year did Ajatshatru kill his father Bimbisara and become the ruler of Magadha?**
(a) 491 AD (b) 493 AD
(c) 495 AD (d) 497 AD

3. **In which year did rail transport start in Bihar?**
(a) 1860 AD (b) 1862 AD
(c) 1864 AD (d) 1866 AD

4. **Buddhist literary texts are known as**
(a) Trivatta (b) Tripitak
(c) Ayukt (d) Aranyaka

5. **What is the total population of Bihar as per 2011 Census?**
(a) 10.2 crore (b) 10.3 crore
(c) 10.4 crores (d) 10.5 crores

6. **What is the name of the river group which has formed the boundary line between Bihar and Uttar Pradesh?**
(a) Gandak (b) Karmanasha
(c) Ghaghara (d) (a), (b) and (c)

7. **Which English commander was defeated by santhals in 1855 AD?**
(a) Legrand
(b) Major Baro
(c) Captain Cook
(d) L Douglas

8. **Kharwar tribe is found in which region of the state of Bihar?**
(a) Rohtas (b) Gaya
(c) Saran (d) Munger

9. **The construction of bronze statues related to Buddhist art was characteristic of which era?**
(a) Sen Period
(b) Pal period
(c) Karnat Period
(d) Gupta Period

10. **Who is the Head of the State Council of Ministers?**
(a) Governor
(b) Chief Minister
(c) Speaker of the Assembly
(d) (b) and (c)

11. **Bakhtiyar Khilji is known as**
(a) Ghazi Shah (b) Ghazi Samad
(c) Ghazi Ikhtiar (d) Ghazi Bakshi

12. **When and where was the first Buddhist Conference held?**
(a) Rajagraha (b) Vaishali
(c) Pataliputra (d) Kundalvan

13. **What is the cause of suffering in Buddhism called?**
(a) Moh
(b) Dakshini
(c) Pratitya Samutpad
(d) Kaivalya

14. **When was the Kalinga War fought?**
(a) 261 AD (b) 263 AD
(c) 265 AD (d) 267 AD

15. **With which ruler of Kaushal Mahajanpad did Ajatshatru fight for Kashi?**
(a) Chhatrasal (b) Prasenjit
(c) Ruddaman-II (d) Miharpal

16. **What is the normal tenure of the Council of Ministers?**
(a) 3 Years (b) 4 years
(c) 5 Years (d) 6 years

17. **What was the name of Mahavir's mother?**
(a) Yashodhara (b) Trishala
(c) Prabhavati (d) Devmati

18. **When was the Chandrabhari Museum established in Darbhanga?**
(a) 1951 (b) 1953
(c) 1955 (d) 1957

19. Who was the last ruler of the Karnat dynasty?
(a) Bhim Singh (b) Hari Singh
(c) Kehar Singh (d) Surya Singh

20. Which river meets the Ganges from south?
(a) Punpun (b) Falgu
(c) Jamunia (d) Baitarani

Answers

1. (c)	**2.** (b)	**3.** (a)	**4.** (b)
5. (c)	**6.** (d)	**7.** (b)	**8.** (a)
9. (b)	**10.** (b)	**11.** (c)	**12.** (a)
13. (c)	**14.** (a)	**15.** (b)	**16.** (c)
17. (b)	**18.** (d)	**19.** (b)	**20.** (a)

SET-56

1. Which tax was taken in Mauryan period to protect animals?
(a) Rajjuk (b) Aprahat
(c) Sankar (d) Vivit

2. What was the male and female literacy rate in the State as per census 2011?
(a) 53 % – 63% (b) 60% – 63%
(c) 73 % – 53% (d) 65% – 57%

3. When was an attempt made by Khudiram Bose and Praful Chaki to kill Kings Ford in Muzaffarpur?
(a) 1906 AD (b) 1907 AD
(c) 1908 AD (d) 1909 AD

4. In which financial year was the Mukhyamantri Shram Shakti Yojana launched in Bihar?
(a) 2006-07 (b) 2008-09
(c) 2010-11 (d) 2012-13

5. Who was the real founder of Magadha empire?
(a) Bimbi Sara (b) Ajatshatru
(c) udayan (d) jarasandha

6. Who was the first passenger to travel to Bihar?
(a) Plato (b) Hnensang
(c) Megasthenes (d) Fahiyan

7. Which is the largest multipurpose project of Bihar?
(a) Gandak (b) Sone
(c) Kosi (d) Ganga

8. When and where was the first sugar mill of Bihar established?
(a) 1901 - Motihari
(b)1902 - Bettiah
(c) 1903 - Gaya
(d) 1904 - Madhora

9. Which district of Bihar is famous for nylon industry?
(a) Munger (b) Gaya
(c) Kaimur (d) Arrah

10. Who was the editor of Bihar's leading newspaper 'Bihari'?
(a) Baikunth Shukla
(b) Hasan Imam
(c) Shir Krishan Singh
(d) Maheshwar Prasad

11. In the seal obtained from Basadhar, Dhruvswami is described as the wife of which ruler?
(a) Ajatshatru
(b) Ashoka
(c) Kalashok
(d) Chandragupta II

12. Prakrit and Jainshastra Shodh Sansthan is located in Bihar in -
(a) Nalanda (b) Pavapuri
(c) Patna (d) Gaya

13. Which is the district with the highest rural population of Bihar as per 2011 Census?
(a) Samastipur
(b) Gaya
(c) Banka
(d) Jamui

14. Which is the main cash crop of Bihar?
(a) cotton (b) sugarcane
(c) Peanuts (d) Sunflower

15. What was the sex ratio in Bihar as per 2011 census?

(a) 916 (b) 918
(c) 920 (d) 922

16. In 2015-16 AD, how many hectares of litchi plantations were there in the State?
(a) 30,000 h (b) 32,000 h
(c) 34,000 h (d) 36,000 h

17. Whose disciples were the parents of Mahavir, the 24th Tirthankara of Jainism?
(a) Parsvanatha (b) Tashbhadev
(c) Arishtanemi (d) Ajitnath

18. Who became the first individual Satyagrahi of Bihar on 27 November 1940?
(a) Hasan Imam
(b) Majhrul Haque
(c) Shri Krishan Singh
(d) Dr. Rajendra Prasad

19. In 322 BC, which ruler defeated Magadha king Ghanananda and abolished the Nandavansh?
(a) Kautilya
(b) Kalashok
(c) Chandragupta Maurya
(d) Ashoka

20. Till when was 350th Prakash Guru parva (Guru Gobind Singh Janma Utsav) was organised in Bihar?
(a) 31 December, 2016 AD
(b) 5 January, 2017 AD
(c) 31 December, 2017 AD
(d) 5 January, 2016 AD

Answers

1. (d)	2. (c)	3. (c)	4. (b)
5. (a)	6. (c)	7. (a)	8. (d)
9. (a)	10. (d)	11. (d)	12. (c)
13. (a)	14. (b)	15. (a)	16. (b)
17. (a)	18. (c)	19. (c)	20. (b)

SET-57

1. On January 4, 1915, Ganesh Shankar Vidyarthi published an article on kisan problem in Pratap by which name?
(a) Bechara Kisan
(b) Champaran mei andhera
(c) Neel hatya
(d) Bedard mil hai

2. At the time of the death of Gautam Buddha in 483 BC, which monk said that today we are liberated?
(a) Anand (b) Jamali
(c) Subhadra (d) Udayan

3. What is the sex ratio in Bihar in the age group of 0-6 years as per 2011 census?
(a) 933 (b) 935
(c) 937 (d) 939

4. Who was arrested in Hazaribagh on 6th August, 1942?
(a) Jayaprakash Narayan
(b) Narayan Singh
(c) Sukhlal Singh
(d) (b) and (c)

5. Where did Parsvanatha attain emancipation after 83 days of penance?
(a) Vindhya Mountain
(b) Nagarjuna Mountain
(c) Mount Kailash
(d) Samvet Hills

6. When did Ikhtiaruddin Muhammad bin Bakhtiyar Khilji launch a successful attack on Bihar?
(a) 1201 AD (b) 1203 AD
(c) 1205 AD (d) 1207 AD

7. Who is the first woman Chief Minister of Bihar?
(a) Prabhavati Gupta
(b) Sarojini Naidu
(c) Rabri Devi
(d) Shailbala Rai

8. Where is the first mention of the word Magadha?

(a) Tatgveda (b) Atharvaveda
(c) Samaveda (d) Yajurveda

9. When did Kunwar Singh, the leader of the revolution of 1857 AD, die?
(a) 1 May, 1858 AD
(b) 5 May, 1858 AD
(c) 9 May, 1858 AD
(d) 13 May, 1858 AD

10. Who composed 'Allahabad Prashasti'?
(a) Harishen (b) Pushyamitra
(c) Kalhana (d) Jeevak

11. Which movement did Gandhiji term as a Himalaya like mistake?
(a) Champaran
(b) Non-cooperation
(c) Kheda
(d) Civil Disobedience

12. Economic planning is in which list of the Constitution?
(a) Association list
(b) Concurrent list
(c) State list
(d) (b) and (c)

13. Who sat on the throne of Magadha after the death of Shishunag?
(a) Ghanananda (b) Shashank
(c) Kalashok (d) Ajatshatru

14. Where was the world's first republican system established in the sixth century BC?
(a) Vaishali (b) Pataliputra
(c) Gaya (d) Anga

15. Famous poet Vidyapati was a resident of?
(a) Munger (b) Saharsa
(c) Madhubani (d) Sitamarhi

16. Which movement started after the partition of Bengal in 1905 AD?
(a) Swadeshi
(b) Champaran
(c) Kheda
(d) Non-cooperation

17. When did Satchidanandsinha, who played an important role in the separation of Bihar from Bengal, become a member of the Bihar, Bengal and Orissa Legislative Assembly?
(a) 1918 AD (b) 1920 AD
(c) 1922 AD (d) 1924 AD

18. Who killed Bakhtiyar Khilji and when?
(a) Ali Mardan-1206 AD
(b) Dilawar Khan-1205 AD
(c) Hasmat Ali-1204 AD
(d) Ibrahim Jung-1203 AD

19. According to census 2011, what was the decadal growth rate of Bihar?
(a) 21.41% (b) 23.14%
(c) 25.07% (d) 27.81%

20. When did Bakhtiyar Khilji attack the Nadia, the capital of Lakshman Sen?
(a) 1202-03 AD
(b) 1203–04 AD
(c) 1204-05 AD
(d) 1205–06 AD

Answers

1. (b)	**2.** (c)	**3.** (b)	**4.** (d)
5. (d)	**6.** (b)	**7.** (c)	**8.** (b)
9. (c)	**10.** (a)	**11.** (b)	**12.** (b)
13. (c)	**14.** (a)	**15.** (c)	**16.** (a)
17. (b)	**18.** (a)	**19.** (c)	**20.** (b)

SET-58

1. Where did Gautam Buddha, the founder of Buddhism, first go after his renunciation?
(a) Vaishali (b) Gaya
(c) Sarnath (d) Shraswati

2. Tin minerals are found in which district in Bihar?

(a) Munger (b) Kaimur
(c) Gaya (d) Buxar

3. **What was the percentage of female literacy in Bihar as per 2011 census?**
(a) 51.12% (b) 53.33%
(c) 55.62% (d) 57.61%

4. **In which century did the Magadha Empire flourish?**
(a) 4th Century
(b) 5th century
(c) 6th Century
(d) 7th century

5. **The statue of the famous Didar Ganj Yajni is related to which museum of Bihar?**
(a) Patna (b) Gaya
(c) Darbhanga (d) Bhagalpur

6. **'Baharisante Gabi' is the creation of**
(a) Mirza Ghalib
(b) Mirza Nathan
(c) Hasan Imam
(d) Pir Ali

7. **Where is the Prabhavati Women's Library located?**
(a) Saharsa (b) Munger
(c) Motihari (d) Patna

8. **What is the name of the oldest university in India?**
(a) Nalanda University
(b) Takshashila University
(c) Vikramshila University
(d) Sompur University

9. **When was Barauni oil refinery established?**
(a) 1960 AD (b) 1962 AD
(c) 1964 AD (d) 1966 AD

10. **Which was the first English newspaper of Bihar?**
(a) The Bihar Times
(b) The Bihar Gazette
(c) The Bihar Herald
(d) The Motherland

11. **Barauni Oil Refinery was established in collaboration with which country?**
(a) Germany
(b) Romania
(c) Soviet Union
(d) (b) and (c)

12. **Which was the smallest kingdom of Magadha empire?**
(a) Kalinga (b) Toshali
(c) Anga (d) Vajji

13. **Which ruler's record has been obtained from Mandar hill at Bansi in Banka district describing digging ponds and installing a statue of Vishnu?**
(a) Kunal Sen (b) Ashwa Sen
(c) Aditya Sen (d) Laxman Sen

14. **What was the percentage of children below 6 years of age in Bihar as per 2011 Census?**
(a) 14.13% (b) 15.62%
(c) 16.82% (d) 17.90%

15. **Who presided over the Congress session at Bankipur, Patna?**
(a) Rajendra Prasad
(b) RS Madholkar
(c) Mahatma Gandhi
(d) Hasan Imam

16. **Who established Sitaram Ashram in Patna?**
(a) Shri Krishna Singh
(b) Mahatma Gandhi
(c) Baikunth Shukla
(d) Swami Sahajananda Saraswathi

17. **Who was the Chairman of the Reception Committee of the Congress Session at Bankipur, Patna?**
(a) Majhrul Haque
(b) Shri Krishna Singh
(c) Rajendra Prasad
(d) Jayaprakash Narayan

18. Where is Baba Brahmeshwarnath's fair held in Bihar?
(a) Kaimur (b) Gaya
(c) Buxar (d) Sitamarhi

19. Most of the area of Bihar is covered with which soil?
(a) alluvial soil
(b) balther soil
(c) scarpsoil
(d) balsundari soil

20. When was the ancient Roman Catholic Church (priest's mansion) built?
(a) 1747 AD (b) 1749 AD
(c) 1751 AD (d) 1753 AD

Answers

1. (a)	**2.** (c)	**3.** (b)	**4.** (c)
5. (a)	**6.** (b)	**7.** (d)	**8.** (a)
9. (d)	**10.** (c)	**11.** (d)	**12.** (a)
13. (c)	**14.** (d)	**15.** (b)	**16.** (d)
17. (a)	**18.** (c)	**19.** (a)	**20.** (c)

SET-59

1. Who was the scholar who led Ashoka into Buddhism?
(a) Upagupta (b) Ananda
(c) Ashwasen (d) Adinatha

2. What percentage of the total area of Bihar is found to be under forest cover?
(a) 5.94% (b) 6.84%
(c) 7.21% (d) 8.29%

3. Where did Bakhtiyar Khilji conquer the regions of Bihar and Bengal and establish the capital?
(a) Lucknowi (b) Bihar Sharif
(c) Hajipur (d) Munger

4. According to 2011 census, what percentage of population lived in villages in Bihar?
(a) 82.14% (b) 84.29%
(c) 86.71% (d) 88.70%

5. What kind of religion is Buddhism?
(a) Ishvarvadi
(b) Pranavadi
(c) Anishvarvadi
(d) (a), (b) and (c)

6. Which district of Bihar is considered to be the district of Vermi Compost?
(a) Begusarai (b) Gaya
(c) Banka (d) Supaul

7. At which place of Bihar did Lord Buddha attain enlightenment?
(a) Pataliputra (b) Rajagraha
(c) Bodh Gaya (d) Vaishali

8. Which revolutionary led Bihar at the Hindustan Socialist Republican Army meeting in September, 1928?
(a) Kheti Naag
(b) Baikunth Shukla
(c) Sachindranath Sanyal
(d) Fanindranath Ghosh

9. What was the minimum age of any person required to enter the Buddhist Union, based on the democratic system?
(a) 11 Year (b) 13 years
(c) 15 Year (d) 17 years

10. What was the percentage of population of Bihar in India as per 2011 census of India?
(a) 6.98% (b) 7.12%
(c) 7.81% (d) 8.58%

11. Which texts come in the tripitak of Buddhist literature?
(a) Sutta Pitak
(b) Vinay Pitak
(c) Abhidhamma Pitak
(d) (a), (b) and (c)

12. Which leader demanded nationalization of land and waterways?

(a) Swami Sahajananda Sarasvati
(b) Mahatma Gandhi
(c) Hasrat Mohani
(d) Shri Krishna Singh

13. Kunwar Singh was the zamindar of which place?
(a) Azamgarh (b) Danapur
(c) Jagdishpur (d) Shahabad

14. Which play is presented with jat-jatin?
(a) Chhau (b) Bhakulibanka
(c) Karama (d) Sarhul

15. What is the main source of liveli-hood for the people of Bihar?
(a) Agriculture
(b) Industry
(c) Manufacturing
(d) (a), (b) and (c)

16. On what basis Mahabodhi temple was established in Bodh Gaya?
(a) Place of birth
(b) Knowledge place
(c) Religious cycle conversion site
(d) Mahaparinirvan site

17. Gandhiji's Champaran Satyagraha was associated with which agricul-tural system?
(a) Tinkathia (b) Bar Bigha
(c) Char Ser (d) Yaman Katha

18. What was the name of the first Railway in the State of Bihar?
(a) Bihar Railway
(b) Eastern Railway
(c) East India Railway
(d) British Railways

19. Which is the most dense district in Bihar as per 2011 census?
(a) Patna
(b) Shivhar
(c) Muzaffarpur
(d) Vaishali

20. Whose seal has been obtained from Basadhar?
(a) Ajatshatru
(b) Harisingh
(c) Laxman Sen
(d) Mahadevi Dhruvswami

Answers

1. (a)	**2.** (c)	**3.** (a)	**4.** (d)
5. (c)	**6.** (a)	**7.** (c)	**8.** (d)
9. (c)	**10.** (d)	**11.** (d)	**12.** (a)
13. (c)	**14.** (b)	**15.** (a)	**16.** (b)
17. (a)	**18.** (c)	**19.** (b)	**20.** (a)

SET-60

1. Buddha died after eating pork at the house of which goldsmith in Pava, the capital of southern Malla?
(a) Nanda (b) Kanand
(c) Chund (d) Chhatrap

2. What are senior level officers called in Kautilya's 'Arthashastra'?
(a) Rajjuk (b) Teerth
(c) Agrahara (d) Sukta

3. When was the new advertising pol-icy implemented by the Govern-ment of Bihar?
(a) 10.4.2016
(b) 15.06.2016
(c) 15.8.2016
(d) 12.09.2016

4. When was the Bihar Student Credit Card Scheme launched?
(a) 2014 AD (b) 2015 AD
(c) 2016 AD (d) 2017 AD

5. When was Buddha born according to Chinese literature?
(a) 483 AD (b) 498 AD
(c) 512 AD (d) 563 AD

6. Which is the district with the highest crop density in Bihar?
(a) Buxar (b) Rohtas
(c) Saran (d) Munger

7. **Where was the first meeting of the Congress Socialist Party held?**
(a) Gaya (b) Ranchi
(c) Bokaro (d) Patna

8. **'Manjusha' style is based on which popular folk tale of Anga Pradesh?**
(a) Karama (b) Jat-jatin
(c) Chhau (d) Bihula-vishhari

9. **Which gurus did Buddha find in Rajagraha to attain knowledge?**
(a) Alar Kalam
(b) Ashwasen
(c) Rudrak Ramputra
(d) Mahasen

10. **With whom was Mahavir's daughter married?**
(a) Jamali (b) Anand
(c) Ashwasen (d) Prasenjit

11. **Which districts of Bihar touch Jharkhand on the southern border?**
(a) Bhagalpur
(b) Banka
(c) Jamui
(d) (a), (b) and (c)

12. **Who was the commander of the warship and merchant ship during Mauryan period?**
(a) Navadhyaksh
(b) Sitadhyaksh
(c) Karadhyaksh
(d) Mavadhyaksh

13. **Who among the following was the first Bihari to come first in first class in Calcutta University?**
(a) Sri Krishna Singh
(b) Abdul Bari
(c) Rajendra Prasad
(d) Gyandev Tripathi

14. **Who was the first Chief Minister of Bihar?**
(a) Rajendra Prasad
(b) Mohd Zubair
(c) Sachchidanand Sinha
(d) Sri Krishna Singh

15. **Which district has minimum crop density in Bihar?**
(a) Darbhanga (b) Banka
(c) Lakhisarai (d) Patna

16. **In which forest did the Buddha perform hard penance with his five companions Kondilya, Aj, Assig, Wapp and Bhadiya?**
(a) Sanvet forest
(b) Usar forest
(c) Uruvela Forest
(d) Magadh Forest

17. **Mahavir Swami was born in which place in Bihar?**
(a) Vaishali (b) Pavapuri
(c) Nalanda (d) Rajagraha

18. **Where is Bettiah Mela held in Bihar?**
(a) Motihari (b) Bettiah
(c) Mehsi (d) Motipur

19. **When was east-central railway established?**
(a) 2000 AD (b) 2001 AD
(c) 2002 AD (d) 2003 AD

20. **What is the second official language of Bihar?**
(a) Urdu (b) Maghi
(c) Angik (d) Bhojpuri

Answers

1. (c)	**2.** (b)	**3.** (d)	**4.** (c)
5. (d)	**6.** (a)	**7.** (d)	**8.** (d)
9. (c)	**10.** (a)	**11.** (d)	**12.** (a)
13. (c)	**14.** (d)	**15.** (a)	**16.** (c)
17. (a)	**18.** (b)	**19.** (c)	**20.** (a)

SET-61

1. **At whose initiative was a vermi compost unit set up at Khudabandpur in Begusarai?**
(a) Ramratan Singh
(b) Dr. RK Sohane

(c) Dr. Abid Ali
(d) Dr. Anand Rai

2. **When did Baldev Prasad resign as Advocate General during the national agitation?**
(a) 1938 AD (b) 1940 AD
(c) 1942 AD (d) 1944 AD

3. **Which was the district with the lowest credit-deposit ratio in Bihar in September, 2015?**
(a) Saharsa (b) Supaul
(c) Sivan (d) Banka

4. **Where is the Brahmanyoni Hill located?**
(a) Gaya (b) Arrah
(c) Kaimur (d) East Champaran

5. **Who was the last ruler of Mauryan dynasty?**
(a) Kunal (b) Harigupta
(c) Brihadratha (d) Harishen

6. **Who was the founder of Karnat dynasty?**
(a) Nanyadeva (b) Gangdev
(c) Hari Singh (d) Surya Singh

7. **What was the percentage of ST population in Bihar as per 2011 census?**
(a) 0.7% (b) 0.8%
(c) 0.9% (d) 1.0%

8. **How many poplar plants will be planted in the next 5 years under Krishi forestry scheme?**
(a) 3.30 Lakh (b) 3.40 lakh
(c) 3.50 Lakhs (d) 3.60 lakhs

9. **What is the conjunction of agriculture, animal husbandry, trade, commerce etc. called in Kautilya's Arthashastra?**
(a) Sangam (b) Varta
(c) Aprahat (d) Jangam

10. **What is the length of concrete dam (Hanuman Nagar Nepal, which is located on the border of Bihar)?**
(a) 1120 meter (b) 1130 meter
(c) 1140 meter (d) 1150 meter

11. **Where is Kakolat Mela held in Bihar?**
(a) Nawada (b) Saran
(c) Madhubani (d) Buxar

12. **Which is the district with highest credit-deposit ratio in Bihar as on September, 2016?**
(a) Buxar (b) Patna
(c) Rohtas (d) Kaimur

13. **Which bank has the highest number of branches in Bihar?**
(a) Allahabad Bank
(b) Central Bank of India
(c) SBI
(d) Bank of India

14. **At which place does the Karmanasha river merge in the Ganga?**
(a) chausa (b) Bihta
(c) Mokama (d) Pehleja Ghat

15. **Who discovered the remains of the ancient Nalanda Mahavihara found in Bargaon?**
(a) Rolf Fitch
(b) Max Mueller
(c) John Marshall
(d) Cunningham

16. **How many Regional Rural Banks are there in Bihar?**
(a) 2 (b) 3
(c) 4 (d) 5

17. **In which year of Ashoka's rule, the Kalinga War was fought?**
(a) 6th (b) 7th
(c) 8th (d) 9th

18. **Irrigation facility arranged by the state in Mauryan period was called:**
(a) Ahar (b) Setubandh
(c) Aprahat (d) Agrahar

19. **Whose creation is 'Kirtilata'?**
(a) Vidyapati
(b) Nagarjuna
(c) Bhikhari Thakur
(d) Ramdhari Singh Dinkar

20. 'Do or Die is related to which movement?
(a) Swadeshi
(b) Champaran
(c) Non-cooperation
(d) Quit India

Answers

1. (b)	**2.** (c)	**3.** (c)	**4.** (a)
5. (c)	**6.** (a)	**7.** (c)	**8.** (d)
9. (b)	**10.** (c)	**11.** (a)	**12.** (d)
13. (c)	**14.** (a)	**15.** (d)	**16.** (b)
17. (c)	**18.** (b)	**19.** (a)	**20.** (d)

SET-62

1. Which artists have contributed significantly to the development of Pal style of construction of bronze statues?
(a) Prempal
(b) Dhiman
(c) Bithpal
(d) (b) and (c)

2. What was the wild army called in the Mauryan period?
(a) Atavi Bal (b) Ganjam Bal
(c) Teerth Bal (d) Rahat Bal

3. Kanwar Lake is constructed by the discharge of which river?
(a) Sone (b) Ganga
(c) Gandak (d) Kosi

4. Rajkumar Shukla, a famous farmer of Champaran, was a resident of which village?
(a) Murli Bharhawa
(b) Mehsi
(c) Amodei
(d) Jiradei

5. In which year was the first meeting of The Congress Socialist Party held in Patna?
(a) 1930 AD (b) 1932 AD
(c) 1934 AD (d) 1936 AD

6. What was the last sentence of Buddha?
(a) Atma Bhava
(b) Aap Deepo Bhava
(c) Moksha Karam Bhava
(d) (a),(b) and (c)

7. When did The Governor of Kashi, Shishunag become the king of Magadha?
(a) 408 AD (b) 410 AD
(c) 412 AD (d) 414 AD

8. What was a landowner called in the Mauryan period?
(a) Shetrak (b) Atavi
(c) Teerth (d) Rajjuk

9. Who was the first Indian Governor of Bihar-Odisha?
(a) Narpat Mishr
(b) Khan Sarwar Jung
(c) Satyendra Prasanna Sinha
(d) Meghnath Shah

10. Where is Kanwar Lake located?
(a) Begusarai (b) Nawada
(c) Saran (d) Nalanda

11. A Bill is sent to the Governor for signature by whom after it is passed in both the Houses?
(a) Chief Minister
(b) Parliamentary Affairs Minister
(c) Speaker of legislative assembly
(d) Deputy Chief Minister

12. Kautilya's 'arthashastra' is divided into how many parts?
(a) 13 (b) 14
(c) 15 (d) 16

13. Which aspect is highlighted in Kautilya's 'Arthashastra'?
(a) Economy
(b) Politics
(c) Religious
(d) (a), (b) and (c)

14. In which year did Buddha die at the age of 80?
(a) 481 AD (b) 483 AD
(c) 485 AD (d) 487 AD

15. Which pillars of Kaushambi and Prayag mention about charity done by a queen of Ashoka?
(a) Sanghmitra (b) Karuvaki
(c) Trishala (d) Yashodhara

16. With the help of which of his ministers did Ajatshatru divide the Vajji Sangh?
(a) Upagupta (b) Chhatrap
(c) Jamali (d) Vasskar

17. What was the silver coin called in the Mauryan period?
(a) Pann (b) Dinar
(c) Apharsh (d) Tishk

18. When was the Kosi project started?
(a) 1951 AD (b) 1953 AD
(c) 1955 AD (d) 1957 AD

19. Who was the first woman to join the Buddhist Union?
(a) Prajapati Gautami
(b) Sanghmitra
(c) Yashodhara
(d) Karuvaki

20. Kosi river is known as
(a) Narayani
(b) Bhairavi
(c) Saptakoshiki
(d) Sariswa

Answers

1. (d)	**2.** (a)	**3.** (c)	**4.** (a)
5. (c)	**6.** (b)	**7.** (c)	**8.** (a)
9. (c)	**10.** (a)	**11.** (c)	**12.** (c)
13. (b)	**14.** (b)	**15.** (b)	**16.** (d)
17. (a)	**18.** (b)	**19.** (a)	**20.** (c)

SET-63

1. Which inscription is the only record which is inscribed on stone plates?
(a) Verat (b) Bhabru
(c) Kalsi (d) Junagadh

2. What is the script of Mauryan records found in Bihar?
(a) Brahmi
(b) Kharosthi
(c) Armic
(d) (a), (b) and (c)

3. Which river is also known as 'Kekat' and 'Bagagadhi'?
(a) Niranjana (b) Punpun
(c) Bagmati (d) Sone

4. Who was the originator of the Federal Buddhist Community?
(a) Ajatshatru (b) Mahakashyap
(c) Jeevak (d) Prasenjeet

5. What is the golden coins called in Buddhist jataka stories?
(a) Nishk (b) Pann
(c) Karsapana (d) Dinar

6. Who was the founder of Pataliputra?
(a) Ajatshatru
(b) Udain
(c) Ghanananda
(d) Chandragupta Maurya

7. What was the name of Mahavir's father?
(a) Siddhartha
(b) Anant Sen
(c) Ashwaghosh
(d) Jeevak

8. Which object was first widely used in the field of art during the Mauryan period?
(a) Stone (b) Brass
(c) Iron (d) Copper

9. What is not similar in Buddhism and Jainism?
(a) Moksha
(b) Kaivalya
(c) Self-suppression
(d) (a) (b) and (c)

10. What was the sex ratio in rural and urban areas in Bihar as per census 2011?

(a) 927-869 (b) 930-872
(c) 935-875 (d) 940-881

11. Where was silk exported in Mauryan times?
(a) Iran (b) China
(c) Mongolia (d) Japan

12. In Nalanda University in Bihar, the Mahayana branch of which religion was specially taught?
(a) Buddhist (b) Jain
(c) Ajeevak (d) Shaiva

13. Who was the first Chief Justice of Patna High Court?
(a) DA riuben
(b) David cooper
(c) Mark Lehmann
(d) George Mattis

14. Since when is the Mukhyamantri Kanya Suraksha Yojana being implemented in Bihar?
(a) 2006 AD (b) 2007 AD
(c) 2008 AD (d) 2009 AD

15. When was Magadh University established in Bodh Gaya?
(a) 1960 AD (b) 1962 AD
(c) 1964 AD (d) 1966 AD

16. Which tax was called 'Bali' in the Mauryan period?
(a) Income Tax (b) Agricultural Tax
(c) Trade Tax (d) Land Revenue

17. Udayan was a follower of which religion?
(a) Jain (b) Buddhist
(c) Ajivak (d) Vaishnava

18. In which posture is the statue of Buddha installed in Bodh Gaya Mahabodhi Temple?
(a) Earth Touch
(b) Padmasana
(c) Chakrasana
(d) (a), (b) and (c)

19. When was the Kunwar Army formed in Bihar?
(a)1972 AD (b) 1974 AD
(c)1976 AD (d)1978 AD

20. Kurkihar' is another name for
(a) Kumharar (b) Chirand
(c) Chechar (d) Mahdah

Answers

1. (b)	**2.** (a)	**3.** (b)	**4.** (b)
5. (a)	**6.** (b)	**7.** (a)	**8.** (a)
9. (c)	**10.** (a)	**11.** (b)	**12.** (a)
13. (a)	**14.** (c)	**15.** (b)	**16.** (d)
17. (a)	**18.** (b)	**19.** (d)	**20.** (a)

SET-64

1. Who was Mahavir married to?
(a) Shivneri (b) Yashodhara
(c) Yashoda (d) Sanghmitra

2. Who created the Kaikeyi process?
(a) Kedarnath Mishra
(b) Baikunth Shukla
(c) Chittaranjan Das
(d) All of the above

3. Who first reported Kesaria stupa and Areraj pillar?
(a) Cunningham
(b) John Marshall
(c) Major Baro
(d) Hotgaon

4. In which inscription has Ashoka described himself as the Emperor of Magadha?
(a) Maski (b) Bhabru
(c) Vairat (d) Junagadh

5. What does Kaivalya mean?
(a) Salvation
(b) Recipient of the highest knowledge
(c) Struggle
(d) Sense of service

6. The Central Potato Research Centre located in Bihar?
(a) Patna (b) Mokama
(c) Gaya (d) Muzaffarpur

7. The conflict between the Pala, Pratihara and Rashtrakuta dynasties

that happened to take over Kannauj is called?

(a) Three - fold battle
(b) Trilateral conflict
(c) Friendship Struggle
(d) (a), (b) and (c)

8. Nav Nalanda Mahavihara is famous for

(a) Pali research center
(b) University
(c) Buddhist Bihar
(d) Chaitya

9. Where did Buddha accept pravajana (renunciation of clothes)?

(a) Bodh Gaya (b) Anoma
(c) Sarnath (d) Shravasti

10. The Republic of Lichchavi was established by

(a) Vishal (b) Anand
(c) Jamali (d) Rajkarna

11. When did Iltutmish take full control of Bihar and Bengal?

(a 1229-30 AD (b) 1230-31 AD
(c) 1231-32 AD (d) 1232-33 AD

12. What is the name of the book written by Kalhana?

(a) Rajatarangini
(b) Alekha
(c) Dimasa
(a) Priyadarshini

13. Bihar falls in which agro-climatic zone of India?

(a) Zone I (b) Zone II
(c) zone III (d) zone IV

14. Under whose leadership was the Bakasht movement launched in Bihar at a place called Barhia?

(a) Karyanand Sharma
(b) Sahajanand Sarasvati
(c) Purvanand Sharma
(d) (a), (b) and (c)

15. In which cycle was the plain of the Intermediate Ganga built?

(a) 4th Mahakalpa
(b) Dharwad Order
(c) Vindhyan Order
(d) Kadapa Order

16. What is the incident of Buddha's death called in Buddhism?

(a) Dharmachakraparivartan
(b) Mahaparinirvan
(c) Kaivalya
(d) Suktashil

17. Who was the founder of Mauryan empire?

(a) Ajatshatru
(b) Bimbi Sara
(c) Bindusara
(d) Chandragupta Maurya

18. According to the Constitution, the governor divides the portfolios among ministers on whose advice?

(a) Governor
(b) Chief Minister
(c) Speaker of legislative assembly
(d) President

19. Which was the district with the lowest sex ratio in Bihar as per 2011 census?

(a) Munger
(b) Sivan
(c) Gaya
(d) Bhagalpur

20. As the Chief Advisor to the Council of Ministers, which post is called the Head of the Government Machinery?

(a) Secretary
(b) Chief Secretary
(c) Joint Secretary
(d) Deputy Secretary

Answers

1. (c)	**2.** (a)	**3.** (d)	**4.** (a)
5. (b)	**6.** (a)	**7.** (b)	**8.** (a)
9. (b)	**10.** (a)	**11.** (b)	**12.** (a)
13. (d)	**14.** (a)	**15.** (a)	**16.** (b)
17. (d)	**18.** (b)	**19.** (a)	**20.** (b)

SET-65

1. **Whom did Iltutmish make his first subedar in Bihar?**
(a) Malik Jani (b) Shaista Khan
(c) Islam Shah (d) Mir Madan

2. **Cabinet Minister in the Council of Ministers, Minister of State for Independent Charge, Minister of State and Chief Minister are selected by**
(a) President
(b) Governor
(c) Chief Minister
(d) Speaker of Assembly

3. **The Council of Ministers is collectively responsible to the State Assembly and to whom personally?**
(a) President
(b) Chief Minister
(c) Governor
(d) Speaker of legislative assembly

4. **Manjusha style was the main style of which mahajanapada?**
(a) Anga (b) Vajji
(c) Lichchavi (d) Magadha

5. **When did Swami Sahajananda Sarasvati established the Bihar Kisan Sabha?**
(a) 1927 AD (b) 1928 AD
(c) 1929 AD (d) 1930 AD

6. **According to Mahipal's Nalanda Stone Article, which mahavihara was burnt by Baladitya?**
(a) Nalanda (b) Takshashila
(c) Vikramshila (d) Sompur

7. **Mahila Samakhya Programme is being conducted since 1992 AD under**
(a) State Commission for Women
(b) Mahila Samakhya Society
(c) Sakhi Centre
(d) State Human Rights Commission

8. **Which was the first capital of Magadha empire?**
(a) Giriraj (b) Bodh Gaya
(c) Patliputra (d) Lucknowati

9. **Which place was first attacked by Mahmud Ghaznavi in 1001 AD?**
(a) Sindh (b) Chittorgarh
(c) Amritsar (d) Udbhandpur

10. **Which was the capital of Mauryan empire?**
(a) Pataliputra (b) Bodh Gaya
(c) Lucknowti (d) Rajagraha

11. **Which dynasty did Mahapadmananda establish by ending the Shishunag dynasty?**
(a) Kanva (b) Hariyank
(c) Nanda (d) Maurya

12. **Who founded the Congress Socialist Party?**
(a) Jayaprakash Narayan
(b) Mukunda Roy
(c) Sri Krishna Singh
(d) Mohd Zubair

13. **Who was the last ruler of the Nanda dynasty?**
(a) Gopal Nand (b) Dev Nand
(c) Ghanananda (d) Keshav Nand

14. **Which tax was Levied on the farmers to prevent the invasion of the Turks?**
(a) Takavi (b) Sondhar
(c) Aprahat (d) Turushkdand

15. **Where did Mahavira die at the age of 72 in 468 BC?**
(a) Pavapuri (b) Bodh Gaya
(c) Varanasi (d) Pataliputra

16. **What is the number of Assembly members in Bihar?**
(a) 240 (b) 243
(c) 246 (d) 249

17. **Which is the district with highest sex ratio in Bihar as per 2011 census?**

(a) Darbhanga (b) Begusarai
(c) Gaya (d) Gopalganj

18. Mahavira's mother was the sister of which ruler?
(a) King Karna
(b) King Siddhartha
(c) King Chetak
(d) King Chhatrasal

19. In which book is there a collection of 549 Jataka stories related to the rebirth of Buddha?
(a) Angutar Nikay
(b) Abhidhamma Pitak
(c) Khuddak Nikay
(d) Vinay Pitak

20. What was the tax rate in Mauryan period?
(a) 1/4 (b) 1/5
(c) 1/6 (d) 1/7

Answers

1. (a)	**2.** (c)	**3.** (c)	**4.** (a)
5. (c)	**6.** (a)	**7.** (b)	**8.** (a)
9. (d)	**10.** (a)	**11.** (c)	**12.** (a)
13. (c)	**14.** (d)	**15.** (a)	**16.** (b)
17. (d)	**18.** (c)	**19.** (c)	**20.** (c)

SET-66

1. Where is Kusheshwar Bird Sanctuary located?
(a) Sivan (b) Saran
(c) Gaya (d) Darbhanga

2. Which is the highest jute producing district in Bihar?
(a) Purnia (b) Munger
(c) Sivan (d) Supaul

3. Mention about which dynasty is found in the article of Davabernaq from Arrah in Bihar province and articles recovered from Shahpur (Patna) and Mandar (Banka)?
(a) Mauryan dynasty
(b) Hariyank dynasty
(c) Gupta dynasty
(d) Later Gupta dynasty

4. Megasthenes was the ambassador of
(a) Seleucus (b) Alexander
(c) Antiocus (d) None of these

5. When was the attempt to murder Kingsford in Muzaffarpur made?
(a) 1906 AD (b) 1908 AD
(c) 1910 AD (d) 1912 AD

6. What was Mahavira's childhood name?
(a) Siddhartha (b) Vardhman
(c) Chetan (d) Kunal

7. Which Buddhist book is in the form of a quiz?
(a) Jataka Stories
(b) Sutta Pitak
(c) Abhidhamma Pitak
(d) Vinay Pitak

8. When was the Nawada Museum established in the State of Bihar?
(a) 1972 AD (b) 1974 AD
(c) 1976 AD (d) 1978 AD

9. When was Jharkhand separated from Bihar and given the status of a new province?
(a) 1 January, 2000
(b) 8 March, 2000
(c) 7 July, 2000
(d) 15 November, 2000

10. Which dynasty was finally conquered in the tripartite conflict?
(a) Gurjar Pratihar (b) Pal
(c) Rashtrakuta (d) Sen

11. Which river separated Magadha and Anga Mahajanapada?
(a) Sone (b) Champa
(c) Saryu (d) Niranjana

12. What is the estimated reserve of coal in present-day Bihar?

(a) 12 million tons
(b) 14 million tons
(c) 16 million tonnes
(d) 18 million tonnes

13. When was the notification for the formation of the State of Bihar issued?
(a) 1 January,1912
(b) 22 March,1912
(c) 13 June, 1912
(d) 15 August, 1912

14. In which district is coal found in present-day Bihar?
(a) Aurangabad (b) Gaya
(c) Jehanabad (d) Kaimur

15. When was the Mukhyamantri Private Nursery Scheme launched by the Government of Bihar?
(a) 2009 AD (b) 2011 AD
(c) 2013 AD (d) 2015 AD

16. When did Jayaprakash Narayan establish the Congress Socialist Party?
(a) 1930 AD (b) 1932 AD
(c) 1934 AD (d) 1936 AD

17. What was the revenue from the city called in the Mauryan administration?
(a) Durg (b) Aprahat
(c) Sondhar (d) Ujra

18. Where the highest rainfall occurs in Bihar?
(a) Purnia (b) Katihar
(c) Kishanganj (d) Gaya

19. Which district of Bihar was the most affected in the Quit India Movement of 1942?
(a) Patna (b) Bhagalpur
(c) Saran (d) Banka

20. Who has composed a book called 'samajvad hi Kyun'?
(a) Rajendra Prasad
(b) Meenu Masani
(c) Hasan Imam
(d) Jayaprakash Narayan

Answers

1. (d)	**2.** (a)	**3.** (d)	**4.** (a)
5. (b)	**6.** (b)	**7.** (c)	**8.** (b)
9. (d)	**10.** (a)	**11.** (b)	**12.** (c)
13. (b)	**14.** (a)	**15.** (c)	**16.** (c)
17. (a)	**18.** (c)	**19.** (a)	**20.** (d)

SET-67

1. Gaya Nagar is situated on the banks of which river?
(a) Sone (b) Lehri
(c) Phalgu (d) Sariswan

2. At which place did Mahatma Gandhi perform the first Satyagraha (Kisan Andolan) in Bihar?
(a) Champaran (b) Saran
(c) Sivan (d) Gaya

3. Pavapuri was the capital of which of the mahajanapada?
(a) Vaishali (b) Anga
(c) Malla (d) Vajji

4. Where is Jayaprakash Narayan University located in Bihar?
(a) Patna (b) Chhapra
(c) Gaya (d) Munger

5. When and where was the great clarinet player Bismillah Khan born?
(a) 1916 AD Dumraon
(b) 1916 AD Gaya
(c) 1916 AD Bihar Sharif
(d) 1916 AD Maner

6. Which river is called the mourning of Bihar?
(a) Bagmati (b) Karmanasha
(c) Kosi (d) Ghaghra

7. What was the real name of the great clarinet player Bismillah Khan?

(a) Jamaluddin Khan
(b) Ibrahim Khan
(c) Kamruddin Khan
(d) Hasmat Khan

8. Mahendra Mishra, Bhikhari Thakur and Babu Raghuveer Nath are litterateurs of which language?
(a) Angika (b) Bhojpuri
(c) Maghi (d) Maithili

9. Where is Mahant Ramsaran Das Library located?
(a) Samastipur (b) Darbhanga
(c) Shivhar (d) Banka

10. Where did Mir Qasim shift his capital from Murshidabad in 1761 AD?
(a) Munger (b) Patna
(c) Bhagalpur (d) Bihar Sharif

11. Whose composition is the Mirtul Ahwal?
(a) Shad Azimabadi
(b) Amir Khusro
(c) Kaifi Azmi
(d) Mullah Bahbahani

12. The sum of budgetary deficit and the sum of market deficit and liability of government is called -
(a) Fiscal Deficit
(b) Capital Deficit
(c) Current Deficit
(d) Primary Deficit

13. How many committees of 5 persons each are there for city administration in The Indica of Megasthenes?
(a) 6 (b) 5
(c) 4 (d) 3

14. What was the state currency of the Mauryan called?
(a) Dinar (b) Pann
(c) Rupees (d) Hun

15. According to the 2011 Census, which state of India has a population of more than that of Bihar?
(a) Karnataka
(b) Maharashtra
(c) Uttar Pradesh
(d) (b) and (c)

16. Which officer ran the army in the war zone in the Mauryan period?
(a) Nayak (b) Karnat
(c) Durgapal (d) Tirtha

17. Where did Buddha establish the Buddhist Union?
(a) Shravasti (b) Bodh Gaya
(c) Sarnath (d) Vaishali

18. Which round table was held in 1931 AD?
(a) 1st (b) 2nd
(c) 3rd (d) 4th

19. Who used to maintain weapons and manage security during the Mauryan period?
(a) Sitadhyaksh
(c) Ayudhgaraadhyaksh
(b) Navadhyaksh
(d) Karadhyaksh

20. When was the Patna High Court established?
(a) 1912 AD (b) 1914 AD
(c) 1916 AD (d) 1918 AD

Answers

1. (c)	**2.** (a)	**3.** (c)	**4.** (b)
5. (a)	**6.** (c)	**7.** (c)	**8.** (b)
9. (a)	**10.** (a)	**11.** (d)	**12.** (a)
13. (a)	**14.** (b)	**15.** (d)	**16.** (a)
17. (c)	**18.** (c)	**19.** (b)	**20.** (a)

SET-68

1. Where is the Ajgabinath Temple located in Bihar?
(a) Bhagalpur (b) Gaya
(c) Supaul (d) Saharsa

2. What was the rental army called in the Mauryan period?

(a) Karnat (b) Navadhyaksh
(c) Bhratak (d) Jaavar

3. Where is the Arabic and Persian Research Institute located in Bihar?
(a) Patna (b) Bhagalpur
(c) Hajipur (d) Bihar Sharif

4. When was the Mukhyamantri Grameen Peyjal (Quality Affected Area) Nirbhaya Yojana launched?
(a) 2014 AD (b) 2015 AD
(c) 2016 AD (d) 2017 AD

5. Eminent news anchor Shweta Singh belongs to which district of Bihar?
(a) Vaishali (b) Patna
(c) Bhagalpur (d) Buxar

6. What was the percentage of male literacy rate in Bihar as per 2011 census?
(a) 70.12% (b) 17.69%
(c) 72.84% (d) 73.39%

7. Where was the capital of Kalinga?
(a) Tosli (b) Ujjain
(c) Pavapuri (d) Mathura

8. Chirag Paswan has been elected as an MP from which constituency in the 2019 Lok Sabha elections?
(a) Jehanabad (b) Bettiah
(c) Jamui (d) Gaya

9. In the movement of 1942, Dr. Rajendra Prasad was arrested and lodged in which jail?
(a) Bankipur (b) Ranchi
(c) Calcutta (d) Hazaribagh

10. When was the Mukhyamantri Vidyut Sambandh Yojana launched?
(a) 2014 AD (b) 2015 AD
(c) 2016 AD (d) 2017 AD

11. Where was the second Buddhist sangeeti held?
(a) Rajagraha (b) Vaishali
(c) Pataliputra (d) Kundalvan

12. What is the name of the book of Megasthenes?
(a) Indica (b) Capital
(c) Samrat (d) Arthneeti

13. What were the widows who lived independently in the Mauryan period called?
(a) Ganika
(b) Rajjuk
(c) Kshandavasini
(a) Konarki

14. From where the remains of the palace of Magadha Emperor Chandragupta were found?
(a) Agamkuan (b) Phulwari Sharif
(c) Kumhar (d) Bankipur

15. From which place the Neolithic remains have been first found in Bihar?
(a) Chirand (b) Gaya
(c) Kumhar (d) Kesariya

16. Where is Kosi Mela held in Bihar?
(a) Gaya (b) Katihar
(c) Madhubani (d) Banka

17. What was the copper coin called in the Mauryan period?
(a) Pann
(b) Hun
(c) Karsapana
(d) Masak and Kakani

18. Where is the Dargah of Makhdoom Shah located?
(a) Maner (b) Bihar Sharif
(c) Patna (d) Munger

19. Who is called Shakespeare of Bhojpuri?
(a) Bhikhari Thakur
(b) Vidyapati
(c) Nagarjuna
(d) Kedar Pandey

20. What percentage of sales tax on imported goods during Mauryan period used to be taken?

(a) 6% (b) 8%
(c) 10% (d) 12%

Answers

1. (a)	**2.** (c)	**3.** (a)	**4.** (c)
5. (b)	**6.** (d)	**7.** (a)	**8.** (c)
9. (a)	**10.** (c)	**11.** (b)	**12.** (a)
13. (c)	**14.** (c)	**15.** (a)	**16.** (b)
17. (d)	**18.** (b)	**19.** (a)	**20.** (c)

SET-69

1. When did the youth of Bihar establish the Bihar Socialist Party?
(a) 1930 AD (b) 1931 AD
(c) 1932 AD (d) 1933 AD

2. How many revenue villages are there in Bihar?
(a) 41,320 (b) 42,630
(c) 43,140 (d) 44,867

3. Where did Mahatma Buddha give his first sermon?
(a) Sarnath (b) Gaya
(c) Shravasti (d) Mathura

4. Mullah Bahbahani was a traveler of which country?
(a) Greece (b) Iran .
(c) Azerbaijan (d) Syria .

5. Bimbisara and Ajatshatru belonged to which dynasty?
(a) Heryak dynasty
(b) Kanva dynasty
(c) Gupta Dynasty
(c) Shishunag Dynasty

6. According to Mahabharata and puranas, which was the first dynasty of Magadha?
(a) Kanva dynasty
(b) Heryak dynasty
(c) Brihadratha dynasty
(c) Kushan dynasty

7. How many times was National Poet Ramdhari Singh Dinkar elected to Rajya Sabha?
(a) once (b) twice
(c) Three times (d) four times

8. In Atharvaveda the word 'vratya' is used for the people of which state?
(a) Vaishali (b) Magadha
(c) Rajagraha (d) Pavapuri

9. In which year was the Tharu caste included in the Scheduled Tribes in Bihar?
(a) 2001 AD (b) 2002 AD
(c) 2003 AD (d) 2004 AD

10. In which festival is The Zhizia Dance performed?
(a) Durga Puja (b) Diwali
(b) Chhath (d) Raksha Bandhan

11. Where did Mahavir Swami give his last sermon?
(a) Gaya (b) Pataliputra
(b) Vallabhpuri (d) Pavapuri

12. Who was appointed as the first Chairman of Bihar human rights commission?
(a) SN Jha
(b) Jamil Asghar
(b) Deepak Mishra
(a) Kailash Nath Katju

13. What were the spies called in the Mauryan period?
(a) Rajjuk (b) Gunnpurush
(b) Teerth (d) Bhratak

14. What is the famous folk dance prevalent in Muslim society on the occasion of Muharram called?
(a) Karam (b) Sohay
(b) Zarni (d) Zhizia

15. Where is Mansi Chaur located?
(a) Purnia (b) Gaya
(b) Nawada (d) Khagaria

16. What was the title of Ramdhari Singh Dinkar's first book?
(a) Urvashi
(b) Maila aanchal
(c) Pramaan Mantra
(d) Khalihaan

17. What is the amount being provided per student to children studying in Class IX under Mukhyamantri Balika and Balak Cycle Yojana?
(a) 2500 (b) 2800
(c) 3000 (d) 3200

18. In which city of Bihar was the first Doordarshan Kendra established?
(a) Muzaffarpur (b) Patna
(c) Gaya (d) Bhagalpur

19. When was the Mukhyamantri Kanya Vivah Yojana launched in Bihar?
(a) 2001 AD (b) 2003 AD
(b) 2005 AD (d) 2007 AD

20. Which dance is particularly prevalent among the tribes?
(a) Karama (b) Chhou
(c) Jat-jatin (d) Zhizia

Answers

1. (b)	**2.** (d)	**3.** (a)	**4.** (b)
5. (a)	**6.** (c)	**7.** (c)	**8.** (b)
9. (c)	**10.** (a)	**11.** (d)	**12.** (a)
13. (b)	**14.** (c)	**15.** (d)	**16.** (c)
17. (a)	**18.** (a)	**19.** (d)	**20.** (a)

SET-70

1. The epics 'Kaikeyi' and 'Ritu-vansh' are composed by
(a) Bhikhari Thakur
(b) Kedarnath Mishra Prabhat
(c) Nagarjuna
(d) Mandan alloy

2. How much incentive is being given to minority students who have passed matriculation examination in first class under Mukhyamantri Vidyarthi Protsahan Yojana?
(a) 6000 (b) 8000
(c) 10,000 (d) 12,000

3. What was the permanent army called in the Mauryan period?
(a) Bhruk (b) Rajjuk
(c) Teerth (d) Maul

4. What is the main slogan of Mukhya-mantri Vidyut Samba Nirbhaya Yo-jana?
(a) bijli 24 × 7
(b) Roshan Bihar
(c) Har ghar bijli lagataar
(d) Ujala Bihar

5. In which city did Mahavir die?
(a) Gaya (b) Vallabhpuri
(c) Pavapuri (d) Vaishali

6. By which another name is the Mukhyamantri Private Nursery Scheme known?
(a) Greening mission
(b) Eco-Friendly Mission
(c) Forest Revolution Mission
(d) None of these

7. Which district had the lowest urban population in Bihar as per 2011 census?
(a) Gaya (b) Samastipur
(c) Munger (d) Vaishali

8. When was the Mukhyamantri Shahari Peyjal Nirbhaya Yojana launched?
(a) 2013 AD (b) 2014 AD
(c) 2015 AD (d) 2016 AD

9. When was the Mukhyamantri Shahari Nali-Gali Pakkikaran Nirbhaya Yojana launched?
(a) 2016 AD (b) 2015 AD
(c) 2014 AD (d) 2013 AD

10. What was free labor meaning 'begar' called in Mauryan period?
(a) Karagam (b) Pann
(c) Vishti (d) Bhrat

11. When was the Mukhyamantri Grameen Peyjal (Non-Quality Affected Area) Nirbhaya Yojana launched?
(a) 2014 AD (b) 2015 AD
(c) 2016 AD (d) 2017 AD

12. When was the Mukhyamantri Gramin Peyjal Nirbhaya Yojana launched?

(a) 2014 AD (b) 2015 AD
(c) 2016 AD (d) 2017 AD

13. When was the Mukhyamantri Grameen Gali-Nali Pakkikaran Nirbhaya Yojana launched?
(a) 2016 AD (b) 2014 AD
(c) 2012 AD (d) 2010 AD

14. What was the purpose of Munger's Barhia Tal protest?
(a) Boycott of project on agricultural land
(b) Demand for return of bakast land
(c) uneven distribution of land
(d) increase in tax

15. The picture of Muslim nikah is made by which artist?
(a) Yamuna Prasad
(b) Shivlal
(c) Hulas Ram
(d) Sevakram

16. Which revolt was committed by the prisoners lodged in the jail of Muzaffarpur?
(a) lota rebellion
(b) indigenous rebellion .
(c) nude rebellion
(d) blanket rebellion .

17. Which was the district with the lowest literacy rate in Bihar as per 2011 census?
(a) Gopalganj (b) Purnia
(c) Sivan (d) Madhepura

18. In which year did Dr. Rajendra Prasad start publishing a weekly paper called 'Bihar Law'?
(a) 1910 AD (b) 1912 AD
(c) 1914 AD (d) 1916 AD

19. Who is the author of the book 'surya Siddhant'?
(a) Aryabhata (b) Vishakhdutt
(c) Kautilya (d) Ashwasen

20. Who was the first foreign traveler to visit Bihar during the Mughal period?
(a) Rolf Fitch
(b) Hawkins
(c) Mullah Pillow
(d) Mullah Bahbahani

Answers

1. (b)	**2.** (c)	**3.** (d)	**4.** (c)
5. (c)	**6.** (a)	**7.** (c)	**8.** (d)
9. (a)	**10.** (c)	**11.** (c)	**12.** (b)
13. (a)	**14.** (b)	**15.** (b)	**16.** (a)
17. (b)	**18.** (d)	**19.** (a)	**20.** (c)

SET-71

1. What was the revenue from rural areas called in Mauryan administration?
(a) Vartman (b) Sita
(c) Rashtr (d) Bhag

2. Where is the fisheries research center proposed to be set up in Bihar?
(a) Mithapur (b) Sonpur
(c) Gaya (d) Muzaffarpur

3. Where was Vidyapati, the supreme poet of Maithili language, born?
(a) Khagaria (b) Darbhanga
(c) Madhepura (d) Sitamarhi

4. Where did Mahavira attain knowledge?
(a) Under the Peepal Tree
(b) Under the Sal Tree
(c) under the banyan tree
(d) Under the Arjuna Tree

5. What did Megasthenes say to Pataliputra in his book 'Indica'?
(a) Palihol (b) Agastan
(c) Palibrotha (d) Patnam

6. What were women who were independently involved in prostitution called in the Mauryan period?
(a) Kamya (b) Rupajiva
(c) Sahasi (d) Amaram

7. **When and where was Majhrul Haque born?**
(a) 1860 AD Bilta
(b) 1862 AD Dumra
(c) 1864 AD Hathua
(d) 1866 AD Maner

8. **The tomb of which Sufi saint at Maner is also known as Chhoti Dargah?**
(a) Makhdoom Shah Daulat
(b) Yahya Maneri
(c) Abdul Samad Shah
(d) Karim Maneri

9. **For what purpose was Golghar constructed in Patna?**
(a) tourism
(b) housing
(c) grain storage
(d) soldiers to live

10. **What was the name of the wife of the famous scholar Mandan Mishra?**
(a) Bharati
(b) Durga
(c) Kalpana
(d) Prabhavati

11. **Basatin-ul-Uns is a valuable source in respect of which region of Bihar?**
(a) Saran (b) Tirhut
(c) Mithila (d) Magadha

12. **Where is the tomb of Malik Ibrahim Bayan located?**
(a) Maner (b) Hajipur
(c) Patna (d) Bihar Sharif

13. **In which Five-year Plan was the Jawahar Rozgar Yojana renamed as 'Grameen Samriddhi Yojana'?**
(a) 7th (b) 8th
(c) 9th (d) 10th

14. **The festival of 'sama- Chakeva' is celebrated in which region of Bihar?**
(a) Mithila (b) Magadha
(c) Tirhut (d) Seemanchal

15. **When and where was the soldier of pen, Ramvriksha Benipuri, born?**
(a) 1897 AD Gaya
(b) 1899 AD Muzaffarpur
(c) 1901 AD Banka
(d) 1903 AD Bhagalpur

16. **When was The Antyodaya Anna Yojana launched?**
(a) 1998 AD (b) 1999 AD
(c) 2000 AD (d) 2001 AD

17. **When was NREGA changed to MGNREGA?**
(a) 2007 AD (b) 2008 AD
(c) 2009 AD (d) 2010 AD

18. **At the time of which ruler of Magadha in 326 BC, did the invasion of India by the Greek ruler Alexander happen?**
(a) Mahapadmananda
(b) Ghanananda
(c) Chandragupta Maurya
(d) Bindusara

19. **What is the original name of Kosi river?**
(a) Saptakosi (b) Narayani
(c) Kaushiki (d) Kalyani

20. **The famous doctor Jivak was in the kingdom of Magadha during whose reign?**
(a) Bimbisara
(b) Ajatshatru
(c) udayan
(d) brihadratha

Answers

1. (a)	**2.** (a)	**3.** (b)	**4.** (b)
5. (c)	**6.** (b)	**7.** (d)	**8.** (a)
9. (c)	**10.** (a)	**11.** (b)	**12.** (d)
13. (c)	**14.** (a)	**15.** (b)	**16.** (c)
17. (c)	**18.** (b)	**19.** (c)	**20.** (a)

SET-72

1. **Which state has announced pension to the JP agitators?**
(a) Telangana (b) Goa
(c) Maharashtra (d) Bihar

2. **What percentage of sale was made on indigenous goods during Mauryan period?**
(a) 2% (b) 3%
(c) 4% (d) 5%

3. **Which ancient state of Bihar was initially outside Aryavarta for a long time and was the residence of the Anarya caste people?**
(a) Magadha (b) Anga
(c) Vajji (d) Kashi

4. **How many stone pillars have been found in the palace of Magadha Emperor Chandragupta?**
(a) 80 (b) 82
(c) 84 (d) 86

5. **For the first time in the history of Bihar, the Economic Survey of the State was presented by**
(a) Lalu Prasad Yadav
(b) Nitish Kumar
(c) Sushil Kumar Modi
(d) Abdul Bari Siddiqui

6. **As per 2011 Census, which district of Bihar has the highest literacy rate?**
(a) Kaimur (b) Patna
(c) Bhagalpur (d) Rohtas

7. **By whom was Kalinga first merged with the Magadha Empire?**
(a) Mahapadmananda
(b) Kalashok
(c) Chandragupta Maurya
(d) Ashoka

8. **What are the followers of Mahavira called?**
(a) Ajeevak (b) Shaiva
(c) Jaini (d) Vaishnava

9. **Who is the first Bihar resident to receive jnanpith award?**
(a) Bhikhari Thakur
(b) Ramdhari Singh Dinkar
(c) Nagarjuna
(d) Mandan Mishr

10. **Who is called the father of the 'Magahi Boli' style?**
(a) Amar Singh
(b) Bhikhari Thakur
(c) Suresh Dubey
(d) Ajay Pal

11. **Where is The Malamas Mela held in Bihar?**
(a) Bihar Sharif (b) Rajgir
(c) Sonpur (d) Kesaria

12. **The second Buddhist sangeeti (conference) was presided over by**
(a) Ashwasen (b) Kanishka
(c) Sarvakami (d) Anand

13. **Barauni Oil Refinery in Bihar was established under which Five Year Plan?**
(a) 1st (b) 2nd
(b) 3rd (d) 4th

14. **The second Buddhist sangeeti was organized during whose reign?**
(a) Kalashok (b)Ashoka
(c) Ajatshatru (d) Kanishka

15. **Who was the first to participate in the tripartite conflict on behalf of the Pala dynasty?**
(a) Devpal (b) Gopal
(c) Dharmapala (d) Mihir pal

16. **Which was the last of the three dynasties involved in the tripartite conflict to rule for the most days?**
(a) Gurjar-Pratihara Dynasty
(b) Pal Dynasty
(c) Rashtrakuta dynasty
(d) Sen dynasty

17. **Kundgram, the birth place of Mahavir, is in which district of Bihar?**
(a) Vaishali (b) Gaya
(c) Nalanda (d) Munger

18. **In how many phases did the tripartite conflict take place?**
(a) Two steps (b) three steps
(c) Four Steps (d) Five Steps

19. **In which scheme period was the Jaiprakash Rozgar Guarantee Scheme launched in Bihar?**
(a) 8th (b) 9th
(c) 10th (d) 11th

20. **Where did a revolt take place during the reign of Bindusara?**
(a) Takshashila (b) Vaishali
(c) Kalinga (d) Mathura

Answers

1. (d)	2. (c)	3. (a)	4. (c)
5. (c)	6. (d)	7. (a)	8. (c)
9. (b)	10. (c)	11. (b)	12. (c)
13. (b)	14. (a)	15. (c)	16. (b)
17. (a)	18. (d)	19. (c)	20. (a)

SET-73

1. **When was the Mauryan Empire established?**
(a) 318 AD (b) 320 AD
(c) 322 AD (d) 324 AD

2. **Which state did Bimbisara win by defeating Brahmadutta?**
(a) Anga (b) Vajji
(c) Videha (d) Kalinga

3. **Who did Bimbisara marry under the matrimonial policy for expansion of empire and attain a fertile region like Kashi as dowry?**
(a) Yashoda (b) Sangh Mitra
(c) Kosala Devi (d) Trishala

4. **Bimbisara sent his king Jivak for the treatment of which ruler?**
(a) Pradyot Sen (b) Amar Singh
(c) Lilavati (d) Charak

5. **What was the infant mortality rate in Bihar as per census 2011?**
(a) 60 per thousand
(b) 62 per thousand
(c) 64 Per thousand
(d) 66 per thousand

6. **When were two separate States called Bihar and Orissa formed?**
(a) 1934 AD (b) 1935 AD
(c) 1936 AD (d) 1937 AD

7. **In the time of which poet of Bihar were the songs of Nacharirag sung from house to house?**
(a) Vidyapati
(b) Bhikhari Thakur
(c) Kamal Mishra
(d) Jagpati Sahay

8. **Who was the ruler who included elephants in his army for the first time?**
(a) Jarasandha (b) Ghanananda
(c) Bimbi Sara (d) Ajatshatru

9. **Which king of Magadha was a contemporary of Alexander the Great?**
(a) Ghanananda
(b) Mahapadmananda
(c) Kalashok
(d) Chandragupta Maurya

10. **When was the Bihar Provincial Kisan Sabha constituted?**
(a) 1923 AD (b) 1925 AD
(c) 1927 AD (d) 1929 AD

11. **Chakravarty Devi of Bihar was a prominent painter of which style?**
(a) Patna Kalam
(b) Madhubani Painting
(c) Jadopati painting
(d) Manjusha style

12. **Which was the district with the highest urban population of Bihar as per 2011 census?**

(a) Patna (b) Gaya
(c) Bhagalpur (d) Munger

13. What was the population growth rate of Bihar in the 1981-91 decade?
(a) 21.12 % (b) 22.19 %
(c) 23.54 % (d) 24.95 %

14. Who is considered to be the first ruler to have a permanent army?
(a) Bimbisara (b) Ghanananda
(c) Ajatshatru (d) Ashoka

15. On which day was Buddha born, died and attained enlightenment?
(a) Chaitra Purnima
(b) Vaisakh Purnima
(c) Ashadh Purnima
(d) None of these

16. When did the construction of the Multipurpose Project, Kosi project of Bihar, start and in which year it was completed?
(a) 1955-1960 AD
(b) 1957–1961 AD
(c) 1959-1962 AD
(d) 1955-1963 AD

17. What was the time period of 12th Five Year Plan?
(a) 2010-15 AD (b) 2011-16 AD
(c) 2012-17 AD (d) 2013-18 AD

18. What was the percentage of industrial growth target set during the 12th Five Year Plan in Bihar?
(a) 10.88 % (b) 11.19 %
(c) 12.12% (d) 13.54 %

19. What was the scheduled tribe population in Bihar as per census 2011?
(a) 10 Lakh (b) 11 lakhs
(c) 12 Lakhs (d) 13 lakhs

20. The picture of 'Begamo ki sharab-khori' is made by which artist?
(a) Yamuna Prasad
(b) Sevak Ram
(c) Shivlal
(d) Ishwari Prasad

Answers

1. (c)	**2.** (a)	**3.** (c)	**4.** (a)
5. (d)	**6.** (c)	**7.** (a)	**8.** (c)
9. (a)	**10.** (d)	**11.** (d)	**12.** (a)
13. (c)	**14.** (a)	**15.** (b)	**16.** (d)
17. (c)	**18.** (c)	**19.** (d)	**20.** (a)

SET-74

1. Which was the first Maithili film of Bihar?
(a) Mithila Gaurav
(b) Mati Hamar
(c) Kanyadan
(d) Ghar-Dwar

2. Which is the district with lowest population density as per 2011 census?
(a) Kaimur (b) West Champaran
(c) Shivhar (d) Supaul

3. What was the number of Scheduled Castes in the State as per census 2011?
(a) 1.40 lakhs (b) 1.50 lakhs
(c) 1.60 lakhs (d) 1.70 lakhs

4. Which is the major river of Bihar?
(a) Kosi (b) Ganga
(c) Gandak (d) Bagmati

5. Prabhavati Devi was a freedom fighter of which region?
(a) Champaran (b) Saran
(c) Patna (d) Bhagalpur

6. Which tribe also considers itself to be Chandravanshi?
(a) Khadiya (b) Chero
(c) Oraon (d) Munda

7. Which ruler built the Rajgraha, the capital of Magadha kingdom?
(a) Bimbisara
(b) Ajatshatru
(c) Udayan
(d) Chandragupta Maurya

8. Which country is situated on the border of Bihar?

(a) Nepal (b) Bhutan
(c) Tibet (d) Myanmar

9. **What is the literacy rate of Bihar?**
(a) 61.12 % (b) 63.82 %
(c) 65.23 % (d) 67.82 %

10. **Which is the highest peak of Bihar?**
(a) Sammed Shikhar
(b) Parasnath
(c) Gurumukhi Mountain
(d) Someshwar Fort

11. **What was the height of Someshwar Fort, the highest peak of Bihar?**
(a) 840 meter (b) 880 meter
(c) 920 meter (d) 960 meter

12. **What was the length of Bihar from north to south?**
(a) 360 Km (b) 362 km
(c) 364 Km (d)366 km

13. **What is the width of Bihar from east to west?**
(a) 483 Km (b) 485 km
(c) 487 Km (d) 489 km

14. **What was the decadal population growth rate of Bihar?**
(a) 21.3 (b) 23.4
(c) 25.7 (d) 27.1

15. **How many persons per square kilometer was the population density of Bihar?**
(a) 1096 persons (b) 1100 persons
(c) 1106 persons (d) 1110 persons

16. **What is the position of Bihar on the basis of population density**
(a) 1st (b) 2nd
(c) 3rd (d) 4th

17. **Bihar College of Engineering, Patna got NIT status in which year?**
(a) 2000 AD (b) 2002 AD
(c) 2004 AD (d) 2006 AD

18. **In which year was the Bihar Football Association established?**
(a) 1984 AD (b) 1986 AD
(c) 1988 AD (d) 1990 AD

19. **What is the percentage of population of Bihar in India as per 2011 census of the country?**
(a) 8.40 (b) 8.60
(c) 8.80 (d) 9.10

20. **What was the position of Bihar in the country on the basis of population growth rate?**
(a) 2nd (b) 4th
(c) 6th (d) 8th

Answers

1. (c)	**2.** (a)	**3.** (c)	**4.** (b)
5. (a)	**6.** (b)	**7.** (b)	**8.** (a)
9. (b)	**10.** (d)	**11.** (b)	**12.** (b)
13. (a)	**14.** (c)	**15.** (c)	**16.** (a)
17. (c)	**18.** (b)	**19.** (b)	**20.** (c)

SET-75

1. **What type of climate prevalils of Bihar?**
(a) Monsoon climate
(b) Cyclonic climate
(b) Temperate climate
(d) Tundra climate

2. **Indira Gandhi Stadium is located in which district of Bihar?**
(a) Purnia (b) Supaul
(c) Gaya (d) Banka

3. **What type of climate prevails of Bihar?**
(a) Hot climate
(b) Humid climate
(c) Temperate climate
(d) Humid subtropical climate

4. **Hemant Trophy is related to which sport?**
(a) Cricket (b) Hockey
(c) Football (d) Chess

5. **What is the average height of Bihar above sea level?**
(a) 51 meter (b) 53 meter
(c) 55 meter (d) 57 meter

6. Amarnath Jha Award belongs to which field?
(a) Journalism
(b) Painting
(c) Children's Literature
(d) Medicine

7. Which was the first open university in Bihar?
(a) Patna University
(b) Gaya University
(c) Vaishali University
(d) Nalanda University

8. Which was the first Hindi newspaper of Bihar?
(a) Bihar (b) Bihar Bandhu
(c) Kaal (d) Prabhat

9. Which district of Bihar has minimum population density?
(a) Gaya (b) Bhabhua
(c) Kaimur (d) Gopalganj

10. Which district of Bihar has minimum area?
(a) Sheikhupura (b) Shivhar
(c) Banka (d) Jamui

11. Which district had the lowest percentage of rural population as per 2011 census?
(a) Munger (b) Vaishali
(c) Patna (d) Bhagalpur

12. In which year was the Bihar State Chess Association formed?
(a) 1931 AD (b) 1933 AD
(c) 1935 AD (d) 1937 AD

13. Dr. Grierson Award is given in which field?
(a) Folk language
(b) Journalism
(c) Medicine
(d) Folk Drama

14. What was the length and breadth of the palace of Magadha Emperor Chandragupta?
(a) 110 × 120 (b) 120 × 110
(c) 130 × 120 (d) 140 × 120

15. In which field is the Mandan Mishra Award given?
(a) Painting
(b) Religion
(c) Philosophy
(d) Both (b) and (c)

16. In which year was the Bihar Lawn Tennis Council constituted?
(a) 1910 AD (b) 1912 AD
(c) 1914 AD (d) 1916 AD

17. In which year were Davis cup matches played in Patna?
(a) 1966 AD (b) 1968 AD
(c) 1970 AD (d) 1972 AD

18. Magadha is first mentioned in which book?
(a) Rigveda (b) Samaveda
(c) Atharvaveda (d) Yajurveda

19. Sanjay Gandhi Mini Stadium is located in which district of Bihar?
(a) Gaya (b) Muzaffarpur
(c) Patna (d) Munger

20. When was Bihar bandhu, Bihar's first Hindi newspaper, started?
(a) 1870 AD (b) 1872 AD
(c) 1874 AD (d) 1876 AD

Answers

1. (a)	**2.** (a)	**3.** (d)	**4.** (a)
5. (b)	**6.** (c)	**7.** (d)	**8.** (b)
9. (b)	**10.** (a)	**11.** (c)	**12.** (d)
13. (a)	**14.** (d)	**15.** (d)	**16.** (b)
17. (c)	**18.** (a)	**19.** (c)	**20.** (c)

SET-76

1. What was the name of the first Urdu daily of Bihar?
(a) Inklab
(b) Qaumi Tanzim
(c) Noor ul Anwar
(d) Khabar Nama

2. When and where was Noor ul Anwar, Bihar's first Urdu daily, published?

(a) 1870 AD Patna
(b) 1872 AD Hajipur
(c) 1874 AD Bihar Sharif
(d) 1876 AD Aara

3. Which village has been declared as the first organic village of Bihar?
(a) Amodei (b) Belvatia
(c) Kothia (d) Dumaria

4. Who was the first Naib Nazim of Bihar?
(a) Alivardi Khan
(b) Mir Qasim
(c) Mir Madan
(d) Islam Khan

5. Where was the third Buddhist Sangiti held?
(a) Rajagraha (b) Vaishali
(c) Pataliputra (d) Kashi

6. When was the Barauni Oil Refinery established?
(a) 1962 AD (b) 1964 AD
(c) 1966 AD (d) 1968 AD

7. Who is the state animal of Bihar?
(a) Bull (b) Cow
(c) Horse (d) Goat

8. How much amount is provided under Muslim Desertion Assistance Scheme in Bihar?
(a) 10,000 (b) 15,000
(c) 20,000 (d) 25,000

9. Which is the largest district of Bihar in terms of area?
(a) Arrah (b) West Champaran
(c) Gaya (d) Buxar

10. Which is the largest hydropower station in Bihar?
(a) Dagmara (b) Obra
(c) Navinagar (d) Bihta

11. What does the word 'Bihar' basically mean?
(a) Buddhist Literature
(b) Buddhist Monastery
(c) Jain Place of Worship
(d) Shaiva Literature

12. Which was the highest rainfall receiving area of Bihar?
(a) Terai region
(b) Plains of ganga
(c) South Bihar
(d) Seemanchal region

13. At what percent loans are provided to unemployed youth under the Mukhyamantri Minority Employment Loan Scheme which has been in force since 2013-2014?
(a) 3% (b) 4%
(c) 5% (d) 6%

14. What is the average temperature of Bihar?
(a) 30°C (b) 32°C
(c) 34°C (d) 36°C

15. In which texts, the first mention of Bihar is made?
(a) Rigveda
(b) Ramayana
(c) Shatpath Brahmin
(d) Aranyaka

16. 'Mukhyamantri Shram Shakti Yojana' is being run by which department of Bihar government?
(a) Department of agriculture
(b) Department of Panchayati Raj
(c) Department of industry
(d) Department of Micro, Small and Central Industries

17. What is the longitudinal expansion of Bihar?
(a) 80° 19 "50" – 83° 11 "40"
(b) 81° 14 "50" – 84° 20 "40"
(c) 82° 14 "60" – 85° 60 "50"
(d) 83° 19 "50" – 88° 17 "40"

18. In which year was the agriculture roadmap first created in Bihar?
(a) 2004 AD (b) 2006 AD
(c) 2008 AD (d) 2010 AD

19. How much stipend will be provided per month to each meritorious student to turn him towards agricultural education?

(a) 2000 (b) 2002

(c) 2004 (d) 2006

20. When was the Indian Institute of Technology (IIT), Patna established?

(a) 2002 (b) 2004

(b) 2006 (d) 2008

Answers

1. (c)	**2.** (d)	**3.** (c)	**4.** (a)
5. (c)	**6.** (b)	**7.** (a)	**8.** (a)
9. (b)	**10.** (a)	**11.** (b)	**12.** (a)
13. (c)	**14.** (b)	**15.** (c)	**16.** (d)
17. (d)	**18.** (c)	**19.** (a)	**20.** (d)

SET-77

1. Which place does Bihar have in India in terms of population?

(a) 1st (b) 2nd

(c) 3rd (d) 4th

2. What is the latitude extension of Bihar?

(a) 24° 21 "10" –27° 31 "15"

(b) 23° 15 "40" – 26° 20 "14"

(c) 22° 40 "12" –25° 16 "14"

(d) 21° 20 "40" –24° 25 "42"

3. Centre of Excellence has been set up in which two districts of Bihar to provide plantation material to farmers?

(a) Gaya (b) Nalanda

(b) Vaishali (d) (b) and (c)

4. In ancient times, Bihar was known as

(a) Anga Pradesh

(b) Magadha Region

(c) Videha Pradesh

(d) Vajji Sangha

5. When was the Bihar Congress Socialist Party formed?

(a) 1930 AD (b) 1932 AD

(c) 1934 AD (d) 1936 AD

6. In the context of Sendai Framework Agreement, which was the first state to prepare a 15-year disaster risk reduction road-map 2015-2030?

(a) Goa

(b) Assam

(c) Himachal Pradesh

(d) Bihar

7. When the first public demonstration of the singing of Vindhyavasini Devi, popularly known as 'Bihar Kokila' was made?

(a) 1941 AD (b) 1943 AD

(c) 1945 AD (d) 1947 AD

8. With which institution has an MoU been signed for implementation of disaster risk reduction roadmap?

(a) UNO (b) IMF

(c) ADPC (d) FAO

9. What was the state-owned land called in the Mauryan administration?

(a) Tushk (b) Sita

(c) Ujra (d) Jawar

10. Which European company first came to Bihar region?

(a) Portuguese (b) British

(c) French (d) Dutch

11. When and where was Phaneeswar Nath Renu, the great zonal novelist of Bihar, born?

(a) 1920 AD Arrah

(b) 1921AD Araria

(c) 1922 AD Gaya

(d) 1923AD Supaul

12. Which state ranks last in literacy rate in the country as per 2011 census?

(a) Assam (b) Bihar

(c) Odisha (d) Manipur

13. **Who was the first great poet of Bihar?**
(a) Bhikhari Thakur
(b) Vidyapati
(c) Nagarjuna
(d) Radhakrishna Mukherjee

14. **When was All India Institute of Medical Sciences (AIIMS), Patna established?**
(a) 2008 AD (b) 2010 AD
(c) 2012 AD (d) 2014 AD

15. **Which districts of Bihar touch Nepal?**
(a) Sitamarhi
(b) Madhubani
(c) Supaul
(d) (a), (b) and (c)

16. **At the time of Buddha's birth, which prophet told King Suddhodhana that this child would become a Sanyasi?**
(a) Jeensen (b) Pradyotsen
(c) Kaldeval (d) Vanaspati

17. **Which districts of Bihar touch Uttar Pradesh on the western border?**
(a) Saran (b) Sivan
(c) Rohtas (d) (a), (b) and (c)

18. **Which districts of Bihar touch West Bengal on the eastern border?**
(a) Katihar (b) Purnia
(c) Kishanganj (d) (a), (b) and (c)

19. **Some areas of which district of Bihar were given to West Bengal?**
(a) Kishanganj (b) Manbhum
(c) Purnia (d) (b) and (c)

20. **What percentage of the total area of Bihar is under water cover?**
(a) 3.6 % (b) 3.9 %
(c) 4.2 % (d) 4.5 %

Answers

1. (c)	**2.** (a)	**3.** (d)	**4.** (b)
5. (c)	**6.** (d)	**7.** (c)	**8.** (c)
9. (b)	**10.** (a)	**11.** (b)	**12.** (b)
13. (b)	**14.** (c)	**15.** (d)	**16.** (c)
17. (d)	**18.** (d)	**19.** (d)	**20.** (b)

SET-78

1. **Where was Gautam Buddha, the founder of Buddhism, born?**
(a) Sarnath (b) Bodh Gaya
(c) Pavapuri (d) Lumbini

2. **What percentage of the total area of Bihar is forest edifying?**
(a) 7.27 % (b) 7.53 %
(b) 7.89 % (d) 8.11 %

3. **Out of the total 56 districts of Bihar, how many districts together formed a new State of Jharkhand?**
(a) 14 (b) 16
(c) 18 (d) 20

4. **When was the third Buddhist sangiti held?**
(a) 251 AD (b) 255 AD
(c) 259 AD (d) 263 AD

5. **How many square kilometers of Bihar has forest area?**
(a) 6214 Sq km
(b) 6485 Sq km
(c) 6616 Sq km
(d) 6845 Sq km

6. **What percentage of the total geographical area of Bihar is forest?**
(a) 6.21 % (b) 6.53 %
(c) 6.87 % (d) 7.27 %

7. **What is the total number of City Councils in Bihar?**
(a) 40 (b) 42
(c) 44 (d) 46

8. **When and where was the Great Litterateur of Bihar Devaki Nandan Khatri born?**

(a) 1860 AD Gaya
(b) 1860 AD Patna
(c) 1861 AD Muzaffarpur
(d) 1861 AD Munger

9. The third Buddhist sangiti was held at the time of which ruler?
(a) Ajatshatru (b) Kalashok
(c) Ashoka (d) Kanishka

10. With what the ambitious scheme called Hariyali Mission related to?
(a) Tree cover
(b) Pollution control
(c) E-Vehicle encouragement
(d) All of the above

11. In which region of Bihar there is evidence of volcanic structure?
(a) Gaya (b) Kaimur
(c) Aurangabad (d) Saharsa

12. In the time of which great poet of Bihar, the songs of Nachari Raag were sung from house to house?
(a) Vidyapati
(b) Saryu Rai
(c) Mandan Mishra
(d) Tapan Tiwari

13. Enhancing Teacher Effectiveness Programme is sponsored by which institution?
(a) IMF
(b) World Bank
(c) Asian Development Bank
(d) Both (a) and (b)

14. With which two sections of society did Buddhism associate to leave an important impact?
(a) Women
(b) Shudras
(c) Vaishnava
(d) Both (a) and (b)

15. Some parts of which district of Bihar were included in West Bengal in the year 1956 AD?
(a) Saharsa
(b) Kishanganj
(c) Purulia
(d) Both (b) and (c)

16. In which district of Bihar is 'dolomite' mineral found?
(a) Bhojpur (b) Gaya
(c) Aurangabad (d) Munger

17. Who was the last important painter of Patna Kalam style?
(a) Yamuna Prasad
(b) Hulas Ram
(c) Shivlal
(d) Ishwari Prasad

18. In which district of Bihar the highest number of families live below the poverty line?
(a) Saharsa (b) Kishanganj
(c) Khagaria (d) Supaul

19. The maximum quality of opium is cultivated in which district of Bihar?
(a) Munger (b) Bhagalpur
(c) Saharsa (d) Shivhar

20. Vikramshila Bridge on river Ganga has been constructed in which district?
(a) Vaishali (b) Patna
(c) Gaya (d) Bhagalpur

Answers

1. (d)	**2.** (a)	**3.** (c)	**4.** (a)
5. (d)	**6.** (d)	**7.** (b)	**8.** (c)
9. (c)	**10.** (a)	**11.** (c)	**12.** (a)
13. (b)	**14.** (d)	**15.** (d)	**16.** (a)
17. (d)	**18.** (b)	**19.** (a)	**20.** (d)

SET-79

1. Which airport in Bihar is used to go to Nepal?
(a) Raxaul (b) Bettiah
(c) Motihari (d) Muzaffarpur

2. Bhagat Singh visited Hajipur several times to meet which nationalist revolutionary leader of Bihar?

(a) Baikunth Shukla
(b) Yogendra Shukla
(c) Arjun Singh
(d) Dilawar Khan

3. The third Buddhist 'Sangiti' was presided over by
(a) Sarvakami (b) Ashwasen
(c) Mogalliput (d) None of these

4. In which city of Bihar the second women employment exchange of the country has been set up?
(a) Patna (b) Bhagalpur
(c) Muzaffarpur (d) Hajipur

5. Gliding Club is in which city of Bihar?
(a) Rajgir (b) Bihar Sharif
(c) Patna (d) Bhagalpur

6. Which texts in Buddhist religious literature is the source of information about the history of ancient Bihar?
(a) Angutar Nikay
(b) Dirgh Nikay
(c) Khuddka Sanstha
(d) Jataka Katha

7. Where did Lord Buddha attain enlightenment?
(a) Bodh Gaya (b) Sarnath
(c) Lumbini (d) Shravasti

8. From where are the inscriptions of the Ottoman dynasty obtained in Bihar?
(a) Patna (b) Bihar Sharif
(c) Muzaffarpur (d) Hajipur

9. Which leader of Bihar led kisan andolan along with Mahatma Gandhi?
(a) Jayaprakash Narayan
(b) Sri Krishna Singh
(c) Rajendra Prasad
(d) Hassan Imam

10. Who was the General Secretary of the Congress Session held at Bankipur, Patna in 1912 AD?
(a) Sachchidanand Sinha
(b) Majhrul Haque
(c) Sri Krishna Singh
(d) Rajendra Prasad

11. In how many categories Megasthenes had divided Indian society?
(a) 4 (b) 5
(c) 6 (d) 7

12. In which district of Bihar is Dr. A.P.J. Abdul Kalam Science City being established?
(a) Vaishali (b) Patna
(c) Munger (d) Bhagalpur

13. From which city of Bihar was the monthly magazine 'Balak' published?
(a) Patna (b) Arrah
(c) Kaimur (d) Jehanabad

14. How many districts of Bihar touch Uttar Pradesh?
(a) 6 (b) 7
(c) 8 (d) 9

15. How many districts of Bihar touch West Bengal?
(a) 2 (b) 3
(c) 4 (d) 5

16. How many districts of Bihar touch Jharkhand?
(a) 5 (b) 6
(c) 7 (d) 8

17. How many districts of Bihar touch Nepal?
(a) 7 (b) 6
(c) 5 (d) 4

18. Which districts of present-day Bihar were included in Anga Mahajanapada?
(a) Katihar
(b) Munger
(c) Bhagalpur
(d) (b) and (c)

19. Which soil is found in Purnia, Saharsa, Darbhanga and Muzaffarpur?

(a) Bhangar (b) Kagari
(c) Balther (d) Balsundari

20. What was the oldest literary source of knowing the ancient history of Bihar?

(a) Rigveda
(b) Angutar Nikay
(c) Atharvaveda
(d) Aranyaka

Answers

1. (a)	**2.** (b)	**3.** (c)	**4.** (a)
5. (c)	**6.** (b)	**7.** (a)	**8.** (a)
9. (c)	**10.** (a)	**11.** (d)	**12.** (b)
13. (a)	**14.** (c)	**15.** (b)	**16.** (c)
17. (a)	**18.** (d)	**19.** (a)	**20.** (c)

SET-80

1. When was the Bihar Legislative Council formed separately from Orissa?

(a) 1936 AD (b) 1937 AD
(c) 1938 AD (d) 1939 AD

2. In which literary work the geographical area of Bihar was first discussed?

(a) Jataka Katha
(b) Khuddak Sanstha
(c) Samaveda
(d) Shatpath Brahmin

3. Which Mahajanapada had a republican system?

(a) vajji (b) Anga
(c) Magadha (d) Kalinga

4. What was the total area of the northern Ganga plain of Bihar?

(a) 52,140 sq km.
(b) 53,840 sq km
(c) 55,921 sq km
(d) 56,980 sq km

5. Patna and Gaya districts were included in which Mahajanapada?

(a) Vajji (b) Magadha
(c) Anga (d) Kashi

6. Who was the editor of the leading newspaper 'Bihari'?

(a) Maheshwar Prasad
(b) Kedar Pandey
(c) Majhrul Haque
(d) Rajendra Prasad

7. Who was the Finance Minister in the first Congress State Cabinet of Bihar (1937-1939)?

(a) Mohd Zubair
(b) Anugrah Narayan Singh
(c) Rajendra Prasad
(d) Vinodanand Jha

8. When did the publication of English newspaper 'The Bihar Herald' begin?

(a) 1871 AD (b) 1873 AD
(c) 1875 AD (d) 1877 AD

9. Who took over as the first Governor of Bihar in the British era?

(a) Lord Meghnath Saha
(b) Lord Satyendra Prasanna Sinha
(c) Lord Ibrahim Shah
(d) Lord Mukund Tripathi

10. Which hospital is being set up by Global Health Private Limited (Medanta), Gurgaon under Public Private Partnership Scheme?

(a) Bihar Medanta Hospital, Patna
(b) Jayaprabha Medanta Hospital, Patna
(c) Ashok Medanta Hospital, Patna
(d) Chanakya Medanta Hospital, Patna

11. In which hospital in Bihar was the facility of kidney transplant introduced in February, 2016 AD?

(a) Jayaprabha Medanta Hospital, Patna

(b) Indira Gandhi Institute of Medical Sciences, Patna
(c) Paras Hospital, Patna
(d) PMCH

12. Which was the first newspaper published in the State?
(a) Sanyog
(b) Amrit Bazar
(c) Bihar Darpan
(d) Taapman

13. 'Videshiya' is a popular dance of which state?
(a) Bihar
(b) Jharkhand
(c) Uttar Pradesh
(d) Chhattisgarh

14. What was the name of the Revolutionary of Bihar who attended the Hindustan Socialist Republican Army meeting in September 1928?
(a) Kheti Nag
(b) Khudiram Bose
(c) Shahid Khan
(d) Fanindranath Ghosh

15. Which river divides the northern plain of Bihar into two parts?
(a) Gandak (b) Kosi
(c) Balan (d) Bagmati

16. In which year was Golghar declared a state protected monument?
(a) 1973 AD (b) 1975 AD
(c) 1977 AD (d) 1979 AD

17. Who was elected as the first Independent Chief Minister of Bihar?
(a) Daroga Prasad Rai
(b) Mahamaya Prasad Sinha
(c) Karpuri Thakur
(d) Lalu Prasad Yadav

18. Which was the main center of Thumri in Bihar?
(a) Gaya (b) Banka
(c) Jamui (d) Lakhisarai

19. What percentage of area of Bihar is covered by the Northern Ganga Plains?
(a) 31.06 % (b) 32.77 %
(c) 33.49 % (d) 34.19 %

20. Where is the State Cancer Centre being set up in the State?
(a) Patna (b) Gaya
(c) Hajipur (d) Bhagalpur

Answers

1. (a)	**2.** (d)	**3.** (a)	**4.** (d)
5. (b)	**6.** (a)	**7.** (b)	**8.** (c)
9. (b)	**10.** (b)	**11.** (b)	**12.** (b)
13. (a)	**14.** (d)	**15.** (a)	**16.** (d)
17. (b)	**18.** (a)	**19.** (b)	**20.** (a)

SET-81

1. The early evidence of the presence of primitive humans in Bihar dates back to which era?
(a) Neolithic age
(b) Pre stone age
(c) The Megalithic Age
(d) (a), (b) and (c)

2. Which dynasty is known from the records obtained from Apsad of Gaya district?
(a) Maurya
(b) Gupta
(c) Parvarti Gupt
(d) Pal

3. When was Magadha University established in Bodh Gaya?
(a) 1960 AD
(b) 1962 AD
(c) 1964 AD
(d) 1966 AD

4. When was the Bihar Prohibition and Products Act, 2016 implemented?
(a) 2014 AD (b) 2015 AD
(c) 2016 AD (d) 2017 AD

5. **Hajipur is the headquarters of which railway zone?**
(a) Eastern Railway
(b) Central Railway
(c) North-Eastern Railway
(d) East-Central Railway

6. **Which of the following was the most famous center of education in Mauryan period?**
(a) Takshashila (b) Nalanda
(c) Vikramshila (d) Pataliputra

7. **Where has a new factory of Sonalika Tractor been set up in Bihar in collaboration with International Tractors?**
(a) Bihta (b) Fatuha
(c) Bankipur (d) Pehleja Ghat

8. **When was Kameshwar Singh Darbhanga Sanskrit University established?**
(a) 1957 AD (b) 1959 AD
(c) 1961 AD (d) 1963 AD

9. **When was the publication of 'Bihar Bandhu' newspaper started in the state?**
(a) 1872 AD (b) 1874 AD
(c) 1876 AD (d) 1878 AD

10. **Tin mineral is produced in which district of Bihar?**
(a) Gaya (b) Banka
(b) Kaimur (d) Lakhisarai

11. **Which two banjaras were first made disciples of Buddha in Bodh Gaya?**
(a) sabar
(b) tapas
(c) Bhallika
(d) (b) and (c)

12. **Hajipur city is situated on the banks of which river?**
(a) Gandak (b) Son
(c) kosi (d) Balan

13. **In which year was Patna museum established?**
(a) 1911 AD (b) 1913 AD
(c) 1915 AD (d) 1917 AD 1917

14. **Who composed the songs 'Phag-Raag'?**
(a) Vidyapati
(b) Saryu Mahato
(c) Bhikhari Thakur
(d) Naval Kishore Singh

15. **Jayaprakash Narayan All India Institute of Medical Sciences is located in which city?**
(a) Patna (b) Saran
(c) Gaya (d) Motihari

16. **Where is Agni-cum-soil mineral found in Bihar?**
(a) Gaya (b) Aurangabad
(c) Vaishali (d) Bhagalpur

17. **Where is mica found in the state?**
(a) Jamui (b) Banka
(c) Gaya (d) Munger

18. **What was the salt tax called which was taken in cash during Mauryan period?**
(a) Pann (b) Hiranya
(c) Karshapana (d) Hun

19. **When was the Gaya Museum established?**
(a) 1966 AD (b) 1968 AD
(c) 1970 AD (d) 1972 AD

20. **When was Lalit Narayan Mithila University established?**
(a) 1970 AD (b) 1972 AD
(c) 1974 AD (d) 1976 AD

Answers

1. (b)	**2.** (c)	**3.** (b)	**4.** (c)
5. (d)	**6.** (a)	**7.** (b)	**8.** (c)
9. (b)	**10.** (a)	**11.** (d)	**12.** (a)
13. (c)	**14.** (d)	**15.** (a)	**16.** (d)
17. (c)	**18.** (b)	**19.** (c)	**20.** (b)

SET-82

1. **Which district is the highest producer of paddy in Bihar?**
(a) Rohtas (b) Bhagalpur
(c) Katihar (d) Sivan

2. **When was Bihar State Road Transport Corporation established?**
(a) 1953 AD (b) 1955 AD
(c) 1957 AD (d) 1959 AD

3. **Where is uranium found in Bihar?**
(a) Banka (b) Gaya
(c) Rohtas (d) Jamui

4. **When was a formal announcement of the formation of 'Kisan Sabha' in Bihar made?**
(a) 1924 AD (b) 1926 AD
(c) 1928 AD (d) 1930 AD

5. **Aadhaar programme is related to**
(a) identity
(b) citizenship
(c) Passports
(d) (a), (b) and (c)

6. **Which is the largest district of Bihar by area?**
(a) Gaya (b) West Champaran
(c) Bhagalpur (d) Vaishali

7. **Which is the smallest district of Bihar by area?**
(a) Sheikhpura (b) Shivhar
(c) Jamui (d) Arwal

8. **On which day the revolt of 1857 AD started in Bihar?**
(a) 21 March
(b) June 12
(c) 13 September
(d) 21 November

9. **Which river brings water into the Triveni Canal?**
(a) Sone (b) Ganga
(c) Kosi (d) Gandak

10. **Who was instrumental in passing the Prohibition of Liquor Bill in 1938 AD in the State?**
(a) Karpuri Thakur
(b) Hassan Imam
(c) Jaglal Chaudhary
(d) Maulana Majhrul Haque

11. **Since when is Bihar Transformational Development Project Jeevika-11 being implemented?**
(a) 2012 AD (b) 2014 AD
(c) 2016 AD (d) 2018 AD

12. **What was the total number of livestock in Bihar as per the animal census of 2012?**
(a) 326.14 lakhs (b) 327.86 lakhs
(c) 328.94 lakhs (d) 329.39 lakhs

13. **What has been renamed as Sittha Motihari railway station in Bihar?**
(a) Champaran Motihari
(b) Bapudham Motihari
(c) Satyagraha Motihari
(d) Kisandham Motihari

14. **Bauxite mineral is found in which district of Bihar?**
(a) Gaya (b) Banka
(c) Jamui (d) Munger

15. **Who was the first Independent Chief Minister of Bihar?**
(a) Mahamaya Prasad Sinha
(b) Karpuri Thakur
(c) Shri Krishna Singh
(d) Vinodanand Jha

16. **Which is the district with the highest urban population of the State as per census 2011?**
(a) Munger (b) Vaishali
(c) Patna (d) Muzaffarpur

17. **Who is known as a 'dialect expert' in Bihar?**
(a) George Giryson
(b) Cunningham
(c) Major Baro
(d) Kevinall Lawn

18. **Who were the archaeologists who carried out large scale excavations in Bihar and discovered many ancient sites?**
(a) George Orwell
(b) Major Baro
(c) Legrand
(d) Cunningham

19. Where was the copper statue of Buddha found in Bihar?

(a) Bhagalpur (b) Banka
(c) Jamui (d) Gaya

20. Which monsoon branch in the state brings rainfall?

(a) Arabian Sea
(b) Bay of Bengal
(c) Gulf of Myanmar
(d) (a), (b) and (c)

Answers

1. (a)	**2.** (d)	**3.** (b)	**4.** (c)
5. (a)	**6.** (b)	**7.** (a)	**8.** (b)
9. (d)	**10.** (c)	**11.** (c)	**12.** (d)
13. (b)	**14.** (d)	**15.** (a)	**16.** (c)
17. (a)	**18.** (d)	**19.** (a)	**20.** (b)

SET-83

1. Which of the following oil refineries is located in Bihar?

(a) Mokama (b) Begusarai
(c) Bihta (d) Barauni

2. Which is the most Sulphur producing district in the State?

(a) Rohtas (b) Gaya
(c) Banka (d) Sivan

3. Where was the first session of the Congress held in Bihar?

(a) Gaya (b) Patna
(c) Ramgarh (d) Ranchi

4. Where did Rajaram Mohan Roy, founder of The Brahma Samaj, get Persian education?

(a) Bihar Sharif (b) Nalanda
(c) Patna (d) Bodh Gaya

5. Where was the first meeting of the Congress Socialist Party held?

(a) Patna (b) Hajipur
(c) Bihar Sharif (d) Muzaffarpur

6. Hindi film actress Neha Sharma hails from which place in Bihar?

(a) Gaya (b) Bhagalpur
(c) Nalanda (d) Saharsa

7. Which dance is organized on the occasion of janma utsav?

(a) Jat-jatin (b) Chhou
(c) Pavadia (d) Karama

8. Atish Dipankar was the acharya of which university?

(a) Nalanda (b) Vikramshila
(c) Takshashila (d) Sompur

9. What is the total number of Zilla Parishads in Bihar?

(a) 36 (b) 37
(c) 38 (d) 39

10. What percentage of the total area of Bihar is under water cover?

(a) 3.0% (b) 3.3 %
(c) 3.6% (d) 3.9%

11. Where is Pali Post Graduate Research Institute located?

(a) Nalanda (b) Munger
(c) Gaya (d) Saharsa

12. How many districts are there in Bihar?

(a) 35 (b) 36
(c) 37 (d) 38

13. What was local in the Mauryan administration?

(a) District Administration
(b) Government
(c) City Administration
(d) Village Administration

14. Which is the main cash crop of Bihar?

(a) Tobacco (b) Soyabean
(c) Sugarcane (d) Cotton

15. Approximately what percentage of the total irrigated area in Bihar is irrigated by canals?

(a) 41% (b) 43 %
(c) 45% (d) 47 %

16. The historic Nepali temple is located in which district of Bihar?

(a) Vaishali (b) Gaya
(c) Aurangabad (d) Bhagalpur

17. What is the total number of Panchayat Samitis in Bihar?
(a) 530 (b) 532
(c) 534 (d) 536

18. What is the number of Panchayats and Gram Kachhari of Bihar?
(a) 8,214 (b) 8,398
(c) 8,452 (d) 8,561

19. What is the total number of municipal corporations in Bihar?
(a) 10 (b) 11
(c) 12 (d) 13

20. What is the total number of Nagar Panchayats in the State?
(a) 83 (b) 84
(c) 85 (d) 86

Answers

1. (d)	**2.** (a)	**3.** (b)	**4.** (c)
5. (a)	**6.** (b)	**7.** (c)	**8.** (b)
9. (c)	**10.** (d)	**11.** (a)	**12.** (d)
13. (a)	**14.** (c)	**15.** (d)	**16.** (a)
17. (c)	**18.** (b)	**19.** (c)	**20.** (d)

SET-84

1. When was the All-India Kisan Sabha established?
(a) 1930 AD (b) 1932 AD
(c) 1934 AD (d) 1936 AD

2. Kala Bhawan is located in which district of Bihar?
(a) Purnia (b) Bhagalpur
(c) Gaya (d) Vaishali

3. Where was the All-India Kisan Sabha organised?
(a) Patna (b) Lucknow
(b) Allahabad (a) Dhanbad

4. In which financial year was the Chief Minister Disabled Matrimony Incentive Grant Scheme launched?
(a)2013-14 (b) 2014–15
(c) 2015-16 (d) 2016–17

5. When was the Bihar Human Rights Commission established?
(a) 2000 AD (b) 2002 AD
(c) 2004 AD (d) 2006 AD

6. Which was the most famous river for diversion in Bihar?
(a) Bagmati (b) Gandak
(c) Kosi (d) Niranjana

7. When was the Mukhyamantri Nirbhaya Swayamsahayata Yojana launched?
(a) 2015 AD (b) 2016 AD
(c) 2017 AD (d) 2018 AD

8. Where is Upendra Maharathi Crafts Research Institute located?
(a) Patna (b) Darbhanga
(c) Bhagalpur (d) Munger

9. Where is Magadh University located?
(a) Vaishali (b) Gaya
(c) Patna (d) Munger

10. JBL Mega Food Park is located in which district?
(a) Rohtas (b) Arrah
(c) Buxar (d) Patna

11. Bihpur in Bhagalpur district belongs to which movement?
(a) indigenous movement
(b) Champaran movement
(c) non-cooperation movement
(d) Quit India Movement

12. In which district in Bihar the highest irrigation is done by canals?
(a) Bhojpur (b) Gaya
(c) Saran (d) Saharsa

13. Where is M/s Pristin Food Park located?
(a) Purnia (b) Saran
(c) Motihari (d) Khagaria

14. Where did Buddha give the most sermons in his life?

(a) Shravasti (b) Sarnath
(c) Gaya (d) Pavapuri

15. Home Defence Corps Office and Training Centre is located in which district?
(a) Gaya (b) Bhagalpur
(c) Munger (d) Muzaffarpur

16. From which place were two Yaksha idols found in Bihar?
(a) Pataliputra (b) Gaya
(c) Bhagalpur (d) Nalanda

17. From which place in Bihar have Neolithic bone equipment been obtained?
(a) Gaya (b) Aurangabad
(c) Saran (d) Champaran

18. In which year was the Bihar State Commission for Women constituted?
(a) 2000 AD (b) 2001 AD
(c) 2002 AD (d) 2003 AD

19. Where is the Bihar State Judicial Academy Training Institute located?
(a) Munger (b) Patna
(c) Hajipur (d) Muzaffarpur

20. When was the National Food Security Act enacted in Bihar?
(a) 2012 AD (b) 2013 AD
(c) 2014 AD (d) 2015 AD

Answers

1. (d)	**2.** (a)	**3.** (b)	**4.** (c)
5. (a)	**6.** (c)	**7.** (b)	**8.** (a)
9. (b)	**10.** (a)	**11.** (d)	**12.** (a)
13. (d)	**14.** (a)	**15.** (d)	**16.** (a)
17. (c)	**18.** (b)	**19.** (b)	**20.** (c)

SET-85

1. What was the ancient name of Bihar Sharif?
(a) Pavapuri (b) Chechar
(c) Chirand (d) Odantpuri

2. When was the Kisan Oil Coupon Scheme in Bihar fully launched?
(a) 2006 AD (b) 2007 AD
(c) 2008 AD (d) 2009 AD

3. Who created 'Phag Raag'?
(a) Naval Kishore Singh
(b) Bhikhari Thakur
(c) Vidyapati
(d) Mandan Mishr

4. In which year was the Bihar Secretariat constituted?
(a) 1910 AD (b) 1912 AD
(c) 1914 AD (d) 1916 AD

5. Where was Swami Sahajananda Saraswati born?
(a) Gorakhpur (b) Sivan
(c) Ghazipur (d) Hardoi

6. Sher Shah's last expedition was
(a) Chittorgarh (b) Kalingar
(c) Bengal (d) Jaunpur

7. How many divisions are there in Bihar?
(a) 6 (b) 7
(c) 8 (d) 9

8. How many universities are there in Bihar?
(a) 10 (b) 11
(c) 12 (d) 13

9. In which year did the Bihar Public Service Commission come into existence?
(a) 1947 AD (b) 1948 AD
(c) 1949 AD (d) 1950 AD

10. How many blocks are there in Bihar?
(a) 534 (b) 536
(c) 538 (d) 540

11. From which places of Bihar black bright pottery has been obtained?
(a) Gaya (b) Chirand
(c) Buxar (d) (b) and (c)

18. **Which is the district with the highest male literacy rate in Bihar?**
(a) Rohtas (b) Patna
(c) Kaimur (d) Munger

19. **Sheelbhadra was the Vice Chancellor of which university?**
(a) Nalanda (b) Takshashila
(c) Odantpuri (d) Vikramshila

20. **Pavapuri was the capital of which of the Mahajanapada area?**
(a) Anga (b) Vajji
(c) Malla (d) Magadha

Answers

1. (b)	**2.** (a)	**3.** (b)	**4.** (a)
5. (b)	**6.** (d)	**7.** (a)	**8.** (c)
9. (b)	**10.** (d)	**11.** (c)	**12.** (d)
13. (a)	**14.** (d)	**15.** (b)	**16.** (d)
17. (c)	**18.** (a)	**19.** (a)	**20.** (c)

SET-89

1. **In which district of Bihar does the production of durri silk happen?**
(a) Purnia (b) Saharsa
(c) Supaul (d) Khagaria

2. **Which is the district with the highest forest cover in Bihar?**
(a) Gaya (b) Rohtas
(c) Bhojpur (d) Saran

3. **Which district has the highest population density in the state?**
(a) Patna (b) Munger
(c) Shivhar (d) Gaya

4. **Which is the most populous district in Bihar?**
(a) West Champaran
(b) Patna
(c) Vaishali
(d) Bhagalpur

5. **Who became the first disciple of Mahavira?**
(a) Jamali (b) Upali
(c) Ananda (d) Shamak

6. **Which district has the highest increase in urban population in Bihar?**
(a) Nalanda (b) Bhagalpur
(c) Begusarai (d) Patna

7. **Which bank was first established in Bihar?**
(a) PNB
(b) SBI
(c) Allahabad Bank
(d) Bank of India

8. **National Jute Manufacturing Mill is located in which district of Bihar?**
(a) Katihar (b) Kishanganj
(c) Purnia (d) Saran

9. **When was the First Prohibition of Liquor Bill passed in Bihar?**
(a) 1936 AD (b) 1938 AD
(c) 1940 AD (d) 1942 AD

10. **Who was appointed as the first Lokayukta in Bihar?**
(a) Sridhar Vasudev Sahni
(b) Chandrakant Jha
(c) Javed Rizvi
(d) Umakant Singh

11. **Where is the office of Commissioner of Industries in Bihar located?**
(a) Hajipur (b) Patna
(c) Kishanganj (d) Muzaffarpur

12. **In north India, during the period of Upanishads, which of these was the great center of Brahminism and knowledge.**
(a) Mathura (b) Videha
(c) Anga (d) Pataliputra

13. **Lohat, Riga and Hasanpur are places associated with which industry?**
(a) Sugar (b) Paper
(c) Jute (d) Silk

14. **Where did Mahavir Swami give his last sermon?**

(a) Pataliputra (b) Gaya
(c) Pavapuri (d) Nalanda

15. What was the name of Mahavir's daughter?
(a) Sangh Mitra (b) Priyadarshini
(c) Trishala (d) Karuvaki

16. The first sugar factory in Bihar was established by which foreign company?
(a) British (b) French
(c) Portuguese (d) Dutch

17. What is the present number of judges in Patna high court including chief justice?
(a) 28 (b) 30
(c) 32 (d) 34

18. Which is the second crop after rice in terms of production in Bihar?
(a) wheat (b) sugarcane
(c) jowar (d) millet

19. Since when is National Mission on Medicinal Plant celebrated every year in Bihar?
(a) 2006 AD (b) 2007 AD
(c) 2008 AD (d) 2009 AD

20. When was the sixth economic census published in the state?
(a) 2014 AD (b) 2015 AD
(c) 2016 AD (d) 2017 AD

Answers

1. (a)	**2.** (b)	**3.** (c)	**4.** (b)
5. (a)	**6.** (c)	**7.** (c)	**8.** (a)
9. (b)	**10.** (a)	**11.** (b)	**12.** (b)
13. (a)	**14.** (c)	**15.** (b)	**16.** (d)
17. (b)	**18.** (a)	**19.** (c)	**20.** (c)

SET-90

1. Darbhanga air station broadcasts in which language?
(a) Maithili (b) Bhojpuri
(c) Angika (d) Maghi

2. Rajpur Canal is a branch of which canal?
(a) Western Kosi
(b) East Kosi
(c) Triveni
(d) Sone

3. When was the Bihar State Cooperative Milk Producers Federation (COMFRED) established to increase milk production in Bihar?
(a) 1981 AD (b) 1982 AD
(c) 1983 AD (d) 1984 AD

4. Durgavati Reservoir Project is located in which district?
(a) Rohtas (b) Arrah
(c) Kaimur (d) Gaya

5. What was the sex ratio of Bihar as per 2011 census?
(a) 918 (b) 920
(c) 930 (d) 960

6. Where was the first Jain sangiti held?
(a) Pavapuri (b) Pataliputra
(c) Vallabhpuri (d) Bodh Gaya

7. The first Jain sangiti was organized during whose reign?
(a) Chandragupta Maurya
(b) Ajatshatru
(c) Kalashok
(d) Ashoka

8. In which year was the Kosi project completed?
(a) 1961 AD (b) 1963 AD
(c) 1965 AD (d) 1967 AD

9. Saran Irrigation Canal originates from which river?
(a) Gandak (b) Sone
(c) Bagmati (d) Ganga

10. In how many categories are the forests divided in Bihar keeping in view the protection of forests?
(a) 2 (b) 3
(c) 4 (d) 5

11. In which district was the Barnar Reservoir Project located?

(a) Jamui (b) Arrah
(c) Buxar (d) Aurangabad

12. In which district, ceremic is produced in Bihar?
(a) Aurangabad (b) Bhagalpur
(c) Munger (d) (b) and (c)

13. Where was the Rice Research and Development Institute located in Bihar?
(a) Arrah (b) Gaya
(c) Jehanabad (d) Patna

14. In which district is the Tassar silk industry exists in Bihar?
(a) Munger (b) Bhagalpur
(c) Aurangabad (d) Saran

15. Which bird sanctuary in Bihar is counted as the wetland of the world?
(a) Kanwar Bird Sanctuary
(b) Kusheshwar Place
(c) Gogabil Bird Sanctuary
(d) (a), (b) and (c)

16. When did the era of Ottoman rule begin in Bihar?
(a) 1201 AD (b) 1203 AD
(c) 1205 AD (d) 1207 AD

17. Who is credited with establishing Ottoman power in eastern India?
(a) Balaban (b) Bakhtiyar Khilji
(c) Iltutmish (d) Razia Sultan

18. Jayaprakash Narayan University is located in which city?
(a) Chhapra (b) Aurangabad
(c) Gaya (d) Patna

19. Which year was called the great separator year of population?
(a) 1911 AD (b) 1921 AD
(c) 1931 AD (d) 1941 AD

20. Which district has minimum female literacy rate in Bihar?
(a) Purnia
(b) Saharsa
(c) Jamui
(d) Banka

Answers

1. (a)	**2.** (b)	**3.** (c)	**4.** (a)
5. (a)	**6.** (b)	**7.** (a)	**8.** (c)
9. (a)	**10.** (b)	**11.** (a)	**12.** (d)
13. (a)	**14.** (b)	**15.** (a)	**16.** (b)
17. (b)	**18.** (a)	**19.** (b)	**20.** (a)

SET-91

1. Which district has minimum male literacy rate in Bihar?
(a) Katihar (b) Kishanganj
(c) Saharsa (d) Khagaria

2. In which year did the publication of 'Amrit Varsha' newspaper in Bihar begin?
(a) 1981 AD (b) 1983 AD
(c) 1985 AD (d) 1987 AD

3. Who was the first editor of 'The Search Light'?
(a) Syed Haider Hussain
(b) Maheshwar Shah
(c) Rajendra Gupta
(d) Kedar Pandey

4. With whose help has the livelihood project for the most deprived sections been launched in Bihar?
(a) IMF
(b) World Bank
(c) Asian Development Bank
(d) Japan Bank

5. Ten symptoms are mainly the festival of which sect?
(a) Buddhist (b) Jain
(c) Ajeevak (d) Shaiva

6. On which currency was the seal of peacock, mountain and crescent marked in Mauryan period?
(a) Pann (b) Karshapana
(c) Aahat (d) Hun

7. Where in Bihar, the ixitial evidence of the primitive man settled there is found?
(a) Gaya (b) Munger
(c) Nalanda (d) Both (b) and (c)

8. What is the average annual rainfall in Bihar?

(a) 10 cm (b) 106 cm

(b) 109 cm (d) 115 cm

9. The Oriental Public Library in Bihar was established by

(a) Rajendra Prasad

(b) Khudabakhsh

(c) Majhrul Haque

(d) Mahatma Gandhi

10. What was the tenant farmer called in the Mauryan period?

(a) Aprahat (b) Naagar

(c) Upvaas (d) Dhekal

11. When was an International Cricket Match held in Bihar?

(a) 1990 AD (b) 1992 AD

(c) 1994 AD (d) 1996 AD

12. Who led the movement for a separate province which resulted in the formation of the province of Bihar and Orissa in the year 1912?

(a) Rajendra Prasad

(b) Sachchidanand Sinha

(c) Mohd Yunus

(d) Jai Prakash Narayan

13. When was the Gaya Museum established?

(a) 1948 AD (b) 1950 AD

(c) 1952 AD (d) 1954 AD

14. When is Buddha Jayanti Parv organized in the state?

(a) Vaisakh Purnima

(b) Kartik Amavasya

(c) Chaitra Purnima

(d) Sawan Amavasya

15. Which is the largest tributary of Ganga in Bihar?

(a) Kosi (b) Bagmati

(c) Gandak (d) Sone

16. Which is the main center of hot water in Bihar?

(a) Kaimur (b) Rajgir

(b) Munger (d) (b) and (c)

17. What is the number of villages in Bihar?

(a) 36,912 (b) 37,876

(c) 39,073 (d) 40,198

18. Who has written the book 'Nagmat Asfi' related to music?

(a) Bismillah Khan

(b) Rajashah

(c) Mehndi Hussain

(d) Amir Khusro

19. On which occasion is the Singheshwar Mela organized?

(a) Shivratri (b) Ram Navami

(c) Durga Puja (d) Raksha Bandhan

20. On which occasion lagni raag is sung in Bihar?

(a) Birth of a baby

(b) Paddy Sowing

(c) Marriage

(d) Holi

Answers

1. (a)	**2.** (d)	**3.** (a)	**4.** (b)
5. (a)	**6.** (c)	**7.** (d)	**8.** (c)
9. (b)	**10.** (c)	**11.** (d)	**12.** (b)
13. (c)	**14.** (a)	**15.** (d)	**16.** (d)
17. (c)	**18.** (b)	**19.** (a)	**20.** (c)

SET-92

1. Patna Book Fair is being organized since which year?

(a) 1970 AD (b) 1971 AD

(c) 1972 AD (d) 1973 AD

2. Out of the total 243 seats in Bihar Legislative Assembly, how many seats are reserved for Scheduled Castes?

(a) 36 (b) 37

(c) 38 (d) 39

3. Out of the total 243 seats in Bihar Legislative Assembly, how many seats are reserved for Scheduled Tribes?

(a) 2 (b) 3

(c) 4 (d) 5

4. In which month is the wedding fair held in Sauwarath?
(a) Chaitra-Vaisakh
(b) Jayeshth-Ashadh
(c) Sawan-Bhado
(d) Ashwin-Karthik

5. Sahodra Mela is held in which district?
(a) West Champaran
(b) Gaya
(c) Banka
(d) Jamui

6. In which month is the Pitrupraksha Mela of Gaya held?
(a) Ashwin (b) Chaitra
(c) Vaisakh (d) Kartik

7. On which day is the festival of Jitiya celebrated in Bihar?
(a) Chaitra Krishna Paksha Saptami
(b) Ashwin Krishna Paksha Ashtami
(c) Sawan Krishna Paksha Navami
(d) Kartik Krishna Paksha Dashami

8. Gunava ji, the holy place of Jain sacraments, is located in which district of Bihar?
(a) Nawada (b) Nalanda
(c) Gaya (d) Banka

9. In which financial year was the Mukhyamantri Maha dalit Rozgar Yojana launched in Bihar?
(a) 2010-11 (b) 2011-12
(c) 20120-13 (d) 2013-14

10. When was Golghar constructed?
(a) 1785 AD (b) 1787 AD
(c) 1789 AD (d) 1791 AD

11. Who founded Bihar Vidyapeeth and Sadakat Ashram?
(a) Majhrul Haque
(b) Mohd Shafi
(c) Hasan Imam
(d) Rajendra Prasad

12. Who was the first Vice Chancellor of Bihar Vidyapeeth?
(a) Rajendra Prasad
(b) Prof. Abdul Bari
(c) Majhrul Haque
(d) Shri Krishna Singh

13. Which province leader's tomb is located in Maner?
(a) Shah Daulat
(b) Pir Ali
(c) Rahmat Baba
(d) Karamat Ali Pir

14. When was the Bihar Cricket Association formed?
(a)1930 AD (b) 1932 AD
(c)1934 AD (d) 1936 AD

15. When was the Bihar Hockey Association formed?
(a) 1984 AD (b) 1986 AD
(c) 1988 AD (d) 1990 AD

16. Makhdoom Kund, the holy place of Muslim religion, is located in which district?
(a) Rajgir (b) Bihar Sharif
(c) Munger (d) Rohtas

17. According to Rajatarangini of Kalhana, Ashoka was a follower of which religion before converting to Buddhism?
(a) Buddhist (b) Ajeevak
(c) Jain (d) Shaiva

18. What is the tag line of Bihar Tourism?
(a) Swachh Bihar, Sundar Bihar
(b) Bihar nahi dekha to kya dekha
(c) Blissful Bihar
(d) Incredible Bihar

19. Who was the first Muslim ruler to conquer Bihar?
(a) Mohd Bin Bakhtiyar Khilji
(b) Mohd Bin Qasim
(c) Balaban
(d) Mohd Gori

20. Where was the evidence of the dominance of the gahadwalas over Bihar found?
(a) Nalanda (b) Maner
(c) Kumharar (d) Champaran

Answers

1. (b)	2. (c)	3. (a)	4. (b)
5. (a)	6. (a)	7. (b)	8. (a)
9. (c)	10. (a)	11. (a)	12. (c)
13. (a)	14. (d)	15. (b)	16. (a)
17. (d)	18. (c)	19. (a)	20. (b)

SET-93

1. Who built a stone mosque in Patna?
(a) Aurangzeb (b) Sher Shah
(c) Parvez (d) Shah Alam-II

2. Who was made the convener of Tilak Swaraj Kosh Samiti constituted by Bihar regional congress committee?
(a) Hassan Imam
(b) Shri Krishna Singh
(c) Majhrul Haque
(d) Jayaprakash Narayan

3. When was the Bihar Provincial Kisan Sabha constituted?
(a)1929 AD (b) 1931 AD
(c) 1933 AD (d) 1935 AD

4. In which year was the Bihar National Language Council established?
(a) 1948 AD (b) 1950 AD
(c) 1952 AD (d) 1954 AD

5. Which is the district with the highest rural population as per 2011 Census?
(a) Supaul (b) Banka
(c) Saharsa (d) Samastipur

6. Where is the Akhara of Jarasandha located?
(a) Rajgir (b) Bihar Sharif
(c) Maner (d) Patna

7. Which state is bordering the state of Bihar?
(a) Jharkhand
(b) West Bengal
(c) Uttar Pradesh
(d) Both (b) and (c)

8. When was the Archaeological Museum established in Bodh Gaya?
(a) 1950 AD (b) 1952 AD
(c) 1954 AD (d) 1956 AD

9. Which was the oldest irrigation project in Bihar?
(a) Sone (b) kosi
(c) Gandak (d) Bagmati

10. Which is the hottest district of Bihar?
(a) Kishanganj (b) Patna
(c) Shivhar (d) Gaya

11. Who presided over the first Jain sangiti?
(a) Sthulbhadra
(b) Bal Bhadra
(c) Digambar Muni
(d) Jinsen

12. Which district was selected for the 'satyen Mitra Literacy' award for outstanding literacy?
(a) Patna (b) Munger
(c) Muzaffarpur (d) Rohtas

13. From which district of Bihar was the 'pro-all' newspaper published?
(a) Bhagalpur (b) Patna
(c) Arrah (d) Munger

14. From which year did the publication of 'The Search Light' begin?
(a) 1914 AD (b) 1916 AD
(c) 1918 AD (d) 1920 AD

15. How many districts of the State of Bihar do not form an international boundary or touch any State?
(a) 10 (b) 11
(c) 12 (d) 13

16. What is the percentage of alluvial soil on the Land of the State of Bihar?
(a) 75% (b) 80%
(c) 1% (d) 90%

17. Who is considered to be the first poet of Magahi dialect?
(a) Ishaan (b) Navkishore Jha
(b) Vidyapati (a) Mandan Mishra

18. Since when has the Maghi Mela started?
(a) 1879 AD (b) 1881 AD
(c) 1883 AD (d) 1885 AD

19. In which year was the 'sandhya Prahari' established?
(a) 1998 AD (b) 1990 AD
(c) 1992 AD (d) 1994 AD

20. Mahavir Swami belonged to which Sangh?
(a) Anga (b) Vajji
(b) Magadha (a) Kashi

Answers

1. (c)	**2.** (b)	**3.** (a)	**4.** (b)
5. (d)	**6.** (a)	**7.** (c)	**8.** (d)
9. (a)	**10.** (d)	**11.** (a)	**12.** (c)
13. (b)	**14.** (c)	**15.** (d)	**16.** (d)
17. (a)	**18.** (b)	**19.** (c)	**20.** (b)

SET-94

1. Where did Gautam Buddha find Kondinya and 5 Brahmins?
(a) Rajgir (b) Pavapuri
(c) Sarnath (d) Uruvela

2. In which district was the branch of Xavier's Fires Safety Academy established?
(a) Muzaffarpur (b) Patna
(c) Gaya (d) Bhagalpur

3. In which year was the Bihar National Language Council established?
(a) 1947 AD (b) 1948 AD
(c) 1949 AD (d) 1950 AD

4. Which place was the birthplace of Vasupujya, the 12th Tirthankara of Jainism?
(a) Rajgir (b) Champa
(c) Bodh Gaya (d) Pavapuri

5. Prakrit Jain Shastra and Ahimsa Sansthan are located in which district?
(a) Vaishali (b) Patna
(c) Gaya (d) Nalanda

6. Aryabhata Gyan University has been established in which district?
(a) Bhagalpur (b) Patna
(c) Gaya (d) Nalanda

7. When was Janani and Bal Suraksha Yojana launched in Bihar?
(a) 2002 AD (b) 2004 AD
(c) 2006 AD (d) 2008 AD

8. Government College of Arts and Crafts is located in which district of the state?
(a) Gaya (b) Patna
(c) Sitamarhi (d) Sivan

9. Which district produces the maximum quantitity Sulphur in the state of Bihar?
(a) Rohtas (b) Bhojpur
(c) Buxar (d) Gaya

10. Where is the State Fruit Research Institute located?
(a) Patna (b) Darbhanga
(c) Bhagalpur (d) Kishanganj

11. When was Chandrabhari Museum, Darbhanga established?
(a) 1951 AD (b) 1953 AD
(c) 1955 AD (d) 1957 AD

12. Simultala Residential School has been established on the lines of which school model?
(a) Kendriya Vidyalaya
(b) Netarhat Residential School
(c) District level school
(d) Divisional level school

13. Gandhi Museum is located in which district?

(a) Patna (b) Gaya
(c) Muzaffarpur (d) Vaishali

14. When was the Rural Livelihood Mission launched in the State of Bihar?

(a) 2009 AD (b) 2011 AD
(c) 2013 AD (d) 2015 AD

15. Which scheme has been launched to make educate women in Bihar?

(a) Mukhyamantri Saakshar Yojana
(b) Mukhyamantri Akshara Anchal Yojana
(c) Mukhyamantri Nai Roshni Yojana
(d) Mukhyamantri Saakshar Bihar Yojana

16. Who was the Chairman of the State Disaster Management Authority?

(a) Governor
(b) President
(c) The Chief Minister
(d) Advocate General

17. When was the State Textile Corporation established?

(a) 1968 AD (b) 1970 AD
(c) 1972 AD (d) 1974 AD

18. In which book is the word Bihar first mentioned?

(a) Rigveda (b) Yajurveda
(c) Samaveda (d) Atharvaveda

19. Which year was declared Bhikhari Thakur year by Bihar Sangeet Natak Akademi?

(a) 1995 AD (b) 1997 AD
(c) 1999 AD (d) 2001 AD

20. In which period did the Aryans arrive in Eastern India?

(a) Harapan period
(b) Vedic period
(c) Post-Vedic Period
(d) Mauryan period

Answers

1. (d)	**2.** (b)	**3.** (d)	**4.** (b)
5. (a)	**6.** (b)	**7.** (c)	**8.** (b)
9. (a)	**10.** (c)	**11.** (d)	**12.** (b)
13. (a)	**14.** (c)	**15.** (b)	**16.** (c)
17. (b)	**18.** (d)	**19.** (c)	**20.** (c)

SET-95

1. On which date is Bihar Foundation Day or Bihar Day celebrated every year?

(a) 10 January (b) 22nd March
(c) 8 June (d) 21st September

2. Who was the wife of Bimbisara, the ruler of Magadha, who became disciple of Buddha?

(a) Kshema (b) Karuvaki
(c) Trishala (d) Sangh Mitra

3. What percentage of reservation has been provided for women in Gram Panchayat in Bihar?

(a) 30 % (b) 33%
(c) 43 % (d) 50%

4. When was the 'Toilet Construction House Honour' scheme launched by the Government of Bihar?

(a) 2014 AD (b) 2015 AD
(c) 2016 AD (d) 2017 AD

5. How many tourist circuits has the Tourism Department of Government of Bihar marked in the State?

(a) 5 (b) 6
(c) 7 (d) 8

6. When did the Bihar Government implement the Mukhyamantri Food Security Scheme?

(a) 2011 AD (b) 2013 AD
(c) 2015 AD (d) 2017 AD

7. When was the State Disaster Management Plan (SDMP) constituted in the State under the Disaster Management Act, 2005?

(a) 2010 AD (b) 2012 AD
(c) 2014 AD (d) 2016 AD

8. When did the Government of Bihar launch the Skilled Youth Programme?
(a) 2014 AD (b) 2016 AD
(c) 2018 AD (d) 2020 AD

9. In which year did the Government of Bihar implement the Bihar State Panchayati Raj Act?
(a) 2004 AD (b) 2005 AD
(c) 2006 AD (d) 2007 AD

10. When was the first Bihar Panchayat Samiti and Zilla Parishad Act, 1961 passed by the Government of Bihar given the status of law?
(a) 1962 AD (b) 1963 AD
(c) 1964 AD (d) 1965 AD

11. In which year was the Chandragupta Institute of Management established?
(a) 2006 AD (b) 2008 AD
(c) 2010 AD (d) 2012 AD

12. Who was the founder of Bihar Socialist Party?
(a) Jayaprakash Narayan
(b) Rajendra Prasad
(c) Majhrul Haque
(d) Hassan Imam

13. How much of the produce was taken as irrigation tax by the state during the Mauryan period?
(a) 1/2 to 1/3 (b) 1/3 to 1/4
(c) 1/4 to 1/5 (d) 1/5 to 1/3

14. Which is the longest National Highway passing through Bihar?
(a) NH-31 (b) NH-28
(c) NH-527 (d) NH–85

15. The first bilingual record obtained from Bihar is related to which ruler?
(a) Aurangzeb (b) Shah Alam-II
(c) Parvez (d) Sher Shah

16. In which year was the Bihar Education Project Council established?
(a) 1989 AD (b) 1991 AD
(c) 1993 AD (d) 1995 AD

17. What are the types of stone equipment recovered from Bihar?
(a) Ashulian (b) Chopper
(b) Hathoda (d) Chhaini

18. Chanakya Award is given for good work in which field?
(a) Journalism (b) Politics
(c) Economics (d) Social Welfare

19. At which place is the hydropower project being constructed by Bihar State Hydroelectric Power Corporation in collaboration with France?
(a) Navinagar (b) Valmiki Nagar
(c) Supaul (d) Srikhindi

20. On which day did Buddha's renunciation take place?
(a) Vaisakh Purnima
(b) Ashadh Purnima
(c) Chaitra Purnima
(d) Sawan Purnima

Answers

1. (b)	**2.** (a)	**3.** (d)	**4.** (c)
5. (d)	**6.** (a)	**7.** (c)	**8.** (b)
9. (c)	**10.** (a)	**11.** (b)	**12.** (a)
13. (d)	**14.** (a)	**15.** (d)	**16.** (b)
17. (a)	**18.** (b)	**19.** (d)	**20.** (b)

SET-96

1. Where was the famous Buddhist Sariputra born?
(a) Vaishali (b) Nalanda
(c) Gaya (d) Saran

2. Where is the giant statue of Lord Buddha being installed in Bihar?

(a) Rajgir (b) Vaishali
(c) Sarnath (d) Maner

3. **Where is the Indian Dance Art Temple located in Bihar?**
(a) Gaya (b) Muzaffarpur
(c) Patna (d) Hajipur

4. **Where is the Mithila Painting Institute being set up?**
(a) Madhubani (b) Darbhanga
(c) Saharsa (d) Madhepura

5. **When was the Bihar Right to Public Grievances Redressal Act, 2015 implemented?**
(a) 2015 AD (b) 2016 AD
(c) 2017 AD (d) 2018 AD

6. **Who was the founder of Magadh district?**
(a) Chandragupta Maurya
(b) Brihadratha
(c) Jarasandha
(d) (b) and (c)

7. **In which century did the first Magadha Empire flourish?**
(a) 4th Century
(b) 5th Century
(c) 6th Century
(d) 7th Century

8. **Where has the Centre for Agriculture and Dairy Development been set up in Bihar?**
(a) Motihari (b) Patna
(c) Munger (d) Bhojpur

9. **Who was the last ruler of the Haryak dynasty?**
(a) Kunal (b) Brihadratha
(c) Chetak (d) Nagdashak

10. **Where is the modern driver training-cum-research institute proposed to be established?**
(a) Aurangabad (b) Patna
(c) Motihari (d) Supaul

11. **From which date the Bihar Prohibition of Liquor and Products Act, 2016 is in force?**
(a) 10 April, 2016
(b) 8 June, 2016
(c) 2 October, 2016
(d) 10 December, 2016

12. **Discount at what percentage has been provided in stamp duty by the State Government to encourage online payments?**
(a) 1 (b) 2%
(c) 3 (d) 4%

13. **Which scheme has been launched to honor eminent and highest Tax Paying professionals in Bihar?**
(a) Tata Samman Yojana
(b) Iranian Samman Yojana
(c) Bihar Samman Yojana
(d) Bhama Shah Samman Yojana

14. **The second Buddhist 'Sangiti' was organized during whose reign?**
(a) Chandragupta Maurya
(b) Ashoka
(c) Kalashok
(d) Ajatshatru

15. **Where was the second Buddhist 'Sangiti' held?**
(a) Vaishali (b) Rajagraha
(c) Pataliputra (d) Bodh Gaya

16. **Which mountaineer has been selected as the State Icon by the Bihar State Election Commission?**
(a) Bachhendari Pal
(b) Arunima Sinha
(c) Tapan Tiwari
(d) Santosh Yadav

17. **The first Buddhist 'Sangiti' was organized during whose reign?**
(a) Ajatshatru (b) Kalashok
(c) Ashoka (d) Kanishka

18. **Where was the first Buddhist 'Sangiti' held?**
(a) Vaishali (b) Bodh Gaya
(c) Pataliputra (d) Rajagraha

19. When was Asian Development Bank (ADB) established?
(a) 1962 AD (b) 1964 AD
(c) 1966 AD (d) 1968 AD

20. Who presided over the first Buddhist 'sangiti'?
(a) Mahakashyap
(b) Mowgliputta Tiss
(c) Ajitam
(d) Sariputra

Answers

1. (b)	**2.** (a)	**3.** (c)	**4.** (a)
5. (b)	**6.** (d)	**7.** (c)	**8.** (a)
9. (d)	**10.** (a)	**11.** (c)	**12.** (a)
13. (d)	**14.** (c)	**15.** (a)	**16.** (d)
17. (a)	**18.** (d)	**19.** (c)	**20.** (a)

SET-97

1. By whom was Kalinga first merged with the Magadha Empire?
(a) Ajatshatru
(b) Ashoka
(c) Mahapadmananda
(d) Kalashok

2. Diamecus came to whose court?
(a) Ashoka
(b) Bindusara
(c) Chandragupta Maurya
(d) None of these

3. Chandragupta Maurya is called the Liberator of India because of his freedom from whom?
(a) Iranians (b) Aryans
(c) Greeks (d) Kushans

4. At which place was Rahul Sansikrityayan active in Bihar during the non-cooperation movement of 1920?
(a) Chhapra
(b) Darbhanga
(c) Madhubani
(d) Champaran

5. Who presided over the session of the Indian National Congress held in Delhi in 1947?
(a) Rajendra Prasad
(b) Maulana Abdul Kalam Azad
(c) GB Pant
(d) Hassan Imam

6. Which was the largest river project in Bihar?
(a) Sone (b) Kosi
(c) Gandak (d) Bagmati

7. When was COMFED Established?
(a) 1981 AD (b) 1983 AD
(c) 1985 AD (d) 1987 AD

8. In which financial year was the Tassar Vikas Yojana launched?
(a) 2010-11 (b) 2011-12
(b) 2012-13 (d) 2013-14

9. Where has jute park been established in Bihar?
(a) Purnia (b) Kishanganj
(c) Katihar (d) Saharsa

10. Where is the Central Leather Research Institute located?
(a) New Delhi (b) Kanpur
(c) Patna (d) Chennai

11. What is the percentage of economic growth aimed at in the Industrial Investment Incentive Policy 2016?
(a) 5% (b) 10%
(c) 15% (d) 20%

12. What did the famous Chinese traveler Fahiyan, who visited the palace of Magadha Emperor Chandragupta, say to him?
(a) God Made
(b) Museum
(c) Supernatural Building
(d) Buddhist Monastery

13. Where is the film city proposed to be built in Bihar?
(a) Patna (b) Darbhanga
(c) Begusarai (d) Rajgir

14. Under the Mukhyamantri Old Age Pension Scheme, pension is

provided to a person above the age of how many years?

(a) 50 (b) 55
(c) 60 (d) 62

15. Which article of the Constitution provides for constitution of finance commission in India?

(a) Article 278 (b) Article 279
(c) Article 280 (d) Article 281

16. When was India's first Human Development Report (HDT) released?

(a) 2000 AD (b) 2002 AD
(c) 2004 AD (d) 2006 AD

17. National Income Units in India are assessed by

(a) PMO
(b) CSO
(c) Niti Aayog
(d) Finance Ministry

18. Who is the Chairman of Island Development Authority?

(a) President
(b) Vice-President
(c) Prime Minister
(d) Finance Minister

19. Where is the Bank Note Printing Press of India located?

(a) Nepanagar (b) Devas
(c) Allahabad (d) New Delhi

20. On which committee's recommendations was National Bank for Agriculture and Rural Development (NABARD) established?

(a) Abid Ali (b) Amit Verma
(c) Sivaraman (d) Narasimha

Answers

1. (b)	**2.** (b)	**3.** (c)	**4.** (a)
5. (a)	**6.** (c)	**7.** (b)	**8.** (c)
9. (a)	**10.** (d)	**11.** (c)	**12.** (a)
13. (d)	**14.** (c)	**15.** (c)	**16.** (b)
17. (b)	**18.** (c)	**19.** (b)	**20.** (c)

SET-98

1. Who has written the book 'Politics of Charkha'?

(a) Mahatma Gandhi
(b) JB Kripalani
(c) Hasan Imam
(d) Jayaprakash Narayan

2. When was the Securities and Regulation Board of India established?

(a) 1982 AD (b) 1984 AD
(c) 1986 AD (d) 1988 AD

3. Where is CAPART's (Council for Advancement of People Action and Rural Technology) main office located?

(a) New Delhi (b) Mumbai
(c) Chennai (d) Kolkata

4. Which bank performs all the functions of the Central Bank in India?

(a) SBI (b) RBI
(c) SEBI (d) IRDA

5. The middle part of the pillar established by Ashoka was built by the stone of

(a) Makrana (b) Jaipur
(c) Chunar (d) Jodhpur

6. Which scheme has been launched to provide scholarships to students belonging to Scheduled Castes, Scheduled Tribes and OBCs?

(a) Rupay Card (b) Visa Card
(c) ATOZ Card (d) E-Z Pay Card

7. According to Bihar Economic Survey 2018-19, what was the percentage growth rate of GDP in the state of Bihar?

(a) 11% (b) 11.3%
(c) 11.6% (d) 11.9%

8. Which scheme has been launched in Bihar to make illiterate women in the age group of 15-35 years literate?

(a) Sabla Scheme
(b) Shiksha Hunar Yojana
(c) Mukhyamantri Akshar Anchal Yojana
(d) (b) and (c)

9. In which financial year was the Nari Shakti Yojana launched in Bihar?
(a) 2006-07 (b) 2007–08
(c) 2008-09 (d) 2009–10

10. Which Prakash utsav was celebrated on the birth anniversary of Shri Guru Gobind Singh at Patna Sahib on 13 January 2019?
(a) 349th (b) 350th
(c) 351st (d) 352nd

11. Who is called the father of the statistical movement in India?
(a) Majhrul Haque
(b) Rajendra Prasad
(c) Shri Krishna Singh
(d) PC Mahalanobis

12. The concept of 'Rolling Plan' in nationalplanningwasimplemented by which government?
(a) Janata Sarkar
(b) Congress Government
(c) UPA Government
(d) NDA Government

13. For which period was President's rule first imposed in Bihar?
(a) 1966-67 AD
(b) 1968–69 AD
(c) 1970-72 AD
(d) 1973–1974 AD

14. How many times has President's rule been imposed in Bihar?
(a) 5 (b) 6
(c) 7 (d) 8

15. In which article of the Constitution the Money Bill is defined in detail?
(a) Article 110 (b) Article 112
(c) Article 115 (d) Article 118

16. Inequality in income distribution is represented by which curve?
(a) Sen curve
(b) Kuntaj curve
(c) Lawrence curve
(d) Mill curve

17. The slogan of 'Garibi Hatao' was first a part of which Plan?
(a) Second Plan (b) Third Plan
(c) Fourth Plan (d) Fifth Plan

18. Unemployment, in which people are seen engaged in employment, but whose marginal utility is zero is called?
(a) Urban (b) Disguised
(c) Educated (d) Cyclic

19. In which year was NABARD established and where are its headquarters?
(a) 1978 AD Delhi
(b) 1980 AD Kolkata
(c) 1982 AD Mumbai
(d) 1984 AD Chennai

20. Which was the top institution of rural credit system?
(a) SBI (b) SEBI
(b) IDBI (a) NABARD

Answers

1. (b)	**2.** (d)	**3.** (a)	**4.** (b)
5. (c)	**6.** (d)	**7.** (b)	**8.** (c)
9. (c)	**10.** (d)	**11.** (d)	**12.** (a)
13. (b)	**14.** (c)	**15.** (a)	**16.** (c)
17. (d)	**18.** (b)	**19.** (c)	**20.** (d)

SET-99

1. What is the name of the stupa built by Ashoka at Takshashila?
(a) Dharmarajika
(b) Boudhayan
(c) Mahayana
(d) Hinayana

2. An agreement with which country has been signed for production of 800 locomotives in Madhopura (Bihar)?
(a) Germany (b) Britain
(c) France (d) Spain

3. Under which category is Nalanda Mahavihara included in UNESCO's World Heritage List?
(a) Cultural
(b) Mixed
(c) Precious Gemstones
(d) Preserved

4. Who has first discovered Nalanda site in modern times?
(a) Cunningham
(b) Buchanan
(c) Legrand
(d) Major Baro

5. When was The Mahabodhi Temple Complex Bodh Gaya included in the world-famous UNESCO list in the cultural category?
(a) 2000 AD (b) 2001 AD
(c) 2002 AD (d) 2003 AD

6. When was the archaeological site of Nalanda Mahavihara included in UNESCO's World Heritage List of Cultural Classes?
(a) 2012 AD (b) 2014 AD
(c) 2016 AD (d) 2018 AD

7. To whom has been given the fertilizer unit at Barauni for revival by the Union Cabinet?
(a) HPCL (b) HFCL
(c) ONGC (d) OIL

8. Which is the state with minimum per capita income in the country?
(a) Sikkim (b) Odisha
(b) Bihar (a) Manipur

9. Which city of Bihar has been first selected for implementation of Smart City Mission?
(a) Patna (b) Bhagalpur
(c) Bihar Sharif (d) Muzaffarpur

10. What was the second name of Sudama Cave?
(a) Nyonati Cave
(b) Aparas cave
(c) Teerth Cave
(d) Nyagrodh Cave

11. During which year of Ashoka's accession the Sudama Cave was built?
(a) 10th year (b) 11th year
(c) 12th year (d) 13th year

12. Which Pal ruler is credited with the establishment of Vikramshila and Sompur Viharas?
(a) Gopal
(b) Devpal
(c) Dharmapala
(d) (b) and (c)

13. Patna Kalam or Patna style is known as
(a) Mughal style
(b) Bihari style
(c) Kampani Style
(d) Rajput Style

14. Ragini Gandhari painting is made by which artist?
(a) Yamuna Prasad
(b) Hulas Ram
(c) Shivlal
(d) Mahadev Lal

15. What is the share of sales tax in total tax?
(a) 45.4% (b) 47.2%
(c) 49.8% (d) 51.6%

16. NAFED has been established to serve the purpose of
(a) Promoting Industries
(b) Marketing of Agricultural Produce
(c) Increasing employment opportunities
(d) Maintaining Law and Order

17. When did Environment Protection Act (EPA) come into force?
(a) 1982 AD (b) 1984 AD
(c) 1986 AD (d) 1988 AD

18. When did National Environmental Tribunal Act (NETA) come into existence?

(a) 1980 AD (b) 1982 AD

(c) 1984 AD (d) 1986 AD

19. Price index aims to measure the change of

(a) Increase in unemployment

(b) Increase in wholesale inflation

(c) purchasing power of currency

(d) Reduction in retail inflation

20. Which is the regulatory body regulating insurance business in India?

(a) SEBI (b) IRDA

(c) IDFC (d) SBI

Answers

1. (a)	**2.** (c)	**3.** (a)	**4.** (b)
5. (c)	**6.** (c)	**7.** (b)	**8.** (c)
9. (b)	**10.** (d)	**11.** (a)	**12.** (d)
13. (c)	**14.** (d)	**15.** (b)	**16.** (b)
17. (c)	**18.** (d)	**19.** (c)	**20.** (b)

SET-100

1. Which city of Bihar has been covered under smart Ganga City Scheme?

(a) Bihar Sharif

(b) Muzaffarpur

(c) Patna

(d) (a), (b) and (c)

2. On 1 September 2016, the Central Government constituted a Committee under whose chairmanship to study silt in river Ganga in Bihar?

(a) AK Sinha (b) Girdhar Malviya

(c) Amit Dubey (d) Javed Hasmi

3. Under whose chairmanship was a committee constituted to deal with the pulse's crisis on 12th July 2016?

(a) Verma Committee

(b) Subrahmanyam committee

(c) Abid Ali Committee

(d) Chandra Bose Committee

4. Under whose chairmanship was a committee constituted on 17th July, 2016 for full review and suggestion of the Financial Responsibility and Budget Management Act?

(a) Ramesh Yadav

(b) Wajahat Habibullah

(c) NK Singh

(d) Yogendra Mishra

5. Who is the Chairman of the Committee constituted by the Supreme Court on corruption and conflict of interest in cricket administration?

(a) RM Lodha

(b) Deepak Gupte

(c) Deepak Mishra

(d) Jagdish Khehar

6. How many kilograms of food grains are provided per month under Antyodaya Yojana?

(a) 30 Kg (b) 35 kg

(c) 40 Kg (d) 45 kg

7. What kind of economy is there in India?

(a) Capitalist

(b) Socialist

(c) Mixed

(d) (a), (b) and (c)

8. Which Patna style connoisseur is called the acharya of 'Portrait of Sarjana'?

(a) Vivek Singh

(b) Jamil Ansari

(c) Radha Mohan Babu

(d) Jagadamba Prasad

9. Sevak Ram and Hulas Lal are painters of which style?
(a) Madhubani Painting
(b) Patna Kalam
(c) Manjusha style
(d) Jadopatia painting

10. Human Development Index was the product of which economist?
(a) Amartya Sen
(b) Irfan Habib
(c) James Mill
(d) Mehboob-ul-Haq

11. Human Development Index is created by which institution?
(a) IMF (b) UNESCO
(c) UNDP (d) FAO

12. On what basis is an economy classified into public and private sectors?
(a) Agriculture
(b) Manufacturing
(c) Service
(d) Ownership of industries

13. The picture of 'begum's alcoholism' is drawn by which artist?
(a) Yamuna Prasad
(b) Mahadev Lal
(c) Hulas Ram
(d) Ishwari Prasad

14. Who propounded the theory of drain?
(a) Tayyab Ji
(b) Surendra Nath Banerjee
(c) Dadabhai Naoroji
(d) Mahatma Gandhi

15. Hindu growth rate is related to
(a) unemployment growth
(b) national income
(c) per capita income
(d) inflation rate

16. If the cash Reserve ratio is reduced by the Reserve Bank of India, what will be its impact on credit generation?
(a) lack
(b) equal
(c) growth
(d) Sometimes decrease, sometimes increase

17. How many districts of Bihar have been included in the New India Vision?
(a) 10 (b) 11
(c) 12 (d) 13

18. Gopashtami Mela is organized in which district?
(a) Khagaria
(b) Supaul
(c) Madhubani
(d) Saran

19. Where is Matsyagandha Raktakali temple located?
(a) Munger
(b) Aurangabad
(c) Gaya
(d) Saharsa

20. Economic planning is included in which list of the Constitution?
(a) Union
(b) State
(c) Concurrent
(d) Both (a) and (b)

Answers

1. (d)	**2.** (a)	**3.** (b)	**4.** (c)
5. (a)	**6.** (b)	**7.** (c)	**8.** (c)
9. (b)	**10.** (d)	**11.** (c)	**12.** (d)
13. (a)	**14.** (c)	**15.** (b)	**16.** (c)
17. (d)	**18.** (a)	**19.** (d)	**20.** (c)

SET-101

1. **In the year 2020-21, what was the per centage increase in gross domestic product of the income of Bihar State?**
(a) 1.5 per cent
(b) 1 per cent
(c) 2.5 per cent
(d) 2 per cent

2. **The Economic survey 2021-22 released by the Bihar state legislative assembly was which survey in ranking?**
(a) 17th (b) 14th
(c) 18th (d) 16th

3. **As per the survey, what was the per capita income of Bihar in 2021-22 ?**
(a) ₹ 50,000 (b) ₹ 60,000
(c) ₹ 55,000 (d) ₹ 50,555

4. **During the last five years (2016-17 to 2020-21), what has been the per centage increase in primary sector in Bihar?**
(a) 2.3 per cent (b) 4.8 per cent
(c) 8.5 per cent (d) 2.1 per cent

5. **During the last five years (2016-17 to 2020-21), by how much per centage did the agriculture and allied sector increase?**
(a) 2.1 per cent (b) 4.8 per cent
(c) 2.3 per cent (d) 8.5 per cent

6. **What is the rate of urbanization in the state currently?**
(a) 11.3 per cent (b) 10.5 per cent
(c) 15.3 per cent (d) 14.2 per cent

7. **As per the Bihar Economic survey 2021-22, what the contribution of primary sector in GSDP in per centage terms?**
(a) 61.2 per cent (b) 19.5 per cent
(c) 20.3 per cent (d) 19.2 per cent

8. **As per Economic survey 2021-22, what percentage is per capita GSDP increase rate at the current price level in Bihar?**
(a) 3.4 per cent (b) 2.5 per cent
(c) 2.1 per cent (d) 4.5 per cent

9. **What district has the least income as per Economic Survey 2021-22?**
(a) Rohtas
(b) Sheohar
(c) Madhepura
(d) Kishsanganj

10. **As per the survey, how much increase there has been in the social security obligation out of the state government's total expenditure during the last 5 years?**
(a) 52.8 per cent (b) 47 per cent
(c) 38.9 per cent (d) 44 per cent

11. **As per Bihar Economic survey 2020-21, in the financial year 2020-21, under the MNREGA scheme of the employment sector, the number of families who have secured jobs has increased to become how many lakhs?**
(a) 15 lakh (b) 55 lakh
(c) 51 lakh (d) 20 lakh

12. **The name of the mobile app launched by Agriculture Department in Bihar is –**
(a) Bihar app
(b) Bihan app
(c) Vihan app
(d) Veer app

13. **According to the survey, what is the per capita electricity (energy) consumption in the state?**
(a) 350 kilowatt
(b) 250 kilowatt
(c) 450 kilowatt
(d) 150 kilowatt

14. **The aim of an ambitious scheme, solar street scheme, ongoing in Bihar is –**
(a) To free the village from defecation in open.

(b) To make available solar energy to villages.

(c) To encourage formation of self-help group in villages.

(d) To open unit of ethanol production in villages.

15. Which App has been launched in Bihar to issue warning atleast 40 minutes before incident of striking of lightning within area of 20 km area?

(a) Indra App

(b) Indrabraj App

(c) Braj App

(d) Twarit App

16. Compared to the last year, the total expenditure of the state increased to become how much?

(a) 1,65,696 crore

(b) 1,28,168 crore

(c) 1,30,126 crore

(d) 1,50,235 crore

17. The revenue receipts of the Bihar government were –

(a) 1,30,216 crore

(b) 1,25,115 crore

(c) 1,28,168 crore

(d) 1,39,493 crore

18. How much did the state government's capital expenditure 2019-20 increase from 3.3 per cent within GSDP?

(a) 3.8 per cent (b) 4.5 per cent

(c) 4.1 per cent (d) 4.2 per cent

19. How much did the revenue of the state government increase from tax and non-tax sources?

(a) 30,521 crore

(b) 32,250 crore

(c) 33,858 crore

(d) 36,543 crore

20. Which statement is correct with regard to inflation in the state in last year?

(a) The rate of inflation in rural areas of Bihar was more than that in India

(b) The rate of Inflation in rural areas of Bihar was less than that in India

(c) The rate of Inflation in urban areas of Bihar was less than that in India

(d) Both (b) and (d)

Answers

1. (c)	**2.** (b)	**3.** (a)	**4.** (a)
5. (b)	**6.** (c)	**7.** (d)	**8.** (b)
9. (b)	**10.** (d)	**11.** (c)	**12.** (b)
13. (a)	**14.** (b)	**15.** (b)	**16.** (a)
17. (c)	**18.** (d)	**19.** (d)	**20.** (d)

SET-102

1. As per last year, which district had the maximum per capita income amongst the ranking of 38 districts?

(a) Rohtas

(b) Kishanganj

(c) Patna

(d) Sheohar

2. How many Krishi Karman Awards is the Bihar state win?

(a) 6 (b) 3

(c) 4 (d) 5

3. How much amount was approved by the state government under pradhan mantra matasya sampada yojna?

(a) 20.31 crore

(b) 30.51 crore

(c) 40.76 crore

(d) 50 crore

4. How many crore rupees were invested in food processing?

(a) 1016 crore

(b) 1605 crore

(c) 1761.28 crore
(d) 1904.78 crore

5. How much amount did the government allocate for Mukhya Mantri Mahila Udyaymi Yojana and Mukhya Mantri Yuva Yojana in 2020-21?
(a) 250 crore
(b) 200 crore
(c) 400 crore
(d) 300 crore

6. The state government's mineral deposits increased by how much in 2020-21?
(a) 100 crore
(b) 150 crore
(c) 120 crore
(d) 172 crore

7. Out of the 270 new branches of major banks opened in the state in 2020-21, what per centage have been opened in urban areas?
(a) 23.3 per cent
(b) 20.5 per cent
(c) 40 per cent
(d) 43.3 per cent

8. According to the survey, the amount approved by the state government for development of a zoo safari in Rajgir is –
(a) 170 crore
(b) 100 crore
(c) 180 crore
(d) 176.8 crore

9. How much is the Bihar Gross State Domestic Product at current price?
(a) 419.88 thousand crore
(b) 566.47 thousand crore
(c) 618.63 thousand crore
(d) 600.10 thousand crore

10. During the financial year 2022-23, how many industrial parks are proposed to be developed in Bihar?
(a) 7 (b) 6
(c) 5 (d) 4

11. Who was the first lady judge of the high court?
(a) Ms. Fatima Bibi
(b) Ms. Ruma Pal
(c) Ms. Sujata Manohar
(d) None of the above

12. The salary and allowances of judges of the Supreme Court are charged from?
(a) Finance Commission
(b) Reserve Bank of India
(c) Consolidated Fund of India
(d) Contingency Fund of India

13. While considering which of the following issues, the supreme court of India acts like a federal court?
(a) Civil matters
(b) Appeals from lower courts
(c) Election petitions
(d) Interstate disputes

14. Under which Regulating Act, the Supreme Court was established in Calcutta?
(a) Charter Act, 1713
(b) Regulating Act, 1773
(c) Charter Act, 1813
(d) Pitts India Act, 1784

15. Which one of the following comes under the jurisdiction of both the supreme court and the high court?
(a) Reservation of Fundamental Rights
(b) Reservation of Constitutional Violation
(c) Dispute amongst States
(d) Dispute between the Centre and States

16. Under what jurisdiction, the supreme court settles disputes between the centre and the states?
(a) Advisory Jurisdiction
(b) Initial Jurisdiction
(c) Appellate Jurisdiction
(d) Constitutional Jurisdiction

17. **The person appointed as a judge of the Supreme Court before assuming the office is administered oath by**
(a) Vice President
(b) President, or any other person appointed by him
(c) Chief Justice of India
(d) None of the above

18. **Who was the first Chief Justice of India?**
(a) Mehar Chand Mahajan
(b) A.K Sarkar
(c) Harilal J Kania
(d) S.R Das

19. **Which one of the following is the oldest High Court of India?**
(a) Bombay High Court
(b) Madras High Court
(c) Calcutta High Court
(d) Andhra Pradesh High Court

20. **The judges of the Supreme Court can tender their resignation by writing to whom?**
(a) President
(b) Prime Minister
(c) Law Minister
(d) Attorney General of India

Answers

1. (c)	**2.** (d)	**3.** (c)	**4.** (c)
5. (b)	**6.** (d)	**7.** (d)	**8.** (d)
9. (c)	**10.** (a)	**11.** (a)	**12.** (c)
13. (d)	**14.** (b)	**15.** (a)	**16.** (b)
17. (b)	**18.** (c)	**19.** (c)	**20.** (a)

SET-103

1. **The Supreme Court of India came into existence on ______**
(a) 26 January 1950
(b) 28 January 1950
(c) 15 August 1949
(d) 26 January 1949

2. **Under whose jurisdiction, the High Courts of India come directly under the Indian Judicial System?**
(a) Parliament
(b) Chairman
(c) Supreme Court
(d) Attorney General

3. **The judges of the Supreme Court can be removed by ______**
(a) Parliament
(b) Law Minister
(c) Supreme Court
(d) Attorney General

4. **Which Part of the Indian Constitution describes Federal Judiciary?**
(a) Part II (b) Part III
(c) Part IV (d) Part V

5. **Who is the interpreter and messenger of Constitution?**
(a) President
(b) Parliament
(c) Supreme Court
(d) Advocate General of India

6. **Under which of the following Supreme Court was established for the first time in India?**
(a) Regulating Act 1773
(b) Charter Act 1853
(c) Government of India Act 1935
(d) Constitution of India 1950

7. **Appointment of judges on adhoc basis in Supreme Court is inspired from the judicial system of which country?**
(a) Australia (b) Canada
(c) USA (d) France

8. **The judges of the Supreme Court can be removed from their post only on what proven bases?**
(a) Misconduct
(b) Incompetence
(c) Both of the above
(d) None of the above

9. **The Supreme Court enjoys right to settle disputes relating to election of President and Vice President. This is its–**
(a) Fundamental Right
(b) Judicial Renew Right
(c) Advisory Right
(d) Versatile Right

10. **The form of Judiciary in India is –**
(a) Decentralized
(b) Unified
(c) Collective
(d) Practical

11. **The Judiciary in India is –**
(a) Independent
(b) Subordinate to Parliament
(c) Subordinate to President
(d) Subordinate to Prime Minister

12. **Who is vested with the power of increasing the Jurisdictional authority of the Supreme Court?**
(a) Supreme Court
(b) President
(c) Parliament
(d) Council of Ministers

13. **After retirement, the judges of the Supreme Court can practice in**
(a) Only in Supreme Court
(b) Only in a High Court
(c) both in Supreme Court and High Court
(d) in any Court

14. **When was the Supreme Court of India established?**
(a) By an Act of Parliament in 1950
(b) Under Indian Independence Act 1947
(c) Under Government of India Act 1935
(d) By Indian Constitution

15. **Who among the following adorned the offices of judge of a high court and Lok Sabha Speaker?**
(a) Subba Rao
(b) P N Bhagwati
(c) M. Hidayatullah
(d) KS Hegde

16. **When were the new states formed in the name of Bihar and Odisha?**
(a) 1910 (b) 1912
(c) 1914 (d) 1916

17. **Who took over as the first governor of Bihar?**
(a) Sir Ali Imam
(b) Satish Chandra Jha
(c) Satyendra Prasanna Sinha
(d) Mandan Mishra

18. **When was the first legislative assembly election held in Bihar?**
(a) 1937 (b) 1935
(c) 1933 (d) 1931

19. **When did the Bihar Public Service Commission start working?**
(a) 1948 (b) 1949
(c) 1950 (d) 1951

20. **What is the tenure of member of Bihar Public Service Commission?**
(a) 4 (b) 5
(c) 6 (d) 7

Answers

1. (b)	**2.** (c)	**3.** (a)	**4.** (d)
5. (c)	**6.** (a)	**7.** (d)	**8.** (c)
9. (a)	**10.** (b)	**11.** (a)	**12.** (c)
13. (d)	**14.** (d)	**15.** (d)	**16.** (b)
17. (c)	**18.** (a)	**19.** (b)	**20.** (c)

SET-104

1. **How many zones are there in the Bihar state?**
(a) 6 (b) 7
(c) 8 (d) 9

2. **Who performs the work of all department of the Bihar Government?**
(a) Governor
(b) Chief Minister
(c) President
(d) All of these

3. **How many square kilometer is the total area of Bihar?**
(a) 94,163
(b) 95,840
(c) 96,113
(d) 97,930

4. **When was the Patna High Court established?**
(a) 1916 (b) 1918
(c) 1920 (d) 1922

5. **When was the Bihar Panchayat Committee and District Council Act passed?**
(a) 1960 (b) 1961
(c) 1962 (d) 1963

6. **How many district councils are there in Bihar?**
(a) 36 (b) 37
(c) 38 (d) 39

7. **During partition, how many districts existed in Bihar?**
(a) 52 (b) 54
(c) 56 (d) 58

8. **Who among the following was the chairman of Bihar-Odisha Council?**
(a) Lord David
(b) James Cook
(c) Sir Walter Mande
(d) Kevin Cooper

9. **When did the legislative councils of Bihar-Odisha come into existence?**
(a) 1919 (b) 1921
(c) 1923 (d) 1925

10. **What is the minimum number of members compulsorily required for Legislative Council?**
(a) 40 (b) 42
(c) 44 (d) 45

11. **What is the tenure of members of Legislative Council?**
(a) 3 (b) 4
(c) 5 (d) 6

12. **How many seats are reserved for the Scheduled Casted in Bihar Legislative Assembly?**
(a) 36 (b) 38
(c) 40 (d) 42

13. **Under which article the speaker of legislative assembly is elected?**
(a) Article 172 (b) Article 174
(c) Article 176 (d) Article 170

14. **When was Human Rights Commission set up in Bihar?**
(a) 1998 (b) 2000
(c) 2002 (d) 2004

15. **Who was the first chairman of Bihar Public Service Commission?**
(a) Rajdhari Sinha
(b) Madan Jha
(c) Pramod Mishra
(d) Asgar Wajahat

16. **When was the Jharkhand Self-Governance Regional Council constituted?**
(a) 1991 (b) 1993
(c) 1995 (d) 1997

17. **Urban local self-governance is a subject of which list?**
(a) State list
(b) Union list
(c) Concurrent list
(d) All of the above

18. **Who is the chairman of district council?**
(a) District chief
(b) District collector
(c) Lok Sabha member
(d) Pradhan

19. **According to the panchayati raj Act, to whom do the panch, upsarpanch, and sarpanch submit their resignation?**
(a) Sub-division Officer
(b) District Chief
(c) Development Officer
(d) District Collector

20. **Who is entrusted with the task of getting conducted elections of Panchayati Raj Institutions?**
(a) Election Commission of India
(b) Panchayati Raj Department

(c) State Election Commission
(d) Chief Election Commissioner

Answers

1. (d)	**2.** (a)	**3.** (a)	**4.** (a)
5. (b)	**6.** (c)	**7.** (b)	**8.** (c)
9. (b)	**10.** (a)	**11.** (d)	**12.** (b)
13. (d)	**14.** (b)	**15.** (a)	**16.** (c)
17. (a)	**18.** (a)	**19.** (c)	**20.** (c)

SET-105

1. Who are the members of village assembly?
(a) All the residents of a village
(b) All the residents of village registered in electoral list
(c) In accordance with list supplied by the state government
(d) Nominated member by the sarpanch

2. The purpose of social accounting is to ensure accountability of –
(a) State Government
(b) Union Government
(c) Local Administration
(d) Rural Local Self-government

3. Panchayati raj system is –
(a) Of local government
(b) Of local self-government
(c) Of local administration
(d) Of rural local self-government

4. When is Panchayat Day celebrated?
(a) 21 April (b) 24 April
(c) 22 March (d) 13 May

5. District planning council has how many elected and ex-official members?
(a) 20 and 5 (b) 20 and 3
(c) 20 and 2 (d) 20 and 10

6. The Panchayat Committee is constituted at –
(a) Village level
(b) Division level
(c) Sub-division level
(d) District level

7. The primary part of panchayati raj three-tier system is
(a) Panchayat Committe
(b) Village Panchayat
(c) District Committee
(d) None of the Above

8. What is the source of income of Village Panchayat?
(a) Land and local taxes
(b) Fair and market taxes
(c) Government grant tax
(d) House and cattle tax

9. In a development block, panchayat committee is –
(a) An Advisory Committee
(b) An Administrative Agency
(c) A Counseling Committee
(d) An Inspection Authority

10. Which is an example of direct democracy in India?
(a) District Panchayat
(b) Nagar Panchayat
(c) Gram Sabha
(d) Regional Panchayat

11. The main performer of Panchayat Committee is –
(a) Pradhan
(b) Sarpanch
(c) District Chief
(d) Block Development Officer

12. Generally, the Panchayat Committee has how many types of members?
(a) Ex-official member
(b) Cooperative member
(c) Associated member
(d) All of the above

13. The Panchayati Raj system was adopted –
(a) To provide political enlightenment to people
(b) For decentralizing the powers of democracy

(c) To educate the farmers
(d) None of the above

14. In the working area of Panchayati Raj, doesn't come –
(a) Rural Roads
(b) Rural Industries
(c) Agriculture Production
(d) Secondary Education

15. Suggestion for democratic decentralization was given by
(a) Mahatma Gandhi
(b) Vinoba Bhave
(c) Jai Prakash Narayan
(d) Balwant Rai Mehta

16. If a Panchayat is dissolved, then within how much time can the elections be held?
(a) 6 months
(b) 3 months
(c) 1 month
(d) 1 year

17. On 15th April 2022, at which place the Chief Minister of Bihar, Nitish Kumar inaugurated the largest Pepsi plant of the eastern India?
(a) Patna
(b) Basaini, Begusarai
(c) Siwan
(d) Munger

18. Soon, the Durgawati Dam will be developed as an eco-tourism spot on which district of Bihar is it situated?
(a) Kaimur
(b) Begusarai
(c) Buxar
(d) Madhubani

19. Bal Hriday Yojna was started on 02 April 2021 in which state?
(a) Chhatisgarh
(b) Jharkhand
(c) Bihar
(d) Uttar Pradesh

20. Village Public Works Scheme and Poor Welfare Employment Campaign were started by the Prime Minister, Narendra Modi in how many states?
(a) 4 (b) 6
(c) 8 (d) 10

Answers

1. (b)	**2.** (c)	**3.** (d)	**4.** (b)
5. (b)	**6.** (b)	**7.** (b)	**8.** (b)
9. (b)	**10.** (c)	**11.** (d)	**12.** (d)
13. (b)	**14.** (d)	**15.** (d)	**16.** (a)
17. (a)	**18.** (a)	**19.** (c)	**20.** (c)

SET-106

1. In which state, Ghar Tak Fibre Scheme was started though video conference?
(a) Uttar Pradesh
(b) Madhya Pradesh
(c) Bihar
(d) Karnataka

2. The Bihar Government has started Child Assistance Scheme for the children who lost their parents due to covid pandemic. The state government will provide financial assistance of how many rupees per month to such children?
(a) ₹ 1500 (b) ₹ 1600
(c) ₹ 1700 (d) ₹ 1800

3. Under which scheme land would be surveyed and mapping done in rural areas?
(a) Property Ownership Scheme
(b) Water Life Greenery Mission
(c) Skilled Youth Programme
(d) Chief Minister Village Transport Scheme

4. The campaign, "Pyar Ka Paudha" was started by Environment and Forest Department of which state?
(a) Chhattisgarh
(b) Rajasthan
(c) Bihar
(d) Jharkhand

5. How much subsidy will the government provides assistance to farmers living in the state under the Bihar Water Life Greenery Mission?

(a) ₹ 60,000 (b) ₹ 65,000
(c) ₹ 70,500 (d) ₹ 75,584

6. In which year was the "Bihar Self-Help Allowance Scheme" started?

(a) 2017 (b) 2018
(c) 2020 (d) 2021

7. How much amount will be provided to the beneficiary for setting up industry under the "Bihar SC/st Entrepreneurship Scheme" ?

(a) 5 lakh (b) 10 lakh
(c) 15 lakh (d) 20 lakh

8. By which state government was the Mukhyamantri Kanya Utthan Yojana (Chief Minister Girls Empowerment Scheme) started?

(a) Bihar Government
(b) Madhya Pradesh Government
(c) Uttar Pradesh Government
(d) Maharashtra Government

9. The inauguration of "Gram Ujala" programme was done from which virtual function?

(a) Araria (b) Arrah
(c) Patna (d) Banka

10. When was "Chief Minister Guaranteed Self-Help Allowance Scheme" started?

(a) 2 October 2016
(b) 12 October 2016
(c) 5 October 2016
(d) 8 October 2016

11. Which of the following scheme was started by the Bihar government with the aim of stopping female infanticide and sex discrimination?

(a) Bihar Unnayan Scheme
(b) Kanya Suraksha Yojana
(c) Chief Minister Sakhi Yojana
(d) Balika Protsahan Yojana

12. How much amount is given to widows per month as pension under the 'Widow Pension Scheme'?

(a) ₹ 400 (b) ₹ 500
(c) ₹ 600 (d) ₹ 700

13. Chief Minister Village Transport Scheme has been started in which of the following states?

(a) Uttakhand
(b) Uttar Pradesh
(c) Bihar
(d) Jharkhand

14. Which of the following schemes are being run in Bihar for social, economic and cultural empowerment of women in bihar?

(a) Mukhyamantri Kanya Suraksha Yojna
(b) Mukhyamantri Kanya Vivah Yojana
(c) Mukhyamantri Nari Shakti Yojana
(d) Mukhyamantri Kanya Utthan Yojana

15. Under which scheme of Bihar, the State Government will encourage those candidates who want a job in government administrative sector?

(a) Vikas Yojna
(b) Civil Sewa Protsahan Yojna
(c) Sewa Yojna
(d) Shram Shakti Yojna

16. Under the Chief Minister Crop Assistance Scheme in Bihar, how much amount will be given per hectare on 20% reduction to actual crop rate

(a) 5000 (b) 6000
(c) 7000 (d) 7500

17. Which scheme is being run in Bihar to give all schools by computer-based education?

(a) Digital Scheme
(b) Life Vision Scheme
(c) Human Development Scheme
(d) e-Samarth Scheme

18. Agro Forestry Scheme has been started by which department in Bihar?

(a) Forest Department
(b) Agriculture Department
(c) (a) and (b)
(d) None of the Above

19. Under the 'Physically Challenged Person Scheme' how much amount will be given per month for daily expenses?

(a) 200 (b) 300
(c) 400 (d) 500

20. Under what scheme mid-day food would be provided to all children belonging to classes 1 to 8 of government schools of the state?

(a) Mid-day Food Scheme
(b) Child Development Scheme
(c) Skill Scheme
(d) Human Development Scheme

Answers

1. (c)	2. (a)	3. (a)	4. (c)
5. (d)	6. (c)	7. (b)	8. (a)
9. (b)	10. (a)	11. (d)	12. (b)
13. (c)	14. (c)	15. (b)	16. (a)
17. (d)	18. (a)	19. (b)	20. (a)

SET-107

1. When was 'Shatabdi Ann Kalash Yojana' started in bihar?

(a) In 2010 (b) In 2011
(c) In 2012 (d) In 2013

2. Which scheme for imparting training for security employment for muslim women is being run by the bihar government?

(a) Naari Shramshakti Yojana
(b) Skill
(c) Mahila Utthan Yojana
(d) Hazrat Begum Mahal Shram Shakti Yojana

3. Recently which state government started Mamta Scheme?

(a) Chattisgarh
(b) Madhya Pradesh
(c) Odisha
(d) Bihar

4. Which state government has started 'chief minister family benefits scheme'?

(a) Assam
(b) Goa
(c) Bihar
(d) Uttar Pradesh

5. How much amount is given in Bihar under the 'Inter Caste Marriage Encouragement Scheme'?

(a) 1 lakh
(b) 2.50 lakh
(c) 3 lakh
(d) 4 lakh

6. How much amount is given per month to member of BPL families (city) under the 'State Social Security Pension Scheme' in Bihar?

(a) 100 (b) 200
(c) 300 (d) 400

7. Which committee operates the 'poorak poshahar programme' in Bihar?

(a) Ann Sravan Committee
(b) Panchayat Committee
(c) District Council
(d) None of the above

8. When was 'Kabir Antyesti Grant Scheme' started in Bihar?

(a) 2005 (b) 2007
(c) 2010 (d) 2015

9. International Booker Prize 2022 was awarded to whom?

(a) Professor Ramdarash Mishra
(b) Gitanjali Shri
(c) Professor Sandeep Sharma
(d) Nilmani Phukan

10. Who was awarded with world food prize 2022?
(a) Cynthia Rosenzweig
(b) Priyanka Dubey
(c) Neelam Sharma
(d) Arfa Khanum Sherwani

11. 57th Gyanpith award 2022 was awarded to whom?
(a) Damudar Manzo
(b) Nilmani Phukan
(c) Ramdarash Mishra
(d) None of the Above

12. Which famous poet and literature was awarded with 'Saraswati Samman 2021'?
(a) Professor Ramdarash Mishra
(b) Professor Sanjay Singh
(c) Professor Sandeep Sharma
(d) Professor Sanket Singh

13. International Gandhi Prize 2021 (in personal category) was awarded to whom?
(a) Dr. G.P Talwar
(b) Dr. M.D Gupta
(c) Dr. Bhushan Kumar
(d) Dr. Atul Shah

14. The first 'Late Dinanath Mangeshkar Prize' was awarded to whom?
(a) Sonu Nigam
(b) Anupam Kher
(c) Vivek Agnihotri
(d) Narendra Modi

15. Special Bangla academy prize 2022 was awarded to whom?
(a) Sanjay Verma
(b) Sumit Sharma
(c) Mamta Banerjee
(d) Sanjeet Mehta

16. Recently, who was awarded with the highest 'British prize'?
(a) Cynthia Rosenzweig
(b) Priyanka Dubey
(c) Ajay Piramal
(d) Arfa Khanum Sherwani

17. Which district of Bihar is the Kurtha division situated?
(a) Gaya (b) Patna
(c) Arwal (d) Siwan

18. How many division are present in the Arwal district?
(a) 4 (b) 5
(c) 6 (d) 7

19. What is the literacy rate of Arwal district?
(a) 60.02% (b) 68.92%
(c) 65.22% (d) 67.4%

20. Which is the main river of Nevada district?
(a) Sakri (b) Sone
(c) Falgun (d) Ganga

Answers

1. (b)	**2.** (b)	**3.** (d)	**4.** (c)
5. (b)	**6.** (b)	**7.** (a)	**8.** (b)
9. (b)	**10.** (a)	**11.** (a)	**12.** (a)
13. (c)	**14.** (d)	**15.** (c)	**16.** (c)
17. (c)	**18.** (b)	**19.** (d)	**20.** (a)

SET-108

1. Hisva and Kashichak divisions are a part of which district?
(a) Patna (b) Jehanabad
(c) Nevada (d) Siwan

2. How many legistative assembly come within Nevada district?
(a) 6 (b) 8
(c) 7 (d) 5

3. How many gram panchayats are included in Nevada district?
(a) 180 (b) 187
(c) 190 (d) 200

4. What is the female literacy rate of Nevada district?
(a) 50% (b) 64%
(c) 48.9% (d) 55.2%

5. In which district is Kakolat waterfall situated?
(a) Nevada (b) Patna
(c) Buxar (d) Vaishali

6. **Rajauli sub-division comes under which districts?**
(a) Siwan
(b) Bhagalpur
(c) Katihar
(d) Nevada

7. **What is the population density of Aurangabad district?**
(a) 841 per km^2
(b) 769 per km^2
(c) 810 per km^2
(d) 911 per km^2

8. **Daudnagar sub-division comes under which district?**
(a) Aurangabad
(b) Gaya
(c) Buxar
(d) Siwan

9. **How many divisions come under the Aurangabad districts?**
(a) 14 (b) 10
(c) 11 (d) 13

10. **Residual soil is mainly found in which district of Bihar?**
(a) Lakhisarai
(b) Buxar
(c) Banka
(d) Aurangabad

11. **What is the literacy rate of Aurangabad district?**
(a) 75.2% (b) 70.3%
(c) 68.1% (d) 73.6%

12. **What is the male literacy rate of Aurangabad district?**
(a) 78% (b) 82.2%
(c) 80.1% (d) 82%

13. **Aurangabad district was carved out from which district?**
(a) Gaya (b) Siwan
(c) Buxar (d) Patna

14. **In which year was Saran district constituted?**
(a) 1985 (b) 1981
(c) 1988 (d) 1983

15. **How many legislative assembly constituencies come under Saran district?**
(a) 15 (b) 12
(c) 8 (d) 10

16. **What is th administrative headquarters of Saran district?**
(a) Chhapra (b) Marhaura
(c) Manjhi (d) Sadar

17. **What is the area of Saran district?**
(a) 2310 per km^2
(b) 2400 per km^2
(c) 2641 per km^2
(d) 2215 per km^2

18. **In which district are the Chhapra included?**
(a) Buxar
(b) Saran
(c) Aurangabad
(d) Gaya

19. **How many divisions are included in Saran district?**
(a) 10 (b) 12
(c) 14 (d) 20

20. **What is the female literacy rate of Saran district?**
(a) 50.2% (b) 52.1%
(c) 54.4% (d) 55%

Answers

1. (c)	**2.** (d)	**3.** (b)	**4.** (c)
5. (a)	**6.** (d)	**7.** (b)	**8.** (a)
9. (c)	**10.** (d)	**11.** (b)	**12.** (c)
13. (a)	**14.** (b)	**15.** (d)	**16.** (a)
17. (c)	**18.** (b)	**19.** (d)	**20.** (c)

SET-109

1. **As per 2011 census, what was the population of Saran district?**
(a) 39,51,562 (b) 38,61,421
(c) 35,00,212 (d) 32,62,412

2. **In which year was the siwan district constituted?**
(a) 1975 (b) 1980
(c) 1972 (d) 1988

3. **Daha and Jharhi are major rivers of which district?**
(a) Aurangabad (b) Gaya
(c) Patna (d) Siwan

4. **Which division doesn't come within the Siwan district?**
(a) Darouli (b) Sapat
(c) Panchrukhi (d) Basantpur

5. **How many Lok Sabha constituencies are there in Siwan district?**
(a) 4 (b) 5
(c) 2 (d) 1

6. **Of which district is Maharajganj Legislative Assembly Constituency?**
(a) Siwan (b) Gaya
(c) Patna (d) Buxar

7. **What is the population density of Siwan district?**
(a) 1555 per square km.
(b) 1501 per square km.
(c) 1600 per square km.
(d) 1580 per square km.

8. **What is the literacy rate (2011) of Siwan district?**
(a) 70% (b) 69.5%
(c) 65.6% (d) 67.8%

9. **As per the 2011 census, what is decadal growth rate in population in Siwan district?**
(a) 27.7% (b) 25%
(c) 20% (d) 23.72%

10. **Zeradei (birth place of Dr. Rajendra Prasad) is situated in which district of Bihar?**
(a) Patna (b) Siwan
(c) Gaya (d) Buxar

11. **What is the female literacy rate of Siwan district**
(a) 60.2% (b) 55.6%
(c) 58.7% (d) 62%

12. **In which year was the Gopalganj district constituted?**
(a) 1966 (b) 1970
(c) 1968 (d) 1973

13. **Gandak is major river of which district?**
(a) Gopalganj
(b) Sitamarhi
(c) Sheohar
(d) Vaishali

14. **Which among the following is division of Gopalganj?**
(a) Panchrukhi
(b) Siwan
(c) Saran
(d) Basantpur

15. **How many sub-divisions are present in Gopalganj district?**
(a) 4 (b) 2
(c) 5 (d) 6

16. **Which of the following divisions is not a part of Gopalganj district?**
(a) Vijaypur (b) Manjhia
(c) Thawe (d) Basantpur

17. **How many Lok Sabha constituencies are there in Gopalganj district?**
(a) 6 (b) 4
(c) 5 (d) 8

18. **What is the latitudinal expanse of Gopalganj district?**
(a) 26º 12' to 26º 39' East
(b) 26º 12' to 26º 39' West
(c) 26º 12' to 26º 39' North
(d) 26º 12' to 26º 39' South

19. **Ramgarhta Deet Tourist Spot is situated in which district of Bihar?**
(a) Buxar (b) Gopalganj
(c) Siwan (d) Gaya

20. **As per 2011 census, what is the population density of Gopalganj district?**
(a) 1310 per square km.
(b) 1285 per square km.
(c) 1325 per square km.
(d) 1260 per square km.

Answers

1. (a)	2. (c)	3. (d)	4. (b)
5. (c)	6. (a)	7. (b)	8. (b)
9. (a)	10. (b)	11. (c)	12. (d)
13. (a)	14. (a)	15. (c)	16. (b)
17. (a)	18. (c)	19. (b)	20. (d)

SET-110

1. **What is the female literacy rate of Gopalganj district?**
   (a) 58% (b) 60%
   (c) 54.8% (d) 52.3%
2. **Tirhut division comes under which district of Bihar?**
   (a) Muzaffarpur
   (b) Gopalganj
   (c) Sheohar
   (d) Gaya
3. **Which of the following divisions does not come within Muzaffarpur district?**
   (a) Shakara (b) Katra
   (c) Paroo (d) Thawe
4. **How many divisions are present in Muzaffarpur district?**
   (a) 10 (b) 16
   (c) 19 (d) 22
5. **Aurai Legislative Assembly constituency comes under which district?**
   (a) Muzaffarpur
   (b) Vaishali
   (c) Madhubani
   (d) Darbhanga
6. **A total of how many divisions come within Muzaffarpur district?**
   (a) 15 (b) 18
   (c) 16 (d) 20
7. **Minapur and Gaighat Legislative Constituencies come under which district?**
   (a) Patna
   (b) Muzaffarpur
   (c) Buxar
   (d) Madhubani
8. **What was the population density of Muzaffarpur district as per the 2011 census?**
   (a) 1410 per square km.
   (b) 1021 per square km.
   (c) 1580 per square km.
   (d) 1514 per square km.
9. **As per 2011 census, what was the male literacy rate of Muzaffarpur district?**
   (a) 65.2% (b) 70.6%
   (c) 71.3% (d) 74.6%
10. **What is the area of Sitamarhi district?**
    (a) 2294 per square km.
    (b) 2310 per square km.
    (c) 2545 per square km.
    (d) 2612 per square km.
11. **Bagmati is a major river of which district of Bihar?**
    (a) Patna (b) Gaya
    (c) Sheohar (d) Sitamarhi
12. **Tirhut division comes under which district of Bihar?**
    (a) Gaya (b) Sitamarhi
    (c) Buxar (d) Vaishali
13. **Which sub-division doesn't come within Sitamarhi district?**
    (a) Gopalganj
    (b) Sitamarhi Sadar
    (c) Belkhand
    (d) Pupri
14. **How many divisions are there in Sitamarhi district?**
    (a) 19 (b) 21
    (c) 17 (d) 12
15. **Which among the following legislative assembly constituencies does not come within Sitamarhi district?**
    (a) Parihar (b) Riga
    (c) Bathnaha (d) Obra

16. **What is the latitudinal expanse of Sitamarhi district?**
(a) 25° 36' to 26° 6' East
(b) 25° 36' to 26° 6' West
(c) 25° 36' to 26° 6' North
(d) 25° 36' to 26° 6' South

17. **As per 2011 census, what was the population density of Sitamarhi district?**
(a) 1492 per square km.
(b) 1526 per square km.
(c) 1610 per square km.
(d) 1819 per square km.

18. **What is the literacy rate of Sitamarhi district?**
(a) 52.8% (b) 50.7%
(c) 52.1% (d) 50%

19. **Punaur Haleshwar Temple is situation in which district of Bihar?**
(a) Sheohar
(b) Sitamarhi
(c) Gaya
(d) Siwan

20. **In which year was Sheohar district constituted?**
(a) 1980 (b) 1985
(c) 1991 (d) 1994

Answers

1. (c)	**2.** (b)	**3.** (d)	**4.** (b)
5. (a)	**6.** (c)	**7.** (b)	**8.** (d)
9. (c)	**10.** (a)	**11.** (d)	**12.** (b)
13. (a)	**14.** (c)	**15.** (d)	**16.** (b)
17. (a)	**18.** (c)	**19.** (b)	**20.** (d)

SET-111

1. **What is the area of Sheohar district?**
(a) 325 per square km.
(b) 340 per square km.
(c) 355 per square km.
(d) 349 per square km.

2. **Burhi Gandak is a major river of which district of Bihar?**
(a) Sheohar (b) Araria
(c) Katihar (d) Buxar

3. **Tirhut division comes under which district?**
(a) Gaya (b) Sheohar
(c) Patna (d) Bhojpur

4. **How many divisions come under Sheohar district?**
(a) 8 (b) 5
(c) 4 (d) 6

5. **What is the strength of panchayats in Sheohar Districts?**
(a) 50 (b) 60
(c) 57 (d) 53

6. **How many revenue villages are there in Sheohar district?**
(a) 210 (b) 215
(c) 207 (d) 205

7. **As per 2011 census, what was the male literacy rate in Sheohar district?**
(a) 61.3% (b) 68%
(c) 58.2% (d) 60%

8. **What was sex ratio of Sheohar district as per 2011 census?**
(a) 800/1000 Male
(b) 850/1000 Male
(c) 900/1000 Male
(d) 893/1000 Male

9. **Shiva temple of Deokuli is situated in which district of Bihar?**
(a) Sitamarhi
(b) Sheohar
(c) Buxar
(d) Madhubani

10. **The administrative headquarters of Western Champaran district is located at which place?**
(a) Gaunaha
(b) Nautan
(c) Bettiah
(d) Tirhut

11. **Which of the following sub-divisions does not come within Western Champaran district?**

(a) Pupri
(b) Bettiah
(c) Bageha
(d) Narkatiaganj

12. Tirhut division comes under which district of Bihar?
(a) Gaya
(b) Buxar
(c) Patna
(d) Western Champaran

13. How many panchayats are there in western champaran district?
(a) 300 (b) 315
(c) 345 (d) 308

14. How many revenue villages are there in Western Champaran district?
(a) 1510 (b) 1545
(c) 1483 (d) 1474

15. Which of the follow sub-divisions do not come within Western Champaran district?
(a) Gaunaha
(b) Ramnagar
(c) Sikta
(d) Nanpur

16. Deposits of mineral feldspar are found in which districts of Bihar?
(a) Jamui
(b) Moungher
(c) Banka
(d) (a) and (b) both

17. The number of divisions in Bihar state are –
(a) 6 (b) 9
(c) 11 (d) 13

18. How many districts are contained in Patna division?
(a) 3 (b) 6
(c) 8 (d) 10

19. How many sub-divisions are contained in Patna district?
(a) 6 (b) 7
(c) 8 (d) 12

20. How many sub-divisions are there in Nalanda district?
(a) 3 (b) 4
(c) 5 (d) 6

Answers

1. (d)	**2.** (a)	**3.** (b)	**4.** (b)
5. (c)	**6.** (c)	**7.** (c)	**8.** (d)
9. (b)	**10.** (c)	**11.** (a)	**12.** (d)
13. (b)	**14.** (c)	**15.** (d)	**16.** (d)
17. (b)	**18.** (b)	**19.** (b)	**20.** (c)

SET-112

1. How many sub-divisions are there in Buxar district?
(a) 4 (b) 2
(c) 3 (d) 6

2. How many districts are there in Magadha division?
(a) 6 (b) 9
(c) 8 (d) 5

3. How many sub-divisions are there in Gaya district?
(a) 3 (b) 4
(c) 5 (d) 6

4. How many sub-divisions are there in Arwal district?
(a) 4 (b) 2
(c) 7 (d) 6

5. How many districts are there in Saran (Chhapra) district?
(a) 4 (b) 2
(c) 6 (d) 0

6. How many sub–divisions are there in Siwan district?
(a) 4 (b) 2
(c) 6 (d) 0

7. How many districts are there in Siwan district?
(a) 5 (b) 4
(c) 7 (d) 11

8. How many sub-divisions are there in Sitamarhi district?
(a) 8 (b) 4
(c) 7 (d) 3

9. **How many sub-divisions are there in Eastern champaran?**
(a) 7 (b) 9
(c) 6 (d) 13

10. **How many districts are there in Darbhanga district?**
(a) 4 (b) 2
(c) 7 (d) 9

11. **How many sub-divisions are there in Darbhanga district?**
(a) 3 (b) 6
(c) 9 (d) 12

12. **How many sub-divisions are there in Madhubani district?**
(a) 4 (b) 7
(c) 11 (d) 5

13. **How many districts are there in Kosi division?**
(a) 2 (b) 3
(c) 4 (d) 5

14. **How many sub-divisions are there in Saharsa district?**
(a) 2 (b) 4
(c) 6 (d) 8

15. **How many sub-divisions are there in Supaul district?**
(a) 5 (b) 8
(c) 7 (d) 4

16. **How many districts are there in Purnia division?**
(a) 6 (b) 4
(c) 7 (d) 9

17. **How many sub-divisions are there in Katihar district?**
(a) 2 (b) 4
(c) 8 (d) 3

18. **How many districts are there in Bhagalpur division?**
(a) 2 (b) 4
(c) 6 (d) 8

19. **How many districts are there in Munger division?**
(a) 8 (b) 9
(c) 6 (d) 11

20. **How many sub-divisions are there in Begusarai district?**
(a) 3 (b) 5
(c) 7 (d) 11

Answers

1. (b)	**2.** (d)	**3.** (c)	**4.** (b)
5. (a)	**6.** (b)	**7.** (a)	**8.** (d)
9. (c)	**10.** (b)	**11.** (a)	**12.** (d)
13. (b)	**14.** (a)	**15.** (c)	**16.** (b)
17. (d)	**18.** (a)	**19.** (c)	**20.** (b)

SET-113

1. **What is the area of Patna district?**
(a) 3208 (b) 3106
(c) 3010 (d) 3202

2. **How many panchayats are there in Patna district?**
(a) 327 (b) 275
(c) 300 (d) 410

3. **What is the population density of Patna district?**
(a) 1848 square km.
(b) 1920 square km.
(c) 1823 square km.
(d) 1942 square km.

4. **In which year was the Nalanda district constituted?**
(a) 1878 (b) 1875
(c) 1881 (d) 1885

5. **The number of divisions in Nalanda district are –**
(a) 20 (b) 25
(c) 30 (d) 40

6. **The population density of Nalanda district is –**
(a) 1303 square km.
(b) 1208 square km.
(c) 1406 square km.
(d) 1222 square km.

7. **In which year was the Rohtas district constituted?**
(a) 1982 (b) 1985
(c) 1972 (d) 1978

8. **The number of divisions in Rohtas district are –**

(a) 15 (b) 19
(c) 21 (d) 23

9. Patliputra Patnasahib are Lok Sabha constituencies of which district?
(a) Patna (b) Gaya
(c) Nalanda (d) Rohtas

10. How many legislative assembly constituencies are there in Patna district?
(a) 12 (b) 8
(c) 14 (d) 18

11. Which of these sub-divisions does not come within Patna district?
(a) Patna Sadar (b) Rajgir
(c) Danapur (d) Masaurhi

12. Falgu and Mohama are major rivers of which district?
(a) Buxar (b) Bhojpur
(c) Nalanda (d) Nevada

13. Which river is not a major river of Patna?
(a) Ganga (b) Sone
(c) Pun pun (d) Falgu

14. Bihar Sharif, Rajgir, and Hilsa are sub-divisions of which district?
(a) Nalanda (b) Patna
(c) Gaya (d) Buxar

15. Red soil and bangar soil are found in which district?
(a) Patna (b) Nalanda
(c) Gaya (d) Kaimur

16. What is the area of Rohtas district?
(a) 3570 square km.
(b) 3110 square km.
(c) 3680 square km.
(d) 3881 square km.

17. Rohtas district has how many legislative assembly constituencies?
(a) 6 (b) 5
(c) 7 (d) 8

18. Sasaram and Karakat lok sabha constituencies come within which district?
(a) Rohtas (b) Gaya
(c) Punpun (d) Bhojpur

19. Which sub-division is not a part of Rohtas district?
(a) Sasaram
(b) Vikramganj
(c) Dehri
(d) Rajgir

20. In which district is Tomb of Shershah situated?
(a) Patna (b) Rohtas
(c) Kaimur (d) Sheohar

Answers

1. (d)	**2.** (a)	**3.** (c)	**4.** (b)
5. (a)	**6.** (d)	**7.** (c)	**8.** (b)
9. (a)	**10.** (c)	**11.** (b)	**12.** (c)
13. (d)	**14.** (a)	**15.** (b)	**16.** (d)
17. (c)	**18.** (a)	**19.** (d)	**20.** (b)

SET-114

1. What is the area of Kaimur district?
(a) 3332 square km.
(b) 3117 square km.
(c) 3610 square km.
(d) 3252 square km.

2. Bhabua and Mohania are sub-divisions of which district?
(a) Patna
(b) Rohtas
(c) Kaimur
(d) Madhubani

3. Which is the Lok Sabha constituency of Kaimur District?
(a) Ramgarh
(b) Bhabhua
(c) Mohania
(d) Sasaram

4. How many legislative assembly constituencies are there in Kaimur district?
(a) 4 (b) 5
(c) 6 (d) 3

5. **How many sub-divisions are there in Kaimur district?**
(a) 12 (b) 14
(c) 11 (d) 15

6. **What is the population density of Kaimur district?**
(a) 382 square km.
(b) 488 square km.
(c) 435 square km.
(d) 395 square km.

7. **Bhojpur district was earlier a part of which district?**
(a) Patna (b) Gaya
(c) Kaimur (d) Shahbad

8. **In which year was the Shahbad district partitioned?**
(a) 1992 (b) 1997
(c) 1993 (d) 1990

9. **How many districts were carved out from Shahabad district?**
(a) 4 (b) 3
(c) 2 (d) 1

10. **What is the area of Bhojpur district?**
(a) 2250 (b) 2180
(c) 2479 (d) 2500

11. **Ganga and Sone are major rivers of which district?**
(a) Shahabad (b) Gaya
(c) Patna (d) Bhojpur

12. **Arrah is a Lok Sabha constituency of which district?**
(a) Bhojpur
(b) Kishanganj
(c) Bhagalpur
(d) Katihar

13. **Which of the following is not an electoral area of Bhojpur Legislative Assembly Constituency?**
(a) Arah (b) Jagdishpur
(c) Gaya (d) Burhata

14. **How many sub-divisions are there in Bhojpur district?**
(a) 5 (b) 3
(c) 6 (d) 7

15. **How many divisions are there in Bhojpur district?**
(a) 16 (b) 18
(c) 15 (d) 14

16. **Which one of the following division does not come within Bhojpur district?**
(a) Dobhi (b) Sahar
(c) Pira (d) Hiya

17. **Buxar district was carved out from which district?**
(a) Gaya (b) Patna
(c) Shahbad (d) Buxar

18. **What is the area of Buxar district?**
(a) 1609 square km.
(b) 1703 square km.
(c) 1735 square km.
(d) 1800 square km.

19. **Ganga, Sone, and Karamnasa are major rivers of which district?**
(a) Patna (b) Gaya
(c) Sitamarhi (d) Buxar

20. **How many sub-divisions are there in Buxar district?**
(a) 2 (b) 4
(c) 6 (d) 8

Answers

1. (a)	**2.** (c)	**3.** (d)	**4.** (a)
5. (c)	**6.** (d)	**7.** (a)	**8.** (b)
9. (c)	**10.** (d)	**11.** (a)	**12.** (a)
13. (b)	**14.** (d)	**15.** (a)	**16.** (c)
17. (b)	**18.** (d)	**19.** (a)	**20.** (c)

SET-115

1. **How many divisions are there in Buxar district?**
(a) 14 (b) 12
(c) 11 (d) 16

2. **Which division is not a part of Buxar district?**
(a) Chausa (b) Arah
(c) Dumraon (d) Rajpur

3. **How many panchayats are there in Buxar districts?**
(a) 124 (b) 132
(c) 138 (d) 142

4. **How many Lok Sabha Constituencies are there in Buxar district?**
(a) 1 (b) 2
(c) 3 (d) 4

5. **Which one of the following legislative assembly constituencies does not come within Buxar district?**
(a) Brahampur
(b) Rajpur
(c) Shahpur
(d) Dumraon

6. **In which year was the Gaya district constituted ?**
(a) 1880 (b) 1865
(c) 1870 (d) 1890

7. **Which is the most important river of Gaya district?**
(a) Ganga
(b) Sone
(c) Karamnasa
(d) Falgu

8. **How many divisions are there in Gaya district?**
(a) 24 (b) 28
(c) 32 (d) 22

9. **Which one of the following divisions does not come within Gaya district?**
(a) Dobhi
(b) Mohanpur
(c) Arrah
(d) Manpur

10. **How many electoral areas are there under Gaya legislative assembly constituency?**
(a) 12 (b) 10
(c) 15 (d) 14

11. **Which sub-division does not come within Gaya district?**
(a) Gaya Sadar
(b) Neemchak
(c) Bathani
(d) Jagdishpur

12. **What is the population density of Gaya district?**
(a) 883 square km.
(b) 903 square km.
(c) 825 square km.
(d) 925 square km.

13. **What is the literacy rate of Gaya district?**
(a) 60.02% (b) 68.61%
(c) 63.70% (d) 70.01%

14. **From which district was the Jehanabad district separated?**
(a) Patna (b) Gaya
(c) Saran (d) Buxar

15. **What is the latitudinal expanse of Jehanabad district?**
(a) 25º0' to 25º15' West
(b) 25º0' to 25º15' South
(c) 25º0' to 25º15' East
(d) 25º0' to 25º15' North

16. **Balthar soil and old soil are found in which district?**
(a) Jehanabad (b) Nawada
(c) Gaya (d) Buxar

17. **How many Lok Sabha constituencies are there in Jehanabad district?**
(a) 4 (b) 5
(c) 3 (d) 7

18. **What is the male literacy rate of Jehanabad district?**
(a) 66.8% (b) 77.7%
(c) 80% (d) 75.2%

19. **Nagarjuna Museum and Balahar Caves are tourist spots of which district of Bihar?**
(a) Buxar (b) Sheohar
(c) Sitamarhi (d) Jehanabad

20. **How many divisions are there in Jehanabad district?**
(a) 7 (b) 9
(c) 11 (d) 13

Answers

1. (c)	**2.** (c)	**3.** (d)	**4.** (a)
5. (c)	**6.** (b)	**7.** (d)	**8.** (a)
9. (c)	**10.** (b)	**11.** (d)	**12.** (a)
13. (c)	**14.** (b)	**15.** (d)	**16.** (a)
17. (c)	**18.** (b)	**19.** (d)	**20.** (d)

SET-116

1. Which district was carved out from Jehanabad District?
(a) Nawada (b) Shibhar
(c) Akhal (d) Siwan

2. What is the area of Akhal district?
(a) 670 square km.
(b) 810 square km.
(c) 820 square km.
(d) 638 square km.

3. Kurtha is a Legislative Assembly Constituency of which district?
(a) Jehanabad
(b) Akhal
(c) Gaya
(d) Buxar

4. What is the longitudinal expanse of Akhal district?
(a) 84°31' to 85°15' East
(b) 84°31' to 85°15' West
(c) 84°31' to 85°15' North
(d) 84°31' to 85°15' South

5. How many legislative assembly constituencies are there in Westen Champaran district?
(a) 8 (b) 7
(c) 9 (d) 10

6. What is the longitudinal expanse of Western Champaran District?
(a) 83°50' to 85°18' West
(b) 83°50' to 85°18' East
(c) 83°50' to 85°18' North
(d) 83°50' to 85°18' South

7. What is the population density of Western Champaran District?
(a) 753 per square km.
(b) 710 per square km.
(c) 615 per square km.
(d) 800 per square km.

8. What is the sex ratio of west Champaran District?
(a) 900/1000 Male
(b) 920/1000 Male
(c) 950/1000 Male
(d) 909/1000 Male

9. The Gandhi Ashram of Bhitiharwa in Bihar is situated in which district?
(a) Patna
(b) West Champaran
(c) Buxar
(d) Vaishali

10. What was the literacy rate of West Champaran as per the 2011 census?
(a) 50% (b) 52%
(c) 55.7% (d) 53.25%

11. When was East Champaran District constituted ?
(a) 1970 (b) 1971
(c) 1973 (d) 1972

12. What is the area of East Champaran District?
(a) 3810 square km.
(b) 3525 square km.
(c) 3610 square km.
(d) 3968 square km.

13. Motihari is administrative headquarters of which district of Bihar?
(a) West Champaran
(b) Gaya
(c) East Champaran
(d) Buxar

14. Tirhut division comes under which district of Bihar?
(a) East Champaran
(b) Madhubani
(c) Vaishali
(d) Patna

15. **How many sub-divisions are there in East Champaran district?**
(a) 6 (b) 8
(c) 5 (d) 4

16. **Which of the following blocks does not come within East Champaran District?**
(a) Areraj
(b) Raxaul
(c) Kotwa
(d) Gaunaha

17. **Dhaka, Pipra, and Govindganj are Legislative Assembly Constituencies of which district?**
(a) West Champaran
(b) Darbhanga
(c) Samastipur
(d) Madhubani

18. **How many panchayats are there within East Champaran District?**
(a) 380 (b) 405
(c) 390 (d) 400

19. **What was the population density of East Champaran District as per the 2011 census?**
(a) 1285 per square km.
(b) 1310 per square km.
(c) 1400 per square km.
(d) 1325 per square km.

20. **Which is the administrative headquarters of Vaishali District?**
(a) Motihari (b) Hajipur
(c) Lalganj (d) Desri

Answers

1. (c)	**2.** (d)	**3.** (b)	**4.** (a)
5. (c)	**6.** (b)	**7.** (a)	**8.** (d)
9. (b)	**10.** (c)	**11.** (d)	**12.** (d)
13. (c)	**14.** (a)	**15.** (a)	**16.** (d)
17. (a)	**18.** (b)	**19.** (a)	**20.** (b)

SET-117

1. **Which sub-division does not come within Vaishali District?**
(a) Hajipur
(b) Mahua
(c) Areraj
(d) Mehnar

2. **How many divisions are there within Vaishali District?**
(a) 14 (b) 18
(c) 12 (d) 16

3. **Which of the following divisions does not come in Vaishali District?**
(a) Bhagwanpur
(b) Sugauli
(c) Mahua
(d) Desari

4. **How many Lok Sabha Constituencies are there in Vaishali District?**
(a) 4 (b) 6
(c) 2 (d) 3

5. **Raghopur is a Legislative Assembly Constituency of which district?**
(a) Patna
(b) Gaya
(c) Madhubani
(d) Vaishali

6. **What is the longitudinal expanse of Vaishali district?**
(a) 84° to 85° East
(b) 84° to 85° West
(c) 84° to 85° North
(d) 84° to 85° South

7. **What is the sex ratio of Vaishali District as per 2011 census?**
(a) 1800/1000 Male
(b) 900/1000 Male
(c) 895/1000 Male
(d) 925/1000 Male

8. **What is the male literacy rate of Vaishali district as per 2011 census?**

(a) 70.2% (b) 72.1%
(c) 78.12% (d) 75.4%

9. **Vishwa Shanti Stupa is a tourist spot of which district of Bihar?**
(a) Vaishali (b) Patna
(c) Shivgarh (d) Gaya

10. **In which year was the Darbhanga district constituted ?**
(a) 1870 (b) 1875
(c) 1880 (d) 1885

11. **Which sub-division is not a part of Darbhanga district?**
(a) Darbhanga Sadar
(b) Benipur
(c) Biraul
(d) Mehnar

12. **How many revenue villages are there in Darbhanga district?**
(a) 1269 (b) 1310
(c) 1274 (d) 1418

13. **Baheri block comes under which district of Bihar?**
(a) Patna (b) Darbhanga
(c) Shibhar (d) Gaya

14. **Which of the following legislative constituency is not a part of Darbhanga District?**
(a) Kusheshwar
(b) Benipur
(c) Pipra
(d) Keoti

15. **How many Lok Sabha Constituencies are there in Darbhanga District?**
(a) 1 (b) 2
(c) 4 (d) 5

16. **What is the latitudinal expanse of Darbhanga District?**
(a) 25º53' to 26º27' East
(b) 25º53' to 26º27' North
(c) 25º53' to 26º27' South
(d) 25º53' to 26º27' West

17. **As per the 2011 census, what is the population density of Darbhanga District?**
(a) 1625 per square km.
(b) 1717 per square km.
(c) 1810 per square km.
(d) 1785 per square km.

18. **Akashvani and Doordarshan Broadcasting Centre is a scenic spot of which district of Bihar?**
(a) Madhubani (b) Buxar
(c) Darbhanga (d) Gaya

19. **Which of the following divisions comes under Madhubani District?**
(a) Benipur
(b) Khatauna
(c) Keoti
(d) Darbhanga

20. **Which of the following sub-divisions come under Madhubani District?**
(a) Benipur
(b) Jainagar
(c) Jhanjarpur
(d) Phulparas

Answers

1. (c)	**2.** (d)	**3.** (b)	**4.** (c)
5. (d)	**6.** (a)	**7.** (c)	**8.** (d)
9. (a)	**10.** (b)	**11.** (d)	**12.** (a)
13. (b)	**14.** (c)	**15.** (a)	**16.** (b)
17. (b)	**18.** (a)	**19.** (a)	**20.** (b)

SET-118

1. **How many divisions are there in Madhubani District?**
(a) 24 (b) 21
(c) 15 (d) 20

2. **Jhanjharpur lok sabha constituency comes in which district of Bihar?**
(a) Samastipur
(b) Darbhanga
(c) Madhubani
(d) Gaya

3. **Which of the following legislative assembly constituencies does not fall under Madhubani district?**
(a) Khajauli (b) Rajnagar
(c) Benipatti (d) Kewti

4. **How many panchayats are there in Madhubani District?**
(a) 399 (b) 350
(c) 367 (d) 385

5. **What is the sex ratio of Madhubani District as per 2011 census?**
(a) 993/1000 Male
(b) 926/1000 Male
(c) 980/1000 Male
(d) 905/1000 Male

6. **Khadi Industry in Loha Kapasia is the major industry of which district?**
(a) Patna (b) Gaya
(c) Madhubani (d) Madhepura

7. **When was Samastipur district constituted?**
(a) 1988 (b) 1992
(c) 1984 (d) 1972

8. **How many sub-divisions are there in Samastipur District?**
(a) 4 (b) 5
(c) 6 (d) 8

9. **Which of the following divisions is not a part of Samastipur District?**
(a) Patori (b) Keoti
(c) Mohanpur (d) Vibhutipur

10. **How many Legislative Assembly Constituencies are there in Samastipur District?**
(a) 12 (b) 13
(c) 10 (d) 8

11. **What is the longitudinal expanse of Samastipur District**
(a) 85° 46' 45" West
(b) 85° 46' 45" North
(c) 85° 46' 45" South
(d) 85° 46' 45" East

12. **What was the literacy rate of Samastipur District as per 2011 census?**
(a) 61.9% (b) 64.4%
(c) 68.1% (d) 70%

13. **Pusa Agricultural University is situated in which district of Bihar?**
(a) Madhepura (b) Samastipur
(c) Sharsa (d) Purnia

14. **What is the area of Saharsa District?**
(a) 1680 sq. km.
(b) 1702 sq. km.
(c) 1687 sq. km.
(d) 1710 sq. km.

15. **Kosi is a division of which district of Bihar?**
(a) Madhepura (b) Madhubani
(c) Gaya (d) Saharsa

16. **Sonbarsa block comes under which district of Bihar?**
(a) Saharsa (b) Supaul
(c) Patna (d) Buxar

17. **What was the decadal (2001-2011) increamental rate in population of district?**
(a) 25% (b) 26%
(c) 27% (d) 28%

18. **What is the male literacy rate of Saharsa District as per 2011 censur?**
(a) 60.2% (b) 65.6%
(c) 63.6% (d) 67.2%

19. **Sonbarsa Van (Harsidhha) is a scenic spot of which district of Bihar?**
(a) Supaul (b) Buxar
(c) Gaya (d) Saharsa

20. **What is the area of Supaul district?**
(a) 2425 sq. km.
(b) 2512 sq. km.
(c) 2601 sq. km.
(d) 2281 sq. km.

Answers

1. (b)	2. (c)	3. (d)	4. (a)
5. (b)	6. (c)	7. (d)	8. (a)
9. (b)	10. (c)	11. (d)	12. (a)
13. (b)	14. (c)	15. (d)	16. (b)
17. (b)	18. (c)	19. (d)	20. (a)

SET-119

1. Which of the following sub-divisions does not come under Supaul District?
(a) Birpur
(b) Saharsa Sadar
(c) Nirmali
(d) Triveniganj

2. How many blocks are there in Supaul District?
(a) 12 (b) 13
(c) 11 (d) 9

3. Triveniganj Legislative Assembly Constituency comes under which district of Bihar?
(a) Madhubani
(b) Katihar
(c) Kishanganj
(d) Supaul

4. What is the population density of Supaul District as per the 2011 census?
(a) 919 per sq.km.
(b) 948 per sq.km.
(c) 902 per sq.km.
(d) 980 per sq.km.

5. When was the Madhepura District constituted?
(a) 1984 (b) 1981
(c) 1985 (d) 1978

6. Uda-kishanganj is sub-division of which district of Bihar?
(a) Supoul (b) Gaya
(c) Madhepura (d) Katihar

7. Which of the following blocks is not a part of Madhepura District?
(a) Chausa
(b) Puraini
(c) Kumarkhand
(d) Pipra

8. What is the latitudinal expanse of Madhepura District?
(a) 25° 31' to 26° 20' North
(b) 25° 31' to 26° 20' South
(c) 25° 31' to 26° 20' East
(d) 25° 31' to 26° 20' West

9. Which type of soil is found in Madhepura District?
(a) Black Soil
(b) Alluvial Soil
(c) Old Alluvial Soil
(d) Khaddar Soil

10. What is the sex ratio of Madhepura District as per the 2011 census?
(a) 932/1000 Male
(b) 902/1000 Male
(c) 911/1000 Male
(d) 948/1000 Male

11. What is the area of Purnia District?
(a) 3510 sq.km.
(b) 3045 sq.km.
(c) 3018 sq.km.
(d) 3229 sq.km.

12. Which of the following sub-divisions is not a part of Purnia District?
(a) Araria
(b) Banmankhi
(c) Dhamdaha
(d) Baisi

13. How many divisions are there in Purnia District?
(a) 12 (b) 14
(c) 16 (d) 18

14. What is the number of Panchayats in Purnia District?
(a) 260 (b) 280
(c) 246 (d) 235

15. Narasumha Avtar Pillar is a scenic spot of which district of Bihar?
(a) Gaya (b) Araria
(c) Buxar (d) Purnia

16. **Araria district was carved out from which district?**
(a) Purnia (b) Buxar
(c) Gaya (d) Patna

17. **Farbesganj is a sub-division of which district of Bihar?**
(a) Banka (b) Araria
(c) Munger (d) Purnia

18. **Which of the following divisions is not a part of Araria District?**
(a) Raniganj
(b) Bhargaon
(c) Chausa
(d) Plassey

19. **How many Legislative Assembly Constituencies does the Araria district have?**
(a) 5 (b) 8
(c) 4 (d) 6

20. **What is the longitudinal expanse of Araria District?**
(a) 87° 28' East
(b) 87° 28' West
(c) 87° 28' North
(d) 87° 28' South

Answers

1. (b)	**2.** (c)	**3.** (d)	**4.** (a)
5. (b)	**6.** (c)	**7.** (d)	**8.** (a)
9. (b)	**10.** (c)	**11.** (d)	**12.** (a)
13. (b)	**14.** (c)	**15.** (d)	**16.** (a)
17. (b)	**18.** (c)	**19.** (d)	**20.** (a)

SET-120

1. **What is the population density of Araria District (as per 2011 census)**
(a) 900 per sq.km.
(b) 993 per sq.km.
(c) 980 per sq.km.
(d) 890 per sq.km.

2. **Flax industry is the major industry of which district in Bihar?**
(a) Saran (b) Siwan
(c) Araria (d) Shivhar

3. **Mahananda River is the most important river of which district of Bihar?**
(a) Bhagalpur (b) Katihar
(c) Gaya (d) Kishanganj

4. **Pothia division comes under which district of Bihar?**
(a) Kishanganj
(b) Buxar
(c) Madhubani
(d) Siwan

5. **How many revenue villages come under Kishanganj District?**
(a) 792 (b) 802
(c) 710 (d) 912

6. **Which of the following Legislative Assembly Constituencies does not come within Kishanganj District?**
(a) Bahadurganj
(b) Thakurganj
(c) Nathnagar
(d) Kochadhaman

7. **Which type of soil mostly occurs in Kishanganj District?**
(a) Alluvial Soil
(b) Tal Soil
(c) Old Alluvial Soil
(d) Terai Soil

8. **What is the female literacy rate of Kishanganj District?**
(a) 46.8% (b) 44%
(c) 50.25% (d) 53.2%

9. **In which year was the Katihar District constituted?**
(a) 1980 (b) 1973
(c) 1985 (d) 1970

10. **Barsoi sub-division comes under which district of Bihar?**
(a) Kishanganj
(b) Bhagalpur
(c) Katihar
(d) Buxar

11. **How many divisions are there in Katihar District of Bihar?**
(a) 18 (b) 14
(c) 12 (d) 16

12. Which of the following divisions is not included in Katihar District?

(a) Bihpur (b) Kurmela
(c) Falka (d) Mansi

13. What is population density of Katihar District as per 2011 census?

(a) 988 per sq.km.
(b) 998 per sq.km.
(c) 1025 per sq.km.
(d) 1005 per sq.km.

14. Jute and Paper industries are the main industries of which district?

(a) Patna (b) Buxar
(c) Siwan (d) Katihar

15. What is the area of Bhagalpur District?

(a) 2569 sq.km.
(b) 2610 sq.km.
(c) 2809 sq.km.
(d) 2408 sq.km.

16. Kahalgaon sub-division comes under which district of Bihar?

(a) Banka
(b) Bhagalpur
(c) Lakhisarai
(d) Khagaria

17. Which of the following divisions does not come under Bhagalpur district?

(a) Bihpur (b) Gopalpur
(c) Pothia (d) Nathnagar

18. How many Panchayats are there in Bhagalpur District?

(a) 280 (b) 310
(c) 298 (d) 242

19. Bihpur and Kahalgaon Legislative Constituencies come under which district of Bihar?

(a) Bhagalpur (b) Gaya
(c) Buxar (d) Banka

20. As per the 2011 census, what is the population density of Bhagalpur district?

(a) 1100 per sq.km.
(b) 1182 per sq.km.
(c) 1210 per sq.km.
(d) 1042 per sq.km.

Answers

1. (b)	**2.** (c)	**3.** (d)	**4.** (a)
5. (b)	**6.** (c)	**7.** (a)	**8.** (a)
9. (b)	**10.** (c)	**11.** (d)	**12.** (a)
13. (d)	**14.** (d)	**15.** (a)	**16.** (b)
17. (c)	**18.** (d)	**19.** (a)	**20.** (b)

SET-121

1. As per the 2011 census what is the male literacy rate of Bhagalpur District?

(a) 75.2% (b) 76.6%
(c) 70.3% (d) 68.1%

2. Banka district was carved out from which district?

(a) Lakhisarai (b) Munger
(c) Madhubani (d) Bhagalpur

3. Which of the following divisions is not a part of Banka district?

(a) Bariarpur (b) Rajan
(c) Dhuriya (d) Chandan

4. What is the number of panchayats in Banka District?

(a) 200 (b) 185
(c) 198 (d) 210

5. Amarpur constituency comes in which district of Bihar?

(a) Patna (b) Buxar
(c) Banka (d) Siwan

6. What is the population density of Banka district?

(a) 600 per sq.km.
(b) 720 per sq.km.
(c) 810 per sq.km.
(d) 674 per sq.km.

7. What is the literacy rate of Banka district?

(a) 58.2% (b) 60.2%
(c) 56.6% (d) 64.4%

8. When was Mungar district constituted?
(a) 1830 (b) 1832
(c) 1836 (d) 1840

9. How many divisions are there in Munger district?
(a) 8 (b) 7
(c) 9 (d) 5

10. Tarapur is a Legislative Assembly constituency of which district?
(a) Banka (b) Lakhisarai
(c) Siwan (d) Munger

11. What is the longitudinal expanse of Munger district?
(a) 85º 45' to 86º 45' East
(b) 85º 45' to 86º 45' West
(c) 85º 45' to 86º 45' North
(d) 85º 45' to 86º 45' South

12. What is the male literacy rate of Munger district?
(a) 72.2% (b) 77.7%
(c) 68.1% (d) 74.3%

13. What is the area of Lakhisarai District?
(a) 1310 sq.km.
(b) 1280 sq.km.
(c) 1228 sq.km.
(d) 1120 sq.km.

14. Which of the following is a division of Lakhisarai District?
(a) Bhagalpur
(b) Purnia
(c) Katihar
(d) Munger

15. Which of the following blocks does not come in Lakhisarai District?
(a) Amarpur
(b) Pipariya
(c) Suryagarh
(d) Halsi

16. Which of the following is legislative assembly constituency of Lakhisarai District?
(a) Munger
(b) Suryagarh
(c) Tarapur
(d) Banka

17. As per 2011 census, what is the male literacy rate of Lakhisarai District?
(a) 988/1000 Male
(b) 810/1000 Male
(c) 902/1000 Male
(d) 890/1000 Male

18. As per 2011 census, what is the male literacy rate of Lakhisarai District?
(a) 75.2% (b) 78.1%
(c) 64.6% (d) 71.3%

19. What is the latitudinal expanse of Lakhisarai District?
(a) 25º to 25º 20' North
(b) 25º to 25º 20' South
(c) 25º to 25º 20' East
(d) 25º to 25º 20' West

20. In which year wasa Sheikhpura District constituted?
(a) 1992 (b) 1994
(c) 1982 (d) 2000

Answers

1. (c)	**2.** (d)	**3.** (a)	**4.** (b)
5. (c)	**6.** (d)	**7.** (a)	**8.** (b)
9. (c)	**10.** (d)	**11.** (a)	**12.** (b)
13. (c)	**14.** (d)	**15.** (a)	**16.** (b)
17. (c)	**18.** (d)	**19.** (a)	**20.** (b)

SET-122

1. How many blocks are there in Sheikhpura District?
(a) 7 (b) 8
(c) 6 (d) 5

2. How many panchayats are there in Sheikhpura District?
(a) 50 (b) 45
(c) 6 (d) 54

3. Barbigha is a constituency of which district of Bihar?

(a) Sheikhpura
(b) Banka
(c) Lakhisarai
(d) Purnia

4. **How much is the total population of Sheikhpura District ?**
(a) 653641 (b) 636342
(c) 703110 (d) 681481

5. **What is the population density of Sheikhpura District?**
(a) 829 per sq.km.
(b) 980 per sq.km.
(c) 924 per sq.km.
(d) 894 per sq.km.

6. **What is the literacy rate of Sheikhpura District as per 2011 census?**
(a) 65.2% (b) 74.3%
(c) 60.8% (d) 63.9%

7. **What is the area of Jamui District?**
(a) 3098 per sq.km.
(b) 3100 per sq.km.
(c) 3210 per sq.km.
(d) 3302 per sq.km.

8. **Which of the following blocks does not come in Jamui District?**
(a) Chakai (b) Araria
(c) Khaira (d) Laxmipur

9. **Jamui district has a total of how many villages?**
(a) 1210 (b) 1400
(c) 1506 (d) 1800

10. **Sikandra is a legislative assembly constituency of which district?**
(a) Patna (b) Gaya
(c) Buxar (d) Jamui

11. **What is the latitudinal expanse of Jamui District?**
(a) 24º 55' North
(b) 24º 55' South
(c) 24º 55' East
(d) 24º 55' West

12. **As per the 2011 census, what was the incremental rate in decadal population of the Jamui District?**
(a) 28.2% (b) 25.8%
(c) 20.2% (d) 24.6%

13. **What is the sex ratio of Jamui District as per 2011 census?**
(a) 960/1000 Male
(b) 900/1000 Male
(c) 922/1000 Male
(d) 934/1000 Male

14. **Chandrashekhar Museum is a scenic spot of which district?**
(a) Munger
(b) Sheikhpura
(c) Buxar
(d) Jamui

15. **In which year was Khagaria District constituted?**
(a) 1980 (b) 1985
(c) 1910 (d) 1924

16. **Gorgi is a sub-division of which district of Bihar?**
(a) Sheikhpura
(b) Khagaria
(c) Jamui
(d) Banka

17. **What is the number of panchayats in Khagaria District?**
(a) 110 (b) 150
(c) 129 (d) 199

18. **Which of the following legislative assembly constituencies is not a part of Khagaria District?**
(a) Atauli (b) 150 Parbatta
(c) Beldaur (d) Suryagarh

19. **What is the longitudinal expanse of Khagaria District?**
(a) 86º 17' to 86º 52' East
(b) 86º 17' to 86º 52' West
(c) 86º 17' to 86º 52' North
(d) 86º 17' to 86º 52' South

20. **What is the population of Khagaria district as per 2011 census?**
(a) 18821241 (b) 1666886
(c) 1992231 (d) 1224321

Answers

1. (c)	2. (d)	3. (a)	4. (b)
5. (c)	6. (d)	7. (a)	8. (b)
9. (c)	10. (d)	11. (a)	12. (b)
13. (c)	14. (d)	15. (a)	16. (b)
17. (c)	18. (d)	19. (a)	20. (b)

SET-123

1. **What is the male literacy rate of Khagaria District as per 2011 census?**
(a) 61.4% (b) 72.4%
(c) 65.3% (d) 68.6%

2. **Slate industry is a major industry of which district of Bihar?**
(a) Madhubani
(b) Purnia
(c) Vaishali
(d) Khagaria

3. **Begusarai district was carved from which other district?**
(a) Darbhanga
(b) Buxar
(c) Gaya
(d) Saharsa

4. **In which year was the Begusarai District constituted?**
(a) 1980 (b) 1972
(c) 1982 (d) 1967

5. **What is the area of Begusarai District?**
(a) 1907 sq. km.
(b) 1981 sq. km.
(c) 1918 sq. km.
(d) 2012 sq. km.

6. **What of the following sub-division does not come under Begusarai District?**
(a) Manjhaul
(b) Belia
(c) Bakhari
(d) Jamui

7. **Dandari block comes in which district of Bihar?**
(a) Begusarai
(b) Saharsa
(c) Madhepura
(d) Supaul

8. **Which of the following legislative assembly constituencies does not come in Begusarai District?**
(a) Bachhawara
(b) Atauli
(c) Matihani
(d) Sahebpur Kamaal

9. **As per 2011 census, what is the population density of Begusarai District?**
(a) 1898 per sq. km.
(b) 1610 per sq. km.
(c) 1549 per sq. km.
(d) 1910 per sq. km.

10. **As per 2011 census, what was the decadal (2001-2011) Incremental rate in population of Begusarai District?**
(a) 28.2% (b) 22.1%
(c) 24.8% (d) 26.4%

11. **Between 2001 to 2011, by how much per cent did the literacy rate of Bihar Increase?**
(a) 17.9% (b) 18.6%
(c) 19% (d) 21.1%

12. **How many universities are there in Bihar state presently?**
(a) 12 (b) 17
(c) 19 (d) 22

13. **Which programme was started in Bihar to encourage vocational education for girls?**
(a) Girls Vocational Test
(b) Chief Minister Girls Education Scheme
(c) Gyan Jyoti Vocational Test
(d) Hunar Programme

14. When was Bihar education project council established?
(a) 1989 (b) 1995
(c) 1988 (d) 1991

15. When was 'Literate India Campaign' started by the central government?
(a) September 8, 2009
(b) September 10, 2009
(c) September 15, 2009
(d) September 6, 2009

16. With what motive was the 'Akshay Aanchal Yojana' started?
(a) For male literacy
(b) For female literacy
(c) For literacy of differently abled
(d) All of the above

17. Which year was the Patna University established?
(a) 1920 (b) 1925
(c) 1917 (d) 1914

18. Bihar Agriculture University is situated in which area of the Bihar state?
(a) Patna (b) Nalanda
(c) Gaya (d) Sabaur

19. Maharaja Laxmishwar Singh Museum is situated in which district of Bihar?
(a) Begusarai
(b) Buxar
(c) Madhubani
(d) Darbhanga

20. A total of how many integrated child development schemes are being run in Bihar state?
(a) 500 (b) 544
(c) 600 (d) 617

Answers

1. (c)	**2.** (d)	**3.** (d)	**4.** (b)
5. (c)	**6.** (d)	**7.** (a)	**8.** (b)
9. (c)	**10.** (d)	**11.** (b)	**12.** (b)
13. (d)	**14.** (d)	**15.** (b)	**16.** (d)
17. (c)	**18.** (d)	**19.** (d)	**20.** (b)

SET-124

1. What is the ratio of expenditure shared between the centre and state in Rajiv Gandhi's Girls Empowerment Scheme?
(a) 70 : 30 (b) 80 : 30
(c) 60 : 40 (d) 75 : 25

2. Which year was the Mithila Lalit Museum established?
(a) 1985 (b) 1983
(c) 1980 (d) 1981

3. Which year was the Bihar State Sports Council established?
(a) 1961 (b) 1964
(c) 1968 (d) 1970

4. Which year did the game of football began in Bihar?
(a) 1902 (b) 1897
(c) 1892 (d) 1880

5. Sanjay Gandhi Mini Stadium is situated in which district of Bihar?
(a) Chhapra (b) Gaya
(c) Patna (d) Buxar

6. Which of the following stadiums is not located in Patna district?
(a) Secretarial Indoor Stadium
(b) Mithilesh Stadium
(c) Moinul-Haq Stadium
(d) Rajendra Stadium

7. With which sport is Jaipal Singh Cup associated?
(a) Hockey
(b) Football
(c) Tennis
(d) Cricket

8. President cup is associated with which sport?
(a) Cricket (b) Football
(c) Volleyball (d) Kho-Kho

9. Hemant Trophy is associated with which sport?
(a) Football (b) Polo
(c) Cricket (d) Hockey

10. **With which sport is Saba Karim associated?**
(a) Football
(b) Hockey
(c) Table Tannis
(d) Cricket

11. **Which of the following players plays football?**
(a) Badri Prasad
(b) Subroto Banerjee
(c) Dinesh Mohan
(d) Rajesh Chauhan

12. **With which sport is Jaipal Singh associated?**
(a) Cricket
(b) Hockey
(c) Carrom
(d) Karate

13. **Pranav Sinha is associated with which sport?**
(a) Football
(b) Basketball
(c) Shooting
(d) Hockey

14. **With which sport is Anjana Jha associated?**
(a) Tennis
(b) Badminton
(c) Softball
(d) Chess

15. **Dinesh Mohan is associated with which sport?**
(a) Tennis
(b) Football
(c) Hockey
(d) Chess

16. **With which sport is Chittranjan Sinha associated?**
(a) Chess
(b) Badminton
(c) Baseball
(d) Archery

17. **Which of the following players is not associated with baseball?**
(a) Sunil Singh
(b) Ajay Tiwari
(c) Helen Soy
(d) Smita Pal

18. **Kumar Shyamnand Sinha is associated with which sport?**
(a) Cricket
(b) Hockey
(c) Wrestling
(d) Billiards

19. **Which of the following is a Carrom player?**
(a) Rashmi Kumari
(b) Shalini Srivastava
(c) Ananya Anand
(d) Pooja Kumari

20. **Nand D. Prasad is associated with which player?**
(a) Carrom
(b) Karate
(c) Hockey
(d) Cricket

Answers

1. (a)	**2.** (d)	**3.** (a)	**4.** (b)
5. (c)	**6.** (d)	**7.** (d)	**8.** (b)
9. (c)	**10.** (d)	**11.** (b)	**12.** (b)
13. (c)	**14.** (d)	**15.** (a)	**16.** (b)
17. (c)	**18.** (d)	**19.** (a)	**20.** (b)

SET-125

1. **Which of the following players is not associated with athletics?**
(a) Saroj Lakda
(b) Shivnath Singh
(c) Satyajit Shakt
(d) Arvind Panna

2. **Prachi sharma is Associated with which sport?**
(a) Kho-kho
(b) Tennis
(c) Carrom
(d) Softball

3. **With which sport is Nirmal Kumar Singh associated?**

(a) Archery
(b) Baseball
(c) Football
(d) Cricket

4. **With which sport is Chetna Solanki associated?**
(a) Karate
(b) Pole Vault
(c) Football
(d) Kho-Kho

5. **With which sport is Nikaj Kumar associated?**
(a) Archery
(b) Cricket
(c) Basketball
(d) Hockey

6. **With which sport is Indrajeet Singh associated?**
(a) Tennis
(b) Chess
(c) Carrom
(d) Weightlifting

7. **With which sport is Sanjeev Shankar associated?**
(a) Table Tennis
(b) Hockey
(c) Cricket
(d) Football

8. **Where is the headquarters of Bihar State Sports Authority located?**
(a) Gaya
(b) Patna
(c) Buxar
(d) Siwan

9. **Which is the highest state of Bihar in terms of area?**
(a) Rohtas
(b) Buxar
(c) West Champaran
(d) Gaya

10. **How many districts of Bihar are contiguous with boundary of Uttar Pradesh?**
(a) 6 (b) 9
(c) 11 (d) 8

11. **Forest are spread in how much area of Bihar?**
(a) 7.21% (b) 10.2%
(c) 15% (d) 18.43%

12. **The name of the mobile app launched by Agriculture Department in Bihar is –**
(a) Bihar app
(b) Bihan app
(c) Vihan app
(d) Veer app

13. **According to the survey, what is the per capita electricity (energy) consumption in the state?**
(a) 350 kilowatt
(b) 250 kilowatt
(c) 450 kilowatt
(d) 150 kilowatt

14. **The aim of an ambitious scheme, solar street scheme, ongoing in Bihar is –**
(a) To free the village from defecation in open.
(b) To make available solar energy to villages.
(c) To encourage formation of self-help group in villages.
(d) To open unit of ethanol production in villages.

15. **Which App has been launched in Bihar to issue warning atleast 40 minutes before incident of striking of lightning within area of 20 km area?**
(a) Indra App
(b) Indrabraj App
(c) Braj App
(d) Twarit App

16. **Compared to the last year, the total expenditure of the state increased to become how much?**
(a) 1,65,696 crore
(b) 1,28,168 crore

(c) 1,30,126 crore
(d) 1,50,235 crore

17. The person appointed as a judge of the Supreme Court before assuming the office is administered oath by
(a) Vice President
(b) President, or any other person appointed by him
(c) Chief Justice of India
(d) None of the above

18. Who was the first Chief Justice of India?
(a) Mehar Chand Mahajan
(b) A.K Sarkar
(c) Harilal J Kania
(d) S.R Das

19. Which one of the following is the oldest High Court of India?
(a) Bombay High Court
(b) Madras High Court
(c) Calcutta High Court
(d) Andhra Pradesh High Court

20. The judges of the Supreme Court can tender their resignation by writing to whom?
(a) President
(b) Prime Minister
(c) Law Minister
(d) Attorney General of India

Answers

1. (c)	**2.** (d)	**3.** (a)	**4.** (b)
5. (c)	**6.** (d)	**7.** (a)	**8.** (b)
9. (c)	**10.** (d)	**11.** (a)	**12.** (b)
13. (a)	**14.** (c)	**15.** (b)	**16.** (a)
17. (b)	**18.** (c)	**19.** (c)	**20.** (a)

❑❑❑

Part–III
Solved Papers

65th, Bihar Combined Solved Papers Re-examination-2020

1. The name of the Union Minister of State for Home Affairs from Bihar is:
(a) RK Singh
(b) Nithyananda Roy
(c) Ashwini Kumar
(d) RV Paswan
(e) None of the above/more than one of the above

2. Where did Gautam Buddha give his first sermon?
(a) Pataliputra (b) Sarnath
(c) Gaya (d) Vaishali
(e) None of the above/more than one of the above

3. Who was the president of the first Jain 'Sangiti' called in Pataliputra?
(a) Vasumitra (b) Sthirmati
(c) Sthulbhadra (d) Sudharman
(e) None of the above/more than one of the above

4. Who was the President of Gaya session of Indian National Congress in 1922?
(a) CR Das
(b) SP Sinha
(c) Dr. Rajendra Prasad
(d) Ras Bihari Bose
(e) None of the above/more than one of the above

5. Who raised the question of Indigo growers of Bihar during the Lucknow Session of the Indian National Congress in 1916?
(a) Rajkumarukla
(b) Dr. Rajendra Prasad
(c) JB Kripalani
(d) Sampoornanand Sinha
(e) None of the above/more than one of the above

6. Which ruler shifted his capital to Pataliputra?
(a) Bimbisara
(b) Ajatshatru
(b) Udayin
(d) Chandragupta Maurya
(e) None of the above/more than one of the above

7. In which movement the farmers of Bihar denied to pay 'chowkidari-kar'?
(a) Champaran Satyagraha
(b) Non-cooperation movement
(c) Indigenous movement
(d) Civil disobedience movement

8. Which of the following is the latest in the geological history of Bihar?
(a) Dharwad rock of South-East
(b) level part
(c) Bihar Maidan
(d) Vast part of south-west
(e) None of the above/more than one of the above

9. In which of the following areas of Bihar old alluvial soil expansion is found?

(a) Patna and Gaya
(b) Purnia and Gaya
(c) Purnia and Patna
(d) Darbhanga and Patna
(e) None of the above/more than one of the above

10. Barauni Refinery in Bihar was built in collaboration with
(a) Germany
(b) South Korea
(c) Soviet Russia
(d) France
(e) None of the above/more than one of the above

11. The famous animal fair of Bihar is held on the day of Kartik Purnima -
(a) In Gaya
(b) in Madhubani
(c) In Bhagalpur
(d) in Sonepur
(e) None of the above/more than one of the above

12. Traditional water conservation irrigation system prevalent in South Bihar is called-
(a) Ahar-pine (b) Nahar-pine
(c) Chahar-Pine (d) Sahar-Pine
(e) None of the above/more than one of the above

13. At which of the following places does the Kosi river merge with the River Ganga?
(a) Kursela (b) Vaishali
(c) Hajipur (d) Jamalpur
(e) None of the above/more than one of the above

14. In which district Vikramshila Gangetic Dolphin Sanctuary is located in Bihar?
(a) Bhagalpur (b) Patna
(c) Buxar (d) Nalanda

15. To ensure 'water in every household' for all rural households, which year has been set as the target year by the Jal Jeevan Mission?
(a) 2022 (b) 2025
(b) 2026 (d) 2024
(e) None of the above/more than one of the above

16. Per Capita Gross State Domestic Product (GSDP) of Bihar in 2017-18 was ₹ 42,242 at the present prices. What is the per capita index on Fixed Prices (Keeping the base year as 2011-12)?
(a) ₹ 31,316 (b) ₹ 30,000
(c) ₹ 21,316 (d) ₹ 20,000
(e) None of the above/more than one of the above

17. Which district of Bihar in 2018-19, was amongst the three richest districts (on the basis of per capita income) at constant prices (keeping the base year as 2011-12)?
(a) Madhepura (b) Supaul
(c) Begusarai (d) Shivhar
(e) None of the above/more than one of the above

18. Approximately what percentage of growth is estimated in revenue surplus in Bihar in 2018-19 as compared to 2017-18?
(a) 40% (b) 50%
(c) 54% (d) 44%
(e) None of the above/more than one of the above

19. Total production of coarse cereals in Bihar (in lakh tonnes) in 2017-18 and its growth rates between 2013-14 and 2017-18 were as under respectively.
(a) 2.15; 5% (b) 4.0; 6%
(c) 3.15; 6% (d) 5.15; 4%
(e) None of the above/more than one of the above

20. Jeevika has achieved unprecedented success in promoting social development in Bihar. The estimated number of Gs formed till September 2018 was

(a) 7.17 Lakh
(b) 9.01 lakh
(c) 9.17 lakhs
(d) 8.17 lakhs
(e) None of the above/more than one of the above

21. Who founded Jamshedpur Labor Association in 1920?
(a) SN Haldar
(b) Byomkesh Chakraborty
(c) Ramesh Paul
(d) Swami Vishwananda
(e) None of the above/more than one of the above

22. Who wrote 'Kisan Kya karein'?
(a) Swami Sahaj Ananda Saraswathi
(b) Karyanandarma
(c) Baba Ramachandra
(d) All of the above
(e) None of the above/more than one of the above

23. Patna Yuva Sangh was established in which year?
(a) In 1917
(b) In 1925
(c) In 1927
(d) In 1930
(e) None of the above/more than one of the above

Answers

1. (b)	**2.** (b)	**3.** (c)	**4.** (a)	**5.** (a)	**6.** (c)	**7.** (d)	**8.** (c)
9. (a)	**10.** (c)	**11.** (d)	**12.** (a)	**13.** (a)	**14.** (a)	**15.** (d)	**16.** (a)
17. (c)	**18.** (d)	**19.** (c)	**20.** (d)	**21.** (a)	**22.** (a)	**23.** (c)	

65th, Bihar Combined Exam Solved Papers-2019

1. Who led the revolt of 1857 in Bihar?
(a) Babu Amar Singh
(b) Hare Krishna Singh
(c) Kunwar Singh
(d) Raja Shahzada Singh
(e) None of the above/above More than one of the above

2. Who led the farmers in Bihar during the Non-Cooperation Movement?
(a) Swami Vidyananda
(b) Rajkumarukla
(c) Sri Krishna Singh
(d) JB Sen
(e) None of the above/ More than one of the above

3. Who is considered to be the creator of modern Bihar?
(a) Sachchidanand Sinha
(b) Kumar Kalika Prasad Sinha
(c) Sir Ganesh Singh
(d) Acharya Narendra Dev
(e) None of the above/above More than one of the above

4. Who constituted the Bihar Provincial Kisan Sabha?
(a) Swami Sahaj Ananda Sarasvati
(b) Ram Sundar Singh

(c) Gangaaran Sinha
(d) Ramanand Mishra
(e) None of the above/above More than one of the above

5. In which year did the Dutch East India Company set up its factory in Patna?

(a) 1601 (b) 1632
(c) 1774 (d) 1651
(e) None of the above/above More than one of the above

6. Who formed Swaraj Dal in Bihar?

(a) Sri Krishna Singh
(b) Ramlalah
(c) Bankim Chandra Mitra
(d) Sachindranath Sanyal
(e) None of the above/above More than one of the above

7. Ashoka is commonly known as

(a) Chakravarty
(b) Priyadarshi
(c) Dharmadeva
(d) Dharmakirti
(e) None of the above/ More than one of the above

8. Which of the following districts is not of Dharwad land level structure?

(a) Munger (b) Rohtas
(c) Jamui (d) Nawada
(e) None of the above/above More than one of the above

9. The number of districts along the Ganga in the State of Bihar is

(a) 21 (b) 17
(c) 12 (d) 6
(e) None of the above/above More than one of the above

10. Which of the following wildlife sanctuaries is located in Munger district of Bihar?

(a) Valmiki (b) Rajgir
(c) Bhimbandha (d) Gautam Buddha
(e) None of the above/above More than one of the above

11. Which district of Bihar has recorded the highest sex ratio as per census 2011?

(a) Siwan (b) Gopalganj
(c) Saran (d) Kishanganj
(e) None of the above/above More than one of the above

12. Which of the following districts is surrounded by the densest autumn forest area?

(a) West Champaran
(b) Gaya
(c) Kaimur
(d) Nawada
(e) None of the above/above More than one of the above

13. River Ganga is the longest in which district of Bihar?

(a) Bhagalpur (b) Katihar
(c) Patna (d) Begusarai
(e) None of the above/above More than one of the above

14. As per census 2011, which district of Bihar has recorded the most dense population (per square km)?

(a) Shivhar (b) Vaishali
(c) Patna (d) Darbhanga
(e) None of the above/ More than one of the above

15. Which of the following is part of river Ganga valley?

(a) Conch
(b) Northern Cuckoo
(c) Southern Cuckoo
(d) Baraker
(e) None of the above/ More than one of the above

16. Where was the Krishi Kumbh Mela, 2019 held in Bihar?

(a) Champaran (b) Motihari
(c) Rajgir (d) Gaya
(e) None of the above/ More than one of the above

17. As per NITI Aayog's Health Index 2019, the state of Bihar has a score of:
(a) 30.12 (b) 30.13
(c) 32.11 (d) 32.12
(e) None of the above/above More than one of the above

18. As per Census 2011, the child sex ratio in Bihar was:
(a) 935 (b) 934
(c) 933 (d) 932
(e) None of the above/above More than one of the above

19. The growth rate of tertiary sector in Bihar during 2017-18 was:
(a) 14.2% (b) 14.6%
(c) 15.6% (d) 15.2%
(e) None of the above/above More than one of the above

20. Antyodaya Programme was first launched in which state?
(a) Bihar
(b) Tamil Nadu
(c) Andhra Pradesh
(d) Rajasthan
(e) None of the above/above More than one of the above

21. Who wrote the book 'Desher Katha'?
(a) Sakharam Ganesh Devaskar
(b) Rajendra Prasad
(c) Nivaran Chandra
(d) Murli Mohan Prasad
(e) None of the above/above More than one of the above

22. Who was the editor of 'Searchlight' newspaper in Bihar?
(a) Abdul Bari
(b) Lambodar Mukherjee
(c) Murli Mohan Prasad
(d) Ramanand Chatterjee
(e) None of the above/above More than one of the above

23. Who formed the Bihar Samajwadi Party in 1931?
(a) Phoolan Prasad Verma
(b) Swami Yogananda
(c) Narhari Parikh
(d) Dadabhai Naoroji
(e) None of the above/above More than one of the above

24. Who was the Chief Justice of Patna high court who administered the oath of office to Fagu Chauhan as governor of Bihar in July 2019?
(a) Hon'ble Mukesh Shah
(b) Hon'ble AP Sahi
(b) Hon'ble Rekha Manharlal Doshit
(c) Hon'ble Deepak Mishra
(d) None of the above/ More than one of the above

25. What is the significance of Bihar Day, which is celebrated on 22nd March every year?
(a) On this day, the State Reorganization Commission announced the state of Bihar
(b) Bihar was expelled from the United Provinces on this day in 1873
(c) To remember Bihar's separation from Bengal presidency in 1912
(d) To celebrate the naming of Bihar by Muslim rulers in the 12th century
(e) None of the above/above More than one of the above

26. Which of the following States has never been granted Special Category Status (SCS) by the Central Government?
(a) Bihar
(b) Sikkim
(c) Himachal Pradesh
(d) Jammu and Kashmir
(e) None of the above/above More than one of the above

27. At which place Yusuf Shah Chak, the last Muslim ruler of the Kashmir Valley who was deported to Bihar by the Mughal Emperor Akbar, is buried.

(a) In Pataliputra
(b) in Rajgir
(c) In Munger
(d) In Nalanda
(e) None of the above/above More than one of the above

28. What is the tagline of Bihar State Tourism Development Corporation?

(a) Bright Bihar
(b) Bihar for all of us
(c) Blissful Bihar
(d) Bihar is the best
(e) None of the above/above More than one of the above

29. On which river did Prime Minister Narendra Modi recently lay the foundation stone of Mandal Dam Project?

(a) Kosi (b) Old Gandak
(c) Phalgu (d) North Cuckoo
(e) None of the above/above More than one of the above

30. Experts visited which of the following districts for the first documentation of Megalithic Site of Bihar in July 2019?

(a) Patna (b) Kaimur
(c) Madhubani (d) Banka
(e) None of the above/above More than one of the above

Answers

1. (c)	**2.** (a)	**3.** (a)	**4.** (a)	**5.** (b)	**6.** (a)	**7.** (b)	**8.** (b)
9. (c)	**10.** (c)	**11.** (b)	**12.** (a)	**13.** (c)	**14.** (a)	**15.** (b)	**16.** (b)
17. (c)	**18.** (a)	**19.** (b)	**20.** (d)	**21.** (a)	**22.** (a)	**23.** (e)	**24.** (a)
25. (c)	**26.** (a)	**27.** (d)	**28.** (c)	**29.** (d)	**30.** (b)		

64th, Bihar Combined Exam Solved Papers-2018

1. In which year Bihar became an Indian State?

(a) In 1911 (b) In 1912
(c) In 1936 (d) In 2000
(e) None of the above/more than one of the above

2. Which of the following is expectedly the oldest one from the geo-theoretical point of view of Bihar?

(a) Rohtas Plateau
(b) North-Western Hills
(c) Khaar Gapur Hills
(d) North Ganga Maidan
(e) None of the above/more than one of the above

3. Till 2018, Patna district was bordered by how many districts of Bihar.

(a) 7 (b) 8
(c) 9 (d) 10
(e) None of the above/more than one of the above

4. The area covered by the abyss of Bihar is
(a) From Pahari Mitti
(b) From Kachari Mitti
(c) From regur mitti
(d) From terai mitti
(e) None of the above/more than one of the above

5. Amongst all the states, according to minimum literacy rate (2011 census), Bihar is at position -
(a) first (b) second
(c) third (d) fourth
(e) None of the above/more than one of the above

6. What is the position of Bihar from the point of view of jute products from among the States of India?
(a) first (b) second
(c) third (d) fourth
(e) None of the above/more than one of the above

7. What are the types of industries in Bihar with expectations and possibilities?
(a) Oil-Refinery
(b) forest-based industry
(c) Sand-Mining Industry
(d) agriculture-based industry
(e) None of the above/more than one of the above

8. As per Census of India 2011, density of population is severe in which of the following States
(a) Kerala (b) Haryana
(c) Bihar (d) Uttar Pradesh
(e) None of the above/more than one of the above

9. What is the proportion of people in the State of Bihar as per Census of India 2011?
(a) 893 (b) 916
(c) 918 (d) 925
(e) None of the above/more than one of the above

10. 'Bihar Financial Survey' was published for which year for the first time?
(a) 2004-05 (b) 2006-07
(c) 2008-09 (d) 2009-10
(e) None of the above/more than one of the above

11. During April-June 2018 in Bihar, which sector attracted maximum FDI Equity in foreign exchange?
(a) service sector
(b) ispat industry
(c) processing industry in agriculture
(d) cement industry
(e) None of the above/more than one of the above

12. What percentage of population is employed in agriculture in 2017-18 in Bihar?
(a) 65 (b) 67
(c) 68 (d) 70
(e) None of the above/more than one of the above

13. What was the rate of economic growth in 2016-17 in the state of Bihar?
(a) 6.3% (b) 7.3%
(c) 8.3% (d) 9.3%
(e) None of the above/more than one of the above

14. At which place did Kunwar Singh participate in revolt of 1857 against Britishers?
(a) Arrah
(b) Patna
(c) Betiyah
(d) Varanasi
(e) None of the above/more than one of the above

15. At which place did the Adivasis revolt against Britishers?

(a) Bihar (b) Punjab
(c) Sindh (d) Kathiaavad
(e) None of the above/more than one of the above

16. During the salt satyagraha, people in Bihar protested against the government by being against salt manufacturing and which other tax?

(a) watchman
(b) elephant
(c) development
(d) debris
(e) None of the above/more than one of the above

17. In February 1938, the elected Government of Bihar resigned for what reason?

(a) India's participation in the war
(b) Being against British rule on being beckoned by Gandhi.
(c) Heavy tax imposed by British
(d) On releasing the political prisoners

18. Who was associated with Bihar Kisan Sabha?

(a) Swami Sahaj Ananda
(b) Karyanand Sharma
(c) Rahul Sanskrityayan
(d) Yadunandan Sharma
(e) None of the above/more than one of the above

19. On March 16, 2018, in which district of Bihar did the Deputy Chief Minister Sushil Modi, inaugurate state's first 'Startup hub'?

(a) Motihari (b) Munger
(c) Patna (d) Arrah
(e) None of the above/more than one of the above

20. On 22 March, 2018, on the 106th Foundation Day of the State of Bihar, who released a book titled 'Neel ke Dhabbe' in Patna?

(a) Vice President of India Venkaiah Naidu
(b) Prime Minister Narendra Modi
(c) Home Minister Rajnath Singh
(d) Lok Sabha Speaker Smt. Sumitra Mahajan
(e) None of the above/more than one of the above

21. Manufactured in Madhepura Locomotive Factory, India's most powerful electric rail engine's potential is :

(a) 9000 horsepower
(b) 10000 horsepower
(c) 11000 horsepower
(d) 12000 horsepower
(e) None of the above/more than one of the above

22. On 22 April, 2018, where did the Prime Minister Narendra Modi, address a national conference of Swachchagrahis?

(a) Motihari (b) Patna
(c) Kishanganj (d) Katihar
(e) None of the above/more than one of the above

23. On which airport did NDMA practice mock drills based on CBRN emergency in April 2018?

(a) IGI-New Delhi
(b) LNJP-Patna
(c) CSI-Mumbai
(d) DABH-Indore
(e) None of the above/more than one of the above

24. As per a report, at which place Patna is placed amongst 20 cities observed between December 2017 to February 2018 from the point of availability of 4G signals?

(a) first (b) second
(c) 19th (d) 20th
(e) None of the above/more than one of the above

25. In which city of Bihar Sulabh International has planned to start a project named 'Sulabh Jal' to provide drinking water at affordable rates?

(a) Patna (b) Bhagalpur
(c) Darbhanga (d) Purniya
(e) None of the above/more than one of the above

26. What is false regarding The Chief Minister of Bihar's, Kanya Utthan Yojana?

(a) 7,221 crore is proposed as annual expenditure for this program.
(b) Education, Health and Social-Welfare – These 3 departments are operating the program.
(c) ₹60,000 will be provided to each girl child on completion of education from first class to graduation
(d) ₹2,000 is provided to the family of the girl child at the time of birth
(e) None of the above/more than one of the above

27. The first Buddhist 'sangiti' was performed after the Mahaparinirvana of Lord Buddha.

(a) In Rajghar (Rajgir)
(b) In Gaya
(c) In Patliputra
(d) In Vaishali
(e) None of the above/more than one of the above

28. Who was the king of the golden land who established a Buddhist vihara in Nalanda and prayed to his messenger, Dwara Devpal, to donate five villages for its maintenance?

(a) Dharnindra
(b) Sangram Dhananjay
(c) Balputradev
(d) Churamarivarman
(e) None of the above/more than one of the above

29. The first description of Bakhtiyar Khilji's attack on Bihar was obtained from -

(a) Tareekh-e-hind
(b) Tabkat-a-Nasiri
(c) Taj-ul-Masir
(d) Tareekh-e-Mubarak from the royal
(e) None of the above/more than one of the above

30. When did the Government of Bengal Act approve the land acquisition in Bengal and Bihar by the tenants?

(a) 1868 (b) 1881
(c) 1885 (d) 1893
(e) None of the above/more than one of the above

31. When Bihar become an independent state in India?

(a) 1897 (b) 1905
(c) 1907 (d) 1912
(e) None of the above/more than one of the above

32. Who invited Gandhiji to Champaran?

(a) Rajendra Prasad
(b) Rajkumar Shukla
(c) Majhrul Haque
(d) Krishna Sahai
(e) None of the above/more than one of the above

33. When was Bihar socialist party formed?

(a) 1921 (b) 1927
(c) 1931 (d) 1934
(e) None of the above/more than one of the above

34. Which of the following led the first Congress Minister's council in Bihar?

(a) Anugrah Narayan Sinha

(b) Abdul Bari

(c) Jayaprakash Narayan

(d) Shri Krishna Sinha

(e) None of the above/more than one of the above

Answers

1. (b)	**2.** (c)	**3.** (c)	**4.** (b)	**5.** (a)	**6.** (b)	**7.** (d)	**8.** (c)
9. (c)	**10.** (b)	**11.** (a)	**12.** (e)	**13.** (e)	**14.** (a)	**15.** (a)	**16.** (a)
17. (d)	**18.** (e)	**19.** (c)	**20.** (a)	**21.** (d)	**22.** (a)	**23.** (b)	**24.** (a)
25. (c)	**26.** (e)	**27.** (a)	**28.** (c)	**29.** (b)	**30.** (c)	**31.** (d)	**32.** (b)
33. (d)	**34.** (d)						

63th, Bihar Combined Exam Solved Papers-2018

1. Swami Sahaj Ananda Sarasvati published a magazine called-

(a) Jan Kranti

(b) Hunkar

(c) Krishak Samachar

d) Vidrohi

(e) None of these/more than one of these

2. Who established a branch of the Anushilan Committee in Patna in the year 1913?

(a) Revathi Nag

(b) Yadunath Sarkar

(c) Sachindranath Sanyal

(d) Majhrul Haque

(e) None of these/more than one of these

3. Who formed the Kisan Sabha at Munger in 1922-23?

(a) Swami Sahaj Ananda Sarasvati

(b) Sri Krishna Singh

(c) Mohammad Zubaid

(d) KN Singh

(e) None of these/more than one of these

4. _____________ was the secretary of Bihar socialist party formed in 1934?

(a) Acharya Narendra Dev

(b) Jayaprakash Narayan

(c) Ramvriksha Benipuri

(d) Karpuri Thakur

(e) None of these/more than one of these

5. Who was a member of the Constituent Assembly of India from Bihar?

(a) AN Sinha

(b) Rajendra Prasad

(c) Jagjivan Ram

(d) Shyamanandan Prasad Mishra

(e) None of these/more than one of these

6. Who led the first Indian Cabinet formed in Bihar in the year 1937?

(a) Sri Krishna Singh
(b) Mohammad Yunus
(c) GS Lal
(d) Wahab Ali
(e) None of these/more than one of these

7. Who had Rajendra Prasad considered to be the originator of Pakistan?
(a) Mohammad Jinnah
(b) Lord Mountbatten
(c) Lord Minto
(d) Liaquat Ali Khan
(e) None of these/more than one of these

8. When was Patna Lawn named as Gandhi Maidan?
(a) During the Quit India Movement
(b) During Simon Commission Anti-Rally
(c) During Champaran Satyagraha
(d) On the occasion of India's independence
(e) None of these/more than one of these

9. Which of the following districts of Bihar do not share border with Nepal?
(a) Madhubani (b) Kishanganj
(c) Sitamarhi (d) Purnia
(e) None of these/more than one of these

10. Which of the following is the only UNESCO World Heritage Site in the State of Bihar, India?
(a) Mahabodhi Vihar
(b) Buddhist Monastery in Nalanda
(c) Ancient site of Vikramshila Monastery
(d) Tomb of Sher Shah Suri
(e) None of these/two are not included in the statement. More than one of these

11. Flood Super Thermal Power Stations (BSTPS) are located in which state?
(a) Bihar (b) Karnataka
(c) Rajasthan (d) Punjab
(e) None of these/more than one of these

12. When was the Bihar Provincial Kisan Sabha constituted?
(a) Year 1929 (b) Year 1930
(b) Year 1931 (d) Year 1932
(e) None of these/more than one of these

13. Under which Act did Bihar become a separate State?
(a) Government of India Act, 1935
(b) Government of India Act, 1919
(c) Indian Council Act, 1909
(d) Indian Independence Act,1947
(e) None of the above/more than one of the above

14. In Panchayati Raj institutions of which states 50% reservation of women has been validated?
(I) Bihar
(II) Uttarakhand
(III) Madhya Pradesh
(IV) Himachal Pradesh
(a) only II
(b) II and III
(c) II, III and IV
(d) I, II, III and IV

15. As per Census of India, 2011, literacy percentage in both men and women is the lowest in which state?
(a) Arunachal Pradesh
(b) Andhra Pradesh
(c) Bihar
(d) Jammu and Kashmir
(e) None of these/more than one of these

16. Average size of agricultural land holdings in Bihar as compared to that in other States is -
(a) minimum
(b) Second to minimum
(c) highest
(d) Second from highest
(e) None of these/more than one of these

17. Which State in India has the lowest latest per capita income at current prices?
(a) Bihar (b) Uttar Pradesh
(c) Odisha (d) Nagaland
(e) None of these/more than one of these

18. The latest annual per capita power consumption in Bihar is
(a) minimum
(b) Second to minimum
(c) highest
(d) Second from highest
(e) None of these/more than one of these

19. The length of road per one lakh population in Bihar is
(a) minimum
(b) Second to Minimum
(c) highest
(d) Second from highest
(e) None of these/more than one of these

20. Which of the following rivers is found meeting Ganga near Fatuha?
(a) Sone (b) Punpun
(c) Sakri (d) Balan
(e) None of these/more than one of these

21. According to the climate classification of Coppen, the climate of North Bihar can be represented by
(a) Cwg (b) Aw
(c) CA'w (d) CB'w
(e) None of these / more than one of these

22. Which soil is mostly found in Muzaffarpur, Darbhanga and Champaran districts?
(a) black soil
(b) new alluvial
(c) ancient alluvial
(d) red soil
(e) None of these/more than one of these

23. Bihar's highest jute producing district is -
(a) Siwan (b) Gaya
(c) Vaishali (d) Purnia
(e) None of these/more than one of these

24. Triveni Canal is built on which river?
(a) Kosi (b) Sone
(c) Gandak (d) Kamla
(e) None of these/more than one of these

25. Which place is the place of salvation of Mahavirji, the originator of Jainism?
(a) Maner (b) Rajgir
(c) Pavapuri (d) Jalan Fort
(e) None of these/more than one of these

26. Kaimur Plateau is famous for
(a) copper (b) limestone
(c) lithium (d) bauxite
(e) None of these/more than one of these

Answers

1. (b)	**2.** (c)	**3.** (e)	**4.** (b)	**5.** (e)	**6.** (b)	**7.** (c)	**8.** (e)
9. (d)	**10.** (e)	**11.** (a)	**12.** (a)	**13.** (a)	**14.** (d)	**15.** (c)	**16.** (b)
17. (a)	**18.** (a)	**19.** (b)	**20.** (b)	**21.** (a)	**22.** (b)	**23.** (d)	**24.** (c)
25. (c)	**26.** (b)						

61st, 62nd, Bihar Combined Exam Solved Papers-2017

1. **Who was the leader of the revolutionaries in Bihar during the revolution of 1857?**
   (a) Namdar Khan
   (b) Babu Kunwar Singh
   (c) Birsa Munda
   (d) Shankar Shah
   (e) None of the above/above More than one of the above
2. **On which day Birsa was caught sleeping?**
   (a) 1 February 1900
   (b) February 2nd, 1900
   (c) February 3rd, 1900
   (d) February 4th, 1900
   (e) None of the above/more than one of the above
3. **Who drew Gandhiji's attention to the exploitation of farmers by European indigo plantation owners?**
   (a) Baba Ramachandra
   (b) Rajkumar Shukla
   (c) Swami Sahaj Ananda Sarasvati
   (d) Shri Krishna Sinha
   (e) None of the above/more than one of the above
4. **Who left Patna College during the Non-Cooperation Movement while only 20 days were left for his examination?**
   (a) Rajendra Prasad
   (b) Braj Kishore
   (c) Jayaprakash Narayan
   (d) Shri Krishna Sinha
   (e) None of the above/more than one of the above
5. **Which lawyer from Bihar gave up his beneficial advocacy during the non-cooperation movement?**
   (a) Jayaprakash Narayan
   (b) Rajendra Prasad
   (c) Sahaj Ananda Sarasvati
   (d) Rajkumar Shukla
   (e) None of the above/more than one of the above
6. **According to census 2011, what is the position of Bihar in the country according to population?**
   (a) 1st (b) 2nd
   (c) 3rd (d) 4th
7. **Who was the founder of Karnat dynasty?**
   (a) Nanyadeva (b) Narasimha Dev
   (c) Vijaydev (d) Haridev
   (e) None of the above/more than one of the above
8. **Who was the first Muslim winner of Bihar?**
   (a) Malik Ibrahim
   (b) Iltutmish
   (c) Bakhtiyar Khilji
   (d) Ali Mardan Khilji
   (e) None of the above/more than one of the above
9. **Who was the last ruler of the Karnat dynasty?**
   (a) Hari Singh (b) Ram Singh
   (c) Mati Singh (d) Shyam Singh
   (e) None of the above/more than one of the above

10. The author of 'Political Ratnakar' is

(a) Chandeshwar
(b) Vidyapati
(c) Jyotireshwar
(d) Haribrahmadev
(e) None of the above/more than one of the above

11. The author of 'Udwant Prakash' is

(a) Molly Kavi (b) Bodhraj
(c) Parmal (d) Vidyapati
(e) None of the above/more than one of the above

12. Nalanda Vihar was demolished by-

(a) Bakhtiyar Khilji
(b) Qutbuddin Aibak
(c) Muhammad bin Tughlaq
(d) Allaudin Khilji
(e) None of the above/more than one of the above

13. Which of the following land figures surrounds the northwestern part of the State of Bihar?

(a) Someshwar Hill Range
(b) Kaimur Plateau
(c) Nawada Hill Region
(d) Rajgir Hill Region
(e) None of the above/more than one of the above

14. Tel River is a tributary of which of the following rivers?

(a) Bagmati (b) Ghaghara
(c) Gandak (d) Kamla
(e) None of the above/more than one of the above

15. Which of the following canal systems leads to irrigation in the region of Bihar?

(a) Upper Ganga Canal
(b) Triveni Canal
(c) Sharda Canal
(d) Eastern Yamuna Canal
(e) None of the above/more than one of the above

16. Which of the following silk textile scent centers is in Bihar?

(a) Motipur (b) Bajari
(c) Bhagalpur (d) Dalmia Nagar
(e) None of the above/more than one of the above

17. Bharat Wagon and Engineering Co., Ltd. is located in which of the following locations?

(a) Madhepura (b) Jamalpur
(c) Haranat (d) Mokama
(e) None of the above/more than one of the above

18. Which connects Chhapra and Gopalganj on the following National Highways?

(a) National Highway No.77
(b) National Highway No.84
(c) National Highway No. 85
(d) National Highway No.80
(e) None of the above/more than one of the above

19. The highest population growth during 2001-11 was in which the following districts?

(a) Kishanganj (b) Araria
(c) Madhepura (d) Khagaria
(e) None of the above/more than one of the above

20. Which district of Bihar is the poorest keeping in view the per capita income criteria?

(a) Begusarai
(b) Madhepura
(c) Supaul
(d) Sheohar
(e) None of the above/more than one of the above

21. Which sector recorded the highest growth rate between 2005-06 and 2014-15 in Bihar?

(a) Agriculture
(b) Banking

(c) Registered Manufacturing
(d) Transport
(e) None of the above/more than one of the above

22. The SPUR project in Bihar is concerned with-
(a) Health
(b) Poverty
(c) Banking
(d) Municipal Finance
(e) None of the above/more than one of the above

23. The total length of National Highways in Bihar is
(a) 3410 kms (b) 3587 kms
(c) 4595 kms (d) 4707 kms
(e) None of the above/more than one of the above

24. In the State of Bihar per capita energy consumption is -
(a) 203kWh
(b) 187 kWh
(c) 161 kWh
(d) 145 kWh
(e) None of the above/more than one of the above

25. Jeevika is an initiative of the Government of Bihar. It is related to:
(a) Employment Generation
(b) Financial Inclusion
(c) Poverty Alleviation
(d) Public Distribution
(e) None of the above/more than one of the above

Answers

1. (b)	**2.** (e)	**3.** (b)	**4.** (c)	**5.** (b)	**6.** (c)	**7.** (a)	**8.** (c)
9. (a)	**10.** (a)	**11.** (a)	**12.** (a)	**13.** (a)	**14.** (e)	**15.** (b)	**16.** (c)
17. (d)	**18.** (c)	**19.** (c)	**20.** (d)	**21.** (c)	**22.** (d)	**23.** (c)	**24.** (e)
25. (e)							

56th, 59th, Bihar Combined Exam Solved Papers-2015

1. Who is called Napoleon of ancient India?
(a) Chandragupta Maurya
(b) Pushy Mitra
(c) Kanishka
(d) Samudragupta

2. Where did Gautam Buddha give his first sermon?
(a) Vaishali (b) Kaushambi
(c) Sarnath (d) Pavapuri

3. Who was the author of 'Indica'?
(a) Vishnugupta (b) Megasthenes
(c) Deimachus (d) Pliny

4. Who was the founder of Nalanda University?
(a) Chandragupta Vikram Aditya
(b) Kumargupta
(c) Dharmapala
(d) Pushyagupta

5. In which place of Bihar did Gandhiji perform his first Satyagraha?
(a) Champaran (b) Chhapra
(c) Bettiah (d) Patna

6. Who was the President of the Indian National Congress session of Gaya in 1922?
(a) Chittaranjan Das
(b) SN Banerjee
(c) Dr. Rajendra Prasad
(d) Hakim Ajmal Khan

7. One of the beliefs prevalent in Bihar during the non - cooperation movement of 1920-22 was that he would win because Gandhi-
(a) Was symbol of religion
(b) Was an accomplished politician
(c) Knew how to defeat the British
(d) Knew English

8. At which place was Rahul Sanskrityayan active in the non-cooperation movement of 1920?
(a) Chhapra (b) Delhi
(c) Lucknow (d) Patna

9. When Swami Sahaj Ananda Sarasvati constituted the All India Joint Kisan Sabha with the demand for 'nationalization of land and waterways'.
(a) Just before his death
(b) At a very young age
(c) In the decade of 1930
(d) In the 1920s

10. Who highlighted the plight of the farmers of Champaran by writing under pseudonyms like 'Unhappy', 'Unhappy Soul', 'Unhappy Heart'?
(a) Pir Muhammad Munis
(b) Rajendra Prasad
(c) Sahaj Ananda Sarasvati
(d) SN Sinha

11. Fill in the blanks:
The rights of tenants on land in Bengal and Bihar in ------- were given by the Bengal Tenancy Act.
(a) 1885 (b) 1886
(c) 1889 (d) 1900

12. How many members are elected to Lok Sabha from Bihar?
(a) 20 (b) 30
(c) 35 (d) 40

13. Dalmia Nagar in Bihar is famous for
(a) Silk (b) Cement
(c) Leather (d) Jute

14. What is the unique festival of Bihar?
(a) Deepawali
(b) Bisu
(c) Vinayak Chaturthi
(d) Chhath Puja

15. Which Sikh Guru was born in Patna?
(a) Nanak (b) Teg Bahadur
(c) Hargovind (d) Govind Singh

16. How much is the forest area in Bihar in square meters?
(a) 2812 square meters
(b) 3612 square meters
(c) 2461 square meters
(d) 2612 square meters

17. Who among the following was a farmer leader of Bihar?
1. Swami Vidyananda
2. Swami Sahaj Ananda
3. Sardar Vallabhbhai Patel
Select the correct alternative from the following:
(a) 1 and 2 (b) 2 and 3
(c) 1 and 3 (d) only 2

18. Jayaprakash Narayan is known by what name?
(a) Lokmanya (b) Loknayak
(c) Lokhitvadi (d) Lokneta

19. Which of the following lakes is located in Bihar?

(a) Anupam Lake
(b) Sambhar Lake
(c) Sukhna Lake
(d) Kama Lake

20. Which of the following cities is located in the easternmost part of Bihar?

(a) Bhagalpur
(b) Patna
(c) Katihar
(d) Purnia

Answers

1. (d)	**2.** (c)	**3.** (b)	**4.** (b)	**5.** (a)	**6.** (a)	**7.** (a)	**8.** (a)
9. (c)	**10.** (a)	**11.** (a)	**12.** (d)	**13.** (b)	**14.** (d)	**15.** (d)	**16.** (*)
17. (d)	**18.** (b)	**19.** (a)	**20.** (c)				

53rd, 55th, Bihar Combined Exam Solved Papers-2011

1. What was the name of the dynasty of Ajatshatru?

(a) Maurya (b) Hariyank
(c) Nanda (d) Gupt

2. Which was the initial capital of Magadha?

(a) Pataliputra
(b) Vaishali
(c) Rajgrah (Girivraj)
(d) Champa

3. At which place was the third Buddhist meeting convened?

(a) Takshashila (b) Sarnath
(c) Pataliputra (d) Vaishali

4. Where did Mahatma Buddha give his dharma chakrapravartan?

(a) Takshashila (b) Sarnath
(c) Bodh Gaya (d) Pataliputra

5. Where was Mahavir Swami born?

(a) Kundgram (b) Pataliputra
(c) Magadha (d) Vaishali

6. How many Industrial Sector Development Authorities were there in the State of Bihar (Pre-Partition)

(a) Six, i.e., Adityapur, Bokaro, Patna Ranchi, Darbhanga and Muzaffarpur
(b) Five, i.e., Adityapur, Bokaro, Darbhanga, Muzaffarpur and Patna
(c) Seven, i.e., Adityapur, Bokaro, Patna, Darbhanga, Muzaffarpur, Ranchi and Bhojpur
(d) Four, i.e., Adityapur, Muzaffarpur, Bhojpur and Khagaria

7. Name the scheme of Bihar which focuses on building the required high level infrastructure facilities for setting up of export-oriented units like Delhi?

(a) Integrated Infrastructure Development (IID)

(b) Export Promotion Industrial Park (EPIP)
(c) Concept of Build-Operate-Transfer (BOT)
(d) Software/Hardware Technology Park (STP/ HTP)

8. Where The office of Commissioner of Industries of Bihar's located?
(a) Patna (b) Gaya
(c) Hajipur (d) Muzaffarpur

9. When was the 16th Session of Bihari Students' Conference held at Hazaribagh.
(a) in 1921 (b) in 1922
(c) in 1923 (d) in 1924

10. North Bihar is famous for
(a) Agricultural Prosperity
(b) Heavy Industry
(c) Flood
(d) Drought

11. Which of the following cities is not located on NH-2?
(a) Aurangabad (b) Sasaram
(c) Mohania (d) Patna

12. In Bihar, air services are provided by the following:
(a) Indian Airlines only
(b) Sahara Airlines Only
(c) Royal Nepal Airlines only
(d) Indian Airlines, Sahara Airlines and Royal Nepal Airlines

13. The Planning Commission in 1993-94 estimated the following percentage of population of Bihar living Below-Povert Line (BPL):
(a) 55 (b) 65
(c) 45 (d) 35

14. Who was the editor of Bihari, the leading newspaper of Bihar.
(a) Babu G. Prasad
(b) Babu Ram Prasad
(c) Babu Gopal Prasad
(d) Babu Maheshwar Prasad

15. In Bihar though zamindari was statutorily removed in 1952, the social basis of land control remained in the hands of the following:
(a) Middle Caste Hindus
(b) Scheduled Caste Hindus
(c) Hindus of the main caste
(d) Scheduled Caste Hindus

16. Rajkumar Shukla was a resident of which village?
(a) Murli Bharhawa's
(b) Murli Bhit
(c) Murli Dhir
(d) Murli Kher

17. Shri Nivaran Chandra Dasgupta was:
(a) From Patna
(b) From Purulia
(c) From Hajipur
(d) from Meenapur

18. Which party's selection is correct in Bihar assembly elections 2010 as compared to that of 2005 elections?

	JDU	BJP	RJD	LJP	Congress	Others
(a)	+40	+25	–30	–10	–7	–19
(b)	+25	+34	–20	–5	–3	–11
(c)	+27	+36	–32	–7	–5	–19
(d)	+17	+46	–15	–10	–10	–10

19. Which State Governments have increased the reservation of women in local bodies to 50% by 2010?
(a) Bihar, Uttar Pradesh, Rajasthan
(b) Bihar, Madhya Pradesh, Himachal Pradesh
(c) Bihar, Madhya Pradesh, Kerala
(d) Bihar, Himachal Pradesh, Uttar Pradesh

20. In August, 2010, Union Cabinet decided to set up an institute equivalent to All India Institute

of Medical Sciences (AIIMS) in which six States?

(a) Bihar, Chhattisgarh, Madhya Pradesh, Orissa, Rajasthan, Uttarakhand

(b) Bihar, Uttar Pradesh, Himachal Pradesh, Haryana, Kerala, Gujarat

(c) Bihar, Uttarakhand, Jharkhand, Orissa, Andhra Pradesh, Maharashtra

(d) Bihar, Tamil Nadu, Karnataka, Uttar Pradesh, Jammu and Kashmir, Assam

21. Where is the headquarters of East-Central Railway Division located?

(a) Patna

(b) Hajipur

(c) Muzaffarpur

(d) Katihar

22. Kunwar Singh was the king of -

(a) Hamirpur (b) Dhirpur

(c) Jagdishpur (d) Rampur

23. Patna International Airport is directly connected to:

(a) Kathmandu (Nepal), New Delhi, Kolkata, Mumbai, Lucknow, Varanasi and Ranchi

(b) Bengaluru, Hyderabad and Dhaka

(c) Islamabad, Dhaka and Bengaluru

(d) Washington, Dhaka and Chennai

Answers

1. (b)	**2.** (c)	**3.** (c)	**4.** (b)	**5.** (a)	**6.** (b)	**7.** (a)	**8.** (a)
9. (c)	**10.** (d)	**11.** (d)	**12.** (d)	**13.** (d)	**14.** (d)	**15.** (c)	**16.** (a)
17. (b)	**18.** (c)	**19.** (b)	**20.** (c)	**21.** (b)	**22.** (c)	**23.** (a)	

48th, 52nd Bihar Combined Exam Solved Papers-2009

1. From which of the following constituencies did RJD's Lalu Prasad Yadav contest the 15th Lok Sabha elections?

(a) Patliputra and Madhepura

(b) Buxar and Patna Sahib

(c) Darbhanga & Saran

(d) Pataliputra & Saran

2. Chandragupta Basdi Temple is located at -

(a) In Shravana Belagola

(b) in Rajgir

(c) In Nalanda

(d) In Bodh Gaya

3. How many districts are there in Bihar?

(a) 27 (b) 34

(c) 45 (d) 38

4. Hajipur is the headquarters of which zone of Indian Railways?

(a) East-Central

(b) North-East

(c) Eastern

(d) South-East

5. What is the name of the director of Super-30 Coaching Institute, Patna where all the thirty candidates passed the 2009 IIT-JEE?

(a) Abhay Anand
(b) Santosh Kumar
(c) Ramanujan
(d) Anand Kumar

6. When was Bihar merged with Bengal as an administrative entity?
(a) 1719 AD (b) 1911 AD
(c) 1819 AD (d) 1636 AD

7. Who invited Mahatma Gandhi for Champaran Satyagraha in Bihar?
(a) Dr. Rajendra Prasad
(b) Rajkumar Shukla
(c) Pandit Jawaharlal Nehru
(d) Jai Prakash Narayan

8. Who built the Fort of Rohtas in Bihar?
(a) Akbar (b) Aurangzeb
(c) Sher Shah (d) Babur

9. Who led the Santhal rebellion in 1757?
(a) Sidhu and Kanhu
(b) Angad and Birju
(c) Bhikhan
(d) Tapesar and Mulai

10. Bihar is the only producer of -
(a) Mica (b) limestone
(c) pyrite (d) Steatite

11. The Heenyan caves of Mauryan period are located on -
(a) Gaya Hill
(b) Rajgiri Hill
(c) Raajmahal Hill
(d) Barabar and Nagarjuni Hill

12. Which of the following districts of Bihar has minimum population density?
(a) Jamui (b) West Champaran
(c) Aurangabad (d) Bhabhua

13. In Mauryan period, one person was appointed as Sitadhyaksh for management of government land and agricultural system. Who was he?
(a) Village Head
(b) Government Employee
(c) Amatya
(d) head of slaves

14. The correct descending order of sex ratio of districts in Bihar is
(a) Siwan, Gopalganj, Saran, Nawada
(b) Gopalganj, Siwan, Jamui, Kishanganj
(c) Siwan, Madhubani, Kishanganj, Gaya
(d) Gopalganj, Siwan, Gaya, Kishanganj

15. In which district Bihar was found to have the lowest female literacy in 2001:
(a) In Araria (b) in Kishanganj
(c) In Supaul (d) in Madhepura

16. In which district Savanna vegetation is found in Bihar.
(a) In Motihari
(b) in Shivhar
(c) In Madhubani
(d) In West Champaran

17. Barauni Oil Refinery was established -
(a) in1940 (b) in 1946
(c) in 1956 (d) in 1966

18. Coal mines are engaged in Bihar -
(a) From Jharia
(b) from Gaya
(c) From Arrah
(d) from Sasaram

19. B.E.B means:
(a) Bihar Economic Board
(b) Bihar Electricity Board
(c) Bihar's prosperous class' bargaining
(d) Bihar Environment Board

20. The ancient university of Bihar is
(a) Bodh Gaya University
(b) Patna University
(c) Nalanda University
(d) Darbhanga University

21. Which state has a greater Number of IAS officers?
(a) Gujarat (b) Maharashtra
(c) Kerala (d) Bihar

22. North Bihar is famous for -

(a) agricultural prosperity

(b) heavy industry.

(c) flood situation

(d) famine

23. Which of the following rivers flows in Bihar?

(a) Ganga (b) Yamuna

(c) Kaveri (d) Mahanadi

24. The State of Bihar is well known for -

(a) Betrayal

(b) Overspending

(c) Greedy Subjects

(d) Simplicity

25. Match cities of Bihar in List-I with tourist place in List-II

LIST-I	LIST-II
A. Motihari	**1. Mahatma Gandhi started independence movement**
B. Mujaffarpur	**2. Tata Steel Plant**
C. Patna	**3. Bihar University**
D. Jamshedpur	**4. Capital of Bihar**

	A	B	C	D
(a)	1	4	2	3
(b)	2	3	4	1
(c)	4	3	2	1
(d)	1	2	3	4

26. In which year did the Gaya conspiracy case take place?

(a) in January 1933

(b) in March 1943

(c) In January 1928

(d) in January 1932

27. Who presided over the Patna Swadeshi League in 1930?

(a) Sir Ali Imam

(b) KB Dutt

(c) Feroz Shah Mehta

(d) Baldev Sahai

28. Where did the Secretariat shooting of August 11 take place in Bihar in the context of the revolution of 1942-43?

(a) Hazaribagh (b) Munger

(c) Patna (d) Sivan

Answers

1. (d)	**2.** (a)	**3.** (d)	**4.** (a)	**5.** (d)	**6.** (b)	**7.** (b)	**8.** (c)
9. (a)	**10.** (c)	**11.** (b)	**12.** (d)	**13.** (b)	**14.** (a)	**15.** (b)	**16.** (d)
17. (d)	**18.** (a)	**19.** (b)	**20.** (c)	**21.** (d)	**22.** (c)	**23.** (a)	**24.** (d)
25. (a)	**26.** (a)	**27.** (a)	**28.** (c)				

46th, Bihar Combined Exam Solved Papers-2004

1. Bihar is the great religious center -

(a) For Sikhs

(b) For Jains

(c) For Buddhists

(d) For all of these

2. When was Jharkhand separated from Bihar?

(a)15 November, 2000

(b) August 25, 1999

(c) 2 August, 1998

(d) July 5, 1997

3. **How many universities are there in Bihar?**
(a) 9 (b) 11
(c) 12 (d) 13
4. **Who is known as 'Loknayak'?**
(a) Mahatma Gandhi
(b) Subhas Chandra Bose
(c) Jayaprakash Narayan
(d) Bal Gangadhar Tilak
5. **What is the painting style of Bihar called?**
(a) Madhubani (b) Srirangam
(c) Pichchwai (d) Mughal
6. **Who is the Governor of Bihar at present?**
(a) Shri Naval Kishore Sharma
(b) Justice MR Ramazois
(c) Shri Madan Lal Khurana
(d) Justice Anshuman Singh
7. **Where was the third Buddhist association held?**
(a) Vatya (b) Pataliputra
(c) Kaushambi (d) Kashmir
8. **In 1932, the All-India Congress Committee was declared illegal by passing one of the following orders. The order is-**
(a) unlawful union ordinance
(b) Violation of peace law
(c) executive rights ordinance
(d) Viceroy's Special Order
9. **The source in which the description of the administration of Pataliputra is:**
(a) divyavadan
(b) economics
(c) indica
(d) Ashoka's Inscriptions
10. **Which of the following areas you will not include in physical map of Bihar?**
(a) Chhotanagpur Plateau
(b) North Ganga Plain
(c) Southern Ganga Plain
(d) Eastern Ganga Maidan
11. **Which of the following groups of rivers in Bihar come from north in Ganga or its tributaries?**
(a) Ghaghara, Kosi, Punpun
(b) Kosi, Mahananda, Karmanasha
(c) Gandak, Kamala, Bagmati
(d) Sone, Kosi, Northern Koel
12. **Bangar soil is found in Bihar in -**
(a) Bodh-Gaya Gaya-East Champaran-Bhagalpur Region
(b) Purnia-Saharsa-Darbhanga-Muzaffarpur area
(c) Gaya-Nalanda-Bodh Gaya-Sasaram Area
(d) East Champaran-Nalanda-Gaya-Sasaram area
13. **Consider the following statements regarding various geographical aspects of Bihar:**
I. In Bihar, about 37 per cent of the total irrigated land is irrigated by canals
II. The North Ganga Plain in Bihar is extended to an area of 33,620 square kilometers.
III. Kishanganj and West Champaran receive the highest annual rainfall in Bihar
IV. The total length of National Highways in Bihar is 2,461 km
Which of the following statements is correct?
(a) I & II (b) II & III
(c) II & IV (d) I, III & IV
14. **In Bihar, correlate list-I (minerals) with list-II (places of receipt) and select the correct answer using the table given below the lists:**

LIST-I	LIST-II
Minerals	Place of Receipt
A. Mica	1. Munger
B. Gold	2. Gaya

C. Dolomite 3. Kishanganj
D. Petroleum 4. Rohtas

	A	B	C	D
(a)	3	4	1	2
(b)	1	2	3	4
(c)	2	1	4	3
(d)	4	3	2	1

15. Associate List-I (Industries)with List- II (Cities) in Bihar and select the correct answer using the table given below the lists:

LIST-I	LIST-II
A. Mica	1. Munger
B. Gold	2. Gaya
C. Dolomite	3. Kishanganj
D. Petroleum	4. Rostas

	A	B	C	D
(a)	3	4	1	2
(b)	1	2	3	4
(c)	2	1	4	3
(d)	4	3	2	1

16. Which of the following group of districts of Bihar represents the correct descending order of population as per census 2001?

(a) Patna, East Champaran, Muzaffarpur, Madhubani
(b) East Champaran, Patna, Madhubani, Muzaffarpur
(c) Patna, Muzaffarpur, East Champaran, Madhubani
(d) Muzaffarpur, Patna, Madhubani, East Champaran

17. What is the rate of female literacy in Bihar as per census 2001?

(a) 60.32% (b) 53%
(c) 33.5% (d) 47.53%

Answers

1. (d)	**2.** (a)	**3.** (c)	**4.** (c)	**5.** (a)	**6.** (d)	**7.** (b)	**8.** (a)
9. (b)	**10.** (a)	**11.** (c)	**12.** (b)	**13.** (d)	**14.** (c)	**15.** (b)	**16.** (a)
17. (c)							

45th, Bihar Combined Exam Solved Papers-2002

1. Who is the Election Commissioner of Bihar state?

(a) ML Majumdar
(b) Renuka Bajaj
(c) LM Sindhvi
(d) None of these

2. Who among the following from Bihar Assembly was elected to the Rajya Sabha?

(a) Sunil Dutt
(b) Rabri Devi
(c) Sahib Singh Verma
(d) None of these

3. The number of wards in Patna Municipal Corporation is

(a) 57
(b) 67
(c) 64
(d) 59

4. Who among the following is the co-governor of Bihar and Jharkhand?

(a) Vinod Chandra Pandey
(b) Vimal Kumar Dubey
(c) Vishnu Kant Shastri
(d) Girish Choubey

5. **Bihar has outstanding loans of -**
(a) ₹ 37,653 crore
(b) ₹ 67,653 crore
(c) ₹ 87,663 crore
(d) ₹ 90,000 crore

6. **Mahavir Jain had died in which of the following cities?**
(a) Rajgir (b) Ranchi
(c) Pavapuri (d) Samastipur

7. **Which of the following places is famous for wildlife in Bihar?**
(a) Bhagalpur (b) Bodh Gaya
(c) Patna (d) Hazaribagh

8. **Some of the areas of which district/s of Bihar were given to West Bengal:**
(a) Jamshedpur
(b) Bhagalpur and Samastipur
(c) Purnia and Manbhum
(d) Rajgir

9. **Mahabodhi Temple was built in Bodh Gaya at the place where-**
(a) Gautam Buddha was born
(b) Gautam Buddha attained enlightenment
(c) Gautam Buddha gave his first sermon
(d) Gautam Buddha died

10. **The total length of National Highways in Bihar is -**
(a)1913 Km (b)1088 km
(c)1313 Km (d)1371 km.

11. **What is the percentage of population of Bihar in the total population of India?**
(a) 9.33% (b)10.21%
(c) 16.44% (d) 8.04%

12. **Jamshedpur is situated on the banks of which river?**
(a) Damodar (b) Brahmin
(c) Suvarnarekha (d) Ajay

13. **The minimum age limit for a person to be elected to the Lok Sabha is**
(a) 18 Year (b) 21 years
(c) 25 (d) none of these

14. **Which new State has been formed recently by separating from Bihar:**
(a) Vananchal (b) Vidarbha
(c) Jharkhand (d) Chhattisgarh

15. **How many districts are left in Bihar after Jharkhand was formed?**
(a) 37 (b) 65
(c) 60 (d) 62

16. **The main foodgrain crops of Bihar are:**
(a) Rice, Wheat & Maize
(b) Sugarcane, Tea & Barley
(c) Peanuts, Coffee & Wheat
(d) None of these

17. **Which of the following is true?**
(a) Bihar has been the main producer of coal and mica
(b) Bihar was separated from Orissa in 1911
(c) Bihar borders Orissa after Jharkhand becomes a state
(d) Bihar has a single-house legislature

18. **Basically the word 'Bihar' means**
(a) Buddhist Monastery
(b) Land of angels
(c) Arya Pradesh
(d) Green region

19. **Which city of Bihar has become the capital of Jharkhand?**
(a) Buxar (b) Dhanbad
(c) Ranchi (d) Hazaribagh

20. **Kunwar Singh led the revolt of 1857 from which province?**
(a) Punjab (b) Bengal
(c) Bihar (d) Maharashtra

21. Where was Shri Yogendra Shukla brought on 7 December,1942?
(a) Ranchi (b) Munger
(c) Patna (d) Bhagalpur

22. Which of the following newspapers was published from Patna?
(a) Indian Nation
(b) Punjab Kesari
(c) Prabhakar
(d) Don

23. Jagat Narayan Lal was sent to which jail?
(a) Bankipur Jail
(b) Camp Jail
(c) Bhagalpur Jail
(d) Hazaribagh Jail

24. Ram Chandra Sharma was from which village?
(a) Gogri (b) Indrapur
(c) Pema (d) Amhara

25. Who was Shri Narasimha Narayan?
(a) A Socialist
(b) A Nationalist
(c) A Internationalist
(d) A Communist

26. Jayaprakash Narayan belonged to which party?
(a) Congress
(b) Kisan Sabha
(c) Congress Socialist Party
(d) Rayavadi

Answers

1. (a)	**2.** (b)	**3.** (a)	**4.** (a)	**5.** (b)	**6.** (c)	**7.** (b)	**8.** (c)
9. (b)	**10.** (a)	**11.** (d)	**12.** (c)	**13.** (c)	**14.** (c)	**15.** (a)	**16.** (a)
17. (a)	**18.** (a)	**19.** (c)	**20.** (c)	**21.** (c)	**22.** (a)	**23.** (d)	**24.** (a)
25. (c)	**26.** (c)						

44th, Bihar Combined Exam Solved Papers-2001

1. The largest city on the banks of river Ganga is
(a) Varanasi (b) Patna
(c) Kanpur (d) Allahabad

2. Which dynasty was established after Mauryan dynasty?
(a) Shaka dynasty
(b) Kushan dynasty
(c) Satavahana dynasty
(d) Shunga dynasty

3. The largest district of Bihar is
(a) Patna (b) Gaya
(c) Darbhanga (d) Samastipur

4. Saran (Nand) Irrigation Canal emerges:
(a) From Sone (b) From Ganga
(c) From Kosi (d) From Gandak

5. Percentage of literacy in Bihar is
(a) 42.85 (b) 37.25
(c) 52.51 (d) 43.56

6. The total population in the State of New Bihar is
(a) 64.434 million
(b) 86.374 million
(c) 72.325 Million
(d) 70.562 million

7. Which of the following rivers have the maximum river path changes:
(a) Sone River (b) Gandak River
(c) Kosi River (d) River Ganga

8. What is the percentage of Urban population in Bihar of its total population:
(a) 10.76% (b) 13.14%
(c) 12.86% (d) 21.56%

9. What percentage of land of old Bihar has been segregated and Jharkhand state is formed?
(a) 38.40 % (b) 45.85%
(c) 42.35 % (d) 51.72%

10. In which year did Bihar get the status of a separate province during British rule?
(a) 1905 (b) in 1912
(c) 1936 (d) in 1946

11. Which of the following kings settled Pataliputra?
(a) Shishunag (b) Bimbisara
(c) Ajatshatru (d) Udayin

12. In which of the following cities is the 'Sun Temple' located?
(a) Gaya
(b) Buddhist Gaya
(c) Dev
(d) Ranchi

13. What is the total forest cover in percentage terms in Bihar state–
(a) 32% (b) 21%
(c) 19% (d) 31%

14. Which is the main cash crop of the State of Bihar?
(a) Tea
(b) Rubber
(c) Sugarcane
(d) Coconut and Coffee

15. Which city of Bihar is famous for wildlife sanctuary and national park?
(a) Hazaribagh (b) Nalanda
(c) Gaya (d) Jamshedpur

16. With whom was Sachchidanand Sinha associated?
(a) Quit India Movement
(b) Dandi March
(c) Civil disobedience movement
(d) Not with any of these

17. Who among the following was associated with the Kisan Andolan in Bihar?
(a) Rajendra Prasad
(b) CR Das
(c) Motilal Nehru
(d) Bhagat Singh

18. Rajendra Prasad was from which place:
(a) Uttar Pradesh
(b) Bihar
(c) Madhya Pradesh
(d) None of these

19. Jayaprakash Narayan was associated with which movement?
(a) Champaran movement
(b) Non-cooperation movement
(c) Satyagraha movement
(d) Quit India Movement

Answers

1. (c)	**2.** (d)	**3.** (b)	**4.** (d)	**5.** (b)	**6.** (*)	**7.** (c)	**8.** (b)
9. (b)	**10.** (b)	**11.** (d)	**12.** (c)	**13.** (c)	**14.** (c)	**15.** (c)	**16.** (d)
17. (a)	**18.** (b)	**19.** (d)					

43rd, Bihar Combined Exam Solved Papers-1999

1. Three thermal power stations running on coal which are located in Bihar are as under:
(a) Chandrapur, Panchait, Barauni
(b) Bokaro, Panchait, Chandrapura
(c) Barauni, Chandrapura, Santaldih
(d) Bokaro, Chandrapura, Santaldih

2. The politics of terrorist army based on casteism is in the following State:
(a) Bihar
(b) Uttar Pradesh
(c) Andhra Pradesh
(d) Maharashtra

3. Which place is the center of steel plants in Bihar?
(a) Dhanbad (b) Ranchi
(c) Mithila (d) Patna

4. Which of the following cities is the largest one?
(a) Dhanbad (b) Gaya
(c) Jamshedpur (d) Ranchi

5. In the East, the river originating from Bihar, which is also called the 'Misery of Bengal', is
(a) Baraker (b) Damodar
(c) Mayurakshi (d) Swarn Rekha

6. The number of States of India bordering Bihar is -
(a) Four (b) Five
(c) Six (d) Seven

7. The population growth rate of Bihar in the decade 1981-91 is:
(a) 19.76% (b) 21.33%
(c) 23.54% (d) 24.06%

8. The state-wise decreasing order in coal production is
(a) Bihar, Madhya Pradesh, West Bengal
(b) Madhya Pradesh, West Bengal, Bihar
(c) West Bengal, Madhya Pradesh, Bihar
(d) Bihar, West Bengal, Madhya Pradesh

9. The National Highway passing through Bihar is
(a) NH 3 (b) NH 8
(c) NH 22 (d) NH 23

10. The center of revolt of 1857 in Bihar from July 15, 1857 to January 20, 1858 was -
(a) Rampur (b) Hamirpur
(c) Dhirpur (d) Jagdishpur

11. The king of Jagdishpur was
(a) Nana Saheb
(b) Tatya Tope
(c) Lakshmi Bai
(d) Kunwar Singh

12. Rambilas Singh was an active member of the Forward Bloc of which district -
(a) Of Darbhanga
(b) Of Jamshedpur
(c) Of Munger
(d) Of Patna

13. The two leaders who were arrested on August 6, 1942 were:
(a) Ramlal and Devi Lal
(b) Narayan Singh and Sukhlal Singh
(c) Ramnath and Devnath
(d) Shiva Kumar and Ramanand

14. The name of the wife of Shri Jagat Narayan Lal was
(a) Smt. Rampyari
(b) Smt. Sundari Devi
(c) Smt. Bhagwati Devi
(d) Smt. Mangala Devi

15. Dr. Rajendra Prasad was arrested and sent on 9th August,1942 in –
(a) Camp Jail
(b) Hazaribagh Jail
(c) Bhagalpur Jail
(d) Bankipur Jail

16. Jayaprakash Diwas was celebrated in -
(a) In January1946
(b) In February1946
(c) In March1946
(d) In April, 1946

17. It is possible to cut off Bihar and form a separate Vananchal (Jharkhand) State.
(a) By passing the law in the State Assembly
(b) By passing the Ordinance by the Governor
(c) By completing constitutional formalities
(d) None of these

18. The reason for state of Bihar to have the maximum number of people below the poverty line is-
(a) Failure of land reforms
(b) Lack of political will
(c) Higher number of working class
(d) All of these

19. The era of establishment of Nalanda University is
(a) Maurya (b) Kushan
(c) Gupt (d) Pal

20. The reasons for the destruction of Nalanda University was:
(a) Muslim
(b) Kushan
(c) Sithyans
(d) Mughal

21. The leader of the 1857 war of independence of Patna was:
(a) Haider Ali Khan
(b) Rajput Kunwar Singh
(c) Judhar Singh
(d) Kushal Singh

22. Mahatma Gandhi and his colleagues were caught in 1942 leading to a lot of riots in Bihar. The train service was completely suspended with the maximum affected district being
(a) Munger
(b) Gaya
(c) Patna
(d) Shahabad

23. Copper plate article shows that ancient _________ had contact with the kings of Bihar:
(a) Burma
(b) Thailand
(c) Cambodia
(d) Java-Sumatra

24. The founder of Vikramshila Shiksha Kendra was
(a) Devpal (b) Dharmapala
(c) Nayanpal (d) Narendra Pal

Answers

1. (a)	**2.** (a)	**3.** (a)	**4.** (c)	**5.** (b)	**6.** (a)	**7.** (c)	**8.** (a)
9. (d)	**10.** (d)	**11.** (d)	**12.** (d)	**13.** (b)	**14.** (a)	**15.** (d)	**16.** (d)
17. (c)	**18.** (d)	**19.** (c)	**20.** (a)	**21.** (*)	**22.** (c)	**23.** (d)	**24.** (b)

42nd, Bihar Combined Exam Solved Papers-1998

1. Which kisan movement did Mahatma Gandhi first participate in?
(a) Kheda (b) Champaran
(c) Bardoli (d) Baroda

2. Which ruler first made Pataliputra his capital?
(a) Chandragupta Maurya
(b) Ashok the Great
(c) Chandragupta Vikram Aditya
(d) Kanishka

3. Nalanda University was world famous for
(a) Medicine
(b) Logic
(c) Buddhist Philosophy
(d) Chemistry

4. Which leader of Bihar led the Kisan Andolan with Mahatma Gandhi?
(a) Baba Ramachandra
(b) Dr. Rajendra Prasad
(c) Rajkumar Shukla
(d) Rafi Ahmed Kidwai

5. Who led the revolt of 1857 in Bihar?
(a) Khan Bahadur Khan
(b) Kanwar Singh
(c) Tantya Tope
(d) Rani Ram Kuwari

6. Which state sends the highest number of representatives to the Lok Sabha?
(a) Bihar
(b) Madhya Pradesh
(c) West Bengal
(d) Uttar Pradesh

7. In terms of production in Bihar, the second crop after rice is
(a) wheat
(b) maize
(c) gram
(d) potato

8. Irrigated area in Bihar has increased after Independence to what extent?
(a) Doubled
(b) Four times
(c) Five times
(d) Ten times

9. Bihar has a monopoly in the production of the following in India:
(a) limestone (b) coal
(c) pyrite (d) graphite

10. At an early stage, the economy of Chhota Nagpur was based on:
(a) On agriculture
(b) On forests.
(c) On mines
(d) On industries

11. Bihar separated from Bengal in -
(a) 1910 (b) 1912
(c) 1921 (d) 1947

12. The total number of Lok Sabha seats from Bihar is
(a) 48 (b) 50
(c) 52 (d) 54

13. Swami Sahaj Ananda was related:
(a) With tribal movements of Bihar
(b) With the ethnic movements of Bihar

(c) With the farmers' movements of Bihar
(d) With the labor movements of Bihar

14. The movement against manning in Begusarai was a part of :
(a) Non-cooperation movement
(b) Civil disobedience movement
(c) Quit India Movement
(d) Khilafat movement

15. There were terrible Hindu-Muslim riots in Shahabad, Gaya and Patna districts of Bihar on the issue of cow protection in -
(a) 1917 (b) 1919
(c) 1939 (d) 1946

16. The Chhotanagpur Kasht Act of 1908 stayed:
(a) Independent use of forest production
(b) On burning forests
(c) On Beggary
(d) On the khuntakatty land system

17. "We will make a big mistake if we leave the people of Bihar and their cabinet reserved in the face of violent and rude attacks by the leaders of the League." Who said this in 1946?
(a) Mahatma Gandhi
(b) Jawaharlal Nehru
(c) Rajendra Prasad
(d) Sardar Patel

18. The movement for a separate province in Bihar which led to the creation of new provinces of Bihar and Orissa in the year 1911 was led by:
(a) Sachchidanand Sinha
(b) Anugrah Narayan Sinha
(c) JB Kripalani
(d) Birsa Munda

19. Sumeshwar hills of Bihar is -
(a) Older than Parasnath hill
(b) Older than Raajmahal Hill
(c) Older than Kharagpur Hill
(d) None of these

20. Damodar flows in Bihar–
(a) In a Karst Region
(b) In a Bhransh Valley
(c) In a kachari area
(d) None of these

21. The forest cover percentage of the total geographical area of Bihar is approximately:
(a) 17% (b) 23%
(c) 27% (d) 33%

22. Heavy machine manufacturing plant is located in Bihar-
(a) In Jamshedpur
(b) In Bokaro
(c) In Barauni
(d) in Ranchi

23. ____________ produces methane in Bihar:
(a) thermal power
(b) waterpower
(c) molecule power
(d) Solar Power

24. Bihar is the leading producer in India of-
(a) glass
(b) manganese
(c) mica
(d) limestone

25. Who was appointed as the Governor of Bihar by the Atal Bihari Vajpayee Government?
(a) Sunder lal Bhandari
(b) Sunderlal Patwa
(c) Swaraj Kaushal
(d) Pramod Mahajan

Answers

1. (b)	**2.** (a)	**3.** (c)	**4.** (c)	**5.** (b)	**6.** (d)	**7.** (a)	**8.** (d)
9. (b)	**10.** (b)	**11.** (b)	**12.** (d)	**13.** (c)	**14.** (b)	**15.** (a)	**16.** (d)
17. (d)	**18.** (a)	**19.** (d)	**20.** (b)	**21.** (a)	**22.** (d)	**23.** (b)	**24.** (c)
25. (a)							

41st, Bihar Combined Exam Solved Papers-1996

1. Which part of Bihar was unaffected by the revolt of 1857:

1. Danapur 2. Patna

3. Arrah 4. Muzaffarpur

5. Munger

Select the correct answer from the following:

(a) 4 and 5 (b) only 5

(c) Only 4 (d) 3, 4 and 5

2. Local time of Patna-

(a) is ahead of Indian standard time

(b) is behind Indian standard time

(c) is same as Indian standard time

(d) is not related to Indian standard time

3. Buddhist monks have been agitating in Bihar over the years to get control of -

(a) Mahabodhi Temple in Gaya

(b) Vishnu pad temple in Gaya

(c) The Sun Temple of God

(d) None of the above

4. Who will preside over the proposed Commission for Women in Bihar?

(a) Governor of Bihar

(b) Chief Minister of Bihar

(c) Chief Justice of Bihar

(d) None of the above

5. Chandragupta's palace in Pataliputra was mainly built:

(a) of bricks (b) of stone

(c) of wood (d) of sand

6. Who was most famous for producing cotton clothes during Xuanzang's visit to India:

(a) Varanasi (b) Mathura

(c) Pataliputra (d) Kanchi

7. Patna was made the provincial capital–

(a) By Shershah

(b) By Allaudin Hussain Shah

(c) By Abraham Lodi

(d) By Prince Azim

8. Where were the gold mines located in Bihar in the 17th century?

(a) Champaran (b) Patna

(c) Sasaram (d) Jharkhand

9. In which year were the Gorakshani Sabhas established to prevent cow slaughter in Bihar?

(a) 1877 (b) 1882

(c) 1893 (d) 1897

10. In which year did Orissa got separated from Bihar?

(a) 1930 (b) 1933

(c) 1936 (d) 1937

11. Iron ore is available in Bihar–

(a) In Lohardaga district

(b) In Dumka district

(c) In Dhanbad district

(d) In Singhbhum district

12. The jute industry strip is located in Bihar–

(1) In the ground of North-West Bihar

(2) In the Ground of North-East Bihar

(3) In the Ground of Central-South Bihar

(4) In the region of Damodar Valley

Select the correct answer from the following:

(a) 1 and 2 both

(b) Only 2

(c) 2 and 3 both

(d) Both 1 and 3

13. Bihar has the lowest population in the district of -

(a) Godda

(b) Gumla

(c) Araria

(d) Lohardaga

14. The Terai region of Bihar is spread:

(a) Parallel to the northern brink of Chhotanagpur plateau

(b) Parallel to Indo-Nepal border

(c) Parallel to the eastern brink of Rohtas plateau

(d) Parallel to the western border of the Raajmahal hills

15. What is the ratio of rural urban population in Bihar?

(a) 40: 60

(b) 20: 80

(c) 50: 50

(d) 80: 20

16. What percentage of the total mineral production of the country is available in Bihar?

(a) Approximately 36%

(b) Approximately 60%

(c) Approximately 16%

(d) None of the above

17. Which is the major financial institution in Bihar which provides industrial financial assistance?

(a) World Bank

(b) Biscoman

(c) Bihar State Finance Corporation

(d) SBI

18. What was the total number of districts in Bihar at the end of 1995?

(a) 55

(b) 52

(c) 50

(d) None of the above

19. What percentage of cultivable land in Bihar is irrigated?

(a) More than 50%

(b) 40-50%

(c) 30-40%

(d) Less than 30%

Answers

1. (a)	**2.** (a)	**3.** (a)	**4.** (d)	**5.** (c)	**6.** (b)	**7.** (a)	**8.** (b)
9. (b)	**10.** (c)	**11.** (d)	**12.** (a)	**13.** (d)	**14.** (b)	**15.** (d)	**16.** (d)
17. (c)	**18.** (a)	**19.** (c)					

40th, Bihar Combined Exam Solved Papers-1995

1. The revolt of 1857 affected many cities of Bihar. Which of these present the correct sequence of eruption of insurgency in various cities of Bihar:
(a) Patna, Muzaffarpur, Rohini, Jagdishpur
(b) Rohini, Patna, Muzaffarpur, Jagdishpur
(c) Muzaffarpur, Patna, Jagdishpur, Rohini
(d) Jagdishpur, Patna, Rohini, Muzaffarpur

2. Identify the area where Santhals announced their Government in 1855-56.
(a) Munger-Bhagalpur
(b) Bhagalpur-Raajmahal
(c) Gaya-Munger
(d) Shahabad-Gaya

3. Identify the area of revolt in Bihar of indigo planters in 1866-67?
(a) Muzaffarpur and Chhapra
(b) Madhubani and Begusarai
(c) Darbhanga and Champaran
(d) Champaran

4. Bihar Congress Socialist Party was formed in -
(a) 1930
(b) 1931
(c) 1934
(d) 1939

5. Identify the areas from which the Europeans received the best Shora and opium:
(a) Bihar
(b) Gujarat
(c) Bengal
(d) Madras

6. The famous Saint of Bihar, Sharfuddin Maneri, belonged to which sect of Sufis?
(a) Chishti
(b) Suhrawardy
(c) Firdausi
(d) Kubravi

7. The city of Bihar Sharif was important in the middle ages–
1. As a business center
2. As a education center
3. As an administrative center
4. As a religious center
Select the correct answer from the following:
(a) 1 & 3 (b) 1, 2 and 3
(c) 2, 3 & 4 (d) 2 & 4

8. Which of the following rivers merges with Ganga in Bihar?
1. Gandak
2. Sone
3. Ghaghara
4. Punpun
Select the correct answer from the following:
(a) 1, 2, 3 & 4
(b) 1, 2 and 4
(c) 1, 3 & 4
(d) 2 & 4

9. According to the area, what is the correct descending order of the following States?

1. Andhra Pradesh

2. Bihar

2. Madhya Pradesh

4. Uttar Pradesh

Select the correct answer from the following:

(a) 3, 2, 4, 1 (b) 1, 2, 3, 4

(c) 4, 3, 2, 1 (d) 3, 4, 1, 2

10. Two statements are given below. One is a statement (A) and the other is a reason (R) -

Statement A - South Bihar is more developed than north Bihar.

Reason R - Industries have developed in South Bihar.

Which among the following is correct in respect of both the above statements?

(a) Both Statement A and the reason R are correct and reason R interprets the statement A correctly.

(b) Both statement A and reason R are correct but the reason R does not interpret statement A correctly.

(c) Statement A is correct but reason R is incorrect.

(d) Statement A is incorrect but reason R is correct

11. First sugar mill was established in Bihar -

(a) in Marhora

(b) in Bettiah

(c) In Motihari

(d) in Patna

12. What is the position of Bihar in the production of raw copper in the country?

(a) 1st (b) 2nd

(c) 3rd (d) 4th

13. The total geographical area of Bihar is

(a) About 1.70 lakh sq km

(b) About 1.72 lakh sq km

(c) About 1.74 lakh sq km

(d) About 1.78 lakh sq km

14. What is the number of MPs in Lok Sabha from Bihar?

(a) 50

(b) 52

(c) 54

(d) None of the above

15. Which is the imminent irrigation potential of Bihar?

(a) 89.20 lakh hectares

(b) 90.30 lakh hectares

(c) 91.64 lakh hectares

(d) 92.11 lakh hectares

16. What is the crop density of Bihar?

(a) 108% (b) 118%

(c) 128% (d) 138%

17. What is the nature of agriculture in Bihar?

1. Life-giving

2. Professional

3. Export-oriented

4. Self-reliant

Select the correct answer from the following codes:

(a) Only 1

(b) 2 and 3

(c) Only 3

(d) Only 4

Answers

1. (b)	**2.** (b)	**3.** (b)	**4.** (c)	**5.** (b)	**6.** (c)	**7.** (d)	**8.** (a)
9. (d)	**10.** (a)	**11.** (c)	**12.** (a)	**13.** (c)	**14.** (c)	**15.** (c)	**16.** (d)
17. (a)							

39th, Bihar Combined Exam Solved Papers-1994

1. What was the purpose of Munger's protest against Barhiatal?

(a) Demand for return of bakast land
(b) Stop exploitation of Muslim farmers
(c) Abolition of Zamindari System
(d) Ushering in a 'Class War'

2. When was Bihar separated from Bengal?

(a) 1911 (b) 1912
(c) 1913 (d) 1914

3. When was the Patna High Court established?

(a) 1916 AD (b) 1917 AD
(c) 1913 AD (d) 1921 AD

4. In 1930 and 1931, the Barhi Congress successfully thwarted the British rule in which district?

(a) Madhubani (b) Bhagalpur
(c) Gaya (d) Munger

5. When did the Chhotanagpur Tribal Mutiny taken place?

(a) 1807-1808 (b) 1820
(c) 1858-1859 (d) 1889

6. Which state is second and third in terms of representation in Lok Sabha?

(a) Bihar and Maharashtra
(b) Madhya Pradesh and Tamil Nadu
(c) Madhya Pradesh and Maharashtra
(d) Bihar and Maharashtra

7. Forests are spread over Bihar–

(a) On an area of 28 lakh hectares
(b) On an area of 29 lakh hectares
(c) On an area of 30 lakh hectares
(d) On an area of 31 lakh hectares

8. A steel factory in Bihar is in–

(a) Darbhanga (b) Gaya
(c) Hazaribagh (d) Jamshedpur

Answers

1. (a) **2.** (b) **3.** (a) **4.** (a) **5.** (b) **6.** (a) **7.** (d) **8.** (d)

38th, Bihar Combined Exam Solved Papers-1992

1. Where did the recent massacre in Bihar occur in which nearly 40 people died?

(a) Near Gaya (b) Near Patna
(c) Near Ranchi (d) Near Bhagalpur

2. **The State of Bihar is located between the following longitudes:**
(a) About 840 east to 880 east
(b) About 800 east to 840 east
(c) About 800 east to 880 east
(d) None of these

3. **The level of literacy in Bihar is approximately-**
(a) 30% (b) 34%
(c) 38% (d) 45%

4. **The population of Bihar in India is**
(a) highest
(b) Second highest
(c) Third highest
(d) Fourth highest

5. **Iron ore is not available in the following Indian State:**
(a) In Bihar
(b) in Madhya Pradesh
(c) In Odisha
(d) In Punjab

Answers

1. (a) **2.** (a) **3.** (b) **4.** (c) **5.** (d)

Miscellaneous

BSSC Ameen (Amanat) Recruitment Exam-2005

1. **In Bihar, the city bride of Vaishali, Amrapali was there during whose reign?**
(a) Lichchavi (b) Maurya
(c) Gupt (d) chola

2. **As per census 2001, what is the population of Bihar?**
(a) 82878796 (b) 92878796
(c) 102878796 (d) 20287796

3. **Where is the Magadha Vishwavidyalaya located?**
(a) In Patna
(b) In Bodh Gaya
(c) In Muzaffarpur
(d) at Nalanda

4. **At what place did Lord Mahavir die?**
(a) Kushinagar (b) Vaishali
(c) Rajagraha (d) Pavapuri

5. **Which district of Bihar has a minimum area?**
(a) Gaya (b) Sheikhupura
(c) Buxar (d) Saran

Answers

1. (a) **2.** (a) **3.** (b) **4.** (d) **5.** (b)

BSSC The Lower-Class Clerk (LDC-PT) Examination-2005

1. **In which place was Mahavir born in 540 AD?**
(a) Vaishali (b) Magadha
(c) Sarnath (d) None of these

Answer

1. (a)

BSSC The Lower-Class Clerk (LDC-PT) Examination-2008

1. Where is the National Rural Manufacturing Institute located?

(a) Patna (b) Delhi
(c) Hyderabad (d) Shimla

Answer

1. (a)

BSSC The Lower-Class Clerk (LDC-Mains) Examination-2005

1. Xuanzang visited India-

(a) During the reign of Chandragupta
(b) During the reign of Harsha
(c) During Ashoka's reign
(d) During the reign of Kanishka

Answer

1. (b)

BSSC Stenographer Examination-2006

1. Where is the National Rural Livelihood Sanstha located?

(a) Patna (b) Delhi
(c) Hyderabad (d) Shimla

2. On what area of Bihar is the northern plains of Ganga spread?

(a) 33670 sq km (b) 56980 sq km
(c) 12670 sq km (d) None of these

3. When was the State of Orissa separated from Bihar and a new province was created

(a) 1912 (b) 1926
(c) 1936 (d) 1956

4. When was the formal announcement of the constitution of Kisan Sabha made?

(a) 4 March 1927
(b) 4 March 1928
(c) 4 March 1929
(d) 4 March 1930

5. India's great astrologer Acharya Aryabhatt was closely associated with which city of Bihar?

(a) Vaishali (b) Patliputra
(c) Odantpuri (d) Nalanda

6. The grandeur of Nalanda Visvavidyalaya was destroyed by whom?

(a) Allaudin
(b) Sher Shah Suri
(c) Ibrahim Lodhi
(d) bakhtiyaar khilaji

7. Which river is called the Mourning of Bihar?

(a) Karma Nasha
(b) Kosi
(c) Sone
(d) Swarna Rekha

8. By what name do the old alluvial soils in the southern part of the Ganga called–

(a) Bhangar mitti
(b) Red clay
(c) Balther mitti
(d) Cratal-Caval mitty

9. When did construction of Kosi project start in Bihar?

(a) 1947 AD
(b) 1948 AD
(c) 1952 AD
(d) 1954 AD

10. In which year a centre of Doordarshan was established in Bihar?

(a) 1947 (b) 1956
(c) 1978 (d) 1983

11. Where is the Salarjung Museum located?

(a) In Patna
(b) In Hyderabad
(c) In New Delhi
(d) In Lucknow

Answers

1. (c)	**2.** (b)	**3.** (c)	**4.** (b)
5. (b)	**6.** (d)	**7.** (b)	**8.** (d)
9. (d)	**10.** (c)	**11.** (b)	

BSSC Welter (Tourism Department) Recruitment Exam-2007

1. What is Nav Nalanda Mahavihar famous for?
(a) Xuanzang Memorial
(b) Museum
(c) Mahavir's birth place
(d) Pali

2. The Bodhi tree in Bodh Gaya belongs to which generation of its offspring:
(a) Third (b) Fourth
(c) Fifth (d) Sixth

3. At which tourism spot in Bihar are there many hot water sources?
(a) Dev (b) Bihar Sharif
(c) Rajgir (d) Pavapuri

4. Where is the Vishnu Pada Temple located?
(a) In Patna (b) in Danapur
(c) In Jamui (d) Gaya

5. In which of the following cities did the Japanese create Global Shanti Stupa?
(a) Dev (b) Rajgir
(c) Gaya (d) Bodh Gaya

6. Mahabodhi Mandir was built in Bodh Gaya at a place where -
(a) Gautam Buddha was born
(b) Gautam Buddha attained enlightenment
(c) Gautam Buddha gave his sermon
(d) Gautam Buddha died

7. Which was the first republic of the World in the sixth century BC?
(a) Vaishali (b) Athens
(c) Sparta (d) Patliputra

8. Which of the following city is famous for Sun temple?
(a) Gaya (b) Bodh Gaya
(c) Dev (d) Ranchi

9. The famous festival of Bihar is
(a) Durga Puja (b) Chhath Puja
(c) Vaisakhi (d) None of these

10. What is the painting style of Bihar?
(a) Madhubani
(b) Shri Rangam
(c) Pichchvai
(d) Mughal

Answers

1. (a)	**2.** (b)	**3.** (c)	**4.** (d)
5. (b)	**6.** (b)	**7.** (a)	**8.** (c)
9. (b)	**10.** (a)		

BSSC Junior Engineer (Public Resources Department) Examination-2007

1. Who among the following did not enforce the silver currency represented by "taka" or "rupee"?
(a) Sher Shah Suri
(b) Akbar
(c) Taimur
(d) Humayun

Answer

1. (a)

BSSC Eye Assistant (Ophthalmic) Examination-2007

1. Who came to India during the reign of Harshvardhan?
(a) Fahyan
(b) Xuanzang
(c) Lord Dalhousie
(d) Hitler

2. Kunwar Singh was a prominent hero of revolt in 1857.
Which of the following is related to him?
(a) Bihar (b) Madhya Pradesh
(c) Rajasthan (d) Uttar Pradesh

3. In which of these states, Council of Ministers of Congress was not formed according to the Act of 1935 AD?
(a) Bihar (b) Madras
(c) Odisha (d) Punjab

Answers

1. (b) **2.** (a) **3.** (d)

BSSC Inspector (Police Sub-Inspector) Examination-2005

1. With which company has the Government entered into an agreement for construction of bridge-road in Bihar?
(a) INDC
(b) Tantia construction
(c) NDCL
(d) Ircon

2. Which district of Bihar is the leading one in jute products?
(a) Kishanganj (b) Purna
(c) Araria (d) Katihar

3. Babu Kunwar Singh led from which region of Bihar in the 1857 war?
(a) Buxar (b) Patna
(c) Arrah (d) Munger

4. Who has been made visitor to the newly constructed Nalanda university?
(a) Amartya Sen
(b) Niti Kumar
(c) DY Patil
(d) A.P.J Abdul Kalam

5. On how much area does agriculture work take place in Bihar?
(a) 80% (b) 86%
(c) 60% (d) 65%

6. What is the rate of literacy in Bihar (as per 2001 census)?
(a) 46.65% (b) 45%
(c) 47.53% (d) 52%

7. What was the name of Sher Shah in his childhood?
(a) Farid (b) Salim
(c) Rahim (d) Murid

8. Who was the founder of Ancient Nalanda University?
(a) Dharma Pal
(b) Chandragupta Dwivedi
(c) Samudragupta
(d) Kumargupta

9. Munger was the capital of who of the following?
(a) Mir Qassim
(b) Kunwar Singh
(c) Sirajuddaula
(d) Virsa Munda

10. What was the name of Guru Govind Singh's mother?
(a) Bibi Jaila (b) Rani Dida
(c) Kajri Devi (d) None of these

11. Where was Phaneeswar Renu born?
(a) In Patna
(b) in Bhagalpur
(c) In Bhagalpur
(d) in Munger

12. Who is the creator of the book Kamayani?
(a) Jaishankar Prasad
(b) Ramdhari Singh Dinkar
(c) Mahadevi Verma
(d) Harivansh Rai Bachchan

13. Who wrote the book Arthashastra?
(a) Chandragupta Maurya
(b) Kautilya
(c) Aryabhata
(d) Kanishka

14. Who gave the slogan of Inquilab Zindabad'?

(a) Subhas Chandra Bose
(b) Mahatma Gandhi
(c) Chandrashekhar Azad
(d) Bhagat Singh

15. The battle of Buxar took place between whom–

(a) Mir Qasim and the Englishman
(b) Englishman and Sirajuddaula
(c) Englishman and Kunwar Singh
(d) None of these

16. Total number of divisions in Bihar–

(a) 11 (b) 10
(c) 9 (d) 12

17. As per census 2001, what is the total population of Bihar?

(a) 82878796 (b) 80278600
(c) 80000700 (d) 81378796

18. Sitara Devi is related to which skill?

(a) Darbhanga Painting
(b) Madhubani Painting
(c) Classical Music
(d) Folk Dance

19. When was Patna high court established?

(a) 1916 (b) in 1926
(c) 1917 (d) in 1920

20. Where did Tirthankara Mahavir die at the beginning of Jainism?

(a) in Kundgram
(b) in Rajghar
(c) In Sarnath
(d) in Pavapuri

21. Lord Buddha was born in Lumbini. Where is Lumbini?

(a) in Gaya (b) in Bihar
(c) in Nepal (d) in Uttar Pradesh

22. The number of Lok Sabha seats in Bihar is?

(a) 44 (b) 43
(c) 42 (d) 40

23. Bimbisara was the king of which dynasty?

(a) Haryak (b) Gupta
(c) Maurya (d) Shunga

24. Where did Gandhiji start the first satyagraha in India?

(a) Hazaribagh (b) Champaran
(c) Sabarmati (d) Bombay

Answers

1. (b)	**2.** (d)	**3.** (c)	**4.** (d)
5. (c)	**6.** (c)	**7.** (a)	**8.** (d)
9. (a)	**10.** (a)	**11.** (c)	**12.** (a)
13. (a)	**14.** (a)	**15.** (a)	**16.** (c)
17. (c)	**18.** (d)	**19.** (a)	**20.** (a)
21. (c)	**22.** (b)	**23.** (a)	**24.** (b)

BSSC Research Examination-2010

1. Mahatma Gandhi's Champaran movement was successful in–

(a) 1920 (b) 1915
(c) 1917 (d) None of these

2. The average height of Bihar from sea level is-

(a) 53 meters (b) 173 meters
(c) 192 meters (d) 203 meters

3. Bihar is the largest state in the country from the point of view of area:

(a)13th (b) 10th
(c)11th (d) 12th

4. The construction of Golghar located in Patna took place during the time of which governor general?

(a) Lord Harding
(b) Sir John Shore
(c) Warren Hastings
(d) Lord Corn wallis

5. When was the State of Orissa separated from Bihar and a new province was created?

(a) 1912 AD
(b) 1926 AD
(c) 1936 AD
(d) 1956 AD

6. **In Bihar, how many blocks are there?**
(a) 400 (b) 150
(c) 534 (d) 200

7. **Where is the Plant Wood factory in Bihar located?**
(a) Arrah (b) Hajipur
(c) Patna (d) Gaya

Answers

1. (c) **2.** (a) **3.** (d) **4.** (d)
5. (c) **6.** (c) **7.** (b)

BSSC First Graduate Level (Secretariat) Exam-2011

1. **Ashoka the Great, ruled India for 40 years, the name of his capital was-**
(a) Takshashila (b) Bodh Gaya
(c) Patliputra (d) Sarnath

2. **Guru Gobind Singh ji, the 10th Guru of the Sikhs, was born in**
(a) In Amritsar (b) in Delhi
(c) In Patna (d) Kolkata

3. **Chinese pilgrim Xuanzang visited India -**
(a) During Ashoka's reign
(b) During the reign of Chandragupta Maurya
(c) During the reign of Harshavardhan
(d) During the reign of Chandragupta Dwivedi

4. **A complete revolution was called by -**
(a) Mahatma Gandhi
(b) Bhagat Singh
(c) Dr. Bhimrao Ambedkar
(d) Jayaprakash Narayan's

Answers

1. (c) **2.** (c) **3.** (c) **4.** (d)

BSSC Excise Sub-Inspector (ESI) Examination-2012

1. **Samrat Ashoka's father was -**
(a) Bimbisara
(b) Bindusara
(c) Chandragupta Maurya
(d) Brihadratha

Answer

1. (b)

BSSC Junior Engineer (Water Resources Division)-2012

1. **As per the data released by the Ministry of State for Statistics of India in June, 2012, which State has emerged as the highest economic finance state?**
(a) Gujarat (b) Punjab
(c) Bihar (d) Maharashtra

Answer

1. (c)

BSSC Auditor Recruitment Exam-2012

1. **Who was the famous ruler of ancient India who converted to Jainism at the end of his life:**
(a) Samudragupta
(b) point abstract
(c) Chandragupta Maurya
(d) Ashoka

2. **Ashoka's inscriptions have been written in:**
1. Greek **2. Kharoshti**
3. Armeek **4. Sanskrit**

(a) 1, 2 & 4 (b) 1, 2 & 3
(c) 2 & 3 (d) 2,3 & 4

3. Which of the following is the oldest gurukul in:
(a) Ujjain (b) Nalanda
(c) Vikramshila (d) Takshashila

4. Sher Shah is well-known for his administrative skills, specifically for -
(a) Buying-selling control system
(b) Land revenue system
(c) Manasabdari system
(d) Justice & Order

Answers

1. (c) **2.** (b) **3.** (d) **4.** (b)

BSSC First Graduate Level (Secretariat) Main-2013

1. What is the current name of the State where the ancient educational place Nalanda was located?
(a) Bihar
(c) Maharashtra
(c) Delhi
(d) Uttar Pradesh

2. The first Vice Chancellor of Nalanda International University School was appointed by–
(a) A.P.J. Abdul Kalam
(b) Sonia Gandhi
(c) Manmohan Singh
(d) P. Chidambaram

3. The State in the north of Jharkhand is:
(a) Chhattisgarh
(b) Bihar
(c) West Bengal
(d) Madhya Pradesh

Answers

1. (a) **2.** (a) **3.** (b)

BSSC Ameen (Amanat) Recruitment Exam-2013

1. Which of the following countries is located in the north direction of Bihar?
(a) Nepal (b) Pakistan
(c) Bhutan (d) Maldives

2. Which of the following States is located in the west direction of Bihar?
(a) Odisha
(b) Uttar Pradesh
(c) Nagaland
(d) Arunachal Pradesh

3. Where is the main headquarters of the Saran district?
(a) Patna (b) Chhapra
(c) Motihari (d) Gaya

4. During British reign, Bihar was the part of which district?
(a) Bombay (b) Madras
(c) Hyderabad (d) Bengal

5. What is the official language of Bihar?
(a) Hindi (b) Oriya
(c) Munda (d) Bihari

6. Which State was separated from Bihar in the year 2000?
(a) Chhattisgarh
(b) Jharkhand
(c) Haryana
(d) Uttarakhand

7. Which river is called the mourning of Bihar?
(a) Yamuna (b) Sindhu
(c) Kosi (d) Bagmati

8. Which of the following presidents of India was born in Bihar?
(a) Zakir Hussain
(b) Neelam Sanjeeva Reddy
(c) KR Narayanan
(d) Dr. Rajendra Prasad

9. **Which coalition came to power in Bihar in 2006?**
(a) NDA (b) UNPA
(c) Left Front (d) National Front

10. **Where was Lord Mahavir born?**
(a) Bodh Gaya (b) Rajgir
(c) Vaishali (d) Lumbini

11. **Patna was known as ________ in the ancient times?**
(a) Patliputra (b) Rajagraha
(c) Patandevi (d) Vaishali

12. **Which of the following was not a centre of education in India?**
(a) Nalanda
(b) Vikramshila
(c) Udaant Puri
(d) Vijayanagar

13. **From which original word was the word 'Bihar' taken?**
(a) Chaitya (b) Vihara
(c) Vaahan (d) Vikramshila

14. **Sher Shah Suri was from which place?**
(a) Patna (b) Gaya
(c) Sasaram (d) Arrah

15. **Who led the 1857 Sipahi Vidroh in Bihar?**
(a) Kunwar Singh
(b) Tantia Tope
(c) Rani Laxmi Bai
(d) Bahadur Shah

Answers

1. (a)	**2.** (b)	**3.** (b)	**4.** (d)
5. (a)	**6.** (b)	**7.** (c)	**8.** (d)
9. (a)	**10.** (c)	**11.** (a)	**12.** (d)
13. (b)	**14.** (c)	**15.** (a)	

BSSC Stenographer Examination-2013

1. **Which state has recorded the highest growth rate in the last decade 2001-2011 in literacy?**
(a) Kerala
(b) Bihar
(c) Meghalaya
(d) Arunachal Pradesh

2. **Where are the moist deciduous forests found?**
(a) Saharsa and Purnia
(b) Patna and Nalanda District
(c) Samastipur and Darbhanga district
(d) Vaishali and Begusarai Districts

3. **Which of the following are the products of Bihar?**
(a) limestone, quartzite and pyrite
(b) Lignite, Mica and Lime Stone
(c) Mica, Gold and Tin
(d) Mitti, Iron-Ore and Sand

4. **The battle of Chausa took place between-**
(a) Babur and Sher Shah
(b) Sangram Singh and Sher Shah
(c) Humayun and Sher Shah
(d) Akbar and Sher Shah

5. **In which script are the Inscriptions of Samrat Ashoka written?**
(a) Brahmi (b) Kharosthi
(c) Devanagari (d) Yunani

6. **The Ancient World School of Nalanda was built during which dynasty?**
(a) Mauryan dynasty
(b) Gupta dynasty
(c) Kushan dynasty
(d) Pala dynasty

7. **Which of the following is a book written by Ramdhari Singh Dinkar?**
(a) Rashmi Rathi
(b) Jhansi ki Rani
(c) Madhushala
(d) Arjuna's Ki Pratigya

8. **Who was Phaneeswarnath Renu?**
(a) mathematics expert
(b) poet
(c) astrologer
(d) None of these

9. **Where was Gautam Buddha born?**
   (a) Vaishali (b) Bodh Gaya
   (c) Rajgir (d) Lumbini
10. **Who out of the following was not the ruler of Magadha?**
   (a) Shishunag (b) Dhanananda
   (c) Bindusara (d) Kanishk
11. **Didarganj Yakshini is of which period–**
   (a) Gupta (b) Kushans
   (c) Maurya (d) Shaka
12. **Who was given the title of Deshratna?**
   (a) Jayaprakash Narayan
   (b) Dr. Rajendra Prasad
   (c) Lal Bahadur Shastri
   (d) Jagjivan Ram

Answers

1. (b) **2.** (a) **3.** (a) **4.** (c)
5. (a) **6.** (b) **7.** (a) **8.** (b)
9. (d) **10.** (d) **11.** (c) **12.** (b)

BSSC Kara Mishrak (Kara Division) Exam-2015

1. **The population density of which State is maximum?**
   (a) Uttar Pradesh
   (b) Bihar
   (c) West Bengal
   (d) Maharashtra
2. **Who among the following Presidents of India was born in Bihar?**
   (a) Zakir Hussain
   (b) Neelam Reddy
   (c) Dr. Rajendra Prasad
   (d) KR Narayanan
3. **The Government of Bihar has prohibited the sale and manufacture of all ________ products for the next one year.**
   (a) Til Oil seeds (b) Tobacco
   (c) Meat (d) Cotton

Answers

1. (b) **2.** (c) **3.** (b)

BSSC Secondary Graduate Level (Secretariat) Exam-2015

1. **The Bihar Panchayati Raj Act has a tenure of five years for gram panchayat. Its calculation-**
   (a) Is calculated from the date of notice of Panchayat Nirvachan
   (b) Is calculated from the date of first meeting of the Panchayat
   (c) Is calculated from the date of declaration of the results of Panchayat Nirvachan.
   (d) None of these
2. **Who established Kisan Sabha in Bihar?**
   (a) Dr. Rajendra Prasad
   (b) Sahaj Ananda Sarasvati
   (c) Jayaprakash Narayan
   (d) Swami Agnivesh
3. **Which of the rivers flowing in Bihar originates in Amarkantak?**
   (a) Koyal (b) Sone
   (c) Punpun (d) Karo

Answers

1. (c) **2.** (b) **3.** (b)

BSSC Secondary Graduate Level (Secretariat) Exam-2015

1. **When was Patna high court established?**
   (a) 1905 AD (b) 1911 AD
   (c) 1914 AD (d) 1916 AD
2. **Bihar has 40 Lok Sabha seats. How many seats does Rajya Sabha have?**

(a) 12 (b) 14
(c) 15 (d) 16

3. **The estimated population of Bihar in the 2011 Census is–**
(a) 8 Crore (b) 9 crore
(c) 10 Crores (d) 14 crores

4. **Total number of districts in Bihar are-**
(a) 40 (b) 35
(c) 38 (d) 39

Answers

1. (d) 2. (d) 3. (c) 4. (c)

BSSC Secondary Graduate Level (Secretariat)-2016

1. **Among Tributaries of Ganga which are described below, which is flowing towards north?**
(a) Kosi (b) Ghaghara
(c) Sone (d) Gandak

Answer

1. (c)

BSSC Ambedkar High School (Teacher) Examination-2016

1. **Which muslim destroyed Nalanda University?**
(a) Allaudin Khilji
(b) Muhammad Bin Tughlaq
(c) Muhammad Bin Bakhtiyaar
(d) Muhammad Bin Qassim

Answer

1. (c)

BSSC 1st Inter Level (PT) Examination-2017

1. **When did Champaran Satyagraha begin?**
(a) 1929 (c) 1917
(c) 1857 (d) 1946

2. **Who drove Dawood out of Patna and Hajipur?**
(a) Humayun (b) Babur
(c) Jahangir (d) Akbar

3. **Who was Megasthenes who came to India during the reign of Chandra Gupta Maurya?**
(a) invader (b) ambassador.
(c) pujari (d) Minister

4. **Where did Guru Gobind Singh study and where did he learn Persian?**
(a) Lahore (b) Amritsar
(c) Patna (d) Ambala

5. **Where is Valmiki National Garden Located?**
(a) Uttar Pradesh
(b) Madhya Pradesh
(c) Bihar
(d) Odisha

Answers

1. (b) 2. (d) 3. (b) 4. (d)
5. (c)

BSSC First Inter Level Exam-2017

1. **Chhau is the folk dance of which other state other than Bihar?**
(a) West Bengal
(b) Mizoram
(c) Madhya Pradesh
(d) Uttar Pradesh

2. **From the point of view of population, the state which is not among the four major states is -**
(a) Bihar
(b) Uttar Pradesh
(c) Maharashtra
(d) Tamil Nadu

3. The population density of which state is maximum every year?

(a) Bihar (b) West Bengal
(c) Kerala (d) Uttar Pradesh

4. Which of these is called the city of palaces?

(a) Patna (b) Kolkata
(c) Chandigarh (d) Lucknow

5. This part of Bihar has a maximum population density?

(a) Eastern (b) Western
(c) northern (d) southern

Answers

1. (a) **2.** (d) **3.** (a) **4.** (b)
5. (c)

BSSC Bihar Inspector (Police Sub-Inspector) Re-Examination-2017

1. Who is the Deputy Chief Minister of Bihar now?

(a) Nitish Kumar
(b) Sushil Kumar Modi
(c) Tejaswi Yadav
(d) Sharad Yadav

2. The state which is dependent on canal irrigation is:

(a) Bihar (b) Uttar Pradesh
(c) Punjab (d) Andhra Pradesh

3. The second official language of Bihar is–

(a) Urdu (b) Mathili
(c) Bhojpuri (d) Maghi

4. Who appointed the Chief Minister of Bihar?

(a) President of India
(b) The party president
(c) The governor of Bihar
(d) Vice President of India

5. The capital of old Lichchiva was?

(a) Patliputra
(b) Nalanda
(c) Vaishali
(d) Gaya

6. Which of these was the capital of Chandragupta Maurya's empire?

(a) Vaishali (b) Rajgir
(c) Patliputra (d) Bodh Gaya

7. Hot water sources are here:

(a) Arrah (b) Rajagraha
(c) Ranchi (d) Vaishali

Answers

1. (c) **2.** (c) **3.** (a) **4.** (c)
5. (c) **6.** (c) **7.** (b)

BSSC Junior Engineer (Water Resources Division) Re-Examination-2018

1. Why was Bihar Prantiya Kisan Sabha formed by Sahajananda Sarasvati in Bihar in 1929?

(a) Demonstration of angst against Nokhali riots
(b) To associate people against the murder of Baikunth Shukla
(c) To bring to light the grievances of the poor in protest against the attack on the rights of the poor by Zamindars.
(d) To wake up people against Gandhiji's arrest in Bihar

Answer

1. (c)

BSSC Bihar Inspector (Police Sub-Inspector) Main Examination-2018

1. Sher Shah's tomb is located at–

(a) Kalinjar (b) Sasaram
(c) Delhi (d) Agra

2. Who was the first expert and astronomer of the Gupta period?

(a) Varahamihir (b) Brahma Gupta
(c) Bhaskar I (d) Aryabhatta

3. **Which State of India does not have a two-member local system?**
   (a) Bihar
   (b) Uttar Pradesh
   (c) Punjab
   (d) Jammu and Kashmir

Answers

1. (b) **2.** (d) **3.** (c)

BSSC Group (GH) to Group (G) Translator Promotion Examination-2018

1. **Which one of the following in Bihar has recently been added as a special place of importance to the World Heritage Committee?**
   (a) Sasaram
   (b) Nalanda Mahavihar
   (c) Vaishali
   (d) Munger
2. **Which of the tribal leaders of Bihar strongly opposed the British rule in India?**
   (a) Chakra Bisoi
   (b) Rupsingh
   (c) Jabonang
   (d) Birsa Munda
3. **In Bihar, farmers were forced to grow indigo, and were not permitted to grow essential food items and were not given adequate payments for growing indigo; due to all these there was a national protest demonstration in 1917. What is this protest known as?**
   (a) Bardoli Satyagraha
   (b) Vicom Satyagraha
   (c) Champaran Satyagraha
   (d) Kheda Satyagraha

Answers

1. (b) **2.** (a) **3.** (c)

BSSC Kara Mishrak (Kara Division) Examination-2018

1. **In what form did the Gupta dynasty establish Nalanda?**
   (a) Business centre
   (b) Buddhist Monastery
   (c) natural tourist destination
   (d) wildlife sanctuary
2. **In 1929, why was Bihar Provincial Kisan Sabha constituted in Bihar by Swami Sahjaanand Sarasvati?**
   (a) To start the publication of a weekly magazine Hunkar
   (b) To bring to light the grievances of the people who are against the cruelty of landlords.
   (c) Against Baikunth Shukla's execution
   (d) Against the cruelty of Fanindranath Ghosh's Revolutionary Party
3. **Which of the following leaders of Freedom fight is called "Bihar Vibhuti"?**
   (a) Baikunth Shukla
   (b) Sathyendra Narayan Sinha
   (c) Anugrah Narayan Sinha
   (d) Jai Prakash Narayan
4. **The Mithila region of Bihar is famous for**
   (a) Pashmina Wool
   (b) Rajgir Dance
   (c) Madhubani Chitrakari
   (d) Patthar Nakkashi

Answers

1. (b) **2.** (b) **3.** (c) **4.** (c)

BSSC First Inter Level (PT) Re-Examination-2018

1. Rail wheel factory is located in Bihar in -

(a) Chhapra (b) Madhora
(c) Gaya (d) Madhepura

2. In which district of Bihar is maximum sex ratio prevails?

(a) Nawada (b) Sivan
(c) Gopalganj (d) Chhapra

3. What is India's global ranking in Global Passport Power?

(a) 81st (b) 75th
(c) 76th (d) 51st

4. In which district of Bihar female literacy is the maximum?

(a) Patna (b) Gaya
(c) Bhojpur (d) Rohtas

5. When was the Bihar Lok Shikayat Act passed?

(a) 5 June 2015
(b) 2nd October 2016
(c) 1 May 2016
(d) June 5, 2016

6. Who is the Chairman of Panchayat Samiti's Audit, Planning and Finance in Bihar?

(a) Deputy Head of Panchayat
(b) Prakhand Vikas officer
(c) District finance officer
(d) Head of Panchayat Samiti

7. Where did the first Congress session take place in Bihar?

(a) Bhagalpur (b) Motihari
(c) Bankipur (d) Gaya

8. Paika dance is related to which state?

(a) Bihar (b) Rajasthan
(c) Punjab (d) Kerala

Answers

1. (a) **2.** (c) **3.** (d) **4.** (d)
5. (d) **6.** (d) **7.** (d) **8.** (d)

BSSC Sub-Inspector Products (ESI) Examination-2019

1. Which birth anniversary of Guru Govind Singh was celebrated in 2019?

(a) 352nd (b) 353rd
(c) 452nd (d) 453rd

2. When was Vardhaman Mahavir born?

(a) 540 AD (b) 562 AD
(c) 440 AD (d) 468 AD

3. Where is the Kaimur Forest Sanctuary located?

(a) Bihar (b) Jharkhand
(c) Odisha (d) Gujarat

4. Arrange these districts of Bihar from North to South –

(a) Mujaffarpur, Sitamgarhi, Gaya, Partna, Jehanabad
(b) Sitamgarhi, Mujaffarpur, Patna, Gaya, Jehanabad
(c) Sitamgarhi, Mujaffarpur, Jehanabad, Patna, Gaya
(d) Sitamgarhi, Mujaffarupur, Patna, Jehanabad, Gaya

Answers

1. (a) **2.** (a) **3.** (a) **4.** (d)

BSSC Bihar Police Forest Guard Examination

1. Lalji Tandon was which Governor of Bihar?

(a) 29th (b) 30th
(c) 32nd (d) 36th

2. Bihar's minimum population district is -

(a) Sheikhupura
(b) Shivahar
(c) Sitamarhi
(d) Vaishali

3. **Which district of Bihar has maximum sex ratio?**
(a) Patna (b) Rohtas
(c) Gopalganj (d) Vaishali

4. **What is the infant mortality rate in Bihar?**
(a) 38 (b) 40
(c) 42 (d) 44

5. **On what percentage of Bihar's land cubic forest exists?**
(a) 0.15 (b) 0.25
(c) 0.35 (d) 0.40

6. **In Bihar, what amount is given to encourage inter-caste marriage?**
(a) ₹ 50,000
(b) ₹ 75,000
(c) ₹ 80,000
(d) ₹ 2,50,000

7. **Which Authority is related to Bihar's sustainable development?**
(a) Planning and development Division
(b) rural development division
(c) urban development division
(d) None of these

8. **Who was the prominent leader of Darbhanga Kisan Movement in 1919-20?**
(a) Babu Krishna Singh
(b) Sahaj Ananda Sarasvati
(c) Babu Braj Kishore Prasad
(d) Babu Ramdayalu Singh

Answers

1. (b)	**2.** (d)	**3.** (b)	**4.** (d)
5. (b)	**6.** (d)	**7.** (b)	**8.** (d)

66th, Bihar Combined Solved Papers Pre-exam-2020

1. **Ram Vilas Paswan started his political career from which political party?**
(a) Janata Party
(b) Bharatiya Lok Dal
(c) Samyukta Socialist Party
(d) Praja Socialist Party
(e) None of the above/More than one of the above

2. **When Did the Election Commission of the India issue a Press Note for the General Election to the Legislative Assembly of Bihar, 2020?**
(a) 23rd September, 2020
(b) 24th September, 2020
(c) 25th September, 2020
(d) 26th September, 2020
(e) None of the above/More than one of the above

3. **In Which state, 'Ghar Tak Fiber' Scheme has been launched on 21st September, 2020 through video conference?**
(a) Uttar Pradesh
(b) Madhya Pradesh
(c) Bihar
(d) Karnataka
(e) None of the above/More than one of the above

4. **Bihar Politician Late Raghuvansh Prasad Singh was for the first time elected to which Lok Sabha?**
(a) Tenth Lok Sabha
(b) Eleventh Lok Sabha
(c) Twelfth Lok Sabha
(d) Thirteenth Lok Sabha
(e) None of the above/More than one of the above

5. **Kol Mutiny of 1831 under Buddho Bhagat took place in which of the following regions?**
(a) Kutch
(b) Singhbhum
(c) Western Ghats
(d) Satara
(e) None of the above/More than one of the above

6. **Who spearheaded the 1857 Revolt in Bihar?**

(a) Nana Saheb
(b) Tatya Tope
(c) Kunwar Singh
(d) Maulavi Ahmadullah
(e) None of the above/More than one of the above

7. Who drew Gandhiji's attention to the plight of Indigo peasants in Champaran?
(a) Rajendra Prasad
(b) Anugrah Narayan Sinha
(c) Acharya Kripalani
(d) Raj Kumar Shukhla
(e) None of the above/More than one of the above

8. Which was the first capital of ancient Mahajanapada Magadh?
(a) Pataliputra
(b) Vaishali
(c) Champa
(d) Anga
(e) None of the above/More than one of the above

9. Swami Sahajananda was realted to which of the following?
(a) Tribal Movement in Bihar
(b) Labour Movement in Bihar
(c) Peasant Movement in Bihar
(d) Caste Movement in Bihar
(e) None of the above/More than one of the above

10. Which of the following was Gandhiji's first Satyagraha Movement in India in which he used Civil Disobedience?
(a) Champaran
(b) Kheda
(c) Ahmedabad
(d) Rowlatt Satyagraha
(e) None of the above/More than one of the above

11. Which of the following rivers flowing in Bihar is a north flowing river?
(a) Bagmati
(b) Kamla
(c) Kosi
(d) Gandak
(e) None of the above/More than one of the above

12. Among the following pairs of mineral and district, which one is correctly matched?
(a) Limestone – Kaimur
(b) Mica – Bhagalpur
(c) Quartzite – Madhubani
(d) Lead – zinc – Gaya
(e) None of the above/More than one of the above

13. Which one of the following pairs of industry and Place is not correctly matched?
(a) Oil refinery – Barauni
(b) Cement – Banjari
(c) Fertilizer – Bhaurahi
(d) Wagon and engineering – Bhagalpur
(e) None of the above/More than one of the above

14. Which one of the following pairs of Administrative Divisions of Bihar, Ganga river does not flow?
(a) Darbhanga – Munger
(b) Purnea – Bhagalpur
(c) Tirhut – Saran
(d) Kosi—Magadh
(e) None of the above/More than one of the above

15. Among the following pairs of tribe and district, which one is not correctly matched?
(a) Santhal – Banka
(b) Munda – Jamui
(c) Oraon – Supaul
(d) Kharwar – Bhagalpur
(e) None of the above/More than one of the above

16. What is the percentage of all types of forest area to the total geographical area of Bihar State?
(a) 7.27 (b) 6.87
(c) 3.21 (d) 12.77

(e) None of the above/More than one of the above

17. Which one of the following districts is having the only National Park of Bihar?

(a) Nalanda
(b) Bhagalpur
(c) Champaran
(d) East Champaran
(e) None of the above/More than one of the above

18. Which company established its factory in 1632 at Patna, Bihar?

(a) British East India Company
(b) Dutch East India company
(c) Portuguese East India Company
(d) French East India Company
(e) None of the above/More than one of the above

19. Bihar Government has introduced the comprehensive Financial Management System (CFMS) on 1st April, 2019. This System

(a) will make all financial activities in the state online and paperless
(b) will solve the problem of NPA of banks
(c) will ensure effective implementation of State projects
(d) will manage State Government finance including local bodies
(e) None of the above/More than one of the above

20. The government of India conferred the Krishi Karman Award to Bihar State on 2nd January, 2020. This award was given for

(a) Production and productivity of maize and wheat
(b) food grain production
(c) production of rice
(d) production of oilseeds
(e) None of the above/More than one of the above

21. Bihar government launched a new scheme 'Satat Jivikoparjan Yojana' in August 2018. The Objective of this scheme is

(a) to provide unemployment allowance to youth
(b) to provide employment in rural areas through local bodies
(c) to provide sustainable income generating assets to extremely poor households
(d) to provide free training for skill upgradation of youth
(e) None of the above/More than one of the above

22. Which of the following is not included in Seven Resolves (Saat Nishchay) of Bihar Government?

(a) Women Employment
(b) Clean Drinking Water
(c) Supply of electricity to all households
(d) Child Welfare
(e) None of the above/More than one of the above

23. The per capita Net State Domestic Product at constant prices for Bihar is less than the country. In the year 2018-19, it was

(a) 75 percent of the national average
(b) 60 percent of the national average
(c) 50 percent of the national average
(d) 33 percent of the national average
(e) None of the above/More than one of the above

24. When was Bihar established?

(a) 1911 (b) 1912
(c) 1913 (d) 1914
(e) None of the above/More than one of the above

25. In Tinkathia System in Bihar, how much land was to be reserved for indigo cultivation?

(a) 01/10 (b) 01/03
(c) 03/20 (d) 03/25
(e) None of the above/More than one of the above

26. Who was the first Chief Minister of Bihar?
(a) Shri Krishna Singh
(b) Satya Pal Malik
(c) Nitish Kumar
(d) Rabri Devi
(e) None of the above/More than one of the above

27. Where was the first Congress Session in Bihar held?
(a) Patna
(b) Gaya
(c) Muzaffarpur
(d) Darbhanga
(e) None of the above/More than one of the above

28. Which title was given to Jayaprakash Narayan?
(a) Praja Hitechhu
(b) Lok Nayak
(c) Lokmanya
(d) Rashtra Nayak
(e) None of the above/More than one of the above

Answers

1. (c)	2. (c)	3. (c)	4. (b)
5. (b)	6. (c)	7. (d)	8. (e)
9. (c)	10. (a)	11. (e)	12. (a)
13. (d)	14. (d)	15. (b)	16. (a)
17. (c)	18. (b)	19. (a)	20. (a)
21. (c)	22. (d)	23. (d)	24. (b)
25. (c)	26. (a)	27. (a)	28. (b)

BPSC Assistant Audit Officer Examination-2022

1. Who started newspaper Motherland in September 1921 to disseminate the Hindu-Muslim unity and Gandhian ideology?
(a) Shah Mohammad Zubair
(b) Mazhar-ul-Haq
(c) Anugrah Narayan Sinha
(d) Shambhu Sharan
(e) None of the above/More than one of the above

2. Who inaugurated Bihar National College and its building 'Bihar Vidyapeeth' in February 1922?
(a) Dr. Rajendra Prasad
(b) Mahadev Desai
(c) Mahatma Gandhi
(d) Chittaranjan Das
(e) None of the above/More than one of the above

3. Who was the first Prime Minister of Bihar under Provincial Autonomy in 1937?
(a) Mohammad Yunus
(b) Sri Krishna Singh
(c) Prof. Abdul Bari
(d) Ramsunder Singh
(e) None of the above/More than one of the above

4. The name of the Hindi Weekly which was the mouthpiece of the agrarian and peasant movements in Bihar in 1940 was
(a) Leader
(b) Lokmat
(c) Hunkar
(d) Sarathi
(e) None of the above/More than one of the above

5. Who was the convener of a branch of Swaraj Dal formed in Bihar?
(a) Raj Kumar Shukla
(b) Shambhu Sharan
(c) Srikrishna Singh
(d) Dharnidhar Prasad
(e) None of the above/More than one of the above

6. According to the Government Think Tank NITI Aayog's Multidimensional Poverty Index (MPI), the percentage of poor population of Bihar is
(a) 50.91%

(b) 51.91%
(c) 52.91%
(d) 53.91%
(e) None of the above/More than one of the above

7. In which game had Pramod Bhagat of Bihar won the gold medal in 'Tokyo Paralympics'?
(a) Para Hockey
(b) Para Football
(c) Para Badminton
(d) Para Cricket
(e) None of the above/More than one of the above

8. The theme of Bihar Diwas, 2022 is
(a) Jal Hi Jeevan Hai
(b) Jal Jeevan Hariyali
(c) Jal Bachao
(d) Jal Jeevan Khushali
(e) None of the above/More than one of the above

9. Eastern Zone Conference, held at Patna on 7th January, 2022, was jointly organized by the Ministry of Railways and the Government of Bihar on
(a) PM Jal Shakti Yojana
(b) PM Gati Shakti Yojana
(c) PM Vidyut Shakti Yojana
(d) PM Bal Shakti Yojana
(e) None of the above/More than one of the above

10. How many talents of Bihar were the winners in the Rashtriya Kala Utsav, 2021?
(a) 2
(b) 3
(c) 4
(d) 5
(e) None of the above/More than one of the above

11. Who was awarded Padma Shri Award for the year 2022 for Social Work in Bihar?
(a) Acharya Ram Krishan
(b) Acharya Chandanaji
(c) Acharya Vishwanath
(d) Acharya Najma Akhtar
(e) None of the above/More than one of the above

12. Who was awarded Pradhan Mantri Rashtriya Bal Puraskar, 2022 in Bihar?
(a) Vikas
(b) Sumit
(c) Dhiraj
(d) Udhyan
(e) None of the above/More than one of the above

13. In which city of Bihar, the country's first Craft Art Museum is being built?
(a) Darbhanga
(b) Gaya
(c) Nalanda
(d) Patna
(e) None of the above/More than one of the above

14. Under 'Bal Sahayata Yojana', how much amount was announced by the Bihar's Chief Minister for the rehabilitation of children orphaned by COVID-19 till the attainment of 18 years?
(a) ₹ 1,000
(b) ₹ 1,200
(c) ₹ 1,400
(d) ₹ 1,500
(e) None of the above/More than one of the above

15. Which Pavilion was awarded a gold medal in the 'Best Pavilion' category during the closing ceremony of the 40th India International Trade Fair held at Pragati Maidan in New Delhi?
(a) The Punjab Pavilion

(b) The Haryana Pavilion
(c) The Assam Pavilion
(d) The Bihar Pavilion
(e) None of the above/More than one of the above

16. Who among the following was not directly related to Champaran Peasant Movement of 1917?
(a) Mahadev Desai
(b) Narhari Parikh
(c) Dr. Rajendra Prasad
(d) Gauri Shankar Mishra
(e) None of the above/More than one of the above

17. Who among the following was hanged on the charge of Muzaffarpur Bomb Case?
(a) Prafulla Chaki
(b) Batukeshwar Dutt
(c) Rajguru
(d) Rajendra Lahiri
(e) None of the above/More than one of the above

18. Which ruler founded the beautiful city, Pataliputra?
(a) Ajatashatru
(b) Bimbisara
(c) Bindusara
(d) Udayin
(e) None of the above/More than one of the above

19. Who was the ruler of Magadha on the eve of Alexander's invasion in India?
(a) Mahapadma Nanda
(b) Dhana Nanda
(c) Chandragupta Maurya
(d) Chandragupta 1
(e) None of the above/More than one of the above

20. In which Sufi order was Sufi Saint Sharfuddin Yahya Maneri associated?
(a) Chishti
(b) Qadiri
(c) Firdausi
(d) Suhrawardi
(e) None of the above/More than one of the above

21. Who did lead the peasant movement in the region of Darbhanga Raj?
(a) Swami Sahajanand
(b) Swami Vidyanand
(c) Baba Ramchandra
(d) Vinoba Bhave
(e) None of the above/More than one of the above

22. Which city of Bihar was made capital in lieu of Murshidabad by Mir Qasim?
(a) Patna
(b) Darbhanga
(c) Sasaram
(d) Munger
(e) None of the above/More than one of the above

23. In which year was 'Bakasht Movement' started in Bihar?
(a) 1936
(b) 1938
(c) 1926
(d) 1928
(e) None of the above/More than one of the above

24. In which inscription did Ashoka show his believe in 'Triratna'?
(a) Maski
(b) Kalsi
(c) Mahesana
(d) Bhabru
(e) None of the above/More than one of the above

25. Which Gupta ruler is mentioned as 'Param Bhagawata' in
(a) Chandragupta I
(b) Chandragupta II
(c) Samudragupta
(d) Skandagupta
(e) None of the above/More than one of the above

26. **The smallest river/tributary in length (in km) is**
(a) Burhi Gandak
(b) Kosi
(c) Punpun
(d) Kamala
(e) None of the above/More than one of the above

27. **Which one of the following agro-climatic zones of Bihar produces maximum Makhana (Foxnut)?**
(a) North-West alluvial plain
(b) North-East aluvial plain
(c) South-West alluvial plain
(d) South-East alluvial plain
(e) None of the above/More than one of the above

28. **Which one of the following pairs of park-sanctuary and district is not matched correctly?**
(a) Bhimbandh – Munger
(b) Nagi Dam – Jamuio
(c) Kaimur – Buxar
(d) Rajgir – Nalanda
(e) None of the above/More than one of the above

29. **Who is the author of the book entitled, The Making of Bihar and Biharis : Colonialism, Politics and Culture in Modern India, 1870–1912?**
(a) Arvind N. Das
(b) K. K. Datta
(c) Narendra Jha
(d) Vinita Damodaran
(e) None of the above/More than one of the above

30. **Which is the most educated district in Bihar in 2011 Census?**
(a) Munger
(b) Patna
(c) Rohtas
(d) Bhojpur
(e) None of the above/More than one of the above

31. **Fast-growing industry in the Bihar State is**
(a) Food processing
(b) Dairy
(c) Sugar
(d) Manufacturing
(e) None of the above/More than one of the above

32. **In which crop production, Bihar State is leading in the country?**
(a) Potato
(b) Onion
(c) Egg plant
(d) Cauliflower
(e) None of the above/More than one of the above

33. **Which of the following is the most populated district in Bihar according to population Census 2011?**
(a) Sitamarhi
(b) Banka
(c) Purnia
(d) Nalanda
(e) None of the above/More than one of the above

Answers

1. (b)	**2.** (c)	**3.** (a)	**4.** (c)
5. (c)	**6.** (b)	**7.** (c)	**8.** (b)
9. (b)	**10.** (d)	**11.** (b)	**12.** (c)
13. (d)	**14.** (d)	**15.** (d)	**16.** (d)
17. (e)	**18.** (d)	**19.** (b)	**20.** (c)
21. (b)	**22.** (d)	**23.** (a)	**24.** (d)
25. (c)	**26.** (c)	**27.** (b)	**28.** (c)
29. (c)	**30.** (c)	**31.** (e)	**32.** (e)
33. (a)			

BPSC Child Development Project Officer (CDPO), Exam-2022

1. **When was the Province of Bihar added to the Province of Bengal?**
(a) 1731 AD
(b) 1732 AD
(c) 1733 AD
(d) 1734 AD
(e) None of the above/More than one of the above

2. **Which British officer reported to the Government of India that the Muslims of Patna were in correspondence with 64th Native Infantry near Peshawar and urged it to revolt against the British?**
(a) Robert Montgomery
(b) John Lawrence
(c) Charles Metcalfe
(d) General Van Cortlandt
(e) None of the above/More than one of the above

3. **Who led the Quit India Movement in Patna city on 11th August, 1942?**
(a) Zamindars
(b) Chieftains
(c) Ricksha Pullers and Ekka drivers
(d) Subaltern sections of the city
(e) None of the above/More than one of the above

4. **The parts of eastern Uttar Pradesh and Bihar are included in which of the following plains?**
(a) Upper Ganga Plain
(b) Middle Ganga Plain
(c) Lower Ganga Plain
(d) Brahmaputra Plain
(e) None of the above/More than one of the above

5. **Which of the following is a centre of textiles?**
(a) Bokaro
(b) Bhilwara
(c) Sanand
(d) Tarapur
(e) None of the above/More than one of the above

6. **Someshwar Range is a part of which of the following mountain ranges?**
(a) Satpura Range
(b) Vindhyan Range
(c) eastern Ghats
(d) Shiwalik Range
(e) None of the above/More than one of the above

7. **The land of Bihar is drained by which of the following river systems?**
(a) Mahanadi
(b) Ganga
(c) Yamuna
(d) Godavari
(e) None of the above/More than one of the above

8. **In Bihar, the terms Balsundari Tal, Karail and Balthar are used for which of the following?**
(a) Agriculture
(b) Crop
(c) Soil
(d) Natural vegetation
(e) None of the above/More than one of the above

9. **Which of the following districts has no land under forest cover?**
(a) Bhojpur
(b) Rohtas
(c) Nawada
(d) Munger
(e) None of the above/More than one of the above

10. **Kahalgaon, Kanti, Barh and Nabinagar are the centres for which of the following?**
(a) Coal mining
(b) Tourism
(c) Thermal power
(d) Cotton textile industry

(e) None of the above/More than one of the above

11. Which of the following districts recorded the highest growth rate of population in the decade 2001–11?

(a) Gopalganj
(b) Katihar
(c) Vaishali
(d) Kishanganj
(e) None of the above/More than one of the above

12. Which of the following is a centre of textile industry in Bihar?

(a) Gaya
(b) Bhagalpur
(c) Patna
(d) Munger
(e) None of the above/More than one of the above

13. Who was the first non-Congress Chief Minister of Bihar?

(a) Karpoori Thakur
(b) Mahamaya Prasad Sinha
(c) Ram Sundar Das
(d) Lalu Prasad Yadav
(e) None of the above/More than one of the above

14. Which political party has four seats in Bihar Vidhan Sabha and one seat in Bihar Vidhan Parishad?

(a) INC
(b) AIMIM
(c) VIP
(d) BVP
(e) None of the above/More than one of the above

15. Which of the following supported the removal of Article 370?

(a) RJD
(b) INC
(c) JD (U)
(d) BSP
(e) None of the above/More than one of the above

16. Which of the following supported the Citizenship Amendment Bill?

(a) JD(U)
(b) RJD
(c) BSP
(d) INC
(e) None of the above/More than one of the above

17. Which political party supported the Muslim Women (Protection of Rights on Marriage) Bill, 2019 in the Rajya Sabha?

(a) JD(U)
(b) RJD
(c) BSP
(d) INC
(e) None of the above/More than one of the above

18. Who is the Chief Justice of Patna High Court?

(a) Justice Sanjay Karol
(b) Justice Ahsanuddin Amanullah
(c) Justice Vikash Jain
(d) Justice Sanjay Kumar
(e) None of the above/More than one of the above

19. Who is the Panchayati Raj Minister in Bihar?

(a) Arvind Kumar Chaudhary
(b) Samrat Chaudhary
(c) Ranjit Kumar Singh
(d) Vijay Kumar Chaudhary
(e) None of the above/More than one of the above

20. Cow slaughter was banned by a law in Bihar in which year?

(a) 1948
(b) 1949
(c) 1954
(d) 1955
(e) None of the above/More than one of the above

21. Who is the leader of the opposition in Bihar Legislative Council?

(a) Tej Pratap Yadav
(b) Tejashwi Prasad Yadav

(c) Rabri Devi
(d) Misa Bharti
(e) None of the above/More than one of the above

22. Who among the following has served as the Governor of Bihar twice?

(a) Akhlaqur Rahman Kidwai
(b) Mohammad Yunus Saleem
(c) Mohammad Shafi Qureshi
(d) Zakir Hussain
(e) None of the above/More than one of the above

23. Bihar has rural literacy rate of

(a) 25%
(b) 33.9%
(c) 38%
(d) 43.9%
(e) None of the above/More than one of the above

24. Jharkhand was an integral part of Bihar in

(a) 1999
(b) 2003
(c) 2001
(d) 2002
(e) None of the above/More than one of the above

25. What is 'Tinkathia' method in Bihar?

(a) Education method
(b) Employment method
(c) Agricluture method
(d) Alms method
(e) None of the above/More than one of the above

26. Who was given the title of 'Loknayak'?

(a) Lalu Prasad Yadav
(b) Karpoori Thakur
(c) Jayaprakash Narayan
(d) Nitish Kumar
(e) None of the above/More than one of the above

27. 'Seven Nishchay Yojana' campaign was started by the State Government for sustainable development in Bihar in

(a) 2014
(b) 2013
(c) 2015
(d) 2012
(e) None of the above/More than one of the above

28. The fiscal deficit of Bihar in the year 2021–22 is _____ percent of the State's GDP.

(a) 2.79
(b) 2.89
(c) 2.97
(d) 2.69
(e) None of the above/More than one of the above

29. Which can be rightly said to be a very significant aspect of the Champaran Satyagraha?

(a) Active all-India participation of lawyers, students and women in the National Movement
(b) Active involvement of Dalit and tribal communities of India in the National Movement
(c) Joining of peasant unrest to India's National Movement
(d) Drastic decrease in the cultivation of plantation crops and commercial crops
(e) None of the above/More than one of the above

30. Who among the following leaders from Bihar appeared before the 'Hammond Commission' at Ranchi to demand voting rights for the Dalits?

(a) Jayaprakash Narayan
(b) Babu Jagjivan Ram
(c) Ram Manohar Lohia
(d) Raj Kumar Shukla
(e) None of the above/More than one of the above

31. Who among the following waged a rebellion against the British in Bihar immediately aftern the Battle of Buxar?

(a) Maharaja Fateh Bahadur Shahi
(b) Babu Kunwar Singh
(c) Govind Ram
(d) Chait Singh
(e) None of the above/More than one of the above

32. Who among the following 'Seven Martyrs' of Patna during Quit India Movement was a student of B.N. College?

(a) Umakant Prasad Sinha
(b) Ramanand Singh
(c) Satish Prasad Jha
(d) Jagatpati Kumar
(e) None of the above/More than one of the above

33. India's first 'Kisan Rail' started its journey on 8th August, 2020 between which of the following two stations?

(a) Ghaziabad and Howrah
(b) Devlali (Maharashtra) and Danapur (Bihar)
(c) Nasik and New Delhi
(d) Nasik and Ahmedabad
(e) None of the above/More than one of the above

34. Who from Bihar has been conferred the Padma Bhushan Award on 26th January, 2021?

(a) Mridula Sinha
(b) Ram Vilas Paswan (Posthumously)
(c) Dulari Devi
(d) Ramchandra Manjhi
(e) None of the above/More than one of the above

35. How many from Bihar were conferred the Padma Shri Award in different fields on 26th January, 2021?

(a) Four
(b) Three
(c) Two
(d) Five
(e) None of the above/More than one of the above

36. Who from Bihar was conferred the Padma Shri Award for great contribution in the field of Medicine on 26th January, 2021?

(a) Dr. Ram Kumar Yadav
(b) Dr. Raj Bahadur
(c) Dr. Randeep Guleria
(d) Dr. Dilip Kumar Singh
(e) None of the above/More than one of the above

37. Who among the following from Bihar has been conferred the Bharat Ratna Award?

(a) Rajendra Prasasd
(b) Nitish Kumar
(c) Karpoori Thakur
(d) Ram Vilas Paswan
(e) None of the above/More than one of the above

Answers

1. (c)	**2.** (a)	**3.** (d)	**4.** (b)
5. (b)	**6.** (d)	**7.** (b)	**8.** (c)
9. (e)	**10.** (c)	**11.** (d)	**12.** (e)
13. (b)	**14.** (e)	**15.** (d)	**16.** (a)
17. (e)	**18.** (a)	**19.** (b)	**20.** (d)
21. (c)	**22.** (a)	**23.** (e)	**24.** (a)
25. (c)	**26.** (c)	**27.** (c)	**28.** (c)
29. (c)	**30.** (b)	**31.** (a)	**32.** (d)
33. (b)	**34.** (b)	**35.** (a)	**36.** (d)
37. (a)			

BPSC Project Manager Examination-2022

1. **During the period of 2010-11 to 2014-15, the production level of cereals in Bihar has grown annually by**
(a) 4.65%
(b) 5.65%
(c) 6.65%
(d) 7.65%
(e) None of the above/More than one of the above

2. **Bihar has created a Land Bank for establishing industries which currently has a Corpus Fund limited up to**
(a) ₹ 1,500 crore
(b) ₹ 2,000 crore
(c) ₹ 2,500 crore
(d) ₹ 3,000 crore
(e) None of the above/More than one of the above

3. **The total installed power capacity in Bihar was 3704.63 MW in 2015. Out of which the share of renewable energy was**
(a) 2.1%
(b) 2.2%
(c) 2.3%
(d) 2.4%
(e) None of the above/More than one of the above

4. **Which wetland in Bihar has been designated as Ramsar Site in October 2020?**
(a) Kabartal
(b) Sur Sarovar
(c) Lonar Lake
(d) Asan Conservation
(e) None of the above/More than one of the above

5. **Bhola Paswan Shastri, the former Chief Minister was from which district of Bihar?**
(a) Purnia
(b) Patna
(c) Bhagalpur
(d) West Champaran
(e) None of the above/More than one of the above

6. **In Bihar, RJD candidates Shakti Singh Yadav lost election (2020) to JD(U) candidate Krishna Murari Sharan with just**
(a) 12 votes
(b) 10 votes
(c) 11 votes
(d) 13 votes
(e) None of the above/More than one of the above

7. **How many maximum ministers according to the law, can be appointed to the 243-Member Bihar Assembly?**
(a) 36
(b) 37
(c) 38
(d) 39
(e) None of the above/More than one of the above

8. **According to the Centre for Monitoring Indian Economy (CMIE) data, Bihar's unemployment rate in October 2020 was**
(a) 9.9%
(b) 9.8%
(c) 8.9%
(d) 9.7%
(e) None of the above/More than one of the above

Answers

1. (b)	**2.** (c)	**3.** (c)	**4.** (a)
5. (a)	**6.** (a)	**7.** (a)	**8.** (b)

❑❑❑

Solved Papers
2025–2020

71st, Bihar Combined Exam Solved Papers-2025

1. How many bronze medals were won by Bihar players in the 38th National Junior Athletics Championship 2025?
(a) 4
(b) 5
(c) 6
(d) More than one of the above

2. Which districts in Bihar will benefit from the Kosi Mechi Link Project?
(a) Patna, Nalanda, Gaya, Siwan
(b) Darbhanga, Muzaffarpur, Sitamarhi, Begusarai
(c) Araria, Purnea, Kishanganj, Katihar
(d) More than one of the above

3. Which organisation recognised the Nagi bird sanctuary Site as an Important Bird and Biodiversity Area (IBA)?
(a) UNESCO
(b) World Wildlife Fund
(c) Bird Life International
(d) More than one of the above

4. What is the primary objective of Bihar's Mission Daksh?
(a) To increase school enrolment in primary schools in rural areas.
(b) To provide vocational training to teachers at senior-secondary level.
(c) To offer personalised mentoring for lagging students to reach grade-level competencies.
(d) More than one of the above

5. Which of the following is NOT one of the components under the YUVA framework of the Bihar Startup Policy 2022?
(a) Vibrancy in the education system
(b) Regulatory enablers for support
(c) International market expansion schemes
(d) More than one of the above

6. Which of the following statement/s is/are correct about Bihar's economic performance in 2023-24?
(a) Bihar's per capita GSDP at current prices increased by 12.8% in 2023-24 over the previous year.
(b) The estimated share of the tertiary sector in Bihar's GSVA (constant prices) in 2023-24 was 58.6%.
(c) The Gross Fixed Capital Formation (GFCF) formed 4.6% of GSDP at current prices in 2023-24.
(d) More than one of the above.

7. Consider the following statements:
1. The proportion of the young population (0-19 years) in Bihar is projected to decline significantly by 2041.
2. Bihar's demographic dividend is expected to peak around 2041.
3. The elderly population (60+ years) in Bihar is expected

to rise more sharply than in India.

Select the correct answer using the codes given below:

(a) 1 and 2 are correct.
(b) 1 and 3 are correct.
(c) 2 and 3 are correct.
(d) More than one of the above.

8. According to PLFS 2023-24, which of the following statements best describe the nature of employment among women in Bihar?

(a) Most women are employed in formal, regular wage jobs.
(b) The majority of women are self-employed, often serving as helpers in household enterprises.
(c) Majority of women were engaged in secondary sector.
(d) More than one of the above.

9. Which Congress leader visited Bihar in 1918 in order to strengthen the activities of Home Rule League?

(a) B.G. Tilak
(b) Annie Besant
(c) Mahatma Gandhi
(d) M.A. Ansari

10. Champaran Agrarian Committee was appointed in agreement between:

(a) Indian Government and Gandhiji
(b) Indian Government and Raj Kumar Shukla
(c) Indian Government and Rajendra Prasad
(d) Indian Government and Anugraha Narayan Singh

11. Who was the prominent leader of Kisan Sabha movement in Bihar?

(a) Raj Kumar Shukla
(b) Sahajanand Saraswati
(c) Acharya Narendra Dev
(d) Baba Ram Chandra

12. Who was murdered while hoisting the national flag under the area of Bikram Police Station?

(a) Raghunath Singh of Gorakhari
(b) Ram Narain of Bikrampur
(c) Satyendra of Gorakhari
(d) None of the above

13. Who became the Chief Minister of Bihar in March 1939?

(a) Anugraha Narain Singh
(b) Rajendra Prasad
(c) Shri Krishna Singh
(d) None of the above

14. Which Buddhist council was not held in Bihar?

(a) First (b) Second
(c) Third (d) Fourth

15. Who among the following was not an Acharya in The Nalanda Vishvavidyalaya?

(a) Nagarjuna (b) Kautilya
(c) Sheelbhadra (d) Shantirakshit

16. Among the following Newspapers of Bihar, which was the first one to get published?

(a) Bihar Bandhu
(b) Patna Harkara
(c) Akhbar-E-Bihar
(d) Bihar Herald

17. Match List-I with List-II.

List-I Event/Organisation	List-II Related Person
A. Champaran Satyagrah	**1. Jayaprakash Narayan**
B. Azad Dasta	**2. Shyam Narayan Singh**
C. Individual Satyagrah in Bihar (1940)	**3. Sahajanand Saraswati**
D. Kisan Sabha Bihar	**4. Dr. Rajendra Prasad**

Select the correct answer using the codes given below:

	A	B	C	D
(a)	4	2	3	1
(b)	2	3	1	4
(c)	1	4	3	2
(d)	4	1	2	3

18. **Which of the following parks/ sanctuaries come under the project tiger in Bihar?**
(a) Valmiki National Park
(b) Udaypur Wildlife Sanctuary
(c) Bhimbandh Wildlife Sanctuary
(d) None of these

19. **Which of the following is the state animal of Bihar?**
(a) Cow (b) Bull
(c) Buffalo (d) Horse

20. **Karmanasa river originates in:**
(a) Kaimur District
(b) Vaishali District
(c) Patna District
(d) Bikram District

21. **Bihar produces ....% of pyrite of whole India?**
(a) 75 (b) 85
(c) 95 (d) 100

22. **Gold is found in which district of Bihar?**
(a) Gaya District
(b) Jamui District
(c) Nalanda District
(d) Bhagalpur District

23. **Most of the Bihar comes under which of the following climate type?**
(a) Subtropical Monsoon
(b) Tropical savannah
(c) Hot and dry
(d) Hot and Semi Arid

Answers

1. (*)	**2.** (c)	**3.** (c)	**4.** (c)	**5.** (c)	**6.** (d)	**7.** (a)	**8.** (b)
9. (b)	**10.** (a)	**11.** (b)	**12.** (a)	**13.** (c)	**14.** (d)	**15.** (b)	**16.** (b)
17. (d)	**18.** (a)	**19.** (b)	**20.** (a)	**21.** (*)	**22.** (b)	**23.** (a)	

70th, Bihar Combined Exam Solved Papers-2024

1. **Match List-I with List-II**

List-I	**List-II**
A. Vaishali	**1. Silk Textile**
B. Bhagalpur	**2. Gold**
C. Jamui	**3. Rail coach factory**
D. Madhepura	**4. Flori culture**

Select the correct answer using the codes given below:

	A	B	C	D
(a)	2	3	4	1
(b)	3	4	1	2
(c)	4	1	2	3
(d)	1	2	3	4

2. **In which of the following years the Bihar state Hydroelectric power corporation was established?**
(a) 1992 (b) 1982
(c) 1998 (d) 1990

3. **In which city of Bihar the recently inaugurated National Dolphin Research Centre is located**
(a) Darbhanga (b) Patna
(c) Munger (d) Gaya

4. **The book Critical of the British Policies *Ghareeb Hindustan* was**

banned in Bihar in 1930 by the British, was written by

(a) Ali Mohd. Shad
(b) Mohd. Wali Hasan
(c) Badrul Hassan
(d) Shaikh Mian Jaan

5. What is the contribution of agriculture in the Gross Domestic Product (GDP) of Bihar?

(a) 19% (b) 17%
(c) 33% (d) 26%

6. The hundred years of Indian National Congress in Bihar was edited by

(a) K.K. Dutta (b) P.N. Ojha
(c) A.R. Desai (d) B.B. Mishra

7. The first Hindi daily newspaper to be published in Bihar was

(a) Kshatriya Samachar
(b) Udyoga
(c) Sarwa Hitaishi
(d) Chaitanya Chandrika

8. Which of the following drainage systems drains the lands of Bihar?

(a) Ghagra (b) Mahanadi
(c) Yamuna (d) Narmada

9. Which of the following districts of Bihar has the highest percentage of Scheduled Tribe in 2011 census?

(a) Katihar (b) Jamui
(c) Purnia (d) Banka

10. Which sector received the highest allocation in the Bihar Budget 2024-25?

(a) Agriculture (b) Health
(c) Infrastructure (d) Education

11. What was the Per Capita Net State Domestic Product at Current Prices for Bihar for the fiscal year 2022-23, based on the base year 2011-12?

(a) ₹54,111 (b) ₹42,083
(c) ₹61,434 (d) ₹47,498

12. Which of the following centres in Bihar is proposed to develop under Vishnupad Yojana for promotion of tourism in Union Budget 2024?

(a) Nalanda (b) Rajgir
(c) Vaishali (d) Gaya

13. The sikh pilgrimage site 'Takhat Sri Harimandir Ji Patna Sahib' which is considered as the second holiest Takhat is located in

(a) Bhagalpur
(b) Gaya
(c) Patna
(d) More than one of the above

14. Bihula Festival is celebrated especially in which one of the following districts in Bihar usually in the month of August each year?

(a) Bhagalpur
(b) Patna
(c) Sitamarhi
(d) Darbhanga

15. Which of the following great ruler founded the "Haryak Vansh" in ancient Bihar?

(a) Bimbisara
(b) Brihadrath
(c) Ajatashatru
(d) More than one of the above

16. Who presented the Bihar Budget 2024-25 in the State Assembly?

(a) Shri Vijay Sinha
(b) Shri Nitish Kumar
(c) Shri Vijay Kumar Choudhary
(d) Shri Samrat Choudhary

17. When did the new province Bihar came into force during British rule?

(a) April 1912
(b) April 1911
(c) March 1912
(d) More than one of the above

18. Which community was categorized as Scheduled Caste (SC) by a 2015 Bihar government notification which was quashed in July 2024 by the Supreme court, ruling that states cannot make changes to the

SC list published under Article 341 of the Constitution?
(a) Lal Begi (b) Tanti-Tantwa
(c) Pano (d) Dabgar

19. What is the sex ratio in Bihar as per the Census 2011 of India?
(a) 918 (b) 916
(c) 933 (d) 922

20. Which dynasty ruled Magadh (Bihar) after Shishunag dynasty?
(a) Maurya Vansh
(b) Sunga Vansh
(c) Nanda Vansh
(d) More than one of the above

21. When did Bihar State introduce the Green Budget for the first time?
(a) Financial Year 2020-21
(b) Financial Year 2018-19
(c) Financial Year 2021-22
(d) Financial Year 2019-20

22. Manvi Madhu Kashyap recently became Bihar's first transgender
(a) Havildar in Bihar Regiment
(b) Bus Driver in state transport
(c) Traffic Police Inspector
(d) Sub-Inspector of Police

23. Shreyasi Singh, Member of the Legislative Assembly, who has represented India in shooting in Paris Olympics 2024 was elected from which constituency in Bihar?
(a) Sugauli (b) Gidhaur
(c) Jamui (d) Kesaria

24. What is the name of the one month long cattle fair organized at the confluence of Ganga and Gandak rivers?
(a) Katihar Mela
(b) Sonepur Mela
(c) Purnia Mela
(d) More than one of the above

25. Munger Hilly region is a part of which of the following physiographic region?
(a) Southern Hilly Region
(b) North Bihar Plain
(c) Someshwar Hilly Range
(d) South Bihar Plain

Answers

1. (c)	**2.** (b)	**3.** (b)	**4.** (b)	**5.** (*)	**6.** (b)	**7.** (c)	**8.** (a)
9. (a)	**10.** (d)	**11.** (a)	**12.** (d)	**13.** (c)	**14.** (a)	**15.** (a)	**16.** (d)
17. (a)	**18.** (b)	**19.** (a)	**20.** (c)	**21.** (a)	**22.** (d)	**23.** (c)	**24.** (b)
25. (a)							

69th, Bihar Combined Exam Solved Papers-2023

1. The Maithili language was started to develop during the reign of which of the following?
(a) Oiniwar dynasty
(b) Karnat dynasty
(c) Pithipatis
(d) Chero dynasty

2. Which city served as the capital of the ancient kingdom of Magadha during the early Vedic period?

(a) Campa (b) Vaishali
(c) Pataliputra (d) Rajagriha

3. When was Bihar first separated from the Bengal Presidency under the British-ruled India?
(a) 1947
(b) 1936
(c) 1912
(d) None of the above

4. In Indian art, the construction of 'Stupa', 'Chaitya' and 'Vihara' is related to which of the following?
(a) Vaishnava sect
(b) Buddhism
(c) Shaiva sect
(d) Ajivika sect

5. In the context of Indian handicrafts, what is 'Sujini' in Bihar?
(a) A metal craft
(b) A type of embroidery
(c) A type of clay pottery
(d) A type of glassware

6. Consider the following statements regarding the Vikramshila University in Bihar:
1. It was located in the present-day Banka district of Bihar.
2. It was established by King Gopala I of the Pala dynasty.
3. The Vajrayana' sect of Buddhism flourished here.
4. Other subjects like Astronomy, Logic, Law, Grammar and Philosophy were also taught here.
Which of the above statements are incorrect?
(a) 1 and 2
(b) 1 and 4
(c) 2 and 3
(d) None of the above

7. Which of the following National Parks/Wildlife Sanctuaries are in Bihar?
1. Valmiki National Park
2. Dudhwa National Park
3. Gajner Wildlife Sanctuary
4. Bhimbandh Wildlife Sanctuary
Select the correct answer using the codes given below.
(a) 2 and 3 (b) 1 and 3
(c) 2 and 4 (d) 1 and 4

8. The other name of river Gandak is
(a) Mahananda
(b) Narayani
(c) Punpun
(d) Burhi Gandak

9. Gold is found in which of the following districts of Bihar?
(a) Saran (b) Siwan
(c) Jamui (d) Munger

10. The Triveni Canal has been constructed on which of the following rivers?
(a) Sone
(b) Gandak
(c) Mayurakshi
(d) Kosi

11. Bihar's geographical structure consists of rock systems. Match the rock systems with their descriptions:

A. Dharwar rock system	**1. Created by the rapid deposition of alluvium by Himalayan and Peninsular rivers**
B. Vindhyan rock system	**2. Can be found in the West Champaran district**
C. Quaternary rock system	**3. Part of the oldest Archaean rock system**

D. Tertiary rock system	4. Sandstone, limestone, dolomite, quartzite and shale are the main constituents of this rock system

Select the correct answer using the codes given below.

	A	B	C	D
(a)	1	3	2	4
(b)	2	3	4	1
(c)	4	2	3	1
(d)	3	4	1	2

12. What is the current population of Gaya district of Bihar?

(a) 320000 (b) 780000
(c) 234000 (d) 598000

13. The Bakasht Movement in Bihar during 1937-1938 was organized by whom?

(a) Jayaprakash Narayan
(b) Swami Sahajanand Saraswati
(c) Peer Ali Khan
(d) Swami Dayanand Saraswati

14. Which treaty was signed after the Battle of Buxar?

(a) The Treaty of Sugauli
(b) The Treaty of Bassein
(c) The Treaty of Salbai
(d) The Treaty of Allahabad

15. The Dutch East India Company established its factory at Patna in which year?

(a) 1632 (b) 1643
(c) 1648 (d) 1635

16. The Quit India Movement in 1942 witnessed significant contributions from leaders of Bihar. Which prominent Bihar leader was known as the 'Bihar Kesari' and actively participated in the Quit India Movement?

(a) Shri Krishna Singh
(b) Anugrah Narayan Sinha
(c) Ram Manohar Lohia
(d) Dr. Rajendra Prasad

17. In response to the mass agitation of the Champaran Movement, the British Government took which step to address the issue?

(a) Enforced strict curfew and imposed Martial Law in the region
(b) Instituted the Champaran Agrarian Committee
(c) Declared Champaran as an independent State
(d) Appointed Mahatma Gandhi as the Governor of Champaran

18. The cook from Bihar who saved Mahatma Gandhi's life from a murder attempt by food poisoning in 1917 was

(a) Mir Bakawal
(b) Batak Mian
(c) Muzaffar Ahmad
(d) None of them

Answers

1. (b) **2.** (d) **3.** (c) **4.** (b) **5.** (b) **6.** (a) **7.** (d) **8.** (b)
9. (c) **10.** (b) **11.** (d) **12.** (*) **13.** (b) **14.** (d) **15.** (a) **16.** (a)
17. (b) **18.** (b)

68th, Bihar Combined Exam Solved Papers-2023

1. **At what percentage has Bihar registered the lowest Female Workforce Participation Rate for the year 2020-2022?**
   (a) 7% in rural and 9.1% in urban areas
   (b) 4% in rural and 6.5% in urban areas
   (c) 6% in rural and 8.1% in urban areas
   (d) More than one of the above
   (e) None of the above

2. **The maximum number of tax industries is in which district?**
   (a) Kishanganj
   (b) Darbhanga
   (c) Purnia
   (d) More than one of the above
   (e) None of the above

3. **According to the National Family Survey-5 released by the Union Ministry of Health and Family Welfare on November 24, 2021, there has been a significant improvement in the sex ratio of Bihar. It has increased from ______ in 2015-2016 to ______ in 2020-2022.**
   (a) 1030, 1050
   (b) 1062, 1090
   (c) 1040, 1070
   (d) More than one of the above
   (e) None of the above

4. **According to the Bihar Economic Survey (2021-2022), what was the rate of growth of Gross State Domestic Product (GSDP) of Bihar in 2020-2021?**
   (a) 2·5%
   (b) 3%
   (c) 2%
   (d) More than one of the above
   (e) None of the above

5. **Which one of the following is correct for Bihar economy?**
   (a) The occupational structure of the economy is stagnant from above.
   (b) The growth rate is one of the lowest in India at 2.5%.
   (c) Bihar produces mostly primary goods.
   (d) More than one of the above
   (e) None of the above

6. **During the Salt Satyagraha in Bihar, in addition to making salt, the people chose to oppose the government by opposing which tax?**
   (a) Malba
   (b) Haathi
   (c) Development
   (d) More than one of the above
   (e) None of the above

7. **The elected Government of Bihar formed by Shri Krishna Singh resigned in February 1938 for which reason?**

(a) Satyagraha against the British at the call of Gandhiji
(b) Participation in the Freedom Struggle of India
(c) For the release of political prisoners
(d) More than one of the above
(e) None of the above

8. Who saved the life of Gandhiji in Bihar during Champaran Satyagraha?
(a) Ravindra Pathak
(b) Batak Mian
(c) Hamid Ansari
(d) More than one of the above
(e) None of the above

9. Who led cultivators in Bihar during the Non-Cooperation Movement?
(a) Shri Krishna Singh
(b) Swami Vidyanand
(c) Raj Kumar Shukla
(d) More than one of the above
(e) None of the above

10. Who established Swaraj Dal in Bihar?
(a) Bankim Chandra Mitra
(b) Shri Krishna Singh
(c) Ramlal Shah
(d) More than one of the above
(e) None of the above

11. Who among the following made an offer to Humayun that he would surrender Bihar and pay an annual tribute of 10 lakh dinars, if he was allowed to retain Bengal?
(a) Bahadur Shah
(b) Sher Khan
(c) Bairam Khan
(d) More than one of the above
(e) None of the above

12. The Vikramshila University was established by
(a) Gopala
(b) Dharmapala
(c) Devapala
(d) More than one of the above
(e) None of the above

13. Who among the following was the first Governor of Bihar?
(a) Sir Maurice Garnier Hallett
(b) Sir James David Sifton
(c) Sir Hugh Dow
(d) More than one of the above
(e) None of the above

14. Who was the author of Mahatma Gandhi and Bihar, Some Reminiscences?
(a) Dr. Rajendra Prasad
(b) J. P. Narayan
(c) Karpoori Thakur
(d) More than one of the above
(e) None of the above

15. Which is the oldest church in Bihar?
(a) Padri Ki Haveli
(b) Luke's Church
(c) Stephen's Church the
(d) More than one of the above
(e) None of the above

16. The late actor Kumudlal Ganguly, also known by his stage name Ashok Kumar, was born in which of the following cities of Bihar?
(a) Patna
(b) Munger
(c) Bhagalpur
(d) More than one of the above
(e) None of the above

17. In 1940, Patna Women's College was founded by which of the following societies?
(a) Sisters of the Apostolic Carmel
(b) Society of Jesus
(c) Irish Christian Brothers
(d) More than one of the above
(e) None of the above

18. According to the NITI Aayog SDG Report for the year 2020-2021, how much did the State of Bihar score?

(a) 52 out of 100
(b) 22 out of 100
(c) 35 out of 100
(d) More than one of the above
(e) None of the above

19. In the year 2020, Bihar gained which position out of 36 States in the Ease of Doing Business, awarded by Business Reforms Action Plan (BRAP).
(a) 25th
(b) 23rd
(c) 24th
(d) More than one of the above
(e) None of the above

20. Ganga Jal Aapurti Yojana was inaugurated by Chief Minister Nitish Kumar on November 28, 2022 at which place?
(a) Bodh Gaya
(b) Lakhisarai
(c) Rajgir
(d) More than one of the above
(e) None of the above

21. The urbanization of the State has increased very rapidly in the last ten years. According to the 2011 Census, the level of urbanization in Bihar was just ______ per cent, which has ________ increased to per cent at present.
(a) 14.4, 15.5
(b) 11.3, 15.3
(c) 12.2, 13.1
(d) More than one of the above
(e) None of the above

22. Which of the following States of India borders with the maximum number of districts in Bihar?
(a) West Bengal
(b) Uttar Pradesh
(c) Jharkhand
(d) More than one of the above
(e) None of the above

23. Which of the following is the last railway station of Bihar in the train route from Bhagalpur towards Mirza Cheuki?
(a) Kahalgaon Railway Station
(b) Pirpainti Railway Station
(c) Ammapali Railway Station
(d) More than one of the above
(e) None of the above

24. With reference to the mineral production in Bihar, consider the following statements :
1. Rohtas has the highest deposit of pyrites.
2. Limestone is found in Kaimur (Bhabhua), Munger (Monghyr) and Rohtas districts.
3. Gold deposits are found in Jamui district.
Which of the statements given above is/are correct?
(a) 1 and 3 only
(b) 3 only
(c) 1 and 2 only
(d) More than one of the above
(e) None of the above

25. Phalgu, a sacred river flowing in Bihar, is formed by the confluence of which of the following rivers?
(a) Mohana and Lilajan rivers
(b) Lilajan and Son rivers
(c) Son and Mohana rivers
(d) More than one of the above
(e) None of the above

26. In Bihar, tea gardens were established for the first time in which of the following places?
(a) Supaul
(b) Thakurganj
(c) Bahadurganj
(d) More than one of the above
(e) None of the above

27. Choose the correct order of the following districts of Bihar as per the ascending decadal population growth (2001-2011).

(a) Kishanganj < Madhepura < Siwan
(b) Siwan < Kishanganj < Madhepura
(c) Madhepura < Kishanganj < Siwan
(d) More than one of the above
(e) None of the above

28. Which food industry dominates among the agro-based industries in Bihar?
(a) Sugarcane industry
(b) Cereal-based industry
(c) Pulses industry
(d) More than one of the above
(e) None of the above

Answers

1. (b)	**2.** (c)	**3.** (b)	**4.** (a)	**5.** (d)	**6.** (e)	**7.** (c)	**8.** (b)
9. (b)	**10.** (b)	**11.** (b)	**12.** (b)	**13.** (b)	**14.** (a)	**15.** (a)	**16.** (c)
17. (a)	**18.** (a)	**19.** (a)	**20.** (a)	**21.** (b)	**22.** (c)	**23.** (c)	**24.** (d)
25. (a)	**26.** (b)	**27.** (b)	**28.** (b)				

67th, Bihar Combined Re-Exam Solved Papers-2022

1. Who was the real founder of Turk rule in Bihar?
(a) Ibn Bakhtiyar Khilji
(b) Ibrahim
(c) Dariya Khan Noohani
(d) Malik Husamuddin
(e) None of the above More than one of the above

2. Who was the first Indian Governor of Bihar?
(a) Dr. Shri Krishna Singh
(b) Brij Kishor Prasad
(c) B. P. Mandal
(d) Satyendra Prasanna Sinha
(e) None of the above/More than one of the above

3. Who were the leaders of Santhal Revolt?
(a) Sidhu and Kanhu
(b) Gaurakshni Bhagat and Keshav Chandra Roy
(c) Shambhunath Pal and Korra Mallaya
(d) Jara Bhagat and Balaram Bhagat
(e) None of the above/More than one of the above

4. In which year the Chuar Revolt of Bihar took place?
(a) 1842
(b) 1798
(c) 1784
(d) 1832
(e) None of the above/More than one of the above

5. In which year was Orissa separated from Bihar?
(a) 1936
(b) 1956
(c) 2000
(d) 1912
(e) None of the above/More than one of the above

6. Where was the first Buddhist Council convened?
(a) Rajagriha
(b) Amaravati
(c) Kanganhalli
(d) Pataliputra
(e) None of the above/More than one of the above

7. Which Gupta ruler assumed the throne after killing his elder brother?
(a) Samudragupta
(b) Chandragupta II
(c) Skandagupta
(d) Shri Gupta
(e) None of the above/More than one of the above

8. Who laid the foundation of Vardhana dynasty?
(a) Rajyavardhana
(b) Adityavardhana
(c) Prabhakarvardhana
(d) Pushyabhuti
(e) None of the above/More than one of the above

9. Where was first coal mine in India mined?
(a) Raniganj
(b) Dhanbad
(c) Asansol
(d) Jharia
(e) None of the above/More than one of the above

10. The total geographical area of Bihar State is
(a) 94316 sq. km.
(b) 94163 sq. km
(c) 94526 sq. km
(d) 94200 sq. km
(e) None of the above/More than one of the above

11. Which river is known as Sorrow of Bihar?
(a) Ganga
(b) Kosi
(c) Sone
(d) Ghaghra
(e) None of the above/More than one of the above

12. In wbich district of Bihar, Telhar Kund Waterfall is located?
(a) Nawada
(b) Kaimur
(c) Rohtas
(d) Sasaram
(e) None of the above/More than one of the above

13. Which is the Asia's largest and freshwater oxbow lake in Bihar?
(a) Kanwar Lake
(b) Anupam Lake
(c) Kusheshwar Lake
(d) Ghogha Lake
(e) None of the above/More than one of the above

14. Which district of Bihar has the largest gold reserve?
(a) Jamui
(b) Banka
(c) Katihar
(d) Munger
(e) None of the above/More than one of the above

15. Which district of Bihar is known as 'silk city'?
(a) Bhojpur
(b) Bhagalpur
(c) Banka
(d) Katihar
(e) None of the above/More than one of the above

16. What is the female literacy rate of Bihar as per the Census 2011 of India?
(a) 71.25%
(b) 50.50%
(c) 51.50%.
(d) 61.80%
(e) None of the above/More than one of the above

17. Choose the correct order of the following districts of Bihar as per the ascending level of urbanization.
(a) Nalanda < Patna < Munger
(b) Patna < Munger < Nalanda
(c) Munger < Nalanda < Patna
(d) Nalanda < Munger < Patna
(e) None of the above/More than one of the above

18. The fiscal deficit is expected to be _ of GSDP of Bihar for the financial year 2022–23.
(a) 12.1%
(b) 3.47%
(c) 9.89%
(d) 3.18%
(e) None of the above/More than one of the above

19. Choose the option which is not part of the "Saat Nischay Part-2 Scheme" of Bihar.
(a) Strong woman, capable woman
(b) Irrigation water to every field
(c) Airways to everyone
(d) Yuva Shakti-Progress of Bihar
(e) None of the above/More than one of the above

20. Choose the correct order of the Bihar State districts in descending order of per capita income.
(a) Sheohar > Araria > East Champaran > Kishanganj > Nawada
(b) East Champaran > Sheohar > Araria > Kishanganj > Nawada
(c) Araria > Nawada > East Champaran > Sheohar > Kishanganj
(d) Nawada > Kishanganj > East Champaran > Araria > Sheohar
(e) None of the above/More than one of the above

21. In which place Khudiram Bose tried to kill Kingsford?
(a) Darbhanga
(b) Muzaffarpur
(c) Gaya
(d) Patna
(e) None of the above/More than one of the above

22. During which Movement 'Azad Dasta' was active in Bihar?
(a) Non-Cooperation Movement
(b) Civil Disobedience Movement
(c) Quit India Movement.
(d) Champaran Satyagraha
(e) None of the above/More than one of the above

23. In 1942, on the occasion of which festival Jayaprakash Narayan escaped from Hazaribagh jail?
(a) Holi
(b) Dussehra
(c) Deepawali
(d) Baisakhi
(e) None of the above/More than one of the above

24. According to the Economic Survey of Bihar 2021-22, what is the level of urbanization in the State at present?
(a) 22.4%
(b) 15.3%
(c) 18.6%
(d) 11.6%
(e) None of the above/More than one of the above

25. Who is the Brand Ambassador of Khadi in Bihar?
(a) Rajesh Tiwari
(b) Manoj Tiwari
(c) Manoj Vajpayee
(d) Pawan Singh
(e) None of the above/More than one of the above

26. In which district of Bihar, the world's tallest (251 m) statue of Mother Sita will be constructed?
(a) Sitamarhi
(b) Bodh Gaya
(c) Patna
(d) Madhubani
(e) None of the above/More than one of the above

27. The 'Operation Prahar' in Bihar is related to
(a) literacy campaign
(b) no smoking
(c) liquor ban
(d) COVID-19 vaccination
(e) None of the above/More than one of the above

28. Hrithik Anand from Bihar has won medal for India at the 24th Summer Deaf Badminton Olympics held in Brazil?
(a) Silver medal
(b) Bronze medal
(c) Platinum medal
(d) Gold medal
(e) None of the above/More than one of the above

29. At which place in Bihar, North India's first bird Ringing Station has been recently opened?
(a) Saran
(b) East Champaran
(c) West Champaran
(d) Bhagalpur
(e) None of the above/More than one of the above

30. Which of the following in Bihar started the Vulture's Conservation Plan?
(a) Rajgir Wildlife Sanctuary
(b) Valmiki Tiger Reserve
(c) Kanwar Lake Bird Sanctuary
(d) Kaimu Tiger Reserve.
(e) None of the above/More than one of the above

Answers

1. (a)	**2.** (d)	**3.** (a)	**4.** (b)	**5.** (a)	**6.** (a)	**7.** (b)	**8.** (d)
9. (a)	**10.** (b)	**11.** (b)	**12.** (b)	**13.** (a)	**14.** (a)	**15.** (b)	**16.** (c)
17. (d)	**18.** (b)	**19.** (c)	**20.** (d)	**21.** (b)	**22.** (c)	**23.** (c)	**24.** (b)
25. (b)	**26.** (a)	**27.** (c)	**28.** (d)	**29.** (d)	**30.** (b)		

67th, Bihar Combined Exam Solved Papers-2022

1. Which type of banks is proposed to be established for agriculture and rural development in Bihar?
(a) Krishi Vigyan Banks
(b) Krishi Yantra Banks
(c) Krishi Vikas Banks
(d) Krishi Utthaan Banks
(e) None of the above/More than one of the above

2. The value of Human Development Index of Bihar in 2019 was
(a) 0.641
(b) 0.613
(c) 0.596
(d) 0.574
(e) None of the above/More than one of the above

3. The fiscal deficit in Bihar during 2021-22 is estimated as

(a) ₹ 22,511 crores
(b) ₹ 27,617 crores
(c) ₹ 20,011 crores
(d) ₹ 21,543 crores
(e) None of the above/More than one of the above

4. Under Digital Bihar Programme, which students will receive computer education and training from 2021-22 onwards?
(a) All students of Class V
(b) All students of Class VI
(c) All students of Class VII
(d) All students of Class VIII
(e) None of the above/More than one of the above

5. According to the 15th Finance Commission's recommendations, how much share will Bihar receive in divisible pool of Central taxes from 2021-26?
(a) 4.12 percent
(b) 4.23 percent
(c) 4.89 percent
(d) 4.06 percent
(e) None of the above/More than one of the above

6. Who is not related to the Champaran Satyagraha of 1917?
(a) J. B. Kripalani
(b) Raj Kumar Shukla
(c) Rajendra Prasad
(d) Ram Manohar Lohia
(e) None of the above/More than one of the above

7. One of the leaders of the Revolt of 1857, Kunwar Singh was related to which place?
(a) Gwalior
(b) Jagdishpur
(c) Jhansi
(d) Meerut
(e) None of the above/More than one of the above

8. During Quit India Movement, who among the following escaped from the Hazaribagh Jail?
(a) Sachchidananda Sinha
(b) Jayaprakash Narayan
(c) Jagjivan Ram
(d) Rafi Ahmed Kidwai
(e) None of the above/More than one of the above

9. Who was the President of Gaya Session of the Indian National Congress held in 1922?
(a) Chittaranjan Das
(b) Hakim Ajmal Khan
(c) Mahatma Gandhi
(d) Maulana Abul Kalam Azad
(e) None of the above/More than one of the above

10. According to 2011 Census, which district of Bihar has more women than men?
(a) Gopalganj
(b) Begusarai
(c) Patna
(d) Siwan
(e) None of the above/More than one of the above

11. In which year was the first sitting of the Bihar Legislative Council convened?
(a) 1911
(b) 1913
(c) 1914
(d) 1919
(e) None of the above/More than one of the above

12. Rashmi Kumari from Bihar is a/ an
(a) international cricketer
(b) international carrom champion
(c) football player
(d) chess player
(e) None of the above/More than one of the above

13. The Digital India Award, 2020' was given to the Bihar Government for

(a) establishing technical institutes in Bihar
(b) bringing IT revolution in Bihar
(c) facilitating e-administration in Bihar
(d) providing services to people stranded outside Bihar during COVID-19 lockdown
(e) None of the above/More than one of the above

14. How many seats are reserved for the SC candidates in the Bihar Legislative Assembly?
(a) 38
(b) 40
(c) 44
(d) 46
(e) None of the above/More than one of the above

15. In which year was 50% reservation to women in Panchayat bodies provided in Bihar?
(a) 2005
(b) 2006
(c) 2009
(d) 2014
(e) None of the above/More than one of the above

16. In which year was Bihar divided to create Jharkhand
(a) 2000
(b) 2001
(c) 2004
(d) 2005
(e) None of the above/More than one of the above

17. The new ministry proposed in the Bihar Budget for the year 2021-22 focuses on
(a) child care
(b) women empowerment
(c) infrastructure development
(d) skill and development entrepreneurship
(e) None of the above/More than one of the above

18. How many departments are covered under the Human Development Sub-Mission in Bihar?
(a) 6
(b) 7
(c) 8
(d) 10
(e) None of the above/More than one of the above

19. From which district of Bihar was the Garib Kalyan Rojgar Abhiyan launched by the Prime Minister in 2020?
(a) Patna
(b) Banka
(c) Madhepura
(d) Khagaria
(e) None of the above/More than one of the above

20. Who invited Gandhiji to come to Champaran?
(a) Raj Kumar Shukla
(b) Rajendra Prasad
(c) Jayaprakash Narayan
(d) Krishna Sahay
(e) None of the above/More than one of the above

21. Who had attained enlightenment in Bodh Gaya?
(a) Mahavira Swami
(b) Gautama Buddha
(c) Simandhar Swami
(d) Parshvanath Swami
(e) None of the above/More than one of the above

22. Who established a branch of Anushilan Samiti in Patna in 1913?
(a) Ramananda Sinha
(b) Satish Jha
(c) Sachindra Nath Sanyal
(d) Bipin Jha

(e) None of the above/More than one of the above

23. Who had formed the Bihar Socialist Party in 1931?

(a) Phulan Chand Tiwari and Rajendra Prasad
(b) Phulan Prasad Varma and Jayaprakash Narayan
(c) Raj Kumar Shukla and Swami Agnivesh
(d) Swami Sahajananda and Swami Yogananda
(e) None of the above/More than one of the above

24. Where is Sher Shah's tomb located?

(a) Sasaram
(b) Maner
(c) Sitamarhi
(d) Pavapuri
(e) None of the above/More than one of the above

25. Which district of Bihar has mica deposits?

(a) Rohtas
(b) Patna
(c) Gaya
(d) Saran
(e) None of the above/More than one of the above

26. The confluence of the rivers Son and Ganga is located in which district of Bihar?

(a) Buxar
(b) Patna
(c) Bhojpur
(d) Nalanda
(e) None of the above/More than one of the above

27. Which is the first Ramsar Site in Bihar?

(a) Kaimur Range
(b) Kharagpur Lake
(c) Kanwar Lake
(d) Rajgir Hill
(e) None of the above/More than one of the above

28. Brahmayoni Hill is located in which district of Bihar?

(a) Gaya
(b) Rohtas
(c) Nalanda
(d) Nawada
(e) None of the above/More than one of the above

29. Which agroclimatic region of Bihar has the highest number of districts?

(a) Northern East
(b) Northern West
(c) Southern East
(d) Southern West
(e) None of the above/More than one of the above

30. What is the most famous feature of Chiria located in West Singhbhum?

(a) Iron Ore Mining
(b) Dam
(c) Bird Sanctuary
(d) National Park
(e) None of the above/More than one of the above

Answers

1. (b)	**2.** (d)	**3.** (a)	**4.** (e)	**5.** (a)	**6.** (d)	**7.** (b)	**8.** (b)
9. (a)	**10.** (a)	**11.** (b)	**12.** (b)	**13.** (d)	**14.** (a)	**15.** (b)	**16.** (a)
17. (d)	**18.** (a)	**19.** (d)	**20.** (a)	**21.** (b)	**22.** (c)	**23.** (b)	**24.** (a)
25. (c)	**26.** (b)	**27.** (c)	**28.** (a)	**29.** (a)	**30.** (a)		

66th, Bihar Combined Exam Solved Papers-2020

1. Ram Vilas Paswan started his political career from which political party?
(a) Janata Party
(b) Bharatiya Lok Dal
(c) Samyukta Socialist Party
(d) Praja Socialist Party
(e) None of the above/More than one of the above

2. When Did the Election Commission of the India issue a Press Note for the General Election to the Legislative Assembly of Bihar, 2020?
(a) 23rd September, 2020
(b) 24th September, 2020
(c) 25th September, 2020
(d) 26th September, 2020
(e) None of the above/More than one of the above

3. In which state, 'Ghar Tak Fiber' Scheme has been launched on 21st September, 2020 through video conference?
(a) Uttar Pradesh
(b) Madhya Pradesh
(c) Bihar
(d) Karnataka
(e) None of the above/More than one of the above

4. Bihar Politician Late Raghuvansh Prasad Singh was for the first time elected to which Lok Sabha?
(a) Tenth Lok Sabha
(b) Eleventh Lok Sabha
(c) Twelfth Lok Sabha
(d) Thirteenth Lok Sabha
(e) None of the above/More than one of the above

5. Who spearheaded the 1857 Revolt in Bihar?
(a) Nana Saheb
(b) Tatya Tope
(c) Kunwar Singh
(d) Maulavi Ahmadullah
(e) None of the above/More than one of the above

6. Who drew Gandhiji's attention to the plight of Indigo peasants in Champaran?
(a) Rajendra Prasad
(b) Anugrah Narayan Sinha
(c) Acharya Kripalani
(d) Raj Kumar Shukhla
(e) None of the above/More than one of the above

7. Which was the first capital of ancient Mahajanapada Magadh?
(a) Pataliputra
(b) Vaishali
(c) Champa
(d) Anga
(e) None of the above/More than one of the above

8. Swami Sahajananda was related to which of the following?
(a) Tribal Movement in Bihar
(b) Labour Movement in Bihar
(c) Peasant Movement in Bihar
(d) Caste Movement in Bihar
(e) None of the above/More than one of the above

9. Which of the following was Gandhiji's first Satyagraha Movement in India in which he used Civil Disobedience?

(a) Champaran
(b) Kheda
(c) Ahmedabad
(d) Rowlatt Satyagraha
(e) None of the above/More than one of the above

10. Which of the following rivers flowing in Bihar is a north flowing river?

(a) Bagmati
(b) Kamla
(c) Kosi
(d) Gandak
(e) None of the above/More than one of the above

11. Piedmont Swamp Soil is found only in which one of the following districts of Bihar?

(a) Madhubani
(b) Bhagalpur
(c) West Champaran
(d) Sitamarhi
(e) None of the above/More than one of the above

12. Which one of the following pairs of Administrative Divisions of Bihar, Ganga river does not flow?

(a) Darbhanga - Munger
(b) Purnea - Bhagalpur
(c) Tirhut - Saran
(d) Kosi—Magadh
(e) None of the above/More than one of the above

13. Among the following pairs of tribe and district, which one is not correctly matched?

(a) Santhal - Banka
(b) Munda - Jamui
(c) Oraon - Supaul
(d) Kharwar - Bhagalpur
(e) None of the above/More than one of the above

14. What is the percentage of all types of forest area to the total geographical area of Bihar State?

(a) 7.27 (b) 6.87
(c) 3.21 (d) 12.77
(e) None of the above/More than one of the above

15. Which one of the following districts have the only National Park of Bihar?

(a) Nalanda
(b) Bhagalpur
(c) West Champaran
(d) East Champaran
(e) None of the above/More than one of the above

16. Which company established its factory in 1632 at Patna, Bihar?

(a) British East India Company
(b) Dutch East India company
(c) Portuguese East India Company
(d) French East India Company
(e) None of the above/More than one of the above

17. The government of India conferred the Krishi Karman Award to Bihar State on 2nd January, 2020. This award was given for

(a) Production and productivity of maize and wheat
(b) Food grain production
(c) Production of rice
(d) Production of oilseeds
(e) None of the above/More than one of the above

18. Bihar government launched a new scheme 'Satat Jivikoparjan Yojana' in August 2018. The objective of this scheme is

(a) to provide unemployment allowance to youth
(b) to provide employment in rural areas through local bodies
(c) to provide sustainable income generating assets to extremely poor households

(d) to provide free training for skill upgradation of youth
(e) None of the above/More than one of the above

19. Which of the following is not included in Seven Resolves (Saat Nishchay) of Bihar Government?
(a) Women Employment
(b) Clean Drinking Water
(c) Supply of electricity to all households
(d) Child Welfare
(e) None of the above/More than one of the above

20. The per capita Net State Domestic Product at constant prices for Bihar is less than the country. In the year 2018-19, it was
(a) 75 percent of the national average
(b) 60 percent of the national average
(c) 50 percent of the national average
(d) 33 percent of the national average
(e) None of the above/More than one of the above

21. When was Bihar established?
(a) 1911 (b) 1912
(c) 1913 (d) 1914
(e) None of the above/More than one of the above

22. In Tinkathia System in Bihar, how much land was to be reserved for indigo cultivation?
(a) 01/10 (b) 01/03
(c) 03/20 (d) 03/25
(e) None of the above/More than one of the above

23. Who was the first Chief Minister of Bihar?
(a) Shri Krishna Singh
(b) Satya Pal Malik
(c) Nitish Kumar
(d) Rabri Devi
(e) None of the above/More than one of the above

24. Where was the first Congress Session in Bihar held?
(a) Patna
(b) Gaya
(c) Muzaffarpur
(d) Darbhanga
(e) None of the above/More than one of the above

25. Which title was given to Jayaprakash Narayan?
(a) Praja Hitechhu
(b) Lok Nayak
(c) Lokmanya
(d) Rashtra Nayak
(e) None of the above/More than one of the above

Answers

1. (c)	**2.** (c)	**3.** (c)	**4.** (b)	**5.** (c)	**6.** (d)	**7.** (e)	**8.** (c)
9. (a)	**10.** (e)	**11.** (c)	**12.** (a)	**13.** (b)	**14.** (a)	**15.** (c)	**16.** (b)
17. (a)	**18.** (c)	**19.** (d)	**20.** (d)	**21.** (b)	**22.** (c)	**23.** (a)	**24.** (a)
25. (b)							

❑❑❑